# HISTORY OF THE BALKANS

## TWENTIETH CENTURY

### VOLUME 2

LEARNED SOCIETIES · the Joint Committee on Eastern Europe Publication Series Number 12 · THE AMERICAN COUNCIL OF · SOCIAL SCIENCE RESEARCH COUNCIL · THE SOCIAL

# HISTORY OF THE BALKANS

*Twentieth Century*

## VOLUME 2

BARBARA JELAVICH

CAMBRIDGE
UNIVERSITY PRESS

PUBLISHED BY THE PRESS SYNDICATE OF THE UNIVERSITY OF CAMBRIDGE
The Pitt Building, Trumpington Street, Cambridge, United Kingdom

CAMBRIDGE UNIVERSITY PRESS
The Edinburgh Building, Cambridge CB2 2RU, UK   http: //www.cup.cam.ac.uk
40 West 20th Street, New York, NY 10011-4211, USA   http: //www.cup.org
10 Stamford Road, Oakleigh, Melbourne 3166, Australia

First published 1983
Reprinted 1984, 1985, 1986, 1988, 1989, 1991, 1993, 1994 (twice),
1995, 1996, 1997, 1999

Printed in the United States of America

Typeset in Galliard

*A catalogue record for this book is available from the British Library*

*Library of Congess Cataloguing-in-Publication Data is available*

ISBN 0-521-27459-1 (vol. 2) paperback

# Contents

## Contents

# Maps

# *Preface*

T HE FIRST VOLUME of this Balkan history covered the main events of the eighteenth and nineteenth centuries. The emphasis was on the national movements leading to the formation of the modern states and the organization of the first independent or autonomous governments. Although the final stages were not completed until after World War I, the major steps toward a national organization and a definition of future goals were taken by the end of the nineteenth century by all of the nationalities except the Albanians. The main issues in the twentieth century were thus to be the completion of territorial unification and internal economic and political development. Problems of great-power interference and rivalry among the nations continued from the previous period.

This volume commences with an introduction designed for those readers whose primary interests lie in the present century, although it is hoped that this factual review of the preceding centuries will also be of interest to those who desire a summary and an overview of the previous volume. The material selected is that which is necessary as a background for the next chapters.

This volume, as well as its predecessor, was prepared as part of a program organized in 1972 by the Joint Committee on Eastern Europe of the American Council of Learned Societies and the Social Science Research Council to provide histories of Eastern Europe. Professor Peter F. Sugar of the University of Washington was the chairman of the special committee that prepared the original proposal; Professor Michael B. Petrovich of the University of Wisconsin became chairman of the supervising committee and was responsible for the subsequent organization. This Balkan history has received generous funding from the Office of Education, including grants that allowed the author the free time necessary to complete the writing and funds to assist in the preparation of the volumes for publication. Dr. Gordon B. Turner, Vice-President of ACLS until 1980, and his successor, Dr. Jason H. Parker, contributed valuable suggestions and assistance. The author is also greatly indebted to Julia A. Petrov of the Office of Education for her advice and support.

As stated in the original project, this book is designed as an introduction to Balkan history; it assumes no prior knowledge. Major European events and political, philosophical, and economic theories necessary to the narrative are also covered. Because of the complexity of the developments being treated, some subjects are touched on in more than one section. Since this area has played such a major role in world affairs, attention is directed not only to internal Balkan events, but also to the great international conflicts in this turbulent century. This book thus covers both Balkan developments and the place of the peninsula in twentieth-century history.

The multiplicity of languages and the varieties of spelling that have been used in the past provide certain difficulties for the historian of the area. In this book the attempt has been made to adopt in the spelling of personal and geographic names the form that is most commonly used and that will be most familiar to the reader. Standard systems of transliteration have been used for Greek and Bulgarian; Serbian words and names appear in their Latin spelling. Complete consistency has not been possible. In addition, names of rulers and Ottoman statesmen and many first names have been anglicized.

Dating also provides some problems, since the Balkan people used three separate calendars until after World War I. The Muslims dated events from the Hegira in A.D. 622. The Orthodox used the Julian, or Old Style, calendar, whereas the Catholics and Protestants adopted the Gregorian, or New Style. In the nineteenth century the Julian calendar ran twelve days behind the Gregorian; in the twentieth century this number increased to thirteen. All dates in this book are in the New Style. The difference in dating produces difficulties principally when a particular day or month is associated with an event. For example, the Serbian Constitution of 1888 was actually passed in January 1889. When such complications arise, they are explained in the text.

For the most part, the footnotes have been limited to identifications of the sources of quotations and of some of the statistical information. The capitalization and spelling of quotations from old sources have been changed to conform to the style of the text. The bibliography is designed to provide the reader with a list of books on various aspects of Balkan history. Books in languages other than English and all articles are excluded, although, of course, these have been used extensively in the preparation of the book.

The author is greatly indebted to her friends and colleagues, specialists in the field, who kindly consented to read the manuscript. Their expert comments and criticisms greatly assisted in the preparation of the final version of the book. All or a major section of the two volumes was read by Professors Richard V. Burks, Wayne State University; Dimitrje Djordjevic, University of California, Santa Barbara; Rufus Fears, Indiana University; John V. A. Fine, Jr., University of Michigan; Keith Hitchins, University of Illinois; Halil Inalcik, University of Chicago; John R. Lampe, University of Maryland; Thomas A. Meininger, York University; John A. Petropulos, Amherst College; Michael B. Petrovich, University of Wisconsin; Dennison I. Rusinow, American Universities Field Staff; Traian Stoianovich, Rutgers University;

and Peter F. Sugar, University of Washington. In addition, this work is in fact the product of the collaboration of the author with her husband, Charles Jelavich, who contributed not only suggestions and criticisms, but also the results of his own research.

The author would like to thank Debbie Chase, who typed the final draft, and Janis Bolster, whose excellent editorial reading and valuable suggestions added much to the manuscript in its final stages of preparation. She also compiled the index. The maps were prepared by William Jaber.

# Introduction

ALTHOUGH THIS VOLUME OF BALKAN HISTORY commences formally at the beginning of the twentieth century, the reader should be aware of the immense influence of past events, including those of classical and medieval times, on contemporary developments. For example, the modern Greek and Romanian national movements look back for inspiration to ancient Greece and Rome. The Albanians of today lay emphasis on their Illyrian ancestry. The Slavic invasions of the sixth through the eighth centuries brought these people into the peninsula as permanent settlers. For the great majority of Balkan inhabitants the conversion to Christianity and the subsequent division of the church after 1054 provided both elements of unity and cohesion and causes of mutual distrust and animosity. In the Middle Ages the Byzantine, Serbian, and Bulgarian empires were states of considerable power and prestige. The thousand-year Byzantine civilization left a deep imprint on Balkan culture. Independent or autonomous political entities, under their own kings, princes, or noble leaders, arose also in Croatia, Bosnia, Albania, Wallachia, Moldavia, and Transylvania in this early period. In approaching twentieth-century Balkan history it is thus essential to remember that all of these people have deep historical roots in the ancient and medieval periods, when they lived under their own rulers, despite their subsequent long period of domination by outside powers.

For the entire history of the peninsula perhaps the deepest mark was left by the five hundred years of Ottoman occupation. By the end of the fifteenth century the Ottoman Empire had gained control of the territory now held by the modern states. Despite this subjugation, the methods of government and the attitude of the Muslim conquerors in fact preserved a feeling of identity among the Christian population. The Ottoman rulers regarded themselves as representing not a national, but a religious, organization. By converting to Islam, any individual among the conquered could become a member of the privileged section of society. Those who retained their faith were indeed not regarded as equals, but they were allowed a great deal of self-government through their churches and their institutions of local government. Under the millet system the majority of the Balkan people, being Orthodox, were under the jurisdiction of their church authorities, of which the most important was

I

the Patriarchate of Constantinople. In general, local communities ran their own affairs under the direction of their traditional leaders. The preconquest Balkan aristocracy had been eliminated except in a few areas, such as Bosnia, Albania, and Crete, where some converted to Islam and thus preserved their privileges. Ottoman officials held the major government offices in the peninsula and controlled the police and, with limitations, the legal system. The Muslim population provided the soldiers for the army, although, at least in the early period, many of these were in fact Christian converts to Islam.

Although this system of administration was in effect in the greater part of the peninsula, different conditions existed in certain border provinces and in the lands that fell under Habsburg control by the beginning of the eighteenth century. The Danubian Principalities of Wallachia and Moldavia always retained a special status. Transylvania, Croatia-Slavonia, and the Vojvodina were similarly to have distinctive governments. In these areas a Christian aristocracy was able to retain a predominant influence, even though in places – Transylvania, for instance – it might not be of the same nationality as the majority of the population.

Most of the Balkan people were peasants who supported themselves by animal husbandry or agriculture. In the lands under direct Ottoman administration they could be sharecroppers or farm laborers on the estates of Muslim or Christian landowners, or they could hold land on what were in practice conditions of virtually free ownership. All were subjected to numerous taxes, whose high rates and methods of collection caused extreme dissatisfaction among both the Muslim and the Christian people. In areas where a native aristocracy existed peasant conditions could in fact be worse than in the other regions. Here the peasants were usually serfs, although most were freed from this bondage in the eighteenth century. Questions of land tenure and taxation were a major cause of social unrest throughout all of the lands under study.

The Treaty of Karlowitz of 1699 provides a convenient landmark with which to begin the modern history of the Balkan peninsula. In this agreement the Ottoman Empire surrendered important territories to Christian powers on a permanent basis. At this time the Habsburg Empire acquired Transylvania, Croatia, and Slavonia, as well as other lands; Venice took Dalmatia and the Peloponnesus. Throughout the eighteenth century the Ottoman Empire waged repeated wars with the European powers, in particular with Russia and the Habsburg Empire, which were usually in alliance. The Balkan lands were also involved in the campaigns of the French Revolution and Napoleon. However, despite the many wars, relatively little Balkan territory changed hands on a long-term basis during this time. In 1775 the Habsburg Empire acquired Bukovina; in 1797 it gained Dalmatia and Istria, annexations that were confirmed in the Vienna settlement of 1815. Russia received Bessarabia in the Treaty of Bucharest of 1812, which brought to an end a century of successful

Russian endeavors to acquire lands north of the Black Sea. In 1815 Britain gained control of the Ionian Islands, which were held until 1863.

The wars of the eighteenth century, although the results were usually to the detriment of the Ottoman overlord, brought few advantages to the Balkan people. Instead, they saw large sections of their lands devastated. In addition, the conflicts had the negative result of involving the European great powers – Britain, France, Russia, the Habsburg Empire, and, on some issues, Prussia – in the events of the Near East. This situation arose not so much because of the conditions within the peninsula as because of the highly strategic position of these lands, especially the Turkish Straits, in world affairs. Not only were Russia and the Habsburg Empire, the neighboring states, determined to protect their interests on their sensitive Balkan borders, but Britain and France, the great imperial powers, were deeply concerned about the balance of power in the Mediterranean, where they had often conflicting interests. Involved in a wider arena, Russia and Britain throughout the nineteenth century were in competition for lands and influence along a broad band of territory running through China, the northern borderlands of India, Afghanistan, Persia, and the Ottoman Empire. Regarding the Ottoman state as a valuable check on Russian expansion in the Near East, the British government usually attempted to maintain its territorial integrity. The Habsburg Empire held a similar view. In contrast, both Russia and France, at least in some crises, were more sympathetic to the national movements. The question of the fate of the Ottoman lands, referred to in the diplomacy of the period as the Eastern Question, was perhaps the major cause of European international controversy in the century from 1815 to 1914.

With the European powers divided, it can be understood why the major initiative for the ending of Ottoman control over the peninsula came from the Christian population itself. Although the leaders of each national movement called for outside assistance, their actions had their basis in domestic considerations. By the end of the eighteenth century conditions were favorable for revolutionary activity. In a period of decline at the center, the Ottoman authorities lost their ability to control the actions of some of the provincial authorities. In these years, and through the first decades of the nineteenth century, anarchy and outlawry ruled in many regions. For the Balkan people the activities of Ali Pasha of Janina and Pasvanoglu of Vidin were particularly important. In addition, by this time many of the ideas associated with the French Revolution, in particular liberalism and nationalism, had penetrated into the Balkans, especially among those groups having connections with the rest of Europe.

The first national revolution, that of the Serbs in 1804, arose directly from the failure of the Ottoman government to curb provincial disorder. Under the first leader, Karadjordje, it turned from a revolt against corrupt local authorities to a movement for national independence. Although Karadjordje

3

was defeated, a second insurrection in 1815, headed by Miloš Obrenović, succeeded in obtaining favorable conditions from the Ottoman government. By 1830 Serbia had attained an autonomous status in the empire. Miloš was forced to abdicate as prince in 1839, when he was succeeded by his sons, first Milan and then Michael. In 1842 Michael was replaced by Alexander Karadjordjević, a son of the revolutionary leader. By this time a bitter controversy over the throne had arisen between the two families. In 1858 Alexander was overthrown and Miloš was recalled for a short reign. After his death he was followed in 1860 by Michael for a second term. When this prince was assassinated in 1868, his cousin Milan became prince.

The second national revolution occurred in Greece and attracted wide attention and sympathy throughout the Christian world. The rebellion had two centers: first, the Danubian Principalities and second, the Greek mainland, in particular the Peloponnesus and Rumeli. Although the revolt in the Romanian lands was crushed, the Greek leaders had more success in Greece proper. After the interference of the powers and after the defeat of the Ottoman Empire in a war with Russia, an independent Greek state was established in 1830, although the territory allotted to it represented only a fourth of the lands inhabited by Greeks. The great powers determined that the first government should be monarchical, and they chose the second son of the king of Bavaria, Othon (Otto), as king.

The third national movement, that of the Romanians in Wallachia and Moldavia, obtained few notable successes until the second half of the century. In 1821, in association with the Greek revolt of that year, Tudor Vladimirescu led an insurrection whose prime aims were more social than political in direction. When he came into conflict with the Greek leadership, he was assassinated and his army disbanded. In 1848 a Wallachian attempt to set up an independent administration, initiated by a liberal, revolutionary leadership, was crushed by a Russian and Ottoman occupation. A great improvement in the political position of the Principalities came only after 1856, when Russia was defeated in the Crimean War. Thereafter, primarily with French aid, the Romanian leaders were able to secure the election of a single prince, Alexander Cuza, for both Wallachia and Moldavia. He then united the administrations and legislatures of the two provinces. During Cuza's reign important reforms to improve the condition of the peasants were introduced. In 1866 this prince was overthrown and Charles of Hohenzollern-Sigmaringen, a member of the Catholic branch of the Prussian royal family, was chosen as ruler.

By the 1860s, therefore, Serbian, Greek, and Romanian national endeavors had achieved a great measure of success. An independent Greece and an autonomous Serbia and Romania had been established. In addition, in the rugged mountains of the western Balkans, another state, Montenegro, under its own rulers, was in existence. Orthodox in religion and Serbian in nationality, the Montenegrin people enjoyed relative independence, largely because of

the poverty and remoteness of their lands. The relationship of the government with Constantinople varied over the years, but the great powers considered the country an Ottoman dependency.

Although all of these states thus achieved a high degree of separation from
Ottoman control, in so doing they fell under increasing great-power influence. Independent Greece was by treaty endowed with three protectors –
Britain, France, and Russia – which could and did interfere constantly in its
internal affairs. After 1826 Russia became the protecting power for Romania
and Serbia. Its representatives in the Danubian Principalities, in particular,
attempted to guide and influence domestic policy. After 1856 the powers signatory to the Treaty of Paris of that year took over the role of guarantors not
only for Serbia and the Danubian Principalities, but also for the Balkan
Christians in general.

Once established, the governments, with the exception of Montenegro's,
followed a similar pattern. Following Western European institutions, they all
acquired constitutions: Serbia first in 1838, Greece in 1844, and Romania in
1866. In general, these documents provided for a strong executive and limited
the franchise to the wealthier and more powerful elements of the society. The
legislatures thus represented primarily their interests. Political parties, based
on loose combinations of individuals with similar aims, also emerged. Usually designated "Liberal" and "Conservative," they fought over issues such as
the relative power of the executive and the legislature, the franchise, and who
should staff the government offices. Much corruption characterized all the
regimes. As far as internal organization was concerned, the new national leaders,
admirers of French administrative practice, favored a strongly centralized system. Power and influence were accordingly taken from the village communities and the local leaders, to the detriment of the interests of the peasant
majorities.

Faced with opposition and rebellion from within and with attacks and
interference from the great powers, the Ottoman government, often referred
to as the Porte, made determined attempts to halt the disintegration of the
empire. From the eighteenth century on the necessity for reform was recognized. The first important measures were taken during the reign of Mahmud
II (1808–1839). The great period of reform, that of the Tanzimat, lasted from
the beginning of the reign of Abdul Mejid in 1839 to 1878, when Abdul Hamid
II suspended the recently introduced constitution and began a period of autocratic rule. Despite the great efforts made in these years and thereafter to
improve the administrative efficiency and military capabilities of the state, the
Ottoman leaders were unable to halt the empire's decline in international
standing or to maintain the integrity of its territories. Nor could they formulate a program of sufficient strength or appeal to combat successfully the
nationalist propaganda of the militant Balkan Christian leaderships.

Meanwhile, national issues had become a major problem in the Habsburg
Empire. By 1815 the monarchy held large areas populated in the majority by

Romanians and South Slavs. A Romanian population, primarily Orthodox in religion and, of course, sharing a similar language with the people of the Danubian Principalities, lived in Transylvania and in parts of Bukovina. Of the South Slavic people, the Croats, Serbs, and Slovenes, the Croats and Serbs shared a common literary language, but were divided by religion. The Croats and Slovenes, both Catholics, were separated by their differing languages. The Slovenes, whose national movement will be described in Chapter 2, lived primarily in Carniola and Styria; the Croats were to be found principally in Dalmatia, Croatia, and Slavonia; and the Serbs lived mainly in the Vojvodina and in the southern border areas of Croatia and Slavonia.

Of these people the Croats in Croatia and Slavonia enjoyed the best political position. With a strong historical background, looking back to the Triune Kingdom of the medieval period, whose lands had included Dalmatia and much of Bosnia as well as Croatia and Slavonia, the Croats had certain autonomous rights, although their definition was a matter of continuous controversy with both the Habsburg and the Hungarian authorities. The relationship of the Catholic Croats to the Orthodox Serbs, who composed about a fourth of the population of the regions in question, also was to become a major problem, as will be discussed subsequently.

The situation in Transylvania was quite different. There the Romanian, Orthodox majority of the population was effectively blocked from political influence. The control of the province lay in the hands of the Hungarians; of the Szeklers, who were related to the Hungarians and spoke the same language; and of the Germans, called Saxons, descendants of twelfth-century immigrants. The Catholic, Lutheran, Calvinist, and Unitarian churches were recognized, but not the Orthodox. In the eighteenth century a Uniate church was established, which attracted some Romanians and played an important cultural role. The Orthodox church and its leaders, in particular Bishop Andreiu Şaguna, were an even greater influence on the Romanian movement in the province.

In 1866 the Habsburg Empire faced a grave internal crisis: the defeat by Prussia excluded it from a major role in German affairs and resulted also in the loss of Venetia, its last major Italian possession. Challenged by the growing claims of the national minorities, the central authorities came to an agreement with the strongest and most vocal of the nationalities, the Hungarians. In the Ausgleich, or Compromise, of 1867 the empire was divided into two sections, which will be referred to subsequently as Austria, with the center in Vienna, and Hungary, with the capital in Budapest. Of the regions with which we are primarily concerned, Dalmatia, Bukovina, and the Slovene lands fell under Austrian authority; Croatia, Slavonia, the Vojvodina, and Transylvania were assigned to Hungary. Franz Joseph stood at the head of both sections, but he was emperor in Austria and king in Hungary. A central authority existed in Vienna, but its duties were limited to foreign affairs, the military, and finance (the third having jurisdiction over only the first two offices). The major problems in the empire until 1914 centered around the difficulties caused by this new political arrangement.

By 1870 the Habsburg Monarchy had thus undergone a radical reorganization; and the Ottoman Empire, despite numerous efforts at reform, had lost effective control of a major portion of the Balkan peninsula. In addition, by this year a Bulgarian national movement had taken shape. Here the first target of the leadership had been the Greek cultural and political control. Some local revolts had also taken place. In 1870 the Bulgarian position was strengthened when an Exarchate, separate from the Greek-dominated Patriarchate, was established to represent Bulgarian religious interests. Thereafter a sharp struggle to gain members ensued between the two ecclesiastical organizations. The major Bulgarian uprising took place in 1876, with its center in the Balkan Mountains. Although this revolt was suppressed with an enormous loss of life, many of its aims were to be achieved within the next two years as a result of other events.

In 1875 a revolt broke out in Bosnia and Hercegovina. The cause lay in the peasants' grievances against their landlords, who were Muslim but of Serbo-Croatian language and nationality. Despite the efforts of the Ottoman government and the great powers, this rebellion could not be subdued. In the summer of 1876 Serbia and Montenegro, taking advantage of a turbulent situation, declared war on the Ottoman Empire. A major international crisis arose, which reached a climax when Russia declared war in April 1877. Once victory had been won over the Ottoman armies, the Russian government was able to impose the Treaty of San Stefano in March 1878. This agreement, which upset the balance of power in the peninsula among both the Balkan states and the great powers, had as its principal achievement the creation of a large Bulgarian state whose lands embraced Macedonia and Thrace as well as those of present-day Bulgaria. The reaction of the powers, in particular Britain and Austria-Hungary, was so strong that Russia was forced to accede to a new settlement that was decided upon at the Congress of Berlin, held in June and July 1878.

The Congress of Berlin is an important landmark in the formation of the Balkan national states. The treaty drawn up at this time is perhaps the most significant single document for the national liberation movements. Three states, Romania, Serbia, and Montenegro, joined Greece as independent nations. An autonomous Bulgaria was also established, but with a much reduced territory. The San Stefano state was divided into three sections: an autonomous Bulgaria in the lands north of the Balkan Mountains; a semiautonomous province, Eastern Rumelia, to the south; and Macedonia, which was returned to Ottoman rule. Serbia and Montenegro each gained some territory. In 1881, as part of the general settlement, Greece obtained Thessaly and part of Epirus.

The great powers also took rewards. Austria-Hungary was given the right to administer and occupy Bosnia and Hercegovina and occupy the Sanjak of

Novi Pazar, a strip of land separating Serbia and Montenegro. Russia took back from Romania three districts of southern Bessarabia lost in 1856; Romania in compensation received southern Dobrudja. Britain, in a separate agreement, compelled the Ottoman Empire to agree to its occupation of Cyprus.

In addition, the Ottoman defeat and the terms of the settlement forced the Albanians to organize and to examine their relationship with the Ottoman Empire. In the majority Muslim, and separated from the other Balkan people by racial background and language, the Albanians had previously fought for local autonomy, but they had not seriously challenged Ottoman sovereignty, at least in the modern period. When the congress awarded Albanian-inhabited lands to Montenegro, the League of Prizren was formed in their defense. Henceforth, the great powers and the other Balkan states had to take Albanian claims into account.

None of the Balkan states was satisfied with the Berlin settlement. The Bulgarian leaders in particular were deeply disappointed about the dismemberment of the San Stefano state. Nonetheless, they devoted the first years after the congress to the establishment of state institutions. Since Russia had been tacitly accepted by the powers as the Bulgarian protector, Russian officials played a major role in the accomplishment of this task. A prince, Alexander of Battenberg, was named by the powers and a constitution adopted. In 1885 a revolt in Eastern Rumelia resulted in the unification of that province with Bulgaria. This event caused an international crisis and a break between the government and its Russian patron. In 1886 Alexander was forced to abdicate, and a new prince, Ferdinand of Coburg, was chosen. He ruled at first in close association with his influential minister Stephen Stambolov, but after Stambolov's assassination, Ferdinand played the major role in state affairs. He was soon able to reestablish good relations with Russia.

Despite its great losses, the Ottoman Empire, under the rule of Abdul Hamid II after 1876, still held Macedonian, Thracian, and Albanian lands, and the island of Crete. Moreover, in theory it held sovereignty over autonomous Bulgaria and Habsburg-occupied Bosnia and Hercegovina. No Balkan government expected this situation to last: each had claims on these areas. Greece looked forward to acquiring Macedonia, Thrace, and all of Epirus; Serbia too looked southward to Macedonia. Moreover, most Serbs were firmly convinced that Bosnia and Hercegovina were rightfully theirs. For Bulgaria the San Stefano boundaries marked the correct borders for the state. Albanian leaders similarly looked to a future when they could unify the regions occupied by their people. Although Romania had no serious claims to Ottoman territory, the nationalists hoped that at some time Transylvania and Bessarabia, both in great-power possession, would be joined to their nation.

In the eighteenth and nineteenth centuries, as we have seen, the great powers directed a great deal of attention toward Balkan events. However, after 1887 they were more concerned with other areas; a major Balkan crisis was not to recur until 1908. In 1887, largely as a result of the Bulgarian affair, the Three Emperors' Alliance, which joined Germany, Russia, and Austria-Hungary, was broken. By the end of the century the Continent was divided into two major alliance systems: the Triple Alliance of Germany, Austria-Hungary, and Italy and the Russo-French Alliance. At this time none of these powers wished another Balkan crisis; all were involved in imperial expansion or in meeting their internal problems. For a period the Balkan peninsula was out of the international spotlight.

Although all of the Balkan states had territorial objectives, their major immediate problems were connected with the necessity of internal economic development and improvements in the living conditions of their people. The national leaders were acutely conscious of the economic backwardness of the region, and they were aware that radical advances were necessary both for the welfare of the population and for defense. Attention was thus directed increasingly to the social and economic issues, which had been relatively neglected in the era when first national liberation had to be achieved and then new independent or autonomous political institutions had to be organized.

# PART I

# War and national consolidation, 1887–1941

# 1

## *The Balkan national monarchies*

THE MAJOR GOAL of the Balkan national liberation movements was largely obtained by the end of the nineteenth century. Much of the peninsula was under the control of native governments (see Map 1). Ottoman rule was limited to Thrace, Macedonia, Epirus, and Albania. Although Bosnia, Hercegovina, and Bulgaria were still theoretically Ottoman possessions, the Ottoman Empire had no voice in their administration. The conclusion of the revolutionary era and the establishment of the national regimes in the peninsula, however, in no sense decreased the problems of Balkan social and economic life. Indeed, in some areas the difficulties of national freedom overshadowed those of Ottoman dependency. A major question concerned finances. The independent states had to bear the full burden of the costs of defense, internal administration, and foreign representation, at least some of which had previously been carried by the Porte. Equally important, as the century progressed and the industrial revolution brought a radical change in European standards of living, the Balkan leadership too revised its goals. With the most technologically advanced sections of the world as their model, successive Balkan governments and the wealthier members of their societies sought to introduce into these backward lands the most modern of European achievements. For this period, the building of railroads and the acquisition of military equipment was to have the first priority in most of the countries.

Unfortunately, none of the states had the economic base for the accomplishment of their aims. First and foremost, there was little domestic capital to invest in new enterprises. The entire peninsula was extremely poor. In the past, wealthy men had preferred to place their earnings in land or in the purchase of state offices, such as the position of tax farmer. More prestige was attached to landholding and official posts than to commercial ventures. In this situation, only two other sources of funds were available: taxation and foreign loans. With an impoverished peasant majority, most governments faced extreme limitations on the amount of taxes that could be collected. The fate of states that relied on outside loans was to be illustrated by the Ottoman and Greek economic disasters.

The economic weakness and the huge expenditures that had to be met forced the independent regimes to face immediately the problem of the in-

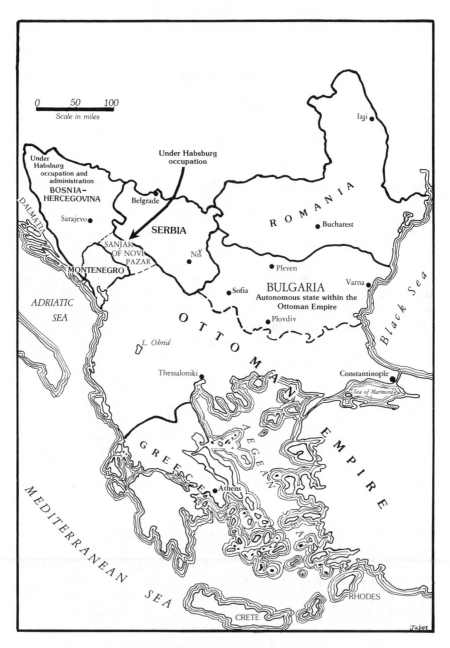

Map 1. The Balkan peninsula in 1900

volvement of the state in the economic life of the country. Decisions had to be made concerning the role to be assumed by the central government in national development and the direction in which the chief efforts were to be made. The situation was complicated by the heritage of corruption in politics. The temptation was great for the influential members of the governments to use their positions for economic gain. The tendency in all of the states to emphasize military preparedness and national expansion over internal development was also to have a tremendous effect on the economic health of the region. Equally important was the fact that all of the governments failed to pay adequate attention to the concerns and interests of the peasantry or to give adequate support to the agricultural sections of their economies.[1]

## ECONOMIC DEVELOPMENTS

### The agricultural base

In the years before World War I agrarian conditions failed to improve at a satisfactory rate. Instead, the urban population was the main beneficiary of any economic advances, and the peasant was exposed to new sacrifices. This situation was largely due to factors outside the control of both the national governments and the general population. As has been previously emphasized, these were peasant societies: in Serbia and Bulgaria at this time 80 percent of the population was engaged in agriculture; the figure for Romania was 75 percent; and that for Greece was 60 percent. Any chance that these people had for an improvement in their living standards was negated by the rapid increase of population that occurred at this time. From the 1860s until the first decade of the next century the numbers more than doubled. For instance, in 1878 Serbia had a population of 1.7 million, a figure that rose to 2.9 million by 1910. Bulgaria and Eastern Rumelia had 2.8 million people in 1881 and 4.3 million in 1910. The Romanian lands had about 1.5 million in 1815 and 6.9 million in 1910. Figures for the other areas rose proportionally. The increase appears to have been due in part to a reduction of the death rate, but the birth rate remained high. There was also a large immigration from neighboring Ottoman territory.

This increase meant, of course, that the land had to support more people. The life of the peasant was made worse by another contemporary development. With the building of the railroads in the American West, wheat from the prairies began to enter the European market. Russian grain was purchased in Germany, and Australia too became a source of supply. With the

---

1 For Balkan economic conditions in this period the reader should consult Iván T. Berend and György Ránki, *Economic Development in East-Central Europe in the Nineteenth and Twentieth Centuries* (New York: Columbia University Press, 1974); and John R. Lampe and Marvin R. Jackson, *Balkan Economic History, 1550–1950* (Bloomington: Indiana University Press, 1982).

availability of cheap transportation facilities and improved methods of production, agricultural products became more abundant on world markets and prices dropped. The Balkan peasant, with the decreasing amount of land available to each individual and with the rise of foreign competition, faced an ever-worsening situation.

Similar problems had, of course, been met in other parts of the world. The solutions adopted had usually been three: agricultural methods could be improved so that the products offered would be more competitive; the industrialization of the country could provide alternate employment for the surplus agricultural population; or a mass emigration to other lands could take place. Before World War I the third choice was most prevalent in many of the Balkan and Habsburg regions with which we are concerned. Beginning in the 1890s these areas – for example, Greece and the Croatian lands of the Habsburg Empire – provided hundreds of thousands of new citizens to the less-populated parts of the world, in particular to the United States.

Despite this outlet, the Balkan governments still had to deal with the problem. Although they all shared certain common difficulties, they chose different methods of coping with them. Most important was the fact that land was distributed in different ways in the various states. Great estates worked by sharecroppers predominated in Romania, whereas small peasant holdings were characteristic of Serbia and Bulgaria. Montenegro and Greece, with a shortage of arable land, were forced either to import food or to export people. A further examination of conditions in these areas will illustrate how each government and society met the continuing agrarian crises.

In Romania, despite the measures taken in the reign of Cuza to provide each peasant with a plot, the landholding aristocracy had been able to maintain its predominant position in the economic as well as the political life of the state. With the increase in the peasant population, accompanied by the inevitable subdivision of the plots, and with the loss of their holdings by the poorer members of the population, a situation arose in which 85 percent of the peasantry had either no land or so little that they had to rent additional plots or work elsewhere. Estates of more than 247 acres (100 hectares) controlled over 55 percent of the land; five thousand large estates held half of the arable land.

In other European states the concentration of landownership had usually led to an improvement in the methods of production. Large farms were better suited to the introduction of the new and expensive farm machinery and to scientific methods. In Romania, however, such possible advantages were seldom utilized. Instead, the majority of the landowners preferred to let out their estates to agents or stewards, who in turn would sublease the lands to peasants on sharecropping arrangements. At the turn of the century it has been estimated that about 60 percent of the estates of more than 247 acres were farmed by this method. The system was not conducive to a rational use of the land or to social harmony. The steward was naturally primarily interested in making a quick and high profit from his investment. He had no stake in long-term improvements. The peasant sharecropper, as in the past, provided the primitive tools and the animals used in cultivating the soil. In Romania the relationship between peasants and stewards was complicated by the fact that many of the latter were Jewish, a variation that introduced a religious and national element into an intrinsically strained situation.

Despite these conditions Romania did provide a large crop for export. At the beginning of the nineteenth century the Principalities had chiefly emphasized livestock raising. The animals were pastured in the hill and mountain areas or in the common land of the estates. With the growth of demand in the industrializing West, the emphasis gradually shifted. After 1870 there was no more uncultivated land available, and most common land had passed into private hands. From 1860 to 1900 the area devoted to grain cultivation doubled; livestock production then dropped sharply. Wheat and corn provided 80 percent of the grains grown; of these about half the wheat and 40 percent of the corn crop were exported. Corn became the basis of the diet of the peasant, to the detriment of general health standards.

In Serbia and Bulgaria virtually the opposite situation existed. Estates of over 247 acres accounted for only 5 percent of the total land. A farm of about 5 acres was regarded as the minimum needed to support a family; 70 percent of the households held at least this amount. Despite this even division of land, conditions of rural impoverishment existed. In both Serbia and Bulgaria the inheritance laws provided for the equal division of the land among all of the children; the result was the prevalence of small plots. The peasant saw the acquisition of more land as the solution to his problem. Living in conditions of poverty, the peasant families could afford only the most primitive implements. In Bulgaria, for instance, only 10 percent of the peasants used iron plows by 1900. There were also few attempts made to educate the peasant to improve his methods of cultivation. The independent national states were not to adopt wide programs of agricultural improvement until after World War I.

Although Serbia and Bulgaria had similar landholding systems, they differed in some of the problems they faced. The Bulgarian peasant, in acquiring former Muslim-held lands, was required to pay a redemption fee; the Serbian government had simply taken the Ottoman land. The individual peasant families in both states were largely self-sufficient, but they needed to raise crops for the market to gain the cash income necessary to pay taxes and buy the colonial and manufactured products they desired. Their products were sold on the local market and were the basis of the foreign trade of this country. In the nineteenth century livestock export, particularly hogs, was the most important item in the Serbian commerce; the major market was the Habsburg Monarchy. Although at first the hogs were driven across the border, later more attention was given to food processing, in particular to the production of lard and bacon. Serbian peasants also had an outlet for their plums and prunes in Germany and the Habsburg Empire. Bulgaria, in contrast, with a less favorable geographic situation, exported primarily wheat.

The Greek problem was particularly difficult. With only 20 percent of the land arable, the rise in population was very hard to handle. In 1881, with the acquisition of Thessaly, Greece did gain a rich agricultural region. An area of large estates, formerly under Muslim control, these lands passed usually into the hands of Greek large landowners. They were worked generally on a share-cropping basis by peasants who surrendered from a third to a half of their produce. The other regions of Greece were characterized by small subsistence farming. The lack of adequate land forced Greece to import wheat to feed its people. The problem of producing an export crop remained. In the late nineteenth century the single largest item of export consisted of currants (raisins); just before World War I tobacco assumed an increasingly important position.

With these conditions it can be understood why the general situation of the agricultural population throughout the Balkans was very bad indeed. In all of these areas the average peasant families were able to do little more than produce enough to feed themselves and to provide a small surplus for state taxation and for the purchase of a limited number of items that they could not make themselves. The economic backwardness of the countryside naturally severely limited the activities and power of the national governments, which depended on this depressed rural population for taxes and healthy recruits for the growing armies. During the Ottoman period the chief complaints against the government had been the high level of taxation and the methods of collection. If anything, the taxes under the independent administrations rose. The methods of collection were also more efficient and often as brutal and corrupt as before. The tax level was very high. For instance, it has been estimated that between 1879 and 1911 the Bulgarian peasant paid 15 to 20 percent of his earnings in taxes. This amount was extremely burdensome for a population living near the subsistence level.

In return, the rural taxpayer received very little from the central government. Of course, it can be argued that a strong army was to the benefit of every individual citizen. Nevertheless, beyond the provision for local administration and the police, the central regimes showed little positive interest in basic peasant problems. In this connection, however, it should be emphasized that national agricultural planning or the provision of special services to peasants was not an attribute common to any nation at the time. No Western government, on which the Balkan regimes were modeled, provided comprehensive programs of this kind. Although it was obvious that Balkan peasants would have benefited from government-sponsored agricultural extension services, irrigation and water control projects, and general financial assistance, few Balkan leaders would have considered these activities a necessary sphere of state activity. Nor did the states have the financial resources for truly effective intervention in the life of the rural population.

With the rising population and the repeated subdivision of the land, the Balkan peasant thus faced a bleak future. There was little he could do to help himself. Easy agricultural credits might have enabled him to improve his land, purchase better equipment, and increase his production. Loans on reasonable terms were not, unfortunately, readily available. Peasant indebtedness was a common problem throughout the peninsula. Loans were usually taken out simply to carry a family from one season to another. They were thus used not to improve the farms, but to meet tax payments and other vital expenses. Since they were generally contracted on usurious terms, the payments could keep a family permanently in debt. In the absence of central agricultural banks, the peasant usually borrowed from local merchants, wealthy landowners, and village notables. When it is remembered that these men had influence in the local political system, the vulnerability of the peasant to financial abuse is apparent.

The lack of political power or real representation in the government was certainly the basic weakness of the peasant position by the late nineteenth century. One of the major results of the formation of the national governments had been the destruction of local self-government and the creation of a bureaucratic class that proved exceedingly unsympathetic to the problems of the rural areas, from which its families often originated. Under the national regimes the peasants were effectively controlled through the restrictive franchises or through police intervention in the elections. Only two of the important political parties, the Serbian Radical Party and the Bulgarian Agrarian Union, both of which were under the leadership of middle-class intellectuals and politicians, even in theory attempted to speak for the peasant.

Throughout the Balkans the peasants themselves could offer only one answer to their problems: they wanted more land. Where large estates and government lands were in existence, they called for their division. The ideal everywhere was the establishment of small individual family farms. The problems connected with the rising population figures, the poor methods of cultivation, and the lack of adequate markets, even if production should increase, were simply not understood in the countryside. Moreover, the peasants as a group proved unable to organize politically to become an effective force in the government. Nor could they carry through the few efforts they made to organize rebellions. Although there were frequent demonstrations and much rural unrest, they achieved no important successes. The one major agrarian revolt, that in Romania in 1907, was crushed. The police and the army of the national regimes proved far more effective than the Ottoman authorities had been in suppressing and discouraging peasant rebellion.

### Industrial development

Problems of overpopulation and insufficient agricultural land had been met in places other than the Balkans by industrialization. At the end of the nineteenth century, unfortunately, the Balkan peninsula lacked some of the most important attributes for a major effort at industrialization. First, the new national states were deficient in many of the raw materials, notably coal and iron, that had provided the basis for the development of heavy industry in countries such as Britain, Germany, and the United States. Second, the lack of domestic capital has already been mentioned. The massive sums necessary could be obtained only by loans from abroad, but the Balkans were not an attractive field for investment at the time. It was possible to borrow, but the terms were not favorable (except under certain circumstances – for instance, when governments sought to use the money to pay for European arms or for railroad construction). A third hindrance to industrial development was the weak internal market. The urban population was less than 20 percent in Romania, Bulgaria, and Serbia and 30 percent in Greece. The great peasant majority purchased few manufactured goods; most items could still be produced at home or obtained from a local artisan. Fourth, and perhaps most important, the population lacked skills. Although we have seen that many Balkan people took part in domestic and foreign commerce, there was still no large sector of the population with the technical training necessary to organize modern enterprises. Ottoman societies had not fostered or honored such occupations. Even more serious was the shortage of trained craftsmen or men who could readily master the technological skills necessary for the new industrial techniques. The experience and education needed had not been available. When new projects such as the building of railroads were embarked upon, foreign advisers, managers, and even workmen had to be imported.

At first, new Balkan enterprises were faced with the problem of foreign competition. Because of the treaties between the Ottoman Empire and the European great powers, the autonomous governments had to abide by these restricting agreements and limit their tariffs. Native industry, particularly textiles, could not compete under these conditions. One of the first aims of the independent or fully autonomous regimes, like Romania's in the 1870s, was to negotiate new arrangements. Tariffs were to continue to be a major issue between the Balkan states and the European governments and to lead to repeated crises. The question of the level of protection to be given manufactured goods was not an easy one to resolve. The Balkan nations needed to export their agricultural surpluses, and therefore they often had to accept conditions unfavorable to domestic industrial development in order to assure the continuation of their markets.

Despite the difficult situation some industries did develop, particularly in the areas of food processing, textiles, and construction materials. Food processing was naturally vital for this agricultural area. Flour mills and breweries were opened; meat-packing plants, particularly for the handling of pork products, were important. The sugar industry, based on sugar beets, developed in each state except Greece. The extensive building, particularly in the

Problems: ag
industrial
no loans

new capital cities, led to the demand for construction materials, including cement, glass, and lumber.

The fate of textile manufacturing varied throughout the century. There was an important native cloth industry based on home production in the Balkan Mountains in the middle of the century. Bulgarian materials had clothed the Ottoman army. Greece too once exported silk and cotton cloth. These centers were not able to meet the competition of foreign, chiefly British and Austrian, machine-produced textiles, but despite these difficult conditions, some cloth and clothing industries did exist.

Of the Balkan states, Romania made the greatest advances. Food processing, with the emphasis on flour and sugar, was the major industry. At the beginning of the twentieth century the oil of the Ploeşti region began to be exploited. Nevertheless, the country remained predominantly agricultural. In 1914 only 1.5 percent of the national wealth was in industry; agricultural products accounted for 75.7 percent of the exports. Bulgaria, Serbia, and Greece, of course, retained their strongly agrarian structures.

### Government action

The Balkan governments were intensely interested in economic development. They well understood its significance for military power and national prestige, and they wished to obtain for themselves the advantages of an industrial society. The great question was how this could be best accomplished. No government of the time thought in terms of a centrally managed economy. The skills, resources, and statistics for such activities were not available, and it is certainly highly unlikely that any sector of the population would have tolerated an unlimited state intervention in economic life such as that which took place after 1945. The peasants in all the countries disliked administrative controls. Nevertheless, the governments did take some steps. Tariffs were introduced, and some aid was given to industry. Internal improvements were made; here the chief attention was paid to the building of railroads, an activity that was also encouraged by the great powers for their own economic and strategic reasons.

Because of the poor condition of the roads and waterways in the Balkans, the railroads could have played an important part in economic development. Their construction started late; by the 1860s, when the major Balkan efforts commenced, the main lines had been completed in Western Europe. The first railroads, running from Constanţa to Cernavoda and from Varna to Ruse, linked Black Sea cities with Danube River ports. These were built by British companies to facilitate their trade interests. The major construction effort was initiated in 1868 when the Ottoman government gave the concession for a line that was ultimately to run from Constantinople through Plovdiv, Sofia, Niš, and Belgrade and then on to Vienna, thus following the historic roadway. The connection between Constantinople and Western Europe was not completed until 1888.

Although all of the Balkan governments were enthusiastic about building railroads, they met with major problems in their financing and construction. Foreign assistance was essential in both. Those who invested in the undertaking were naturally primarily interested in making a profit. The foreign governments that became involved wished to assure that the lines would follow routes that would benefit their own economic and strategic interests. In fact, once in existence, the railroads served to bring in European manufactured goods, which tended to drive out of the domestic market the local handicraft products. Like other aspects of state life, railroad building became the cause of repeated scandals. There was much corruption both in their financing and in their construction. Although the railroads were built by foreign entrepreneurs, they became state-owned. There were no private lines in Bulgaria after 1885, in Romania after 1888, or in Serbia after 1892.

In addition to showing concern over railroad construction, the states gave some limited aid to industrial development. The negotiation of commercial treaties and the question of tariff schedules became a major part of the international relations of all of the governments. Assistance was given to individual industries in the form of tax benefits and the allowance of duty-free imports on machinery, raw materials, and fuels. The states also granted low rates on the railroads, gave free land for factories, and offered government contracts on good terms. In general, the support offered was on a minor scale and was designed to create an atmosphere that would be favorable to the attraction of domestic and foreign investment. Romania, whose Liberal Party emphasized industrial development in its political program, went furthest of the Balkan countries in assisting such undertakings.

With the absence of native capital and expertise, the participation of foreign financiers, businessmen, and technicians was essential for economic progress. In later years, however, their activities were to be strongly criticized. Much current Balkan historiography places the blame for the backward conditions primarily on outside influences, presenting the Ottoman rule as the basic cause of the lack of development and explaining the failure to advance with independence by alleged foreign exploitation and imperialism in the years before World War I. Although much damage was indeed done to native production by foreign competition, the picture should not be made darker than it actually was. Balkan enterprises did not in fact attract massive outside investment; in comparison to the other opportunities offered in these years, the peninsula was not a favorable place in which to make a profit. There was indeed much participation by foreigners in the new enterprises. However, these men often came as experts and managers in fields where the Balkan nationals lacked expertise; many remained permanently in the region and became citizens. Naturally, others came to the Balkans to make profits and to earn their livings. Although many individual instances of exploitation and corruption can be found, the total picture shows evidence of positive contributions to Balkan prosperity and development.

The one area of the national economies that was subject to massive foreign influence was the state loans. The new national governments all followed in the path of the Ottoman Empire and contracted huge debts that proved beyond their capacities to handle and resulted in the establishment of some kind of foreign supervision over their finances. With the gaining of autonomy or independence the national leaders soon discovered that their internal financial resources were not adequate to cover the expenses that they considered necessary for their state. Administrative costs rose rapidly, and, in addition, they needed funds to pay for the large armies and internal improvements, such as railroads. By 1914 the government loans contracted by all of these states had reached heights incommensurate with their real wealth: Bulgaria owed 850 million francs, Serbia 903 million francs, Romania 1.7 billion francs (American billion), and Greece 1.25 billion francs. The payments connected with these debts soon absorbed a large proportion of the national incomes. In Greece and Bulgaria the interest consumed 30 percent of the government revenue. The loans were often attached to political considerations, and the European governments used them to achieve objectives in foreign policy.

These economic questions played a major role in the political life of each state. In the subsequent pages, the political, social, and economic developments unique to each nation are discussed, and issues in foreign policy involving that state's interest are covered. However, because of the great powers' determination to prevent an Eastern crisis from arising, and because of their concentration on other regions of the world, the Balkan peninsula did enjoy a period of comparative peace from the Serbo-Bulgarian war of 1885 until 1912. There were indeed crises, such as the Greek-Turkish war of 1897, the turmoil in Macedonia, and the Habsburg annexation of Bosnia-Hercegovina in 1908, but these did not lead to major conflicts. In general, all of the Balkan governments in this period had the opportunity to turn their attention primarily to their internal political and economic problems.

## ROMANIA

In the years before World War I Romania was the most advanced of the Balkan states. Although still essentially agrarian, it took important steps toward a modern industrial economy. The political situation was also stable. Prince Charles was to prove one of the most successful of the European monarchs. Extremely active in running the government, Charles was concerned with the economic development of the country. During the crisis of 1875–1878 he had been an enthusiastic supporter of the national interests and the achievement of independence. In 1881, with the assent of the Romanian chamber and with the approval of the powers, Romania became a kingdom and Charles took the title of king. Since he had no living children – his only daughter

23

had died in childhood – he named his nephew, Ferdinand of Hohenzollern, as his successor. Ferdinand married Princess Marie of Edinburgh, who was the granddaughter of both Alexander II and Queen Victoria.

Romania was, of course, a constitutional monarchy. The two political parties, the Liberals and the Conservatives, continued to alternate in power. Both were essentially coteries of men with common interests and a desire to hold power in the government. The Conservatives are usually considered the party of the large landowners, with the Liberals representing the professions and the bureaucrats. It appears, however, that the boyars were equally represented in both parties. Certainly the basic conceptions of the two groups were not strikingly different, although they disagreed on some issues. The highly restrictive franchise assured that political control would rest in the hands of a small minority and that the great mass of the peasant population would be excluded from participation in political life.

After the achievement of independence, Charles continued to govern in cooperation with Ion Brătianu and the Liberal Party. The two men had by then worked together for a long period, despite their frequent conflicts. Brătianu had been chiefly responsible for bringing Charles to the throne, and he was to remain the most prominent Romanian statesman until his replacement in 1888. In this period the Conservatives continued in the opposition. A faction known as the Junimists, after the literary movement *Junimea* (Youth), broke away. This group included such prominent political leaders as Peter Carp, Titu Maiorescu, Teodor Rosetti, and Alexander Marghiloman, all of whom were to play major roles in Romanian politics.

In 1884, under Liberal sponsorship, a bill on electoral reform was passed. Although the franchise was made broader, the system of voting by electoral colleges, which served to exclude the majority of the population from real political influence, was retained. Moreover, as previously, the government in power was able to control the elections through patronage and the police. The king could appoint a new ministry of his choice and then dissolve parliament and hold a new election. The government in office could assure itself of a victory in the voting by use of the centralized administrative system, and thus win sufficient support in the chamber. This procedure gave the king a pivotal role between the two parties.

In 1888 the long period of Liberal rule ended with the appointment in March of a Junimist government, which remained in office until 1895, when the Liberals again assumed control. Both Brătianu and Mihail Kogălniceanu, another influential statesman, died in 1891, and the leadership of the party was taken by Dimitrie A. Sturdza. Until World War I the parties alternated in office: the Conservatives were in power from 1899 to 1901, from 1905 to 1907, and from 1911 to 1914; Liberal ministries controlled between 1901 and 1905, from 1907 to 1911, and again at the beginning of 1914. Both parties formed a firm support to the monarchist government and to the social and economic system in existence.

Although the two parties shared many ideas, they did differ over the question of the role of government in the development of industry and over the amount of protection that should be given against foreign competition. In the 1880s, during a period of Liberal control, the entire question became a matter of intense debate. The tariff issue is discussed later in connection with the disputes with the Habsburg Monarchy. On the question of direct aid to industry, a series of laws was enacted of which the most significant was that of May 1887. Firms employing twenty-five or more workers received exemptions from import duties and some state taxes, and they were allowed the use of state lands. No equivalent measures were passed in other states, and this action was an indication of the Romanian government's attempt to encourage industrial development. This period also marks the beginning of the exploitation of the Ploeşti oil deposits, which were to be very important in the future. Here foreign investment – in particular German, Habsburg, Dutch, British, French, Belgian, and American – was to play a major role.

While this attention was devoted to questions of industrialization, conditions on the land became worse. Despite the fact that the peasantry had no direct political influence, the dissatisfaction and unrest in the countryside were known. Most Romanian leaders had some rural property or connections with the agricultural problems. Certain groups, such as the Junimists, showed a concern for peasant issues. Some measures to regulate agricultural contracts were taken by the government, and state land was sold, but no major effort was directed toward meeting the basic difficulties. Peasant rebellions had been common in the past; another occurred in 1888. However, none of these compared to the great uprising of 1907.

The revolt of 1907 appears to have come as a surprise to the government, despite the many previous signals of peasant discontent. The movement commenced in Moldavia in March 1907 and spread throughout the country. As in the time of Tudor Vladimirescu, the peasants burned manor houses and barns. Their violence was turned as much against the stewards as against the landowners themselves, and since many of the stewards were Jewish, the actions had strong anti-Semitic overtones. The revolt was so widespread and involved so many people that the local police forces could not contain it. The government thus called in the regular army, which was commanded by General Alexander Averescu. He put down the rebellion with extreme force, destroying villages and killing at least 10,000 people. About 120,000 soldiers were needed to quell the uprising.

Although the revolt itself failed, it did succeed in calling attention to the bad conditions of peasant life. The chamber subsequently passed some laws to ameliorate the situation. These again took the form of a regulation of the agricultural contracts and the release of more state land, but the basic problem was not met. Nevertheless, by the beginning of World War I there was a growing recognition that the division of the great estates might be necessary and that the government did have a responsibility in regard to the peasant population. This attitude was to prepare the way for the practical measures taken in the 1920s.

In foreign relations Romania faced no major crises until 1913. As earlier, an active foreign policy was not practical, since the Romanian irredentas – Transylvania, Bukovina, and Bessarabia – remained under the control of great powers. The reaction to the Berlin settlement was, as could be expected, highly negative. Southern Bessarabia had been lost, and the boundary drawn in Dobrudja had not met the Romanian claims. Even Romanian independence had been linked to Article XLIV of the Treaty of Berlin, a stipulation requiring the government to accept the condition that "difference in religious beliefs and confessions" should not exclude anyone from the "enjoyment of civil and political rights, admission to public employments, functions, honors, or the exercise of the various professions and industries in any locality whatsoever."[2] Similar provisions had been attached to the sections of the treaty relating to Serbia and Eastern Rumelia, where they protected principally the Muslim inhabitants of those regions. In Romania the regulation affected primarily the status of the Jews.

At the beginning of the nineteenth century, the Danubian Principalities had no problem with minorities as such. Their population was in the vast majority Romanian in nationality and Orthodox in religion. This situation changed, however, in the second half of the century, when Russian Jews moved in ever-increasing numbers into the Habsburg Empire and the Principalities. In 1859 about 118,000 Jews lived in Moldavia and 9,200 in Wallachia. By 1899 the number had increased to 210,000 in Moldavia and 68,000 in Wallachia. They thus formed a minority of about a quarter of a million in a population of 6 million. The constitution of 1866 provided that the only foreigners who could become citizens were those belonging to the Christian faith. Jews were also prevented from buying rural property. Because of these limitations, they tended to congregate in the large cities, particularly in Bucharest and Iaşi, where they took up occupations such as that of merchant or small trader. In the countryside they could be found as stewards on large estates, as owners of inns selling alcoholic drinks, and as moneylenders – occupations that could bring them into conflict with the peasant population. The stipulations of the Berlin Treaty, which contravened the provisions of the constitution, thus required a special act of the assembly. Most Romanian leaders regarded the measure as an unwarranted interference in their internal affairs, an issue on which they were particularly sensitive. In fact, the government never fully complied with the intent of the treaty. In 1879, under great pressure, it was agreed that Jews could become naturalized citizens, but special action would have to be taken on each individual case. The Jewish question was to remain controversial and to cause many problems in the future.

2 The text of the Berlin treaty is printed in W. N. Medlicott, *The Congress of Berlin and After* (London: Methuen, 1938), pp. 409–419.

Romanian dissatisfaction with the Berlin settlement extended to other points. One of the chief effects of the Balkan crisis of 1875–1878 was the subsequent Romanian estrangement from Russia. Not only had that state taken a piece of territory, southern Bessarabia, that was regarded as both nationally and historically Romanian, but the Russian actions had led to fears that the former protectorate might be reestablished. The formation of the Bulgarian state, which at first appeared to be under Russian domination, offered further dangers. In addition, Romania at that point had no ally or real friend among the great powers. With independence the former great-power guarantee lapsed. The Ottoman government also had no more obligations toward its former vassal. It was quite clear that the country could not remain isolated, but the choice of an alliance partner was not easy.

The Romanian government itself would have preferred Germany, but the German chancellor, Otto von Bismarck, insisted that the chief link must be with Vienna. The difficulty here was the many points of friction between Romania and the monarchy. After the Ausgleich the situation of the Romanians in Transylvania had become worse; this condition was bound to affect the relations between the two states. There were also continuing conflicts over commercial relations and the regulation of the Danube. However, since no other alternative appeared feasible, in October 1883 the Romanian government signed with Austria-Hungary a defensive treaty directed against Russia. Germany adhered at once, and Italy joined in 1888. The terms of the agreement required the Romanian allies to go to war in case of a Russian attack, but Romania was obligated to fight only if Russia or Serbia should attack the Habsburg Empire, not if a conflict were limited to Russia and Germany. The treaty was kept highly secret, being known only to the king and a few of his chief ministers. It was not placed before parliament or made known to the public. Regularly renewed, it was in effect at the outbreak of war in 1914.

The Romanian position was, of course, improved after the break between Bulgaria and Russia in 1885, although relations with the southern neighbor never became close. In the next years the chief Romanian difficulties were to be with allied Austria-Hungary. The first major friction occurred over commercial relations. Romania had signed a disadvantageous convention in 1875 primarily for political reasons. This agreement had allowed the import of Habsburg-manufactured goods under very favorable conditions – in fact, an almost free entrance into the Romanian market. In contrast, Romanian agricultural products were taxed by the monarchy to protect Hungarian interests. Unable to secure a revision of these arrangements, the Romanian government denounced the treaty in June 1885. This action meant that the high tariffs adopted in 1874 came into effect. A new tariff law was enacted in May 1886 that was protectionist in intent. This measure was passed only after intense debate among Liberal and Conservative representatives, who differed chiefly on the issue of how much protection should be given to Romanian products. In this period, it will be remembered, laws were passed to aid in the development of Romanian industry.

The Romanian tariff legislation resulted in a customs war with the monarchy that lasted from May 1886 to December 1893. In retaliation, the Habsburg government forbade the import of Romanian livestock, and tariffs were raised on Romanian imports. The trade war injured some agricultural interests, and there was an alteration of Romanian trade patterns. Even after the conflict was settled, commercial relations did not go back to the previous condition. Germany replaced Austria-Hungary as the chief supplier of industrial goods; Romanian agricultural products went more to Belgium, Germany, Britain, and France than to the monarchy. Another highly protective tariff was introduced in 1904. It must be remembered that Romania's neighbors and closest associates, Russia, Austria-Hungary, and Germany, were protectionist at this time, and Bucharest was merely following their example.

Despite these controversies and the peasant rebellion, Romanian internal and foreign affairs pursued a smoother course than those in other Balkan countries. The country suffered from none of the severe internal crises or foreign adventures that were experienced by Serbia, Bulgaria, or Greece, all of which were to become involved in conflicts with each other and with the Ottoman Empire.

## SERBIA

If the Romanian government was disappointed with the results of Berlin, the settlement faced the Serbian leaders with a virtual castastrophe. For Serbia the period from 1875 to 1878 had been characterized by hesitation, internal division, and military defeat. The revolt in Bosnia and Hercegovina in 1875 had aroused much excitement within the country. Bosnia was a land that most Serbs regarded as a part of their national heritage. Although the Russian government officially advised against intervention, a contrary influence came from the representatives of the Slavic Benevolent Society, whose membership was drawn from among the most influential sections of Russian society. The uprising in Bulgaria and the revolt of May 1876 in Constantinople similarly strengthened the position of those who saw this crisis as an opportunity for national advancement. The war, which commenced in July 1876, was undertaken against the judgment of Prince Milan and the Conservative Party, but it had the enthusiastic support of Serbian public opinion. A Liberal government under Jovan Ristić and Jevrem Grujić was responsible for the conduct of the war. The Serbian leaders went into battle with a most optimistic attitude. They hoped for another Bulgarian uprising, and they thought they could defeat the Ottoman forces. They had the assistance of about five thousand Russian volunteers. In addition, General M. G. Cherniaev, who had won a great reputation in Central Asia, came to take command of the army. Unfortunately, none of their expectations were realized. The Serbian peasant soldiers were no match for the better-trained, -equipped, and -led Ottoman forces. There was no second Bulgarian uprising. The Russian volunteers proved to have in their numbers a large percentage of drunks and incompetents; they were an embarrassment and a source of friction with Russia. The war proved to be both a military and a psychological disaster. The country suffered about fifteen thousand casualties before a peace was finally signed in March 1877.

Russia's declaration of war on April 24, 1877, caused at first no difficulties; that government did not want Balkan allies. Only after the Russian army experienced great difficulties at Pleven was Serbian assistance sought. Since the previous conflict had completely exhausted Serbian resources, Milan asked for money, supplies, and assurances about exactly what territory he would receive in the future. The negotiations dragged on and Serbia did not enter the war until December 13, three days after the fall of Pleven. In the peace the Serbian government hoped to get the territory to the south, in "Old Serbia," including the vilayet of Kosovo and the Sanjak of Novi Pazar to the river Lim. With these expectations, Serbia found the Treaty of San Stefano a real shock. Serbia was given about two hundred square miles, including the cities of Niš, Pirot, and Vranje, altogether less territory than was assigned to Montenegro. An even greater disaster in Serbian eyes was the creation of the large Bulgarian state, which with the inclusion of Macedonia would clearly be the predominant power on the peninsula. The Serbian leaders saw this as a clear threat to their future, and they were bitter to see such gains go to a people whom they regarded as having maintained a passive attitude in the past, instead of to the Serbs, who had fought for centuries.

Although the large Bulgarian state was divided at the Congress of Berlin, the new treaty contained equally disastrous provisions. Austria-Hungary was awarded control of Bosnia, Hercegovina, and the Sanjak of Novi Pazar, areas that the Serbian nationalists had hoped to obtain. The agreement gave the monarchy only the right to occupy and administer these territories, but the probability that they would ever fall into Serbian hands was now remote indeed. Moreover, in the negotiations preceding the congress, the Russian government had made it clear that it would stand sponsor for Bulgarian interests; Serbia should look to Vienna. The Russian attitude, of course, was in line with the division of the Balkans into spheres of influence implicit in the prewar agreements made with the Habsburg Empire. This latter state, with predominance in the western Balkans, would assume the role of the Serbian patron.

The relationship with Austria-Hungary became the main question in Serbian foreign relations in the next years. Both economic and political agreements were made. The Serbian government consented to the monarchy's desire for an extension of the rail lines from Belgrade south through Niš and Vranje, and a new commercial convention was signed. As in the negotiations with Bucharest, the Habsburg diplomats sought an agreement that would give favorable terms to their manufactured goods. Despite their possible negative effect on Serbian industrial development, these demands were met. The Habsburg market was essential to the Serbian peasant: the country had chiefly agricultural products to sell, and there were few manufactured goods to protect. The issue, nevertheless, caused a division in the government. The Liberal ministers resigned, and a Progressive cabinet under Milan Piroćanac and Čedomil Mijatović signed the pact.

Even more significant was the political treaty concluded in June 1881. By it both states promised to remain neutral should the other become involved in a war. The Habsburg Empire agreed to assist Serbia in expanding southward if the proper occasion arose. For its part, the Serbian government gave two highly significant assurances. The first declared that Serbia would not allow any "political, religious, or other intrigues" directed against Austria-Hungary either on its territory or in Bosnia-Hercegovina. The second, even more controversial, stated that "without a previous understanding with Austria-Hungary, Serbia will neither negotiate nor conclude any political treaty with another government, and will not admit to her territory a foreign armed force, regular or irregular, even as volunteers."[3] This statement, which made Serbia's satellite position all too clear, caused a ministerial crisis. Milan Piroćanac was ready to resign, but he received an assurance from the Habsburg government that this stipulation would not impair the ability of the Serbian state to negotiate treaties with other powers. Prince Milan, however, secretly, without notifying even his ministers, sent a declaration to Vienna that he would not enter into any treaties without Habsburg approval. With the conclusion of these agreements, he obtained Habsburg support for his desire to elevate Serbia to the status of a kingdom, an action that was accomplished in March 1882, when Milan took the title of king.

The Progressive Party, which now ran the government and was to remain important for seven years, was one of two new political alignments. An offshot of the left wing of the Conservatives, it supported a standard liberal program. Its members were strong admirers of Western Europe, and they wished Serbia to adopt its institutions. The other party, the Radicals, was more democratic and socialist in orientation and had more in common with the populist, socialist, and anarchist parties of the time. It supported the introduction of universal manhood suffrage, direct taxation, and legislative dominance in the government, and it was the first Serbian party to try to involve the peasantry in the political process. Its leader, Nikola Pašić, was to play henceforth a leading role in Serbian politics and later in the formation of Yugoslavia. During the period of Progressive rule, reforms concerning the freedom of the press, compulsory universal education, and the independence of the judiciary, and measures designed to promote economic growth, were enacted in ac-

3 The agreement can be found in Alfred F. Pribram, *The Secret Treaties of Austria-Hungary, 1879–1914* (Cambridge: Harvard University Press, 1920), I, 51–55.

cordance with the party's liberal program. A National Bank was founded in January 1883. The Progressive government was, however, damaged by repeated scandals, of which the most important were connected with railroad construction.

The Progressives also did not have strong popular support. When elections were held in September 1883, the Radicals won by a large majority. Milan, however, was not willing to accept a Radical ministry. Instead he called the Conservatives back into office, and the newly elected assembly was dissolved. The government then attempted to confiscate weapons owned by individuals, an act that was resisted in eastern Serbia. The Timok Rebellion, which broke out at this time, was caused both by the bad economic conditions of the period and by Radical Party agitation. The largest Serbian peasant revolt of the century, it indicated that this section of the population continued to be dissatisfied with its conditions, even though the country was ruled by an independent national government. The revolt was crushed by the army, and the leaders were either executed or imprisoned. In 1884 the Progressives were restored to power by Milan. The next major crisis was in foreign policy.

Although the great Bulgaria of San Stefano had been divided and the personal relations of Milan and Alexander of Battenberg were good, a great deal of bad feeling separated the two governments. The first dispute came over boundary questions. When the Timok River, which formed part of their mutual frontier, shifted its course, clashes occurred between the countries over the territory involved. The major conflict came in 1885 at the time of the union of Bulgaria and Eastern Rumelia. Since the unified Bulgarian state would be larger and more populous than Serbia, Milan felt that he was entitled to compensation. He thus launched an attack in November 1885. Despite widely held convictions that the Bulgarian army, deprived of its higher officers by the Russian withdrawal, would be crushed, it in fact defeated the invaders. The Habsburg Empire had to intervene to save Milan. Peace was made on the basis of the maintenance of the former boundaries; Serbia had to accept the Bulgarian unification. The entire episode was an enormous blow to the king's prestige.

At this point Milan was confronted with serious problems. The Obrenović dynasty was under attack. The previous years had brought no spectacular national gains, and the king was a weak leader. In the background there was always the threat of his rival, Peter Karadjordjević, the third son of Alexander and the grandson of the revolutionary leader. He had much support in Serbia. He had fought in Bosnia during the conflict of the 1870s, and he was politically very active. In 1883 he married Zorka, the daughter of Prince Nicholas of Montenegro. To many he appeared a much preferable alternative to Milan, whose personal life had become a public scandal. His wife, Natalija, disapproved of her husband's policies, and the couple quarreled in public. The issue of a divorce split the country. In 1887 Natalija left Serbia, taking with her the heir to the throne, Alexander.

The situation became so difficult that Milan, discouraged and disheartened, decided to abdicate. First he summoned a constitutional assembly. It met in December 1888 and was dominated by the Radical Party, which won five-sixths of the seats; the Liberals took the rest. The constitution drawn up at this time was more democratic than the document it replaced. The assembly was given more power, and local government was strengthened. Elections were secret, and all taxpayers received the right to vote. With this action completed, Milan abdicated in favor of his thirteen-year-old son, who was to rule under the direction of a regency headed by Jovan Ristić.

As might be expected, the reign of Alexander Obrenović was another period of weak government. The king's childhood was poisoned by the quarrels of his parents, a strict upbringing, and this early responsibility. The Radical Party controlled the government. Although its power rested on peasant votes, the leadership was in the hands of middle-class politicians and intellectuals. Some reform measures were put through, but no radical changes were made in the system. As in the past the winning party filled the official positions and the civil service with its adherents. In 1892 the Radicals were replaced by a Liberal ministry. In the next year the king, then sixteen, with the cooperation of the army took a major step. The constitution of 1869, which gave the executive more authority, was reinstated. The Radicals remained the strongest party, but Alexander proved adept at playing one political faction against the other. Elections were controlled through the police and the central administration. In April 1901 the king made a further constitutional change, this time on his own authority. A new document was issued, providing for a two-house legislature. The assembly would be elected, but Alexander could appoint three-fifths of the members of the upper house.

Such methods naturally aroused opposition. Moreover, Alexander, like his father, had family troubles. His mother and father fought to gain influence over him. Far more of a problem, however, was his marriage. He met and fell deeply in love with a widow, Draga Mašina, who was more than ten years his elder and who had earned an extremely scandalous reputation. It was believed that she could not have children, which was a serious difficulty in any royal marriage. He first made her his mistress and then married her. This marriage was extremely unpopular with the Serbian public. The queen's relatives subsequently involved themselves in public affairs and won more enemies for the dynasty. These events, combined with Alexander's obvious weakness as a national leader, strengthened the determination of those who wished to remove the Obrenović family from power. In June 1903 a successful military coup was organized, with about 120 involved in the plot. The conspirators killed the queen, the king, the war minister, and both of the queen's brothers under circumstances that shocked European opinion. The overthrow of the dynasty, however, met with public approval and caused little internal unrest.

# The Balkan national monarchies

With the assassination of the Obrenović king, there was one obvious alternative candidate – Peter Karadjordjević. The new king was almost sixty years old at the time of his accession; he had spent his life in exile and was not closely acquainted with internal conditions in Serbia. Educated in Paris and Geneva, he felt close to France. In the future the ties of his government were to be with France and Russia, who were in alliance, rather than with the Central European powers. His reign was thus to bring about a radical shift in Serbian foreign policy. He first governed with two parties, the Radicals and the Independent Radicals, which were both offshoots from the original Radical Party. The Radicals won the elections in 1906 and remained in power through World War I. This ministry, under the leadership of Nikola Pašić, was thus to make the important decisions that led the country into war in 1912, 1913, and 1914.

The new regime was bound to be unacceptable to the Habsburg Monarchy. Controversies arose at once over the question of railroads, loans, and the purchase of military equipment. The commercial conflicts were even more serious. In 1905 Serbia and Bulgaria concluded an agreement that provided for a virtual economic union by 1917. Since the Habsburg government felt that this combination would be detrimental to its economic and political interests, it interrupted the discussions that were being carried on with Belgrade over a trade treaty and other mutual concerns, and then applied pressure to force Serbia to break the pact with Bulgaria. The most important action was the embargo placed on the transportation of Serbian livestock into the monarchy.

This conflict, known as the "Pig War," had very serious consequences for Serbia. Alternative markets were difficult to find, but there were some successes. Germany, for instance, made significant purchases. Moreover, the embargo encouraged the Serbs to process their own meat. This commercial war dragged on from 1906 to 1911, merging with the parallel friction between the two countries over the Habsburg annexation of Bosnia-Hercegovina in 1908, a crisis that will be discussed in detail later. In the end the Habsburg policy failed. Instead of intimidating the Serbian government, the pressure merely served to encourage it to rely even more on France and Russia. French, not German or Austrian, military equipment was now purchased. Once Russia had concluded in 1905 the disastrous war with Japan, its government was in a better position to offer support.

Serbia had thus gained a strong national government. The new regime had effectively drawn away from Vienna and toward Paris and St. Petersburg. With the restraining influence of Austria-Hungary removed, renewed interest was to be shown in matters of national expansion and in the acquisition of territory still under Ottoman rule. Soon the ideas of Balkan cooperation, which we have seen previously in the reign of Michael, were to reemerge and to lead to negotiations among the Balkan states.

## MONTENEGRO

After 1860 the political life of Montenegro was dominated by the strong personality of Prince Nicholas. Conditions in the country remained extremely primitive. The main problem of the central government was that of acquiring and maintaining control over the mountain clans. As far as the relations with the neighboring states were concerned, two considerations predominated. First, Montenegro was always under some degree of danger from the Ottoman territories. The Porte claimed jurisdiction over the land until 1878, and Nicholas suffered a military defeat in 1862, at the beginning of his reign. An ambitious Albanian or Bosnian pasha, or the Ottoman government, might again undertake an offensive. However, the second, and contrary, consideration was the obvious fact that Montenegro needed more agricultural land. The temptation to exploit Christian and peasant discontent in the adjacent Ottoman provinces was thus strong.

Despite its small size and poverty, Montenegro continued to play a conspicuous role in international relations. For some time the state had balanced between Russia and the Habsburg Monarchy. Since the eighteenth century successive rulers had been able to extract a great deal of money from the Russian government, and this policy was to continue. In its relations with the Serbian government, Montenegro had adopted attitudes that were both friendly and competitive. During Michael's reign, Nicholas and the Serbian prince cooperated. Both men were Serbian patriots, and they had a common interest in securing an Ottoman defeat. Although at this time Nicholas was willing to recognize Michael as the ruler should the two states unite, a basic dynastic rivalry did influence their relations. After the death of Michael, this condition was to become of increasing importance.

In 1875 and 1876 Montenegro naturally found itself at the center of events. Refugees from Hercegovina crossed into the country; Montenegrin volunteers left for Ottoman territory to join the rebellion. The Panslav societies devoted a great deal of attention to the Russian protégé. The temptation to go to war was extremely strong. It appeared that a victory was possible, and the state had a clear goal in the acquisition of Hercegovina and other Ottoman lands. Once an agreement with Serbia had been concluded and the battle begun, however, matters did not proceed so smoothly. The reformed Ottoman army had better-trained troops and far superior equipment than desperately poor Montenegro, which suffered from a deficiency of ammunition – in fact, of supplies of all kinds. The Montenegrin fighters were also not trained for modern warfare. They were usually successful, nevertheless, because their mountainous terrain gave them a great deal of natural protection and the Ottoman forces were concentrated elsewhere, at first primarily against Serbia and later, when the war with Russia began, against their main adversary.

When Serbia made peace in March 1877, Montenegro remained at war.

34

Thus, when Russia entered in April, the two states were fighting a common foe. After the Ottoman attempt to conquer Montenegro failed, the Montenegrin forces were able to take the offensive and occupy the coast from the Bojana River to Budva. They were thus in possession of a strip of seacoast that had been a major objective of their policy previously. At the peace negotiations the Russian government made a particular effort to strengthen Montenegro, and the Treaty of San Stefano allotted the state territory that would have increased its size 3.5 times. Even though some land was lost in the Treaty of Berlin, Montenegro nevertheless doubled in size. The desired outlet to the sea was also gained with the acquisition of territory on the Adriatic, including the port of Ulcinj. In return, however, Montenegro did have to accept some Habsburg supervision. That government was deeply concerned that any concessions of coastal territory to Montenegro would signify simply that Russia had acquired a port on the Adriatic. All of the powers, in fact, were concerned about a Russian naval intrusion into the Mediterranean. In the treaty this possibility was excluded by the provision that Montenegrin waters were to be closed to the warships of all nations. Montenegro was not to have a fleet, and Austria-Hungary was entrusted with the policing of the shores. This provision gave the Habsburg Empire a type of naval protectorate in the region.

From 1881 to 1913 Montenegro of necessity enjoyed a period of peaceful foreign relations. Surrounded on three sides by Habsburg possessions or occupied territories – Dalmatia, Bosnia, Hercegovina, and the Sanjak of Novi Pazar – there was little that Nicholas could do. In this period some administrative changes were introduced to make the government resemble more closely that of the other European states. Nicholas was, of course, an autocratic ruler. His chief advisers were the twelve senators whom he chose and who were usually the heads of the major tribes. The senate served as a high court. In 1879 the prince reorganized his state. He appointed members to a state council that acted as a legislative body, and there was also a council of ministers and a high court. The country was divided into twelve provinces, which were subdivided into districts, headed by captains who had both administrative and judicial power. In 1888 a new law code was introduced. At the same time the prince reorganized his army on the Russian model.

Despite the territorial gains made in the war, the basic problem of the state remained the fact that the land simply could not support the population. The basis of the economy was livestock raising; two-thirds of the exports were animals or animal products. Both wheat and textiles had to be imported. In other words, the population could not be adequately fed or clothed from the produce of the land. Most of the people lived in extreme poverty. Since there was no possibility of industrialization or territorial expansion, the only solution was large-scale emigration. In 1912 it is estimated that a third or more of the men of working age had to leave the country to take seasonal jobs or emigrate permanently, usually to the United States. Their remittances to their families were a great aid to the state. Montenegro, in other words, did not have the economic base to provide the essential attributes of a modern state.

Because of this situation Montenegro lived on loans and subsidies. The prince took absolute control in these matters too. He established regular budgets only after 1907. The financial basis of the state was the Russian subsidy, which covered half the budget and thus paid the major military and administrative expenses. In 1910 the amount was raised from 800 thousand to 1.6 million kronen.[4] The Russian government also sent wheat. Despite this subsidy, relations were not always smooth with St. Petersburg. An independent and eccentric ruler, Nicholas did not allow himself to be dominated by any foreign power; he also took loans from the Habsburg Monarchy and encouraged Italian investment.

Despite Nicholas's relative success, his autocratic rule naturally aroused much opposition and resentment, particularly among the younger generation, some of whom had studied abroad. Many students went to Belgrade and there came in touch with the general political ideas of the age, which, of course, had little application to the prince's patriarchal regime. These men too wanted liberal reform and constitutional government. In 1905 Nicholas finally did issue a constitution. His motive was to change the outward appearance of his government so that he could more easily attract foreign loans; he had no intention of surrendering his autocratic powers. He made it clear that he did not want any political parties, and he would not tolerate an opposition of any sort. Certainly the document he sponsored left the control of the state in his hands. According to this constitution the prince had to approve all the laws, he could initiate legislation, and he named the ministers; he could also issue decrees. The representatives to the assembly were chosen partly by the prince and partly through elections in which there was open voting. This body was empowered to discuss and draft laws and to review the budget.

Despite all of the safeguards, an assembly was chosen in 1906 that did try to check the prince. The opposition was organized in the National Club. The prince suppressed the group and dissolved the assembly in 1907, and then brought his supporters together and formed the "True National" Party. The opposition liberals boycotted the subsequent elections. Although Nicholas succeeded in dominating the situation, there was much underground opposition to his policies. These actions caused strained relations with Belgrade because the prince believed that support for his opponents was coming from that direction.

Although he could make no major advances, Nicholas continued to carry on an active foreign policy. He was very successful in arranging marriages for

---

4  Iu. V. Bromlei et al., eds., *Istoriia Iugoslavii* (Moscow: Izdatel'stvo Akademii Nauk SSSR, 1963), I, 526.

his daughters: two married Russian grand dukes and thereafter played an important role in the Russian court; one became the wife of Peter Kara-djordjević, but died in 1890 before he became the Serbian king; and a fourth, married to Victor Emmanuel III, became queen of Italy. Nicholas in 1910 proclaimed Montenegro a kingdom, and he too became a king.

Throughout this period Russia remained the major support of the state. The Habsburg Empire was, however, the market for Montenegrin livestock, and Italian influence was increasing. Italian enterprises gained the right to develop the port of Bar; they also held a monopoly on tobacco and the concession to build a narrow-gauge railroad from Bar to Virpazar. This line, the only one in the country, was opened in 1909.

Montenegro in the early twentieth century was thus an extremely poor country with little hope of development within the boundaries assigned to it. It depended on financial subsidies from Russia, but that power was far away and could render little direct assistance in a time of war or internal crisis. The immediate neighbors, Austria-Hungary and Italy, looked upon the country as a possible area of exploitation, and they were determined not to allow the state any sort of influence on the Adriatic. They also regarded with distrust the Montenegrin links with the Serbs in Bosnia, Hercegovina, and the Serbian kingdom. With the Habsburg Empire in occupation of Bosnia-Hercegovina and the Sanjak, the only direction in which Montenegro could expand was southward into Albanian-inhabited lands. And this indeed was where the Montenegrin hopes lay, as was to be shown in the events of 1912.

## BULGARIA

After the dismissal and assassination of Stephen Stambolov, Prince Ferdinand was able to assume control of the Bulgarian political system. No other individual or party was successful in challenging his position. He was immensely aided by the splintering of the original Liberal and Conservative parties into, by 1914, nine competing factions. Although there were some differences among them on issues in foreign and domestic policy, they shared the major goal of seeking to win the elections and thus of acquiring the subsequent spoils of office. Ferdinand was able to play these parties against each other for his own advantage.

In 1894 a government was formed by Constantine Stoilov of the National Party, formerly the Conservatives, which lasted until 1899. During this period a rapprochement with Russia was undertaken. Interest was also shown in the modernization of the country, although no significant industrialization occurred. Tariffs were raised, but foreign goods continued to be imported to the detriment of local production, particularly textiles. In 1894 a law designed to assist native industries was passed: loans were to be made available to firms that had capital of over 25,000 leva and that employed at least twenty workers. Railroad construction was similarly approved. The main line running from Constantinople to the West had already been completed in 1888; Bulgaria was thus linked with Western Europe. Nevertheless, the country faced the same difficulties as the neighboring states: the railroads were built at a great expense, and they did not contribute significantly to the prosperity of the country.

In 1899 Stoilov was compelled to resign over a question of corruption in regard to the railroads. The Liberals, led by Vasil Radoslavov, came to power and remained in office from 1899 to 1901. This ministry had to deal with a major problem in the countryside. The fact that the great majority of Bulgarian peasants owned their own farms had scarcely lessened the difficult conditions of rural life. Those who acquired land as a result of the expulsion of the Muslim landholders had been required to make payments. Subsequently, the peasantry had to bear the costs of the national administration, the army, the payments on the loans contracted abroad, and the internal improvements, such as the railroads. They too had felt the effects of the rise of population and the continual subdivision of family lands that we have seen elsewhere. In 1897 and 1899 bad weather caused disastrous harvests. The peasants were thus in no mood to accept passively a new tax that the government attempted to collect in 1899. It amounted to 10 percent of the peasant production, and it was to be paid in kind. When massive demonstrations broke out, the government replied with force. Peasant leaders were arrested, and there were some deaths. The opposition was so strong, however, that in 1901 Ferdinand appointed a new ministry under the direction of Petko Karavelov, which canceled the tax.

This unrest and discontent formed the background to the formation of one of the few purely peasant organizations in the Balkans in the prewar period – the Agrarian Union. As we have seen, despite the overwhelming predominance of the peasantry, peasant participation in Balkan politics was almost totally absent. The Serbian Radical Party, which had endeavored to appeal to this group, had by 1914 become a typical middle-class organization. The first steps in founding the Agrarian Union were undertaken not by peasants, but by intellectuals. A particularly active role was played by the Bulgarian teachers, who numbered as many as six thousand at the end of the century.[5] Assigned often to rural areas, they were both educated and in direct touch with the miserable life in the countryside. They were supported by other disaffected sections of Bulgarian society – such as writers, journalists, lower civil servants, doctors, and priests – which were not a part of the narrow clique enjoying the major benefits of Ferdinand's regime.

The Agrarian Union was at first an association of various groups and individuals; it thus did not have a single ideology or a common program. Many of the members were strongly influenced by current populist doctrine, in

5   See John D. Bell, *Peasants in Power: Alexander Stamboliski and the Bulgarian Agrarian National Union, 1899–1923* (Princeton, N.J.: Princeton University Press, 1977), p. 17.

particular by the views held by Russian radicals. They believed that it should be their task to raise the intellectual and moral level of the peasant. They thus placed a strong emphasis on education. Others saw the prime necessity of practical actions, such as steps to improve agricultural productivity and to find a solution to the burden of peasant indebtedness. This last problem was particularly urgent. Many peasants had become heavily in debt to local moneylenders who charged exorbitant rates. They were often in a position where they could never clear their loans.

The first congress of the Agrarian Union, held in December 1899, was attended by about eight hundred delegates. The central issue was the tax that had just been levied. At this meeting the aims of the organization were declared to include the reform of the tax system, the guarantee of the availability of cheap credit, the education of the peasantry, and the further study of rural problems. There was disagreement over the question whether the Union should constitute a political party and enter the elections. This course of action was adopted only in 1901, at which time the name of the organization was changed to the Bulgarian Agrarian National Union, or BANU.

Despite the lack of a single program, the Agrarian Union did from the beginning oppose the government and support certain reforms. The movement was not successful, however, until Alexander Stamboliski took over a leading role after 1906. Under his direction it was given a tighter organization and an ideology. Supporting the interests of the peasant smallholders, the party adopted a program calling for government aid to agriculture, better educational facilities, and state loans. It was argued that tax money should be devoted to economic development rather than to strengthening the army. Stamboliski had no hesitation about attacking the king personally, as well as the political conditions in the country. In May 1908 BANU gained a significant victory. Despite the corruption in the electoral system, it won 100,000 votes and thus became the strongest opposition party. Its major victories were to come after the conclusion of World War I.

Foreign affairs were bound to be the chief concern of the government. Although the state was only autonomous, it functioned as if it were fully independent. Diplomatic relations were established with other governments, and the Porte was not able to exert influence either on foreign or on domestic policy. Naturally, the prince and the parties wanted complete independence, and they continued to hold the ideal of the San Stefano boundaries. The principal attention was still on Macedonia. However, in the first decade of the twentieth century there was little hope of territorial advancement. Both Austria-Hungary and Russia were determined to maintain the status quo in the Balkans. Moreover, after 1878 Bulgaria faced the problem of the suspicion and enmity of its neighbors. Greece and Serbia, in particular, feared Bulgarian influence in the Macedonian lands, which were also the object of their ambitions. The Romanian government similarly opposed the formation of a great Bulgarian state.

The Bulgarian leaders were nevertheless able to make one major national advance in this period. In 1908 a revolt in the Ottoman Empire brought to power a revolutionary government. Using the opportunity thus conveniently provided, Bulgaria and Austria-Hungary took actions that further weakened the Ottoman position in the Balkans. The Habsburg Empire annexed Bosnia-Hercegovina, and Ferdinand declared Bulgaria's independence, at the same time taking the title of tsar and thus recalling the memory of the medieval Bulgarian empires. The Ottoman government could do little to reverse these moves. After negotiations, it was agreed that Bulgaria would pay compensation, part of which was to come from a Russian loan.

Bulgaria thus joined the ranks of the independent Balkan states. With the separation from the Ottoman Empire complete, the government could turn its full attention to the Macedonian problem, an issue that dominated the internal and foreign policy of the nation thereafter. The Macedonian conflict, the major Balkan issue in the period immediately prior to World War I, is discussed in detail in a subsequent chapter.

## GREECE

Like Serbia and Romania, Greece was deeply disturbed by the Treaty of San Stefano and the formation of a Bulgarian autonomous state. Thereafter, Bulgaria was in a position to challenge Greek claims on territory that most Greeks regarded as part of their historical possessions. The Bulgarian Exarchate was similarly in a better position to dispute the authority of the Patriarchate of Constantinople in the lands still under Ottoman control. Prior to the 1870s the Greek statesmen had expected at some time in the future to acquire not only Thessaly and Crete, but also Epirus, Thrace, and Macedonia. Now there had appeared Bulgarian and Albanian national movements that threatened the Greek position in these three areas. After 1878 repeated crises occurred concerning Crete. Although much attention was given to events there, Greek attention was centered primarily on Macedonia. Crete would inevitably sometime fall under the control of Athens; there were no other claimants to this Greek island. In Macedonia, in contrast, Bulgarian, Serbian, Albanian, and even Romanian rivals had to be combated.

The basic Greek problem prior to 1914 was the familiar one that we have met elsewhere. The Greek leaders would ideally have liked to conduct both an active, expansionist foreign policy and a strong program of internal development. Basically a poor nation, Greece did not have the resources to pursue either alternative successfully. From the days of the revolution the country had been plagued with apparently insoluble financial problems. The state had always experienced great difficulty in raising money. It used tithes on agricultural products, indirect taxes on consumer goods, and duties – all extremely unpopular with the people – for revenue. The government also continued to borrow heavily; between 1879 and 1890 the amount of the foreign indebtedness was increased by 630 million gold francs. The service on this debt, combined with the payments on previous loans, absorbed a large part of the national budget. Since the state income, in addition, had to cover the costs of administration, the military, pensions, education, and some other essential services, there was little if anything left over for internal improvements.

After the middle of the century, the Greek political parties were primarily groups of individuals who supported a leader. The aim was to win public office and the benefits that came through the spoils system. The parties usually did not represent a political viewpoint, nor did they have a distinctive class base. In 1875 King George agreed to appoint his ministry from the party with a majority in parliament, and thereafter a more stable situation emerged. Instead of a multiparty system, two blocs formed around the rival personalities of Charilaos Trikoupis and Theodoros Deligiannis. Recognizing that Greece could not adopt both strong foreign and domestic policies, they supported opposite views concerning the path that their state should follow.

Trikoupis was in office from March 1882 to April 1885 and from May 1886 to November 1890. He called for a program of internal development and the postponement of foreign adventures until the country was better prepared both militarily and economically. His ministries had the backing of the British government, which regularly discouraged any move that might lead to a reopening of the Eastern Question. During his years in power Trikoupis carried through a reorganization of the police, the army, and the navy, and he had a strong program of road, railroad, and harbor construction. His principal accomplishment was the building of the Corinth Canal, which linked the Ionian and Aegean seas. The great difficulty that his ministries faced was the high expense of these projects. The money had to come from taxes levied on the peasants and the poorer classes of the population, who were not in a position to experience any direct advantages from these improvements. They saw instead the high taxes that were levied on items, such as matches and tobacco, that they did use. Moreover, no advances were made in foreign policy. In 1895 Trikoupis finally retired from politics.

His rival, Deligiannis, was in office repeatedly from 1885 until his assassination in 1905. He was able to exploit the sensitivity over national questions and the general enthusiasm for expansion. His views won favor when a series of crises arose that deeply aroused Greek national passions. All of these were connected with the Cretan and Macedonian questions, two issues that were extremely important in Greek public opinion. The events on Crete involved chiefly Greek relations with Constantinople, whereas the Macedonian struggle touched upon the interests of all of the Balkan states.

Like the Serbian, the Greek government had been upset by the unification of Bulgaria and Eastern Rumelia. A state of considerable size and population had been created. In general, the Greek leaders had great difficulty in coming to terms with this nation. The Bulgarian challenge to the Greek position was relatively new; in the previous centuries the Greek-dominated Patriarchate and the Phanariots had held predominance over the Bulgarians, and Greek attitudes had been formed by this relationship. The Greek people were influenced by their "picture of Bulgarian inferiority and backwardness. Taken in by their own oratory, most Greeks could not understand how it was possible for civilized Europe to look with favor on these 'savages.'"[6] When Serbia went to war in November 1885, there was considerable enthusiasm in Greece for a similar action. The compensation desired was the rest of Epirus – in other words, lands with a great many Albanians. Deligiannis, then in office, mobilized the army, but the great powers, which were afraid of another serious crisis, established a naval blockade in May 1886. As a result Deligiannis was forced out of office. He had accomplished nothing, and the mobilization had been expensive.

The fate of Crete had remained an almost continual problem since the island passed from Egyptian control back to the Ottoman Empire in 1840. The Cretan leaders and the majority of the population naturally wished to join the Greek state. The island had certain conditions similar to those in Bosnia. After the Ottoman conquest about a fifth of the inhabitants had converted to Islam; these people thereafter held the large estates and had the best positions in the local administration. Repeated uprisings during the century had strong social as well as national connotations. The rebels' principal grievances were against Muslim landholders and administrators who might be Greek in language and national origin. The Ottoman government, under strong great-power pressure, attempted to introduce certain reforms. The most important of these were contained in the Halepa Pact of October 1878, which was concluded after an insurrection that lasted three years. In this agreement the Porte surrendered the administration of the island to the Christian majority. An assembly was to be elected under conditions guaranteeing Christian control, and the sultan was obligated to choose a Christian as governor. These concessions did not bring peace. The Greek population was divided into conservative and liberal factions that fought for political predominance; Eleftherios Venizelos, a liberal, was among the most prominent of the Cretan politicians. Continued unrest on the island led the Porte to break the Halepa accord. Muslim governors were appointed, and the assembly did not meet.

Neither the Greek government nor the Orthodox Cretans could allow this situation to continue. Both followed a policy of *enosis*, that is, of seeking union with Greece. In 1894 the *Ethniki Etairia*, or National Society, was organized to forward Greek national aims. Three-quarters of the officers of the Greek army were among its members. Exceedingly active, it was responsible for sending arms and volunteers to aid in the fight for unredeemed national territories. Both Crete and Macedonia were centers of its activities. In 1897

6 D. George Kousoulas, *Modern Greece: Profile of a Nation* (New York: Scribner's, 1974), p. 72.

the Cretan issue flared up again. In February the leaders of yet another rebellion declared the union of the island with Greece. The government, under
Deligiannis, prepared to act. Despite repeated warnings from the great powers, the army was mobilized. Greek naval units under the command of the
king's second son, Prince George, went into combat; fifteen hundred men
were landed in Crete. At the same time, the Greek army, led by the heir to
the throne, Prince Constantine, began operations on the mainland.

The military campaign directed against the adjacent Ottoman lands was a
complete disaster. The fighting lasted about a month. The Ottoman army
soon defeated the Greek forces and crossed into Greek territory. The great
powers then intervened and prevented a further Ottoman advance. Although
the war itself was a humiliating failure, the peace terms were a Greek victory
as far as Crete was concerned. Under great-power pressure, the Ottoman
government was forced to give the island an autonomous status; Prince George
became the governor. Few vestiges of Ottoman rule were left; the Porte could
not collect a tribute or name the governor. The Greek government, however,
was compelled to pay an indemnity and to surrender a few points on the
border to the Ottoman Empire.

Although the war had brought Crete one step closer to an eventual unification with Greece, it had contributed to the severe economic problems that
faced the state. The indebtedness, to which the indemnity had to be added,
had increased to such a degree that the government had to accept foreign
control over its finances. An International Finance Commission, on which
representatives of the bondholders of the six great powers sat, was given
authority over certain funds. The foreign creditors were thus protected, and
Greek finances were brought into better order. The action was nevertheless
regarded as a national humiliation, since it involved a severe limitation of
Greece's fiscal sovereignty. As previously, the Greek public and politicians
made a scapegoat out of the ruler. Both the king and the crown prince were
strongly criticized, as was the role of the princes in military affairs.

At this time the Greek political system itself came under sharp attack, particularly by foreign observers, and with much justification. With men of the
stature of Trikoupis lacking, the country did not have firm direction; the
parties simply alternated in office. The British representative on the International Finance Commission commented: "No difference of principle divides
one party from the other; some of the smaller groups have a faintly percep-
tible anti-dynastic tinge, but otherwise the difference is of men, not measures
– the sweets of office versus the cold shades of opposition."[7] Bribery and
corruption continued to characterize political life.

The general economic situation remained bad. The taxes, which have been
estimated at 23 percent of the average income, were too high for this impov-

7  Quoted in S. Victor Papacosma, *The Military in Greek Politics: The 1909 Coup d'état* (Kent,
   Ohio: Kent State University Press, 1977), pp. 16–17.

erished population. With the increasing pressure of the population on the land, emigration, which had already commenced, became an increasingly significant factor in national life. The greatest numbers left after the 1897 defeat. Between 1900 and 1921, 383,993 emigrated, of whom the great majority were males between the ages of fifteen and forty-five, the most active and productive sector of the population. Greece had the largest proportion of emigrés of any of the Balkan countries. Although the remittances sent back greatly aided the Greek economy, the mass movement weakened the state and was, of course, detrimental to the military forces, since in theory the youngest and strongest men were those who left.

Dissatisfaction was especially strong in the army. Not only had it suffered a defeat in the war with the Ottoman Empire, but the Greeks appeared to be losing ground in Macedonia. This period marked a rise in violence in that region. Although some reforms were made, the bad financial conditions precluded the strengthening of the Greek army, which was weaker than that of Serbia or Bulgaria. This situation could be dangerous in the future. The discontent of the army increased even further with the apparent setback to Greek national objectives that occurred in 1908, when, it will be remembered, Bulgaria declared its independence. The question of compensation for Greece arose at once. At the same time the Cretans declared their union with Greece. Once more under close great-power control, the Greek government could not move. The entire episode made the weakness of the political system even more apparent.

In August 1909, the army, deeply disturbed by these events, resorted to a coup to correct what it regarded as an impossible political situation. Colonel N. K. Zorbas led three thousand men from the Athens garrison in a demonstration against the government. He represented a new organization, the Military League, which had been formed by young officers who were highly discontented with Greek politics. Although the coup succeeded, the League had neither a candidate to head the government nor a political program of its own. It therefore turned to Venizelos for guidance.

Eleftherios Venizelos, one of the outstanding Greek statesmen of the modern era, had gained his political experience in Cretan politics. There he had clashed with the governor, Prince George, and in 1905 he had led a revolt that forced the prince to return to Athens. In January 1910 he accepted the invitation of the League and came to Athens as its political adviser. Recognizing the necessity of reform, he favored the idea of summoning a special national assembly to change the constitution. He was, however, concerned about the influence of the military in politics. When the king agreed to call the assembly, Venizelos persuaded the League to accept the condition that it dissolve and withdraw from politics.

The first elections held for the assembly resulted in the victory of the old parties, which were not enthusiastic about reform. A second election, held in December 1910, returned representatives who would cooperate with Venizelos. He was now in a strong position. He had the support of the king and the assembly, and he was very popular with the public. Under his leadership a revision of the constitution of 1864 was undertaken. The aim was to preserve the existing system, so no fundamental changes were made. The king still held strong powers. The fifty-three amendments were designed primarily to introduce some necessary reforms and to improve the functioning of the administration. For instance, the position of the government officials was made more secure, a ministry of agriculture was established, and education was made compulsory on the elementary level. The alterations in the constitution and the reforms introduced through regular legislation placed Greece in a much better position to meet the great period of crisis that lay ahead. Although the Liberal Party, once in power, did not prove reluctant to share in the spoils of office, it did provide strong leadership. Venizelos was to play a predominant, but often controversial, role in Greek political life until his death in 1936.

## THE "EUROPEANIZATION" OF BALKAN LIFE

In this chapter the weaknesses of the new national states have often been discussed – their economic deficiencies, the instability of some of the governments, and the corruption of many aspects of national life. Comparisons are usually made between Balkan conditions and those in Western and Central Europe, where indeed standards were higher. When the Balkans are contrasted to other regions, for instance, Asia, Africa, South America, and Russia, the picture is not so bleak. If the Balkan regimes did not always function smoothly, at least institutions of progressive government had been introduced that could serve as a base for future improvement. National administrative systems were in existence that covered the entire nation and provided police and security services. Although illiteracy was high, primary and secondary schools had been opened even in remote areas, and at least the ideal of universal education had been accepted. Greece, for example, developed an educational system that compared advantageously with those of larger and wealthier European states and that was remarkable in view of the country's limited domestic resources.

Moreover, certainly after 1878, most of the Balkan states did enjoy much freedom of action. Although the great powers when united could indeed still compel obedience to their dictates, the small nations were at times able to exploit the mutual rivalries and jealousies of the European governments. Strong economic influences were exerted, particularly in connection with the loans, but great-power conflicts prevented the establishment of any lasting economic domination by a single state. We have seen how Austria-Hungary was largely unsuccessful in its attempts to put pressure on Romania and Serbia in connection with the commercial agreements. Despite its dependence on the Habsburg livestock market, Serbia was able to resist successfully during the Pig War, although, of course, initially at a high cost. Great-power imperialism did exist, but it contained so many internal contradictions and was weakened by such bitter rivalries that it did not result in the political or economic subjugation of the peninsula.

In addition to establishing independent regimes, the Balkan states made the great transition from what was an Eastern or Ottoman pattern of life to one based on European models. The effects of this change can be overestimated, and it did apply primarily to the upper levels of national life, but it altered radically the appearance in particular of the larger Balkan cities over the century. As we have seen, the Balkan leadership was acquainted with Western Europe. Some of its members had traveled widely, and others had been educated abroad. It accepted not only ideology and political institutions from the West, but also its styles. This attitude was accompanied by a great deal of contempt for past patterns of life, which were regarded as "Oriental," backward, and barbarous.

The new elite in particular wanted the capital cities to resemble Paris, Vienna, London, and Munich. There was a great deal to be done. At the beginning of the nineteenth century Athens, Bucharest, Sofia, and Belgrade were provincial cities; the great Balkan centers were Constantinople and Thessaloniki. Changes, however, were soon to be made. Once a national state had been established, the new government had to be housed. The nation had to provide palaces for its princes, offices for the bureaucracy, and a large building for the national assemblies. Soon afterward cultural centers – libraries, opera houses, theaters, museums, and universities – were constructed. New churches and cathedrals were also expressions of national pride. After the establishment of formal diplomatic relations, the powers usually competed to construct impressive embassy and consulate buildings. Hotels were built to accommodate the increasing number of foreign visitors. Native and foreign commercial enterprises, especially the banks, erected large offices. Everywhere the civic leaders desired to get rid of the narrow streets, small houses, and cramped quarters of the Ottoman period and replace them with wide boulevards and large buildings. There was great admiration for the changes made in Paris at the time of Napoleon III. Not only were European styles in architecture brought in, but the architects were often foreigners.

The first city to be reconstructed on a plan was Athens. Chosen as the national capital because of its classical associations, the city in the 1830s was little more than a small Ottoman town crowned by the impressive ruins of the Parthenon. The Philhellene Bavarian regents naturally chose to emphasize the classical rather than the Byzantine heritage of the state. Unencumbered by previous building, they were able to lay out a city with straight streets and squares. They favored a form of neoclassical architecture that was also reflected in some contemporary buildings in Munich. They thus adopted a style of architecture not associated with either Ottoman or Byzantine patterns, but at least not typically European.

Bucharest was, of course, already a large city before the union of the Principalities. Long the Wallachian capital, it had many impressive churches, monasteries, and boyars' residences. After 1862, when it became the Romanian capital, government buildings, a residence for the prince, and cultural and educational establishments had to be erected. A great deal of attention was paid to city planning and to the provision for immense stretches of parkland. Because of the close connections with the France of Napoleon III, Romanian architects were greatly influenced by contemporary Parisian ideas. The great boulevards of modern Bucharest were laid out on the French model.

Sofia suffered from the fact that it had not in the recent past been as important a city as either Plovdiv or Varna. The logical capital of San Stefano Bulgaria, but not of the state as it was finally established, Sofia had only about twelve thousand inhabitants when Alexander of Battenberg became prince. It grew swiftly thereafter, and once again the European imprint was unmistakable. A contemporary observer described with approval "the palace, which is a very fine structure of modern French Renaissance . . . resembling portions of the Louvre and Tuileries." Although Sofia too soon acquired the attributes of a modern city, the same writer complained about the conditions of the 1880s: "There is no theatre, no concerts, and, as far as I could learn, no lectures nor systematic entertainments of any kind, except a military band, which plays very well, and one or two *cafés chantants* [cabarets]."[8]

Belgrade, which had long been an Ottoman military and administrative center, underwent many changes after 1867, when the final vestiges of Ottoman authority were removed. The great fortress, Kalemegdan, remained and was later made into a park. Since the city was built on the hills overlooking the Danube, it suffered from the difficulties of having few wide or straight streets. The first modern boulevard, Terazija, was finished only in 1911. All of the major government buildings were subsequently constructed on European models; the churches, of course, remained Byzantine in design.

The preference for Western styles in building was reflected in other outward forms of life. The wealthy and influential members of Balkan society imported their furniture, their carriages, and their clothes from the West, preferably from Paris or Vienna. They kept in close touch with fashionable trends in these centers and with European art and literature. Not only the intellectuals, but most of those with political and economic power, wished their country to acquire what they regarded as the highest accomplishments of world civilization in the cultural as well as in the political and economic fields.

The Balkan capitals, even though the majority of the population lived in rural areas, became the centers of national life. They were the seats of the centralized administrations and of all of the universities and institutions of higher education. Their inhabitants had a level of literacy far above the na-

8 James Samuelson, *Bulgaria, Past and Present* (London: Trübner, 1888), pp. 117, 118.

tional average. Most of the books, newspapers, and journals were published there; for instance, half of Bulgaria's newspapers appeared in Sofia and almost all of Serbia's in Belgrade. Their inhabitants also enjoyed a far higher standard of living than most of the rest of the country.

When the modern conveniences of urban life became available, the large Balkan cities were not far behind Western Europe. These improvements included the provision of pure water; sewer systems; police and fire protection; better communications, including paved roads and streetcars; and, finally, gas and electric lighting. Bucharest had sewers and running water by the 1880s, Belgrade and Sofia by the first decade of the twentieth century. Bucharest acquired streetcars in 1871, first horsedrawn, then in 1894 electric. A Belgian company built similar lines in Belgrade and Sofia. By 1914 all of these cities had electric lighting.

These extensive innovations were financed by the state or the municipalities, usually with funds borrowed abroad. The costs connected with these loans were high. Moreover, the tax burden for improvements often fell upon those who were not in a position to appreciate their benefits. Many of the advantages were enjoyed almost exclusively by the privileged sections of society. For instance, streetcar fares were so high in Bucharest and Sofia that a worker could use them only irregularly.[9] The lighting of the streets in the center of a city similarly was a convenience enjoyed by a relative minority.

With these changes in styles of life, the separation between the city and the country became increasingly more pronounced. The city population, holding the political power and the economic advantages, lived, dressed, spoke, and thought in a manner different from that of the peasant majority, but ever closer to the equivalent social class in Western Europe. The centralized administrative systems and the use of the police to control elections guaranteed that the cities would dominate the countryside. Politicians and bureaucrats, themselves only a generation or so away from the village, tended to look down on and despise their peasant constituents.

Meanwhile, as we have seen, peasant life was not improving. There had been no great strides forward in food, housing, or education. The individual, even where he had the franchise, was prevented from using it freely because of the corruption at the center and the misuse of police power. Although he still responded to patriotic appeals in times of crisis, the peasant was usually suspicious and mistrustful of those in power. As one scholar has written:

> Practically the only contact that the peasantry had with the state was while paying taxes and fines, rendering military service, and render-

---

9  For the growth of Belgrade, Bucharest, and Sofia see John R. Lampe, "Modernization and Social Structure: The Case of the Pre-1914 Balkan Capitals," *Southeastern Europe* 5, no. 2 (1978): 11–32.

ing *corvée* for various public purposes. The state was not an institution that the peasantry, and this is to say the overwhelming portion of the people, considered their own, but it remained to them a foreign, fearful, and often hated organization. The wrath that the peasantry felt through the centuries against the feudal class was now transferred to the state bureaucracy and the representatives of the new socio-economic order from the city . . . there was little cause for the peasants to look at the newly emerging state of the nineteenth century either with confidence or benevolence.[10]

The difficult situation in the countryside disturbed at least some Balkan leaders. It also became a subject of debate in intellectual circles. Many writers, teachers, and journalists, particularly those who did not have political power, became concerned with the results of the establishment of the centralized state system and the ensuing separation of the mass of the people from the political leadership. The problems inherent in bureaucratic rule were similarly attacked. Even more disillusionment was apparent toward the end of the century when it became clear that independence and constitutional government were not producing the expected results. A series of writers and journalists, some of whom were to have an active political role, concentrated their attacks on the structure of the government, particularly on the centralized bureaucracy that they saw as an imported institution, basically foreign to their own people. In the Slavic states the movement was part of the Panslav-Slavophil current, but it had its equivalent in Romania and Greece. Most of these writers paid particular attention to the condition of the peasants and the poverty and ignorance that they found in the rural areas. They deplored the decline of village and patriarchal life and the decay of local handicraft industries. The disappearance of the former communal administration and the substitution of the new bureaucracy were similarly severely criticized.

Some of these critics – writers on both the right and the left of the political spectrum – saw the salvation of their countries in the return of institutions that had been prevalent under Ottoman rule. For instance, the leading Serbian socialist of the second half of the nineteenth century, Svetozar Marković, called for the reorganization of his state on the "basis of a community of individuals with equal legal rights. The form of the state is the *opština* [commune] and the state is considered a collection of free *opštinas*."[11] In Greece the conservative politician and writer Ion Dragoumis, highly disillusioned by the failures of contemporary Greek society, also supported the restoration of communal authority, which he believed was the natural form of government

---

10  Jozo Tomasevich, *Peasants, Politics and Economic Change in Yugoslavia* (Stanford, Calif.: Stanford University Press, 1955), p. 144.

11  Woodford D. McClellan, *Svetozar Marković and the Origins of Balkan Socialism* (Princeton, N.J.: Princeton University Press, 1964), p. 130.

for his people. "Hellenism," he wrote, "is a family of Greek communities."[12] Similar views were expressed by Bulgarian populist writers, who criticized "the poverty and ignorance of the Bulgarian peasants, the decline of village patriarchal life, the decay of local industries, the spread of careerism and corruption in the new civil service."[13]

Concern for the peasant had a central place in the program of the Junimea circle in Romania, whose leading figure was the greatest Romanian poet, Mihail Eminescu. Another member, the historian Titu Maiorescu, played an active role in Romanian politics. He believed that the political system introduced by the Liberal Party and by the constitution of 1866 was based on ideas that did not fit the Romanian situation. Eminescu also held a conservative and traditional viewpoint. Considering the peasants as the basis of the state, the true Romanians, he sought institutions that would best serve their interests. He favored an autocratic monarchy and the end of the party system. The leading Romanian Marxist theoretician, Constantine Dobrogeanu-Gherea, placed a similar emphasis on the peasantry.

Most of the solutions offered by these writers were entirely impractical under the existing conditions and represented a sentimental longing for a world that had never existed. A return to a communal system, although idyllic in principle, could not have solved the problems of the modern Balkan societies and the competitive world system. The doubts thus expressed, nevertheless, did show the dissatisfaction felt by many, and not only among the peasants, about the way in which national life was evolving. These criticisms were to be important for the future. The writers had attacked the basic principles on which the political institutions of the new nations had been based – Western liberalism and nationalism. The failure of the independent regimes to satisfy the dreams and aspirations of intellectuals, peasants, and other disaffected groups left the door open to other ideological influences. Socialist, communist, anarchist, populist and, later, fascist doctrines were to offer alternative solutions to the problems of modern existence.

12  Quoted in Gerasimos Augustinos, *Consciousness and History: Nationalist Critics of Greek Society, 1897–1914* (Boulder, Colo.: East European Quarterly, 1977), p. 101.

13  Vivian Pinto, "The Civic and Aesthetic Ideals of Bulgarian Narodnik Writers," *Slavonic Review* (London) 32 (June 1954): 356.

# 2

---

# *The Dual Monarchy:*
# *Austria-Hungary*
# *from 1867 to 1914*

I N CONSIDERING THE HISTORY of the Habsburg Empire after 1867, it is important to emphasize that the state had in fact three governments. At the top stood the joint Austro-Hungarian administration with the common ministries for foreign affairs, war, and finance. In addition, separate governments existed for Austria and for Hungary. The major unifying figure in this arrangement was Franz Joseph, who was emperor in Austria and king in Hungary. A constitutional monarch throughout his realm, he nevertheless had different powers in each half. In practice, his influence on military affairs and foreign policy was strong, but he could not effectively control domestic events in any part of his domain. A further unifying element was provided by the fact that delegations of sixty members each from the Austrian Reichsrat and the Hungarian parliament met alternately in Vienna and Budapest to handle certain common problems. However, for the majority of the Habsburg population, the decisions of the separate Austrian and Hungarian governments were more important than the work of the joint institutions. It will be remembered that Austria was assigned Bukovina, Dalmatia, and the Slovenian lands; the great majority of the Habsburg Croats, Serbs, and Romanians, however, lived in the Hungarian crownlands (see Map 2).

Although this narrative deals primarily with the South Slav and Romanian populations, their specific problems did not dominate the political life of the monarchy. From the point of view of domestic concerns, the overriding issue until 1914 was the doubt felt over the strength and durability of the Ausgleich. In a sense the original pact had been based on a misunderstanding. Franz Joseph and his advisers had accepted the terms as the maximum that they were prepared to concede. They therefore regarded the understanding as final. In contrast, the Hungarian government kept attempting to negotiate further improvements in its own position. Hungary already had a disproportionate influence in the entire country, and it could prevent changes in the political structure of the Austrian partner. If the Hungarian leaders felt that their interests were threatened by any action in Vienna, they could and did control the situation by simply threatening to call the entire arrangement into question if they did not obtain their desires. Under no condition would they allow a strengthening of the central institutions. No Hungarian party would

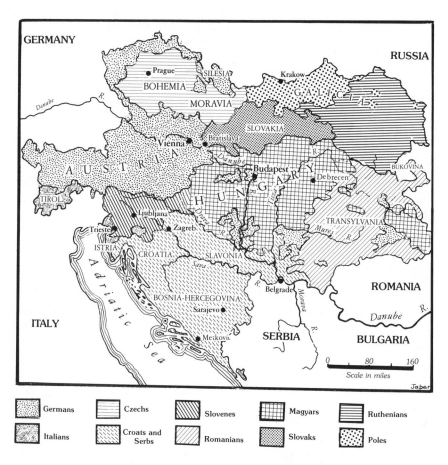

Map 2. Nationality map of Austria-Hungary

accept a change in the relationship unless it allowed Budapest even more freedom of action.

It is often written that the Ausgleich handed the control of Austria to the Germans and the Hungarian crownlands to the Magyars. This statement is in fact an oversimplification, in particular as regards the Austrian sections. The Germans in Austria never enjoyed the same position as the Hungarians in their territories. The Germans were not firmly united nationally; only some groups sought to establish a centralized German-dominated administration in Vienna. They certainly were never in a position to exert full control over the educational system or to follow an open policy of seeking to turn the other nationalities into Germans. Although militant nationalist parties were to arise, the German population was essentially on the defensive by the end of the century. In the early 1860s Germans had been indeed the most favored people. German was the state language; the Hungarian opposition had not yet recovered from 1849. At the time Germans of all parties assumed that this situation would continue. The Prussian victories and German unification gave them additional prestige. Their aim, however, was simply to preserve what they had. Hungary was lost in 1867, and the German position in the Austrian lands began to decline in relation to the other nationalities, a trend that was to continue to 1914. The challenge did not come from the South Slavs – they constituted only 7.3 percent of the population of Austria – but rather from the Czechs, Poles, and Italians.

In both parts of his empire, Franz Joseph should have attempted to remain above the national struggles and to have dealt equally with all his people. An extremely conscientious ruler, he placed his main emphasis on foreign policy and military matters, but he was also deeply involved in the domestic controversies. He attempted to uphold historic traditions and institutions, and he thought constantly about the prestige of the Habsburg dynasty. Internal pressures were, however, often too much for him. In the end, in his discussions with the Budapest government, he often submitted to Hungarian national demands and thus deserted his non-Hungarian subjects. In Austria, in contrast, he did not uphold German privileges with equal rigor. As we will see, he agreed to the appointment of ministries that rested on non-German constituencies. The entire national question, of course, was deeply intertwined with the social and economic issues of the time.

## THE NATIONAL PROBLEM IN AUSTRIA

In 1868 Austria had a two-house central parliament, and all of the seventeen provinces elected their own diets. The emperor had wide powers, including the appointment and dismissal of ministers, but in theory the ministry was responsible to the lower house. The strongest political party was that of the German Liberals. Although they were not in favor of a democratic franchise, they did place an emphasis on civil liberties. Political control in the state remained in the hands of the aristocracy and the wealthy. As far as the nationalities were concerned, the government received the support of the Polish leaders, who were given full authority in Galicia. A similar understanding was not reached with the Czech parties, who were dissatisfied with their position. German remained the principal language of administration, but the bureaucracy was multinational. Polish and Czech officials were becoming more common throughout the Austrian lands and in Bosnia-Hercegovina.

The 1860s, a period of economic upsurge, mark the beginning of industrial development in the monarchy. Bohemia became the main industrial region, with an emphasis on textiles, leather goods, shoes, beads, and jewelry. Vienna was at this time a major banking and financial center. In 1873 a crash followed by a depression had political as well as economic repercussions. It was, however, the issue of the occupation of Bosnia and Hercegovina in 1878 that led to the political crisis ending German Liberal predominance. Violently opposed to the addition of more Slavic people to the empire, this party refused to vote the funds for the occupation.

Politically conservative, Franz Joseph had never personally favored the Liberals, but he had tolerated their rule as long as they let him determine foreign policy. Now that they were opposing him, he was willing to turn the government over to their enemies. Although he signed the Dual Alliance with Germany, he followed a policy in domestic affairs that was not to the advantage of his German subjects. He appointed his friend Count Eduard von Taaffe to head a ministry based on conservatives, clerical groups, and certain Slavic parties, chiefly from among the Czechs and the Poles. This government, known as the Iron Ring, lasted from 1879 to 1893. Germans were included in it, but they came from conservative regions such as Styria and the Tirol.

The main internal issue during this period was the status of the Czechs in the population. Their demands introduced the broader question of the position of the Slavs in the empire as compared to that of the Germans and Hungarians, a matter that was to be the subject of continual and bitter debate thereafter. The Czech leaders themselves did not call for anything like united Slavic solidarity. They fought instead for the attainment of specific Czech goals. Their program, in fact, had much in common with the Hungarian attitude toward the lands of the crown of St. Stephen. The Czech nationalists wanted to obtain control of the Bohemian crownlands, which consisted of Bohemia, Moravia, and part of Silesia, where Czechs constituted about 60 percent of the population. They did not want a division on the basis of nationality. They were naturally opposed by both the Germans and the Poles. The focus of the Czech attack was to be the question of the use of German as the administrative language.

Faced with this challenge, as well as with other problems, the Germans too entered a period of revived national enthusiasm. Like the Slavic peoples and the Hungarians, they were forced to define their goals and develop national programs. They also had to consider their relationship with the German Empire. In these questions, the Germans did not form a single block but split on class, religious, and ideological lines. Most important for the next period were to be the Christian Socialists, who were conservative, clerical, and loyal to the dynasty; the Social Democrats, a Marxist party; and the small group of Pan-Germans who wished to break up the empire and join the Austrian and Bohemian lands to the German state.

After 1893 Austrian politics was dominated by national and social questions. In 1907 Franz Joseph took the radical step of agreeing to the introduction of universal male suffrage into Austria; the measure was never adopted in Hungary. This move solved few of the problems. In 1911, in the last election before the war, over fifty parties fought for the control of 516 seats. All of these events were reflected in the South Slav lands that were a part of Austria, the Slovenian regions and Dalmatia, as well as in Bukovina.

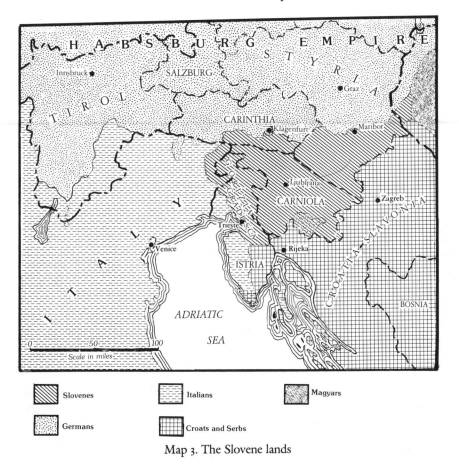

Map 3. The Slovene lands

## The Slovenes

Political activity among the Slovenes was to a degree hampered by the fact that, although they lived in a fairly compact group, their lands had never comprised a historic province. They had more than a 90 percent majority in the central province of Carniola, but they lived also in Styria, Carinthia, Istria, Gorizia, and Gradisca (see Map 3). A peasant population, strongly attached to the Catholic church, the Slovenes were conservative in political inclination and never carried through a major revolutionary movement. Although their region was not among the most prosperous of the empire, the peasantry in general owned their own farms, and they did not suffer from the bad rural conditions that have been noted in other Balkan areas. In fact, the average Slovene peasant was much better off than his equivalent elsewhere in Eastern Europe. As one authority has noted: "By 1914 the Slovenes were culturally and economically by far the most advanced South Slav nation."[1] If a Slovene became wealthy and moved up the social ladder, his inclination was to assimilate with the German population. The combination of political conservatism, strong Catholic influence, and relative prosperity explains why Slovenian political activity was limited and moderate in nature.

From the eighteenth century onward, however, a national cultural movement did develop. Its aim was to advance the use of the Slovenian language in education, literature, and administration. When compulsory primary education was introduced into the Austrian lands, the government provided textbooks that were either bilingual, that is, in German and Slovene, or completely in Slovene. Although the national language was thus used on the elementary levels, German was the language of higher education as well as of state administration. In the first part of the nineteenth century Slovene writers were concerned with their own history and with the Slavs in general. Anton Linhart wrote a history of Carinthia in German. France Prešeren, the greatest Slovenian writer, and another poet, Valentin Vodnik, worked at this time.

During the revolutions of 1848 the Slovenian peasants were primarily interested in ending the vestiges of the feudal system. Some Slovenian liberals became involved in the political events, advocating the unification of the lands inhabited by their co-nationals and the formation of a Slovenian province within the empire. Austro-Slav in convictions, they wished to transform the monarchy into a federal state of which Slovenia would be one part. After 1849 Slovenian nationalists concentrated on obtaining the use of their language in education and administration. Catholic influences remained strong. The Clerical Party held the allegiance of most of the peasant population, but a Liberal Party was also active. Both political organizations were hostile to the Ausgleich, which had divided the Slovene population, with the great majority assigned to Austria. Some national objectives were accomplished, however, during the Taaffe government. The use of Slovenian in the schools and administration increased; more Slovenes entered the bureaucracy. The national question was further complicated toward the end of the century by the increasing pressure of Italian nationalism. Italy laid claims to Habsburg territory, including Istria, which had a large Slovenian minority. Given the choice, the Slovenes preferred Austrian to Italian rule.

In the 1880s and 1890s changes were made in the Austrian voting regulations, culminating in the introduction of universal manhood suffrage in 1907. With this reform, the Slovenian population was in a better position to exert political influence. National feeling throughout the empire was becoming more intense. Unable to work with the German conservative parties, the Slovenian Clericals began to cooperate with the Croatian Party of Rights. In 1912 in the declaration of Ljubljana the two groups agreed to support each

---

1 Jozo Tomasevich, *Peasants, Politics and Economic Change in Yugoslavia* (Stanford, Calif.: Stanford University Press, 1955), p. 130.

other. Neither was Yugoslav in orientation; they did not wish to act together with the Orthodox Serbs of the monarchy.

The Slovenian Liberal Party also increased in influence, and eventually a section broke away to form the National Radical Party. Although both wings were concerned with the national question, neither had a plan to solve it. Both wished to keep the Slovenian lands in the Habsburg Empire. The only truly radical faction was the youth group *Preporod* (Renaissance), which favored the dissolution of the monarchy and the joining of Slovenia, Croatia, and Serbia to form a Yugoslav state. This organization represented, however, only a small minority of the conservative, Catholic, and peasant population. Prior to 1914 there was no Slovenian movement of consequence that stood for the breakup of the Habsburg Empire and the formation of a Yugoslavia.

## Dalmatia

After the acquisition of Dalmatia, the Habsburg Empire did little to disturb the existing social and political order. The chief political influence thus remained in the hands of the Italians and Italian-speaking Slavs who lived in the coastal towns. The franchise guaranteed their preeminent position. In the diet held in 1861 the 15,672 Italian-speakers elected twenty-nine deputies; the over 400,000 Croats and Serbs had only twelve. The fundamental controversy at this time was over the political future of the region. The Autonomist Party called for a separate provincial administration for Dalmatia. This group, which was sympathetic to Italian predominance, consisted primarily of officials, together with some professional men and large landowners. The rival National Party wished to be united with Croatia to form a reconstituted Triune Kingdom. It naturally received enthusiastic support from Zagreb.

The Autonomists, who fought such an annexation, had at first the support of the Austrian authorities. After the unification of Italy, when the new state continued to claim other Habsburg lands, Vienna became less sympathetic to the Italian dominance in Dalmatia. The National Party thus gained in influence in the 1870s. In the diet, which met in Zadar, this group held twenty-six seats; its opponents had fifteen. In 1883 the official language was changed from Italian to Serbo-Croatian.

Meanwhile, friction had developed between the Serbs and the Croats. The 1910 census gave the total population of Dalmatia as 634,855, of which 82 percent were Croats, 16 percent Serbs, and 2 percent Italians and others. During the 1860s the Croats and Serbs had cooperated against the Habsburg authorities. Soon, however, the conflicts arose between them that we shall see also in Croatia. The major quarrel was over the future of Bosnia-Hercegovina and the question of its national composition. The Serbian National Party, organized in 1879, strongly opposed Croatian proposals to unite Dalmatia and the newly acquired Bosnia-Hercegovina with Croatia. The party had a journal, *Srpski List* (Serbian News). Because of the disagreements with the Croats, the Dalmatian Serbs cooperated with the Autonomist Party. At the same time the Dalmatian Croats were attracted increasingly to Ante Starčević's Party of Rights; they were sympathetic with its clerical, conservative, and Croatian-national stand. The situation changed, however, at the beginning of the new century. At this time events in Dalmatia led to the joining of the Serbian and Croatian parties in the Croatian-Serbian Coalition, an action that was to have great effects in Croatia proper. This development will be discussed in connection with the political controversies in the Hungarian crownlands.

A poor land, consisting principally of a narrow strip of rocky soil between the Dinaric Alps and the sea, Dalmatia did not have the resources for a prosperous economy. As in Montenegro, the land could not support the people, and there was a large emigration from the area. Not only was there little economic advancement, but even the existing industry declined. Shipbuilding, which had been a major occupation in the past, fell rapidly with the advent of steamships, because the region did not have the resources or skills for their construction. Wine making and grape production were damaged by the prevalence of the plant disease phylloxera and by the competition of the cheaper Italian products. In 1891 a narrow-gauge railroad linked Metković with Sarajevo, but this line brought little economic advantage. Both Bosnia and Dalmatia were backward and poor.

## Bukovina

Bukovina was the most nationally mixed of the Austrian possessions. According to the 1910 census there were 305,000 Ukrainians, 273,000 Romanians, 168,000 Germans, and 102,000 Jews, together with sizable numbers of Poles and Hungarians. When the region was first annexed to the empire in 1775, it had been joined with Galicia, and a Polish administration predominated. The local leadership was strongly opposed to this association, and in 1848 demands for separation were part of the revolutionary programs. In 1853 the province received its own diet and a separate organization. Romanian and Ukrainian were both recognized as official languages within the province, with German, of course, remaining the language of imperial administration and higher education.

The very complexity of the national structure virtually forced the population to adopt a position of moderation. By the beginning of the twentieth century a system of local administration on a national basis had been set up, which functioned satisfactorily. It was clear by this time that the Ukrainian population was increasing and the Romanian was declining. The fact that this region was relatively remote from the center of the Austrian state appears to have been an advantage; it was never the scene of the bitter national conflicts that took place elsewhere.

# The Dual Monarchy

## BOSNIA-HERCEGOVINA

After 1878 Bosnia and Hercegovina were the subject of vehement disputes between the Austrian and Hungarian governments and similarly between Serbian and Croatian national leaders. As we have seen, Austria-Hungary acquired the right to occupy both regions at the Congress of Berlin; the Sanjak of Novi Pazar similarly passed under Habsburg control. The monarchy joined the two provinces into one administrative district, Bosnia-Hercegovina. It should be noted that although only the right of occupation was conceded, the Habsburg government treated the area as if it were a permanent possession, and the administrative provisions were worked out on a long-term basis.

The Habsburg Empire had asserted its claims to the region in the negotiations with Russia that resulted in the signing of the Reichstadt agreement in 1876 and in the two understandings of January and March 1877. The provinces were to be the Habsburg compensation for Russia's gains in reannexing southern Bessarabia and establishing a Bulgarian state. The action was favored in particular by Franz Joseph, who saw the acquisition of these lands as balancing the surrender of Lombardy and Venetia at the time of the unification of Italy, and by the army, which wished to acquire the Dalmatian hinterland. In contrast, the occupation was strongly opposed by the German Liberals and many Hungarians, who did not want the addition of more Slavs to the empire. The Hungarian leaders, however, were faced with unpleasant alternatives. It was obvious that if the monarchy did not assume responsibility for Bosnia and Hercegovina, the provinces would eventually fall to Serbia. This addition of territory would make Serbia a strong power and a formidable point of attraction to the Habsburg South Slavs. With these considerations in mind, the Hungarian government agreed to the empire's acquisition of the region, but with considerable reluctance. It was because of the sensitivity of the subject in internal affairs that the Habsburg representatives at the Congress of Berlin asked for an occupation rather than a full annexation.

The actual occupation of the provinces was accomplished only with great difficulty. At the Congress of Berlin the Porte vehemently opposed the surrender to outside control. When the Habsburg authorities entered the land, they had to contend with similar violent opposition from the Bosnian Muslims and Serbs. The army had to literally fight its way into the land, an undertaking that proved expensive in men and money. The government had to use a sum of 60 million florins that had been voted for defense at the time of the crisis following the conclusion of the Treaty of San Stefano. Once the region had been secured, the problem of how it should be administered immediately arose.

The military occupation was carried through by divisions of the Croatian Thirteenth Army Corps, stationed in Croatia, under the command of General Josip Filipović. He set up a provisional government, staffed largely by Croatian civil servants, and the laws and legal system of Croatia were introduced. As could be expected, Croatian opinion was most enthusiastic about the occupation. It was hoped that the territory would be joined to Croatia's, an action that was essential for Croatian national aims. Both the Croatian assembly, the *sabor*, and the *ban* (governor), Ivan Mažuranić, requested the unification. Similar points of view were held in Slovenia. The increase in the South Slav population of the empire was supported by the Slovenes and Croats for the political reasons that led the Germans and Hungarians in the opposite direction: in an age when national passion was increasing and the franchise was becoming more democratic, numbers counted in the fight for predominance.

The Hungarian government was, of course, adamant on the question of the joining of Bosnia-Hercegovina to Croatia; the action would strengthen the Croatian national position too much. Similar objections to placing the territory under an Austrian administration were raised. In fact, the addition of the region to either half of the Dual Monarchy would have upset the delicate balance established between Vienna and Budapest. A compromise was finally reached. The lands were placed under the crown and the direct authority of the joint minister of finance. This official had, in fact, few duties, and there seemed no alternative arrangement possible. A system of administration was worked out in which this minister received what were in fact dictatorial powers. The titular head of the government of the province was the commanding general of the army corps stationed there. He had, however, associated with him a civil official, who exercised the real authority. The Habsburg government retained the Ottoman administrative divisions, but simply gave them German names. The basic social and economic order was also preserved.

From June 1882 until his death twenty-one years later Benjámin Kállay, the joint minister of finance, headed the administration of Bosnia-Hercegovina. Well acquainted with the Balkans, he had been consul-general in Belgrade, and he had written a history of Serbia. A good administrator, he organized a bureaucratic system similar to that in the rest of the monarchy. Since Bosnia was an extremely backward area, however, he had difficulty in attracting able men, and some of his officials were not competent to deal with the difficult problems of the region. The introduction of Habsburg institutions also caused a sharp rise in the number of state employees. Under Ottoman rule Bosnia had been governed by 120 officials; this number rose in 1881 to 600 and finally in 1908 to 9,533.[2] This bureaucracy was staffed by men from all over the empire. In 1907, of the 9,106 members, only 2,493 were natives. However, in the administrative level that had the closest contact with the population, most of

2  Peter F. Sugar, *Industrialization of Bosnia-Hercegovina, 1878–1918* (Seattle: University of Washington Press, 1963), p. 29.

the officials were Slavic in national background. The Croats filled about half the posts, but there were also many Czechs, Poles, and Slovenes.

The basic reason for the uprising in 1875 had been the bad system of land-holding and resentment felt by the peasants, or *kmets*, who worked on the large estates. The Habsburg authorities did little to remedy this situation. The landholding Muslim agas and begs, who were largely Serbo-Croatian in language and nationality, were the dominating political element in the prov-ince. The Austrian authorities maintained the 1859 Ottoman land regulations, which favored this group. Some measures were passed to assist the kmets in buying land, but by 1914 there were still 93,368 kmet families, the great ma-jority of them Serbian Orthodox, who worked a third of the cultivated land. At the time of the occupation it was estimated that there were about 85,000 kmet families, of which 60,000 were Orthodox and 23,000 Catholic, with only some Muslims. These peasants worked the land of the 6,000 to 7,000 agas and begs.[3]

There was naturally much disappointment at the Habsburg attitude; it had been expected that there would be major changes under the Habsburg ad-ministration. A few limited efforts were indeed made to help agriculture, and some projects, such as reforesting, were undertaken, but the basic problem of land distribution was not met. The large landed estates were not farmed as a unit. As in Romania, the lands were divided among the kmets and other tenants, who worked their plots by the same inefficient methods as in the past.

The Habsburg government in justifying its claim to the region had cited the backward conditions, and despite the failure to deal with the agricultural problems, the Habsburg authorities did try to make improvements in other areas. The great block to reform, here as elsewhere, was the question who would pay for the modernization of this primitive region. At the beginning of the occupation, the decision had been made that Bosnia-Hercegovina would have to be self-supporting. This action not only sharply curtailed what could be done, but made an increase in local taxes inevitable. New taxes were added, the rates on the old ones were increased, and the methods of collection be-came more efficient. It has been estimated that the taxes paid by the individ-ual during Kállay's administration rose fivefold.[4] In return, the population did receive a better administration, and a modern school system was intro-duced. The government encouraged the development of mineral and timber resources. Railroads financed by Habsburg and foreign loans were built. The problem here was similar to that which we have met elsewhere: the improve-ments that were made were often of no direct value to the peasant taxpayer. In addition, there was criticism of the fact that, in the construction of roads

---

3 Tomasevich, *Peasants, Politics and Economic Change*, p. 108.
4 C. A. Macartney, *The Habsburg Empire, 1790–1918* (London: Weidenfeld & Nicolson, 1969), p. 745.

and railroads, Habsburg military considerations and Hungarian economic interests were usually given precedence over the needs of the local population.

The most controversial aspect of Habsburg policy during the Kállay administration was the treatment of the national question. The acquisition of Bosnia-Hercegovina held a first priority on the programs of both the Serbian government and the Croatian nationalist leaders in Zagreb. The Hungarian government, in contrast, could allow neither alternative. Under Ottoman rule the people had been considered only by their religious affiliation, that is, as Orthodox, Catholic, or Muslim. With the increasing emphasis on national origin, the great question in Bosnian politics was the nationality of the Muslims, who were Slavic and Serbo-Croatian speaking. Both Serbs and Croats put forth claims to these people. Their allegiance was essential to both sides, since each needed this group to be able to claim a majority of the population. Kállay was able to exploit the rivalry in the government interest. He also tried to promote the idea of a separate Bosnian nationalism, but, although the concept appealed to some Muslims, it was not attractive to most of the population.

Since the Serbian threat was seen as the most dangerous, the Habsburg authorities usually favored Croatian interests. In addition, as the majority of the Habsburg subjects were Catholic, the imperial authorities naturally gave the Catholic church special privileges and favored Catholic applicants for official positions. There was an increase of church building and in the number of Catholic educational establishments. In 1882 Dr. Josip Stadler became archbishop of Sarajevo. An active, militant leader, he wished to replace the predominant Franciscan influence over the Bosnian Catholics, and he brought in Croatian clerics from Croatia. This period thus witnessed an increase in Croatian influence and a rise of enthusiasm in support of the union of Dalmatia, Bosnia, Croatia, and Slavonia. The opposition to this idea among the Serbs had, as we have seen, become an issue in Dalmatian politics. It was to play an even greater role in Croatia.

Many Habsburg officials had desired to annex Bosnia-Hercegovina after 1878. The temporary nature of their authority had many drawbacks. The principal block remained, not the opposition of the great powers, but rather the strong objections raised by the Hungarian leaders, joined by many Germans, to the acquisition of more Slavs in the monarchy. In 1908 Hungary agreed to an annexation only after the promise had been given that the region would not be joined with Croatia. The final action, taken in this year, led to a major crisis with Serbia, which will be discussed in the next chapter. Bosnia-Hercegovina was thereafter given a provincial organization and its own diet. The laws regulating its affairs were issued in 1910, and an election was held. The franchise strongly favored the wealthier, conservative elements in the population. A curia system was introduced that gave the large landowners one representative for 80 voters; the city inhabitants had one for every 2,300 and the peasants one for every 10,000. The diet had only limited legislative rights. Bills it passed could be vetoed by the joint Ministry of Finance, under whose control the province remained, and by the Austrian and Hungarian parliaments. In the diet the Muslim and Croatian parties tended to cooperate, leaving the Serbs in a minority. As we shall see, the area became the center of violent Serbian feeling and the focus of the attention of the Serbian state.

## THE KINGDOM OF HUNGARY

Until 1914 the principal controversies in the Hungarian part of the Dual Monarchy continued to center around the national question and relations, on the one hand, with Vienna and, on the other, with the other national groups in the lands of the crown of St. Stephen. The nineteenth century had witnessed two great national unifications – the German and the Italian. In these movements territories were brought together in which the great majority of the population belonged to a single nationality. The Hungarian movement had also been singularly successful, but the leadership was attempting an almost impossible task in the modern world. Its goal remained that of 1848–1849: it wished to establish a unitary Hungarian-national state in lands where the Hungarian population was not in the majority and where the other nationalities had a historic tradition of resistance to rule from Budapest. The concurrent Hungarian attempt to lessen the ties with Vienna contained other dangers; should Hungary secede from the monarchy, even with full control of the Hungarian crownlands, the state would be too weak and small to stand alone without a powerful ally. In seeking to loosen the links with Vienna, and thus to reduce the power and prestige of the monarchy as a whole, the Hungarian kingdom was working toward its own destruction. Nevertheless, the leadership continued to pursue the national struggle on these two levels.

It should be strongly emphasized that Hungarian policy was determined by but a small proportion of the entire population. According to the franchise provisions in effect in 1874 only 5.9 percent of the people voted. Political control thus rested safely in the hands of the Hungarian landowners. It has been estimated that three thousand individuals or institutions held almost half the land.[5] Since their prosperity rested on agriculture, they exerted a strong influence on commercial policy in the entire empire; it was pressure from this group that had caused difficulties in the negotiation of the commercial treaties with Romania and Serbia. A small minority of the Hungarian citizens thus wielded disproportionate economic and political influence. The Hungarian peasants, as well as the other national groups, were placed in a subordinate position in the state.

After the conclusion of the Ausgleich, Ferenc Deák and Gyula Andrássy,

5  Robert A. Kann, *A History of the Habsburg Empire, 1526–1918* (Berkeley: University of California Press, 1974), p. 463.

who had been responsible for the agreement, remained in power. They were soon challenged by others who did not like the settlement and who demanded further advantages for Hungary or even a complete separation from Vienna. A group led by Kálmán Tisza favored an arrangement by which the single link would be the person of the ruler, with a separate Hungarian army and diplomatic service. Tisza's opinions, however, changed when he became prime minister, a post that he held from 1875 to 1890. During his period in office, the Liberal Party, which favored the Ausgleich, dominated the government and was the strongest Hungarian party.

Although Tisza's successors maintained his general policy after 1890, the opposition increased. The chief center was the Independence Party, which based its program on the ideals of the old revolutionary Lajos Kossuth, who still lived in exile. Its main objective was to weaken the connection with Vienna. In 1895, after Kossuth's death the year before, his son Ferenc returned and took the leadership of the party. A much weaker man, the younger Kossuth was no replacement for his father. The major crisis in the relations between Austria and Hungary occurred in 1902 when an army bill was introduced in the diet. The Independence Party, asserting the stand of the strong nationalists, would not accept it unless it provided that the regiments recruited in the kingdom would be led by Hungarian officers, fly their own flags, and have Hungarian as the language of command. These demands had been a part of the party program in the past. In addition to asserting independence from Vienna, these measures would have had the advantage of aiding in the magyarization of the recruits, who would, of course, be taken from Slavic and Romanian regions as well as from Hungarian-speaking districts. It would, of course, be of no advantage for a Romanian or Croatian soldier to receive orders in Hungarian rather than German.

Although Franz Joseph had allowed Hungary almost complete internal autonomy, he was adamant on questions regarding his authority in military matters. He now exercised his powers as king of Hungary. He appointed Stephen Tisza, the son of the former minister and a supporter of dualism, as prime minister, and the army bill was forced through the parliament. The problem, however, was not yet solved. The elections held in 1905 gave a victory to the opposition. Franz Joseph met this challenge by threatening to introduce universal male suffrage and the secret ballot, measures that were to be applied in Austria in 1907. Such an action, if carried through in Hungary, would have ended both Hungarian national dominance and the rule of the landed class. The opposition crumbled before this threat, and the Ausgleich remained unaltered. Although the issue stayed open, there were to be no more major crises regarding the political relationship of the partner states.

Meanwhile, the conflict with the other nationalities continued. The Hungarian objective remained the establishment of a true national state. Every effort was made to bring more members into the Hungarian fold. As we have seen, national background was not a bar to Hungarian citizenship if the individual renounced his past and adopted the language, including the use of a Hungarian form of his name. Under these circumstances, he could enjoy all the privileges of a citizen with full civil rights.

The schools were to become the chief vehicle for magyarization. The Nationalities Law of 1868, passed after the Ausgleich, was moderate and liberal in conception. In theory, it granted every nationality the right to use its language in its political and cultural life. Primary and secondary schools were to be taught in the mother tongue of the pupils. Local courts and the lower levels of the administration were to follow similar rules. However, these regulations were never truly implemented. By the turn of the century, national feeling had become more intense throughout the kingdom. The political leaders of all the groups believed either that their goals had not been achieved, or that they were being weakened and compromised. Great resentment was felt over the measures passed by the Hungarian government to influence the nationalities, in particular those which involved the language to be used in education and the emphasis placed on instilling Hungarian patriotism in the schools. These actions struck directly at the efforts of the leaders of the non-Hungarian population to implant feelings of national self-consciousness and pride in their own people.

The attitude toward the nationalities severely limited the political evolution of the Hungarian nation itself. There could be no franchise reform, since that would increase the influence of the national groups. Thus a small percentage of the Hungarian inhabitants limited the opportunities of all of the people of the kingdom, including the majority of the Hungarians. These policies were not to succeed. By 1914 there had been no significant change in the ethnic balance in the lands. There had been, however, a great intensification of the bitterness felt by the principal non-Hungarian people of the kingdom – Croatians, Romanians, Serbs, and Slovaks alike – toward Budapest. This development will be discussed here as it affected the Croats and Serbs in Croatia and the Romanians in Transylvania.

### Croatia

Despite the Hungarian determination to dominate the other nationalities, the government did concede a special position to Croatia, whose territory included also Slavonia. According to the Nagodba (Agreement, Compromise) of 1868, the state had its own diet and Croatian was the language of local administration. Budapest nevertheless was able to keep a firm hold through the ban, who was appointed by the central government, and through the control that was exercised over finances. In Croatia, as in Hungary, only a minority of the population had political power. The franchise was limited to those who paid 60 kronen in direct taxes in the rural areas and 30 kronen in the city. Up to 1910, 2 percent of the inhabitants were able to vote, a number that was raised to 8.8 percent in that year. Croatian politics was thus to be a matter of concern for only a small section of the population, consisting primarily of the city middle class, members of the professions, and prosperous landowners.

To 1914 Croatian political life was dominated not only by the conflict with the Hungarian central authorities, but also by the alternate friendship and antagonism between the Croat and Serb parties, whose relationship was made more difficult by disagreements over Bosnia-Hercegovina. Both Croatian-national and Yugoslav programs had previously won adherents in Croatia. Among the nationalists, the most popular was Ante Starčević, the head of the Party of Rights, whose doctrines had strong anti-Serbian overtones. Although he has often been criticized as holding extreme views, his attitude toward the Serbs was no more violent than that of some Hungarian parties toward the state's other nationalities, of Greeks toward their Slavic-speaking citizens, of Serbs towards Albanians, or of Panslav Russians toward Poles.

The basic goal of the Croatian nationalist was the establishment of a Croatian state, either within the confines of the empire or as an independent unit. However, before this objective could be accomplished, certain tough problems had to be faced. Most serious was the fact that the Croats had the most difficult geopolitical situation of any major East European nationality. They lived preponderantly in Dalmatia, Croatia, and Slavonia, provinces that formed a semicircle around Bosnia-Hercegovina. Even within these lands, a high percentage of Serbs was to be found, particularly in the area of the Military Frontier. In Croatia-Slavonia the population consisted of 62.5 percent Croats and 24.6 percent Serbs. The ideal Croatian state for the nationalist would have included the lands of the Triune Kingdom with the addition of Bosnia-Hercegovina, which was now, of course, also under Habsburg rule. With these boundaries Croatia would form a respectable East European power with sufficient territory and rational frontiers. The main hindrance to a Bosnian annexation, considered on a national basis, was the fact that the Catholic, or Croatian, section of the population was only 20 percent, compared to the 43 percent that was Orthodox and Serbian. The national affiliation of the Muslim third of the inhabitants was thus a vital question. Even should this issue be met, the problem of what should be done with the Serbian population remained. Starčević and those with similar views regarded the Serbs simply as second-rate Croats. They could be "croaticized," just as the Hungarians were attempting to magyarize their minorities. The entire situation was further complicated by the great attraction that the kingdom of Serbia offered to the Bosnian Serbs. The majority of these people, like the Serbs of Serbia proper, felt that Bosnia-Hercegovina was their heritage and should be joined in a great Serbian state.

The issue of the annexation of Bosnia-Hercegovina to Croatia arose immediately after the region became a Habsburg possession. The ban at this time was Ivan Mažuranić, who held office from 1873 to 1880. The uprising in Bosnia and Hercegovina had been followed with great interest in Croatia.

Once the Habsburg occupation became known, the sabor sent an address to Franz Joseph requesting the unification of the provinces with Croatia, Slavonia, and Dalmatia. The abolition of the Military Frontier, a region under the direct control of Vienna, and the adding of the port of Rijeka to this state was also desired. The Hungarian reaction to such a proposal was not in doubt. Such an action would have involved a major readjustment in the political and national balance in the Habsburg Empire and would have also met the firm opposition of the German parties. The Military Frontier was amalgamated with Croatia in 1881, but no further steps were taken by the imperial government to meet the Croatian wishes.

From 1883 to 1903 Count Károly Khuen-Héderváry was ban of Croatia. A Hungarian landowner, he was able to maintain effective control over the country. The extremely limited franchise allowed him to obtain a cooperative sabor. Like the Transylvanian diet, this body contained some members who held their seats because of their birth or position, such as the archbishop of Zagreb and the great nobility, who usually gave their support to the government. Khuen-Héderváry was aided by the fact that at this time the Unionists, the party that favored cooperation with Budapest, were joined by a part of the National Party, whose program had previously emphasized Illyrian or Yugoslav ideas. With this added support the Hungarian-dominated regime won successive victories in the elections held in 1884, 1887, and 1892.

The Khuen-Héderváry administration was further strengthened by its ability to exploit the antagonism that had developed between the Serbs and the Croats. Whereas previous governments had favored the Croats, this regime reversed the situation. With the incorporation of the Military Frontier into the state, the proportion of Serbs had increased. They were encouraged to enter the civil service and the professions. The major Serbian political organization was the Serbian Independent Party; it published a newspaper, *Srbobran* (Serb Defender), and it had an anti-Croat orientation. It will be remembered that in this period independent Serbia was in close alliance with, in fact had become a dependent of, the Dual Monarchy. The policy of cooperating with the Serbs of the empire thus corresponded with the friendly relations established with Belgrade.

The Croatian nationalists responded as could be expected. Their most popular leader, Starčević, remained extremely influential until his death in 1896. The goal of his Party of Rights was the creation of an independent Croatian state, and he rejected cooperation with either Vienna or Budapest. He continued to regard the Serbs as Orthodox Croats, and he referred to the Slovenes as "mountain Croats." In 1894, however, his party split into two groups. The new alignment, called the Pure Party of Rights, was led by Josip Frank. Although this party was even more antagonistic toward the Serbs than Starčević's organization, it was more favorable in its attitude toward the Habsburg Monarchy. It called for the establishment of a Croatian state, including both the Triune Kingdom and Bosnia-Hercegovina. Croatia was to remain in the empire, but to have the same status as Austria and Hungary. This Trialist solution provided a place for the Catholic Slovenes, but not for the Orthodox Serbs. The demand for the creation of an autonomous kingdom of Croatia was also supported by the Croatian Social Democratic Party, formed in 1894, and the Peasant Party, organized in 1904. The emphasis on Croatian political rights was accompanied by growing animosity between the Serbs and Croats by the end of the century. Riots occurred, and the press of both sides exchanged violent recriminations. The major focus of Serbian and Croatian discontent was thus directed against each other and not against the dualist system.

The year 1903 brought great changes to the South Slav lands of the monarchy, as well as to Serbia. At this time, it will be remembered, the Obrenović dynasty was overturned in Belgrade. Relations between Serbia and the Habsburg Empire subsequently deteriorated. Simultaneously, Kállay's death ended his long rule in Bosnia-Hercegovina, and Khuen-Héderváry left Zagreb to become the Hungarian prime minister. A new generation had also come to influence Croatian politics. Two earlier leaders, Franjo Rački and Bishop Strossmayer, died in 1894 and 1905, respectively, but their Yugoslav orientation was to be favored by others who realized the dangers and futility of the continuing Serb–Croat conflict. These convictions were held in particular by Serbian and Croatian intellectuals and by students, some of whom had studied in Prague with Thomas G. Masaryk, a strong proponent of Slavic unity. These young men had witnessed directly the sharp German–Czech conflict over the control of Bohemia, and they were very critical about many aspects of the Habsburg government.

The first major step toward reconciling at least some Serbian and Croatian parties was taken in Dalmatia. Although a degree of Serb and Croat antagonism had developed there, it had never attained the levels reached in Croatia. In 1905 the Dalmatian South Slav political leaders decided to try to exploit the crisis that had arisen in Budapest over the army question. They therefore offered to give their support to the Hungarian Independence Party in its defiance of the imperial government. In return, they wanted the Hungarian authorities to make changes in the Nagodba to the Croatian advantage and to agree to a restoration of the Triune Kingdom. Once again Croatian parties were willing to give their approval to Hungarian resistance to Vienna in return for political assurances. Although they gained nothing directly by this tactic, the action had the important effect of leading to cooperation between Serbian and Croatian parties, first in Dalmatia and then in Croatia.

In October 1905 representatives of some Croatian parties met in Rijeka, where they adopted a resolution supporting the position of the Hungarian opposition. At the same time they sought the incorporation of Dalmatia into Croatia and a strengthening of the autonomous position of the state. A similar meeting was held by Serbian groups in Zadar. They approved the same program and agreed to cooperation with the Croats in return for equal political rights. They thus expressed their willingness to become a part of a reconstituted Triune Kingdom. In December a similar course of events followed in Croatia. Several Croatian and Serbian parties joined to form the Croatian-Serbian Coalition. The major goal was to secure the unification of Croatia and Dalmatia; the question of the future of Bosnia-Hercegovina was avoided.

Extremely important for the future was the Yugoslav orientation of the coalition's program. Both the Serbian Independent Party and the Croatian Party of Rights, to cite the two major examples, had emphasized the differences between the two South Slav peoples. By implication, the conflicts could end only with the victory of one over the other in the Habsburg lands. The Croatian-Serbian Coalition returned instead to the ideas of the early Illyrian movement and of men like Strossmayer, arguing that both Serbs and Croats formed one Yugoslav nationality. The program of the Dalmatian coalition stated:

> Both clubs stand on the premise that the Croats and Serbs are one people, that they are equal in relation to one another and that . . . they must consolidate their strength and their national forces in order that events do not find them unprepared.
>
> Consequently, the Croats and Serbs in Dalmatia will work shoulder to shoulder as blood brothers in national political questions and separately will endeavor with united forces to realize as soon as possible the union of Dalmatia with Croatia and Slavonia as the chief condition for securing a better common future for us . . . As regards national designation and language, which for the Croats and the Serbs is one and the same, the Croats and Serbs will adhere unalterably to the decision of July 21, 1883, in the Dalmatian Sabor according to which our common language is called Croatian or Serbian . . .
>
> As regards the public schools in Dalmatia, both parties will insist on and work [towards the goal] that the names Croatia and Serbia occupy a position of honor, that Croatian and Serbian history will be taken into consideration in schoolbooks, that Serbian and Croatian students will be able to study the chief events of each other's histories, and that both the Latin and Cyrillic scripts will be taught and learned in order that the students may become versed in the reading and writing of each other's scripts.[6]

In May 1906 the Coalition gained an important victory when it won forty-three out of eighty-eight seats in the Croatian sabor. The original objective

---

6 Viktor Novak, *Antologija Jugoslovenske Misli i Narodnog Jedinstva, 1390–1930* [Anthology of the Yugoslav idea and national unity, 1390–1930] (Belgrade: Štampa Državne Štamparije, 1930), pp. 515–517.

of the Dalmatian parties in cooperating with the Hungarians failed, of course, when their resistance on the military question was abandoned. The Budapest government not only would not give concessions to Croatia, but attempted to limit further what rights the state possessed, passing, for instance, a law concerning the use of the Hungarian language on the state railroads that contradicted the provisions of the Nagodba.

Despite this failure to make immediate advances, the Croatian-Serbian Coalition became the major political bloc in Croatian politics. In the next years it followed a highly opportunistic course of action. Since it was a coalition, it included parties and individuals with differing programs. Some of the more radical members went so far as to seek the complete reorganization, even the breakup, of the empire, whereas the more moderate wing simply wanted increased autonomy for Croatia. Major political parties remained outside its ranks. The National Party, which gave support to the Hungarian-dominated regime, of course did not join. Even more significant, both sections of the Party of Rights retained an independent position.

The strength and popularity of the Coalition, as well as some aspects of its program, thoroughly disturbed the Habsburg authorities. A crisis came at the time of the annexation of Bosnia-Hercegovina, a move that the Coalition opposed. In 1909 two court processes, the Agram (Zagreb) and Friedjung trials, were conducted against members of the Coalition to try to prove treasonous connections with the Serbian state. Both were propaganda disasters for the government officials, who used forged documents and improper evidence to attempt to gain convictions. Instead of injuring or destroying the Coalition, the trials drew its members closer together.

In the years preceding World War I the Coalition and the government modified their attitudes toward each other. Although the Frank party never abandoned its hostility toward the Nagodba arrangements, the Coalition did come to an agreement with the government in 1910. A new electoral law, increasing the number of voters from 49,796 to 190,096, was passed. In the elections the Coalition won thirty-seven seats; the parties supporting the government received eighteen; the two branches of the Party of Rights had twenty-four; and the Croatian Peasant Party won nine. Although the Coalition did not always support the government, it did work within the dualist system prior to the war. Its immediate aim was the widening of Croatian autonomous rights, in particular in financial questions, but within the existing political framework.

The Coalition's moderate policy naturally gave rise to much criticism. In 1912, for the first time, terrorist activities became a part of the Croatian political scene. In that year Slavko Cuvaj was ban; the majority in the sabor, including the Coalition, were in opposition to his government. Čuvaj dismissed the assembly and, after he was named royal commissioner, ruled as a dictator. Two efforts were made to assassinate him during the year. Similar attempts on other officials were organized by small groups of young men who sought a more radical solution to the South Slav problem and who disapproved of the compromises made by the politicians.

On the eve of World War I it can thus be seen that the strongest political group, the Croatian-Serbian Coalition, was working within the limits of the Nagodba and not actively attempting to break the link with Budapest. The great contribution of this group was its attempt to end the Serb–Croat feuding that had been evident in the previous periods. It stood strongly for cooperation among all of the South Slavs within the empire. Although some elements in the Coalition had close ties with Serbia and dreamed of an eventual independent Yugoslav state, the majority were moderate and limited in their objectives. In opposition to this standpoint, other Croatian parties sought a radical reorganization of the empire. The two branches of the Party of Rights, as we have seen, opposed cooperation with Hungary and proposed the establishment of a Greater Croatia, including Bosnia-Hercegovina and the Slovene lands. The Croatian Peasant Party had a similar desire to unify all of these regions into a kingdom of Croatia. These parties thus stood for a Trialist solution to the Habsburg nationality problems, in which a Croatian or South Slav state would be created to serve as a balance to Austria and Hungary. In contrast to the program of the Coalition, these plans did not allow the Orthodox Serbs an equal position with the Catholic Croats and Slovenes.

In the prewar years Croatia was a moderately prosperous area economically. Agriculture remained predominant; the region did not industrialize, as did Bohemia and Upper Austria. In 1910, 78.4 percent of the population was engaged in agriculture and only 9.6 percent in manufacturing, where small craft enterprises played the principal role. All of the Croatian lands, in particular Dalmatia, suffered from the problems connected with the rise in population and the subdivision of the land. As a result, there was much emigration in the prewar years. Nevertheless, general conditions of life were superior to those in Serbia and much better than those in Bosnia-Hercegovinia.

## Transylvania

The political situation in Transylvania contrasted sharply with that in Croatia. Although both regions were a part of the lands of the crown of St. Stephen, the Hungarian government had allowed Croatia a limited autonomy. It had a diet as well as token representation in the Hungarian parliament. Serbo-Croatian was the language of local administration and elementary education. A Croatian school system was in existence. As we have seen, a lively political life had developed, and many parties with different views were organized. There were thus national institutions that could represent the views of the nation despite the restrictions existing in some spheres of political activity. A similar situation had developed in Dalmatia and Bukovina, which also had diets and national representation.

In contrast, after the Ausgleich, Transylvania became an integral part of Hungary. Not only the Romanians, but also the Saxons and the Szeklers lost their provincial rights, and they had only a limited representation in the legislature in Budapest. In 1865 Franz Joseph had surrendered to the Hungarian demands. The old franchise had been reintroduced in Transylvania, a move resulting in the election of a diet in which the Hungarians, with 29 percent of the population, elected eighty-nine delegates, whereas the Romanian majority were represented by only thirteen. As could be expected, this assembly voted union with Hungary, an action that both Budapest and Franz Joseph subsequently approved. This annexation deeply affected the position of the Romanians. Although they constituted a majority in Transylvania, they were but 15 percent of the total population of the entire Hungarian kingdom. The influence of the Saxons and the Szeklers was similarly diminished.

After the union Transylvania was divided into districts with prefects and subprefects at their head. These officials of the centralized system naturally represented the interests of the Budapest government, and they often did not know the languages of the region. In 1874 a new electoral law placed the qualifications for voting so high that most of the Romanian population was effectively excluded. The regulations also gave the franchise to those who had a school diploma or who were officials, and it excluded illiterates. These measures were to the clear detriment of the Romanian peasant, who did not have the income or the educational opportunities necessary to participate in the political activities of his region. He thus had no state institutions through which he could make his demands known or state his grievances. Political action thus had to be organized in another manner, and, as in the past, it was to take the form of the summoning of special assemblies and appeals to the emperor.

Until 1914 most Romanian activities were defensive in nature and were aimed at combating the ever-increasing pressure for magyarization that came from Budapest. The major Hungarian influence was exerted through the schools. In the Nationalities Law of 1868 provision had been made for the use of local languages. Hungary was declared to be one state, but the existence of several nationalities, with the division based on language, was recognized. In other words, Romanians were considered to be Hungarian citizens speaking the Romanian tongue. Hungarian was to be used for the government, but the other languages were to be allowed in education, cultural affairs, and local administration under certain conditions. Private secular or religious schools could be opened, but their programs had to be approved by the Ministry of Education. A similar measure of state control was shown in the laws concerning the press and publications. Despite the fact that the wording of the regulations allowed much room for the development of the national cultures and languages, the laws were administered in an ever more oppressive fashion. The aim of the Hungarian administration was to win over as many individuals as possible. The school system was recognized as the most efficient means of turning the non-Hungarian nationalities into Hungarian citizens.

Moves toward magyarization increased after 1875 when Kálmán Tisza and the Liberal Party came to power. In 1879 a new law on education was passed that mandated the teaching of Hungarian in all primary schools. The teachers were required to be fluent in the language. At the same time pressure was applied to change public signs and place names into Hungarian. Families were encouraged to adopt a Hungarian form of their names. The attempt to magyarize through education was continued with the passage of the Apponyi Laws in 1907, which increased the requirements for the use of Hungarian for both students and teachers. Students were given four years to master the language; if they failed, their teachers were to be dismissed. Moves were also made against the private schools, where teaching in other languages was more prevalent. The level of teachers' salaries was set so high that some church institutions could not pay them and were forced to close. Other measures followed in the next years. By 1914 all state upper- and middle-level educational institutions were taught in Hungarian. The Orthodox and Uniate churches, however, did have upper-level schools in which the instruction was in Romanian.

These laws had an extremely detrimental effect on the educational level of the Romanian population. It has been estimated that there were 2,756 Romanian elementary schools in 1880 and only 2,170 by 1914. Fifty-three percent of the Hungarians could read and write at that time, but only 14 percent of the Romanians.[7] If a Romanian student wanted an advanced education in a language other than Hungarian, he had to go to Romania or to a European university.

One of the great limitations on Romanian political activity in Transylvania remained, as before, the character of the people, the great majority of whom were peasants. Although many owned their own farms, a large number worked on the estates of the Hungarian great landowners. The issue of social as well as national antagonism was thus introduced. As we have seen, in no part of the lands under discussion did the peasants play an important political role. The 1910 census gave the total Transylvanian population at 5,257,249, with 53.8 percent Romanian, 28.6 percent Hungarian, and 10.8 percent German. These figures show that the Romanians had a clear majority, but most of them could not vote under the franchise in effect in Hungary. The danger posed by Franz Joseph's threat to introduce universal manhood suffrage in 1905 is shown by these figures: such a measure would have given political control to the non-Hungarian nationalities and the peasantry; the official parties would have been swamped.

As before, the Romanian national leadership remained in the hands of the

---

7 Constantin Daicoviciu and Miron Constantinescu, ed., *Brève histoire de la Transylvanie* (Bucharest: Éditions de l'académie de la république socialiste de Roumanie, 1965), p. 331.

educated section of society and was composed chiefly of middle-class intellectuals and church leaders. The Ausgleich had disillusioned most of those who had hopes for national advancement through cooperation with Vienna, but attempts were still to be made in this direction. There seemed to be no other alternative. Unlike the Slavs, the Romanians could have no romantic illusions about outside great-power assistance. Moreover, little could be expected from Romania, since that state was in alliance with Vienna after 1883. Even more important, Romania was not a strong state; it obviously did not have the political or military capability of defying Austria-Hungary. Nevertheless, the Habsburg Foreign Ministry was very apprehensive about Romanian influence in Transylvania, and it watched the relationship closely. It understood the attraction that the independent kingdom could exert on the Habsburg Romanian population.

Until 1914 the Transylvanian national leadership concentrated on a basically defensive program and, like the Croatian opposition, used legal and not revolutionary means to obtain its aims. The major objectives were a return to the political conditions of the period when Transylvania had been autonomous and a change in the franchise so that the Romanian majority would be reflected in the elections. The nationalists thus denounced the Ausgleich and the union with Hungary and demanded instead a status equivalent to that of Croatia in the Hungarian kingdom. The application of the laws voted by the diet of Sibiu in 1863–1864 was similarly sought. The Romanian leaders also questioned the right of the Budapest parliament to legislate for Transylvania.

Although there was much common agreement on a national program after 1865, there was disagreement on the tactics that should be adopted. Some favored an active, others a passive, policy. Bishop Şaguna was in the forefront of those who believed that the Romanians should participate in the political life of the state despite the highly unfavorable conditions. In contrast, others, such as George Bariţiu and Ioan Raţiu, favored an attitude of passivism and the refusal to take part in such activities as the elections to the Budapest parliament. The second was to be the more influential group. In two meetings held by Romanian representatives in 1869, one at Timişoara and another at Miercurea, general policy was discussed and passivism was approved. Participants expressed doubt about the effectiveness of petitions to the emperor or reliance on Vienna for assistance.

In May 1881, after years in which little action was taken, a major move toward the renewal of an active stand was taken. At this time 153 delegates met at Sibiu and formed the first Romanian political party in Transylvania, the National Party. The conference was under the leadership of the lay intellectuals rather than the clerics; George Bariţiu, Vincentiu Babeş, and Ioan Raţiu became the presidents of this new organization. Its program restated the basic Romanian aims: provincial autonomy; the use of Romanian in the schools, the administration, and the courts in the areas where the Romanians were the majority of the population; the requirement that officials know the language in the areas where they served; and a widening of the franchise. On the question of the tactics to be pursued to obtain these objectives, there was still disagreement between the activists and the passivists, so no single policy was adopted. It will be noted that the concentration was on the national question. The condition of the peasants and the social and economic problems of Transylvania were not subjects of deliberation.

The Romanian leaders were thoroughly aware of the value of publicity and propaganda. As did the leaders of other national movements, they wished to attract the attention of European public opinion to their problems and to make political conditions in Transylvania a topic of international discussion. Accordingly, it was decided that a general declaration of Romanian grievances would be drawn up with this intent. Barițiu therefore wrote a statement on the abuses of the Transylvanian administration, a document that was published in Romanian, Hungarian, French, and German.

In 1887 another National Party conference was held in Sibiu. Here the policy of passivism was reconfirmed, but it was also decided that another petition should be sent to Franz Joseph. Divisions within the party delayed action, but finally in 1892 the document was completed. It was expected that this memorandum would be rejected, but the aim was simply once again to present the Romanian case. It was taken to Vienna in May 1892 by a delegation of three hundred headed by Ioan Rațiu. Franz Joseph declined to accept it on constitutional grounds and forwarded it to the Hungarian authorities, who treated the matter as an illegal activity and arrested the signators. After a trial lasting eighteen days, held in May 1894, they were given sentences of up to five years in prison. This Transylvanian protest was paralleled by similar actions in Romania. In 1891 a group of students and university instructors in Bucharest formed the League for Cultural Unity. This group drafted a memorandum calling attention to conditions in Transylvania. Both Hungarian and Romanian student associations in the Habsburg Empire responded to its accusations. Again police action was taken against the Romanians. The Hungarian measures of repression achieved very little; in fact, they confirmed many of the Romanian claims of mistreatment. Although the National Party was temporarily dissolved and many of its leaders were imprisoned, the basic objective of drawing European attention to Transylvania had succeeded. The Romanian leadership also took steps toward cooperation with national organizations representing Serbs and Slovaks, nationalities that had the same status as the Romanians in the Hungarian state.

In 1905 the National Party changed its tactics and embarked on an active policy of participation in the political system. In the elections of 1906 fifteen Romanian delegates were elected to the Budapest parliament. There they cooperated with the Serbian and Slovakian representatives. Very little was achieved. In fact, the pressure on the nationalities became worse.

Meanwhile, the intellectuals were as active in the cultural as in the political sphere. In 1861 the Association for Romanian Literature and the Education of the Romanian People (ASTRA) was established, with the objective of giving support to Romanian education and encouraging publication in the Romanian language. Şaguna was the first president; the program was formulated by Bariţiu. The organization offered scholarships and published school books. It encouraged research in Romanian folklore, history, and ethnography. Its review, *Transylvania*, appeared from 1868 to 1945. The Romanian population also had other journals and newspapers in their own language. The first daily paper, *Tribuna* (The Forum), which maintained high literary standards and printed the works of major Romanian writers, was published in Sibiu from 1884 to 1903. Economic, political, and cultural themes were covered in its pages; in all, the emphasis was on the national issue. Transylvanian writers and journalists kept in touch with their colleagues in Romania, and they were, of course, well aware of the cultural and political developments there.

By 1914 the Romanian national movement, despite all of these efforts, had reached an impasse. There had been a great rise in national self-consciousness, particularly among the intellectuals, but no practical advances had been made. Some Hungarian statesmen had given vague assurances about possible changes in the future, but the policy of magyarization continued. In the period before World War I, projects for the reconstruction of the Habsburg Empire were a common preoccupation of both politicians and intellectuals within and without the monarchy. Most of the plans would have given the non-Hungarian nationalities a better position. None, however, was on the point of realization. The Romanian leadership and the National Party had similarly stated their objectives. Their goal was the creation of an autonomous Transylvania, with its own diet elected on a wide franchise. This measure would, of course, have given the Romanians the predominant position in the province, but their objectives were in fact moderate. The programs consistently called for reform within the bounds of the Hungarian state. Given the conditions of the time, there was little hope that even these limited goals could be obtained through peaceful means and in agreement with Budapest.

Unlike Croatia, where some parties, such as that of Starčević, had radical programs directed against control by either Vienna or Budapest, Transylvania had no important group standing either for an independent state or for union with Romania. Such a policy was not practical given the international conditions of the time. Romania, in alliance with Germany and Austria-Hungary in 1914, was unwilling and unable to foster Romanian nationalism in Transylvania. No power, including Romania, desired or foresaw the breakup of the Habsburg Empire. The monarchy was regarded by most statesmen as necessary to political equilibrium on the Continent. Although some Romanians in both Transylvania and the independent kingdom looked to union in the distant future, few considered it a possibility close to realization.

## CONCLUSION: AUSTRIA-HUNGARY UNDER THE AUSGLEICH

The Ausgleich, as we have seen, had been accepted by the emperor and the Habsburg statesmen after a major military defeat and as the best of the practical and possible alternatives available at that time. It had not led to a stable situation. Not only had succeeding generations of Hungarian leaders attempted to modify the arrangement in their own interest, but the other nationalities had refused to acquiesce in their permanent assignment to a secondary political position. The Ausgleich thus in fact served to intensify the national conflicts in the monarchy and to awaken the national self-consciousness of previously passive citizens. By 1914 these controversies dominated the internal life of the empire and weakened its position in international affairs.

Although the general question of the national struggles within Austria-Hungary are outside the framework of this narrative, it should be emphasized that the great majority of the political parties called for the reform and reorganization of the empire within the existing boundaries. Some national leaders and intellectuals did indeed look with favor on the division of the state into its national components. Polish patriots, for example, had dreams of a time when the historic Polish lands, which were under Russian, German, and Habsburg control, might be united in a great Polish state. However, such an action, which implied the military defeat of the three powers, seemed remote indeed. Romanian acquisition of Transylvania and Bessarabia similarly appeared impossible. Under these conditions, the national leaderships had to concentrate on the immediate questions of the day. Most of these concerned practical questions such as the franchise and the language of administration and education. Thus, despite the fact that there was indeed much dissatisfaction with Habsburg rule, the nationalities directed their attention primarily to the issues that directly affected their daily lives. No major leader or party called for the destruction of the monarchy.

The nationality question in the Habsburg Empire, as in the Ottoman lands, was exceedingly complex. In the Balkan peninsula, as we have seen, the achievement of autonomy or independence by the national states was accompanied by an increase of animosity and friction among them. A similar condition existed in the monarchy. For the future, two major relationships were to have a particular significance: first, that of the Hungarians and Romanians in Transylvania and, second, that of the Serbs and Croats in Croatia and Dalmatia. In Transylvania the Hungarians and Szeklers joined against the Romanians, who were usually supported by the Germans. These national cleavages were never healed. The question of the Serbs and Croats was far more difficult because of the similarity, if not the identity, of the two people. In the nineteenth century, as we have seen, two points of view were expressed on this question. The majority of the political parties were organized on a separate and national basis. The Illyrian movement, however, had contained the idea that there might indeed be a Yugoslav nationality embracing Serbs, Croats, and Slovenes. The National Party in Croatia and the Croatian-Serbian Coalition supported the idea of cooperation and some aspects of the Illyrian doctrines. Whether the Serbs and Croats were two nationalities, or two divisions of one, was to remain a controversial political issue.

It is a great impediment to understanding the national developments that in the Hungarian kingdom the majority of the inhabitants were excluded from the political process by the restrictive franchise. The spokesmen for all of the national movements, and, of course, for the Hungarian government, came from a small percentage of the population. They claimed to speak for the "nation" and the "people," but they were often in fact personally as divided from the peasants of their own nationality as they were from those of another ethnic background. What the people really thought could not be determined until after the war, when peasant parties finally came to power.

# 3

## The end of Ottoman rule in Europe: the Albanian and Macedonian questions

### THE OTTOMAN EMPIRE

THE DECISIONS OF THE CONGRESS OF BERLIN greatly reduced the Ottoman territories in the Balkan peninsula. Although the ability to control the domestic politics of Romania, Serbia, and Montenegro had long been lost, the fact that these states were still part of the empire had given prestige to the Porte as well as some practical advantages in foreign relations. In addition, Thessaly, a part of Epirus, and lands bordering on Serbia and Montenegro had been surrendered. Bulgaria, Eastern Rumelia, Bosnia, Hercegovina, and the Sanjak of Novi Pazar, still under Ottoman suzerainty, were no longer under the direct authority of Constantinople. Nevertheless, despite these severe losses, the empire held extensive Macedonian and Albanian territories, most of Epirus, and Thrace. Hope was also never abandoned that the Habsburg occupation of Bosnia-Hercegovina might at some time be ended and these provinces returned. The question facing the Ottoman government was how the remaining possessions could best be administered and defended against further claims from either the Balkan people or the great powers.

The sultan at the time, Abdul Hamid II, had come to the throne in 1876 at the age of thirty-four at a time of revolution and war. He had seen his two predecessors removed by palace revolts, and he had been forced to wage war with the Balkan states and with Russia during his first year in power. These events obviously made a deep impression on his attitude toward the powers and those around him. Early in his reign he showed signs of fear and suspicion in his relations with his advisers and the foreign representatives. At the time of his accession he had promised to establish constitutional government, but he personally had no faith in the system. As soon as his own position was secure he dismissed the assembly and exiled the major reformers. Thereafter, he reestablished his autocratic powers and the centralized government that he believed would be the best solution to the imperial problems. As he declared: "I made a mistake when I wished to imitate my father, Abdulmecit, who sought to reform by persuasion and by liberal institutions. I shall follow in the footsteps of my grandfather, Sultan Mahmut. Like him I now understand that it is only by force that one can move the people with whose protection God has entrusted me."[1]

The center of authority was now the palace, not the bureaucracy. The sultan took personal control and directed the affairs of state. He read all of the major reports of his officials, and he made the principal decisions. His rule was in fact more autocratic than those of his predecessors. He imposed a strong police control; those who were suspected of opposition were arrested, imprisoned, or even executed. Rigorous censorship was similarly instituted. Not only was criticism of the sultan barred, but literature was carefully scrutinized: "The writings of some 'seditious' authors were banned . . . and of European authors such as Racine, Rousseau, Voltaire, Hugo, and Zola. Certain suggestive words could not be used, such as 'anarchy', 'liberty', 'strike', 'constitution', 'revolution', 'assassination', 'socialism', 'dynamite', and 'Murat'. Newspapers and presses were fined and/or suspended whenever they violated the law."[2] Abdul Hamid encouraged his officials to report on each other's activities, and he played them against each other. He used his network of spies to help hold down his opponents.

Despite these methods, Abdul Hamid was a determined reformer. He paid a great deal of attention to the administration of his lands, and he wanted efficient centralized control. Like neighboring Balkan monarchs he had enormous financial problems. The salaries of his officials often fell far in arrears. This weakness also limited the internal improvements that could be undertaken. The sultan was especially interested in better communications, in particular in building railroads; by 1908 the empire had 5,883 kilometers of rail lines. The road system, however, remained primitive. Although there were some paved highways, most of the roads were little more than dirt tracks.

The empire remained a primarily agricultural state, dependent on Europe for manufactured goods. Throughout the nineteenth century the British government, in particular, had persuaded the Porte to maintain free-trade policies. The commercial treaties prescribed low tariffs. The country thus had a lively commerce, but based on the exchange of agricultural produce and raw materials for manufactured goods and colonial products. Thus items such as grapes, figs, olive oil, opium, silk, and minerals were exported; clothing, textiles, medical supplies, and sugar were imported.

Despite the serious territorial losses, particularly in Europe, the Ottoman Empire at the turn of the century was still an important power. If the inhabitants of all of the dependent lands were included, the population in 1897 was 39,096,294. If only those people who were under the direct control of the

---

1 Quoted in Stanford J. Shaw, *History of the Ottoman Empire*, 2 vols. (Cambridge: Cambridge University Press, 1967, 1977), II, 213.
2 Shaw, *History of the Ottoman Empire*, II, 251.

government for tax purposes are counted, the number is 19,050,307.[3] After 1878 the state still had the problem of providing for Muslim refugees, most of whom were forced to leave their homes by the advance of the Christian nations. From 1878 to 1884 the government had to care for 812,193 of these people; from 1884 to 1897 the figure was 202,822. It was difficult to settle these families in the dwindling Ottoman territories. Most of them arrived in a destitute condition and thus without the means to build new lives.

Constantinople was still the center of the Ottoman government and the empire. In 1844 its population was 391,000, but by 1913, after the Balkan Wars, the number had risen to 909,978. Like the large Balkan cities, the Ottoman capital acquired the attributes of a modern metropolis, with paved streets, gaslights, and horse-drawn streetcars. After the unification of Bulgaria, the city was in an extremely vulnerable position; the border of the potentially enemy state was but a short distance away.

Abdul Hamid's entire reign was to be marked by a series of military and diplomatic disasters. Acutely aware of the dangers to the state, the sultan was greatly concerned about strengthening his army. He preferred to rely on German military advisers, since they appeared more disinterested, at least at the beginning of his rule. He also purchased German arms. In 1885 and 1888 Krupp cannons were obtained to guard the Straits, an act that limited in particular the British capabilities of influencing the government. The extreme financial weakness of the country, however, blocked effective military reform. The armed forces were thus not in a condition to protect the Ottoman territories adequately. Under these circumstances it is in no way surprising that the Berlin treaty and its associated agreements did not mark the end of the Ottoman retreats. In 1882 Britain took effective control of Egypt; in 1885 Bulgaria and Eastern Rumelia united. In the 1890s a crisis over the Armenian population of the empire attracted international attention. The one bright point was the defeat of the Greek army in 1897, but the Porte was prevented from exploiting this victory by the great powers. Crete was for all practical purposes lost. By the beginning of the twentieth century conditions in the Albanian and Macedonian lands were becoming increasingly unstable. The anarchy in Macedonia was to lead to a Habsburg and Russian diplomatic intervention.

Throughout this period the pressure from the great powers and the Balkan nationalities thus increased. The Ottoman Empire could no longer count on British support, as it had done in the past. With the acquisition of Egypt, this area and the Suez Canal became the focus of British policy, rather than the Straits and Constantinople. However, the Porte was aided by the aversion of the great powers to a revival of the Eastern Question. Participating in the great imperial expansion of the age, they concentrated their attention on Africa and the Far East and on their mutual rivalries in these regions. They

3 Shaw, *History of the Ottoman Empire*, II, 238.

nevertheless did not abandon their intention of intervening in Ottoman affairs in times of crisis. The revival of interest in imperial conquest made the control of the Mediterranean sea-lanes even more important. The worldwide clash of Britain and Russia gave continued significance to the status of the Straits.

Abdul Hamid II himself was extremely suspicious of the activities of the great powers and the non-Muslim nationalities in his empire. Seeking a firm ideological basis for the state, the sultan turned back to Islam and Pan-Islamic ideals. Monuments and mosques were restored; he showed a great interest in the affairs of other Islamic nations, and encouraged visits from their leaders. In the 1870s and 1880s the Islamic world was under attack from most of the Christian great powers. Of great significance was the Russian penetration of Central Asia, culminating in the fall of Geok Tepe in 1881 and the capture of Merv, near the Afghan border, in 1884. As we have seen, many Muslim refugees entered the Ottoman Empire as a result of the Russian conquests.

In domestic affairs the emphasis was still placed on Ottomanism and the idea of equal citizenship within the empire. Nevertheless, there was an increasing interest in specifically Turkish affairs. Since this trend was in contradiction to both Ottomanism and Pan-Islamic ideas, it did not receive official support. It represented, however, the Turkish equivalent of the type of nationalism that we have seen in the Balkans. It also had an international significance. Pan-Turanism, the concept of the unity of all the Turkic people, could influence events in Russia, where large numbers lived.

The autocratic rule of Abdul Hamid II, as well as the continued decline of the empire, naturally aroused a great deal of opposition, particularly among the educated and intellectual sections of the population. Teachers, students, government officials, and army officers were all well aware of the domestic difficulties, and they were in touch with European political and social thought. Although these people had widely different opinions about what should be done, they did not support the idea of most of the Tanzimat reformers of the years 1838 to 1876 that change and modernization could come successfully from above. They thus wanted the restoration of the 1876 constitution and an end to the autocracy. Most of them strongly desired the maintenance of the territorial integrity of the empire, and they were thus not sympathetic to the claims of the Balkan nationalities.

Many intellectuals and politicians had been forced to emigrate owing to the repressive measures of Abdul Hamid's reign. Living in centers such as Paris, London, Geneva, Bucharest, and Egypt, which was under British administration, they remained in touch with each other, they held meetings, and they published newspapers. At the end of the century the opposition groups joined together to form the Committee of Union and Progress (CUP), a party that was commonly referred to as the Young Turks. Its program called for the restoration of constitutional government, by revolution if necessary.

Abdul Hamid II was to be deposed and replaced by another member of his family. The state was thus to become a constitutional monarchy.

The opposition's demands were able to win much support among the military. The continual record of failure in foreign policy, together with the intervention of the powers in the Macedonian problem, increased dissatisfaction with the government, particularly in the officer corps. Like their Greek colleagues in the Military League, they came to believe that the politicians were endangering the safety and progress of their country. The discontent centered in the Third Army of Macedonia, which had directly witnessed the failure of the government to calm the situation and which resented the presence of the foreign inspectors who had arrived after 1903. The officers did not wish to launch a violent revolution, but only to force the sultan to restore the constitution. Events, however, compelled them to act in another direction.

Reports of the conspiracies in Macedonia soon reached the sultan. When he sent agents to investigate the rumors, some of these men were killed. Spontaneous revolts broke out in June and July 1908. The loyal troops were not strong enough to suppress the movement, so Abdul Hamid in July agreed to the demand of the CUP and the Macedonian army that the constitution be restored. The Young Turk revolution had thus succeeded: the sultan remained on the throne, but the Young Turks held the real power.

From the beginning the revolutionary regime faced great difficulties. Although at first there was much enthusiasm throughout the empire, it was based largely on a misunderstanding of the goals of new leaders. The members of the CUP believed in Ottomanism; they wished to uphold the empire. They offered all the citizens of the empire an equal position, but they were not prepared to make special concessions to the nationalities on an individual basis. This attitude affected particularly the Albanians, many of whom had cooperated in the revolt in the expectation that their national demands would be met. Another weakness of the movement was its failure to produce a single, respected leader or to formulate a clear revolutionary program. The participants were divided among themselves on their aims. Moreover, the leadership failed to act decisively. The headquarters remained in Thessaloniki, but the CUP sent a committee of seven to Constantinople to advise the government. Thus the administration of the state remained in the hands of the former officials, and the committee had little influence in the actual running of the government.

The revolution was also injured by the action of the powers. In October, as we have seen, the Habsburg Monarchy annexed Bosnia-Hercegovina, and Bulgaria declared its independence. Although the Sanjak of Novi Pazar was returned to Ottoman rule, its recovery was little compensation for the final loss of the other provinces. Nevertheless, elections were held for a general assembly. In the voting, which was apparently not free from pressure from the victorious party, the CUP won all but one seat. As far as national distribution was concerned, the assembly was to contain 147 Turks, 60 Arabs, 27 Albanians, 26 Greeks, 14 Armenians, 10 Slavs, and 4 Jews.

Abdul Hamid II was not, however, without his supporters, and in April 1909 a counterrevolution took place in Constantinople. Its basis was the Muslim population of the city, including the merchants, artisans, peasants, and others of the poorer classes. They held demonstrations and presented demands, which the sultan accepted. The Macedonian army then moved in and crushed the uprising. Abdul Hamid was deposed and replaced by Mehmed V.

The CUP was still not in complete control of the state. The army did not intervene directly in the government, although its influence was apparent. The new regime at first made the assembly the center of authority, and the centralized administrative system was retained. The revolution, of course, had yet to deal with the external problems and the unrest within the empire. A new series of crises was soon to arise, commencing with an Italian attack on Tripoli, an Ottoman vassal, in 1911. Defeated in this war too, the Ottoman government had to agree to the surrender of the African province and an Italian occupation of the Greek-inhabited Dodecanese Islands. Even greater dangers were to be faced in Albania and Macedonia.

## THE ALBANIAN NATIONAL MOVEMENT

In the past the Albanian region had often been the center of strong resistance to Ottoman authority. The Muslim pashas who sought to establish autonomous political units under their own control did not, however, represent an Albanian national movement comparable to that of the Christian nationalities in the neighboring areas. Although there was a strong desire for local self-government and much resistance to taxation by the Porte, the population, which was 70 percent Muslim, was in the great majority in favor of remaining within the Ottoman Empire, certainly as long as traditional rights and privileges were maintained. The League of Prizren of 1878 had been formed primarily to prevent encroachment by foreign powers on Albanian national lands; the aim had not been the establishment of an independent Albania.

With the obvious decline of the Ottoman Empire and the obtaining of independence by the Christian states, some elements of the Albanian leadership did develop programs that were more in line with contemporary European nationalism. Emphasizing the cultural and linguistic unity, rather than the religious divisions, they called for the creation of an Albanian state composed of the four vilayets of Janina, Kosovo, Bitola, and Shkodër. The language of administration and education would be Albanian. Such a plan was very difficult to implement. Obviously, the areas in question were in no sense purely Albanian; Greeks and Slavs had valid historic and ethnic claims to at least a part of these territories. Moreover, both the Porte and the Patriarchate could be expected to resist measures that would diminish their influence and authority. The language question was to be particularly difficult. In the period of the Tanzimat reforms the principle had been recognized that elementary education should be in the national languages. In the Albanian-inhabited areas, however, the millet religious basis was preserved. Thus the Muslim students were taught in Turkish-Islamic institutions and the Orthodox in Greek schools, whereas the Catholics were instructed in Italian, but with some classes in Albanian. Quite naturally this system suited the religious authorities, Catholic, Muslim, and Orthodox alike, as well as the Ottoman government.

An Albanian national revival was thus not easy to accomplish. The people had no common religious or geographic center; they had historically been separated into various Ottoman administrative districts. There was no recognized national leadership after the destruction of the League of Prizren. The great unifying element was the spoken language, but it lacked a standard literary form or even a generally accepted alphabet. The choice to be made in this question would have great implications for the future: The various scripts, Latin, Cyrillic, and Arabic, represented different directions in political orientation.

As with the other Balkan national revivals, an Albanian cultural movement preceded and accompanied the political struggle. During the nineteenth century there had been much curiosity about Albania among European intellectuals, who regarded it as an exotic and romantic region. The Austrian scholar J. G. von Hahn published a grammar, a vocabulary, and a collection of folklore. Great interest in Albanian history was shown particularly in the Albanian colonies abroad. European historians had by this time become convinced that the Albanians were the direct descendants of the Illyrians, the oldest known Balkan inhabitants. Like the Greeks and the Romanians, the Albanian nationalists could take pride in an ancient heritage.

With the suppression of the League of Prizren, national activity had to be directed toward the cultural rather than the political field. The emphasis was placed on developing the language and securing its use in education. There was far to go. In 1878 in the most advanced sanjaks of Gjirokastër, Berat, and Vlorë there were 80 Turkish schools, 163 Greek schools, but none with classes in Albanian. Two Catholic institutions in Shkodër taught the language, but it was second to Italian. A great boost to Albanian cultural development occurred in 1879 with the formation in Constantinople of the Society for the Printing of Albanian Writings. Like similar Balkan societies, its aim was the publication of books, journals, and newspapers in the national language and the translation of foreign works. The president was Sami Frashëri. His brother, Naim Frashëri, the greatest Albanian poet, played an important role in the organization and prepared school texts. The cultural movement continued to find strong support among the Albanians in Italy, Egypt, Romania, Bulgaria, Constantinople, and the United States. Books were printed and national pride and self-awareness increased. There were, however, few successes in Albania proper. Some schools were conducted secretly. In 1887 the first officially authorized institution, a private school in Korçë, was opened. Others followed, but they were soon suppressed by the Ottoman officials. In 1902 the Korçë school similarly closed its doors.

The preference shown by Abdul Hamid II for a centralized administration met with firm opposition in the Albanian lands both from the nationally minded and from the mountain clans who were used to running their own affairs. The latter intensely disliked reforms that could result in the regular collection of taxes or efficient recruitment for the army. This resistance was supported by Muslims and Christians alike; neither wished to be dominated by Constantinople. For the three decades after the Congress of Berlin the Porte continued its efforts to control the political situation in the region. It closed the provincial organizations of the League of Prizren and it made arrests of suspected nationalist agitators. The Ottoman government was, however, afraid to go too far; it was correctly apprehensive that it might stir up a revolt. In 1885 it made a few concessions and released the political prisoners; some of the reforms were suspended in the mountain regions. As we have seen, the use of Albanian was authorized for a few schools. Many of these measures were reversed around the close of the century, however, during a period of reaction in Constantinople.

Observing the continuing Serbian, Bulgarian, Montenegrin, and Greek competition over what remained of the Ottoman Empire in Europe, the Albanian leaders had good reason to fear that their national lands were in danger of partition. The situation in which they were placed at the time of the Congress of Berlin might again recur. The lack of a single Albanian political unit was especially dangerous. The demand for the union of the four vilayets was thus the expression of a national necessity. When the Porte did not respond, the Albanians themselves again began to organize. Meetings of their representatives took place at Pejë in November 1897 and again in January 1899. There was still no general agreement on the program to be adopted. Many were still loyalists and accepted the government position. Among those who wished changes, two general currents of opinion prevailed. The first, more moderate, wanted the five vilayets (this would include Thessaloniki) that were inhabited by Albanians to be united in a single province. Both Albanian and Turkish would be taught in the schools, but Turkish would still remain the official language. This plan received the support of the conservatives. The more radical groups desired the unification of just four vilayets, but with full administrative autonomy. Albanian would be the language of government and education. This program won the approval of the majority of the Albanian leaders. Its principal proponent, Haxhi Mulla Zeka, became president of a new Albanian League. This organization had but a short life. The Ottoman government immediately moved against the national opposition, and in 1902 Haxhi Mulla Zeka was executed.

Albanian nationalism received a new impetus in 1903 as a result of the

Macedonian uprising of that year and the increase of antagonisms in that area. The Albanian population at this point felt itself in real danger. As Muslims, Albanians were repeatedly the target of attacks from Bulgarian, Serbian, and Greek terrorist groups. The continued agitation and the intervention of the great powers brought with them the threat that the Macedonian Albanians might be assigned to the Balkan states in another partition plan. In self-defense the Albanians were forced to form their own armed bands. A new generation had also come to the fore, one that had much in common with its contemporaries in other Balkan lands. In November 1905 a group of young intellectuals established a secret society in Bitola, with branches throughout the Albanian lands, called the Committee for the Liberation of Albania. In January 1906 guerilla units were formed under the leadership of Bajo Topulli, and trained to fight both the Ottoman army and the Christian terrorists. In September 1906 the organization was responsible for the assassination of the Greek metropolitan of Korçë, whose actions had angered the Albanian nationalists.

The Young Turk movement from the beginning attracted support among some of the Albanian leadership. Like the Turkish members, these Albanians too were disgusted with the regime of Abdul Hamid II, which not only did not meet the Albanian demands, but was obviously unable to handle the anarchical situation in Macedonia. The cooperation was based on a fundamental misunderstanding. The Albanian leaders expected the CUP to give them autonomy once their cause was victorious. When the revolt succeeded in July 1908, demonstrations of support occurred, and there was much hope for the future. At first, indeed, there were improvements. Emigrés returned, and Albanian-language newspapers appeared. Expectations ran high that a unified, autonomous Albanian state would be created.

The Young Turk movement, however, as we have seen, was devoted to the strengthening, not the further dissolution, of the empire; its leaders supported Ottomanism, not the rights of the nationalities. They certainly did not intend to set up a federal organization. In dealing with the Albanian leaders, the Young Turks faced certain limitations. Since they too represented a secular movement, they could not easily call for Albanian support on a religious basis. In fact, the counterrevolution of 1909 expressed Muslim dissatisfaction with CUP principles; yet Islam was the principal Albanian link with Constantinople. Religious predominance had been acceptable; political rule was not. A clash between the CUP and the Albanian nationalists was inevitable. In fact, soon after its victory the new Young Turk government adopted many of the attitudes of its predecessor. National political activity was suppressed, and the Young Turk candidates received police support in the elections to the assembly that was summoned to meet in Constantinople. Nevertheless, the foremost Albanian leader of this period, Ismail Kemal Vlora, was chosen as a delegate.

Meanwhile, cultural as well as political activities continued. In November

87

1908 Albanian representatives met in Bitola, where they formally adopted the Latin alphabet as the standard form. At the same time, political discussions were carried on, and the desire for political and cultural unity was reaffirmed. Albanian opposition was further heightened when the Young Turk regime continued many of the practices that had caused so much controversy in the past. Taxes were raised and again the attempt was made to control the mountain regions and to obtain recruits there. Laws were also passed against the organization of guerilla bands and national societies.

The background was thus prepared for the outbreak of a major revolt against Constantinople. In the spring of 1909 signs appeared that preparations were being made by local communities for an armed uprising. The Albanian leaders were disenchanted with the new regime and very fearful about the intentions of their neighbors. It will be remembered that Bulgaria had just declared its independence and Austria-Hungary had annexed Bosnia-Hercegovina. Once again the Ottoman government had proved unable to handle an attack on its territorial integrity and its international position. The situation in Macedonia, despite the great-power interference, remained in the same precarious state.

In September 1909 another meeting was held by the Albanian leaders, this time in Elbasan. The choice of the Latin alphabet was reaffirmed; provision was made for the establishment of a teacher-training school, which opened that year. The mountain tribes were also organizing to resist the central government. The Ottoman government, despite warnings, kept its unyielding attitude. It expected loyalty and it opposed the Latin alphabet, preferring that the Arabic script be adopted. Finally, in March 1910, a revolt, commencing in Priština and soon spreading over the entire vilayet of Kosovo, did break out. It was suppressed only after three months of fighting. This event had repercussions throughout the Albanian lands. At the end of the revolt, the Ottoman government closed the Albanian national organizations and schools and stopped the publications. The leaders were imprisoned. The mountaineers, however, a group that the Porte had never been able to control, remained in rebellion.

The Ottoman government was in no position to contain Albanian opposition by force. Faced with problems throughout the empire, it made an attempt to conciliate these people, who, after all, were in the majority Muslim and who sought autonomy, not independence. In June 1911 the sultan himself visited Kosovo. At the same time, concessions were offered over education and some measures were taken to reduce taxes. It was further agreed that army recruits would serve only in the Albanian provinces and that officials assigned to these regions should know the language. Although these measures were at first applied only in the north, they soon extended to the south. The Porte had thus given important concessions concerning schools, the Albanian language, recruits, and taxation. The Latin alphabet was also accepted. The Ottoman government did not, however, concede on the question of the union of the four vilayets.

When war broke out between the Ottoman Empire and Italy in September 1911, the opportunity for further gains appeared at hand. The Albanian national movement still suffered from the fact that it had no central leadership with real authority and the ability to direct activity in all of the Albanian territories. In January 1912 the Young Turk regime dissolved the assembly and announced the holding of new elections, which were again accompanied by fraud and violence. In April revolts began in some parts of the Albanian lands; by June they had become widespread. The Ottoman government had by this time lost effective control of the region. Nevertheless, there was still a deep division among the Albanian leaders on the national goals; some sought little more than the ouster of the Young Turk regime, whereas others demanded the union of the four vilayets with full administrative autonomy. In August 1912 the rebels took Skopje, an action that shocked the Porte. In September it accepted some of the insurgent demands, but before a final settlement could be completed, the First Balkan War commenced in October. This event was to produce an emergency situation for the Albanian leaders. Their national lands were again in grave danger of partition among the Christian Balkan states.

## MACEDONIA

The fate of the Macedonian lands not only was to be a major issue in the late nineteenth century, but was to remain a principal dividing point among the Balkan states thereafter. An area covering 25,000 square miles with about 2 million people, Macedonia had no definite political boundaries, but it was part of the three vilayets of Selanik, Kosovo, and Bitola. The region is generally considered to be bounded on the north by the Šar Mountains; on the east by the Rhodope Mountains; on the south by the Aegean Sea, Mt. Olympus, and the Pindus range; and on the west by Lake Ohrid. The ethnic divisions cannot be given with any degree of accuracy. After the Congress of Berlin, when the fate of this area became a major concern, many statistics were collected, with the results usually reflecting the interests of those who made the study. At least eight different people lived in Macedonia: Turks, Bulgars, Greeks, Serbs, Albanians, Vlachs, Jews, and Gypsies. In addition, undoubtedly some individuals considered themselves primarily Macedonians. The Muslim element, including Turks, Albanians, and South Slavs from Bosnia and Hercegovina, was large, perhaps almost half of the population. Muslim people expelled from Russia or the Balkan states had moved there, and the substantial Albanian population was predominantly Muslim.

The great significance of the area was its strategic location. It was the heart of the peninsula, and it included the Vardar and Struma river valleys. The major Ottoman and Balkan port after Constantinople was Thessaloniki, which was also the economic center of Macedonia. A rail line connected this city with Belgrade by 1888. Austria-Hungary, in occupation of Bosnia-Hercegovina and the Sanjak of Novi Pazar, had the same interest in the lands south to the Aegean as Russia had in Bulgaria. Russia and Britain had a stake in the fate of the region because of its proximity to the Straits and its role in the balance of power in the Balkans. For the Balkan nationalities, the issue was even more immediate and vital: whoever held Macedonia would have the predominant strategic position in the peninsula. The chief objection, it will be remembered, to the great Bulgaria of San Stefano had been that the boundaries assigned, incorporating Macedonia, would make the state the strongest in the Balkans, and given the conditions of the time, it would be expected to act as a Russian surrogate.

Macedonia was not an economically productive area. The landholders of its many chiftlik estates, who were usually Muslim, often lived in Constantinople or Thessaloniki and left the running of the lands to stewards, a practice that led to the abuses we have seen elsewhere. The peasants worked their plots under much the same conditions as those that prevailed for the kmets of Bosnia. They were expected to surrender a third to a half of their produce and to render labor services. They could own their own houses and gardens, or they could live in villages provided by the landowner. Some rented land and paid either in money or kind. There were also agricultural laborers who held no land at all. Before 1914 the chiftliks were in the process of dissolution, with more land passing into the hands of the peasants. In addition, there had always been free peasants, many of them Muslims of Albanian, Turkish, or Slavic backgrounds, holding their own farms. The settlement of Muslim refugees from Bosnia, Hercegovina, and Bulgaria added to their numbers.

The principal products of the area were wheat, barley, corn, rye, tobacco, opium poppies, cotton, and rice; cattle, sheep, and goats were also raised. The poor condition of the land and the massive deforestation that had occurred in the past meant that this area too could not support its increasing population. The poverty and the land problems meant that social and economic unrest, as well as national and religious rivalries, contributed to the difficulties of the region.

In the late nineteenth century four states put forward claims in Macedonia – Bulgaria, Greece, Serbia, and Romania. In addition, Albanian national leaders, at a minimum, wanted the vilayets of Bitola and Kosovo to form part of their future autonomous region. As in the past, the arguments were based on three main principles: the historical background, the ethnic composition of the population, and the necessity of maintaining the balance of power. The third consideration involved the idea of compensation: should one state gain an increase of territory, then its neighbors should receive equal acquisitions. If history were used as the basis for modern ownership, then the Greeks had the advantage. The lands had been associated with ancient Greece and Byzantium, and they had been under the jurisdiction of the Patriarchate of Constantinople, which functioned as a Greek national organization. The Bulgarians and the Serbs also had, of course, historical claims dating back to the pre-Ottoman period.

The really difficult question was the determination of the national divisions of the population. The Ottoman census of 1906, which was based on the millets, reported 1,145,849 Muslims; 623,197 Greek Orthodox, who were under the jurisdiction of the Patriarchate; and 626,715 Bulgarian Orthodox, or members of the Exarchate.[4] The figures for Muslims, of course, included the Albanians. The numbers given for the Patriarchate and Exarchate were also misleading. The Serbs, without a strong national organization, could join either church; Bulgarians could be counted among the Greek Orthodox if they lived in an area outside the jurisdiction of the Exarchate.

The major problem in drawing national lines was not separating the Albanians, Greeks, and Turks, who could be differentiated by language, but distinguishing among the Slavs. Macedonia was a transition zone between Bulgaria proper and the Serbian kingdom. The majority of the Christians of Macedonia were indeed South Slavic, but they spoke dialects, and they had customs and traditions drawn from or common to each of their neighbors. The population was largely illiterate, so there was no written language to assist in the determination of nationality. Since there had been no Slavic Macedonian state in the past, historical records could not be appealed to for an answer. As we have seen, the region had been part of the medieval Serbian, Bulgarian, and Greek empires. The antagonists of old thus reemerged on the modern stage.

Because of this confused situation, it was also possible to argue that the Macedonian Slavs were neither Serbian nor Bulgarian, but formed a unique nationality of their own. This issue was to be of great importance after World War II. However, in the nineteenth century the term *Macedonian* was used almost exclusively to refer to the geographic region; the Macedonians were usually not considered a nationality separate from the Bulgarians, Greeks, Serbs, or Albanians. The diplomatic records of the period make no clear mention of a separate Macedonian nation. At the time of the Constantinople conference of 1876 and the Congress of Berlin, as we have seen, the representatives of the great powers considered the region to be of an extremely mixed ethnic composition, but predominantly Bulgarian. The second major claimant was believed to be Greece, with Serbia in a weak third place. At the end of the century the Romanian government began to show a great interest in the Vlach population, which spoke a Romance language and was scattered throughout the area. Although Romania obviously could not advance claims for Macedonian territory, the issue could be used to gain compensation elsewhere. The Albanian position received very little outside recognition. As long

---

4  Shaw, *History of the Ottoman Empire*, II, 208.

as an Albanian state was not in existence, its rights had to be defended by the Ottoman Empire, and that government was neither able nor willing to undertake the task. The advantage in the area was thus held by the Greeks, the Bulgarians and, to a lesser extent, the Serbs.

The Greek national leaders had long expected eventually to absorb the entire area. Their arguments were based chiefly on the historical association of Greece, both classical and Byzantine, with the region. In a time before serious ethnographic studies were made, these leaders could sincerely believe that the population was indeed Greek. Certainly Greeks and Muslim Turks formed the majority of the city inhabitants. The ecclesiastical jurisdiction exercised by the Constantinople Patriarchate after the abolition of the Peć and Ohrid authorities in the eighteenth century had given the Greeks control over cultural as well as religious matters. They thereafter tended to count all the Orthodox who were under the control of the Patriarchate as Greeks. As we have seen, the establishment of the Bulgarian Exarchate was bitterly resented, because it ended the advantages previously held by the Greek churches. Even after it became apparent that the majority of the Christian people were Slavic, the Greek leaders continued to claim the area on a national basis; they argued that many of the inhabitants were what they called Slavophone Greeks, that is, individuals who were Slavic in language, but Greek in national sentiment.

The Greek fears concerning the Exarchate were soon fully justified. Wherever two-thirds of a district voted for it, the Orthodox population could join this organization. This possibility naturally appealed to many Slavic-speaking people, for whom the attractions of a service in Church Slavic were much greater than those of one in Greek. The areas under the jurisdiction of the Exarchate thus expanded rapidly; the San Stefano boundaries were not greatly different from the lines of this religious authority. In the 1890s the Exarchate was able to add more districts. If nationality was to be used as the basis of assigning ownership, Bulgaria had the advantage at the end of the century. Most Bulgarian leaders and the Bulgarian people were passionately convinced Macedonia was indeed rightfully theirs.

Of the major rivals, Serbia was in the weakest position. Until 1878 its chief attention had been directed toward Bosnia, Hercegovina, and Old Serbia, which covered part of the Kosovo vilayet. After the Habsburg occupation of the two provinces, Serbia could expand only southward. In the agreement of 1881 with Vienna, Milan had received assurances of support for such a move. Serbia thus entered with enthusiasm into the struggle for Macedonian lands, and exerted great efforts to demonstrate that the Macedonian Slavs were Serbs. Studies were made of the local languages and customs, and statistics were collected. Serbia opened consulates in 1887 in Thessaloniki and Skopje, and soon afterward in Bitola and Priština. A major propaganda campaign was launched inside Macedonia. From the beginning the efforts of the Serbs were hindered by their lack of an ecclesiastical organization equal to that of the

Patriarchate or the Exarchate. They nevertheless made considerable advances before 1912.

The tragedy of Macedonia was that the basic issues were of such a serious nature that they could indeed lead to war among the Balkan nations. No matter what the national composition or the desires of the population, neither Greece nor Serbia could allow Bulgaria to annex the territory. Romanian interests were similar. The entire question was further complicated not only by the controversies over the division of the population, but also by the fact that the nationalities did not live conveniently in compact districts. Although the concentration of the Greeks in the south was clear, the other groups were thoroughly intermixed. With this situation, it can be understood why it was difficult for the Balkan states and the great powers to settle the question, and why the fate of the region was finally to be decided by violence.

In their attempts to win supremacy, the rival nationalities relied on organizations operating within Macedonia. Their activities were of two kinds: the first concentrated on a cultural approach and relied upon propaganda and indoctrination to gain success; the second was military in nature. Small bands were formed throughout Macedonia. Essentially groups of armed guerilla fighters, these men used force and terror. They attacked both the Ottoman forces and their rivals among the other national organizations. By the turn of the century the situation in Macedonia was indeed chaotic. All the sides had armed bands except the Muslim Turks, who had to rely on the increasingly ineffective Ottoman army.

The first organizations of importance emphasized cultural propaganda. In 1884 the Bulgarians established the Cyril and Methodius Society; the Serbs followed in 1886 with the formation of the Society of St. Sava. The Greek National Society has already been mentioned. Far more effective than these, however, were to be the military organizations, composed usually of dedicated fanatics, who used direct and violent methods. The Committee for the Liberation of Albania has been discussed previously. However, the best known was the Internal Macedonian Revolutionary Organization, or IMRO, which was founded in Thessaloniki in 1893. Its leading members came from the groups that we have seen playing an important part in national revolutionary movements elsewhere; they were small merchants, artisans, teachers, and professional men.

At first, IMRO supported the formation of a South Slav federation in which Macedonia would have a place. Despite the fact that the motto of the organization was "Macedonia for the Macedonians," at times certain of its members had close connections with Bulgaria. IMRO was extremely effective in organizing and recruiting members. Its main activity was the preparation of a great Macedonian rebellion, and it formed a kind of state within a state in Macedonia. The Bulgarian government could not control its activities effectively, because so many of its citizens were involved in the movement. They exerted influence on the government and aided in Macedonian conspiracies. Certain armed bands used Bulgarian territory as a base for their operations in Macedonia.

The chief rival of IMRO was the Macedonian External Organization, also known as the Supreme Committee, or the Supremists, which was organized in 1895. This society was frankly and openly for the annexation of Macedonia by Bulgaria. Its membership contained many Macedonian refugees, and it had the support of the Bulgarian army and government. The Supremists also organized bands that were dispatched over the Ottoman border. The Macedonian question was the main issue in Bulgarian politics before World War I. It determined the direction of foreign policy, and it was deeply involved in the domestic conflicts.

The chaotic and violent situation caused by the activities of the bands and the unrest in the population was beyond Ottoman capabilities to control. The great powers repeatedly pressed the Porte to make reforms in the area, under the mistaken assumption that the basic cause for the tension was the economic and political conditions. The agitators, however, did not seek a better administration; in fact, they had an interest in making the situation as bad as possible. The Balkan states too were disturbed by the course of events. Obviously, the Bulgarian government enjoyed certain advantages in this contest for control. Seeing Sofia as the party to beat, the Serbian and Greek governments attempted to come to an understanding in the 1890s. However, their inability to divide the territories in question made an agreement impossible at that time.

Of the great powers Russia and Austria-Hungary were most directly involved in the area. Although the Three Emperors' Alliance had been allowed to lapse in 1887 after the dispute over Bulgaria, neither power wished a Balkan crisis to occur. The Habsburg Monarchy was absorbed with its domestic problems; Russian attention had begun to turn increasingly toward the Far East. In April 1897 Franz Joseph and Nicholas II therefore reached an understanding on Balkan affairs. Both their governments had a strong interest in maintaining the status quo in the area. Their agreement to cooperate in this endeavor assured that the Macedonian question would not be exploited by either state and that it would not endanger the general peace.

Meanwhile, IMRO continued its preparations for a general revolt. Its aim was either the freeing of the region from Ottoman control or, at the least, the provoking of foreign intervention. The entire undertaking was extremely badly organized. The most able leader of IMRO, Gotse Delchev, was captured and executed even before the rebellion began. The organization, nevertheless, was able to launch a massive uprising in August 1903. The Ilinden (St. Elijah's Day) revolt was at first successful. Soon most of the Bitola vilayet was under the control of the revolutionaries. The tide then turned, and by December the Ottoman army had crushed the movement. Some of the leaders had misjudged the international situation and had not foreseen the reluctance of the great powers to become involved. The Bulgarian government too had been unprepared to act. After this failure, IMRO split into two rival factions.

To some extent, however, IMRO's desire for outside intervention was to be met. In October 1903 Franz Joseph and Nicholas II met at Mürzsteg and approved a program for Macedonia that provided, in addition to other reforms, for foreign advisers and for a gendarmerie under great-power control. It also had a clause stipulating that Macedonia should be divided into districts based on ethnic divisions. This provision simply gave rise to further battles between armed groups, each attempting to secure control of a distinct area. In 1905 the Porte with great reluctance agreed to an international supervision of Macedonian finances.

Reform, as has been emphasized, was not the answer to the problem. Neither was armed repression. By 1908 the Ottoman government had concentrated most of its army in the region. Its failure to control the situation had the effect of demonstrating to the army officers the apparent incapacity of Abdul Hamid's government. The Young Turk revolution, as we have seen, commenced in Thessaloniki and was carried through by the Third Macedonian Army.

## THE BALKAN WARS, 1912, 1913

By the beginning of the twentieth century two major diplomatic alignments had been formed. The first, the Triple Alliance, joined Germany, Austria-Hungary, and Italy; the second brought together Russia and France. The agreements on which the alignments were based were all defensive in nature. Although these combinations existed, they did not in fact signify that Europe was divided into two armed camps. The alliance partners often disagreed on specific issues. The agreement between Russia and the Habsburg Empire in 1897 on preserving the status quo in the Balkans demonstrated that members of opposing systems could reach important political understandings. The continued cooperation of the states on the Macedonian question has also been shown.

In the nineteenth century one great power, Britain, had consistently refused to sign general alliances. Its attitude was to be modified in the next century. In 1904 and 1907, in separate understandings with France and Russia, Britain settled outstanding colonial disputes with its major rivals in this field. These agreements – the Russo-French alliance and the colonial treaties made by Britain with France and Russia – formed the basis for the diplomatic combination known as the Triple Entente. Although Britain was not tied to France or Russia by actual alliances, its government henceforth tended to work with theirs in international affairs.

Between 1878 and 1908 the status quo in the Near East had been successfully preserved, largely through the cooperation of the powers in calming crises that arose over such events as the Cretan uprisings and the Greek-

Turkish war of 1897. In 1908 this international accord was broken when Austria-Hungary annexed Bosnia-Hercegovina under circumstances that caused strong resentment in both St. Petersburg and Belgrade. Previously, Habsburg and Russian relations had been good. Both states had ambitious foreign ministers. Both the Russian statesman Alexander Izvolsky and his Habsburg colleague, Alois von Aehrenthal, wanted to make gains for their countries and to advance their own careers. In September 1908 they met in Buchlau in Moravia. The Young Turk revolution had just occurred, and the status of the Ottoman Balkan territories was in question. The diplomats thus made a bargain. Russia would support a Habsburg annexation of Bosnia-Hercegovina in return for Habsburg assistance in opening the Straits to Russian warships. Later there was much controversy over this understanding, particularly on the timing of the actions. Izvolsky was exceedingly surprised when he learned on October 6 that the monarchy had announced the annexation of the Ottoman territory. Bulgarian independence was proclaimed at the same time.

The annexation was a bitter blow for Serbia, which, since the accession of Peter Karadjordjević, had ceased to have close relations with Vienna. Despite the fact that the Habsburg government had taken over the administration of Bosnia-Hercegovina, Serbian nationalists still hoped that at some time, somehow, they would be able to acquire what they regarded as national lands. The annexation made this possibility even more remote. A real crisis occurred. The Serbian leaders turned to Russia for support, whereas the Habsburg Empire expected assistance from Berlin. The Russian government, however, was not in a position at this time to come to the aid of its Balkan friend. Its defeat by Japan in 1905 and the internal problems caused by the revolution of that year had weakened the state in international relations. Serbia, faced by an ultimatum, was thus forced to alter the position first taken on the annexation and to give the assurance that the country would "change the course of her present policy towards Austria-Hungary and . . . live henceforth with the latter on a footing of good neighborliness."[5]

The episode was thus a humiliation not only for the Serbian government, but also for the Russian. The policy of cooperation with the Habsburg Monarchy in Balkan affairs was abruptly terminated. Russia was henceforth willing to make agreements and to support policies that in fact implied the reopening of the Eastern Question. In October 1909 Nicholas II and King Victor Emmanuel III of Italy, together with their foreign ministers, meeting at Racconigi, came to an agreement about their mutual interests in the area. This understanding enabled Italy in 1911 to go to war with the Ottoman Empire over Tripoli. Even more serious was the encouragement given by Russia to the Balkan states to commence negotiations for an alliance among themselves. The Russian aim was to establish a front against the Habsburg

---

5 Barbara Jelavich, *St. Petersburg and Moscow: Tsarist and Soviet Foreign Policy, 1814–1974* (Bloomington: Indiana University Press, 1974), p. 266; see also p. 265.

Monarchy, not to foment a war or the final partition of the Ottoman lands in Europe.

Nevertheless, with the active assistance of the Russian diplomatic agents, the Balkan governments concluded a series of agreements that were in fact war alliances directed against the Ottoman Empire. The negotiations thus progressed completely beyond the control of the Russian government. The first agreement was made between Bulgaria and Serbia in March 1912. Relations between the two governments had improved after 1903, but it was still very difficult for them to come to an understanding on the territorial division of Macedonia. The Bulgarian representatives in these negotiations supported the establishment of an autonomous Macedonian state with the expectation that it would eventually join Bulgaria. Serbia, in contrast, wanted a partition arrangement. The treaty signed at this time was on the surface a mutual defense pact; secret clauses, however, provided for a division of the territory in question. It was agreed that the land north of the Šar Mountains would be assigned to Serbia, with the area east of the Struma River and the Rhodope Mountains given to Bulgaria. Much of Macedonia was thus left unassigned (see Map 4). The two governments agreed that if they could not reach an understanding over this region, the tsar would be asked to mediate. It was further settled that, in the future war with the Ottoman Empire, Bulgaria would furnish 200,000 troops and Serbia 150,000.

In May 1912 Greece and Bulgaria made a similar pact, although no territorial provisions were included. In October Montenegro signed agreements with Serbia and Bulgaria. The Balkan states were now organized for war. These negotiations, if not their exact details, were known to the great powers, all of which were becoming increasingly apprehensive. They did not want another Eastern crisis. On October 8 Russia and the Habsburg Monarchy, acting for all of the powers, sent a warning to the Balkan states. The intervention came too late; on that same day Montenegro launched an attack on the Ottoman Empire and was immediately joined by its Balkan allies. Greece, Bulgaria, Serbia, and Montenegro were thus for the first time linked in a Balkan alliance and fighting together against the Ottoman Empire.

The victory over the Ottoman army was to prove relatively easy. The Balkan forces numbered about 700,000, against 320,000 for their adversary. The Ottoman military power had been weakened by the domestic political controversies and the financial problems that left the army short of modern equipment. Moreover, during the war the Greek fleet controlled the seas; troops could thus not be moved from Anatolia to Macedonia by the quickest and most direct route. The Ottoman government had feared the outbreak of such a conflict and, in preparation for the event, had reached settlements with the Albanians in September and with Italy in October. The Italian government not only received Tripoli and Cyrenaica, but used the excuse of the Balkan Wars to keep the Dodecanese Islands, which had been occupied previously. Despite these actions, the Young Turk regime was not ready for war.

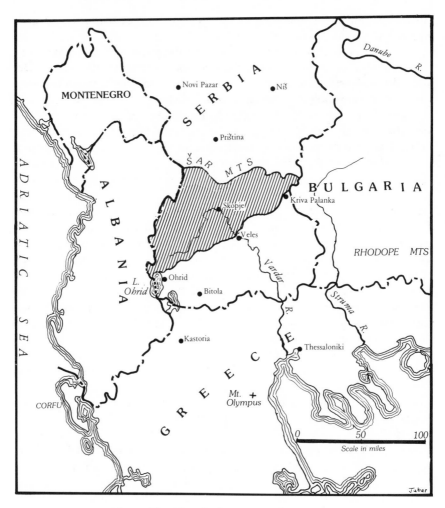

Map 4. The Macedonian contested zone, 1913

Although in previous years the Ottoman armies had usually been able to defeat the Balkan military forces, the combination at this time was too powerful.

On the side of the Balkan states the major fighting was done by the Bulgarian army, which had to face the principal Ottoman forces in Thrace. The Bulgarian command was forced to concentrate its efforts there. Meanwhile, the Serbian and Greek allies advanced into the controversial Albanian and Macedonian territories. Montenegro moved against Shkodër, while the Greek army attempted to take Janina. Both the Greek and the Bulgarian armies raced for Thessaloniki; the Greeks arrived first, on November 8, thus depriving the Bulgarians of the principal Macedonian city.

With this obvious collapse of Ottoman rule, the European great powers hastened to intervene. In May 1913 they compelled the belligerents to stop fighting and to accept the terms of the Treaty of London. This agreement established the Enos-Media line for the Ottoman possessions in Europe, which were reduced to Constantinople and some surrounding territory. Bulgaria was given Adrianople; Crete was finally ceded to Greece. The great problem of the division of Macedonia remained. At this point an issue arose that had not been foreseen by the Balkan allies. In their agreements they had proceeded under the assumption that they would partition the Albanian lands among themselves. Instead, they found that the great powers would insist on the formation of an Albanian state.

The major supporters of an independent Albania were Italy and Austria-Hungary; Russia, in contrast, backed the claims of the Balkan states. One of the major Serbian objectives in the war had been the acquisition of a port on the Adriatic, preferably Durrës. As before, the Habsburg Empire, supported by Italy, opposed any Serbian extension toward the Adriatic. Both of these powers were determined to secure the establishment of an Albania with strong national boundaries that could serve as a check on the neighboring Slavic states. Since this action would deprive both Serbia and Greece of land that they had expected to annex, they sought compensation in the Macedonian territory given to Bulgaria or as yet unassigned. The issue was not the national character of the lands in question, but the balance of power among the Balkan allies. Once again fearing Bulgaria as the chief competition, Serbia and Greece came to a secret agreement on the division of the area in question and on mutual aid in case of war. These two governments were also in touch with Romania, Montenegro, and even the Ottoman Empire.

Meanwhile, the dangers in the situation became increasingly apparent in Sofia. Not only had Bulgaria incurred the jealousy and enmity of its former allies, but it had no great-power supporters. Misjudging the situation and convinced that it could win a military victory, the Bulgarian government on the night of June 29–30 ordered an attack on Greece and Serbia. The action was a disastrous mistake. Romanian, Montenegrin, and Ottoman troops also joined in the battle against the Bulgarian army. The Second Balkan War resulted in the complete defeat of Bulgaria; an armistice was signed on July 31.

The Treaty of Bucharest of August 1913 partitioned Macedonia and established an independent Albania. The great victors were Serbia and Greece. With the addition of Macedonian territory, Serbia almost doubled in size. Montenegro and Serbia divided the Sanjak of Novi Pazar, which the Habsburg Monarchy had returned after the annexation of Bosnia-Hercegovina; the states thus secured a common border. Greece gained southern Macedonian lands and part of Epirus, with the city of Janina. Greece's boundary in the east was extended to include Kavalla. Despite the defeat, Bulgaria received land in the Struma Valley and an eighty-mile section of the Aegean coastline, including the port of Dedeagatch (Alexandroupolis). Both the Ottoman Empire and Romania made gains: the Porte took back Adrianople, and Romania acquired southern Dobrudja. The final agreement, as can be seen, was an extreme setback for Bulgaria and the Ottoman Empire.

The two Balkan Wars thus brought to an end Ottoman rule in the peninsula except for a strip of Thrace and Constantinople. The Young Turk regime had been unable to halt the further decline of the empire. It remained, nevertheless, in control of the government. Although it had been challenged by opposition parties from 1909 to 1911, it attained a full victory in June 1913 and established a dictatorship. The other parties were suppressed.

## ALBANIAN INDEPENDENCE

As soon as the First Balkan War broke out, the Albanian leaders recognized the danger of their situation. At first they adopted an attitude of neutrality. The Ottoman army, however, collapsed faster than had been anticipated, and the Balkan armies occupied Albanian territory. The leadership in defending the Albanian position was taken by Ismail Kemal, whom current Albanian historiography sees as the father of Albanian independence.[6] From Constantinople at the beginning of the war, he traveled first to Romania to obtain the support of the influential Albanian colony there. He then continued to Vienna, where he spoke with the Habsburg foreign minister, Leopold von Berchtold, and the British and Italian ambassadors. He secured Habsburg support, but for Albanian autonomy rather than independence. He returned to Albania by the ports of Trieste and Durrës and then proceeded to Vlorë, which became the Albanian headquarters. On November 28, 1912, a national assembly was opened there, composed of eighty-three Muslim and Christian delegates who came from all the Albanian regions. Kemal became the president of a provisional government that included a ministry whose members were both Muslims and Christians. The situation was precarious. The Balkan armies were pressing forward, and the provisional regime was not represented in all sections of the country. The Albanian leaders were also well aware that the great powers would make the final decisions about their status and the borders of any future state. Their major fear was that Greece and Serbia would partition the country at the Shkumbî River. The government thus remained in touch with the great powers and the Balkan states and sought their recognition for its authority. To assure that the Albanian position would be understood, Kemal went to London to negotiate directly with the European representatives. An attitude of neutrality in the war was maintained.

The major decisions concerning Albania were made by a conference of ambassadors held under the presidency of the British foreign secretary, Sir Edward Grey, which opened in London in December 1912. As we have seen,

6 Stefanaq Pollo and Arben Puto, *Histoire de l'Albanie des origines à nos jours* (Roanne: Éditions Horvath, n.d.), pp. 172, 173.

Austria-Hungary and Italy were strong supporters of the establishment of an Albanian state with ethnic boundaries. Russia stood behind the demands of Serbia and Montenegro, who wished to extend their territories as far as possible at the Albanian expense. Britain and Germany remained neutral. The representatives first decided that an autonomous Albania under continued Ottoman rule but with six-power protection would be organized. This decision had to be changed in the spring of 1913, when it became obvious that the Ottoman Empire would lose all of Macedonia and thus its territorial connection with Albania. Therefore, in July 1913, the conference came to the conclusion that independence was necessary. Albania was to be a neutral state under a great-power guarantee. Its form of government was to be a constitutional monarchy.

Despite the fact that a provisional government under Kemal was in existence, the powers refused to recognize it. Instead they established an International Control Commission composed of the representatives of the great powers, together with one Albanian. The gendarmerie was placed under Dutch control. The determination of the national frontiers caused, as could be expected, great difficulties. In the final settlement the state was deprived of areas with large Albanian majorities, most significantly the Kosovo region, with Priština as its center, which had been a major national focal point (see Map 5). The powers did, however, force Montenegro to evacuate Shkodër, which its troops occupied. As finally constituted, the state was about 11,000 square miles in size and contained 800,000 people.

Two authorities claimed jurisdiction at this point: the Kemal regime and the International Commission. Both had their headquarters in Vlorë. The International Commission began gradually to take more control and to replace the provisional authority. In addition, a rival Albanian center was established by Esad Toptani, who had been minister of interior in Kemal's government and had the support of the great landowners. In the ensuing political struggle, both Kemal and Toptani were forced to step aside. Kemal subsequently left the country and died in Nice; Toptani remained active in politics, and he was part of the commission sent to greet the prince chosen by the powers.

Once it was in charge of the country, the International Commission prepared a draft constitution. It provided for the establishment of a national assembly, which would be composed of three representatives from each of the seven administrative districts, to be chosen by direct suffrage, and certain notables, such as the heads of the three churches and ten nominees of the prince. The assembly was to have a four-year term. The ministers would be appointed by the prince and responsible to him.

To head the state the powers chose Prince William of Wied, a thirty-five-year-old captain in the German army. An Albanian delegation was sent to offer him the crown. Since the German emperor, William II, was not enthusiastic about the idea, the prince also hesitated before finally accepting. He

MONTENEGRO

Priština

Peć

Cetinje

Djakovica

Prizren

*Drin R.*

Shkodër

Skopje

Debar

Durrës
(Durazzo)

★Tirana

*Shkumbî R.*

Ohrid

Bitola

L.
Ohrid

L.
Prespa

Lushnjë

Berat

Kastoria

SASENO
ISLAND

Vlorë

*Vijosë*

Frashër

Tepelene

*R.*

Gjirokastër

CORFU

Janina

A D R I A T I C

S E A

S E R B I A

G R E E C E

0      40      80
*Scale in miles*

Map 5. Albania, 1913

was given a loan of 75 million francs, guaranteed by the powers, to assist in the financing of his new government. Arriving at Durrës in March 1914, he faced a complicated situation. Toptani, serving as minister of both defense and the interior, dominated the new Albanian government. The prince similarly had to deal with the International Commission and the foreign advisers, who remained in the country and who had a great deal of authority. The Italian and Habsburg representatives in Albania also fought each other for superior influence.

The new regime was faced from the beginning with opposition from various sections of the country. The Greek government was not satisfied with the settlement it had gained in Epirus; it wanted more territory. It therefore encouraged the resistance to the government that arose in the southern Albanian districts. The area was finally given a special administration. Even more serious were uprisings whose origins were to be found in the bad economic conditions.

The Albanian peasant had indeed much to complain about. Half of the arable land belonged to the great estates. Moreover, most of the peasants were devout Muslims, deeply attached to their faith and the religious leaders. They were thus willing listeners to Ottoman propaganda that attacked the new regime as a tool of the beys and the Christian powers. Soon the government was faced with a major peasant revolt. The Italian and Austrian representatives played roles in intrigues surrounding this event, and Toptani took part in the rebellion. When he was captured, he was deported to Italy and there received with honor. The peasant revolt, however, continued. It had no clear organization, program, or center. The movement simply gathered together all of those who opposed the new political organization, including those who remained pro-Ottoman. Its attacks were directed mainly against the prince and the International Commission.

In 1914 the situation was thus extremely unfavorable for Albanian national interests. The central government was opposed by strong rebel groups. In the south Greek-supported bands were active. Austrian and Italian adherents fought among themselves for predominant influence. The new prince, inexperienced in Albanian affairs, could not handle the situation. His control over the countryside was soon lost, and his government actually administered little more than the two cities of Durrës and Vlorë. Finally, deprived of the support of the Habsburg government and of many Albanian leaders, William left the country in September 1914, after only six months on the throne.

During the first months of World War I Albania was thus reduced to a condition of political anarchy. This situation was to last throughout the war. Despite these dangerous developments, the Albanian national movement had achieved important successes. The powers had made the decision to establish the state; most of its major territories had not been partitioned among the neighboring Balkan states. At least a basis for the future had been prepared.

The final decisions on the government were not, however, to be made until the postwar period.

## THE OTTOMAN LEGACY

By 1914 the Ottoman possessions in the Balkans had been reduced to the city of Constantinople and a Thracian hinterland. The goal of the Balkan national revolutionary movements had thus been attained: the Ottoman Empire had been expelled from the peninsula. In one sense, however, much had not changed. For five hundred years the Balkan people had lived together under one flag. They had been part of one world, and they had influenced each other. They had all shared in an Ottoman civilization that was quite different from, for instance, that of neighboring Orthodox Russia or Catholic Austria. Despite the constant criticisms by Balkan intellectuals concerning the "Ottoman yoke," the empire had produced a culture with many positive as well as negative traits. What follows here is an attempt to summarize briefly a few of the aspects of this civilization that became a permanent part of the Balkan heritage.

No matter how nationalistic a Balkan state wished to be, the legacy of Ottoman rule was an intimate part of the life of each individual and one that could not be easily obliterated. For instance, many Turkish words had entered into the vocabulary of all of the nationalities. In 1966 a dictionary of 657 pages was published in Sarajevo listing the Turkish words in Serbo-Croatian.[7] The other languages were similarly affected. In Volume I we saw how the Ottoman conquest and the subsequent battles between Christian and Muslim provided the great themes of Balkan literature from the Kosovo cycle and the ballads of the klephts and haiduks until modern times. Similarly, Balkan cooking shares similarities with that of other Near Eastern countries and is again different from that of, let us say, Russia, Italy, or Austria.

The Balkan citizen has also benefited from the fact that many aspects of Ottoman life were extremely beautiful. Ottoman architecture, both for public buildings, such as mosques, bridges, inns, and offices, and for private homes, was far superior to anything that replaced it. The Ottoman culture also placed high value on gardens and on nature, in particular on rivers and running water. European travelers were much impressed by the romantic beauty of the Balkan landscape. One famous travel account states: "A Turkish city has a charm of its own whatever its situation, and looked at from what point you please. True to the pastoral instincts of his ancestors, the Turk ever seeks to absorb the prosaic town into the poetry of nature; he multiplies spires to atone for roofs, and wherever he builds a house he plants a tree."[8]

7  Abdulah Škaljić, *Turcizmi u srpskohrvatskom Jeziku* [Turkisms in the Serbo-Croatian language] (Sarajevo: "Svjetlost" Izdavačko Preduzeće, 1966).
8  G. Muir Mackenzie and A. P. Irby, *Travels in the Slavonic Provinces of Turkey-in-Europe* (London: Alexander Strahan, 1866), p. 5.

Although modern architecture is quite different – and in fact often drab and ugly in contrast – efforts have been made to preserve what remains of the Ottoman past. It must be remembered that even with the expulsion of Ottoman rule, a large Muslim population remained, including approximately 2 million Albanians and a similar number of Slavs. In regions, such as Bosnia, where the Muslims retained a powerful political position, Ottoman traditions were retained as a part of the national heritage.

In addition to these positive aspects of life, the Balkan inhabitants acquired certain traits that were to be a particular hindrance to the adoption of modern institutions:

> The Ottoman social system fostered many undesirable habits . . . that lived on after the Empire's demise. Centuries of feudal bondage contributed to the prevalence of *yavashlik*, a state of being characterized by lethargy, indifference, indecision, and a tendency toward submissiveness which grew out of the necessity for survival. This can be easily detected in the attitude toward authority – apprehension but at the same time humility and acquiescence. Coupled with subservience is cleverness, expressed in attempts to get around obstacles, including those erected by authority, by using none-too-ethical . . . or even illegal means. The notion persists that it is perfectly permissible to cheat and steal from the government . . . The future being uncertain, the subjects of the Ottoman Empire developed a rather hedonistic attitude toward life and a great appreciation of leisure. Work as such is in general little prized . . . Many writers believe that fatalism (*kismet*), deeply rooted in Balkan Christians, is a product of Islamic influence. Fatalism derives from the doctrine of predestination, namely, that everything has been ordained by Allah or God and that no mortal can do anything to change his destiny. The Christians, like their Muslim neighbors, accepted the notion that upon everyone's forehead is written how long he will live![9]

Both the positive and the negative aspects of the Ottoman heritage were to be reflected in the history of all the states in the succeeding years. The fact that they shared in a common culture was to be the principal link among Albania, Bulgaria, Greece, and Romania, to be joined by Turkey and Yugoslavia after the war.

9   Wayne S. Vucinich, *The Ottoman Empire: Its Record and Legacy* (Princeton, N.J.: Van Nostrand, 1965), pp. 120–121.

# 4

## World War I

### SARAJEVO

ORLD WAR I, an event that was to complete the unification of the Balkan states, had its immediate origins in an event closely linked to the national and international controversies that have been previously examined. At the beginning of 1914 there was no indication that the year would end in unparalleled disaster. In fact, the Balkan scene was relatively calm; after two years of conflict no power – victor or vanquished – was in a position to face a renewed period of warfare. Nor was the general diplomatic field unusually troubled. Two alliance systems, the Triple Alliance and the Triple Entente, were in existence, but they were basically defensive alignments, designed to preserve the status quo on the Continent. They had not prevented their members in the past from cooperating closely with states in the opposite camp on specific issues. Within the Triple Alliance, the allegiance of Italy was coming ever more into doubt. The Entente powers were weakened by the growing conflict of Britain and Russia over the control of Persia, despite their previous agreement on spheres of influence. Germany was the strongest single military power on the Continent, but Britain and France clearly predominated in the world imperial field. The British navy still ruled the seas. Although many minor disagreements plagued the relations of the great powers, none were worth the launching of a major war.

With this general situation the question naturally arises what Balkan issue could have precipitated a devastating conflict, one that was to conclude with the final dissolution of the Habsburg and Ottoman empires, the downfall of the tsarist regime in Russia, and the disruption of world relations to the extent that a second even more devastating war was soon to follow. In the Balkan peninsula the danger spots remained the national questions that had not yet been resolved and domestic political conflicts that resulted in a high degree of instability. As far as the first problem is concerned, after the division of Macedonia and Thrace and the establishment of Albania, the Balkan nationalities had finally overturned Ottoman rule (see Map 6). The next national demands could only involve Habsburg territory or, in the case of Romania, Russian Bessarabia. There was little chance that the Romanian government would press its claims against either of its great neighbors. Ro-

Map 6. The Balkan states, 1914

manians lived in large numbers in Transylvania, Bukovina, and Bessarabia. Romania, however, was in alliance with Austria-Hungary, and it was not in a position to intervene actively in any of these regions. In contrast, the attitude of the Serbian government toward the Habsburg South Slavs was far more complicated.

With the expulsion of the Ottoman Empire from Europe, the next immediate national problem concerned the South Slavic inhabitants of the monarchy, the Serbs, Croats, and Slovenes, in particular their relations with the Serbian state and with the central authorities of the Dual Monarchy. Two trends have already been noted among these people. Some parties emphasized the national interests of their particular nation – for instance, the Croatian parties of Starčević and Frank, both of which called for the unification of what they defined as the Croatian lands, including Croatia, Slavonia, Dalmatia, and Bosnia-Hercegovina. Their goal was the formation of a Croatian national state that could be associated in a federal relationship, but on an absolutely equal footing, with Austria and Hungary. The Catholic church would play an important role here. These Croatian nationalists tended to have an antagonistic attitude toward Orthodox Serbs, whom some regarded merely as renegade Croats. The superiority of Habsburg civilization over that of Orthodox, ex-Ottoman Serbia was also emphasized.

The second trend of opinion was that represented by the Croatian-Serbian Coalition, which, as we have seen, was extremely active in Croatian politics at this time. Since it was a combination of parties, the group had no single program. Basic to all sections, however, was the conviction that Serbs and Croats within the empire should work together and not allow either Vienna or Budapest to play one against the other as had often been done in the past. The coalition was indeed the strongest single political organization, but it is difficult to judge its influence throughout the country because of the limited Croatian franchise. It is very important to note that the coalition stood for cooperation *within* the monarchy. Some students and intellectuals might indeed have foreseen a time when the Habsburg South Slavs would join Serbia, but this was certainly not the objective of the majority.

The choices before the Serbs of the Serbian kingdom and the monarchy were wider. The Habsburg Serbs could obviously work with the Yugoslav parties seeking to establish a separate South Slav unit within the empire, or they could emphasize specific Serbian goals and seek an eventual annexation by Serbia. The Serbian government had even more options. First, it could follow past procedures and attempt to build a greater Serbia. This policy would set as a national goal the annexation of Habsburg lands considered Serbian, especially Bosnia, Hercegovina, the Vojvodina, and the sections of Croatia, Dalmatia, and Slavonia that had Serbian populations. Second, the concept of a Balkan federation had long been a standard item in revolutionary and national programs. Such an organization could unite Serbia with Bulgaria, Montenegro, and the Slavs of Austria-Hungary, should that state dissolve. A wider union could include Greece and Romania. Third, the Serbian leaders could adopt a Yugoslav program calling for the unification of all Serbs, Croats, and Slovenes in a single nation. It should be noted here that the absolutely vital question whether this should be a federal or a centralized state received very little attention.

Of the three paths, that of a Balkan federation had the least chance of success. Its impracticality had been repeatedly demonstrated, most recently by means of the mutual conflicts and jealousies among the states apparent during the Balkan Wars. The complete break in relations and the deep animosity that had developed between Serbia and Bulgaria excluded a union between them at this time. The Yugoslav idea, however, did indeed receive a great deal of support from some sections of Serbian society, particularly from intellectuals and students, immediately prior to the war. A great attraction was the obvious fact that the program was both idealistic and practical. Should Belgrade be able to unite all of the South Slav lands, the resulting nation would have the potential of becoming a great power. It would, moreover, clearly be the predominant force in the Balkans. The doctrine was also a weapon in the hands of the Serbian government. After 1903 it did all it could to encourage and attract the support of the South Slavs of the Dual Monarchy. Since political agitation was dangerous after the 1909 crisis, the emphasis was placed on cultural activities. Belgrade became the center of exhibitions and meetings of artists, teachers, and writers. Close contact was maintained with groups within the monarchy that had Yugoslav programs. There was thus some support in Serbia for the creation of a great South Slav state, a concept that naturally involved the dissolution of the monarchy. Representing the opinion of only a small percentage of the population, largely the educated minority, the proponents of a Yugoslavia never adequately met the problem of the basis on which the unification would take place. This failure was to have disastrous consequences in the postwar period.

Though some were thus attracted to the wider concept, the great majority of Serbs thought in terms of traditional nationalism. This attitude was completely understandable. Serbia was an independent state; it had long historic and religious traditions that were not shared with the Croats or the Slovenes. After 1870 most national movements followed the previous Italian and German examples. Serbian nationalists thus wanted their kingdom to be "the Piedmont of the Balkans," a phrase that could have many meanings. Their major objective throughout the nineteenth century had been the unification of the lands they regarded as Serbian, including Bosnia, Hercegovina, Old Serbia, Macedonia, and the Serbian-inhabited lands of the Habsburg Empire. They also sought a union with Montenegro – a practical objective, given the conviction of most Montenegrins that they were indeed Serbs. Some groups, the equivalent of the greater Croatian parties in the monarchy, wished to obtain all of the South Slavs lands, including the Croatian regions. Many had attitudes comparable to those of their Croatian-nationalist counterparts: they regarded the Croats as apostate Serbs.

The greater Serbian goal, like the Great Idea of the Greeks, was thus a state based not on strictly ethnic principles, but on the acquisition of lands that had historic associations or that had at some time been under the jurisdiction of the Serbian Orthodox church. The ideal was the territory included in the empire of Stephen Dušan, the greatest of Serbia's medieval rulers. The nationalists could be encouraged by the rapid progress that Serbia had recently made. As a result of the Balkan Wars the population of the kingdom had increased from 2.9 million to 4.4 million. Thus, despite the great disappointment over the Habsburg annexation of Bosnia-Hercegovina, much had indeed been accomplished during the past century.

As we have seen, almost all Balkan national movements had carried an element of revolutionary conspiracy. Violence and terror, justified with high romantic rhetoric, had a major role in the accomplishment of specific objectives. Secret societies, with distinctive symbols, flags, oaths, and elaborate ceremonies, were also prevalent. Some of these, such as the Filiki Etairia, the Bulgarian committees, and IMRO, were extremely successful in the organization of conspiracies that had important consequences for their national movements. This tradition was alive and flourishing in the Balkans at the end of the century.

Moreover, the intellectual youth in the Balkans was often attracted by the more radical social and political doctrines of the day. Like their peers elsewhere, not only were they nationalists, but they attacked the institutions created by previous generations. As a Bosnian writer expressed it: "Our fathers, our tyrants, have created this world on their model and are now forcing us to live in it."[1] The extreme factions placed great emphasis on personal involvement and praised assassination and terrorism as expressions of creativity and liberation. Between 1910 and 1914 members of these groups in the monarchy achieved an impressive record of acts of violence against Habsburg officials. Their efforts included an attempt to assassinate Emperor Franz Joseph during his visit to Bosnia in May 1910. Further,

> on June 8, 1912, a Bosnian student, Luka Jukić, fired at the ban of Croatia, Slavko Cuvaj, killing a high-ranking official and a policeman and wounding two other policemen; a student of Zagreb, Ivan Planinšćak, tried to kill Ban Cuvaj in Zagreb on October 31, 1912; a Croatian youth, Stjepan Dojčić, who had emigrated to the United States of America, returned to his homeland to kill Cuvaj. In the meantime Baron Ivo Škerlec had become ban of Croatia; Dojčić attempted to kill him but succeeded only in wounding him in the hand on August 18, 1913. On May 15 another Zagreb student, Jakov Šefer, made an attempt on the life of Archduke Salvador and Ban Škerlec as they were leaving the National Theater in Zagreb.[2]

1 Quoted in Vladimir Dedijer et al., *History of Yugoslavia*, trans. Kordija Kveder (New York: McGraw-Hill, 1974), p. 464.
2 Dedijer et al., *History of Yugoslavia*, pp. 465–466.

Added to this ready availability of young fanatics, the unstable political conditions in Serbia contributed to the dangers of the situation. After the Balkan Wars a major conflict developed between the Serbian military and the government headed by Nikola Pašić. The army, as could be expected, was the center of strong national enthusiasm; its spirit was high after the recent victories. Some Serbian officers, with sentiments similar to those of their colleagues in Greece who joined the Military League or those in the Ottoman Empire who supported the Young Turks, felt that the civilian government was holding back the nation. They disliked in particular the Radical Party, which they saw as a group of corrupt politicians endangering the state. The immediate issue in 1914 was the administration of the newly annexed Macedonian lands, over which the army wished to retain jurisdiction. In June King Peter was forced for reasons of health to hand over his authority to his second son, Alexander, as regent. In the spring and summer of 1914 Serbia thus faced a domestic crisis, a major ingredient of which was the question of the ability of the government to control the military.

The intensification of Serbian national sentiment prior to World War I had led to the formation of two societies. The first, the *Narodna Odbrana* (National Defense), was founded in December 1908 at the time of the annexation crisis. It set up a network of agents in the South Slav lands. The second organization, *Ujedinjenje ili Smrt* (Union or Death), commonly known as the Black Hand, appeared in 1911. Primarily under military direction, it was headed by Colonel Dragutin Dimitrijević, known under the pseudonym Apis. He had been one of the participants in the 1903 revolution; in 1913 he was chief of intelligence of the Serbian General Staff. He personally distrusted the civilian leaders. Like the Narodna Odbrana, the Black Hand had a Pan-Serb program. The aim, as stated in its constitution, was "the idea of unification of Serbdom; all Serbs, regardless of sex, religion or place of birth, can become members, and anyone else who is prepared to serve this ideal faithfully." It intended to use "revolutionary action rather than cultural," and therefore it was to remain secret. Its elaborate initiation ceremony was complete with candles, daggers, revolvers, and hooded figures. Like the Etairia in the previous century, the initiates had to swear an oath, which if taken seriously, implied wide commitments:

> I . . . becoming a member of the organization Ujedinjenje ili Smrt, swear by the sun which is shining on me, by the earth which is feeding me, by God, by the blood of my ancestors, by my honor and my life, that from this moment until my death, I will serve faithfully the cause of this organization and will always be ready to undergo any sacrifices for it. I swear by God, by honor and my life, that I will carry out all orders and commands unconditionally. I swear by God, honor and life, that I shall take to the grave all secrets of this orga-

nization. May God and my comrades in this organization judge me, if intentionally or unintentionally, I break or fail to observe this oath of allegiance.[3]

The two societies had many members in common, and the Black Hand could make use of the Narodna Odbrana's agents in Bosnia-Hercegovina.

The incident that precipitated a chain of events leading to the outbreak of World War I has been often recounted. On June 28, 1914, Franz Ferdinand, the heir to the Habsburg throne, and his wife were assassinated in Sarajevo. The visit had been badly organized; adequate safeguards had not been taken to protect the visitors. The date was the anniversary of the battle of Kosovo, the Serbian national holiday. Many warnings had been given on the dangers of such a trip. The archduke was an obvious target for the six young men who succeeded in killing him. The actual assassination was carried out by Gavrilo Princip, who was in many ways typical of the revolutionary Bosnian youth. He had read widely in radical literature, and he especially admired Bogdan Žerajić, who had committed suicide after failing to assassinate a Habsburg official. They were all strong Serbian nationalists, and they were steeped in Serbian history. When one of the conspirators was arrested, he announced, "I am a Serbian hero."[4] They had decided to murder the archduke because they associated him with the program of Trialism, which would have joined Bosnia with the other South Slav lands in a separate autonomous state within the monarchy. The acquisition of the province by Serbia would thus be further hindered.

The students had been assisted in their preparations by Dimitrijević, and they had received their weapons from Serbian government arsenals. Although all the details are not clear, it appears that the young Bosnians approached Dimitrijević in Belgrade in May. He provided them with pistols and bombs and smuggled them back into Habsburg territory. When the central committee of the Black Hand heard about the action, it tried to intervene, but it was too late. Pašić too received reports that some young Bosnians intended to take action against the archduke and that they had been aided by Serbian officials in crossing the border illegally. No open and official action was taken. The Serbian representative in Vienna did, however, warn the joint minister of finance, who was, it will be remembered, responsible for Bosnia-Hercegovina, in an oblique fashion. His words were not understood.

The Habsburg government had always been extremely sensitive about outside influences on the nationalities. In the 1850s and 1860s the unification of the Danubian Principalities and the accession of a foreign prince had been opposed because of the effect of a strengthened Romanian state on Transyl-

---

3 Quoted in Vladimir Dedijer, *The Road to Sarajevo* (New York: Simon & Schuster, 1966), pp. 374, 375.
4 Quoted in Dedijer, *The Road to Sarajevo*, p. 319.

vania. In the 1870s strong opposition had been expressed to the creation of a large Slavic Balkan state for fear of the influence that it might exert over the South Slavs in the monarchy. During the years prior to the assassination ample evidence had been found concerning the ties between Serbia and some elements of the monarchy's Slavic population and the measures that had been taken in Belgrade to strengthen them. The Habsburg leaders were convinced that the assassination had been plotted within the Serbian government and that they would have to act decisively. The Habsburg foreign minister, Berchtold, and the chief of staff, Conrad von Hötzendorf, were the first to believe that a war with Serbia was necessary. They then persuaded Franz Joseph and Count Stephen Tisza, the Hungarian premier. Tisza would agree to strong measures only when he was assured that no Serbian territory would be annexed to the empire. The Habsburg officials, before taking decisive action, attempted to prove a direct connection between the Serbian government and the assassination; this they were not able to do. They also consulted with their German ally.

Having decided upon war, the Habsburg leaders handled the diplomatic preparations in an exceedingly inept manner. The assassination of the archduke had caused shock and disgust among the European statesmen. Had the Habsburg government acted at once, it might have exploited the general revulsion at this act of violence. Instead the entire matter dragged on from June 28 to July 23, when an ultimatum was finally delivered to Belgrade. The intermediate time was not used to prepare the ground adequately. Obviously, it was to the Habsburg interest to keep the war localized. The danger point was a possible Russian intervention in support of Serbia. After 1903 the relations between the two Slavic states had been extremely cordial, and Russia could be expected to react in some manner to a Habsburg threat to Belgrade. In their past Balkan policies the Russian and Habsburg governments had usually observed the principles of the balance of power: when one made major gains, the other should have compensation. Before going to war with the Ottoman Empire in 1877, Russia had negotiated the secret treaties that assured Vienna of advances in the western Balkans. In 1908, prior to the annexation of Bosnia-Hercegovina, Aehrenthal had sought to make a similar bargain with Izvolsky. An Austrian defeat of Serbia in 1914 would have completely upset the diplomatic balance in the region. Romania was still tied to the Central Powers, and after the Balkan Wars Bulgaria too turned to these states. The Young Turk regime in Constantinople was about to sign an alliance with Germany. Should Serbia be forced into a position of vassalage to Vienna, Russian influence would be excluded from the peninsula. If the Habsburg leaders felt that they could no longer tolerate what they were convinced were Serbian provocations, then the tsarist regime could not be expected to accept a humiliating defeat in a region where it had expended so much blood and money in the past.

Not only did the monarchy fail to come to an understanding with Russia, but, even worse, it did not consult its ally, Italy, despite definite treaty obligations. When the Triple Alliance was renewed in 1887, the two powers had agreed that, should it prove impossible to maintain the status quo in the Near East, then they would make changes only after consultation and on the basis of mutual compensation. Only a Habsburg annexation of Bosnia-Hercegovina was excluded from this arrangement. The Habsburg government did not communicate its intentions regarding Serbia to Rome precisely because it feared that Italy would demand some compensation. The violation of the treaty was to be one of the reasons why Italy was able to remain neutral after the fighting began.

The steps to be taken were also not adequately discussed in Berlin. William II and his chancellor, Theobald von Bethmann-Hollweg, assured the Habsburg government that Germany would back whatever decision it reached concerning Serbia. This "blank check" allowed Vienna to determine policy for both alliance partners. The choice of methods was that adopted against Serbia in 1909: an ultimatum that was presented on July 23. However, since the objective was war, not further negotiations, the document was designed to be rejected. It included the demands that strong action be taken to repress anti-Habsburg activities within Serbia and that Habsburg officials participate in the investigation of the assassination. In its reply the Serbian government agreed to all of the terms except this last point. In answer, the Habsburg government broke off relations, and on July 28 war commenced between the two countries. The question remained whether the conflict would be localized or whether it would draw in all of the powers.

Once Serbia was at war, the state that had to make an immediate decision was Russia. With great reluctance, the tsar ordered mobilization on July 29. Since the success of its plans depended on a quick victory against France before the Russian armies were ready to fight, the German government answered the Russian mobilization with a declaration of war on the two powers. Britain entered in support of its allies on August 4. In August 1914 Europe was thus finally dragged into a major war over issues closely connected with the Eastern Question and the Balkan national unification movements. Arguing over the question of "war guilt" is a futile exercise. In 1914 each state acted in the crisis on the basis of what it felt its best interests demanded. A fatal chain of events involved all of the belligerents in a type of warfare that they had not expected and for which they were not militarily, economically, or psychologically prepared.

## THE WAR

The major battles of World War I were fought in northern France and along the extensive eastern front. The military decisions were to be reached there rather than in the Balkans, where the campaigns served as a sideshow to the main conflicts waged elsewhere. Therefore this section places more emphasis on the diplomatic negotiations than on the military planning or the actual battles. Despite the fact that final victory depended on the armies of the great powers, these governments throughout the war sought the support of small allies, particularly when it became apparent, as it soon did, that a long war lay ahead. At the beginning of the conflict, the general staffs of the powers had planned on short, decisive campaigns. When these had all failed by the beginning of 1915, and when the western front settled into trench warfare, the leaders on both sides attempted to win the assistance of the Balkan countries, which occupied strategic locations and had respectable armies. The Balkan governments, with the exception of the Serbian, which was already at war, thus found themselves courted by the belligerents, and they used the opportunity to bargain for the maximum advantages. Each nation also wished to make certain that it would choose the winning side.

At the beginning of the war Serbia was in a very dangerous position in both a military and a political sense. Although the government had hoped to avoid a conflict, this state of 4.5 million found itself fighting an empire of 50 million. It had powerful allies, but they were far away and chiefly concerned with defending their own frontiers against a German attack; they had no troops or arms to spare for Serbia. It was generally expected that the Habsburg army would quickly be victorious. Instead, the first successes were on the Serbian side. The army was, in fact, able to repel two attacks in 1914 and even to go on the offensive and enter Habsburg territory. The Russian advance into Galicia forced the monarchy to shift troops to this zone. Moreover, the Serbian soldiers had gained experience in the Balkan Wars, and they fought well. In early December they suffered a reversal and Belgrade was taken. They then won a major victory on the Kolubara River and in mid-December regained Belgrade. The Serbian losses during the fighting were extremely high. The government had no way of replacing these men or of acquiring more military supplies. Not only were immense casualties suffered by the army in the battles, but a serious typhus epidemic hit the country. Despite the military achievements, the future looked bleak.

The previous Habsburg doubts about the loyalty of their national groups in war soon proved unfounded. The South Slavs, as well as the majority of all the nationalities, fought bravely. Measures of control and repression were, of course, introduced in the monarchy, as in all of the belligerent states. Newspapers were closed, and suspected traitors were imprisoned. Some acts of resistance occurred, but nothing like the French army mutinies of 1917 or the wholesale desertions of the Russian forces at the time of the revolution. Until the last months of the war, the empire held together. In fact, some parties, such as the conservative and clerical parties in Croatia and Slovenia, supported a war against Orthodox Serbs. Even the Serbian detachments of the Habsburg army remained loyal to the traditions of the Military Frontier.

Among the troops that launched the attack on Serbia in August 1914, some corps consisted of 20 to 25 percent Serbs and 50 percent Croats. A contemporary Yugoslav historian writes:

> In the battle of Mačkov Kamen in September 1914, fighting on one side was the Fourth Regiment of Užice [Serbian] and on the other a regiment from Lika including a large number of Serbs from that area whose forebears had for centuries been the most faithful soldiers of the Habsburg emperors. Commander Purić of the Užice regiment led his men in fourteen charges, to which the men from Lika responded with lightninglike countercharges. In one of these Purić shouted to them, "Surrender, don't die so stupidly," and they replied, "Have you ever heard of Serbs surrendering?"[5]

Such romantic national traditions were to yield high casualty figures on all sides.

After the beginning of the war the first state to come to a decision about its allegiance was the Ottoman Empire. Under the influence of Enver Pasha, the pro-German minister of war and one of the most influential of the Young Turk leaders, the government signed a secret alliance with Germany on August 2, 1914, the day before Germany declared war on France. Although the Porte did not immediately enter the fighting, it did offer sanctuary to two German warships, the *Goeben* and the *Breslau*, which it claimed to have purchased. In November the empire was formally at war with the Allies. With the closure of the Straits to Allied shipping, sea communications between Russia and its Western partners were effectively severed. In an effort to remedy this situation and to improve the Allied military position in the Near East, the British government adopted a controversial plan to attempt to open the Straits. The responsibility for the action was largely that of Winston Churchill, who at that time was first lord of the Admiralty. The Dardanelles and Gallipoli campaigns were military disasters, and they were extremely damaging to the career of that politician. In the first effort, carried out in February 1915, a squadron of eighteen British warships tried to force its way through the Straits. After four ships were lost, the commander ordered a withdrawal. In fact, had he pressed on, he might have won a victory, since the Ottoman forts had run short of ammunition. The Gallipoli campaign had even worse results. The objective was to secure a land base from which attacks could be launched on the Ottoman Empire. Allied troops were able to take a beachhead, which they held from April 1915 to January 1916. Ottoman forces remained entrenched on the heights above the Allied soldiers, whose

---

5   Dedijer et al., *History of Yugoslavia*, p. 480.

losses, particularly among the Australian and New Zealand contingents, were immense.

The Allied failure at the Straits was balanced by the entrance of Italy into the war in May 1915. Although this state had been a member of the Triple Alliance, the terms of the treaty were defensive. This fact, together with the failure of the Habsburg Empire to keep Rome informed of its intention to attack Serbia, gave the Italian government ample excuse to remain neutral. It could therefore bargain with both sides and sell its support to the highest bidder. Italian national aims were quite extensive; they included the South Tirol, Trentino, Trieste, Gorizia, Gradisca, Istria, most of Dalmatia, and some Albanian territory, in particular the island of Saseno (Sazan) and the port of Vlorë. Needless to say, these lands had a majority of Albanian, South Slavic, and German people. In the negotiations the Allies had a great advantage because they could freely use Habsburg territory to satisfy Italian demands. The Habsburg representatives could offer only Trentino in return for neutrality. The Allied governments were, however, hampered to an extent by the problem of the South Slav territory. The war had commenced ostensibly to save Serbia. If Italy received the Dalmatian coast, Serbia would not gain the outlet to the sea that was a major war aim. Moreover, if Italy acquired Dalmatia and Istria, it would have under its control about 700,000 South Slavs. Such problems caused difficulties mainly in Britain, where war propaganda was conducted with a high moral tone.

In the spring of 1915, however, the Allied powers believed that they needed Italian support. Although the Russian government was reluctant to make concessions at the expense of Serbia, the needs of the war took precedence, and Italy was promised almost everything it wished. The agreement was secret, and the terms were not published until the Bolshevik regime came to power in Russia in 1917. The Treaty of London of April 1915 required Italy to enter the war within thirty days. In return for its participation, it was to receive the South Tirol, Trentino, Gorizia, Gradisca, Trieste, Istria, part of Dalmatia, and Saseno and Vlorë from Albania. It could also keep the Dodecanese Islands, which had been occupied in 1911, and it was promised a share in any Turkish lands or German colonies that were to be partitioned. In May 1915 Italy declared war on Austria-Hungary, but delayed a similar act in regard to Germany until August 1916.

The next state to enter the war was Bulgaria. The goal remained, as in the past, the recreation of the San Stefano state. The specific objective was thus the acquisition of Macedonian territories, which were in the possession of Greece and Serbia, and the section of southern Dobrudja that Romania had taken in 1913. The Bulgarian decision was of great significance to both sides because of the strategic position of the country in relation both to the Straits and to Serbia, which had not yet been conquered. The Bulgarian action would also influence Greece and Romania, whose ultimate allegiance was still in doubt. In these negotiations the Central Powers held the high cards, since they could offer the Macedonian territory held by Serbia. The Allies could not compete here, nor could they offer compensating land in the possession of Greece or Romania.

Opinion in Bulgaria was divided on the question of entering the war. A disastrous conflict had just ended. The country was not prepared to fight again so soon. Both the Agrarian Union and the socialists opposed intervention. King Ferdinand and the premier, Vasil Radoslavov, in contrast, were sympathetic to the Central Powers, and the desire for Macedonia was very strong. Obviously, the Allies had nothing to offer. Russia, it was quite clear, would aid Serbia in the future. Under these circumstances, the decision was made to join the Central Powers. In September 1915 Bulgaria signed an agreement by which it was promised Macedonia and, in addition, assured of further territorial acquisitions should Greece and Romania join the Allies. This action sealed the fate of Serbia. In October a major offensive was launched by the German, Habsburg, and Bulgarian armies. In that same month, with the approval of the premier, Venizelos, but not of King Constantine, the Allies landed four divisions at Thessaloniki, but they were unable to move north.

Caught between the invading forces, the Serbian army had little chance. The battle lasted about six weeks. Hopelessly outnumbered, the soldiers attempted to retreat across northern Albania. Marching in winter without adequate supplies through a hostile countryside, the troops suffered huge casualties. Once they reached the Adriatic, they were evacuated by Allied ships to Corfu, where a Serbian government-in-exile headed by Prince-Regent Alexander and Nikola Pašić was established. Montenegro shared a similar fate. In January 1916 a Habsburg army conquered the country, and Nicholas fled to Italy. In this month the Allies were forced also to withdraw from Gallipoli. The Central Powers had thus achieved a commanding position in the Balkans. Bulgaria and the Ottoman Empire were allies; Serbia had been subdued. A small Allied army was encamped in Thessaloniki, but it could do little. Under these circumstances the allegiance of Romania and Greece acquired particular importance for the Allies.

Like Italy, Romania in 1914 was linked to the Central Powers through a defensive alliance. It had been renewed five times, most recently in 1913. King Charles favored honoring the commitment, but this opinion was not shared by Ion C. Brătianu, the son of the great minister of the nineteenth century and the most influential Romanian statesman of the period. Pro-French in attitude, he wished to exploit the situation to make gains for his country. In the immediate prewar period, relations between Romania and Austria-Hungary had worsened, primarily because of conditions in Transylvania, whereas those with Russia had improved. In June 1914 Nicholas II had visited the country. The Romanian government could bargain with both sides, and it had much to offer. The army was believed to be strong, and Romanian oil and wheat were in demand by all the belligerents.

The Romanian representatives were, in fact, in an excellent position to negotiate. At the end of July 1914, without consulting its allies, Russia offered Romania the possession of Transylvania in return for remaining neutral. Germany simultaneously promised the acquisition of Bessarabia on similar terms. In a meeting held on August 3, 1914, to discuss the question, the king and a single minister chose to join Germany; the others supported a policy of neutrality. The country was in the favorable situation of having received the assurance that it would obtain either Bessarabia or Transylvania, depending on who won, in return for doing absolutely nothing. Having conceded the major Romanian demands, neither side was left with much to bargain with. Obviously, Russia would not surrender Bessarabia nor the monarchy Transylvania. Nevertheless, during the next months the Romanian government did make some moves in the Allied direction. In October 1914 an agreement was made with Russia that permitted the passage of supplies to Serbia; similar German deliveries to the Ottoman Empire were blocked. In return, Russia conceded both Transylvania and the Romanian sections of Bukovina. Negotiations also continued with the Central Powers, who remained good customers for Romanian wheat and oil. King Charles died in October 1914 and was succeeded by his nephew Ferdinand. This event made easier Romania's entrance into the war on the side of the Allies.

The Romanian decision, however, did not come until 1916. In June the Russian army launched its last great push for victory, the Brusilov offensive. At first this drive was very successful, and Brătianu feared that if Romania did not enter the war, the government would be at a great disadvantage at the peace table. He, nevertheless, would not move without the assurance of maximum benefits. The Allied powers, who needed Romanian aid, agreed to extensive demands, including the annexation of Transylvania and the Banat up to the Tisza River as far as Szeged, that is, beyond the ethnic boundary and including a large piece of present-day Hungary. Romania was similarly assured of part of Bukovina and participation on an equal basis in the future peace conferences. Having won these promises, the country entered the conflict in August. Its army was to operate in Transylvania; there was no coordination with the Russian command. No sooner had these troops gone into action than the tide turned along the entire eastern front. The Russian offensive failed, and the army commenced a retreat. The Romanian forces in Transylvania and Dobrudja were similarly defeated. In December Bucharest fell into the hands of the Central Powers, and the Romanian government moved to Iaşi.

The entire eastern theater of war was deeply affected by the events that now took place in Russia. The first revolution occurred in March 1917; in November the Bolshevik victory assured that Russia would withdraw from the war. In December negotiations with Germany commenced, and in March 1918 the Treaty of Brest Litovsk was concluded. The complete collapse of the Russian ally made the Romanian position impossible. In February 1918 Brătianu was replaced, first by General Alexander Averescu and then by Alexander Marghiloman. In May the government signed the Treaty of Bucharest. Although it acquired Bessarabia, it was forced to cede Dobrudja and certain Carpathian regions. Germany gained full control over the oil production. Thus Romania, like Russia, in early 1918 had made peace and was out of the conflict.

The Greek entrance into the war was to provoke the most controversy and to be the longest delayed. Here the division in the government was to have more serious consequences for the future than elsewhere. Constantine I, who became king in 1913, was the brother-in-law of William II and, like Charles, he supported a pro-German policy. He was backed by those whose sympathies were with the Central Powers or who judged that they would be victorious. This group advised the maintenance of strict neutrality. Greece was not strong enough to stand up against British and French sea power in the Mediterranean, so an open support of Germany was not possible. In contrast, Venizelos, still the principal minister, was convinced that the Allies would win. Like Brătianu, he wished to use the opportunity to gain territory. Despite the advances made in 1912 and 1913, Greece still had claims involving Epirus, Thrace, western Anatolia, certain Aegean islands, in particular the Dodecanese, and Cyprus. The discussions on these issues were to extend over three years.

After the Ottoman Empire entered the war, the Allies were very anxious to win Greek support. During their negotiations with Bulgaria, they attempted to obtain Greek assistance in influencing that government, urging Greece to give concessions to Bulgaria in return for territory to be taken later from the Ottoman Empire. Venizelos was willing to concede the Drama-Kavalla area but only in return for the assurance that Greece would be given the Izmir (Smyrna) region in Anatolia, which had a population of about 800,000 Greeks. The acquisition of this area would give Greece effective control of the Aegean. Venizelos also wished the country to participate in the Dardanelles and Gallipoli enterprises, but he was opposed by the king and the chief of staff. In March 1915 the minister resigned, only to return to office following a major victory in the elections.

After Bulgaria entered the war, the Allies put great pressure on the Greek government to assist the Serbs. Greece did have alliance obligations from a treaty signed in 1913. In October 1915, as we have seen, Allied troops were landed in Thessaloniki, ostensibly to aid Serbia. Meanwhile, tension increased between the two factions in Athens, and Venizelos again resigned. In October 1916 the country faced a major domestic crisis. Venizelos formed a separate government in Thessaloniki, which was backed by the Allied forces there; in December Britain recognized it as the legitimate authority in Greece.

At the same time, as so often in the past, a British and French fleet gathered at Piraeus. In June 1917 Constantine surrendered this throne to his second son, Alexander, and Venizelos returned in triumph to Athens. In the same month Greece entered the war. However, unlike the other states, the Greek government had received no assurances about future gains. The events of this period and the flagrant Allied intervention in Greek domestic affairs were to have lasting effects on the internal politics of the country.

Meanwhile, the decisive military campaigns were being waged in northern France. The arrival of increasing numbers of American troops, together with the failure of the German summer offensive of 1918, turned the tide of battle. In September 1918 the Allied army in Thessaloniki finally went into action. Of the twenty-eight divisions in this force, nine were Greek and six were Serbian. They were to face little opposition. The victory had already been won; the Central Powers were no longer capable of putting up an effective resistance. Bulgarian morale was understandably extremely low. From 1912 to 1918 the army had suffered huge casualties – 160,000 dead and 300,000 wounded out of a population of 5 million. On September 29 the Bulgarian government surrendered; the remaining German and Habsburg troops in the peninsula were forced to withdraw quickly northward. In November Belgrade was taken and Serbian troops occupied Bosnia-Hercegovina and the Vojvodina. On November 10 Romania reentered the war, and its armies marched into the territories that it claimed.

The end of the fighting was at hand. Under extreme pressure, the Habsburg Empire simply fell apart into its national components. An Austrian Republic was established on November 13, and a Hungarian Republic three days later. On December 1 the Kingdom of the Serbs, Croats and Slovenes came into existence. Already, on October 30, the Ottoman Empire had surrendered. The war thus ended with the full victory of the Allied powers, whose numbers included the Balkan states Romania, Serbia, and Greece. Bulgaria and the Ottoman Empire were among the defeated. The Albanian government had collapsed in the first part of the war, and its territories were under foreign occupation. Whether the state would be reestablished would be determined during the peace negotiations.

## THE PEACE SETTLEMENTS

With the conclusion of the war the fate of the Balkan peninsula was again in the hands of the victorious great powers. The peace treaties were to be the work of the representatives of Britain, France, Italy, and the United States, a newcomer to European affairs. In a sharp break with previous tradition, the defeated states – Germany, the Ottoman Empire, Bulgaria, and the successor states of the Habsburg Empire, Austria and Hungary – were excluded from the deliberations. Not only did Russia, under a new revolutionary regime, not take part in the negotiations, but Allied forces were in occupation of certain parts of its territory. Their aim was the overthrow of the Bolshevik regime. Although delegates from the victor Balkan governments – Greece, Romania, and the Yugoslav state, which had just been formed – did attend some meetings, the major decisions, as in the past, were made by the large powers.

The victors had two roads to peace. First, they could base the terms of the treaties on the idealistic principles enunciated during the war by the Socialist parties, the Bolshevik government, and Woodrow Wilson in his Fourteen Points. The aim would be a just peace based on self-determination and conciliation between the victor and the vanquished. Once the fighting had stopped, the chief supporters of this type of settlement were the defeated states and Soviet Russia. These principles would defend their territories from foreign occupation and annexation. The second alternative, almost the opposite in intent, would be to apply the secret treaties and impose a punitive peace on the defeated governments. After all, no state in either camp had shown much interest in self-determination in the formulation of its own wartime objectives, unless indeed the principle would advance its own claims. Such a settlement would also mark a continuation of the imperial policies previously adopted by the powers in Asia and Africa. The secret agreements provided for the division of former Ottoman territories into spheres of influence and the distribution of the German colonies. As far as the Balkans were concerned, the area where the two principles of peacemaking would be chiefly in conflict was the Albanian and South Slav lands slated by the Treaty of London to be given to Italy. As we shall see, in general the peace treaties followed the second alternative – that is, the victor states took the spoils – but with the stipulations often clothed in the idealistic language of national self-determination and justice. The terms themselves and the justifications that accompanied them were to be the cause of much of the extreme interwar unrest and bitterness.

Among the Balkan states the clear winner at the peace table was Romania (see Map 7). This government, under the clever leadership of Brătianu, proceeded to make the maximum gains. The state had reentered the war on November 10, a week after the surrender of the Habsburg Empire and one day before the German capitulation. On the basis of this action the Romanian representatives claimed the territories promised in the agreement of 1916 with the Allies, despite the fact that the government had subsequently made a separate peace with Germany. The Romanian army was in occupation of most of the lands in question, including Bessarabia. In April 1919 the Romanian forces penetrated into Hungarian territory and launched a drive against the Communist regime of Béla Kun. They were soon in occupation of Budapest.

In the final agreement, the Treaty of Trianon of June 1920, Romania received Transylvania, Bessarabia, Crişana, and Bukovina. The Banat was di-

Map 7. The Balkan states after World War I

vided, with part going to Romania and part to the new Yugoslav state. The drawing of the frontier with Hungary caused a major conflict at the peace conference. Brătianu wished the boundary to be at the Tisza River, which would have meant the annexation of solidly Hungarian territory. Although the maximum Romanian demands were not met, the treaty did incorporate 1.7 million Hungarians into Romania. The war thus gave the Romanian nationalists just about everything they could desire – Transylvania, Bessarabia, Bukovina, and a part of the Banat. The disadvantage of this settlement was that minorities now comprised 28 percent of the total Romanian population, a condition that was to complicate domestic politics in the future.

The steps by which the Kingdom of the Serbs, Croats and Slovenes, which we will call Yugoslavia despite the fact that the name did not become official until 1929, came into existence are discussed in greater detail later. Briefly, however, at the beginning of the war the Serbian war aims were not clearly defined, but they included at a minimum the acquisition of Bosnia-Hercegovina and an outlet on the Adriatic; the government also desired some other Habsburg territories. Despite the fact that there was no major resistance in the monarchy during the war, a number of Croatian political leaders had emigrated, among them Ante Trumbić and Frano Supilo, who had been extremely active in the Croatian-Serbian Coalition. They played a major role in the formation of the Yugoslav Committee, which had its headquarters in London and which was committed to the unification of the South Slavs in a single state. The first experiences of the emigré politicians were not encouraging: they heard rumors of the negotiations that led to the Treaty of London and they received little assistance from the Allied governments, which were not at the time in favor of the dissolution of the Habsburg Empire.

At first the Serbian government did not accept the Yugoslav Committee as the representative of the Habsburg South Slavs. Quite naturally, the Serbian leaders would have preferred to be themselves the spokesmen for all of the Yugoslav people. However, after the defeat and the retreat to Corfu, Serbian officials commenced discussions with the Committee. An agreement was reached in 1917 that the South Slavs of the monarchy would join with the Serbs to form one state under the Karadjordjević dynasty. No decision was made about the political organization of the state, that is, about the crucial issue of whether it should have a federal or a centralized administration. The future constitution was to be drafted by an assembly elected on the basis of universal manhood suffrage through a secret ballot. A Montenegrin committee in Paris, similarly composed of emigrés, endorsed this pact. Throughout the conversations, apprehension over Italian designs on South Slav territories was a major factor in encouraging the Serb, Croat, and Slovene representatives to come to an agreement.

In October 1918, immediately preceding the Habsburg collapse, political leaders in Zagreb formed a National Council of Slovenes, Croats and Serbs.

It subsequently voted to join with Serbia and Montenegro. When Prince-Regent Alexander accepted the proposals of the National Council on December 1, the first steps toward unification had been taken. Similar actions followed in Montenegro, despite the opposition of King Nicholas, who did not want to lose his kingdom. Before the opening of the peace conference, local committees had thus taken action to lay the foundation for a Yugoslavia. It should be strongly emphasized that the South Slavs of the monarchy were under extreme pressure, and they had no real practical alternatives. Austrian Germans and Hungarians were in the process of organizing republics on a national basis. The imperial framework no longer existed. The realistic alternatives appeared to be either the establishment of a South Slav state or a possible partition of Croatian and Slovenian lands among Italy, Serbia, and perhaps even Austria and Hungary.

The Albanian settlement was closely connected with the Yugoslav question. During the war the central government had broken down completely, and each region had been forced to fend for itself. Foreign troops were in occupation during the entire war. Greece, Serbia, and Montenegro, of course, intended to keep what they held. Italy had occupied the island of Saseno and the port of Vlorë in anticipation of the realization of its claims under the Treaty of London. At the peace conference the major danger to Albania came from Italy. After much controversy that government finally agreed to the restoration of the 1913 borders in return for the acquisition of the port of Rijeka. The problem of the establishment of a stable Albanian national government had yet to be solved.

As a defeated power, Bulgaria, of course, could expect only to lose territory. In October 1918 Ferdinand abdicated in favor of his son, Boris III. A coalition government was then formed. In August 1919 the Agrarian Union received a plurality in the elections, and Alexander Stamboliski became premier. His government then signed the Treaty of Neuilly in November 1919. This document provided for the surrender to Greece of the territories in western Thrace that had been gained in the Balkan Wars and the cession to Serbia of four militarily strategic regions that were in ethnic composition largely Bulgarian. The state also had to pay an indemnity of $450 million and to agree to the limitation of its army, police, and border guards to 33,000.

Although Greece was on the winning side, its fate was to be closely tied to events in Anatolia. In the Treaty of Neuilly the state received territory in Thrace from Bulgaria. In the Treaty of Sèvres it gained from the Ottoman Empire the strategic islands of Imbros and Tenedos and, in a most controversial provision, the right to occupy a region around Izmir. Except for Thrace, the gains of this settlement were to be lost as a result of a military campaign in Anatolia. Greek postwar history thus was to be strongly influenced by the great-power controversies over Asia Minor and, in particular, by the establishment of the Turkish Republic.

## THE FALL OF THE OTTOMAN EMPIRE: THE TURKISH REPUBLIC

A major result of World War I was the final downfall of the Ottoman Empire, headed by a sultan from the house of Osman and based on Islamic principles, and its replacement by the Turkish Republic, a secular national state. After the Second Balkan War the Young Turk regime remained in power; association with the victorious side and the return of Adrianople gave it added prestige. The government functioned as a party dictatorship. The strongest CUP leader was Enver Pasha, the minister of war. An army officer, he had fought in Macedonia and in Tripoli against the Italian invasion; he had been the commander of the troops that retook Adrianople in 1913. Three other statesmen were of particular importance: Jemal, the navy minister; Talat, the minister of interior; and Said Halim, the grand vezir.

With the loss of the Balkan Christian territories in 1912–1913, the religious balance in the empire had decisively shifted. Although large Christian minorities remained, in particular the Armenian, the empire was preponderantly Islamic. However, in internal politics the emphasis changed from Ottomanism, which was now defunct, not to Islamic or Pan-Islamic doctrines, but to Turkish nationalism. This trend was also shown in the religious practices, where there was a movement to replace Arabic with Turkish in prayers, and in the teaching of the Koran. Measures were also taken to secularize Muslim institutions and to reduce religious influence; the effects were particularly apparent in justice and education. Traditional Muslim groups naturally opposed this direction of affairs, but it was an important step toward the formation of a modern state. Turkish nationalists were thus following in the same path as their Balkan counterparts. Like the Balkan governments, the Young Turk regime copied Western models for its reforms; these were, after all, the only progressive systems available for imitation. Foreign advisers were also extensively used.

The extent of the foreign influence and the presence of European experts were major problems for the government not only because of the resultant outside interference in state affairs, but also because of the intense jealousy among the great powers. The attempt was made to preserve a balance among them. Military reform was a particularly sensitive area. The Porte preferred to rely on German advisers, because Germany did not offer a direct threat to the territorial integrity of the empire, as did Russia, Britain, and France. Berlin also had less direct economic power. France had the paramount position in the Public Debt Commission, which administered a large section of the Ottoman finances, whereas Britain had the major influence in the Ottoman Bank, which issued money. The powers kept a particularly close watch over the German military advisers. A major crisis occurred at the end of 1913 when General Liman von Sanders became commander of the Ottoman First Army Corps in Constantinople, the force that defended the Straits; he was compelled to take a lesser position. British advisers were used for the Ottoman navy.

Enver Pasha was the primary supporter of the policy of allying with Germany and entering the war. His training in Germany made him sympathetic toward that power. His attitude, however, was chiefly influenced by the possible threat to Ottoman territory from Russia. Since Russia was allied with France and Britain, he could expect no assistance from the Entente powers against this traditional danger. The Crimean situation would not be repeated. In the summer of 1914 Enver approached Germany. At the time, France and Britain were pursuing imperialist objectives in Egypt and Mesopotamia; Russia and Britain had made an agreement to divide Persia into spheres of influence. Since neither Germany nor Austria-Hungary was involved in these actions, they seemed the safest allies. The negotiations with Germany were kept very secret. On August 2, 1914, an alliance directed against Russia was signed. The ministry was not informed until after its conclusion; the sultan had prorogued the assembly so that there would be no open discussion of the negotiations.

Despite the conclusion of the agreement, the government delayed entering the war. There was still great division on the question, and doubt was expressed whether the state was prepared for another conflict. Some measures were taken, nevertheless, to aid the Central Powers. In August two German warships, the *Goeben* and the *Breslau*, fled into the Straits despite the prohibition in the treaties, which closed this waterway to warships when the empire was at peace. The Ottoman officials answered the Allied objections by saying that their government had purchased the ships. The German sailors and officers continued on duty, but they wore Turkish fezzes. In September, in a major move against the Western Allies, the Porte abolished the capitulations. Under constant German pressure, Enver in October finally took a decisive action: the Ottoman fleet was ordered to bombard the Russian Black Sea ports. In November Britain and France declared war on the Ottoman Empire.

During the war the Ottoman forces were generally on the defensive, and they were usually unsuccessful. Like the other belligerents, the government had certain war aims. Most of these involved a reversal of the previous defeats suffered at the hands of the Balkan states and the European imperial powers. The Porte thus wished to win back land in Macedonia, Thrace, and the Caucasus and to regain control over Egypt and Crete. The end of European economic domination was another goal. Enver also had certain Pan-Turanian plans for the Turkic people of the Caucasus and Central Asia who were under Russian control. Once Bulgaria became an ally, the Ottoman objectives in Europe were curtailed; that state was to receive the desired Macedonian lands. Bulgarian participation also excluded an Ottoman campaign in the Balkans.

As in previous wars with Russia, heavy fighting took place on the Ottoman eastern front. The war in this theater was characterized by Russian victories until 1917. Even greater disasters occurred in the Arab lands. At the beginning of the war, the sultan proclaimed a *jihad*, or Holy War. Not only did the Muslim Arabs not respond to the religious appeal, but major tribal leaders supported British conspiracies in the area directed against Constantinople. The single greatest Ottoman military victory was that achieved against the British forces in the Dardanelles. Liman von Sanders, again commander of the First Army Corps, directed the Ottoman defense, with Mustafa Kemal, whose career now began a swift ascent, present as a colonel with the Turkish forces.

The Russian Revolution of 1917 and the end of the fighting on the eastern front relieved much of the pressure on the Porte. When the Bolshevik regime published the secret treaties, the Ottoman government was clearly informed about the Allied partition arrangements. Nevertheless, the empire was crumbling. The army had been fighting since 1911. Typhus epidemics and repeated shortages of food and military supplies had weakened its abilities to resist. A British army was advancing in the Arabian lands, and an Allied force was encamped in Thessaloniki. The German and Habsburg allies were obviously facing defeat. Placed in an impossible situation, the Ottoman army surrendered in October 1918. Allied troops stationed in Thessaloniki marched across Thrace and entered Constantinople. The city was then put under a joint British, French, Italian, and American occupation. Thus, after the centuries of conflict between Christian Europe and the Muslim Ottoman Empire, it was to be the Western powers, not the Russian army, that first occupied the capital.

Once the fighting had ended, the Allies had difficulty in finding a government with which to discuss the armistice terms. The ministry in office resigned, and a successor was hard to organize. Finally, Ahmed Izzet Pasha took the responsibility, and the negotiations to end the fighting began. The agreement, which was concluded on October 30, was really an unconditional surrender. According to its provisions, the Allied forces were free to operate throughout the country; the Straits were opened to the passage of warships, so that expeditions could be sent against the Bolshevik forces in Russia. The Allied governments then occupied the zones in Anatolia that they had assigned themselves in the secret wartime agreements. The Russian claims to Constantinople and the Straits, which had been recognized in these treaties, had been nullified by the Bolshevik revolution. On November 13 an Allied fleet arrived in the Straits. Under Allied occupation, Constantinople was governed by a High Commission with British, French, and Italian members; the British influence, however, was the strongest. Once in control, the Allied authorities reconfirmed all of the instruments of international intervention. The capitulations were restored, and the Ottoman Public Debt Commission went back into operation.

Meanwhile, the British, Italian, and French forces had taken up their occupation duties. The Arab lands were withdrawn from Ottoman administration and placed under French and British control. Despite Italian objections,

Greece received a zone in the Izmir area and occupied all of Thrace. In eastern Anatolia, Armenian and Kurdish leaders were actively preparing for the organization of independent or autonomous states. Had all of these plans been implemented, the Turkish-controlled area would have encompassed only a small region in north-central Anatolia.

Faced with these devastating demands, the Ottoman leaders had to decide what position they would take. In July 1918 a new sultan, Mehmed VI Vahideddin, succeeded to the throne. He and his grand vezir, Tevfik Pasha, were convinced that there was no alternative but to cooperate with the Allies, which in practical terms meant the British. The occupying powers, with the vindictiveness and shortsightedness that they showed elsewhere, favored a policy of persecution of the members of the former Young Turk government. The CUP was disbanded, and its leaders were arrested. Although it had used dictatorial methods, it had also been the party of reform. Many of the changes that it had introduced were now reversed. Religious authority was restored in areas, such as the courts, where it had been previously curtailed. A period of reaction, accompanied by a sharp rise in taxes, followed. The sultan dissolved the parliament and ruled by decree. None of these measures were apt to win popular favor for either the government or the victorious Western powers.

The Allied policies had thus gone too far; the Turkish nationalists had little to lose. The land was partitioned, and an increasingly unpopular and incompetent government ruled under obvious British supervision. Moreover, the national movement had won a gifted leader. Mustafa Kemal had been the only really successful Ottoman commander in the war; he now proved to have great political abilities. He was able to bring dissident factions together and find a common base for cooperation. In the spring of 1919 he obtained the post of government military inspector for eastern Anatolia. Arriving in Samsun in May 1919, he immediately sought to bring together the opposition forces and the Turkish guerilla bands that had formed. In June the British government, aware of his activities, pressed the government to dismiss him. He resigned but continued to keep in touch with some of the friendly officials in Constantinople.

The Turkish nationalists, taking a practical point of view, did not attempt to make a real issue about the loss of the Arab lands. Instead they concentrated on holding Anatolia. The major task there was to block the formation of Armenian or Kurdish states and to prevent Greece from annexing the Izmir area. The Armenian question was finally settled through negotiations with the Soviet government, which had a friendly attitude toward the Turkish nationalist movement. The Kurds, without influential foreign supporters, were more easily suppressed. The major difficulty was the blocking of Greek expansion in Anatolia. Greek troops, which the Allies, lacking sufficient manpower, hoped to use to impose the peace terms on the Ottoman Empire and to defeat the Turkish opposition, arrived on British, French, and American warships. In a sense, the arrival of the Greek forces aided the nationalists: the new threat from an enemy Christian, foreign state served to bring all of the factions together and to strengthen national sentiment.

Like similar Balkan groups, the Turkish nationalists presented their programs and organized their first governments in special assemblies. Two were held in 1919. The first opened in Erzurum in July 1919. Composed of delegates from the eastern provinces of Anatolia, it had as its chief concern the blocking of Armenian and Greek territorial claims. This congress did not repudiate the sultan's government. A second, more important, conference was convened at Sivas in September and attended by representatives from all over Anatolia. A program calling for the protection of the territorial integrity of the state and complete independence from foreign domination was adopted. The rule of the sultan was still accepted. At this time Mustafa Kemal made Ankara his center of operation.

Meanwhile, the occupation authorities had agreed to the election of a new Turkish parliament in the fall of 1919. In the voting the nationalist candidates won the majority of the seats. Therefore, when the assembly opened in January 1920, their plans received general support. The nationalist delegates asked for and obtained the acceptance of the Sivas program, which was called the National Pact, with its statement on territorial integrity and independence. The Allied governments would not permit this defiant attitude. They forced the government to arrest the nationalist leaders, and Constantinople was placed under martial law. In March the assembly was dissolved. The central administration and the sultan were thus under full Allied control. The occupying powers were determined to suppress the opposition completely.

Ankara had by then become the nationalist capital. Although the authority of the sultan was recognized, the leaders there declared that they were the Turkish government. Many of the deputies of the dissolved assembly gathered in the city. In April 1920 a Grand National Assembly, composed of 100 of the deputies who had been elected to the Constantinople assembly and 190 representatives chosen throughout the country, was convened. Mustafa Kemal was elected president, and Ismet Pasha (later Ismet Inönü) became commander of the army. In January 1921 the assembly issued a constitution. The Ankara regime, however, still had far to go. A government that ruled with foreign support held Constantinople. Its reaction to the events in Ankara was strong: Kemal and many of his supporters were condemned to death.

In August 1920 a peace settlement for the Ottoman Empire, the Treaty of Sèvres, was finally signed. The sultan's acceptance of its harsh terms was to seal the fate of the Constantinople government. The agreement called for the dismemberment of the Ottoman Empire in favor of the Christian and Arab populations and the imperial great powers. It took little account of the interests or the "self-determination" of the Turkish Muslims. Not only were the Arab lands detached for the benefit of the Western imperial powers, but much of Anatolia was divided among the victors. An independent Armenia and an autonomous Kurdistan were set up in the east. Greece was to receive territory in Thrace and the right to occupy Izmir and a hinterland. After five years a plebiscite, whose results could be foretold, would determine the fate of the land. Constantinople remained in Turkish possession, but the Straits were internationalized. All of the capitulations were restored, and the Allies kept financial control. The British and French had also agreed on their mutual spheres of influence. These terms left very little of Anatolia under full Turkish authority. Italy was also to keep the Dodecanese Islands. The Allies had thus applied to the Ottoman lands the same principles and methods they had used in the partition of Africa.

In this moment of crisis the Turkish nationalist forces had to meet another Greek threat. In March 1921, with Allied approval, the Greek army in Anatolia began to widen its sphere of control and launch what was to become a major offensive against the new Turkish capital. The nationalist troops were forced to withdraw into the country until a stand was finally made in September at the Sakarya River, the last natural barrier before Ankara. The battle lasted three weeks. The result was a great Turkish victory and the swift withdrawal of the Greek army to the west. Kemal's army was not yet strong enough to exploit the situation and pursue the retreating Greeks; another year of preparation was to be necessary before such an action could be attempted.

The Kemalist regime was greatly assisted by changes that took place in the diplomatic situation. In March 1921 Kemal signed a treaty of friendship with the Soviet government. The Russian representatives agreed not to recognize the Sèvres settlement, and they declared null and void all of the agreements that had been signed between the tsarist government and the Ottoman Empire. Russia kept Batum, but returned Kars and Ardahan, which had been annexed in 1878. The pact ended the Armenian threat and stabilized the Turkish eastern frontier. In the next years the Soviet government continued to supply the nationalists with guns and ammunition. Because Allied forces were fighting on Russian soil against the Bolshevik regime, the Turkish opposition was much favored by Moscow.

As valuable as the Soviet support was, Kemal was aided perhaps even more by the split that occurred in the Allied camp. In the scramble for control after the war, it was inevitable that the imperial powers would come into conflict over the spoils. By October 1921 France and Italy, in a move directed against Britain, had in effect recognized the Ankara government, and they withdrew their troops from Anatolia. Britain and Greece were thus left to defend the sultan's government and the impractical and unpopular peace treaty.

At this time Kemal was head of the government, but he did not have dictatorial powers. Although there was disagreement over policy among the leaders, the continued Greek military presence contributed to national unity. The new regime was faced with the difficult task of organizing an administration from a city that did not have the facilities of a national capital. Ankara did not have suitable office buildings, nor were the communications with the rest of Anatolia adequate. The government's major effort had to be directed toward preparing for an offensive to drive the Greek forces out of Anatolia. These activities continued into the summer of 1922. Finally, in August, the campaign commenced, and in the first part of September the principal objective, Izmir, was taken. The Greek army had little chance of success. It had appealed in vain for assistance to the British, who in turn called upon the French and Italian governments. After the Turkish victory, the Greek soldiers, accompanied by thousands of Greek civilians, long-time residents of Izmir and other Anatolian towns, were forced to make a hasty retreat by sea.

With Anatolia secure, the Turkish army continued on into Thrace. The British forces were concentrated at the Straits and in Constantinople. Both sides took care not to provoke hostilities. After continued Turkish victories, an armistice was signed at Mudanya in October 1922; the negotiations were carried on between Kemal and British and Greek representatives. The Greek army was now withdrawn beyond the Maritsa River. The Turkish conquests assured that the Ankara regime would become the legal Turkish government and that the terms of the Treaty of Sèvres would have to be revised.

Despite the fact that most of the great powers had accepted Kemal's authority, a government with the sultan at the head still functioned in Constantinople. In November 1922 the National Assembly at Ankara first voted to separate the office of sultan from that of caliph, or religious leader, and then abolished the sultanate. Meanwhile, in Constantinople the Tevfik ministry resigned and was not replaced; Mehmed VI fled on a British warship. The assembly therefore chose Abdul Mejid II, a son of Abdul Aziz, as caliph. The revolution had thus achieved a full victory. The old Ottoman government had fallen, and the national regime had the recognition of the foreign powers. The Turkish Republic was officially proclaimed in October 1923. A new constitution was then issued; Mustafa Kemal remained as president, with Ismet Inönü as prime minister. In March 1924, in a final break with the past, the assembly abolished the caliphate.

Meanwhile, the new peace treaty had been concluded. The negotiations commenced in November 1922 in Lausanne. Ismet Inönü, who proved a very stubborn and able negotiator, obtained almost all the major Turkish goals against the Allied representatives, who had neither the will to secure their desires nor the means of doing so. The Treaty of Lausanne was signed in July 1923. The Turkish representatives made no attempt to keep possession of Syria, Mesopotamia, Arabia, or Egypt, which had been lost at Sèvres, but they were successful in defending the Anatolian and Thracian territories. They also obtained the abolition of the capitulations, and they paid no reparations despite the fact that they had supported Germany in the war. New terms were set for the payment of the Ottoman debt. The provisions for the Straits remained as they were in the previous treaty: the waterway was demilitarized and placed under an international commission with a Turkish chairman. These provisions were to last only until 1936, when in the Treaty of Montreux Turkey again regained full sovereignty over the Straits.

## CONCLUSION

The effect of the war and the peace settlement on the Balkan states is discussed at length in the following pages. Two empires, the Ottoman and Habsburg, had become a part of history. Of their successor states, Turkey, Austria, Hungary, and Czechoslovakia have henceforth only a peripheral place in this narrative. In contrast, the developments in the former Habsburg regions of Transylvania and Bukovina (which joined Romania) and Dalmatia, Croatia, and Slovenia (which became a part of Yugoslavia) will be followed in detail. The conflicts that arose there are of particular interest since they demonstrate many of the problems inherent in the application of the national principle to Eastern Europe. After World War I this ideal had apparently achieved a victory in the Balkans. Although the two great multinational empires had been dissolved, there was still a question whether the Balkan states could adjust their mutual relations and resolve their internal difficulties, which had been made even more acute by the years of warfare and privation.

# 5

## The first postwar decade

### IMMEDIATE POSTWAR PROBLEMS

THE PERIOD BETWEEN the two great world wars was one of persistent crisis both in Europe and in the Balkans. In fact, only a few years of relative tranquility or prosperity were to be given the Balkan people between 1918 and 1940, when the area again became the scene of major military campaigns. The conflicts among the states and the internal social, political, economic, and national tensions were to be made more intense at the end of the 1920s by the effects of the Great Depression, the most severe period of economic crisis known to the Western world. In the immediate postwar period all of the Balkan states had to meet four major problems: (1) the continuation of the national struggles both within and among the nations; (2) the new economic problems caused in part by the war and the agrarian question; (3) the Bolshevik revolution and its effects on both international relations and the internal politics of the states; and (4) the necessity of readjusting international relations as a result of the removal of Ottoman-Turkish, German, Russian, and Habsburg great-power influence. After a brief review of these issues, we can turn to a discussion of the events in each state in the decade after the war.

### The national issues

The peace settlements in no way settled the national conflicts in Eastern Europe; in fact, in many respects these were to become more tense and bitter. Although some problems were indeed solved, many were to arise to replace them. It was, of course, impossible to devise a treaty that would fairly divide the Balkan people on purely national lines; the border areas were too intermixed. Nevertheless, despite the emphasis on self-determination, the peace treaties in the end were more often based on the historical and strategic claims of the victors than on the national principle. The defeated states had called for self-determination to save themselves from greater losses, whereas the victors had concentrated on the spoils of war. As a result, the national problems in the postwar period were to be most acute in the two states that gained the greatest success at the peace table and hence the largest number of ethnic minorities: Yugoslavia and Romania. Yugoslav internal affairs, in particular, were to be dominated by these unresolved struggles.

The major conflicts in Yugoslavia were to be among the predominant groups, the Serbs, Croats, Slovenes, and Bosnian Muslims. In addition, the Serbian-dominated regime attempted to hold the Kosovo district, which was overwhelmingly Albanian; the Vojvodina, which had a mixed population; and Macedonia, whose national allegiance was in question. The Yugoslav state also had claims against Italy and Austria, both of which had regions inhabited by South Slavs, either Slovenes or Croats. The Romanian government had similar problems. After the war over 5 million of its citizens out of a total population of 18 million were not Romanian. The chief area of friction was Transylvania, where a compact Hungarian minority lived in the central section. Problems were also encountered in southern Dobrudja, which had a large proportion of Bulgarians, and in Bessarabia and Bukovina, with their large Ukrainian populations. The prewar kingdom, known as the Regat, had been overwhelmingly Romanian; the new Greater Romania was never to solve its basic national problem.

The entire national question was complicated by the extremely harsh attitude that each Balkan government was to adopt toward its nonnational citizens or, particularly in the case of Yugoslavia, toward those parties that did not agree with the central regime. They were regularly regarded as a source of weakness and disloyalty, which indeed they were often forced to become. As we have seen, the nineteenth century witnessed the organization of successful national movements among the Greeks, Bulgarians, Serbs, Albanians, Romanians, and South Slavic people of the Habsburg Empire. During the period of national revival, the Balkan leaders had constantly attacked the Habsburg and Ottoman empires for their alleged oppression of national minorities. Yet, in fact, both empires, neither of which was organized on the national principle, gave all of their people a part in state life. The millet system and the community governments allowed most Balkan people under Ottoman rule to run their own affairs on the personal and local level; if an individual wished to convert to Islam he could rise to the highest offices. Within the Habsburg Empire status was often determined more by class than by nationality. The small Croatian nobility stood on an equal footing with the Hungarian or German, or any other. Even among the Romanian and Serbian populations, which, because they consisted predominantly of peasants, were in a definitely weaker position, national religious institutions were available, and education in the national language could be acquired. Needless to say, the general treatment of all minorities was anything but ideal, but the picture was not completely bleak.

The new national regimes were to adopt a much more unconciliatory view. The position of a member of a minority could be much worse under their rule than under the old empires. In general, any action against the central regime or in support of a change of status could be regarded as treason. We shall see in the next pages how members of the Croatian Peasant Party were sent to jail for favoring a program that called for the revision of the centralist Yugoslav constitution, not for seeking a breakup of the state. Strong police repression was applied against any sign of Albanian or Macedonian sentiment. The national leaderships throughout the peninsula acquired the habit of applying the word *foreign* to minority citizens, even when the families might have lived in the region for centuries. Hungarian, Turkish, German, Albanian, and Italian nationals in Yugoslavia were often regarded in this light; Hungarians, Germans, Ukrainians, and Jews shared the same fate in Romania.

The postwar period was also to witness what was perhaps the worst solution to this problem short of outright expulsion or the extermination of national groups. The mandatory exchange of populations, first inaugurated between Greece and Turkey and then extended on a voluntary basis to the Bulgarian–Greek problem, was an action with possibly disastrous consequences for the future. Although the exchanges could produce more homogenous populations and lessen some domestic tensions, the often complete disregard of individual personal and property rights could be tragic for the people involved. The system, for instance, allowed the forced transfer of prosperous Greek merchants and professional men from Ottoman territory to a Greek state where they often ended as starving peasants on inadequate Macedonian farmlands or as shantytown inhabitants in Athens or Piraeus.

The peace settlements also did nothing to lessen international tensions. Neither Bulgaria nor Hungary accepted the treaties that left large numbers of their nationals under foreign control. Most Bulgarians still regarded the San Stefano boundaries as the true borders of their state. Italy, Greece, and Yugoslavia continued to look with acquisitive eyes toward Albanian lands. The Romanian government faced the difficult problem of trying to hold onto all of its gains, which had aroused great Soviet, Hungarian, and Bulgarian resentment. Yugoslavia's neighbors all had claims on parts of its territory.

### Economic and social problems

The poverty and economic backwardness of the Balkan societies has been repeatedly emphasized. The war, of course, made the situation even worse. In September 1914 few expected the war to continue much beyond Christmas. Europe, after all, had not fought a major conflict since Napoleon. No state, and certainly not the Balkan governments, was prepared for the military and economic consequences of a long struggle. The material damage was immense, particularly for Serbia, Albania, and Romania, which were the scene of intense fighting. Casualties were also enormous. Serbia lost 275,000 men, almost 40 percent of the number who were mobilized. Bulgaria suffered 300,000 casualties, of which 100,000 died. The period of warfare commenced, it must be remembered, for the Balkan states in 1912. Greece fought until 1922.

Before the war the Balkan governments had a high rate of indebtedness; to these debts were added the costs of the war, which were met with further borrowing. Not only had these debts to be paid, but Bulgaria as a defeated power was burdened with a perfectly nonsensical reparations bill. In addition, the war and peace settlements broke old trade patterns. For example, before the war Germany and the Habsburg Empire had been the major trading partners of Romania and Serbia, despite the points of friction that existed between them. Replacements had to be found for these markets; Germany, Austria, and Hungary, as defeated states, were temporarily in no position to provide suitable trade outlets. A major hindrance to commerce, both international and inter-Balkan, was to be the determination of the national regimes to develop industrial economies. They accordingly imposed high tariffs on manufactured goods and adopted policies that hampered trade while not attaining the domestic objectives. The interwar period was thus an era of intense economic as well as political nationalism.

The major economic question after the war was, however, that of land distribution. During the fighting and immediately after the conclusion of the peace it was obvious that the peasant soldiers' demand for agrarian reform would have to be met. The governments were also apprehensive about the effect of the Bolshevik revolution on their people, and they had to move to counteract the effect of communist propaganda. Land-reform measures were introduced in all of the states except Albania. The postwar years similarly marked the rise to political prominence of parties based on mass peasant support. Only Stamboliski's Agrarian Union was ever in a position to introduce a positive program, but Stephen Radić's Croatian Peasant Party and the Romanian Peasant Party played major roles in their countries' political lives. Their activities are discussed in more detail in later sections of this chapter.

### The Russian Revolution and the Balkan Communist parties

The victory of the Bolsheviks in November 1917 and the subsequent Russian withdrawal from the conflict had a shattering effect on the conduct of the war and the subsequent peace treaties. Even more disturbing for the Balkan governments was to be the presence in the interwar period of a great power that stood for a radical revision of the political, economic, and social organization of the European states. At the close of the war the Bolshevik leaders had expected a revolutionary wave to engulf Europe. In fact, only Hungary experienced such an event. In 1919 this nation was in a desperate condition; it faced impossible Allied demands in reparations and severe territorial losses. After the collapse of the Habsburg Empire, a moderate republican government first took office in Budapest; it was succeeded by a coalition between the Communists and the Social Democrats. In March 1919 Béla Kun presided over the only Communist government to be established outside Soviet territory at this time. The Romanian government used the opportunity to solidify its position, and in April it sent an army into Hungary. As a result of this invasion, the radical regime was overthrown and Kun fled abroad.

Despite the failure of the Communist parties to win further victories in any state, the Balkan governments remained deeply apprehensive about the movement as such and about Soviet Russia. Their attitude, as well as that of the great powers, resembled in many respects that of monarchical Europe toward the French Revolution. In both cases the revolutionary movement was seen as a threat to the established social order and to the balance of power in international relations. No Balkan government recognized the Soviet Union until the 1930s. The fears appeared justified when newly organized Communist parties, based on the prewar Marxist Socialist and Social Democratic parties, won surprising victories in elections in both Yugoslavia and Bulgaria.

Socialist organizations with Marxist programs developed in particular in Bulgaria and Romania. It is interesting to note that the country with the weakest industrial base, Bulgaria, was to have the strongest socialist movement. In 1891 Dimitŭr Blagoev founded the Bulgarian Social Democratic Party. The organization soon split on questions of doctrine. One section, led by Ianko Sakazov and known as the "Broads," wished to concentrate on the gaining of reforms for the workers, such as a shorter workday and higher wages, and wanted to cooperate with the peasants. Blagoev, at the head of the "Narrows," believed that the party should be based on the workers alone and supported a more radical program, including the confiscation of all private property. The socialist parties, whose strength in fact depended on peasant votes, were able to elect members to the Bulgarian assembly. Their position was weakened after the formation of the Agrarian Union, which attracted away some peasant support. However, in 1913 the Broads and Narrows together won thirty-seven seats in the assembly. Their victory expressed the discontent of the voters with the conduct of the war that had just been lost. Both socialist parties were active in labor organizations, and each had its own union.

In 1893 a Social Democratic Party was founded in Bucharest. At the end of the century it too split on matters of doctrine, with many members joining the Liberals. After a period of eclipse, the party was reestablished in 1910 under the leadership of Christian Racovski. Similarly, there was organized in Serbia in 1903 a Social Democratic Party that was subsequently involved in labor organization and the initiation of strikes. The Social Democratic movement was relatively strong in the Habsburg Monarchy, and both Croatian and Slovenian parties were established. In all of these there were frequent disagreements over issues such as cooperation with middle-class parties, labor union activity, social reform, and the attitude to be taken toward the peasantry. Greece did not have a significant socialist movement until after the war, but workers' organizations were formed as early as the 1880s.

After the Bolshevik revolution the Social Democratic parties had to take a position toward the Soviet government and its ideological program. They then split into two factions, with the more extreme taking the name *Communist* and the rest retaining the original designation. Thus in 1919 the Bulgarian Narrows became the Communist Party. Similarly, in the same year, the left wing of the Serbian socialists united in the Workers' Party of Yugoslavia, which subsequently joined the Communist International. Both the socialist and the Communist parties had to contend with certain basic problems. Because of the low level of industrialization in the Balkans, a strong workers' party could not be formed. An industrial working class did exist, but it was not large and it still had close ties with its peasant background. The "masses" in all of these countries were peasants, and Marxists have always had a great deal of difficulty dealing with an agrarian population. The parties were thus primarily intellectual in leadership and membership. During the interwar period they were illegal most of the time. Their existence, open or underground, served often as an excuse for the adoption of repressive police measures and the abolition of civil liberties. They were thus a convenient justification for the adoption of anticonstitutional measures by the rightist governments in power.

The Communist movements in the Balkans, as in all Europe, were immensely weakened by their obvious subservience to the national interests of a foreign power. The parties were directly connected with and dominated by the Soviet government. Many of the actions of the international organization of the Communist parties, the Comintern, were extremely damaging to the local groups. The greatest blow came in 1924, when the fifth congress of the Comintern took a radical stand on the national question and called for self-determination for the "oppressed people" of Macedonia, Thrace, Croatia, Slovenia, Transylvania, Dobrudja, Bessarabia, and Bukovina. Bessarabia and Bukovina were to be given to the Soviet Union; the rest of the territories were to be organized into separate states that would be part of a Communist federation and obviously under Soviet domination. It was very difficult, for instance, for a Romanian Communist to accept the return of his country to its prewar boundaries, nor was a program with this objective likely to attract supporters to the party. Similarly, the Greek and Yugoslav positions on Macedonia, which had wide domestic support, guaranteed that any such suggestions would be met with fear and hostility.

### The new alliance systems: France and Italy

With the temporary weakening of the power of Germany and the Soviet Union in the 1920s, the door was open for the exertion of influence by other governments. France became the principal great power with a diplomatic program to implement. The primary aim of French policy after the war was to preserve the status quo as expressed in the peace treaties. The major problem was to prevent the resurgence of Germany, with a much larger population than France and a potentially much stronger economy. The imposition of reparations, which proved beyond the capabilities of both the German and the European financial system to bear, and the formation of a circle of alliances of victor states were among the means used to attain this goal. The treaties also provided for the strict limitation of German arms and a demilitarized zone in the German Rhineland. In the severity of the terms and the measures enacted against the defeated, the Paris treaties marked a new departure in international relations. The settlements made among the great powers in previous centuries had been directed toward reestablishing stable relationships. The terms had usually been moderate. In 1815 France had taken an equal place at the peace table; the Treaty of Paris of 1856 had done no severe damage to Russia, aside from questions of prestige. The peace between Prussia and France in 1871 involved primarily a recognition of German unification; the reparations figure was set at an amount that could be paid in a decade, and the controversial annexation of Alsace-Lorraine involved a region of divided but primarily German national composition. Although the great powers had often been quite ruthless in their treatment of weak states, as demonstrated by the partition of Poland in the eighteenth century, they were more careful in their attitudes toward each other. In contrast, the peace settlement of 1919–1920 created two camps: one of victors intent upon preserving their gains and another of those states which had been severely damaged by the treaties or felt that they had been deprived of lands that were justly theirs. With the withdrawal of the United States from European affairs, this situation was to leave Britain and France to defend the peace settlement against Germany and the Soviet Union, soon to be joined by Italy. Although these powers did not act together at once, the deep rifts between the great powers were a major cause of the constant unrest in diplomatic affairs in the two decades after the war.

As the strongest Continental power in the immediate postwar period, France naturally took the lead in the diplomatic organization of Europe. Its policy was to join in a firm alliance the states that had benefited from the peace treaties against those which could be expected to seek a revision of the settlement. In Eastern Europe four states obviously qualified as good allies – Poland, Czechoslovakia, Romania, and Yugoslavia. All were victors, but all had significant minority problems. Poland had reappeared on the map of Europe with the territories that had been taken in the partitions of the eighteenth century by Prussia, Russia, and the Habsburg Empire. The boundaries, as finally drawn, contained a large Ukrainian and White Russian minority in the east and a sizable German population concentrated on the border in the west. Czechoslovakia combined the Czechs of Austria and the Slovaks of

Hungary, with a compact German minority on the western periphery and a Ukrainian population in the east. In the future, the Czechs were to follow many of the same policies as the Serbs in Yugoslavia and to create the same types of national antagonisms within the state. The national problems of Yugoslavia and Romania are discussed in detail in the following sections. It is necessary to note here only that all of these states were vulnerable on the national issue.

Like the French, these governments immediately saw the necessity of standing together in defense of their gains. In August 1920 Czechoslovakia and Yugoslavia signed an alliance directed primarily against Hungary. After the attempt by Charles, the last Habsburg emperor, to regain his throne in Hungary in 1921, the states made further agreements. In April 1921 Czechoslovakia and Romania concluded a treaty, which was paralleled by a similar understanding between Yugoslavia and Romania in June. These pacts were primarily defensive alliances directed against Hungary and Bulgaria; together they formed the basis of the so-called Little Entente. This alignment had the firm support of France, which signed separate treaties with Poland in 1921, with Czechoslovakia in 1924, with Romania in 1926, and with Yugoslavia in 1927. The entire system bore a close resemblance to the policy of the Eastern Barrier in previous centuries, and it was directed as much against the Soviet Union as against Germany. The League of Nations similarly served to bolster the French position. Although it was originally conceived, at least in the intentions of Woodrow Wilson, its most enthusiastic advocate, as an institution that could solve international issues and avoid war, it became principally an instrument for preserving the status quo constructed by the Paris treaties.

The union of victors was bound to produce a counter-alliance. It should first be noted that after the peace French and British interests divided; Britain had entered the war originally to preserve the balance of power on the Continent. The state had no interest in substituting French for German supremacy. The two great colonial powers had quarreled over the spoils of war in that field as well; an example of this rivalry has already been shown in the events in Anatolia. Thus, Britain did not give full support to French diplomatic efforts on the Continent. Of the revisionist states, the potentially most dangerous was the Soviet Union, because its leadership opposed not only the territorial settlement, but also the political and social order of Europe. The second aggrieved power, Germany, similarly sought changes in the territorial, economic, and military sections of the treaties, but its government, of course, did not stand for a policy of social revolution. Using the argument of self-determination, German nationalists attacked the agreements that put large blocs of Germans under Polish and Czech control, and they sought union with Austria, whose population favored a similar action at this time. In Eastern Europe, Austria, Hungary, and Bulgaria were revisionist states. Within Yugoslavia the majority of Croats were similarly dissatisfied with their position. In addition, Greece and Albania were discontented both with their borders and with their general international positions. It was thus obvious that a vast potential for trouble existed. With neither Germany nor the Soviet Union in a position to exploit this situation, the leadership of the camp of the discontented fell first to the weakest of the great powers, Italy.

Although technically a victor in the war, the Italian government was not happy with the peace settlement. Whereas Britain and France had reaped immense rewards for themselves in the imperial field, Italy appeared to have been left by the wayside. The goal was not, as previously, "self-determination" or national unification, which was fully accomplished, but the construction of a Mediterranean empire that would both challenge and emulate the imperial rule of Britain and France. As far as Eastern Europe was concerned, this policy included the domination of the Adriatic and the exerting of major influence in the Balkan peninsula. In the 1920s relations were bad with both Yugoslavia and Greece, with whom Italy had quarrels dating from the time of the peace negotiations.

Tension was particularly high with Belgrade. In the Treaty of London of 1915, it will be remembered, the Italian government had been promised large areas inhabited by South Slavs. It had obtained Istria, but not Dalmatia. A conflict also arose over the port of Rijeka. In November 1920 the Italian and Yugoslav governments signed the Treaty of Rapallo, which was intended to settle their frontier problems. Italy received the port of Zadar, and Rijeka was to be independent. In 1922 Rijeka was seized by a band led by the Italian poet Gabriele D'Annunzio, who proceeded to set up a comic-opera regime. Italian troops subsequently occupied it, and in January 1924 the Yugoslav government accepted the Italian annexation.

Italian expansionist policies were further stimulated by the accession to power of Benito Mussolini in October 1922. Thereafter his Fascist regime undertook an open and frank program of conquest with the ultimate aim of establishing a new Roman empire in the Mediterranean. France stood as the principal power blocking Italian expansion. The obvious policy for Italy to adopt was the organization and encouragement of the states that stood outside the French alliance system: Austria, Hungary, and Bulgaria. In addition, assistance was given to emigré Croatian and Macedonian groups that were in opposition to the Yugoslav government. An active policy was immediately embarked upon. In August 1923 some members of the Italian delegation to a commission delimiting the Greek–Albanian border were murdered. In retaliation, the Italian government delivered an ultimatum to Greece, and Corfu was occupied. After a Greek appeal to the League of Nations, a settlement was arranged that provided for the Italian evacuation of the island.

The major Italian efforts, however, were directed not against Yugoslavia or Greece, but against Albania. Although only the island of Saseno had been given to Italy in the treaties, the powers had recognized the special Italian position in Albanian affairs, which meant in effect that they recognized an Italian protectorate over the country. The interwar history of this state, which will be discussed later, was to have as its predominant theme penetration and later occupation by Italy.

In a parallel with its Adriatic policy, the Italian government sought close ties with the other revisionist states. In April 1927 a treaty was made with Hungary, to be followed by an agreement with Austria in 1930. That same year, King Boris of Bulgaria married Princess Giovanna of the Italian house of Savoy. This alliance system was to be continued and strengthened in the 1930s, when Italy was to enter into a partnership with Nazi Germany.

## PROBLEMS OF NATIONAL ORGANIZATION AND INTERNAL DEVELOPMENT

Despite the active diplomatic policies of both France and Italy, no major international crises occurred in the Balkans in the postwar decade. In fact, for a short period the peninsula remained outside the great powers' major areas of conflict. The states thus had a brief period of repose in which they could devote their efforts to the solution of the internal problems that had arisen both from the peace conditions and from the social and economic difficulties of the time. The major attention of all the governments was directed toward domestic rather than international issues. There were attempts to make the treaties work and to adjust to the new conditions.

### Yugoslavia

Yugoslavia had the most complex internal history of any Balkan nation at this time, and its problems illustrate many of the basic difficulties and contradictions in the national movements. Since the major steps toward the organization of the state were taken during the war and in the month following the armistice, a closer examination of the events before December 1, 1918, is necessary, with particular attention to the role of the three organizations that were most active in these developments: the Serbian government, the Yugoslav Committee, and the Zagreb National Council.

After the defeat by the Habsburg army and the deadly march across Albania, a Serbian government-in-exile under Prince-Regent Alexander, with Nikola Pašić continuing as premier, established residence on the island of Corfu. The Serbian leaders were in an extremely weak position. The army had been defeated; they had no assurances about the future from their allies. The terms of the Treaty of London were known. The Serbian aims remained much what they had been before the war. Pašić and most of his colleagues thought primarily in terms of the furtherance of Serbian national unity. The immediate goal was the acquisition of Bosnia-Hercegovina and an outlet on the Adriatic. If possible, they desired to obtain Serbian-inhabited lands under Habsburg rule, in particular the Vojvodina. Postwar Serbia would thus remain a centralized, Orthodox state under the Karadjordjević dynasty. As we have seen, there had been some enthusiasm for cooperation or even union with other South Slav peoples in the past. Before the war intellectuals and students had been in the forefront of those who held Yugoslav programs. Nevertheless, Serbia did not need a Yugoslav state; the government controlled a compact national territory, and it had influential foreign allies.

The Croatian and Slovenian national leaders in the Habsburg Empire were in a different position. During the war most South Slavs were loyal to the monarchy; Croatian officers distinguished themselves on the battlefield. Although there were desertions, particularly when defeat appeared inevitable, in general South Slav soldiers and sailors carried out their tasks. In the same manner the political leaders continued to perform their functions. Within the monarchy the chief effort was directed toward winning a reorganization on a Trialist basis. The Slovenian People's Party under the leadership of Dr. Anton Korošec was active in the Austrian Reichsrat. Such efforts were naturally strongly opposed by the Hungarian statesmen, who even during the war did not abandon their endeavors to weaken the bonds of the Ausgleich even further. They had, of course, no intention of giving up the Romanian or Slavic lands.

Nevertheless, some prominent men chose to emigrate. The most important emigré group for the future organization of Yugoslavia was the Yugoslav Committee, led by Ante Trumbić and Frano Supilo, both Dalmatians, who had previously played a major role in the formation of the Croatian-Serbian Coalition. Its headquarters were first in Italy and subsequently in London. The Committee was entirely unofficial; it represented little more than the opinions and influence of its members. However, it did maintain links with individuals in the monarchy and with Croatian and Slovenian politicians. It was also in touch with the large emigrant organizations in Europe and America. Its major task was to carry on a propaganda campaign to inform the Allies of the position of the South Slavs within the empire and to agitate for South Slav unification. The members were acting on the assumption of an Allied victory. Their greatest fear thus concerned the threat offered to Yugoslav territory by Italy. After the conclusion of the Treaty of London, whose terms confirmed these apprehensions, the actions of the Committee were dominated by the necessity of combating Italian expansion in the Adriatic.

The relations between the Yugoslav Committee and the Pašić government were bound to be uneasy. Pašić, as we have seen, would have preferred to play the role of spokesman for all of the South Slavs. There was no immediate reason for him to recognize the Yugoslav Committee, which had no official standing or international backing. Nevertheless, after the outbreak of the war, some Serbian leaders had spoken in general terms of the necessity of the liberation of the South Slavs of the Habsburg Empire; Serbs, Croats, and Slovenes had all been named. The question of a future unification had thus been brought up. Pašić saw any such action as involving little more than the extension of the Serbian administrative system over a wider territory.

In contrast, within the Habsburg Empire the Croatian and Slovenian leaders, despite their many points of disagreement, were united in the desire to create first a political unit composed of the Habsburg South Slavs. Once in existence, this authority could come to an understanding with the Serbian government. Should the Habsburg Empire be maintained and separation prove impossible, a similar course of action was to be pursued in the relations with the monarchy, with Trialism as the basic policy. In May 1917 the thirty-three South Slavic members of the Austrian parliament formed a coalition, and their president, Korošec, made the following declaration:

> The undersigned national deputies who are banded together in the Yugoslav Caucus declare that, on the basis of the national principle as well as of Croatian state rights, they demand the unification of all the lands of the Monarchy which are inhabited by Slovenes, Croats, and Serbs, into a single, autonomous political body, free from the rule of an alien peoples and founded on a democratic basis, under the scepter of the Habsburg-Lotharingian Dynasty, and that they will bend all their efforts to the realization of this demand by their united people.[1]

Despite many contradictions in their attitudes toward unification, events forced Pašić and the Yugoslav Committee to come to an understanding. The Serbian government on Corfu was itself beset with serious problems. Prince Alexander had difficulty controlling his military leadership, in particular Colonel Dimitrijević and the Black Hand. In an effort to undermine this threat, the regent formed his own organization, called the White Hand. In 1917 he was in a strong enough position to charge Dimitrijević with treason, mutiny, and the plotting of an assassination against his person. In June 1917, in a fine example of judicial murder, Dimitrijević and two of his colleagues were tried and executed. About two hundred others were imprisoned.

In addition, Pašić and Alexander faced problems in foreign relations. King Nicholas not only showed no signs of a willingness to accept Serbian guidance, but also put forward Montenegrin claims on territory desired by Belgrade. The Macedonian issue similarly showed signs of reemerging. Most dangerous, however, was the fall of the tsarist regime in March 1917. The Russian government had previously been the strongest Serbian supporter; without this backing from a patron great power, the Serbian position in international relations was tremendously weakened. Because of these considerations Pašić in March got in touch with Trumbić and suggested that he and other representatives of the Yugoslav Committee come to Corfu. Trumbić and his colleagues held discussions with Pašić and the Serbian leaders from

---

1  Michael Boro Petrovich, *A History of Modern Serbia, 1804–1918*, 2 vols. (New York: Harcourt Brace Jovanovich, 1976), II, 642.

June 15 to July 30. The basic question under debate was the form of the future state, that is, whether it should be organized on a centralized or on a federal basis. In the conversations Pašić was in the stronger position, since Trumbić's colleagues did not give firm support to his desire for a federal solution. The results of these negotiations were contained in the Declaration of Corfu of July 1917. Here it was agreed that the Serbian government and the Yugoslav Committee would cooperate to establish a Yugoslav state; it was to be a constitutional monarchy under the Karadjordjević dynasty. The constitution was to be drafted by a constituent assembly elected on the basis of universal manhood suffrage. Since the decisions were to be reached by majority vote, the Serbs, with the larger population, would have an advantage. The preamble of the declaration stated that the Croats, Serbs, and Slovenes were one people: "the same by blood, by language, both spoken and written."[2] The document, it will be noted, took into account only these three people; Macedonians, Montenegrins, Albanians, and Bosnian Muslims were not considered separately. The declaration was no more than a statement of intent; it had no legal force. It did nevertheless morally bind the Serbian government to a Yugoslav solution of some kind should the war lead to the breakup of the Habsburg Empire – an open question at the time.

In the year that followed the conclusion of this agreement, there was no clear indication that the Allied great powers sought the destruction of the monarchy. The Serbian leaders themselves remained primarily concerned with assuring adequate territorial compensation in the peace. Pašić would still have preferred to have handled all South Slav affairs himself. The final events were precipitated more by the actions of the national organizations within the Habsburg Empire than by the decisions of either the Committee or the Serbian leadership. In the final weeks of the war the monarchy in fact fell apart into its national components. In an effort to hold his lands together, Emperor Charles, who succeeded Franz Joseph in November 1916, declared in October 1918 that Austria would be reorganized as a federal state. In the same month, Czech national organizations in Prague issued a declaration of independence. In November similar actions were taken by the revolutionary leaderships in Austria and Hungary, where republican governments were set up. The empire had thus in effect dissolved itself. A solution within the Habsburg fold was therefore no longer a practical alternative for any nationality.

In an action paralleling that of the other national associations, a National Council of Slovenes, Croats and Serbs was formed in Zagreb in October 1918. This organization declared its support for the establishment of a state composed of the South Slavs of the monarchy on a democratic basis. The Slovene clerical leader, Korošec, became president of the Council, with Serb and Croat vice-presidents. At the same time, the Croatian sabor declared Croatia independent; it then entered into the union created by the National Council. This

---

2  Petrovich, *History of Modern Serbia*, II, 644.

group authorized the Yugoslav Committee to act as its representative in international relations, thus giving that body real authority for the first time. Similar actions were taken in Slovenia and Bosnia-Hercegovina. By November 3, when an armistice was signed between the Habsburg representatives and the Allies, the South Slavs of the monarchy had established a political organization that had effective control of the national lands. The Council also sent a note to the Allies expressing a desire to join with Serbia and Montenegro.

At this point a choice had to be made about the direction in which to proceed. The period was marked by great turmoil and confusion. All of the South Slav leaders strongly feared Italian intentions; they wished to block if possible an Italian occupation of any part of their territory. It was thus necessary to settle the political status of these lands as soon as possible. There was, nevertheless, a division of opinion in Zagreb. Trumbić believed that it would be better first to establish a firm union of the former Habsburg lands and then to enter into negotiations with Belgrade on what would be an equal basis. Another group, led by Svetozar Pribičević, the head of the Serbian Independent Party, pushed for an immediate union. In the meeting of the National Council that accepted this latter point of view, only one man, Stephen Radić, spoke out in strong opposition. The Council then appointed a delegation to go to Belgrade to negotiate the unification.

The acceptance of the Council's proposals was primarily the responsibility of Prince Alexander, who acted as regent for King Peter. Pašić was not in Belgrade; the members of the Serbian assembly were scattered. Once in the Serbian capital, the representatives of the National Council presented the regent with an official declaration; he in turn accepted it. December 1, 1918, thus marked the official birthday of the Kingdom of the Serbs, Croats and Slovenes, which, as we have seen, was the official designation of the Yugoslav state until 1929 (see Map 8). These actions by the Croatian, Serbian, and Slovenian leaders had the support of national revolutionary organizations in Montenegro and the Vojvodina. In November a national assembly in Cetinje had declared the deposition of Nicholas and union with Serbia, and similar events had occurred in the Vojvodina. Thus the organization of the Yugoslav state was primarily the work of national committees, and the initiative came from the Habsburg South Slavs.

In the two years following the unification the country was governed from Belgrade under what was in fact an extension of the Serbian administrative system. The Serbian army was the sole defense of the land. Croatian units in the Habsburg army were disbanded, and former Croatian officers did not receive commands in the national military forces. In January 1919 Stojan Protić of the Serbian Radical Party became premier, with Korošec as vice-premier and Trumbić as minister of foreign affairs. A provisional assembly was appointed whose members were drawn from the Serbian assembly, the Zagreb National Council, and other bodies representing the nationalities. The most

Map 8. The formation of the Kingdom of the Serbs, Croats and Slovenes

important task of this transitional regime was to prepare for the constituent assembly.

Conflict, of course, arose at once. Under even the best of circumstances the fusion of two different political systems is difficult. There were quarrels about the drawing of the electoral districts and about the basis of representation. Many of the old political parties remained in existence, but new ones also appeared. Forty political organizations, of which only the most important are discussed here, were to participate in the elections.

The most influential political party in postwar Yugoslavia was, as could be expected, the Serbian Radicals under the leadership of Pašić. Although it had once been based on the peasantry, it was by this time led by and representative of the interests of the Serbian middle class, including the businessmen, the merchants, the bureaucrats, the professional men, the military, and the court. Nevertheless, it still attracted the votes of the great majority of the

Serbian peasants, since it stood so clearly for the Serbian national idea. In 1919 a section of the left wing broke off to form the Democratic Party under the leadership of Ljubomir Davidović and Svetozar Pribičević; they had previously played a major role in the political organization of the Serbs of the Habsburg Monarchy, who continued to be known as *prečani*. The party thus spanned Serbia and the former Habsburg lands. Since the Radical Party and the Democrats both supported a centralized government, they were able to cooperate.

In Croatia the Croatian-Serbian Coalition disappeared from the scene. The group that became predominant instead was the Croatian Peasant Party, which had been formed in 1904 by the brothers Ante and Stephen Radić. Because of the extreme narrowness of the franchise at this time, the party was able to elect only a few representatives to the sabor. The situation was to change radically after the war with the introduction of universal manhood suffrage. After the death of his brother in February 1919, Stephen Radić became the undisputed leader. A difficult and stubborn man, he was able to command the allegiance of the vast majority of the Croatian peasants. His attitude toward union with Serbia is indicated by his having been the only man in the National Council to object to the actions that led to the unification of December 1918.

In the subsequent months Radić and the Peasant Party maintained their attitude of extreme opposition. A meeting of the party was held in Zagreb in February 1919, during which the creation of a Peasant Republic of Croatia was supported. In an effort to present the question to the Paris Peace Conference, a petition was drawn up that was signed by 200,000 people. In March Radić was arrested; he remained in jail almost without interruption until the elections of November 1920, and other leaders of the party were similarly treated. The imprisonment on what were indeed very dubious grounds of the most popular political leader in Croatia, and one who retained a strong personal hold over the peasantry, was not a good beginning for the Yugoslav state. Radić's stand in favor of an autonomous organization for Croatia was, of course, firmly seconded by the two branches of the Croatian Party of Rights, which were still in existence. No purely Croatian party, it will be noted, accepted a centralized organization of the state.

Exploiting the antagonistic Serb and Croat stands, the Slovenes and the Bosnian Muslims were able to strengthen their influence in the political system. Slovenian interests continued to be represented primarily by the People's Party, which was still under the leadership of Korošec. Conservative, clerical, and highly opportunistic, it was able to win the solid backing of the Slovenian electorate. A strong position in the state was also held by the Yugoslav Muslim Organization, representing in particular the Bosnian Muslims, who had, it will be remembered, always dominated the political life of their province.

In addition to the Croatian Peasant Party, another organization, the Communist Party, rose to prominence immediately after the war. Established in

1919, it played a major role in the strikes and labor agitation that occurred at this time. Fearful of further revolutionary activities, the government in December 1920 attempted to dissolve the Communist organizations and to repress their publications. Nevertheless, in the elections held for the constituent assembly, the party emerged as the third strongest. It won support particularly from those who were dissatisfied with the political and social system, and it therefore exerted the most attraction in backward areas, such as Macedonia and Montenegro, where it received two-fifths of the votes cast. These regions, of course, had no industrial proletariat, the social class on which the party was theoretically based. The Communists had little chance to function openly or legally. In 1921 an attempt was made on the life of Prince Alexander; in the same year the minister of interior was assassinated. In July 1921, after a strong Law for the Defense of the State was enacted, the party organization was broken up or driven underground. By a majority vote of the assembly, the Communist delegates were deprived of their seats. Thereafter, the party functioned illegally or through the cover of front organizations.

In November 1920 elections for the constituent assembly were held. The franchise was open to all except those of German or Hungarian national background on the basis of universal manhood suffrage. There was no police interference, and 65 percent of those eligible cast their ballots. Of the 419 seats available, the Serbian Democrats won 94, the Serbian Radicals 89, the Communist Party 58, the Croatian Peasant Party 50, the Slovenian and Croatian clerical parties 27, the Bosnian Muslims 24, and the Social Democrats 10.[3] The remaining places went to representatives of other small parties. With these results a new government was formed by the Serbian Democrats and Radicals, with Nikola Pašić as prime minister. Its major task was to be the supervising of the drawing up of the constitution.

After the elections the delegates of the Croatian Peasant Party met in Zagreb and decided not to participate in the assembly. As we have seen, the Communist Party was excluded by a vote of the assembly itself. A quarter of the elected representatives thus did not attend. Under these circumstances the Serbian centralists had a clear field, and the constitution, which was completed in June 1921, expressed their interests. Even then the government had difficulty in securing its passage. In order to get a majority, special promises had to be made to the Muslim delegates to win their support. In the final vote only 258 representatives out of the original 419 were present. The constitution was accepted by a margin of 223 to 35. All of the Croatian parties, the Communist Party, and the Slovenian delegates opposed the decision.

The government established at this point was a constitutional monarchy with much authority given to the king. The unicameral National Assembly

3  Joseph Rothschild, *East Central Europe between the Two World Wars* vol. IX of Peter F. Sugar and Donald W. Treadgold, eds., *A History of East Central Europe* (Seattle: University of Washington Press, 1974), p. 215.

was to be composed of 315 delegates elected for four-year terms by direct, secret ballot. The principle of proportional representation was adopted. Despite the fact that the document gave the familiar assurances of civil liberties, the government retained the ability to limit the exercise of these rights should they prove inconvenient. Alexander took an oath of allegiance to the document on June 28, 1921, the anniversary of the battle of Kosovo, the important date in Serbian history. The new Yugoslav state was organized on a pattern closely resembling that of prewar Serbia. Power was to be centralized in Belgrade and to remain largely in the hands of Serbian political leaders.

The law passed in April 1922 concerning the administration of the country confirmed this tendency. The territory was divided into thirty-three departments, which were administered by prefects appointed by the king. Although some limited autonomy was given on the lower levels of administration, the important decisions were in the hands of the prefects. The historic provinces were eliminated. Croatia and Slavonia were divided into four districts and Dalmatia into two.

Serbian centralism had thus triumphed, but at a tremendous cost. A major proportion of the Yugoslav population simply never accepted this arrangement. Although the fiercest opposition was to come from Zagreb and the Croatian Peasant Party, many Slovenian, Muslim, Montenegrin, Macedonian, and Albanian groups were similarly unhappy with the unitary structure. Unfortunately, the Serbian leadership, in defending its position, tended to treat any criticism of the constitution as "treason," even when it was aimed at the restructuring and not the destruction of the state. Legal opposition thus became very difficult. At the same time, the central authorities were increasingly compelled to use force to control the situation. The repressive measures taken and the general suppression of civil liberties, of course, affected the Serbian population almost as adversely as it did the other nationalities, but they at least had the advantage of belonging to the predominant nationality.

The basic problem of the state was that, despite the hopes of some intellectuals and political leaders before 1914, a Yugoslav nationality did not come into existence. At this time the national balance was approximately 43 percent Serbian, 23 percent Croatian, 8.5 percent Slovenian, 6 percent Bosnian Muslim, 5 percent Macedonian Slavic, and 3.6 percent Albanian, with the final 14 percent composed of minorities such as Germans, Hungarians, Vlachs, Jews, and gypsies.[4] Despite much previous rhetoric, these people never considered themselves one nation. The most intense national struggle was that which broke out between the Serbs and the Croats and which was to paralyze the state. At this time the almost insuperable obstacles involved in bringing together two people with different historic and religious backgrounds became apparent. Previously, most Croats had lived under an autonomous adminis-

4  Rothschild, *East Central Europe*, pp. 202, 203.

tration; they had their own assembly and local leaders. They had been associated with the Habsburg Empire, which represented a civilization on a higher level than that of Serbia, a fact they repeatedly impressed upon the Serbs. Their objections to Habsburg rule had been primarily due to the repeated attempts of both Vienna and Budapest to destroy what independence they had. Having fought literally for centuries for an autonomous administration, they were not about to abandon this stand in favor of Belgrade. These feelings were shared by many of the prečani Serbs, who also did not like their position in the unified state.

Most Serbian leaders felt a deep resentment against Croatian obstruction. They saw themselves as the liberators of the South Slavs from foreign oppression, both Ottoman and Habsburg; this idea was part of their national mythology. They also felt that they had suffered more than the other nationalities in the war, and they wished to be repaid at least in part for their heavy losses. They were firmly united in their national convictions and in the Orthodox church. Many of them never lost a feeling of profound distrust for the Croats because of their Catholic faith and their former Habsburg associations. A feeling that the Croats were somehow treasonous was bound to arise. In any case, the Serbian leadership made a determined and successful effort to control the government. Their domination of subsequent Yugoslav national life has been well described:

> Only one interwar government was headed by a non-Serb prime minister, and for the most part only Serbs were given the key portfolios in the government (i.e., the ministries of foreign affairs, interior, and army and navy). All seven prime ministers of the twenty-four cabinets holding office between December 1918 and January 1929, the period of parliamentary democracy, were Serbs. In the subsequent period, from January 1929 to March 1941, there were fifteen different cabinets of whose ministers three-fifths (73) of the total of 121 were Serbs. The Slovene Anton Korošec was prime minister from July 27, 1928 until January 6, 1929. Only in the six cabinets immediately after the war (December 20, 1918 to January 1, 1929) did a non-Serb (Croat Ante Trumbić) hold the post of foreign minister. Korošec was the only non-Serb to hold the ministry of interior (on two occasions: July 27, 1928 to January 6, 1929; June 24, 1935 to December 21, 1938). In all thirty-nine cabinets, the minister of army and navy was always a Serb general on the active list. Again, of the 165 generals in 1938 only two were Croats and two Slovenes; all others were Serbs.[5]

5  Wayne S. Vucinich, "Interwar Yugoslavia," in Wayne S. Vucinich, ed., *Contemporary Yugoslavia: Twenty Years of Socialist Experiment* (Berkeley: University of California Press, 1969), pp. 10–11.

In this unitary organization both the Slovenes and the Bosnian Muslims were able to find themselves a comfortable place, largely because their support continued to be necessary to maintain the Serbian position. The Slovenian leaders were able politicians; they had gained experience in the Austrian parliament. Since their language was decidedly different from Serbo-Croatian, they did not fear an invasion of outside administrators. They had in effect local autonomy. Because of their mastery of the state language, they were able to win more than their share of the positions in the state bureaucracy. Although they too opposed centralism, they had gained much under the new government. The Slovenian attitude was excellently summarized by Korošec in a conversation with a prominent member of the Croatian Peasant Party in 1924:

I understand and respect the Croats. The territory of Croatia and Slavonia was recognized under the Austro-Hungarian Monarchy as a political nation, and succeeded in preserving its autonomy to a considerable extent. The Croats, therefore, have lost so much to the new state that their unyielding opposition to it is most understandable. But you should understand us, too. We lost nothing – on the contrary, we have achieved noteworthy gains under the new order. Under Austria-Hungary, we Slovenes did not have our own high schools and a Slovenian university seemed a utopian dream. The Croats had their own schools from first grade through university, Croatian was the official language on Croatian territories. In the Slovenian provinces, German had been imposed. In the new State, the Slovenes received all they had previously lacked, high schools and a university to boot. As long as my party is represented in the government, Belgrade will allow us to administer Slovenia according to our own wishes. Although I realize that this centralizing system cannot maintain itself very long, I consider it wise to profit from the circumstances as they exist and to obtain a few favors in the bargain.[6]

Korošec also recognized that only a united Yugoslavia would be able to detach the half million Slovenes under Italian control.

The Muslim leaders in a similar manner gave their support in return for political favors, particularly in connection with land reform, and for cultural and religious privileges. It will be noted that in the interwar period the question of the status of the Montenegrins, Macedonians, and Albanians was not an important issue in domestic politics. Montenegrins were treated as Serbs;

---

6 Quoted in Vladko Maček, *In the Struggle for Freedom* (University Park: Pennsylvania State University Press, 1957), pp. 93–94.

Macedonia was "Southern Serbia." The sensitive Albanian question played a role in foreign relations, but not in internal affairs.

Despite the severe political crises that were to disturb the subsequent political scene, one important issue was met: that of land reform. No action was taken in Serbia or Montenegro, since lands there were already dominated by peasant farms. The chief attention was given to former Habsburg and Ottoman territories. In all of these, large estates, usually under Muslim, German, or Hungarian ownership, were still prevalent. In February 1919 a basic law established the principle of the abolition of peasant obligations, the expropriation of large estates, and the indemnification of the landowners. In general, the goal was to assure that the land would belong to those who farmed it. The agrarian reforms took a long time to complete; some measures had not been fully implemented by the beginning of World War II. Nevertheless, land distribution was no longer a sensitive political issue.

The conditions of landholding differed in former Ottoman and Habsburg areas; so the same methods could not be used in both. It will be remembered that in Bosnia-Hercegovina under Habsburg administration no attempt had been made to change the relationship between landowners, who were usually Muslim, and the kmets, who were mostly Christians. The weight of obligations had been particularly heavy there. Since the estates had not been worked as units, but rather by peasant tenants holding individual plots, the distribution of land caused few problems. It was usually possible to transfer the ownership and simply abolish the payments. The owners were indemnified. As we have seen, the Muslim party was able to win special consideration in this regard in return for political support of the government.

Land reform in the Habsburg lands had been promised even before the unification. In November 1918 the Zagreb National Council declared in favor of the expropriation of the estates, with an indemnity. This action was made easier by the fact that a large percentage of the lands in question were in the possession of owners with a German or Hungarian national background: it was not difficult to dispossess "foreigners."

In the end a massive change of landownership took place. The results have been described as follows:

> A total of perhaps 500,000 peasant families (until about 1935), or more than one out of every four peasant families, benefited from the agrarian reform at the expense of about 10,000 to 12,000 landlords and various institutional landowners. The amount of land involved in the reform, including the land which was earmarked for that purpose by the mid-1930s, was well over two million hectares, not counting forest land. This approximated one-fourth of all cultivated land in 1938.[7]

7 Jozo Tomasevich, *Peasants, Politics and Economic Change in Yugoslavia* (Stanford, Calif.: Stanford University Press, 1955), pp. 368–369.

With the most urgent demands for agrarian reform met, economic questions were not the major political issues. All of the parties concentrated on the national question. From 1921 to 1928, when the country was governed under the constitution, political life was dominated by the theme of Serb–Croat rivalry. The opposition to the entire political system had its center of support in Zagreb, with the Peasant Party, backed by the Party of Rights and other groups, the spokesman for those who wished a federal structure for the state. Elections were held again in March 1923. Once again the strongest nationalists in both camps, Radić in Croatia and Pašić in Serbia, were victorious. As previously, the parties and candidates who favored a centralist government won about half the seats in the assembly. The delegates of the Peasant Party maintained their refusal to attend the sessions.

In July 1923 Radić left the country in an attempt to win foreign support for the Croatian federalist position. During his travels he visited the Soviet Union in the summer of 1924, when the fifth congress of the Comintern was in session. In Moscow he arranged for the affiliation of the Peasant Party with the Communist Peasant International, or Krestintern, which was connected with the Comintern. It will be remembered that at this time Yugoslavia had not recognized the Soviet government, and the Communist Party had been outlawed. In August 1924 Radić returned home and immediately embarked on an active policy. Mass meetings were held, and the Belgrade regime was strongly attacked. In the previous month the Pašić ministry had resigned, to be replaced by a Democratic Party government headed by Ljubomir Davidović, but Pašić regained power in November. At this point he decided to adopt firm measures against the Peasant Party. It was outlawed in December, and Radić, with his principal associate, Vladko Maček, went back to jail. The government used the very flimsy basis of the Law for the Defense of the State to deal with its opponents: the measure had been designed to deal with the Communists, and the charge against the Peasant Party and its leaders was cooperation with the Comintern.

The elections of February 1925 were thus held with the major Croatian party declared illegal and its leaders, who had a massive personal following, in prison. Nevertheless, the results at the polls remained the same. It should be emphasized that the outlawing of a party did not necessarily mean that its members and supporters could not remain on the ballot. The voters knew the candidate's political allegiances, and they could vote on this basis. Once again the elections returned the same proportion of representatives for the major parties. Radić, however, decided to change his tactics. Soon after the elections, in March 1925, Pavle Radić, the nephew of the Peasant Party leader, announced that his uncle would accept the constitution and work within the political system. A complete reversal was thus accomplished. The Peasant Party leaders left prison; their delegates took their seats in the assembly. Even more important, the party gave its support to the Pašić government. Four of its members received places in the ministry, with Radić holding the post of minister of education.

This new cooperation was anything but smooth. A temperamental man, Radić had the habit of characterizing his opponents as "'swine,' 'gamblers,' 'gangsters', 'tyrants,' and 'foreign agents.'"[8] By April 1926 he had withdrawn from the government. At the same time his great rival, Pašić, was forced to resign because of charges of corruption made against his son. The Serbian leader died in December 1926. By February 1927 the cooperation between the Radical and Peasant parties had completely broken down. Elections followed in September 1927. Another political reversal occurred, this time in the camp of the Democratic Party, when Pribičević, the Serbian prečani politician, broke with Davidović and switched to the federalist position. Thereafter the Radicals based their control of the government on the support of the Democrats who did not leave the government bloc and on the Bosnian Muslims. The opposition was composed principally of the Peasant Party and the Democrats who backed Pribičević, groups that at this point adopted obstructionist tactics. The political balance in Yugoslavia was thus most unstable. Factional disputes occurred even within the purely Serbian parties.

The entire situation came to a crisis in June 1928 when a Radical Party delegate from Montenegro shot five Croatian Peasant Party representatives, including Stephen Radić, during a session of the assembly. Two men, one of whom was Pavle Radić, died at once. Stephen Radić at first appeared to recover, but finally died on August 8 from the effects of the wound. Since official collusion in the shooting was strongly suspected by the Croatian representatives, the event ended their cooperation with the government. They withdrew again from the assembly. In July a ministry was formed that was headed by the Slovene Korošec – the single exception to the general rule that the premiership was always held by a Serb from Serbia. The tenth anniversary of the founding of the state in December was marked by riots and demonstrations in Zagreb.

In this time of extreme tension the leadership was taken by Alexander, who had become king in 1921, although he had exercised the powers of the office long before. The alternatives were clear; the constitutional system was breaking down and another system had to be adopted. The opposition, represented by the Peasant Party under Radić's successor, Maček, and the Democrats under Pribičević, demanded a thorough revision of the government. They proposed a federal system based on the historic provinces, which would be given almost complete autonomy. According to this plan, which closely resembled the Habsburg Ausgleich, the local governments would be subordinate to the central authority only for foreign policy, defense, customs, and currency. The military forces would be based on the provinces and organized in national units. As in the Habsburg Monarchy previously, the person of the

8  Rothschild, *East Central Europe*, p. 226.

king would serve as the chief unifying symbol. Such a solution would, of course, have ended the Serbian domination and have fundamentally altered the balance of the national forces. On January 6, 1929, Alexander solved the problem with a radical action. He ended the constitutional regime, abolished the political parties, and dissolved the assembly, thereby inaugurating a period of personal dictatorship that was to last until his assassination in 1934.

The national conflicts thus brought an end to constitutional government in Yugoslavia. In this decade national attention was focused chiefly on these bitter antagonisms. Foreign policy issues, to be discussed subsequently, involved relations with Italy, Bulgaria, Greece, and Albania. Some disputes did arise, but they were settled without a major conflict or a crisis. With the establishment of the royal dictatorship, it remained to be seen whether an able and experienced monarch could create a Yugoslav nation where a parliamentary regime had failed.

### Romania

The immense success of Ion C. Brătianu at the Paris Peace Conference in obtaining a recognition of the maximum Romanian national gains has been recounted. Moreover, his diplomacy was accompanied by events in Transylvania and Bessarabia that showed the desire of the local Romanian population for unification with the old kingdom, Wallachia and Moldavia, also called the Regat. During the war the primary goal of the Romanian leadership had been the acquisition of Transylvania. Here the Bucharest government had a powerful ally in the Transylvanian National Party, which had led the Romanian struggle against Hungarian control. During the war the attitude of the Romanians in Transylvania had been similar to that of the other nationalities. They too had conducted negotiations with the Habsburg government and had met similar Hungarian intransigence. Hungarian nationalists, as we have seen, sought to loosen the ties with Vienna, but to maintain a firm hold on the lands of the crown of St. Stephen. At the close of the fighting, with the collapse of the empire, the Romanian population was left with the choice limited in practical fact to a continued union with Hungary or unification with the Regat. With these alternatives there was little doubt what the decision would be.

In December 1918 a Grand National Assembly was held at Alba Iulia under the sponsorship of the National Party. This meeting was attended by delegates elected from the various districts and by representatives from the Orthodox and Uniate churches and other national organizations. Among the 1,228 present, some came from the Crişana and Maramureş districts, as well as from Transylvania proper. A wide participation was sought, and about 100,000 Romanians gathered in a show of national solidarity. The assembly passed a resolution calling for unification with the Regat, but, most important, conditions were attached. Transylvanian autonomy was to be respected;

the union was to be based on a representative government with full manhood suffrage and a guarantee of civil liberties. In addition, the minorities were to be assured of their political and cultural rights, and measures were to be passed to benefit the peasants and workers. A provisional government was then formed, headed by a council under the direction of Iuliu Maniu, the leader of the National Party. A Great National Council of 150 members was also established. The decision to join in a Greater Romania was supported by the Transylvanian Germans, who showed a preference for Romanian over Hungarian rule. The unification thus had the support of the clear majority of the inhabitants, although it was bitterly opposed by the Hungarian minority.

Events were to be more complicated and controversial in Bessarabia. This province had a population of about 3 million, of which the Romanians constituted over 60 percent. They lived principally in the central portion of the country, with a Ukrainian concentration to the north and a mixed Bulgarian and Tatar population to the south. With the greater part of the territory under Russian rule since 1812, Bessarabia had not experienced a true national movement. Because of the severe policies of russification in force prior to the war, there were no Romanian-language schools or cultural organizations, and no provisions for the publication of Romanian materials. Like the Romanian kingdom, Bessarabia was dominated by great estates worked by peasant labor. Romanians as such did not face prejudice, and there were Romanian as well as Russian large landowners. The widespread discontent was economic and social more than national. The position of the peasants was regulated by the Russian emancipation laws of the 1860s and subsequent reform measures, but, as in other parts of Russia, these had not solved the basic agrarian problems. Since conditions were roughly the same in the Regat, independent Romania did not hold a great attraction for the peasant majority. The main demand of all peasants was a breakup of the large estates and a distribution of their lands. Bessarabia was thus a backward, impoverished area; it had not produced the type of religious and intellectual Romanian leadership that we have seen in Transylvania.

Because of these conditions, the Russian revolutions in March and November 1917 were bound to have a great effect. They influenced not only the disaffected peasants, but also the many soldiers in the province who had deserted the rapidly disintegrating Russian army. After the downfall of the tsarist regime, two types of political activity appeared. First, as in Russia, soviets, or councils, of workers, peasants, and soldiers were formed; second, the Romanian majority organized. As early as July 1917 the peasants began to seize the land; by the end of the year they had appropriated about two-thirds.

In October 1917 a provisional government for Bessarabia was organized, with its center at Kishinev. Subsequently, a National Council, *Sfatul Țărei*, was established to govern the province until a constitutional assembly could be called. This council had 120 members, the majority of whom represented Romanian peasants and soldiers; the president was Ion Inculeț. This government remained in control of the province from November 1917 to November 1918. In December 1917 it declared itself the Democratic Moldavian Republic and expressed the desire to join a Soviet federative republic.

The worst problem for this new Moldavian government was its extreme weakness in the face of outside pressure. The main threat came from the direction of the Ukraine, where a similar autonomous movement was in progress. There was great apprehension that this regime would occupy northern Bessarabia, which had a Ukrainian majority. Just as fears over Italian intentions influenced Croatian and Slovenian actions, uncertainty over the Ukrainian attitude pushed the Moldavian leaders toward more radical decisions. When the Ukraine declared its independence, Bessarabia was isolated from Russia and its position became even more dangerous. In January 1918 the Moldavian government, too, declared its independence.

Meanwhile, the Romanian government, having been defeated by the German army, was in the process of negotiating a peace. Premier Alexander Marghiloman hoped to use the opportunity to obtain a German acceptance of the Romanian annexation of Bessarabia. By the terms of the Treaty of Bucharest of May 1918 Romania was allowed to occupy the land. The Romanian army and an administrative corps moved in. In April 1918 the National Council, in an open vote, accepted union; the division was eighty-six in favor, three against, and thirty-six abstentions. However, as in Transylvania, conditions were attached to unification: Bessarabia was to retain an autonomous administration; the Council was to remain in power; civil liberties and the rights of the minorities were to be protected; land reform was to be introduced. In November 1918, with the Romanian army in full control, the Council withdrew the conditions. The general in command of the occupying troops then dissolved this body, and the autonomous Bessarabian administration disappeared.

The steps toward unification were later to be strongly contested by the Soviet government. In 1924 a Moldavian People's Republic that claimed to be the legitimate authority for Bessarabia was organized on Russian soil. Its argument was that the local soviets, not the National Council, represented the people of the province. Nevertheless, as can be seen, the Council did function much as similar assemblies in other territories did. All of the national organizations at this time were in a sense self-appointed. Under wartime conditions it would have been impossible in any area to have set up provisional governments that were based on open elections and that clearly represented the will of the people. Bukovina, it should be noted, joined Romania by a similar process. In November 1918 a congress was held that voted for union.

Although the national program had thus been attained, Romania after the war had a population that was 28 percent minorities. The 1930 census gave the division as: Romanian, 71.9 percent; Hungarians, 7.9 percent; Germans, 4.1 percent; Jews, 4 percent; Ukrainians, 3.2 percent; Russians, 2.3 percent;

Bulgarians, 2 percent.[9] The Romanian government, despite these figures, never faced problems of the intensity and danger of those in Yugoslavia. Romanians constituted a clear majority of the population; the minorities were divided, and each alone constituted a small fraction of the total number. Of the three strongest groups, the Hungarians, Germans, and Jews, the Germans caused the fewest problems, at least before the rise of National Socialism in Germany. Most Jews too were satisfied with their conditions, largely because of their favorable economic conditions.

Despite the intense feelings that the immigration of Jews had aroused in the nineteenth century, these people had won a commanding position in certain areas of Romanian economic life. The aversion of the Romanian boyars and even of many of the educated middle class to business had left this field open traditionally to foreigners. The previous role of Greeks, Germans, and others has been recounted. The principal "foreign" element in the Romanian economy had by the early twentieth century become the Jewish. As one authority describes the situation:

> By the middle of the interwar era, Jews controlled the bulk of the private capital in the export, transportation, insurance, textile, leather, electrotechnical, chemical, housing, printing, and publishing industries. Though their access to the universities was restricted by statutory limitations and extralegal violence, they were also strongly represented in the legal, medical, dental, journalistic, and banking professions. Though only 4.2 percent of the total population, they constituted 30.1, 27, and 23.6 percent, respectively, of the town populations of Bukovina, Bessarabia, and Moldavia, and 14.3 percent of the entire country's urban population. In such cities as Chişinău (Kishinev) and Cernăuţi, . . . where the Jews accounted for 52.6 and 44.9 percent of the population, most store signs were in Hebrew letters.[10]

Although Germans and Jews thus accepted their position within the Romanian national state, the Hungarian population never did. Prior to the war, they had been the ruling nationality in Transylvania; they were now subjected not only to an administration that was Romanian, but to one that they considered distinctly inferior to that which they had previously enjoyed. Concentrated in the center of Transylvania, separated from Hungary proper by lands largely inhabited by Romanians, they had little hope that their problems would be met by a future territorial transfer. There was no logical way to divide the province on national lines. The Hungarians remained a dissatisfied and disaffected group, and usually with good reason. The treatment of minorities

9  Rothschild, *East Central Europe*, p. 284.
10  Rothschild, *East Central Europe*, p. 289.

was a weakness of all succeeding Romanian governments. Just as the Yugo-slav parties were subsequently to regard Germans, Hungarians, and Italians resident in their lands as foreigners, the Romanian authorities extended this attitude to most of their non-Romanian population. Using historical argu-ments based on the contention of the Daco-Roman origin of their people, they tended to regard any later settlers as intruders on their national lands.

With the unification completed, the major national task ahead was the amalgamation of the new provinces with the old kingdom. In the coming decade Romanian politics was to be dominated by the activities of three par-ties; two, the Liberal and the Transylvanian National, we have already met. The third, the Peasant Party of the Regat, like the Peasant Party of Croatia, rose to prominence with the introduction of universal suffrage. The leader-ship was in the hands of the intellectuals, but its base was the peasant major-ity. Ion Mihalache, a teacher of peasant origin, and Nicolae Lupu, a doctor, played important roles in its organization. The party program supported the principle that the peasant should own the land he worked and that the basis of the agrarian system should be the small peasant farm. In the political struggles of the day, the Peasant Party was able to cooperate well with the National Party of Transylvania. It will be remembered that this latter party, despite its middle-class leadership and membership, had also represented the interests of the Romanian peasants against the Hungarian authorities. The Conserv-ative Party, which had played so important a role in previous Romanian pol-itics, disappeared from the scene after the war. It had been compromised by the fact that it had favored a German alignment. Moreover, its membership had included many large landowners, and with the division of the estates, this class diminished in influence.

As in Yugoslavia, the immediate postwar years saw renewed labor agitation and the formation of a Communist Party. It had little success among the workers and virtually no appeal to the peasants. Moreover, it was the object of immediate government attention. It will be remembered that the Roma-nian government had sent its army against the Hungarian Communist re-gime of Béla Kun; thereafter, Romanian leaders prided themselves on pro-viding a "bulwark" against communism. After the Comintern called for the separation of Transylvania, Dobrudja, Bessarabia, and Bukovina, the party won the intense dislike of Romanian nationalists. In the future the Com-munist Party leadership was to be drawn not from the Romanians as much as from the minority Hungarians, Bulgarians, and Jews, many of whom were acutely unhappy with their position in the state.

In November 1918, when the Allied victory was clear, Ion C. Brătianu re-placed Alexander Marghiloman as premier. In September 1919 he resigned, and a temporary government conducted in November one of the few honest elections in the postwar period. The result was a clear victory for the National Party and the Peasant Party. A coalition government was then established with the National Party leader, Alexander Vaida-Voievod, as premier and Ion

Mihalache as minister of agriculture. The regime, which had a program more radical than that of the deposed Liberal Party, stood for agrarian reform and a decentralized national administration. Even though its proposals were comparatively moderate, the old political leadership of the Regat was profoundly disturbed. Acting in their interest, King Ferdinand dismissed the National–Peasant ministry and appointed General Alexander Averescu as premier. This officer, who had been responsible for the suppression of the peasant revolt of 1907, had nevertheless been a trusted and popular general during the war. As was the custom in Romania, the premier organized new elections; the results were a complete contradiction of the previous elections. The victory went to the People's Party, a personal organization of the general's that had recently been formed. Although much more conservative in orientation, the new regime did proceed on measures of land reform. The socialist labor movements, however, were repressed, and the leaders arrested.

Radical land redistribution had become an absolute necessity by the end of the war. In April 1917 Ferdinand had promised such action in order to keep his peasant soldiers fighting; a further assurance was given in December 1918. The Romanian leaders believed that something had to be done to prevent the peasants from being attracted to communism. In fact, the major aim of the reforms was to preserve the peasantry from political radicalism, not to assure social and economic advancement. The events in Bessarabia, where the peasants had seized the land, made action even more imperative. In December 1918 the first measures were taken; land belonging to the state and to foreign and absentee owners was distributed. In addition, it was decided that the holdings of large landowners would be expropriated, but with compensation. In July 1921 some changes were made in the laws, but the principles remained the same. The Romanian agrarian reform was to be the most extreme in Europe outside Russia. About 14.8 million acres (6 million hectares) were expropriated; of these, 9.6 million acres were given to 1.4 million peasants. The remaining 5.2 million acres consisted of community-controlled pastures and forests.[11] The amount of land expropriated and the payments made differed in the various sections of the country. In general, the measures were more radical in Bessarabia and Transylvania, where many of the large estates had been in the hands of non-Romanian landowners. Compensation was paid on different bases, and the peasants made payments over a twenty-year period.

The land reform satisfied the major demand of the peasants, who formed a majority of 72.3 percent of the population. With the accomplishment of these measures, the government did very little more in the interest of this group. Agricultural production remained about the same, since the estates had always been farmed on an individual basis by peasant tenants. The old farming methods continued; the scattered strips were not consolidated. The

---

11   L. S. Stavrianos, *The Balkans since 1453* (New York: Rinehart, 1958), p. 691.

peasant families did not have the financial means or the knowledge to introduce modern agricultural methods. Moreover, as a class, they were excluded from political power. Even the ostensibly Peasant Party had a middle-class, largely Transylvanian, leadership and was eventually to represent primarily the interests of that section of society.

In January 1922 a Liberal government, again under the premiership of Ion C. Brătianu, returned to office. Except for a short period from March 1926 to June 1927, the Liberal Party was to remain in power until 1928. As was customary, the new ministry held elections. In March 1922, as a result of obviously corrupt procedures, it achieved a great victory, by winning 260 seats as against 17 in the previous election. At this point the Liberals were in a position to implement their policies; their members and supporters staffed the major administrative posts, and they effectively dominated the political system. The new constitution, which was completed in March 1923, thus expressed the Liberal desire for a unitary, national state. Based on the constitution of 1866, the document gave extensive powers to the king and again provided for a bicameral legislature. The lower house was to be elected by universal male suffrage, with elections held every four years. The senate was composed of both elected and appointed delegates, among the latter the heir to the throne, church dignitaries, high officials, army officers, and other prominent men. This constitution, which obviously did not conform to the desires of the newly annexed territories for more local autonomy, was put through only against strong opposition.

The centralizing tendency was also clearly apparent in the regulations issued in June 1925 for the administration of the state. The country was divided into 71 prefectures, which were to be staffed by appointees from Bucharest. Officials from the Regat were thus in control throughout the nation. Less competent than their Habsburg predecessors and often corrupt, they were the source of much dissatisfaction and criticism. It will be noted that the situation was very similar to that in Yugoslavia, where Serbs from Serbia effectively controlled the state. In Romania bureaucrats representing the central government similarly held posts throughout the country. Even though there was, strictly speaking, no national conflict, their actions often jolted local sensibilities.

As before the war, the Liberal Party was concerned with economic advancement. Its program reflected the desires of the commercial, industrial, and banking interests that had the predominant influence in the party. These people expected the government to provide support and leadership and to adopt a policy of economic nationalism. Although they wanted Romania to follow the example of the industrial West, they were most concerned that outside interests not win a preponderant place in the Romanian economy. Foreign investment and technical assistance were to be accepted, but with definite limitations. Measures were thus introduced to prohibit foreign capital from exceeding 40 percent in any one concern; the rest had to be Romanian, either state or private. In addition, at least three-fourths of the personnel and two-thirds of the directors of any enterprise were required to be Romanian. In a further effort to prevent foreign domination, the constitution contained a provision declaring that the national resources of the country were state property; this stipulation allowed the government to control the mines and oil concessions.

The determination to avoid economic dependence on foreign investors had a direct effect on the welfare of the peasants. With the refusal to accept large-scale outside assistance, industrialization was of necessity carried out at the peasant's expense. In order to protect domestic manufacturers, the government raised the tariffs, and the new rates increased the prices of items such as farm implements and textiles, which were purchased by the peasants. Even more serious was the export tax placed on agricultural commodities, which raised the price of Romanian products on the world market. The measure provided an increased revenue for the state and ensured a cheap food supply for the workers. In return for these sacrifices, the peasants received virtually nothing from their government. Some laws were passed to prevent the fragmentation of peasant property, but little else was done.

The Liberal Party's control of the state was made even more firm by a law passed in March 1926, which provided that any party receiving 40 percent of the votes would control half of the seats plus a proportion of the rest. The use of the police and other measures of repression gave added assurance of electoral victories. The Liberals were further aided by the fact that their leaders cooperated well with the king. There were, however, dynastic problems. The heir to the throne, Charles, led a dissolute private life, and he had established what was to be a remarkably long-lasting relationship with a woman, Magda Lupescu, who was the source of continual controversy. Because of this situation, in January 1926 Charles's young son Michael was designated the heir to the throne; his father subsequently lived abroad.

The Liberal policies and the corruption in the government naturally aroused violent protests. In October 1922 Ferdinand was crowned king of Greater Romania in Alba Iulia, an action that was supposed to symbolize the unity of the land. The National Party and the Transylvanian leaders who had been most active in the national cause boycotted the ceremony. In October 1926 the National Party merged with the Peasant Party of the Regat to provide a more effective opposition. The position of the National Peasant Party became much stronger after the death of King Ferdinand in July 1927, followed by that of Ion C. Brătianu. The Liberal Party had lost its most able leader, and Ion's brother Vintilă was not an adequate replacement.

Since the heir to the throne, Michael, was only five years old, a regency was appointed. Opposition to Liberal rule was rising throughout the country; there were peasant demonstrations in some areas. When Vintila Brătianu resigned in November 1928, Iuliu Maniu was asked to form a government. Elections were held in December, this time without official interference. Much

enthusiasm attended the inauguration of the new regime. Maniu gave assurances of aid to the peasants, more autonomy to the local administrations,
true representative government, and a change in general economic policy. In
the voting, the National Peasant Party, which ran in a coalition that included
the German party of Transylvania and the Social Democrats, won control of
349 seats; the Liberals took 13. The National Peasant government was to last
from November 1928 to October 1930. It offered what was undoubtedly the
best opportunity that had arisen in Romania to establish a true constitutional
system: a reform party was in power, and the king was a minor.

The National Peasant Party, despite its middle-class leadership, did introduce an economic policy which contrasted with that of its predecessor. It
certainly showed an increased interest in the peasantry, but in its more prosperous section. Its goal was in fact the establishment of a strong class of
middle peasants. The laws that prevented the sale of land, which had been
passed to prevent the further fragmentation of the small farms, were repealed
so that more property would be available for purchase. Measures were also
taken to encourage the consolidation of the strips of land, to provide sources
of agricultural credit, and to offer a practical education of value to farmers.
At the same time, the government ended the high export duties on grain and
lowered the tariff on farm implements and other items that the peasant purchased. These actions did indeed improve the position of the class for which
they were designed, although the problem of the peasants with only dwarf
holdings or with no land at all was not met.

A radical change was also made in industrial policy. Foreign investment
was welcomed. Restrictions on the percentage of foreign investment and the
nationality of the directors were removed, although the limits on the persons
who could be employed were kept. A foreign loan of $102 million was con-
tracted. Unfortunately, the economic policies concerning both agriculture
and industry were damaged by the effects of the Great Depression of the early
1930s. Romania, like all the Balkan countries, suffered from the worldwide
economic crisis.

In accordance with its previous assurances, the Maniu government did
attempt to introduce true parliamentary government and to end police control and censorship. Efforts were made to improve the national administration and to allow more freedom of action to local authorities. Despite the
numerous reform measures, the National Peasant regime was to fall on an
issue of relative triviality connected with the royal family. In June 1930 Charles
II returned to Romania and assumed the functions of a monarch. The action
was carried through with the approval of Maniu, and it probably had wide
popular support. In accepting Charles's assumption of the throne, the premier, however, had made the condition that he not bring back his mistress,
Magda Lupescu. When she did indeed rejoin Charles, Maniu resigned the
premiership. The ill-considered resignation, over a matter that was not of
great significance for much of Romanian society, whose more privileged

members had never had a strict standard of sexual morality, ended the period in office of the party that best represented the opinion of the majority of the Romanian electorate.

Charles II thereafter dominated Romanian politics. An able and clever ruler, he was able to manipulate the political parties and their leaders in his own interest. As in Yugoslavia during the reign of Alexander, the court became the center of government. Although a true royal dictatorship was not established until 1938, the king henceforth controlled the politicians.

## Bulgaria

As the only Balkan state that had supported the defeated Central Powers, Bulgaria faced no problems caused by amalgamation of new territories. After the Second Balkan War, it will be remembered, southern Dobrudja had been surrendered to Romania and the majority of the Macedonian lands had been partitioned between Greece and Serbia. Later, in the Treaty of Neuilly of 1919, Bulgaria had been forced to give up four border districts to Yugoslavia, and western Thrace to Greece. Although Bulgaria lost its territory bordering on the Aegean, the pact provided for negotiations with Greece concerning access to the sea. Further, the Allies levied a reparations bill of $450 million, an amount equivalent to a quarter of the national wealth, in addition to payments in kind including 13,500 cows, 125 bulls, 12,500 horses, and 2,500 mules.[12] Severe restrictions were also put on the number of men who could serve in the army or the police.

These charges could obviously not be met by a nation that was completely exhausted by long years of fighting. Toward the end of the war the government had not been able to provide its troops with sufficient food, ammunition, or medical supplies. Grain production had fallen to 47 percent of the prewar average, since the young men were taken into the army. By the end of this period 900,000 men had been conscripted, that is, 40 percent of the male population. The enormous casualties have already been noted; together with caring for the wounded, the state had to provide for about 200,000 refugees who were forced to flee from lands under Greek or Serbian control.

The heavy burden of the war on national life and the sufferings of these years were reflected in Bulgaria, as in the other states, in a strong growth of popular support for parties to the left. Both the Agrarian Union of Alexander Stamboliski and the new Communist Party were henceforth to play an important role in Bulgarian political life. Major changes occurred immediately after the ending of the war. In May 1918 the Radoslavov government had been replaced by another under Alexander Malinov. By September it was

---

12  John D. Bell, *Peasants in Power: Alexander Stamboliski and the Bulgarian Agrarian National Union, 1899–1923* (Princeton, N.J.: Princeton University Press, 1977), pp. 188, 194.

clear that the Central Powers would lose the war; as the Allied army advanced from Thessaloniki, the Bulgarian army crumbled. Not only did mutinies and desertions weaken its fighting ability, but it became a danger to the government. On September 29 an armistice was signed, and on October 4 Ferdinand abdicated in favor of his son, who became Boris III, the number implying a direct link with the rulers of the medieval Bulgarian empires.

Although an armistice had been made and a new monarch was on the throne, domestic unrest continued. A revolt in the military forces, the Radomir Rebellion, caused particular apprehension. Under these circumstances the government sought the cooperation of Alexander Stamboliski, who had spent the war in prison because of his strong opposition to Bulgarian participation. He was released, and Agrarian Union representatives joined the ministry. Stamboliski became a member of the delegation that went to Paris to negotiate the peace. While he was away, new elections held in August 1919 gave a clear victory to the left parties; the Agrarian Union received 28 percent of the vote, the Communist Party 18 percent, and the Socialists 13 percent. Stamboliski was thus at the head of the coalition government that signed the peace treaty.

The Bulgarian Communist Party, which, it will be remembered, was formed in 1919 from the Narrow faction of the Socialists, not only did not join the government, but soon clashed with the Agrarians. Communist leaders were very active in labor agitation and in the organization of strikes, the most important of which was the general strike of December 1919. Stamboliski opposed these actions with great energy. His party organized the Orange Guard, composed mainly of peasants armed with clubs, which was used to break up Communist-led strikes and demonstrations. The army ran the transport and communication facilities when the strike activities interfered with them. After the arrest of the leaders, the strikes collapsed.

In March 1920 Stamboliski again scheduled elections, with the hope of gaining an absolute majority so that he could govern without having to rely on a coalition. In the returns the Agrarian Union won 110 of the 229 seats; the Communist Party received 50. Since he was short of a majority, Stamboliski had some mandates invalidated, including those of nine Communist delegates. He was thus able to form an entirely Agrarian ministry in May that rested on a majority of four in the assembly. With this support, he proceeded to move forward toward introducing his political program. What he hoped to achieve is perhaps best described by an article he wrote in March 1922, predicting Bulgarian conditions after twenty years of Agrarian rule:

> Bulgaria would be a "model agricultural state," whose towns and villages would be free of both muddy, crooked streets and human bloodsuckers. They would be furnished with healthy, drinkable water, wooded parks, modern fertilizers, the telegraph and telephone, and electric lights. They would also have highly developed cooperative

organizations, and there would be an extensive rail network with every station having storage facilities for grain and tobacco. Every village would have a "Home of Agrarian Democracy," where lectures, plays, and films would be presented, and where peasants could hear recordings of "the best speeches of the best orators."[13]

In many respects, Stamboliski's ideas, aside from these natural desires for an enormous improvement in Bulgarian daily life, were radical. He personally preferred a republic to a monarchy. He foresaw the end of the political parties and their replacement by a "coalition made up of the Agrarian Union, uniting all peasants in the country's largest political grouping, an organization of proletarians, freed from the control of lawyers and other intellectuals, and an artisan's organization."[14] All of his plans were based on the assumption that Bulgaria would remain an agrarian state. He hated the city and thus was not interested in industrial advancement or the welfare of the worker.

Despite his failure to attain his more radical objectives, Stamboliski was able during his period in office to pass important measures, covering land reform, the introduction of labor service, and the improvement of education on the village level. Since Bulgaria already had the most egalitarian land system in the Balkans, no radical measures or expropriations were necessary. Nevertheless, the government did distribute what land it could acquire, including property owned by the state, the monasteries, and the village governments. A limit of about 74 acres (30 hectares) was set on the amount of landed property that an individual could hold. The consolidation of strips was encouraged. The goal of the government was to assure the health and prosperity of small and medium-sized farms. Measures were also taken to provide better rural credit facilities, and assistance was given to cooperatives. A progressive income tax was introduced so that land taxes could be reduced.

Stamboliski's primary concern with the agrarian community was similarly reflected in his labor service and education reforms. In June 1920 a measure was introduced requiring all men to give a year of labor service at the age of twenty; the obligation for women was six months at the age of sixteen. They were to live in tents in the countryside and work on projects such as roads, railroads, and public buildings. The intention was to bring the youth in touch with the land and to intermix the social classes. The first draft of the plan had to be modified when the Allied governments objected that it contravened the prohibition on military conscription contained in the treaties. Further changes allowed individuals to buy their way out of the service.

As could be expected, the Stamboliski regime in its educational reforms was principally interested in improving the rural schools. Less attention was given to the universities and the institutions of higher education. To the four

13   Bell, *Peasants in Power*, p. 160.
14   Bell, *Peasants in Power*, p. 160.

years of basic education available to the student in the village, another three years was added, with the emphasis on practical subjects. Concern over possible Communist influence was also shown: the teachers were placed under the control of local authorities who could assure that they did not spread Communist doctrines.

In foreign relations the Agrarian government had some unique policies. Here Stamboliski came into conflict both with the older parties and with the Communists. In general, he supported a policy of fulfillment as far as the peace treaties were concerned, and he tried to negotiate for concessions. Bulgaria was the first of the defeated nations to enter the League of Nations. On these matters Stamboliski had no real alternative. The state had neither the armed power nor the outside support to defy the victors. In two other areas, that of supporting an international agrarian organization and that of seeking an agreement with Yugoslavia, the government was following more original paths.

During his period in office Stamboliski gave strong support to the International Bureau of Agriculture, called the Green International, which had its headquarters in Prague. Its aim was to unite the peasant parties of Europe and to form a front against both the Red International of the Bolsheviks and the White International of the "reactionaries." The Romanian National Peasant Party and the Croatian Peasant Party, as well as others, eventually joined. Some information was exchanged and the leaders met, but the organization was never effective. As we have seen, peasant parties were not able to maintain themselves in power in any state.

More controversial, in view of the past relations of Bulgaria with Serbia, was Stamboliski's emphasis on improving relations with Yugoslavia. Here, however, major hindrances were encountered. At this time the Pašić government was not in a similar mood of reconciliation. Moreover, the enormous problem of Macedonia and IMRO continued to stand between the two countries. The assimilating policies of the Belgrade government in its Macedonian lands and the insistence placed on the Serbian character of the population further inflamed Bulgarian opinion. The matter was not easy to handle; in the postwar as in the prewar years the Macedonians had an enormous influence within Bulgaria. The practice of organizing raids from Bulgaria was continued, although now it was Yugoslav and not Ottoman territory that was the target of the attacks. Obviously this question had to be dealt with before relations between the two countries could be improved. In March 1923 the governments signed the Treaty of Niš. In it they agreed that both sides of their common frontier would be cleared of brush to a depth of 109 yards and that major efforts would be made to prevent the crossing of armed bands. With the signing of this pact Stamboliski won the undying hatred of IMRO and thus increased the already considerable number of his opponents.

Similar arrangements to settle outstanding conflicts could not be made with Greece. The major issue was the Bulgarian desire for an outlet on the

Aegean, as provided for in the peace settlement. Greek offers of free zones at the ports of Dedeagatch and Thessaloniki were refused. The Bulgarian government insisted on the establishment of a corridor to the sea under its own control. The differences on this matter were never overcome.

Meanwhile, opposition to Agrarian Union policies and to Stamboliski personally continued to mount. The premier's overbearing and abrasive character, together with his doctrinaire attitude, won him many enemies. In addition, many members of the Agrarian Union were not prepared for their task of running the government. As a new party with a peasant base, the Agrarians did not have a reservoir of trained, capable administrators at their service. Many of their adherents abused their positions and were as corrupt as the officials of any preceding regime. The Agrarian program also had many influential opponents, including both the military and the Communist Party. In April 1923 a new election was scheduled. The Agrarian leadership did not hesitate to use repressive methods to maintain itself in office. Communists and other opposition leaders were put in jail. Stamboliski even supported the purging of some of the moderates of his own party. In the voting the Agrarian Union won 53 percent; the Communists received 18.9 percent.

In 1922 the opposition parties of the center and right had joined in the National Alliance. Political organizations had also been formed in the army. As previously in Greece and Serbia, a Military League composed of officers had been established. Equally influential was the Union of Reserve Officers, whose membership consisted chiefly of officers who had lost their posts because of the restrictions placed on the size of the Bulgarian army in the peace treaties. In June 1923 these groups organized a military coup; the army occupied Sofia. Boris III, whose relations with Stamboliski had been strained, accepted the result as soon as it became obvious that it had succeeded. The action was quick and almost bloodless. Some police and Orange Guards attempted to resist, but they were quickly subdued. The Agrarian Union leaders were arrested.

Stamboliski was at the time in Pazardzhik. The leaders of the revolt knew the importance of his apprehension, so that he could not serve as a center of resistance. He was captured by an IMRO band and tortured. His right hand, which had signed the Treaty of Niš, was cut off, and he was stabbed sixty times. Both he and his brother were decapitated before they were buried.

The conspirators, in complete control, then formed a government with Alexander Tsankov as premier. A bloc of parties called the Democratic Concord, which naturally did not include the Agrarian Union, provided the support necessary. The revolt had been a disaster not only for the Agrarians, but also for the Communists. Since they had no particular reason to support Stamboliski, because of his previous measures against them, they had stood aside during the coup and the subsequent suppression of the Agrarian Union. Their attitude, however, was denounced by the Soviet and Comintern leadership, which belatedly ordered a rebellion. Although the Communist Party obeyed, its members knew that they had no chance of success. The government discovered their intentions at once. The revolt of September 1923 was badly organized and easily suppressed. The party was outlawed in April 1924, but it continued to function thereafter through front organizations.

Elections were held again in November 1923, with the victory going to Tsankov's coalition of parties. Attempts were made to restore parliamentary government. Communist activity, despite the failure of the revolt, remained a problem. In April 1925 a bomb exploded in the Sofia Cathedral and killed 128 people; two Communist Party members were held responsible. The government thereafter made a determined effort to crush the movement, and mass arrests followed.

The chief disturbing influence in domestic affairs, however, remained the uncontrolled activities of IMRO. This organization was split between the Federalists, who wished an autonomous Macedonia in a Balkan federation and the Centralists under Ivan Mihailov, who wanted annexation to Bulgaria. Official support naturally went to Mihailov. The two factions fought among themselves and continued to terrorize the government officials. The Macedonians were in control of the Petrich district, and they formed an important element in the population of Sofia. The activities of the organization disturbed, in particular, relations with Yugoslavia. Bulgaria was at this time isolated in diplomatic affairs; all of its Balkan neighbors were hostile.

In January 1926 Andrei Liapchev succeeded Tsankov as premier. In elections held in May 1927 the Democratic Concord was able to maintain its control, but in June 1931 it was defeated by a coalition of left parties, called the People's Bloc, which included the Agrarians. A government was formed by Alexander Malinov, who was succeeded in October by Nikola Mushanov. This coalition was to hold power for almost three years. It had to deal with the problems associated with the Great Depression, and it too could not control IMRO. It also faced a renewed challenge from the Communist supporters. After the party had been declared illegal in 1924, some of its members had emigrated; others joined a front organization, the Bulgarian Workers' Party, which was formed in 1927. The Communists continued to have their own trade unions. In the election of 1931 the Workers' Party elected thirty-one deputies; in 1932 it gained a plurality in the Sofia city elections. The government then took action and deprived the representatives in the assembly of their seats. Like other Communist parties and front organizations, the Bulgarian party gained its strength from discontented peasants in the rural areas; the leadership was provided by intellectuals. Workers played a relatively small role in party activities.

The election of 1931 was to be the last in which the voters were relatively free to vote for candidates of their choice. The combination of political, economic, and social problems that beset the nation was to lead to another military coup in May 1934, and in 1935 to the establishment of an authoritarian regime under Boris III.

## Greece

Although technically a victor power, Greece had lost more than it had gained during the war. In the postwar decade Greek politics was dominated by issues that had arisen during and immediately after the conflict and that caused bitter, deep divisions in the country. The first problem concerned the controversy between Venizelos and King Constantine I over participation in the war. It will be remembered that Greece abandoned the policy of neutrality only after the British and French governments intervened in support of Venizelos. This action was resented by those Greeks who favored the exiled king, Constantine, or who disliked the continued foreign dictation.

A second, even more serious, division of opinion came when the Venizelos government embarked upon a policy of seeking major territorial gains in Anatolia. A firm adherent of the Great Idea, Venizelos dreamed of a Greece of "two continents and five seas." The opportunity for the realization of these goals seemed at hand immediately after the conclusion of the war. Moreover, the Allies appeared to encourage Greek expansion. Since they had no available troops to enforce their decision on the Ottoman government, they welcomed the Greek intervention. Greek forces were landed in Anatolia with British, French, and American assistance. Until the final disaster, the Greek government continued to believe that it had firm British backing.

At first, Venizelos was very successful. He conducted the negotiations at Paris personally, and in the Treaty of Sèvres of 1920 he gained most of his objectives. Greece received Thrace to the gates of Constantinople, important Aegean islands, and the right to administer Izmir and its hinterland for five years. After that time a plebiscite was to be held, whose result could be assumed. Venizelos had been fortunate in his dealings with the Allied statesmen, especially with the British prime minister, David Lloyd George. Greek troops were committed to the Allied intervention against the Bolshevik regime in order to win Western favor.

After being away for almost two years without interruption, Venizelos came back to Greece from Paris with what appeared to be a favorable peace. Elections were scheduled for November 1920, soon after his return, and he had every reason to expect a satisfying victory. However, a great deal of opposition had developed in the country during his absence. There was much bad feeling left from the events of the war period. Moreover, an army of 300,000 remained mobilized to carry out the conditions of the peace treaties. Not only was this a great expense, but the Greek people were tired of war. They wanted their relatives home. The entire situation was made much worse when King Alexander was bitten by a pet monkey. The wound became infected, and he died unexpectedly on October 25. This event opened the question of the royal succession. Alexander had been the second son of Constantine; Prince Paul, the next in line, refused to take the throne while his father and his elder brother George were still available. The question of the return of

Constantine became the major issue of the day. The elections were to be a contest between Venizelos and the deposed king.

The results were a shock for the Greek premier. The Royalist candidates received 340,000 votes; Venizelos's Liberal Party obtained only 300,000. Moreover, under the system of distribution of seats that was in effect, the Liberals were allotted just 120 of 370 places. Since he did not have a sufficient basis on which to form a government, Venizelos resigned and left the country immediately. In December a plebiscite brought Constantine I back with a large majority.

The immediate question facing the new regime was what to do about the situation in Anatolia. The previous government had planned an advance against the forces of Mustafa Kemal, whose position has been described in a previous section. The international aspects of the intervention had, however, become less favorable for such an action. Both the French and the Italians were in the process of recognizing the Turkish nationalist regime, which was already receiving assistance from the Bolshevik government. The Greek leaders, nevertheless, felt that they still had British approval. The attraction of winning a great victory was also overwhelming; a similar opportunity might never come again. In addition, they had to consider the possible fate of the large Greek population in the Izmir region. Intervention had already occurred; Greek soldiers were in Anatolia. The question what would happen to the Greek inhabitants should the Turkish nationalists be victorious was serious. The long history of mutual atrocities left little hope that such events would not be repeated.

With these considerations in mind, the government ordered the Greek army of 100,000 men to start a campaign against Kemal in July 1921. The objective was to surround and then annihilate the enemy troops. This policy proved unworkable when the Turkish forces simply withdrew back into Anatolia before the Greek advance. The Greek army was soon operating far from its bases in a desert countryside, with insufficient supplies, and in the midst of a hostile population. The reports of apparent victories, followed by the retreat of the Turkish army, were greeted with wild enthusiasm in Greece. The government decided to push forward to capture Ankara, the nationalist headquarters.

As we have seen previously, the Greek army was stopped at the Sakarya River; the campaign was brought to a halt by September 5. The Greeks, who had suffered casualties of 3,897 dead and 20,000 wounded, retreated to the west.[15] No attempt was made to evacuate the troops back to Greece; both the government and public opinion opposed such an action. Owing to its own military weakness, the Turkish government was unable to act for a year. Finally, in August 1922, the Turkish army attacked. The Greek forces quickly

---

15   D. George Kousoulas, *Modern Greece: Profile of a Nation* (New York: Scribner's, 1974), pp. 124, 125.

fell back, and in two weeks the nationalist soldiers entered Izmir. The Greek troops were evacuated in great haste and disorder by every means possible. The Greek inhabitants who could obtain transportation similarly fled to the nearby Greek islands. A fire broke out in the city, which was gutted. Thus, after 2,500 years of occupation, the Greek inhabitants of Anatolia were forced to leave. The Great Idea had brought a catastrophe upon them. An exchange of populations was to come later, but the final outcome had been decided; Mustafa Kemal's troops, as we have seen, after this victory advanced toward the Straits and Thrace.

This disaster made a change in the Greek government inevitable. There now occurred the first of the series of interventions by the army in the political life of the country that was to characterize the interwar period. At this time Colonels Nikolaos Plastiras and Stylianos Gonatas took control; Constantine abdicated in favor of his son, George II. The new regime not only made the king a scapegoat, a tradition in Greek politics, but exacted vengeance from those who appeared to have been chiefly responsible for the debacle. The government proceeded to try, condemn, and execute six men, including the commander-in-chief of the defeated army and Dimitrios Gounaris, who had been premier at the time. These executions added another controversial issue to the volatile Greek political situation.

The Treaty of Lausanne, which replaced the Treaty of Sèvres, deprived Greece of its major gains. Eastern Thrace and the Izmir area were lost. In a separate understanding the Greek and Turkish governments agreed on a massive exchange of populations. This agreement was the first of such treaties and was to establish an unfortunate precedent for the future. As a result of the war and the exchange arrangements, 380,000 Turks and 1.3 million Greeks were displaced from homes where their families had often lived for centuries. The settlement left about 100,000 Turks in Thrace and a similar number of Greeks in Constantinople.

The question whether the monarchy should be retained was the first political issue of the day. The military regime held elections in December 1923. The Populist Party, which represented the monarchists, abstained. Venizelos's supporters won a clear victory, with the election of 250 representatives, but the Republicans also showed considerable strength, with 120 delegates. Venizelos became premier in January 1924 and held office only about three weeks. He preferred the maintenance of a constitutional monarchy, and when it became apparent that the assembly would vote for the expulsion of the king, he resigned and returned to Paris. The assembly then, by a vote of 259 to 3, passed a resolution in favor of a republic. A comparatively free plebiscite was held in April 1924 in which 758,000 voted for a republic and 325,000 for the king.[16]

The first year of the republic was marked by great instability. Greece, as

---

16   Stavrianos, *The Balkans since 1453*, p. 663.

before, had a multitude of parties, most of which were little more than factions grouped around an individual. From January 1924 to June 1925 six governments held power. No single party was strong enough to command a majority, and coalitions had to be formed. In this unsettled situation, conditions became most favorable for another military coup. In June 1925 General Theodoros Pangalos seized control and subsequently established a military dictatorship. Pangalos, who represented that element in Greek military opinion which was extremely critical of civilian leadership and the constant petty quarrels and rivalries, was able to obtain a vote of support from the assembly of 185 to 14, but with 189 abstentions. Despite the fact that the general kept the outward political forms of the republic – he had himself elected president – his government was in fact a dictatorship.

In August 1926 Pangalos was overthrown by another general. The victor, George Kondylis, recognized that he did not have sufficient personal support for a dictatorship and therefore returned the country to the legal system. Elections were held in November 1926 in which the general did not participate. The vote was divided between supporters of Venizelos and those of his opponents. A coalition government was then established under Alexander Zaimis, which lasted until June 1928. In 1927, during a period of relative tranquility, a new constitution was drawn up. It was republican in form, but the president, who was to hold office for five years, was given about the same powers as were previously allotted to the king. A two-house legislature was established, with the ministry dependent on the majority of the lower house.

Although Venizelos was not at this time personally active in Greek politics, his influence was still pervasive. He remained the foremost Greek statesmen of his period. In April 1927 he had returned from Paris to Crete; in July 1928 he was called back to power in Athens. He immediately held elections, and his party won 223 out of the 250 seats in the assembly. Holding office until 1933, Venizelos carried through a moderate policy. The Liberal leader had become more conservative after his long experience in Greek politics, and his principal concern was to maintain tranquil internal conditions. His party was in a strong position. He faced no opposition from the left; the Greek Communist Party was not to play an important role until later. Some reforms were introduced, for example, a program of public works that included provisions for draining the swamps. An Agricultural Bank was established to give the peasants a better source of credit. The number of primary schools was increased, and workers and peasants were encouraged to send their children to the new technical schools, which were just opened.

The Venizelos government also had to deal with the effects of the Great Depression, which hit Greece by the end of 1931. Always sensitive to world economic fluctuations, Greek trade naturally suffered in this period. The demand for raisins, tobacco, and olive products, none of which were necessities, dropped sharply. The bad conditions in the United States had a particularly harmful effect on Greece. Remittances from emigrants fell drastically, and the tourist trade similarly declined. Loans were not available, and Greek shipping lacked customers.

The single greatest domestic social problem in Greece in the interwar years, the care and resettling of the Anatolian refugees, was made far more difficult by the economic decline. After 1922 the Greek government had been forced to handle the consequences of a sudden and massive increase in population. The refugees, who numbered 1.3 million, had to be integrated into a pre-1914 population of 4.3 million. Some assistance was given by agencies of the League of Nations and the Red Cross, but the main burden was carried by the nation. The result was a national and human tragedy. The problem was compounded by the fact that many of the immigrants from Anatolia were used to a higher general standard of living than the inhabitants of Greece proper. Among them were many skilled men – doctors, lawyers, teachers, merchants, and artisans – who could find no employment and whose skills were not needed in their new homes.

The government placed as many of the refugees as possible in the rural areas, particularly in Macedonia and Thrace. The population balance in these areas changed unquestionably in the Greek favor as a result of this policy. The new settlers received some land from the division of the large estates that was a part of the land-reform program adopted after World War I. Former Bulgarian and Turkish property was also used. Efforts were made to develop the cultivation of tobacco as an important export crop. In addition to those settled in the countryside, a large colony, numbering about 400,000, was established near Athens and Piraeus. Here the facilities for housing, sanitation, and water supplies were in no sense adequate; the population lived in shacks and shanties. Employment in the cities was also difficult to find. Although Greek industrialization had commenced under Trikoupis and had increased during the interwar period, it still was relatively limited. In 1940 industry provided 18 percent of the national income and employed only 15 percent of the population. Obviously, the new immigrants could not be absorbed there. Some, however, were able to use their old skills. Favored by an abundant supply of cheap labor, they opened small factories or workshops. The refugees were for the most part republican in political sympathy; they blamed the king for their sad plight.

By far the major event in Greek foreign policy after the war was the Anatolian disaster. Other matters were minor in significance. In its relations with the great powers, the Greek government came into conflict in particular with Italy, which continued to hold the Greek-inhabited Dodecanese Islands. The Italian occupation of Corfu in 1923 naturally caused much ill feeling. Relations were also very bad with Bulgaria. In October 1925 a border incident resulted in the death of two Greek officers. In retaliation Greek troops invaded Bulgaria, an action for which an investigating commission of the League of Nations subsequently fined Greece 45,000 pounds. Negotiations carried on with Yugoslavia about the use of Aegean ports had more favorable results.

The arrangements ultimately made gave Yugoslavia the use of a free port at Thessaloniki. After his return to office, Venizelos made an effort to improve Greek relations with Italy, Yugoslavia, and Turkey. In October 1930, in the Treaty of Ankara, Greece and Turkey recognized the existing territorial settlement and accepted naval equality in the eastern Mediterranean.

Meanwhile, criticism not only of Venizelos, but also of the republican regime, was increasing. The Royalist forces were again gaining in popularity. In elections held in September 1932 the Liberal and Populist parties received about the same number of votes. Since Venizelos lost his majority, he was replaced for a short time by Panagis Tsaldaris, a Royalist. In January 1933 Venizelos formed his last government. The Greek political conditions were again highly unstable. The groundwork had been laid for another military coup and a radical change in the government.

## Albania

Although the independence of Albania had been recognized in 1913, the outbreak of the war in 1914 created conditions that allowed the neighboring states to occupy the lands they desired. Serbia and Montenegro were at first chiefly concerned with the defense of their own frontiers, but Greece and Italy, still neutral, were free to act. In October and November 1914, Greece occupied southern Albania, including Korçë and Gjirokastër. Subsequently, in January 1916, deputies from these districts were chosen to sit in the Greek assembly. In April 1916 the territory was incorporated into Greece by a royal decree. The Italians moved at the same time. In October 1914 they occupied Saseno and in December the port of Vlorë, lands that they were to be assigned by the Treaty of London. In June 1915 Montenegro seized Shkodër, while Serbia moved into central Albania, including Tirana. After the defeat of these two states, their place was taken by the Habsburg Monarchy, which took possession of the north and central part of the country. At the same time, the French forces at Thessaloniki extended their jurisdiction to Korçë. When the Habsburg troops were withdrawn at the end of the war, those of the victorious powers remained. The Italian government was in the best position to exploit the situation, but the French and Serbian armies could also exert influence.

In the secret treaties, it will be remembered, Albania had been partitioned among the powers with only a small central section left for the creation of an Albanian state under Italian protection. Although most of the powers were quite willing to consent to a dismemberment, conflicts between Italy and Serbia made a division difficult to arrange. Serbia sought principally to acquire the port of Durrës; Italy wished to dominate the entire country. In July 1919, during the negotiations over the peace treaties, Italy came to an understanding with Greece. That state agreed to support Italian claims on Vlorë and the establishment of an Italian protectorate over the rest of the country in return for southern Albania and all of Thrace. Both the French and the British governments were willing to allow Serbia to annex a section of northern Albania as part of a territorial deal involving Italy. All of these bargains, however, were opposed by Woodrow Wilson.

Meanwhile, the situation within Albania remained dangerous. There was no recognized single authority within the country, nor was there a government-in-exile. The Albanian colonies abroad, however, continued to show active concern over these developments. Once again an obvious threat to their national existence forced the Albanians to act in their own defense. After the Bolshevik government published the secret treaties, the leaders learned the details of the partition agreements. The organization of an opposition movement was difficult because the Italian army was in occupation of most of the territory, and its permission had to be obtained for any major political action. However, the Italian desire to control the entire area actually aided the Albanian endeavors. The Italians agreed to the holding of a national assembly because they believed that they could control it.

The first postwar congress, attended by fifty delegates, opened at Durrës in December 1919. A government that included a senate with legislative powers was established under the leadership of Turhan Pasha. This government dispatched a delegation to Paris to defend the Albanian interests before the great powers. Although the representatives at Durrës had differing viewpoints on the attitude to be assumed toward Italy, they were all primarily concerned with preserving the land from partition. They were thus willing to accept Italian protection, and even an Italian prince as ruler, if that would keep their territory intact. Although the Italian authorities did not interfere with this congress, they also did not allow it to assume administrative functions.

Meanwhile, the reports from Paris concerning the bargaining with Albanian lands caused a strong reaction, and opposition to the Italian occupation similarly rose. In January 1920 another congress convened, this time at Lushnjë. This meeting was more successful. Its members stood both for the preservation of Albanian territorial integrity and for the end of the Italian presence. What was to be a stable government was organized under the leadership of Suleiman Delvina, who became prime minister. It was decided that the state would be governed provisionally by a Supreme Council of four members and that the legislative power would be exercised by a National Council of thirty-seven representatives. In February 1920 this government moved to Tirana, which henceforth became the national capital. Here the National Council, the first Albanian parliament, met in March 1920. Another delegation was sent to Paris.

With an Albanian administration in office, the next problem was forcing the Italians to evacuate the country. The Albanian cause was aided by strikes and demonstrations that broke out in Italy. At the same time the National Council encouraged the peasants to attack the Italian forces. In June 1920

Esad Toptani, who had played a major role in the formation of the state and who had cooperated with Italy, was assassinated in Paris. Faced by this pressure and the opposition of the other powers, the Italian government in September accepted a settlement in regard to its claims on Albanian and Dalmatian territories. It abandoned its wider pretensions in return for Istria, Rijeka, and Zadar. The Italian forces in Albania were withdrawn, and only the island of Saseno was kept. In 1920 Albania was admitted to the League of Nations over the protests of France, Italy, and Yugoslavia.

Despite this agreement the borders of the state were not yet secure. Yugoslavia and Greece still were not satisfied. Finally, in November 1921, another conference of ambassadors was held, this one attended by the representatives of Britain, France, Italy, and Japan. Although the boundaries of 1913 were retained and Albanian independence again was affirmed, the special Italian interest was implicitly recognized. Nevertheless, Albania had escaped partition. Its relations with its neighbors remained anything but tranquil, but they had not been able to acquire large sections of Albanian territory.

With these matters settled, the Albanian leaders could turn to the question of domestic organization. Although there had been full agreement on the national independence, there was much disagreement on the form of government to be established. The first task to be accomplished was the framing of a constitution and the formation of a permanent administration. Two groups, representing opposing points of view, appeared at this point. The more conservative was the Progressive Party, led by Shefqet Verlaci. It represented the interests of the southern districts and the mountains of the north. The beys, property owners, and clan leaders were its chief supporters. It opposed land reform and wished to maintain social conditions as they were. Its rival, the Popular Party, was open to ideas of reform, although it too had conservative members. In its ranks were the two men who were henceforth to be most influential in Albanian political life, Bishop Fan S. Noli and Ahmed Bey Zogu (Zog).

The first, Noli, represented those who favored reform. He had enjoyed an interesting career. Born in 1882 to an Orthodox family in Thrace, he had attended Greek schools. He had lived in Athens and had taught in a Greek school in Egypt, where he came in touch with the Albanian national movement. He then went to the United States and there earned a Harvard degree. In 1908 he became the bishop of the Albanian Orthodox church. In 1920 the American Albanians chose him to be their representative to the national assembly at Lushnjë. He thus came to Albania with little direct experience of political life in the country.

In contrast, Zog had a background typical of a member of the dominating class. Born in 1895, he was the son of the chief of the Mati district in central Albania. His family was Muslim, and it had distinguished itself in Ottoman service. Zog was twenty-four when he attended the congress of Lushnjë as a delegate. He became minister of interior in the Delvina government in February 1920. In the manner of earlier tribal leaders, he had a body of armed men at his service. He was a strong, determined leader with influential connections.

The first elections were held in April 1921. From this date until 1924 the country underwent a period of great internal instability, with frequent changes in the government. Both Noli and Zog held high posts. In the Popular Party regime of December 1921 Zog was minister of interior and Noli foreign minister. In December 1922 Zog took the offices of both premier and minister of interior. At the same time, he became engaged to the daughter of Shefqet Verlaci and thus allied himself with the conservative forces. Much opposition had meanwhile arisen to his policies: he used the police and forceful measures to put through his desires, and his links were obviously with the beys and landlords. The progressive elements of his party pressed for agrarian reform and the summoning of a constitutional assembly. Noli, Suleiman Delvina, and others with these opinions left the Popular Party and formed an opposition organization.

Elections held in December 1923 gave Zog only a plurality. In February he resigned in favor of Verlaci. Although he was no longer premier, and although there was growing dissatisfaction with his policies, Zog still controlled the government. The situation was exacerbated when Zog's supporters were believed responsible for the assassination of Avni Rustem, a national hero and the man who had murdered Esad Toptani. Rustem's funeral was the occasion of a large demonstrations. In May the reformers, those who opposed Zog personally, and his other opponents organized a successful rebellion, with peasant assistance. Zog fled the country, and Noli formed a government.

Since Noli's administration lasted only the short period from June to December, he did not have sufficient time to carry out his policies. He did, nevertheless, attempt to lay the basis for a Western constitutional government. His program included agrarian reform, the assurance of political liberties, the provision of social services, the encouragement of outside investment, and resistance to Italian pressure. His position was very difficult. Many of those who had participated in the revolt against Zog simply wished to get rid of this leader, not to introduce extensive changes in the country. Domestic opposition thus forced Noli to retreat on some issues. He himself later said that he had made a mistake in not taking a stronger position on the agrarian question: he had won the distrust of the landowners, but not the backing of the peasants.[17] His major error, however, was his failure to organize a military defense for his regime.

Zog did not make a similar miscalculation. After his overthrow, he went to Yugoslavia and immediately set about recruiting a mercenary force. De-

17  Stefanaq Pollo and Arben Puto, *Histoire de l'Albanie des origines à nos jours* (Roanne: Éditions Horvath, n.d.), p. 227.

lighted with the opportunity to exert influence in Albanian affairs, the Yugoslav government gave him assistance. He was thus able to assemble a little army, which included one thousand soldiers and sixteen officers of the Yugoslav forces, and forty officers who were Russian refugees and who had fought with General Wrangel against the Bolsheviks. Zog also received guns from Yugoslav arsenals.[18] In December he invaded Albania. The government was unable to resist this attack; Noli and his adherents were forced to flee the country. In January 1925 the members who were left in the assembly declared Albania a republic and elected Zog president for seven years.

At the same time the country finally received a constitution, but one that was designed to enhance Zog's power. As president he had the authority to name and dismiss ministers, veto bills, and make the major administrative appointments. He nominated a third of the eighteen members of the senate of the two-house parliament. Although his regime was a dictatorship, it did give Albania a stable government. In the next years the nation was run by an extremely conservative administration whose principal concern was the maintenance of order. There were no serious reform measures and no civil liberties, and a strong censorship was imposed. The regime represented the interests of the landowners, the clan leaders, and those who wished to preserve the old system intact.

Once back in power, Zog had to deal with the two states, Yugoslavia and Italy, who had been so dangerous in the past. In aiding Zog, the Yugoslav government had naturally expected to be repaid and to exert great influence over his regime. Zog, however, was largely successful in resisting this pressure. In a territorial settlement made in July 1925, the Albanian government handed over St. Naum on Lake Ohrid; the border dispute was thus ended for the present. Relations with Italy involved other questions. Like any small state, Albania could benefit from a great-power sponsor, and the government was also in great need of foreign economic assistance. Since there was no alternative state to which to turn, a large measure of Italian influence had to be accepted. In the spring of 1925 a policy of cooperation with Rome was thus adopted.

Thereafter Albania received massive economic assistance and in so doing, of course, accepted political interference. Italian financiers established the National Bank of Albania, which issued currency. The bank in turn organized the Society for the Economic Development of Albania (SVEA), which gave loans to pay for such public works as roads, bridges, ports, and Zog's palace, but which also kept the administration running. The conditions of the loans were very favorable, with low or no interest charges. They were in fact subsidies to Zog's regime.

The economic penetration was paralleled by increasing Italian political domination. In November 1926 the two states signed a pact of friendship. In

18   Stavrianos, *The Balkans since 1453*, p. 720.

this agreement the Italian government promised to protect the political and territorial status quo in Albania. Zog's position was thus in effect guaranteed. Since Italian relations with Yugoslavia were tense at this time, the pact caused a strong reaction in Belgrade. In November 1927 Yugoslavia signed a treaty with France directed in part against Italy. In reply, in November 1927, a second Italian–Albanian accord was concluded. A defensive alliance, it had a duration of twenty years. Albania was thus bound closely to Italy in both economic and foreign policy. Italy also provided arms and military instructors, and the port of Vlorë was open to the Italian navy.

Zog had a further ambition. In September 1928 he convened another constitutional assembly, which made him a king. In December a new constitution was issued. Although the government was in theory a limited monarchy, Zog had nearly absolute powers. All laws had to have his approval, and he appointed the ministers. The legislature consisted of a single chamber of fifty-six members. Since Zog had promised reforms, he did take some measures in this direction. New civil, penal, and commercial codes based on Western models replaced the Ottoman laws. There was, however, no agrarian reform or move to divide the great estates. Nor was an effort made to provide an adequate educational system. The king's support rested on the large landowners, the chieftains, and the traditional political leadership; these men did not want their local authority disturbed.

At the time when he was consolidating his power at home, Zog found himself faced with increasing difficulties in his relations with Italy. He strongly needed Italian financial aid. In 1931 he obtained a loan of 100 million gold francs, which was to be paid in installments of 10 million francs a year on extremely easy terms. In 1932 the Italian government presented its bill for this subvention; its demands included increased economic privileges, in particular a customs union, and measures that would strengthen the Italian hold on the country, such as the teaching of Italian in the schools and the admission of Italian colonists. Zog made an initial effort to resist this pressure. Italian Catholic schools were closed, and the military advisers were dismissed. Trade agreements were concluded with Yugoslavia and Greece. Zog also made a vain attempt to win French assistance, but the conditions for support from Paris were as high as those from Rome. In June 1934 the Italian fleet paid a visit to Durrës. The government called this a "courtesy" visit, but it certainly had not been invited. Financial pressure was applied at the same time: the Italian government could always withhold the installments on the loan. Finally, Zog had to give in, and the former relations were restored. The king continued to receive his money, but there was no customs union.

Albania remained in many respects an extremely primitive country. Zog made many personal enemies, and the tradition of the blood feud was still alive. He thus always had to fear assassination. There was also much internal opposition, and frequent local uprisings occurred, including the serious Fieri revolt of August 1935. In this year Zog again gave assurances of a reform program. In October a new ministry under Mehdi Frashëri was formed with the intention of introducing reforms. Some concessions were made, including the granting of more freedom to the press. This regime lasted only a year; in November 1936 a conservative government was back in control under Koço Kota. At the same time the Italian penetration intensified. Italian advisers now held posts in the civilian administration as well as in the military, and some Italian colonists had settled in the country. The full domination of Albania remained Italy's final objective.

The interwar history of Albania cannot easily be compared to that of the other Balkan nations. Because of its late unification and its turbulent first years, this state was at a stage of development similar to the Serbia of Prince Miloš or to Montenegro at the beginning of the nineteenth century. There were no real political parties with developed programs. The traditional conservative interests remained well entrenched. Unlike the surrounding states, Albania had neither an agrarian nor a Communist movement. Nevertheless, because of the events after 1945, some mention should be made of the weak Communist and socialist activity that did occur and the relations with the Soviet Union.

In the 1920s Albania was the only Balkan nation without a Communist Party. In fact, after the advent of Zog, no opposition parties of any sort existed. The actions organized against the king all had their bases outside the country. After Italy became a supporter of Zog, Austria became the major center for the emigrés. In Vienna the National Liberation Committee, or CONARE, was formed with Fan Noli as president. This group, which published a journal in Geneva, was a coalition of people with widely differing views. There was much dissension within its ranks, and it had little influence on events inside Albania.

Like the other Balkan governments, Albania's hesitated to recognize the Soviet regime. During his first ministry Zog refused to take the step because he feared the reaction of the great powers. Noli was braver; in June 1924 his government started negotiations. In December a delegation arrived from Moscow, but strong protests ensued from Britain and Yugoslavia, which feared that Albania would become a Soviet and Communist base. Because of this pressure Noli asked the delegation to leave after only two days. There were no official relations during the Zog period.

Nevertheless, the Soviet Union and the Comintern were concerned with Albanian affairs. In 1927 Noli visited the Soviet Union, and he appears to have been sympathetic to some of the Soviet goals. In 1930, however, he retired from active political life and returned to the United States to resume his religious duties. The left factions of CONARE regularly maintained some links with other Communist parties and with the Comintern. In 1930 the Comintern sent Ali Kelmendi to establish party cells in the Balkan Albanian areas; some were evidently set up. As elsewhere, the Communist leadership and membership came mainly from the intellectual and lower middle classes.

Albania had only a minute working class. There was some labor organization activity, particularly among the miners, in which the Communists participated. In 1939 the government made a determined effort to suppress the movement and arrest the leaders.

## THE GREAT DEPRESSION

For the Balkans the 1920s were a period of comparative peace. The decade ended with the economic catastrophe of the Great Depression. It is difficult to overestimate the effects of this crisis; it may have had an even greater role in determining the future course of the European states than the national and international controversies that have been described previously. At the end of the war all of the participants needed a period of tranquility to recover from the immense losses of that disaster, but by 1926 most of them had regained the level of production of the prewar years and could look forward to a more prosperous future. The West, in particular, had a most optimistic outlook. New technological advances and more efficient systems of industrial organization held out great promises for a better life for all. Unfortunately, the period of hopefulness and confidence was to last but a short time. In October 1929 the crash of the stock market in the United States heralded the beginning of a prolonged period of crisis. Economic conditions in Europe declined until 1933. Recovery was slow; only in 1936 was there a return to stable conditions and the industrial level of 1929.

The immediate effects of the depression were shown in the sharp fall in prices and the decline in production. The indexes of industrial production measure the extent of the problem. If 1929 is taken as 100, industrial production in 1932 had fallen in Britain to 84, in France to 72, in Italy to 67, and in Germany and the United States to 53. The result of this catastrophe was massive unemployment, with the strongest effects felt in the United States, where 15 million were out of work, and in Germany, where the figure was 5 to 6 million. Bad as conditions were in the industrial countries, the situation was even worse in regions that depended on agriculture. Prices of food and raw materials fell as much as 50 percent.[19]

Since the Balkan states were primarily producers of agricultural goods and raw materials, they found the base of their economies profoundly shaken. The drop in prices commenced in 1929. By 1932–1933 the prices of most grains were between one-third and one-half of those of 1929. Agricultural income in the depression years is estimated to have declined 57.6 percent in Romania and 51.8 percent in Bulgaria.[20] The high level of peasant indebtedness and the

---

19  See Raymond J. Sontag, *A Broken World, 1919–1939* (New York: Harper & Row, 1971), pp. 202, 203.
20  Iván T. Berend and György Ránki, *Economic Development in East-Central Europe in the Nineteenth and Twentieth Centuries* (New York: Columbia University Press, 1974), pp. 244–245.

marginal existence of most of this population have been discussed previously. With the fall in agricultural prices the peasants could not meet either their taxes or the payments on their debts. They were also adversely affected by the widening gap between the values of agricultural and of industrial goods. The peasant majorities of the peninsula were thus faced with a continually deteriorating situation.

Confronted with this disaster, the Balkan governments did take some initiatives. Their principal action was to establish state agencies that purchased grain from the peasant at prices well above the world level. Although these measures were helpful in the short run, they did not meet the basic problems of the Balkan agrarian system. The economic crisis brought into bold relief the enormous difficulties that still had to be met by governments. Although the national regimes had been established and a satisfactory urban standard of living had been achieved by a minority, the great majority of the population lived in material conditions that had changed relatively little over the period covered by this narrative. Before continuing to the events of the 1930s. and 1940s – two decades of severe crisis and revolutionary change – it would be well to review the pattern of traditional peasant life. It was this society whose manner of living was to be so profoundly altered in the next half century.

## TRADITIONAL PEASANT LIFE

Although the position of the peasants has been discussed previously, the emphasis has been primarily on the great events – the wars, revolutions, and catastrophes – that changed the political status of the lands they inhabited. Less attention has been devoted to those aspects of their lives that were relatively unchanging over the centuries, in particular village and family relationships. Although it is difficult to offer valid generalizations for the entire Balkans, an attempt will be made here to summarize the material conditions of peasant life and to comment briefly on family and village relationships.

Balkan peasants lived in village communities whose patterns of settlement differed among the various regions. In some areas the houses followed the line of the main street; in others they were built on radiating side streets. In some regions the dwellings were scattered over a wide distance and surrounded by the owners' fields and orchards. The village center, depending on the size of the population, contained the church, the government offices, and the school, as well as inns, coffeehouses, stores, and workshops of craftsmen. The stores in this impoverished society usually had small stocks and specialized in the sale of colonial wares, such as sugar and coffee, and the small number of items that the peasant family could not produce itself. The craftsmen similarly provided the services that required skills or equipment not possessed by the peasant farmer; among this group were tailors, carpenters, masons, and ironsmiths.

The individual houses were built of whatever materials were available locally. They could thus be constructed of logs or stone, but they were usually made of mud or clay bricks, baked in the sun and then perhaps whitewashed. Roofs could be thatched, tiled, or made of stone. By Western standards peasant housing was very bad. The average dwelling consisted of just two rooms: a principal communal room and another where the cooking was done. Some had a covered porch. A farm would, of course, have additional barns or sheds to house animals and poultry and to protect the farm implements. Members of the family also lived in outlying buildings. Large numbers of people were housed in what seem very cramped quarters, a situation that prevailed also, it must be noted, in middle-class city dwellings. Furniture was also primitive, although, of course, conditions differed widely according to the wealth of the family and the traditions of the region. Poor families might have only a low table and a few benches; their members would sleep on rugs on the floor. Their wealthier neighbors could have regular beds, tables, and chests. The houses were also decorated with carpets, pillows, and embroidery done by the women. Conditions, even for the more fortunate, were primitive – at least when judged by Western standards. An observer writing in the 1920s describes a relatively prosperous household:

> In the village of Capari, near Bitolj, I found a new stone house with a tiled roof and an upper story. On the ground floor was a kitchen-living-room with a board floor, furnished with bed, tables, chairs, and a stove. On the first floor, four communicating rooms opened out of the *hodnik*, or wide passage, three bedrooms, with beds, tables, and chairs, and, as in towns, a "*slava*-room" or kind of best parlour, with stencilled walls, green armchairs, ordinary bentwood chairs arranged round the walls, pictures and photographs on the walls, a large table, and a round occasional table, covered with knick-knacks. Yet in this very "modern" house there was no *nuznik* (closet), and the sleeping arrangements were still primitive. Trajko (42) and his wife Malina (42), with their four sons (16–2) and one daughter (9), occupied one room. His brother Anamće (52), with his wife Donka (52), their two sons (12 and 8) and their daughter (10), slept in another.[21]

The same author describes also extremely primitive housing, where peasants and their animals shared single rooms, measuring "24 by 17 or 28 by 18 feet":

> In one such stable-room the village herdsman, Djordje (45), his wife Stojanka (30), and Radislav, their four-year-old child, slept round

21 Olive Lodge, *Peasant Life in Jugoslavia* (London: Seeley, Service, n.d.), pp. 66–67.

the fire, while their pair of oxen, their donkey, their pigs, and their chickens shared the stable half. Another gave shelter to a widow, Velika, of 75 . . . , her son Stojan (28), the sole survivor of ten children, his wife Dosta (28), and their little boy of 5, Atanas, and baby-girl six weeks old, Cona. The old mother slept on one side of the fire, the son and his family on the other. Their sheep, goats, oxen, and chickens occupied the stable part. Under another roof of this kind abode a man, Jože (65), his wife Menka (62), and their two surviving sons, the elder, Milan (25), with his wife Božana (30), their two little boys, Aleksije and Risto (9 and 7), and Pauna, their little girl of two, and the younger, unmarried son Marko (19). In the stable half the thirty sheep rested on straw; while an ox and an ass reposed behind a low partition.[22]

As far as food was concerned, the choice was seasonal and, of course, largely limited to what the family could grow. The basic foods for the entire year were bread, cornmeal, beans, onions, garlic, peppers, and cabbage. To this were added the products of the local orchards and gardens, including vegetables of different varieties and such fruits as apples, pears, peaches, cherries, and plums. The plums, which were particularly prized, were made into slivovica, a potent brandy. Meat was relatively scarce since it was expensive. However, poultry (including chickens, ducks, and geese), cows, goats, pigs, and sheep were all raised; sheep provided wool as well as meat. The average family bought very little food and then usually items such as sugar, coffee, and salt that could not be produced at home.

By the 1930s clothing was in the process of transition. As elsewhere, most people preferred manufactured products. Traditionally, of course, clothes had been made at home. Spinning and weaving with wool, cotton, or hemp had been a major responsibility of the women in the family; clothing was then cut and sewn at home, although some men's outfits were made by the village tailor. Sandals were bought in the market. Clothing styles were traditional, but as manufactured thread and cloth became more widely available and as people became more aware of European styles, village dress gradually changed. Where possible, people adopted what they regarded as more modern – usually also more practical and comfortable – clothing.

The housing, dress, and food of the average family thus reflected the life of a farm population that was largely self-sufficient. These standards were enforced by the low income of these people. From 1925 to 1930 it has been estimated that the average annual income in Romania was $243, in Bulgaria $284, in Yugoslavia $330, and in Greece $397, whereas in the United States the sum was $1,368. Cash was, of course, needed for taxes and a few other necessities; there was little surplus for manufactured goods or food grown

22  Lodge, *Peasant Life in Jugoslavia*, pp. 67, 68.

outside the home farm. When considering these figures it must, however, be remembered that prices were also low. In 1937 at a village near Sofia a pair of sheep could be purchased for $3.60, a bull for $25 to $35, a cow for between $35 and $45, and a horse for from $12 to $60.[23]

These conditions of life, which remained relatively stable over the years, were accompanied by an attitude toward the world and a social organization that served to protect the community during the turbulent periods that have been described previously. No matter what political authority had held sway, the peasants had family and village connections that gave them support and served their interests. For the peasant farmer life centered on the land he cultivated, on his family, and on his village.

Land and land ownership were of particular importance. The prestige and honor of the individual family was largely determined by this standard. When extra money was available, additional plots were acquired. The attachment was also emotional:

> Life in these scattered fields . . . was hard and laborious, but to the peasant, life without the fields would not be worth living, for these narrow strips of land were his children growing under his painstaking care. The land was his companion and friend, as he shared with it the thoughts and dreams of a starlit summer night, with a cloak for a pillow and dew for a blanket. Land meant more to the peasant than money in the bank; it meant more than food on the table; it meant life itself.[24]

We have seen in previous sections how this attitude toward the land affected the peasant's political and economic views. In each crisis he saw his salvation in the acquisition of more land. The emphasis was put not on the better use of what property he had – that is, on developing methods of intensive farming – but on increasing his personal possessions. By the 1930s this struggle had become almost hopeless. With the division of most of the large estates in the interwar reforms, and with the continuing rise in the rural population, there was increasingly less land for more people.

For most Balkan people the family, not the nation or the community, compelled the strongest allegiance and devotion. In the interwar period throughout most of the Balkans the standard organization was the family farm, which usually included three generations: grandparents, parents, and children. Although some variations might occur, the basic relationships were remarkably similar throughout the peninsula. Within the family there was a recognized hierarchy and a division of labor. Under patriarchal standards, all males held more authority than females; within the sex divisions, age usually determined

23  Irwin T. Sanders, *Balkan Village* (Lexington: University of Kentucky Press, 1949), p. 104.
24  Sanders, *Balkan Village*, p. 49.

position. Parents held full control over and responsibility for their children. In everyday working conditions, the tasks were divided. In general, the men were responsible for the heavy work in the fields and the care of large animals like horses, oxen, and sheep. They were also the hunters and the defenders of the family. Women undertook the lighter farm tasks, such as the cultivation of the fields and the care of small animals, such as poultry and pigs. They also raised vegetables. The basic responsibility of the women in the family was the care of the household. They raised the children and tended to the sick and the aged. Household tasks were often arduous. Not only was there no electricity, but water and fuel could be a major problem. Water had to be carried from a well, spring, river, or other source, sometimes for considerable distances. Although women and children were the principal water carriers, men, women, and children were all occupied with the gathering and cutting of wood. Family life in the Balkans thus closely resembled that in any frontier or impoverished region. Much of the time of the average family was consumed by the multiple tasks necessary for simply existing.

Although the family farm, worked by a man, his wife, and their children, with perhaps a grandparent present, was most common, other arrangements also existed. There was, of course, a large population of farm laborers, shepherds, and seasonal workers who were principally employed in caring for others' property. In the South Slav lands, another institution, the *zadruga*, was for some time a prevalent form of agricultural organization. This extended family farm was based on the principle that the male members never left their parents' lands. Instead, they and their wives farmed the property on a cooperative basis. Except for clothes and a few personal items, there was no private property. In theory, all males had an equal right to participate in any general decisions concerning the farm. The principal authority was held by an elder, chosen by the group. Tasks on the land were divided again by age and sex. This organization was well suited to primitive areas engaged in subsistence farming. By the late nineteenth century the zadrugas had for the most part been broken up in the more prosperous areas, but some were still in existence in the 1930s.

Everywhere in the Balkans the family relationships, which had been developed to protect and care for the members, were tight. The individual was regarded primarily as a family member; the family of a person who committed a crime or suffered dishonor was similarly shamed. If an outsider harmed a relative, honor bound the family to seek redress. The blood feud, common to the most primitive areas, was an extreme form of this common obligation. In this situation, marriage was a serious affair and was generally a matter arranged by parents, who had the practical interests of the family as a whole in mind. When marrying, a girl in effect gave up her own family and entered that of her husband. The close living conditions and traditional family obligations caused much friction. Problems between young wives and their mothers-in-law were recognized as major difficulties in marriages. Close ties between families and individuals were also developed through other institutions, in particular that of the godparent. Most Balkan children at birth were given a godparent, who in theory was responsible for the well-being of his or her ward. In some areas, especially in Greece, a prominent local leader might have innumerable godchildren; their families supported his candidacy while he defended their interests with the government. All of these relationships, of course, served a practical purpose and were adopted to defend the family in times of danger and against tyrannical political authorities.

Second to their families, individual peasants were dependent on their village communities. Throughout much of Balkan history, no matter what outside authority ruled the land, local notables had a major role in the administration of their district. We have seen how important they were in the Ottoman system. After the establishment of centralized national regimes they still retained much of their prestige and authority, which enabled them often to protect the local inhabitants against rapacious officials of the central bureaucracy. Despite all of the propaganda efforts of the national leaderships, most villagers retained a feeling of deep mistrust toward the large cities and their representatives, who still in their eyes represented a grave danger. Government officials, for instance, demanded taxes and recruits for the army; as yet they offered little in return for these sacrifices.

The village was, of course, the communal center for the population. Its heart was usually its church. Whether they were Orthodox, Catholic, or Muslim, it is difficult to overestimate the part that religious institutions and clergy played in these rural societies. A priest was present at every major turn of a person's life – birth, marriage, and death being the most important. The agricultural calendar was marked by saints' days. Religious doctrine explained life and the individual's role in it. Conservative and fatalistic, it usually instilled a willingness to accept difficult conditions and a reluctance to change established practices. The attitude prevailed that what existed, however bad, was somehow God's will and that natural disasters, like sickness, death, war, floods, and drought, were somehow a just punishment for human sins. The churches also enforced a very strict code of moral conduct, in particular in sexual and marriage relationships. These rules too were designed to protect a population vulnerable to outside invasion, natural epidemics, and other catastrophes.

The reader can tell from this superficial description that although agricultural conditions in the Balkans were primitive, they were very similar to those which existed in other nonindustrialized areas. Too often foreign observers compared Balkan peasant conditions with middle-class life in Western cities. Difficult as the situation was, Balkan peasant farmers were not much worse off than their counterparts in other areas, for instance, Ireland, Scotland, and many parts of rural America. Moreover, the framework of traditional life had already shown serious weaknesses by 1930; in fact, all of those processes which were to accelerate after 1945 had already begun to act upon rural society. Most important was the increasing impingement of the outer world upon village life. The young men were forced to leave their families to serve in the army; many were compelled to leave home to find work. Others, particularly in Greece, emigrated, but kept in touch with their families. In addition, the national governments did begin to concern themselves to a greater degree about their rural populations. Schools were, of course, a most important instrument for the communication of ideas and knowledge about other places. Although the efforts were to prove insufficient, the state did begin to provide some social services. Unfortunately, the world situation was not to allow the peninsula an opportunity for the peaceful development of new institutions and relationships.

## CONCLUSION

During the years after the war, as can be seen, the Balkan governments, with the exception of the Albanian, whose situation was unique, faced many similar problems. All in one manner or another had to deal with serious national issues involving not only the treatment of minorities, but also the integration of co-nationals in the new territories. Even Bulgaria, who lost lands in the peace treaties, had a Macedonian problem. In addition, each state had to meet the domestic political consequences of the enfranchisement of the mass of the population. Because of the hardships of the war and the prevalence of revolutionary ideologies in this period, no government could maintain the previous restrictive franchises. As we have seen, these measures brought to the forefront Agrarian and Communist parties that challenged the hold of the traditional groups, which were nevertheless able to maintain their power. The trend toward the right was to continue in the next decade.

# 6

## Balkan authoritarian regimes: the outbreak of World War II

DESPITE THE EFFORTS MADE to meet the enormous problems caused by World War I and the subsequent controversies, any achievements were largely negated by the recurrent crises of the 1930s in both domestic and foreign relations. The internal politics of all of the Balkan states were deeply affected by the repercussions of the Great Depression and the rise in influence of the European dictatorships. In foreign relations the adoption by the Soviet Union of an active policy in European affairs and the establishment of the National Socialist regime in Germany, with its militant revisionist program, forced the Balkan governments to adjust their attitudes to the changed relationships of the great powers. By 1939 the international situation had so deteriorated that each state had to face the probability that Europe would again be engulfed by war, scarcely two decades after the conclusion of the previous catastrophe.

### THE RISE OF SOVIET AND GERMAN INFLUENCE

The predominant French and Italian role in East European diplomacy in the 1920s had to a large extent been a result of the abnormal situation created by the revolution in Russia and the defeat of Germany. With recovery from these shocks, and with the dissolution of the Habsburg Empire, these two states, because of their large populations and their strategic locations, were in a position to exert a strong influence on the thirteen small countries that stretched from the Baltic to the Mediterranean – Esthonia, Latvia, Lithuania, Poland, Czechoslovakia, Austria, Hungary, Romania, Yugoslavia, Bulgaria, Greece, Albania, and Turkey. The radical shift in the power balance resulting from the war and the territorial settlements was in the long run satisfactory neither to Germany nor to the Soviet Union, but both states needed time to recover from the past upheavals before they could act. Since they sought to change the provisions of the peace treaties, they had interests in common with the other members of the revisionist camp: Italy, Hungary, Austria, and Bulgaria.

Although in theory the postwar boundaries had been based on the doctrine of self-determination, this principle, as we have seen, had been very dubiously applied, and then primarily to the benefit of the victor powers.

Germany and the Soviet Union had indeed been deprived of territory that was of another national composition, particularly in the reconstruction of the Polish state, but they had also lost land that contained millions of their own people. Over 1 million Germans were assigned to Poland; Alsace-Lorraine, which was given to France, had in 1910 contained 1,634,260 German-speakers and only 204,262 French. The strongly expressed wish of 6 million German Austrians to unite with Germany had been stifled at French insistence. In the same manner, over 3 million Bohemian Germans, who were former Habsburg citizens and who lived close to the border, were incorporated into Czechoslovakia. The Soviet Union had similar territorial grievances. In the peace the Baltic states, the Polish lands, and Bessarabia, regions that contained a minority of Ukrainian and White Russian inhabitants, were taken away. Moreover, in the future the Soviet regime was to adopt a policy remarkably similar to that of its tsarist predecessor: a land once possessed by the Russian state should never be definitively surrendered in the future.

Germany and the Soviet Union shared a similar experience in another area. The victor powers, led by France, treated them as pariahs and attempted to exclude them from normal international relations. The attitude toward the Bolshevik regime, which represented an ideological as well as a military danger, was particularly harsh. Allied troops remained on Russian soil to support the anti-Bolshevik forces until 1922. Even after the Soviet victory, all of the governments hesitated to establish regular diplomatic relations. Among the Balkan states the Bolshevik regime was recognized by Bulgaria in 1934 and by Yugoslavia in 1940, but not at all by Greece, Albania, and Romania. This policy was part of the general anti-Communist hysteria that swept much of Europe in the immediate post–World War I period as the result of the rise of the local Communist parties and the sharp increase of labor unrest. In the years right up to the outbreak of World War II, the Bolshevik revolutionary threat, both real and imagined, played a vital part not only in international relations, but also in the domestic politics of all of the states.

The possible spread of the Communist movement, which so frightened the European politicans, was, of course, regarded in quite another light by the Soviet regime. In fact, after 1918 its leaders expected that revolutions would occur in other countries. Their main hope lay in Germany, which was the Continent's foremost industrialized state and which, in the Social Democrats, had the world's strongest workers' party. Soviet ideology, discussed in detail in a later section, taught that Marxism as a doctrine was most applicable to highly industrialized economies. As we have seen, in the interwar period a Communist regime came to power only in Hungary, where it lasted but a short time. There was also an unsuccessful revolt in Bavaria. Despite the fact that the Soviet Union was to remain the single Communist government in existence until after World War II, attempts to bring the revolution to other countries were not abandoned, and an international organization was established.

The First International, which brought together all of the small Communist groups then in existence, was organized by Karl Marx in 1864 and functioned until 1876. The Second International, a loose association of socialist parties, was founded in 1889 and dissolved at the beginning of World War I, when the socialist parties all took a patriotic stand and supported their governments. In March 1919 the Soviet government took steps to form a Third International, to be known as the Comintern. The first conference was composed almost without exception of representatives resident in the Soviet state. The second congress, held in July and August 1920, was more significant. It was attended by 200 delegates from forty-one countries; German was spoken, since it was the language most common among the delegates and, of course, that of the "founding fathers," Karl Marx and Friedrich Engels. The major accomplishment of the conference was the adoption of the Twenty-One Conditions, which laid down the basic requirements for membership in the organization. Primarily the work of Vladimir Ilich Lenin, at the head of the Soviet government, the program placed strong emphasis on the predominant and controlling position of the Soviet Union. World Communist parties were to follow the Soviet example in ideology, organization, and methods of operation; the Soviet state was the model for the future. Since it was the single Communist power, it was to be the duty of the Communist parties everywhere to give their first allegiance to Soviet interests. With such a program, the Comintern naturally aroused much suspicion among the other governments. The Soviet leaders consistently denied responsibility for Comintern actions, declaring that it was an independent organization that just happened to meet on Soviet soil. The obviously false nature of this declaration served to cause even further suspicions. The Comintern was supposed to have yearly meetings, but only seven were ever held.

When it became apparent that a revolutionary wave was not to engulf Europe, the Soviet government was faced with the necessity of establishing regular relations with other states. Since it had not been represented at the Paris Peace Conference and it was not a member of the League of Nations, it could exploit the mistakes of the postwar settlement and the resultant international animosities. Relations with France, the supporter of the international system, were at this time very bad. The fact that the Soviet regime had refused to honor the tsarist debts, a major percentage of which were owed to French citizens or the French government, increased the tension between the countries. The nationalization of foreign property carried through after the revolution also involved a large number of French investors. France nevertheless recognized the Soviet government in 1924, as did Italy, despite the anti-Communist attitude of its Fascist regime.

Britain and Germany were more favorable toward the Soviet Union, but here too difficulties were caused by the revolutionary nature of its policies. Although the Communist issue became involved in British domestic politics, normal relations were established in 1924; they were then broken, and finally resumed in 1929. Negotiations with Germany were concluded earlier and led to far closer ties. As has been noted, the two powers shared certain common interests, and they suffered from similar disabilities. Both had been damaged as a result of the war, and they wished to make extensive changes in the status quo. They were also excellent commercial partners. The Soviet Union needed German industrial goods and technical assistance. Neither was favorable to the new Polish state, and each had claims on a part of its territories. Full diplomatic and consular relations were established in the Rapallo Agreement of 1922. Thereafter the German army was able to use Soviet facilities to get around the arms-limitation provisions of the Versailles Treaty.

In January 1924 Lenin died; after a struggle for power, his position was taken by Joseph Stalin in 1927. More interested in economic development than in exporting revolution, Stalin placed his main emphasis on the quick industrialization of the country. With its efforts directed primarily toward internal improvements, the Soviet government had a major interest in the preservation of world peace. Like its tsarist predecessor after the Crimean War, it wanted no foreign disturbances until it was in a position to exploit them. As a result, Soviet diplomacy concentrated on international reconciliation. Maxim Litvinov was appointed foreign minister with this policy as his goal; the Soviet diplomats now talked in softer tones. Although this was the age of the Great Depression, the Soviet government did not attempt to take advantage of the widespread unrest and economic misery. It established regular diplomatic relations with the United States in 1933 and joined the League of Nations in the next year.

The major disruptive event in European diplomacy in the 1930s was, of course, the revival of Germany under the National Socialist leadership. The hardest hit of any of the powers by the Great Depression, Germany could be expected to experience the most violent political consequences of the world disaster. The major beneficiaries of the popular disillusion with the republican government were the extreme parties of the right and left. In elections held in July 1932 the National Socialist Party won 37.5 percent of the vote, and the Communists received 14.5 percent. In other words, the majority of the German electorate had lost confidence in the constitutional regime. The steps by which Adolf Hitler came to power have been often recounted. In January 1933 he became chancellor by a perfectly legal procedure. Once in office, with the support of the right, he was able to gain from a newly elected assembly extraordinary powers to deal with the internal crisis. He and his party then proceeded to liquidate both the Communist and the Social Democratic opposition and to institute a dictatorial regime.

For the Balkan states the great significance of the Nazi victory was its implications for foreign policy. Hitler's basic ideas were stated in his book *Mein Kampf*, written in 1924 when he was in jail after an unsuccessful attempt to seize power. An expression of extreme nationalist ideology, this work declared that the Nordic, or Germanic, peoples were the most gifted of all mankind; they alone were the true creators and discoverers. If they acquired sufficient power and resources, they could create a civilization – what Nazi propaganda was to call a New Order – that would be far superior to any other. Hitler placed an enormous emphasis on land and the relation of a people to the territory it occupied:

> Never regard the Reich as secure while it is unable to give every national offshoot for centuries his own bit of soil and territory. Never forget that the most sacred right in this world is the right to that earth which a man desires to till himself, and the most sacred sacrifice that blood which a man spills for this earth.[1]

Quite obviously the Germany of the 1930s lacked the proper territorial base for the future. An industrial state, dependent on outside sources for food and raw materials, it had been gravely hampered by the British blockade in the war. The question, however, was where these lands could be found. *Mein Kampf* makes this clear too: "But if we talk about new soil and territory in Europe today, we can think primarily only of *Russia* and its vassal border states." This land would have to be conquered: "Just as our forefathers did not get the land on which we are living today as a gift from Heaven, but had to conquer it by risking their lives, so no folkish [national] grace but only the might of a triumphant sword will in the future assign us territory, and with it life for our nation." According to these doctrines, the foreign policy of the German state should thus be directed in the final analysis toward a single goal: It should aim to "bring the land into consonance with the population."

> The foreign policy of a folkish State is charged with guaranteeing the existence on this planet of the race embraced by the State, by establishing between the number and growth of the population, on the one hand, and the size and value of the soil and territory, on the other, a viable, natural relationship . . . Only a sufficiently extensive area on this globe guarantees a nation a freedom of existence.[2]

Although the book was widely circulated, Hitler's most extreme statements were often disregarded or not taken seriously. Certainly, disarmed and impoverished Germany was in no position to launch an imperial drive against Eastern Europe. These doctrines were not a major part of the German electoral campaigns, and they were not used in the diplomatic negotiations. In internal politics the Nazi leaders directed their primary attacks on the Jews, the Communists, and the Versailles Treaty, which were made the scapegoats

1 Adolf Hitler, *Mein Kampf* (New York: Reynal & Hitchcock, 1939), p. 964.
2 Hitler, *Mein Kampf*, pp. 935–951.

for all of the nation's ills. Some measures were taken against the Jews at once, but extreme actions did not come until later. The mass exterminations were carried out only after the war had started. After the Nazi seizure of power and the subsequent suppression of the Communist Party, it was difficult for the German and Soviet governments to retain their former friendly relations. Contacts between the two regimes were, however, never completely severed.

The years between 1934 and 1939 were a period of intense diplomatic activity. Although the Balkan states were not directly involved in the major crises, each event had an effect on their diplomatic position. As we have seen, the basis of the French security system had been the alliances with Poland and the Little Entente, an alignment that could function against the Soviet Union as well as against Germany. In 1934 Poland signed a nonaggression pact with Germany that weakened this front. The French government, however, at this point changed its attitude toward the Soviet Union. Since that state was at least temporarily no longer a revisionist power, and since both France and the Soviet Union felt endangered by the new German policy, these two governments were able to cooperate. In 1935 the Soviet Union concluded mutual assistance pacts with both France and Czechoslovakia. It should, however, be noted that the Soviet government was not obligated to come to the aid of the Czechs unless France acted first. Although Britain was not a part of this combination, its government usually worked with France to maintain the European equilibrium.

The reestablishment of a French–Russian tie naturally had a direct effect on the relations of the two major revisionist powers. Although their regimes had much in common, Hitler and Mussolini were not at first compatible. Their initial meeting in 1934 was certainly not very successful in laying a basis for their future friendship. Mussolini at this time made clear his opposition to a German absorption of Austria, with whose conservative government he was on good terms. He soon, however, was forced to modify his attitude. In October 1935, in a step toward the establishment of his new Roman Empire, Mussolini commenced an attack on Ethiopia. This venture drew strong denunciations from the Western powers, despite the fact that they held vast colonial domains. A blockade applied by the League of Nations, although limited and ineffective in nature, and the antagonism of the other states compelled the Italian leaders to seek support in Berlin. Henceforth the two dictators worked together toward their common imperial goals.

In October 1936 the states joined in the so-called Rome–Berlin Axis. The alignment was based on assurances of mutual support and a division of Europe into spheres of interest. Greece, Albania, and Yugoslavia were recognized as falling into the Italian section; Austria and Czechoslovakia were in the German zone. Germany then widened its diplomatic system and concluded the Anti-Comintern Pact with Japan in November. On the surface, the agreement was directed against the international Communist organization, but it included secret clauses that applied specifically to the Soviet Union.

Both signatories agreed to remain neutral should either become involved in a war with that power. Italy adhered to the treaty in November 1937; Hungary, Spain, and Japan's satellite Manchukuo were to join later. When the Soviet Union objected to the pact, the signatories pointed to the repeated Soviet disclaimers of responsibility for Comintern activities.

Even before these agreements had been signed, Germany had taken major steps toward reasserting its position in Europe. In March 1936 the demilitarization of the Rhineland was ended, and the country embarked on a full program of rearmament. This violation of the Versailles Treaty was of major significance for the French alliance system and thus for the security of the Little Entente members. France could come to the aid of its Eastern allies only by launching an attack on the German western frontier. A demilitarized Rhineland made such an undertaking possible; a strongly fortified border was another matter. In fact, France now put its major effort into the construction of the Maginot Line; money thus went into fixed fortifications and defensive armaments rather than into offensive weapons like planes and tanks. The change marked what had been a gradual alteration in the French attitude. By this time many French leaders had become tired of attempting to uphold the Versailles Treaty single-handed; others had become convinced pacifists. Leon Blum, the Socialist leader, expressed a common opinion in declaring, "We do not believe – as did our forefathers in 1792 and 1848 – that there can be some good to war, nor that war can be an instrument for Liberty or for Revolution."[3] Georges Bonnet, who became foreign minister in 1938, expressed a similar idea: "Let's not go in for heroism . . . France cannot afford another blood-letting. Our vital statistics are getting steadily worse."[4]

The Axis camp meanwhile made notable advances. When a civil war broke out in Spain in July 1936, the two dictators came to the aid of General Francisco Franco. With the assistance of German and Italian equipment and volunteers, he achieved a victory in March 1939. In March 1938, with the assent of Italy, Germany carried through the annexation of Austria. This act was accomplished with the approval of most of the population and could be justified on the grounds of the principle of self-determination. Still exploiting this doctrine, Hitler then turned to the question of the German population of the Sudeten region of Czechoslovakia. In September 1938 the French premier, Edouard Daladier, and the British prime minister, Neville Chamberlain, met with Mussolini and Hitler in Munich. There the German areas of Czechoslovakia were given to Germany. Hungary and Poland similarly took small sections of territory that they claimed. The transaction was accomplished without the presence of Czech representatives, and it involved the territory of a close French ally.

By the end of 1938 the Balkan states were thus faced with a diplomatic

---

3  Quoted in Pierre Lazareff, *Deadline* (New York: Random House, 1942), p. 130.
4  Quoted in Lazareff, *Deadline*, p. 175.

balance entirely different from that which had existed in the early postwar years. Germany had rearmed, while France had invested in the Maginot Line. Despite a firm alliance, France had not supported the interests of a member of the Little Entente. With the annexation of the Austrian and the Sudeten territories, Germany was in a good position to dominate the Danubian region. The prestige of the dictatorships was also at a high point. They had won repeated victories in their confrontations with the Western powers. All of the Balkan governments had to adjust to the new conditions. Their internal political balance as well as their foreign policies were to be deeply affected by the Axis diplomatic victories.

## THE ESTABLISHMENT OF THE BALKAN AUTHORITARIAN REGIMES

The Balkan states not only had to adopt policies to meet international challenges, but also had to deal with the disastrous effects of the Great Depression. The economic crisis put an additional burden on the Balkan governments, which had not been able to handle their problems of internal development even in more prosperous times. The question was whether the new economic problems would place too great a strain on what remained of the parliamentary systems for them to survive, with their multiple parties, their fighting leaderships, and their deep corruption. As we have seen, internal political conflicts had already by the early 1930s enabled Alexander in Yugoslavia and Boris in Bulgaria to assume strong roles in the direction of state affairs. Although the tendency toward increasingly authoritarian regimes was obvious, it was not clear what alternate political system would be adopted should the last vestiges of liberal, constitutional government disappear.

In the past the Balkan leaderships had consistently looked to the European great powers for political institutions. At this time both the Soviet Union and Fascist Italy offered alternate patterns for the reorganization of government and society. The rejection of the Communist program and the fear that its doctrines aroused among many sections of Balkan society have been mentioned. Fascism was another matter. Italy, as we have seen, exerted a major influence on the foreign relations of the region. In addition, fascist doctrines in their Italian variant had certain points of attraction. They were highly nationalistic, and they were based on the maintenance of traditional social patterns. The fact that representative institutions and civil liberties were abolished did not cause great concern in an area where the majority of the population had really never enjoyed the advantages of a functioning constitutional government based on universal suffrage and a secret ballot. In fact, to many Balkan citizens dictatorial regimes had the advantage of putting an end to the ceaseless squabbling among political parties that represented only a minority of the population. Moreover, dictatorships apparently could achieve social cohesion among all elements of the population in a time of crisis. Fascist movements also provided for their members an array of ceremonies, salutes, songs, and special uniforms, and a simplistic nationalistic ideology, all of which had carried a wide appeal in this area in the past.

Despite these attractions and the fact that the Axis powers gained considerable prestige from their foreign policy victories, the Balkan governments did not adopt Italian Fascist or German Nazi patterns. Only Romania's Legion of the Archangel Michael, usually called the Iron Guard, had the attributes of a true fascist party, and even it had specific Romanian features. General Ioannis Metaxas in Greece was the single Balkan political leader whose position resembled that of Franco or Mussolini, although the differences were perhaps as great as the similarities. The Balkan authoritarian regimes of the 1930s were instead a return to the nineteenth century, to the era when the leadership of each nation rested in the hands of the monarch and his close advisers. There were no mass political movements organized to back these regimes, nor did they attempt to alter the traditional social, economic, or political relationships. Their chief task was to hold the state together in a time of increasing international tension. Except in Greece, the power in the government was taken by the king, who decided the major policies and manipulated the politicians. Royal dictatorships were introduced into Albania by Zog and into Yugoslavia by Alexander before 1930; Bulgaria and Romania were soon to follow.

## Yugoslavia

In January 1929, as we have seen, King Alexander of Yugoslavia, instead of attempting to satisfy the demands of the Croats and the other opposition political parties, chose a radical change of direction. He suspended the constitution and established a personal dictatorship. His powers were virtually limitless: he was in command of the army and the state, and he chose all the high officials. Political parties and organizations such as trade unions were abolished; the guarantees on civil liberties disappeared. Not only was the rigid centralized administration maintained, but the historic divisions with their nationalistic associations were eliminated. The country was divided into nine provinces, called *banovinas*, the boundaries of which were drawn with the intention of weakening or destroying traditional loyalties. The banovinas were given the names of rivers and other geographic features. Placed under a strongly centralized control, they were allowed no local autonomous rights. This action was justified as an attempt to create a feeling of supranational, or Yugoslav, unity, and the official name of the country was changed from the Kingdom of the Serbs, Croats and Slovenes to Yugoslavia. In fact, once in practice, these measures served to enhance Serbian domination. The boundaries of banovinas were gerrymandered so that Serbs formed a majority in six, Croats in two, Slovenes in one, and Muslims in none. The principal offices in the state continued to be held by Serbs from Serbia, with the Slovenes receiving an adequate share. Muslims were allotted the lowest positions, whereas the Croats remained inadequately represented.

In September 1931 Alexander issued another constitution, which was little more than a cover for his dictatorship. It established a bicameral legislature; the king appointed half of the members of the upper house. The elected representatives were chosen by voice vote and not secret ballot. The assembly could propose measures and express its opposition to them, but it did not have the power to legislate independently. A limited amount of political activity was allowed, although it was strictly watched. In the elections the party that received a plurality was given two-thirds of the seats and a proportional share in the remaining third. All national or regional parties were forbidden. In order to run, a party had to demonstrate that it had sufficient supporters in all of the districts. This regulation, of course, made it almost impossible for Croatian, Slovenian, or other national groups to present a slate of candidates. All of the advantages were thus held by the official government party, called the Yugoslav National Party. It is therefore not surprising that in 1931, with the support of the police, the government candidates won all 306 seats in the assembly.

These actions could not be carried through without serious opposition. The loss of civil liberties affected the Serbs of Serbia as well as all of the other nationalities. The government maintained a strict supervision over its critics. The Croatian Peasant Party leader, Vladko Maček, was condemned for treason in April 1933 and sentenced to three years in jail. Other important statesmen, including Trumbić and Korošec, had similar experiences. Although the prominent men were usually detained under good conditions, many others died in jail or suffered under extremely harsh treatment. Macedonians, Albanians, suspected Communists, and Croatians had a particularly difficult time.

In order to escape the repressive regime, many political leaders emigrated. Pribičević, at the head of the prečani Serbs, was first imprisoned and then allowed to go for medical treatment to Czechoslovakia, where he died of cancer in 1936. The most controversial Croatian politician, Ante Pavelić, a member of the Frank wing of the Croatian Party of Rights, left the country in January 1929 and with the support of Mussolini organized the *Ustaša* (Insurrection) movement, centered in Italy. The goal was the achievement of Croatian independence, if necessary by means of revolution and violence. This group was able at times to cooperate with IMRO, which had the similar aim of overthrowing Serbian domination in Macedonia. Both organizations received Italian and Hungarian assistance. Mussolini, in particular, used the Ustaša as a weapon in his diplomatic arsenal with which to threaten Belgrade. When he was able to come to an agreement with the Yugoslav government, he had no hesitation about suppressing Croatian emigrant activity.

Alexander's dictatorship enjoyed the full support of France and the Little

Entente. As usual, a Western constitutional government was quite willing to encourage a dictatorship when its own interests were served. Determined to maintain the Versailles system, and opposed to Italy, the French leaders believed that Alexander's centralist regime contributed to the military strength of the allied state. In October 1934 the association came to an end with the assassination of King Alexander and French foreign minister Louis Barthou in Marseilles. The assassin was a Macedonian, but the act was part of a conspiracy with links to the Ustaša and Italy. Alexander was succeeded by his son, Peter II, who was only eleven years old. A regency was thus established, headed by Alexander's cousin, Prince Paul. Bogoljub Jevtić became premier.

The new regent was not dictatorial in temperament. A great admirer of British institutions, he felt that his main task was to keep the state together until Peter's majority. Therefore, although he hesitated to make major constitutional changes, he had no desire to maintain the previous authoritarian system intact. Moreover, criticism of the dictatorial policies had grown to such a degree that some relaxation was necessary. Maček was released, as were other political prisoners. There was less police supervision and censorship. The constitution, however, was kept, and the elections were still controlled. Within these limitations, the political parties were able to resume some of their activities. The Croatian Peasant Party united with the Serbian opposition to challenge the government candidates at the polls. In elections held in 1935, despite police interference and fraud, the opposition was able to win 37.4 percent of the votes. Although they participated in the campaign, the Croatian Peasant Party delegates did not take their seats in the assembly.

In June 1935 a new government was formed under the premiership of Milan Stojadinović. It was to last for over three years and to bring a period of relative calm in Yugoslav internal affairs. Press censorship was further relaxed, and many political prisoners were released. Returning to the former system, Stojadinović based his rule on a government party, the Yugoslav Radical Union, which was composed of the Serbian Radical Party, the Bosnian Muslims, and the Slovene People's Party. There was an attempt to make some sort of an agreement with the Croatian representatives, but any reconciliation proved impossible as long as the government stood for the maintenance of the unitary state and the constitution of 1931.

In foreign policy, closer relations were established with Germany and Italy. Stojadinović himself adopted a few of the outward signs of the fascist movement. He, for instance, organized youth groups appropriately clothed in green shirts. Other organizations with fascist attachments were also in existence at this time. In addition to the Croatian Ustaša, already mentioned, a Serbian group, the Yugoslav National Movement, known as *Zbor* (Rally), was organized under the leadership of Dimitrije Ljotić. It was strongly centralistic and Serbian-nationalistic in ideology, and its goal was the establishment of a corporate regime similar to that in Italy. It had a youth organization known as the White Eagle.

Despite the comparative relaxation in this period, the national conflicts continued to dominate political life. The bitterness in feeling was displayed again when the government, in a move to appease Croatian opinion, concluded a concordat with the Vatican that defined the privileges of the Catholic church in Yugoslavia and placed it on a footing of equality with the Orthodox. This agreement met with such violent opposition from the Orthodox hierarchy, which charged that the Catholics would receive superior privileges, that it had to be withdrawn. As members of the national church of the dominant nationality, the Orthodox were not willing to accept a modification of their position. The Orthodox–Catholic hostility shown in this issue was to break forth in full force during World War II.

The Yugoslav state obviously could not afford the continuation of these bitter national divisions. The international situation was becoming increasingly ominous. After March 1938, when Austria joined Germany, that state had a common border with Yugoslavia. The Munich agreement demonstrated that the Western allies could not be relied on to prevent the Axis from exploiting the national controversies. The Italian relations with and encouragement of the dissident Croatian factions were well known. In this situation a solution to the Croatian problem was an immediate necessity.

The Croatian position had remained consistent and firm. The political leaders demanded a federal and not a centralized state. In 1937 the opposition bloc consisted not only of the Croatian Peasant Party, but also of some Serbian parties including the Democratic and sections of the Radical. They all demanded the holding of a constituent assembly to reorganize the state institutions, an action that Prince Paul refused to take before Peter became of age. In December 1938 elections were again held, and with the usual police supervision. The results were really a defeat for the government. Despite the illegal procedures, the Maček opposition list gained 44.9 percent of the votes, against the government's 54.1 percent. Stojadinović was dismissed, but primarily for reasons connected with foreign policy, which will be discussed later.

In February 1939 a new ministry was formed under Dragiša Cvetković with the objective of coming to an understanding with the Croatian opposition. Prince Paul played a leading role in this effort. Negotiations commenced in April 1939 and proceeded under the influence of a threatening international situation. An agreement was finally worked out between Maček and the government representatives only days before the outbreak of World War II. In the Sporazum (Understanding) of August 1939 Yugoslavia was reorganized to give Croatia an autonomous position within the state. Its lands included Croatia, Slavonia, Dalmatia, and some Bosnian and Hercegovinian territory inhabited by Croats. The autonomous region had a population of 4.4 million, of which 866,000 were Serbs. It was thus 77 percent Croatian in nationality. Autonomous Croatia controlled about 30 percent of the population and territory of the entire country. It had its own assembly, or sabor, and its chief executive officer, the ban, was appointed by the king. This official was, however, responsible to the sabor. Croatia was linked to Belgrade for foreign affairs, defense, transportation, and communications, but was self-governing in almost all other matters.[5] The agreement thus resembled closely the Ausgleich that had been concluded between Austria and Hungary in the previous century and also to a degree the arrangements that had linked Zagreb and Budapest until 1918.

With the completion of this agreement the Croatian Peasant Party joined the government. Maček became vice-premier of Yugoslavia, and four of his colleagues entered the ministry. Ivan Šubašić was appointed ban of Croatia. Although the major problem had thus been met, the other national conflicts remained. Slovenes, Muslims, Macedonians, and Albanians had similar grievances. Moreover, as could be expected, the Serbian nationalists were deeply discontented; they wanted a Serbian state composed of the areas where they had a majority. The outbreak of World War II was to hinder further attempts at reconciliation.

## Romania

After the resignation of Iuliu Maniu as Romanian premier in October 1930, a government under George Mironescu held office until April 1931. The king remained the center of the political power of the state. A clever and unscrupulous ruler, Charles II was able to manipulate the politicians and the system. He kept control through rapid changes of political leadership: between 1930 and 1940 there were twenty-five different ministries, with eighteen different premiers, sixty-one ministers, and thirty-one undersecretaries. At the same time, the post of chief of the general staff changed hands nine times.[6] It is not necessary to review these administrations in detail since they introduced no notable changes in the state. The system of first appointing a ministry and then holding the elections was retained, and free use was still made of the police by the faction in power. Romania, it will be remembered, had electoral regulations that gave the party receiving a plurality of votes a majority in the chamber. The most stable government was that formed by George Tătărescu, which lasted from January 1934 to December 1937.

During this period the Romanian Iron Guard was the only political party in the Balkans with a program similar to that of other European fascist movements which was able to attract a mass following. Its leader, Corneliu Zelea Codreanu, was born in Moldavia in 1899. His father, who was probably of Ukrainian or Polish national origin, changed his original name of Zelinski to

---

5  Joseph Rothschild, *East Central Europe between the Two World Wars* vol. IX of Peter F. Sugar and Donald W. Treadgold, eds., *A History of East Central Europe* (Seattle; University of Washington Press, 1974), pp. 260, 261.

6  Rothschild, *East Central Europe*, p. 305.

Zelea and then added the surname Codreanu, from the word *codru*, meaning "forest." His son had a strongly nationalistic and religious upbringing and entered into political activity at a young age. In 1927 he organized the Legion of the Archangel Michael. A charismatic leader, Codreanu at first supported no set ideology, but instead emphasized the moral regeneration of the individual. His program and the spirit in which it was presented are well illustrated by a speech he gave in December 1929:

> Let us all unite, men and women, and fashion another fate for our nation and for ourselves. The hour of Romanian revival and salvation is drawing nigh. He who believes, he who will fight and suffer, will be rewarded and blessed by the nation. New times are knocking at our doors. A world with a sterile, dried-up soul is dying and another is being born: the world of those whose souls are full of faith. In this new world, everybody will have his place, not according to his schooling, not according to his cleverness or learning, but above all according to his character and his faith.[7]

The movement placed a great emphasis on religion, and each meeting was opened by an Orthodox service.

Codreanu's doctrines appealed to a wide audience, but in particular to the peasants and the youth who were outside the Romanian political system; they also attracted workers, intellectuals, and civil servants. In a country where political corruption was deeply rooted, the movement offered the alternate values of poverty, sacrifice, and service. It also had the attractions of the other romantic and revolutionary ideologies that we have examined previously. With its emphasis on action and the sacrificial deed, it provided the opportunity for idealistic and violent exploits similar to those of other terrorist organizations. The great Romanian poet, Mihail Eminescu, had written: "A political crime ... committed by a private person, ceases to be a crime when it is based on higher views and dictated by the clean notion, even if it be mistaken, of saving the state." Adopting this principle, the Legion accepted the necessity of violence, but only if the deeds were committed for the good of the cause and subsequently expiated. There were many examples of Legionnaires surrendering to the police after committing acts of terror. The party doctrines also placed an emphasis on death and dying quite unusual among the political doctrines of the day. These morbid preoccupations were clear in the songs and poems of the movement, as illustrated in the following verses:

> Legionary do not fear
> That you will die too young

7 Quoted in Eugen Weber, "Romania," in Hans Rogger and Eugen Weber, *The European Right: A Historical Profile* (Berkeley: University of California Press, 1966), pp. 541–542.

> For you die to be reborn
> And are born to die
>
>    .  .  .
>
> With a smile on our lips
> We look death in the eye
> For we are the death team
> That must win or die.

And from the Legionary hymn:

> And wind blows over the waters
> And the willows weep
> We do not forget you, brother
> But you go on, asleep.[8]

The Legionary organization was based on local units, called nests, each of which was composed of from three to thirteen members. The Legion also acquired a military section, the Iron Guard, which consisted of armed bands formed to combat Communists and other opponents; this name was subsequently applied to the entire movement. The bands committed numerous acts of violence and resisted government control. In December 1933, after repeated provocation, the police moved against the organization. The Guard was dissolved and hundreds of its members were imprisoned; some were killed. The Legion, however, continued to function through a front organization called All for the Fatherland.

Among the Legion's negative features was the intense chauvinism of its program; it attacked all elements in the state that were considered foreign, in particular the Jews. Anti-semitism, as we have seen, was always an extremely sensitive question in Romanian politics. The chief rival of the Guard, the National Christian Party, had many similar doctrines, especially in regard to the Jewish issue. Although Charles II strongly resisted Legionary influence, he was willing to entrust the government to the National Christian Party, whose leaders were Octavian Goga and Alexander Cuza. In elections held in December 1937 Tătărescu's supporters received only 35.9 percent of the votes, with the National Peasants winning 20.4 percent, the Iron Guard 15.5 percent, and the National Christians 9 percent. Unable to form a majority coalition, the king asked Goga to form a ministry; his regime lasted only until February 1938.

Until this time Charles had exerted great political influence, but he had not assumed dictatorial powers personally. He had worked through the cor-

---

8 All quoted in Weber, "Romania," pp. 522, 523.

rupt system and through the politicians whom he could dominate. In 1938, with the growing disarray of the internal political situation and the increase of the external dangers, he, like Alexander in Yugoslavia before him, took full charge of the government and established a royal dictatorship. The Orthodox patriarch Miron Cristea became premier. In February 1938 a new constitution was issued, which gave the king full powers; only he could amend the constitution, and he appointed and dismissed the ministers. The assembly was organized on a corporatist basis, and the administrative system was reorganized. The constitution was approved in a plebiscite by a vote of 4,289,581 to 5,483; the voting, needless to say, was not secret. In a reorganization of the local government designed to weaken local loyalties, the seventy-one prefectures were divided into ten regions. In December 1938 the king organized his own party, the Front of National Rebirth. The royal government at the same time adopted many of the Legionary themes, such as work, patriotism, religion, and personal dignity.

Meanwhile, the government had again moved against the Iron Guard, which had regained considerable influence since its suppression in 1933. In April 1938 Codreanu was arrested and his organization again disbanded. A treason trial followed. Although the charges were never proven, Codreanu was condemned to ten years in prison. In November 1938 he and twelve of his followers were shot "while trying to escape." These violent reprisals did not deeply injure the influence of the movement. Horia Sima took Codreanu's place as the leader of the organization. In September 1939 members of the Guard assassinated Armand Călinescu, the king's closest associate. Although Charles temporarily had full control of the government, the Iron Guard was to become a major political force after the commencement of the war.

### Bulgaria

A similar conservative, rightist trend was shown in Bulgarian politics. In May 1934 a military coup led by Colonel Damian Velchev of the Military League took over the government. This revolt resembled similar actions of the past in which army officers had organized to overturn civilian governments that they believed were following policies ruinous to the country. The movement was supported by the civilian association *Zveno* (the Link), which had been formed in 1927 and was under the direction of Colonel Kimon Georgiev, an officer in the reserves. Small in numbers, Zveno's members

> perceived themselves as an elitist group set on modernizing Bulgaria by means of political guidance from above. They were averse to mass action and remained committed to the concept of direct political intervention by the enlightened few. In their estimation, parliamentarianism, as well as the role of political parties, was withering away. Bulgaria's fundamental ills were not related to the maladministration

of her wealth but to the economic scarcities of the country and the underdevelopment of her economic resources. The only way the country could be modernized was by means of an efficient technocracy accountable to itself. The top-heavy state bureaucracy had to be streamlined and rationalized.[9]

Once in power the leaders of the revolt proceeded to implement the Zveno program. Georgiev became the head of the government, but Velchev did not take an official post. As could be expected, the new leaders attempted to make radical changes in the political institutions that they believed to be the cause of many of their nation's problems. The constitution, which dated from 1879, was abolished; the political parties and organizations such as trade unions were suppressed. Unlike the leaders of similar regimes in other Balkan countries, Georgiev and Velchev did not attempt to create a government party or an official coalition. An assembly met, but its members were appointed. The regime governed by decree.

Some domestic reforms were introduced, particularly in the countryside, but the main accomplishments were in foreign policy. Like the majority of Bulgarians, the Zveno members were convinced that the Macedonians were Bulgarian in nationality. However, they believed that the IMRO activities had been so detrimental to national interests that they could not be allowed to continue. The new regime wished to establish better relations with France, a matter that could best be handled through Yugoslavia. Yet as long as the Macedonian issue remained a constant sore point, the cooperation of Belgrade could not be obtained. With the assistance of the army and the moderate wing of IMRO, the government was able to disband the terrorist organization; its leader, Ivan Mihailov, fled. The action was accomplished with no major internal repercussions and made closer relations with France and the Little Entente possible. In 1934 formal relations were also established with the Soviet Union.

The new leadership, however, suffered from the absence of a mass base of support, and its program did not enjoy wide popular approval. There was no official party or national organization. Moreover, the Military League did not represent a single point of view; its members disagreed on the policies that should be adopted. These circumstances allowed Boris III to move against a regime that he had never been able to control. In January 1935, in a bloodless coup, Boris was able to secure the removal of Georgiev. In April the king returned the country to civilian control and abolished the Military League. Bulgaria too was now under a royal dictatorship. An assembly was still elected, but it had only consultative powers. Elections were held in 1938; the candidates could run only as individuals and not as members of parties, although

9  Nissan Oren, *Revolution Administered: Agrarianism and Communism in Bulgaria* (Baltimore: Johns Hopkins University Press, 1973), p. 20.

the voters, of course, knew their affiliations. Even with close police supervision, the voting resulted in the election of 32 Agrarians, 8 Social Democrats, and 5 Communists now organized in the Bulgarian Workers' Party, in a house of 160 members. All of these parties were in opposition to the regime. The Communists and some Agrarians were expelled. Bulgaria thus had a government very similar to that of its neighbors on the eve of the war.

## Greece

Greek politics, as we have seen, suffered from the chronic failure to find a stable combination of parties and from the bitter antagonism of the republicans and monarchists. Venizelos, the most experienced Greek politician, formed his last government in January 1933. In elections held in March the new government suffered a sharp defeat. The Populists, representing the monarchist cause, received a majority of 135 against the Liberals' 96. Tsaldaris became premier once again. These electoral results, with their obvious implications, were a shock to the army and its Republican officer corps. It must be remembered that in Greece a change of government always brought with it a turnover of both civilian and military personnel. Should the king be restored, the Republican officers in the army would similarly be replaced by royalists. As soon as he heard of the Liberal defeat, General Plastiras organized a revolt and proclaimed himself dictator. The rebellion, however, was easily suppressed. Although Venizelos had not participated in this action, many suspected his complicity. In June 1933 his car was attacked by men armed with machine guns. Venizelos escaped unharmed, but his driver was killed. It was subsequently discovered that the assassin's car belonged to the chief of police of Athens.

A second conspiracy was organized by the Republican officers in March 1935. This time Venizelos did know of the plans, and he supported them. However, once again the military revolt failed. Although there was some support from Macedonia and from the navy, Athens could not be taken. The action considerably strengthened the Royalist position. The government, under the leadership of Tsaldaris and the Populist Party, now had ample excuse to remove Venizelos's supporters from the state offices and the army. Venizelos, who had left the country, was sentenced to death.

New elections were held in June 1935. Since the Venizelist party abstained, the Populist Party won a clear victory. The only challenge came from the Royalist Union Party, led by General Ioannis Metaxas, which won only a small percentage of the votes. Tsaldaris next wished to arrange a plebiscite on the question of the return of the king. His proposals were opposed by those Royalist generals who wished to accomplish the restoration in a more reliable manner; they forced Tsaldaris to resign and placed General Kondylis in the office of premier. Kondylis then forced through the assembly, where only a minority of the members were in attendance, measures providing for the abolition of the republic. In full control of the police and the administration, the new government proceeded to hold a plebiscite that produced the amazing return of a 97.8 percent vote in favor of the restoration of the monarchy.

George II, after his return to Athens in November 1935, soon showed that he had no intention of becoming a tool of the faction that had brought him back. He replaced Kondylis with Constantine Demertzis, a professor of law at the University of Athens, who formed a nonparty government. An amnesty was granted to the Republican opponents who were in jail, and many regained the positions that they had lost previously. Preparations were then made to conduct an honest election. The voting, which took place in January 1936, produced a result that clearly reflected the close division in Greek politics. The four Royalist parties received 143 seats; the five Republican won 141. The balance was held by the 15 Communist representatives. This party, which previously had played a minor role in Greek politics, thus held a crucial position.

Although neither the Royalists nor the Republicans were enthusiastic about cooperation with the Communists, they could not come to an understanding with each other. At stake was the control of the spoils of office, including the posts in the army as well as those in the administration. The Liberals were led by Themistoklis Sofoulis, replacing Venizelos, who remained in exile; Tsaldaris continued at the head of the monarchist camp. In February the Liberals made a bargain with the Communists that engaged the latter to vote for Sofoulis as president of the chamber in return for Liberal support of certain moderate reform measures. The arrangement was secret. Sofoulis, however, was not willing to take a further step and organize a government in coalition with the Communists. Since it was impossible to form a ministry with majority backing, Demertzis was authorized to appoint another nonparty government. In April the premier died. George II chose as his successor General Metaxas, who had been minister of war. Not only did his ministry win a vote of confidence from the assembly, but that body, with Liberal acquiescence, agreed to adjourn for five months and to allow Metaxas to govern by decree. The assembly then recessed, presumably for the summer; it was not to meet again.

Once in control Metaxas moved quickly. He acted first against the labor unions and their leaders; strikes were declared illegal. In reply, the Communist Party, together with other labor organizations, attempted to organize an opposition. A general strike was proclaimed in Thessaloniki in May; it was suppressed by the army. Another was announced for the entire country for August 5. This threat gave Metaxas the justification he needed to take full control of the country. Although the other political parties had certainly no interest in strengthening the general's position, they still could not come to an understanding, and they showed a lack of leadership in this time of crisis.

Kondylis had died in January and Venizelos in March 1936. Sofoklis Venizelos, the son of the Liberal statesman, although inheriting his father's prestige, was not an adequate replacement. On August 4 George II agreed to the establishment of a Metaxas dictatorship. A state of emergency was declared, and the assembly was dissolved. Although Greece too was now a dictatorship, the strong man was the general and not the king. Metaxas was not only premier, but also minister of foreign affairs, of the armed forces, and after 1938 of education.

The Metaxas government was subsequently known as the Regime of the Fourth of August, after the date of its inauguration. Although its leader had previously played an important role in both military and political affairs, he did not have a large personal following; his party had drawn only a small vote in previous elections. His position thus depended on the support of the king, who in turn held the allegiance of the army. Like dictatorships elsewhere, this government first turned to suppressing possible sources of opposition. The political parties were outlawed; their leaders either were put in prison or declared their allegiance to the new regime. The Communist Party was driven underground. The press was tightly controlled and education supervised.

Nevertheless, despite many of the harsh methods adopted against the left, some reform measures were enacted. Although strikes were made illegal and the unions closed, the government did set a minimum wage and tried to guarantee certain other benefits for the workers, such as regular yearly two-week vacations. There were also attempts to aid the villages. Most important, however, were the actions taken to improve the Greek military forces. Under the direction of General Alexander Papagos, new arms were acquired for the army, navy, and air force, and the frontier fortifications were strengthened. Supplies were stockpiled in preparation for a possible war. When the catastrophe finally came in 1940, Greece was able to resist an Italian invasion successfully.

Metaxas's regime resembled in many ways those in Italy and Spain. The general took the title of *Archigos*, or leader, in imitation of the other dictators. His movement, which never won a mass following, also had its special uniforms, slogans, salutes, and songs. With no particular ideology at the beginning, it soon developed a strongly nationalistic program. His followers declared that there had been three great periods in Greek history: the classical, the Byzantine, and the Regime of the Fourth of August. Much emphasis was placed on the familiar conservative virtues of family, religion, stability, and social and political order. A National Youth Organization, intended to bring together the children of the different social classes, was formed to provide military training for boys and teach domestic skills to girls. At the commencement of World War II, then, Greece, like the other Balkan states, had a strong authoritarian regime.

## INTER-BALKAN RELATIONS

It can thus be seen that the internal evolution of the Balkan states in the interwar period was very similar. Constitutional governments were overturned in every case. Another negative aspect of Balkan life at this time was the failure to find a firm basis on which the states could cooperate with one another and resist great-power encroachment. As we have seen, one of the principal hindrances to Balkan national development had been the extreme pressure exerted on the populations by outside influences. After 1919 the downfall of the tsarist, Habsburg, and Ottoman empires removed from the scene three of the major powers that had been deeply involved in Balkan affairs. Britain too played a less active role in the postwar period than before. Although France and Italy attempted to form competing alliance systems in Eastern Europe, neither had the military power necessary to enforce its will against a united opposition. With this general situation, the Balkan governments, perhaps for the first time, had the opportunity to adjust their mutual relations and to form some sort of a front to protect their regional interests.

Despite the fact that the possibilities for constructive organization existed, the heritage of past hatreds proved too strong an influence. All of the Balkan states had territories over whose jurisdiction they conflicted with their neighbors, and these disputes took precedence over desires for reconciliation. Albania had claims on Greek Epirus and on the Kosovo district of Yugoslavia, where a quarter of the Albanian people lived. Bulgaria had never accepted the loss of Thrace or Dobrudja, and the majority of the people remained firmly convinced that the Macedonians were Bulgarians. Greece had not only quarrels with Bulgaria and claims on southern Albania, but disputes with Yugoslavia on the use of the port of Thessaloniki, which was the natural outlet for Macedonia. The Romanian government was continually conscious of the necessity of defending Bessarabia, Bukovina, Transylvania, and Dobrudja against its neighbors. Yugoslavia, whose major problems were internal, nevertheless had to face similar designs on its territories, particularly on the regions with an Albanian, Macedonian, or Hungarian population.

Immediately after World War I the major concern of the victor powers had been to preserve their gains. The Little Entente had been organized as a French diplomatic instrument to uphold the status quo and was directed against Hungary and Bulgaria. As such, it was not suited to promote inter-Balkan or general Eastern European conciliation. In the 1930s, however, an effort was made to form an organization to promote closer ties among the Balkan states. The initial major step in this direction occurred in October 1930 when the first Balkan Conference was held in Athens. This meeting, which was not official, was attended by representatives from cultural and professional organizations and the universities as well as by political leaders. Commissions were established and cultural exchanges arranged. The Balkan Entente, the name by which it became known, was composed of Greece,

Yugoslavia, Romania, and Turkey; Albania and Bulgaria did not join. Efforts were made to secure Bulgarian participation, but these proved unsuccessful when none of the other governments would grant concessions to this revisionist state.

With the exclusion of two nations, the Balkan alignment soon became little more than another means of preserving the existing frontiers of its members against challenges from Bulgaria. In February 1934 a pact of mutual security and consultation was signed. One of the greatest weaknesses of this combination was its failure to provide adequate protection against great-power interference in the peninsula. None of the participants in the Balkan Entente was willing to defend the interests of another member against a great power. Greece, for instance, had no intention of becoming involved in an Italian–Yugoslav conflict; Turkey did not wish to be drawn into a Russian–Romanian war. Under these circumstances the understandings had no real utility. They could be of value only should one of the states be attacked by Bulgaria, and there was little likelihood that this state would adopt an offensive policy without great-power backing.

The Balkan states were thus unable to find a firm basis for cooperation and mutual defense in a time of relative peace and security. The situation was to become even more dismal with the rise of German and Italian power and the retreat of France in Eastern European affairs, events that forced all of the small states to readjust their foreign policies. Although the Balkans remained out of the center of great-power attention until 1940, each major change in the European balance had repercussions in this area. The establishment of authoritarian regimes in all of the states reflected the ideological current in Central Europe. A similar drift toward the Axis camp was to be seen in foreign relations.

## THE AXIS ADVANCE: THE CONQUEST OF ALBANIA

In the last analysis the maintenance of the Paris peace settlement depended upon the will of the French government to enforce its provisions and the willingness of the British to back France's action. As we have seen, both these states had become disillusioned over the rewards of diplomatic supremacy. Public opinion in neither country was willing to pay the price necessary to maintain the military level that would permit domination of Continental affairs. As a result the French Eastern alignment soon began to crumble. In 1934 the Polish government made a pact with Hitler. The remilitarization of the Rhineland and the rearmament of Germany in 1936 placed a dangerous barrier between France and its Eastern allies. The French alliance with the Soviet Union did not win favor among the conservative regimes in power in Eastern Europe. The greatest blow to the French position, however, was undoubtedly the Munich agreement. It showed France's attitude toward its treaty commitments, and it broke the Little Entente. The French Eastern Barrier had collapsed.

Deprived of firm outside direction, the Balkan states had to readjust their relations with the great powers and maneuver between the rival blocs. None of the governments, not even the revisionists, wanted a major crisis in the region. Their position was very difficult, and they chose different roads in their quest for stable and reliable alignments. Although some of the statesmen were indeed attached to a great power – that is, genuinely pro-British, pro-French, or pro-German – most of them were simply patriots who attempted to find the best policy for their nations. Some believed it was best to remain close to the Western powers; others turned to the Axis. It will be noted that Soviet Russia played no part in these calculations. No East European government trusted or was tempted to work with it. Support for Soviet policy came only from the Communist parties, which had been driven underground and whose leaders had either emigrated or been imprisoned.

In the Axis camp the major role in Balkan politics was still played by Mussolini. The German diplomats repeatedly stated that they had no political objectives in the Balkans. Until 1940 they did indeed give priority to Italian interests. In addition, two other outside states, Hungary and Turkey, were to play a major role in the region in the next years. Hungary, with a strongly revisionist policy, worked with the Axis powers and, along with Poland, had shared in the rewards of the Munich pact. Although the Hungarian leaders tried to maintain as independent an attitude as possible, they wanted Transylvania and other territories that had formerly been under the control of Budapest. Turkey, in contrast, at least at first chose to cooperate with the Western powers and aid in the attempt to maintain the status quo. The main concern of the Turkish government was, however, the Soviet Union, and not the German and Italian advances.

The weakening of the French alliance system placed the Little Entente powers, Romania and Yugoslavia, in a particularly exposed position. Both were faced with the irredentist demands of their neighbors, and they had no firm great-power backing. The Romanian difficulties were not to become acute until after the outbreak of the war. The Yugoslav government, more immediately and directly threatened, attempted to come to an understanding with Italy during the Stojadinović ministry.

The principal influence in the Yugoslav government was held by Prince Paul, who, it will be remembered, was regent during the minority of King Peter. He was pro-British, and his wife was a Greek princess. Although personally inclined toward the West, he had an extremely realistic attitude about foreign policy. He also had to deal with the major internal problem of Croatian opposition and the ties of extremist Croatian and Macedonian groups to Italy. In an attempt to ensure a stable diplomatic situation Stojadinović, with the prince's approval, negotiated two agreements outside the Little Entente and the Balkan Entente. In neither case did the Yugoslav government consult with its allies concerning its intentions, and the new pacts broke both the letter and the spirit of the previous understandings. First, in January 1937, Stojadinović and the Bulgarian premier George Kioseivanov negotiated a treaty of friendship which included the pledge that the two states would not use force against each other, a provision that contradicted Yugoslavia's obligations under the Balkan Entente. Second, in March 1937, an even more significant nonaggression and arbitration agreement was signed with Italy. This government gave concessions to the Yugoslav minority in Italy and agreed not to support the Ustaša; Yugoslavia, in return, gave tacit assent to the Italian domination of Albania. In the succeeding years Stojadinović was in close touch with the Italian leadership, in particular with Mussolini and his son-in-law Count Galeazzo Ciano, who was Italian foreign minister. The partition of Albania was discussed. These plans were, however, interrupted when Paul in February 1939 dismissed his minister. The two men had personal disagreements, and the regent did not want the ties with the Axis to become too close. Dragiša Cvetković became the next premier, with Alexander Cincar-Marković, who had formerly been ambassador to Berlin, as foreign minister. The new premier continued the policy of close relations with the Axis, but he wished to keep Yugoslavia out of the major crises. The principal task of this government was coming to an understanding with the Croatian opposition.

Whereas Yugoslavia tended to tilt toward the Axis, Greek policy under Metaxas took a slightly different direction. After the Anatolian disaster the Greek government had no major immediate territorial objectives. The Italian possession of the Dodecanese Islands caused much resentment, and there were still claims to the southern part of Albania; however, any moves toward the acquisition of these lands were obviously impossible and dangerous. Greece was itself the object of attack from its revisionist neighbors. Albania desired Epirus, and Bulgaria Thrace. Moreover, despite the fact that Greece participated in the Balkan Entente, Metaxas distrusted Yugoslavia almost as much as Bulgaria. The fear that these two Slavic states would join together was always present, and their friendship treaty in 1937 was looked upon with suspicion.

Since Greece was predominantly a Mediterranean country, its foreign policy in the twentieth, as in the nineteenth, century was bound to be influenced principally by the strongest naval power in the area, which was still Britain, acting in cooperation with France. Italy was obviously the chief danger. Because Greece was unable to afford to build a large navy of its own, the Greek leaders judged that their best policy was to attempt to remain neutral in the great-power conflicts, but to obtain British protection against outside attacks. At this time Metaxas worked most closely with the Turkish government, under the leadership of Mustafa Kemal, by then called by the honorary title of Atatürk (father of the Turks). When he died, Metaxas cooperated well with his successor, Ismet Inönü. Although Greece and Turkey were both members of the Balkan Entente, they remained firm in their refusal to undertake obligations that might involve them in war with a great power. Neither, for instance, wished to fight Russia for the sake of Romania, or Italy for Yugoslavia. This attitude, of course, made the Balkan Entente virtually useless for purposes of inter-Balkan defense or for the protection of either Turkey against Russia or Greece against Italy.

Bulgaria, the target of both the Little Entente and the Balkan Entente, carried on an essentially negative policy. Its statesmen remained convinced that the Treaty of San Stefano correctly stated the true extent of its national lands. In conflict with all of its neighbors on territorial issues, but too weak to act, Bulgaria could do little. Its leaders did, however, sign a treaty in 1937 with Yugoslavia, and they were open to negotiations with the Balkan Entente. Obviously, the failure of that alignment to include Bulgaria was a weakness in its organization. In an attempt to bolster the diplomatic defenses of the Balkans, the Western powers put pressure on the Entente members to come to some sort of an understanding with Sofia. In July 1938 Metaxas, as president of the council of the Balkan Entente, signed a treaty of friendship and nonaggression with Bulgaria. In this pact the Entente members recognized the Bulgarian right to rearm; Bulgaria agreed to submit any disputes with its neighbors to arbitration. The agreement, of course, met none of the Bulgarian territorial claims.

Although Italy continued to carry on the more active diplomatic policy in the Balkans, Germany played the major role in the region's commercial relations. One of the greatest weaknesses in the French Eastern alliance system had been French economic policy. Not only did France and its allies have little to buy or sell to each other, but French financiers and government officials were extremely shortsighted in their general attitude toward Balkan loans and investments. The German economic preeminence, established in the 1930s, was the direct result of the Great Depression, which hit both Germany and the Balkan states with devastating effects. Germany had industrial goods that it could not sell; the Balkan countries had surpluses of agricultural products and raw materials. Neither had the means to pay for the goods they needed. This situation was ably exploited by the Nazi government, which simply organized barter agreements.

Viewing the economic situation from a political perspective, the German diplomats used trade agreements to advance their national goals. Their aim was not a short-range economic advantage, but a long period of future political domination. With a totalitarian system and full control of the economy, the German government could offer very attractive terms to the Balkan customers. The problem of payments was met by barter arrangements and blocked currency accounts. All of the states found the arrangements to their advantage. They, of course, had no alternate markets. The German orders were large and the prices favorable. The Balkan countries needed the industrial goods and machinery that Germany could and did supply. By 1938, after the annexation of Austria and the Sudetenland, Germany had won a predominant position in the trade of all of the Balkan nations. In that year 57.9 percent of Bulgarian imports came from Germany; the figures were 31.1 percent for Greece, 50 percent for Yugoslavia, and 48.5 percent for Romania. In the export column, 63.6 percent of the Bulgarian products, 43.2 percent of the Greek, 49.9 percent of the Yugoslav, and 35.9 percent of the Romanian went to the German market.[10] This economic situation, of course, greatly influenced the foreign policy of each state.

Until 1938 the Axis powers had been able to make major advances without provoking a military retaliation from the Western powers or Russia. In taking Austria and the Sudetenland Hitler had emphasized the right of self-determination of the German population, a principle that in theory the other governments accepted. In March 1939 he stepped out of this framework when he sent the German army into Czechoslovakia and partitioned the rest of its territory. He was able to exploit the Slovak resentment of Czech domination, a relationship that resembled in some ways that of the Serbs and Croats in Yugoslavia. At this time Slovakia was established as an independent state under close German control; Hungary annexed Ruthenia. The rest of the territory was taken over by Germany and organized as the Protectorate of Bohemia and Moravia. This action had an electrifying effect. It precipitated an Italian invasion of Albania and the commencement of a concerted effort by the Western powers to build a diplomatic alignment against further German conquests.

The relationship between Hitler and Mussolini had not been smooth despite the many ostentatious public displays of mutual esteem. As the senior dictator, Mussolini resented the quick rise and apparently easy successes of his partner. He knew that Italy was fast becoming the lesser member of the Axis and that the German leaders were well aware of it. The German destruction of Czechoslovakia was accomplished without consultation with Rome and with little prior warning. Mussolini was furious; his reaction was, "Every time Hitler occupies a country he sends me a message."[11] Sensitive to the effect of the events on Italian public opinion, Mussolini decided to proceed with the annexation of Albania as compensation. In the past years the Italian government had often considered the question of moving against either Albania or Yugoslavia. As we have seen, negotiations on the question of the partition of Albania had been carried on with Stojadinović. The next Yugoslav ministry, under Cvetković, had not wished to participate in such a transaction; Prince Paul believed that his country had too many Albanians as it was. Mussolini therefore acted on his own. He notified Berlin of his intentions, and the German government, having repeatedly assured its ally that it had no interests in the area, was in no position to object. The project was

---

10  L. S. Stavrianos, *The Balkans since 1453* (New York: Rinehart, 1958), p. 600.
11  Hugh Gibson, ed., *The Ciano Diaries, 1939–1943* (New York: Doubleday, 1946), p. 43.

not received favorably by the Italian king. Victor Emmanuel III saw no point in taking a risk in order to "grab four rocks." His reaction caused Mussolini to comment: "If Hitler had had to deal with a nincompoop of a king, he would never have been able to take Austria and Czechoslovakia."[12]

The Italian conquest was quickly completed. An ultimatum was delivered on March 25, 1939; its terms included the demand that an occupation by the Italian army be accepted. King Zog attempted to delay the proceedings, but, seeing the hopelessness of the situation, he fled with his family to Greece. He was not willing to become an outright Italian puppet. The Italian troops landed in the country on April 7; they encountered little resistance and suffered few casualties. Preparations for such an action had been made during the previous years, and Italy had supporters within Albania. On April 12 the Albanian assembly met and, under Italian direction, voted union with Italy; it was then dissolved. The administration was now headed by Shefqet Verlaci, whose prominent role in Albanian politics has been described previously. Albania was no longer an independent state; its army and foreign service were placed under Italian direction. On April 16 a delegation presented the crown to Victor Emmanuel III. Count Ciano commented on this last step in the full conquest of the country:

> The ceremony of offering the Albanian crown to the King of Italy takes place at the royal palace. The Albanians, who seem to be lost in the great halls of the Quirinal, have a depressed air. Verlaci especially appears depressed as he pronounces, with a tired air and without conviction, the words he has to say in offering the crown. The King answers in an uncertain and trembling voice; decidedly he is not an orator who makes any impression on an audience, and these Albanians who are a warrior mountain people look with amazement and timidity on the little man who is seated on a great gilt chair beside which stands a gigantic bronze statue of Mussolini. They cannot understand what this is all about.[13]

In view of the predominant position that Italy had previously held in Albania, the annexation caused little stir in international circles. The second chain of events arising from the German occupation of Prague, however, was of major consequence for European diplomacy and for the eventual outbreak of the war. The original justification for the policy of appeasement adopted toward the dictators by the Western states was the hope that the recognition and satisfaction of legitimate grievances would placate the Axis powers and lead eventually to peace and stability on the Continent. Neville Chamberlain, the British prime minister who stood for this program, willingly admitted

12  Gibson, *The Ciano Diaries*, p. 53.
13  Gibson, *The Ciano Diaries*, pp. 66–67.

the justice of some of the demands. He believed that the treatment of Germany previously had been "neither generous nor wise" and that, "unless this strong and virile people can be induced, in partnership with others, to improve the general lot, there will be neither peace nor progress in Europe in the things that make life worth living."[14] Even after Munich he was willing to consider further concessions if they could be accomplished in a peaceful, orderly fashion. The means by which any further changes would be carried through were of prime importance. In September 1938 Chamberlain expressed an opinion that remained the basis of his policy until the beginning of the war. "If I were convinced that any nation had made up its mind to dominate the world by fear of its force, I should feel that it must be resisted."[15]

The German destruction of Czechoslovakia violated all of the principles on which the Munich concessions had been based. The Western powers therefore proceeded to prepare to block any further German moves. Since it was obvious that German claims would next be directed against Poland, because of its large German minority, the British in March gave a unilateral guarantee to that state: "In the event of any action which clearly threatened Polish independence, and which the Polish Government accordingly considered it vital to resist with their national forces, His Majesty's Government would feel themselves bound at once to lend the Polish Government all support in their power."[16]

In April similar statements were accepted by Greece and Romania. The French government associated itself with all of these declarations. It will be noted that the guarantees were unilateral; the recipients undertook no obligations in return. These were thus not, technically speaking, alliances. In May the Western position in the Mediterranean was considerably strengthened when Britain and Turkey signed a mutual assistance pact. An even stronger agreement was concluded between them in October after the beginning of the war. Although Turkey was willing to join with France and Britain against the Axis, it refused to accept any obligations that might involve a war with Russia.

With the stiffening of the attitude of the Western powers, Hitler was faced directly with the possibility of a European war. In April 1939 the military preparations for a campaign against Poland commenced; the date for the invasion was set for September 1. At the same time, the German diplomats attempted to obtain closer ties with their allies. They wished in particular to conclude a strong military alliance with Japan. Since there was a probability that a war would break out with Britain and France, they wanted the terms

14 Keith Feiling, *The Life of Neville Chamberlain* (London: Macmillan, 1946), p. 392.

15 Arnold Wolfers, *Britain and France between Two Wars* (New York: Harcourt, Brace & Co., 1940), p. 282.

16 Statement by Chamberlain, March 31, 1939, in *Documents on International Affairs, 1939–1946* (London: Oxford University Press, 1951), I, 125–126.

of the agreement to apply to the colonial powers. Japan, however, would not accept a treaty directed against the West, but only one against the Soviet Union. The negotiations with Italy were more successful. In May a close military alliance, called the Pact of Steel, was signed by the two dictators. Its terms appeared to call for unconditional support should either signatory become involved in a war, even as an aggressor. Article III stated: "If, contrary to the wishes and hopes of the contracting parties, it should happen that one of them is involved in hostilities with another power or powers, the other contracting party will come immediately to its side as ally and support it with all its forces on land, sea and in the air."[17]

The immediate value of this alliance to Germany was, however, virtually negated by the fact that Mussolini sent a covering letter to Hitler in which he stated that Italy would not be ready to fight for three years. Thus for all practical purposes Germany had no effective allies. If Hitler attacked Poland, he could count on no outside assistance should the Western powers honor their guarantee.

Like the Germans, the Western governments were faced with major difficulties in implementing their policies. Through the guarantees to Poland, Romania, and Greece, they had made clear their intention of reacting should these states be victims of an unprovoked attack. The problem remained how to stop the German army should it move east. With the remilitarization of the Rhineland, any Allied force would face great obstacles in attempting to invade German territory. Neither the British nor the French military establishment was strong enough to prevent Germany from defeating Poland. In this situation, Soviet assistance was absolutely essential. In fact, only by facing Hitler with the inevitability of a two-front war could the Western powers hope to check further German advances or to assure a victory should war break out. Major obstacles, however, prevented close Soviet and Western cooperation. The chief hindrance was the perfectly justified apprehension felt by all of the Soviet border states concerning their powerful neighbor's intentions. In order to engage the German army, the Soviet forces would have to march through these lands. Finland, Poland, the Baltic states, and Romania were none of them willing to have a Soviet army cross their borders. They feared that they would then face political subjugation and territorial losses. All of these states held former tsarist lands, and Stalin had shown a remarkable sense of history. The conservative regimes in power were thoroughly aware of the Communist threat to their domestic systems.

Even with these obstacles, the Soviet Union was in the pleasant position of having two choices. Despite the strident anti-Communism of the Axis states, the possibility of an agreement was never entirely out of the question. In the spring of 1939 approaches from both camps were received in Moscow.

17   Text of the German–Italian Pact of Steel, May 22, 1939, in *Documents on International Affairs, 1939–1946*, I, 168–170.

In May the Soviet foreign minister Maxim Litvinov, who was pro-Western and Jewish, was replaced by Viacheslav M. Molotov. Despite the previous policy of agreement with France, the Soviet government had no particular reason to trust the West more than the Axis. The Munich agreement had been made without Russian participation. It appeared that the Western states were trying to push Germany eastward and into conflict with the Soviet Union. Thus when the discussions with the West were stalled, the Soviet leaders were willing to turn to the German alternative. The negotiations here proceeded with utmost speed. On August 14 the Soviet government accepted the German proposal of a conference in Moscow; on August 21 Stalin agreed to receive Joachim von Ribbentrop, the German foreign minister. The road was clear for a major diplomatic revolution.

## THE OUTBREAK OF THE WAR: THE PERIOD OF BALKAN NEUTRALITY

The Nazi–Soviet Pact of August 1939 is undoubtedly the most important agreement concluded in the interwar period. It laid the groundwork for World War II, and it gave a clear indication of future Soviet and German intentions. A German delegation under the leadership of Ribbentrop arrived in Moscow on August 23. The negotiations were conducted by Stalin personally for the Soviet side. There was surprisingly little difficulty in arranging the terms, despite the fact that there had been little diplomatic preparation. Two documents were signed at this time: a published nonaggression pact and a secret territorial agreement. Because of the importance of these understandings, they will be quoted at length. In the first article of the nonaggression pact the two governments obligated "themselves to desist from any act of violence, any aggressive action, and any attack on each other, either individually or jointly with other powers." Article II set the stage for the German invasion of Poland: "Should one of the High Contracting Parties become the object of belligerent action by a third power, the other High Contracting Party shall in no manner lend its support to this third power." Article III provided that the two signatories would remain in "continual contact with one another for the purpose of consulation in order to exchange information on problems affecting their common interests." Article IV was in contradiction to the secret protocol of the Anti-Comintern Pact: "Neither of the two High Contracting Parties shall participate in any grouping of powers whatsoever that is directly or indirectly aimed at the other party." Finally, the two powers agreed to adjust any future conflicts "exclusively through friendly exchange of opinion or, if necessary, through the establishment of arbitration commissions."[18]

18  The two treaties are in Raymond James Sontag and James Stuart Beddie, eds., *Nazi–Soviet Relations* (Washington, D.C.: Government Printing Office, 1948), pp. 76–78.

In the secret agreement Germany and the Soviet Union partitioned Poland and the Baltic states and arranged for the return of Bessarabia to Russian control. The exact terms were:

1 In the event of a territorial and political rearrangement in the areas belonging to the Baltic States (Finland, Estonia, Latvia, Lithuania), the northern boundary of Lithuania shall represent the boundary of the spheres of influence of Germany and the U.S.S.R. In this connection the interest of Lithuania in the Vilna area is recognized by each party.

2 In the event of a territorial and political rearrangement of the areas belonging to the Polish state the spheres of influence of Germany and the U.S.S.R. shall be bounded approximately by the line of rivers Narew, Vistula and San.

The question of whether the interests of both parties make desirable the maintenance of an independent Polish state and how such a state should be bounded can only be definitely determined in the course of further political developments.

In any event both Governments will resolve this question by means of a friendly arrangement.

3 With regard to Southeastern Europe attention is called by the Soviet side to its interest in Bessarabia. The German side declares its complete political disinterestedness in these areas.[19]

These political understandings were supplemented by economic agreements that assured to Germany the raw materials it needed to embark upon a war. German purchases included lumber, cotton, feed grain, phosphate, platinum, furs, and petroleum. In return, Germany sent machines, industrial installations, machine tools, and weapons, including airplanes, tank patterns, patents for war materials, and similar items. Since German industry was increasingly organized for war, it was easier for Germany to supply military equipment than other goods, despite the negative effect of strengthening the Russian war potential.

The pact was obviously of enormous advantage to a country determined to risk a general European war. It assured that the German army would not have to meet a major enemy on two fronts once an attack on Poland was launched. Furthermore, after the signing of the agreement the world Communist parties and their supporters turned their attacks away from the Axis and concentrated on the "imperialists" as the major disturbers of the peace. The agreement also opened great geopolitical vistas. As one Berlin paper

19   Sontag and Beddie, *Nazi–Soviet Relations*, p. 78.

wrote: "Eighty million Germans . . . and a hundred and eighty million Russians. Their union represents a combination possessing the greatest military and industrial strength in the world, and an empire which stretches over Europe and Asia, far greater than the greatest mass of territory . . . that has ever existed."[20]

The objectives of the Soviet government are not so easy to determine, since adequate documentation does not exist outside the USSR. Stalin, however, obviously did not want to be involved in the "capitalist" wars, and he certainly did not wish to be left with the main burden of meeting the German army on the Polish front, as he might have been had an agreement been made with the West. The Soviet Union, of course, received immense territorial advantages that it could never have won from France and Britain except under conditions similar to those which arose after 1941. The way for future gains was also open. It will be noted that the partition arrangements stopped at the Danube; the fate of the rest of the Balkans had yet to be settled.

On September 1 the German army invaded Poland. The British and French governments then honored the guarantee and declared war. On September 17, when the decisive German victories showed that the campaign in Poland would soon end, the Russian forces moved up to the line of demarcation of the secret treaty; the Soviet government declared that it was protecting the Ukrainian and White Russian population. The Western nations did not apply the guarantee to the Russian seizure of territory. On September 28 the German and Russian governments made a new agreement, which involved some changes in the boundary between their spheres. They then established administrations in their respective Polish zones. The Soviet authorities conducted a plebiscite and subsequently annexed their regions into the Ukrainian and White Russian Soviet republics. They next put pressure on the Baltic states and Finland. At the end of November, after encountering resistance from the Finnish government, the Soviet army attacked the country. This campaign, which proved difficult and costly, was damaging to the prestige of the Soviet military forces, even though it secured the territorial changes desired.

After the defeat of Poland a period of inaction on the battlefields followed. Then, in April 1940, the German army occupied Denmark and Norway, and in May a major offensive was commenced against France. The German victories placed a great burden on Mussolini, who remained intensely unhappy about his subordinate relationship with Berlin. He had not been consulted about the Soviet pact, and he did not like it. Using the excuse that Italy was not ready, he had not entered the war. Hitler had been angered by this lack of support. Mussolini was well aware of the weakness of his position. In

---

20 Quoted in Grigore Gafencu, *Prelude to the Russian Campaign* (London: Frederick Muller, 1945), p. 43.

October 1939 he commented to Ciano: "The Italians . . . after having heard my warlike propaganda for eighteen years, cannot understand how I can become the herald of peace, now that Europe is in flames."[21] Italy was in fact in no condition to wage a major war after the Ethiopian campaign and the intervention in the Spanish civil war. The position of neutrality, however, could not be maintained after the rapid retreat of the French army presented the possibility that the war might soon be over. If Italy did not act, it might receive little when peace was made. Mussolini thus entered the war on June 10, after the French had been decisively defeated. Italian soldiers went into combat on June 21, a day before the armistice was signed. Mussolini, wishing to extract the maximum gains from the defeated neighbor, objected strongly to the mild terms of the surrender. The German policy was far wiser; until the fighting was indeed over, it was better to follow a policy of conciliation.

The swift and devastating defeat of France was as significant for the Balkan governments as the signing of the Nazi–Soviet Pact. Both events radically changed the diplomatic balance and upset the presuppositions of previous policies. Although Greece could still hope for some assistance from Britain, the other Balkan states could not expect support from the West. Moreover, the Soviet Union had adopted a radically different policy and was in alliance with the strongest military power on the Continent. No Balkan state could hope to resist the combination of Germany and the Soviet Union, backed by Italy. After the Polish campaign the Balkan region had enjoyed a period of respite while the German armies were concentrated in the West and the Soviet Union was occupied with the Finnish, Polish, and Baltic problems. In the summer of 1940, with the Western front quiet, the Balkans became the center of attention of both the Axis and the Soviet government. The Balkan states had to decide how best to protect their interests against the pressure of the victorious great powers.

The first state to be adversely affected by the new events was Romania. From December 1938 to May 1940 the foreign minister, Grigore Gafencu, attempted to follow a policy of balance between the rival camps. He thus accepted the guarantee of France and Britain, but he maintained close commercial relations with Germany, with which a five-year trade pact was signed in March 1939. The German government agreed to assist in the expansion of Romanian agricultural production and in the construction of food-processing plants. Among other items, Romania was to acquire German armaments. The terms were favorable to Bucharest, particularly when it is considered that no alternative market existed. Since Romanian relations with the Soviet Union had always been bad, the Nazi–Soviet Pact had been an unpleasant shock. The defeat of Poland, with whom Romania was on excellent terms, was even worse. Although the two states had a mutual assistance agreement, Poland did not request its implementation. The Soviet invasion and occupation of

21  Gibson, *The Ciano Diaries*, p. 157.

Polish territories intensified Romanian fears of Soviet intentions. Inquiries in London made it clear that only under unusual circumstances would Britain honor its guarantee if the Soviet Union and not Germany threatened Romanian territory.

The French surrender and the Italian entrance into the war made the Romanian position even more dangerous. It was clear that drastic alterations were to be made in the map of Europe, and Romania was surrounded by neighbors that had claims on its territory. The first to act was the Soviet Union, which wanted to take compensation for the great German gains in the West. In the middle of June 1940 Soviet troops entered the Baltic states; puppet regimes were set up that conducted plebiscites and then requested admission into the Soviet Union. At the same time, the Soviet government informed the Germans that Bessarabia and Bukovina would also be taken. After Germany protested that Bukovina was not part of the original bargain, the Soviet diplomats agreed to limit their seizure to the northern section. The Soviet annexation was carried through in the direct and brutal manner that Italy had used in taking Albania. On June 26 an ultimatum with a twenty-four-hour time limit was delivered. When the Romanian government consulted Berlin, it was advised to accept the Soviet demands. Only a few days after the Romanian capitulation and before the authorities could arrange an orderly evacuation, the Soviet troops entered Bessarabia.

This crisis forced a reorganization of the government. In July Ion Gigurtu became prime minister, with Mihail Manoilescu as minister of foreign affairs. Since the Soviet threat seemed far more dangerous, this regime turned to Berlin for support. The British guarantee was renounced, and its replacement by a German assurance was sought. The government also moved to the right. All political parties with the exception of the official Party of the Nation were abolished. In an effort to appease the Axis camp, imprisoned members of the Iron Guard, including its leader, Horia Sima, were released. This tilt toward the German side in no way prevented further Romanian territorial losses. Both the Hungarian and the Bulgarian demands were now presented. The Romanian government had not previously adopted an adamant attitude on Dobrudja, but it was prepared to offer strong resistance to the loss of Transylvania.

Although Hungary had not entered the war on the Axis side, that state had adopted a highly revisionist policy and had shared in the division of Czechoslovakia; it now wanted Transylvania. Its army was mobilized. Since Germany wished to retain the cooperation of both Bucharest and Budapest and to avoid further complications in the area, its diplomats urged both sides to negotiate. When the discussions reached an impasse, the German government decided to impose a settlement, if necessary. After both Hungary and Romania agreed to accept arbitration, a conference was held in Vienna in August that was attended by the Romanian, Hungarian, German, and Italian foreign ministers. The Vienna Award, which divided Transylvania, was pri-

Map 9. The partition of Romania, 1940.

marily the work of Ciano and Ribbentrop. The Hungarian claims were cut down a third; Romania retained three-fifths of Transylvania, but lost the major city of Cluj. The two states agreed to an exchange of populations. In September southern Dobrudja was returned to Bulgaria.

These cessions, which involved a loss of a large percentage of the Romanian territory (see Map 9), caused enormous public indignation, especially the surrender of the Transylvanian lands. In September Charles II was forced to abdicate and leave the country; his son Michael, now nineteen, again became king. The government was dominated by General Ion Antonescu, a conservative, strongly nationalistic leader, who was to play the major role in Romanian politics until the end of the war. Formerly the Romanian military attaché in London, he admired British institutions. He had been minister of war from 1934 to 1938, when he left office after a disagreement with the king. Remaining politically active, he established links with the Iron Guard. With Antonescu at the head of the government, this party was given its first chance to exercise political power. From September 1940 to January 1941 the Guard was able to establish a "National Legionary" regime. It was the sole party in the state, and Antonescu adopted the title of *conducator* (leader), the equivalent of *duce* in Italy, *Führer* in Germany, or *Archigos* in Greece. The period of Legionary control was a disaster. The Guard embarked upon a series of violent acts against its former opponents and the Jews. Prominent men, such as the historian Nicolae Iorga and the economist Virgil Madgearu, were murdered. A condition of political anarchy reigned in the country.

Meanwhile, Antonescu, backed by the army, acted to win German support. After the partitions were accomplished, the German government did guarantee the new boundaries of the state. In order to implement this assurance, to prepare for further military actions in the East, and to protect this vital source of grain and oil, German troops moved into Romania in October; Hungary agreed to the transit of these forces. In January 1941 Antonescu met with Hitler and assured him that if war broke out between Germany and Russia, Romania would participate in the fighting. He also expressed his concern about the activities of the Iron Guard. Since the Germans could not tolerate political strife or anarchy in this strategic area, they backed Antonescu in his desire to suppress the Guard. In January a Legionary uprising took place that was crushed by the Romanian army with the assistance of the German forces. Antonescu then organized a cabinet composed of army officers and technicians. Romania was firmly in the German camp; Hitler admired Antonescu's "glowing fanaticism."

Despite the spectacular German victory over France, the fighting was far from over. In the summer of 1940 the German leadership was faced with major decisions. Britain was still at war; an invasion of that island was obviously dangerous with the Soviet Union at the rear. There was no mutual trust between Berlin and Moscow, despite their alliance. Although Italy was a belligerent, its armies had yet to play a part on the battlefields. With Britain now judged the main target, Hitler wished to induce Franco to bring Spain into the war, so that he might use the military resources of his two fellow dictators to clear the British forces out of the Mediterranean and North Africa. Spain was to aid in taking Gibraltar; Italy was to advance against the British North African strongholds. The very last action that the German command wished to inaugurate was a disturbance of the status quo in the Balkans. Relations with the Soviet Union were declining, and the German government wanted no more complications in Eastern Europe.

Mussolini, however, had other intentions. He remained disconsolate about his role in the war and the lack of glorious Italian achievements. Hitler's attitude toward him also made him very angry. Not only was the senior dictator not asked for advice, but he was not even informed in advance of the German moves. The final blow was the German military occupation of Romania, an event that Mussolini evidently heard about on the radio. Thoroughly enraged, he told Ciano on October 12:

Hitler always faces me with a *fait accompli*. This time I am going to pay him back in his own coin. He will find out from the papers that I have occupied Greece. In this way the equilibrium will be re-established . . . I shall send in my resignation as an Italian if anyone objects to our fighting the Greeks."

In Ciano's judgment, such an undertaking would be "useful and easy."[22]

Since the outbreak of the war the Greek government, like that of the other Balkan states, had attempted to maintain a policy of neutrality. Like Romania, Greece had accepted a guarantee from Britain and France, but it had close trade ties with Berlin. The Italian occupation of Albania had worsened the Greek strategic position considerably; both the Albanian and the Bulgarian frontiers had to be watched. After the French defeat the situation became even more precarious. It was clear that Britain did not have sufficient military forces to spare to aid Greece. Although relations with Yugoslavia and Turkey were still satisfactory, these states in the past had made it clear that they would not assume obligations against a great power.

In preparation for an attack the Italian government and press commenced a press campaign directed in particular against Greece's alleged mistreatment of its Albanian population. Finding itself the object of these accusations and of other provocations, the Greek government turned to Berlin. As a result, and as had happened repeatedly since the beginning of the war, the German diplomats once again warned the Italians not to act in the Balkans, but they seem to have regarded this as another routine precautionary measure. They were certainly surprised by the Italian attack on Greece. On October 28 Hitler arrived in Florence for a previously scheduled meeting. There Mussolini informed him that the campaign had commenced only a few hours before. The Italian dictator completely succeeded in his desire to stun his partner.

Meanwhile, the Greek government had taken a courageous decision. When delivering an ultimatum to Athens before the declaration of war, the Italian leaders had expected the Greeks either to surrender at once or to collapse after a short war. Not only did Metaxas stand firm and reject the Italian demands, but the Greek army put up a surprising resistance. In fact, one month after the invasion began, the last Italian soldier had been driven from Greece, and the Greek army was fighting in Albania. The Greek military adopted intelligent tactics and exploited the rugged mountain terrain. The Italian army, with its heavy mechanized equipment, was effective only in the valleys. The Greek troops remained in command of the heights, and they had the advantage of mobility. The weather was also unusually bad for the time of the year, and the Italian operations soon bogged down in rain, snow, and mud. The Greek army was able to make use of the large amounts of war matériel that its enemy abandoned while retreating.

---

22  Gibson, *The Ciano Diaries*, p. 300.

Although no other Balkan state openly joined Greece in the fighting, Turkey did give diplomatic assistance by warning Sofia that if Bulgaria entered the war, it would also intervene. This action, which checked Bulgaria, meant that Greece could move troops from the Macedonian to the Albanian front. More important, however, was the aid received from Britain. Metaxas did not want to provoke a German intervention; he wished only to repel the Italian invasion. He was aware that once a British army arrived in Greece, this force would constitute a grave danger to Germany. He therefore requested only air and naval assistance, not an expeditionary force. On November 11, in their major action in support of Greece, British planes, operating from an aircraft carrier, succeeded in sinking half of the Italian fleet anchored in the port of Taranto. Metaxas wanted to avoid using not only a British force, but also Albanian aid. Zog was at this time in London, and with British assistance some cooperative action might have been organized. Nevertheless, the Greek government maintained its previous hostile attitude toward the Albanian national objectives.

Metaxas thus carried through a highly rational policy. Although he believed that the West would win in the end and that Germany and Russia would eventually fight, he had attempted to keep his country out of a war from which little could be gained. However, when Italy attacked, he organized a strong resistance. He had no illusions that Greece could defeat the Axis. A traditional nationalist, he argued that: "Greece is not fighting for victory. She is fighting for glory, and for honor. She has a debt to herself to remain worthy of her history . . . There are times in which a nation, if it wishes to remain great, gains by being able to fight, even if it has no hope of victory."[23]

Despite the fact that the Greek army was able to defend its own territory, it was unable to force the Italians out of Albania. During this entire period Metaxas was very careful about his relations with Germany; Hitler appears to have admired the Greek resistance. In January 1941, however, Metaxas died and was replaced by Alexander Koryzis. To support its own strategic interests in the Mediterranean and Africa, the British government wanted to send an expeditionary force; it therefore assured the Greek government of far more assistance than it could actually deliver. The new premier changed the Greek policy and welcomed the British army. Only 58,000 of the promised 100,000 British troops ever arrived, and only part of the war matériel was delivered. Of the soldiers sent, only 35,000 were combat troops. However, the arrival of the British force had a deadly significance for the German war plans. British aircraft based in Greece could bomb the oil fields at Ploeşti and interrupt German supply lines. A British stronghold on the Continent had great implications for general Mediterranean and North African strategy.

---

23  Quoted in Bobby John Macris, "The Foreign Policy of the Metaxas Regime, 1936–1941" (Ph.D. diss., Indiana University, 1979), p. 343.

Although one German ally had thus opened an entirely new front, another friend, Japan, had finally consented to enter into a tighter alignment. With the major opponent identified as Britain, the German diplomats could well use the support of this power against the British Empire and as a check on the United States. In contrast to its previous attitude, the Japanese government was now willing to undertake obligations against these states. Therefore, in September 1940, Germany, Italy, and Japan signed the Tripartite Pact. In this agreement the participants defined their spheres of influence, with Japan recognizing "the leadership of Germany and Italy in the establishment of a new order in Europe," while these powers agreed to respect Japan's role in "the establishment of a new order in Greater East Asia." The pact was directed primarily against the United States. Article III stated that the signatories would "assist one another with all political, economic and military means when one of the three contracting powers is attacked by a power at present not involved in the European war or in the Chinese-Japanese conflict," but Article V specifically exempted the Soviet Union from the application of this section.[24] The Tripartite Pact henceforth replaced the Anti-Comintern Pact as the center of the Axis alliance system.

Meanwhile, relations between Russia and Germany had begun to deteriorate seriously. At first the partnership had functioned well. In February 1940 the two powers signed a commercial treaty in which the German government was able to secure most of its desires. Particularly advantageous was the Soviet representatives' agreement that German deliveries could lag considerably behind their own. In the first year of the twenty-seven-month duration of the agreement the Soviet deliveries were to include, among other items, food and raw materials essential to the German war effort, for instance:

> 1,000,000 tons of grain for cattle, and of legumes, in the
> amount of 120 million Reichsmarks
> 900,000 tons of mineral oil in the amount of approximately
> 115 million Reichsmarks
> 100,000 tons of cotton in the amount of approximately 90
> million Reichsmarks
> 500,000 tons of phosphates
> 100,000 tons of chrome ores
> 500,000 tons of iron ore
> 300,000 tons of scrap iron and pig iron
> 2,400 kg. of platinum [25]

The first notable friction occurred in the summer of 1940. The sudden

24  Text of the Tripartite Pact, September 27, 1940, in *Documents on International Affairs, 1939–1946*, II, 81, 82.

25  Foreign Office memorandum signed by Schnurre on the German–Soviet commercial agreement of February 11, 1940, in Sontag and Beddie, *Nazi–Soviet Relations*, pp. 131–134.

collapse of France appears to have surprised the Soviet government, which, as we have seen, moved swiftly to collect its part of the bargain. If Britain had made peace, the Soviet Union would have been isolated. In addition, the Soviet diplomats made clear their interest in the Danubian area and the Balkans. At the time of the Vienna Award, Molotov protested the lack of a prior agreement and asserted that Article III of the 1939 pact had been violated. In reply, the German government denied that a matter of common interest had been involved, arguing that "after the settlement of the Bessarabian question a like interest in the rest of Romanian territory on the part of the Soviet Union is not evident and has not been expressed to the Government of the Reich, either at the Moscow settlement or later."[26] The Soviet government showed a similar concern over the administration of the Danube River and the commissions that regulated the waterway. It first proposed that a single body be established for the entire river, an action that would have extended Soviet influence deep into Central Europe. After the annexation of Bessarabia, of course, the Soviet borders reached this river.

The divergences between the Soviet and the German positions became particularly clear when Molotov visited Berlin in November 1940. The Soviet government had been upset by the signing of the Tripartite Pact; only a day's notice of the event had been given to Moscow. In reply to its objections, Hitler proposed that the Soviet Union adhere to the agreement and participate in the future division of the British Empire. A sphere of influence to the south, in the direction of the Persian Gulf and the Arabian Sea, was offered, with the aim of directing Soviet attention away from the Danube and the Balkans. Molotov, taking an extremely practical attitude, was not to be diverted by airy dreams of future empire. He was perfectly willing to accept the German offer, but he was more interested in settling certain misunderstandings that had arisen. He thus wished to learn the exact status of the German relations with Finland, the significance of the Tripartite Pact, and the extent of the guarantee to Romania. On this last question, Molotov pointed out that the Soviet Union still had claims to southern Bukovina.

From the German viewpoint, however, the most dangerous aspect of the conversations lay in the foreign minister's new proposals concerning the Balkans. The Soviet government demanded not only the right of free passage through the Turkish Straits, but also bases in the region. In addition, it wanted to give a guarantee to Bulgaria similar to that which Germany and Italy had provided for Romania. In other words, Stalin was attempting to implement many of the fundamental aspects of previous tsarist policy. The Soviet government, despite the fact that it had in the 1920s and 1930s played no important role in Balkan affairs, thus made it clear that it intended henceforth to wield a major influence in the peninsula. It was not to be diverted to the

---

26  Ribbentrop to Schulenburg, Berlin, September 3, 1940, in Sontag and Beddie, *Nazi–Soviet Relations*, pp. 181–183.

Indian Ocean, but insisted on being consulted on all matters relating to the Balkan and East European area.

On November 26 Germany received the reply to its suggestion that the Soviet Union adhere to the Tripartite Pact. The Soviet government agreed to join if four main conditions were met. The first concerned the withdrawal of the German troops that were at that time in Finland; the fourth dealt with the Japanese coal and oil rights in northern Sakhalin. The second and third stated that the agreement would be signed

> 2 Provided that within the next few months the security of the So-
> viet Union in the Straits is assured by the conclusion of a mutual
> assistance pact between the Soviet Union and Bulgaria, which
> geographically is situated inside the security zone of the Black Sea
> boundaries of the Soviet Union, and by the establishment of a
> base for land and naval forces of the U.S.S.R. within range of the
> Bosphorus and the Dardanelles by means of a long-term lease.
>
> 3 Provided that the area south of Batum and Baku in the general
> direction of the Persian Gulf is recognized as the center of the
> aspirations of the Soviet Union.

The Soviet government also proposed a secret protocol that would

> guarantee a base for light naval and land forces of the U.S.S.R. on
> the Bosphorus and the Dardanelles by means of a long-term lease,
> including – in case Turkey declares herself willing to join the Four
> Power Pact – a guarantee of the independence and of the territory
> of Turkey by the three countries named.
>
> This protocol should provide that in case Turkey refused to join
> the Four Powers, Germany, Italy and the Soviet Union agree to work
> out and to carry through the required military and diplomatic mea-
> sures.[27]

An official German reply to this message was never sent. Instead, plans were expedited for a campaign against the Soviet Union and in the Balkans. Already in the summer of 1940 Hitler had decided that it would be necessary to defeat Russia before an invasion of Britain could be undertaken. He wished to commence the action in May 1941, and he evidently expected a victory within five months. After the failure of the negotiations with Moscow and the presentation of the Soviet demands, Hitler issued two directives. The first, number 20, dated December 13 and called Operation Marita, provided

27 Schulenburg to the German Foreign Office, Moscow, November 26, 1940, in Sontag and Beddie, *Nazi–Soviet Relations*, pp. 258, 259.

for the invasion of Greece. The second, directive 21, issued on December 18, set the basis for Operation Barbarossa and stated: "The German Armed Forces must be prepared *to crush Soviet Russia in a quick campaign* . . . even before the conclusion of the war against England."[28]

With this decision taken, the German diplomats proceeded to develop the Tripartite Pact as an anti-Soviet coalition, although, as we have seen, it had originally been designed as an alliance against Britain and the United States. Hungary, Slovakia, and Romania joined at once. The allegiance of Bulgaria, Yugoslavia, and Turkey, however, was desired before the attack on Greece was undertaken. The attitude of Bulgaria was particularly important, since the German plans called for the launching of the invasion through this country. Yugoslavia was expected to remain neutral.

The Bulgarian reaction was, however, strongly influenced by the dismal performance of the Italian troops in Greece. At the beginning of the war Boris III had adopted a policy of neutrality. Bulgarian interests, unlike those of the other Balkan states, were favorably affected by the Nazi–Soviet Pact, since the agreement united the two powers having a primary position in the country. The last war had been fought in alliance with Germany. There was also a strong German cultural influence; half of the Bulgarian professors had studied in Germany, and German works accounted for the majority of the foreign books in the Sofia library.[29] The past ties with tsarist Russia have been discussed previously. The Soviet interests in Bulgaria were aided by the presence of a strong Communist element in the political system. It will be remembered that, after the Communist Party was outlawed in 1924, it reappeared as the Bulgarian Workers' Party. Operating under close Comintern supervision, party members had been shocked by the Nazi–Soviet Pact, but thereafter, following central directives, they concentrated their major attacks on the Western powers. In this period Soviet books, films, and newspapers entered Bulgaria with less hindrance than previously. Soviet concern with Bulgarian events was demonstrated immediately after the war started. In September 1939 the Soviet government offered to conclude a pact of friendship and mutual assistance; Boris refused on the basis that Bulgaria at this time was a part of no diplomatic system and had not signed similar treaties with other powers.

In the winter of 1939–1940 new elections were held. As before, there was considerable police interference, and the government won all but twenty seats in the assembly. In February Bogdan Filov became premier, with Ivan Popov as foreign minister. A former professor of archaeology, Filov had been rector of the University of Sofia and president of the Bulgarian Academy of Sci-

---

28  Directive No. 21: Operation Barbarossa, December 18, 1940, in Sontag and Beddie, *Nazi–Soviet Relations*, pp. 260–264.

29  Marshall Lee Miller, *Bulgaria during the Second World War* (Stanford, Calif.: Stanford University Press, 1975), p. 6.

ences. Germanophile in sentiment, he favored cooperation with the Axis. Boris, however, remained in full control of the government, and he determined policy.

As long as Germany and the Soviet Union acted together, the Bulgarian government faced no real choices. The influence of the West had never been strong in the country in comparison to that of Russia or Germany. Even after the fall of France, the situation remained favorable. When the Soviet Union took Bessarabia, tacit Axis approval was given to the Bulgarian and Hungarian claims against Romania. Under German prodding, the Romanian government agreed to cede to Bulgaria the southern part of Dobrudja, which had been taken after the Second Balkan War. Bulgaria regained this territory in September 1940 as a result of negotiations between the two Balkan states. The annexation followed the principle of self-determination: in 1930 the ethnic composition of the area was 38 percent Bulgarian, 21 percent Romanian, and 34 percent Turkish.

Although the Axis gained the credit with public opinion for this action, the Bulgarian government hesitated to join the German camp openly. When Hitler spoke with Boris in November about adhering to the Tripartite Pact, the king attempted to delay any decision. He argued that Bulgaria was not prepared for war and that he feared the Turkish and Soviet reaction. Bulgaria would sign later. At this time, the Soviet government again pressed its desire for the conclusion of a mutual assistance pact. In November 1940 Arkadi I. Sobolev arrived in Sofia on a special mission. In return for an agreement, he offered Bulgaria lands in Thrace that were in Turkish and Greek possession. He made no objections to Bulgaria's joining the Tripartite Pact, declaring that the Soviet Union might also sign. At first, Boris was able to reject both the German and the Soviet approaches. He excused his failure to join the Axis by reiterating the possible Turkish reaction and Bulgarian public opinion. The Italian defeat in Greece, however, also influenced his decision.

Although Bulgaria did not sign the Tripartite Pact, the government did not oppose the entrance of small numbers of German troops; their presence was, however, publicly denied. In December several thousand soldiers, mostly in civilian clothes, arrived with the task of preparing for the attack on Greece. The Soviet government, of course, learned of the action at once. This gradual occupation of a region that it considered as within its sphere drew a strong protest. In January 1941 a note was delivered to Berlin emphasizing that Bulgaria was part of the "security zone of the U.S.S.R" and that "the appearance of any foreign armed forces on the territory of Bulgaria and of the Straits" would be regarded as "a violation of the security interests of the U.S.S.R."[30] The Bulgarian Communists were now supporting a policy of strict neutrality and the avoidance of war.

---

30 Weizsäcker memorandum to Ribbentrop, Berlin, January 17, 1941, in Sontag and Beddie, *Nazi–Soviet Relations*, pp. 268, 269.

Despite the obvious Soviet disapproval, the Bulgarian government continued to strengthen its ties with the Axis. Like Hungary, Bulgaria was a strongly revisionist country. Changes in its frontiers were more likely to be achieved in agreement with Germany than with any alternate available ally. The Bulgarian position was made much easier when in February 1941 the government signed a nonaggression pact with Turkey; Bulgaria would no longer need to fear an attack from this direction should war break out with Greece. In the same month an agreement on military passage that did not obligate Bulgaria to fight was signed with Germany. On March 1 the final step was taken, and Bulgaria finally adhered to the Tripartite Pact. In return for the signature, an outlet on the Aegean between the Struma and Maritsa rivers was assured. The treaty was accepted by the assembly by a vote of 140 to 20, but there was absolutely no enthusiasm about the new alliance. As could be expected, the Soviet government protested at once. Bulgaria broke relations with Britain in this same month. Although his country was still not at war, Boris III had chosen the Axis camp.

In February 1941, with the entrance of British troops into Greece, Hitler took the final decision to implement Operation Marita. However, before this campaign could be launched, he had to be absolutely certain of the Yugoslav attitude. Despite the fact that Yugoslavia was in the Italian sphere, the German government carried the main burden of the negotiations. Prince Paul and his ministers were asked to join the Tripartite Pact, and they were informed about the intended campaigns against the Soviet Union and Greece. In return for the signing of the agreement, they were offered the port of Thessaloniki. The country could remain neutral; it would not have to participate in the fighting, or even allow a passage of the German military forces.

The German demands placed the Yugoslav leaders in a very difficult position. Although they were in touch with the British, Greek, and Turkish governments, it was obvious that no assistance could be won from them. Formal diplomatic relations had finally been established with the Soviet Union in 1940, but there was little hope of effective assistance from this state. A refusal to sign the agreement would obviously lead to war, and the military aspects of the problem were grim indeed. Yugoslavia could not defeat Germany alone; the Yugoslav guns and munitions were of German origin, so replacements could not be obtained. Faced with these unpleasant alternatives, the Yugoslav diplomats, like their Bulgarian counterparts, attempted to win time. They proposed the substitution of a simple nonaggression pact for the more compromising Tripartite agreement. The German government, however, remained adamant, insisting on an outright Yugoslav adherence to the Axis camp. Some concessions were offered. When objections were made to Article III of the treaty, which might have obligated Yugoslavia to fight the United States or perhaps even Russia, the Germans agreed not to insist upon this stipulation.

In a meeting held on March 21 the Yugoslav leaders discussed the possible alternatives. It appeared clear that either the pact had to be signed or the country would face a war that it could not win. The ministry then voted sixteen to three to accept; Cvetković and Cincar-Marković left for Vienna to conclude the agreement. The document, dated March 25, had both public and secret sections. In the published text Yugoslavia adhered to the pact, and the Axis powers agreed that they would not ask for the passage of troops through Yugoslav territory. In the secret sections Germany and Italy promised not to demand Yugoslav participation in the war despite the wording of Article III, and the assurance was given that the country would receive territorial advantages – that is, Thessaloniki – in the peace settlement.

After the announcement of the signing of the agreement there was much excitement in the country. Rumors circulated concerning the extent of the secret arrangements and the obligations that had been assumed. On the night of March 27 a group of officers, led by General Dušan Simović, took over the government. The conspirators declared the seventeen-year-old Peter to be of age and formed a government. Prince Paul was at the time on a train bound northward. When he heard the news, he returned to Belgrade and resigned. General Simović became premier, but many of the former ministers, including Maček, remained. The foreign minister was Momčilo Ninčić, who favored an agreement with Germany. Once in control, the new regime announced that it would accept all of the previous state obligations, including the Tripartite Pact.

Like all revolutionary coalitions, the participants in this government disagreed on the course that they should take. Simović, whose attitude was much like that of Metaxas, gave a speech to his ministers in which "he recalled page after page of Serbian history. He saluted the bones of Serbia's militantly heroic ancestors, the battle of Kosovo, the legendary princes of early Serbia, and Serbia's epic struggle against the Turks." Maček, who wished the maintenance of peace, replied that "they could not develop a sound national policy by stirring up strong emotions."[31] The majority of the ministers had a similar attitude; they did not want to provoke a German attack.

Despite the Yugoslav hesitations, Hitler made up his mind as soon as the news came from Belgrade. Demonstrations were taking place in Belgrade that were clearly directed against the pact. Hitler decided to invade the country no matter what policy the new government adopted. The plans for Operation Marita were thus altered to include Yugoslavia. The diplomatic preparations for the conquest then commenced. The Hungarian, Romanian, and Bulgarian governments were all approached. Since Yugoslav lands could now be partitioned, the territorial demands of these states could be satisfied. The Bulgarians were told, for instance, that "*this had settled the question of Mace-*

---

31  Dragiša N. Ristić, *Yugoslavia's Revolution of 1941* (University Park: Pennsylvania State University Press, 1966), pp. 118, 119.

*donia."*[32] During the negotiations the Hungarian prime minister, Pál Teleki, shot himself rather than participate in the action; Hungary had signed a friendship treaty with Yugoslavia in the previous December.

In planning the invasion the German command expected to meet the major resistance in Serbia. Croatia and Slovenia were not to be bombed; instead, attempts were made to gain Croatian collaboration. On April 3 Maček received a representative from Ribbentrop offering assistance in separating Croatia from Yugoslavia. When the Peasant Party leader refused, German support went to the Ustaša movement. Indeed, immediately after the arrival of the German army in Zagreb, an independent Croatian state was proclaimed on April 10 and a Ustaša regime installed.

The campaign commenced on April 6, with the main burden carried by the German and Italian forces. Hungarian troops entered the Vojvodina, and later, after the fighting was over, Bulgarian soldiers took over occupation duties in Macedonia and Thrace. The Yugoslav army collapsed with a rapidity that surprised even the German command. Its main forces had been concentrated on the border; when these were defeated, there was little possibility of further resistance. The original plan of a retreat to Thessaloniki and a possible evacuation, as had happened in World War I, was thwarted by the fact that the main German thrust came from Bulgaria, so that the avenues of escape were cut off. In addition, the Croatian and Slovene units often put up little if any resistance. Serbia thus paid the price for the bitter national conflicts that had continued since 1918. On April 14 and 15 the king and most of the government left for Greece. An armistice was signed in Belgrade on April 17.

The Yugoslav resistance in fact weakened the Greek defenses. Lacking the necessary money for a complete defensive system, the Greek government had concentrated on fortifying the border with Bulgaria. The Vardar valley was thus left unprotected, and the German troops swept through this open doorway. On April 18 the Greek premier, Koryzis, committed suicide and was succeeded by Emmanuel Tsouderos, who attempted to continue fighting. An armistice was signed, however, by General George Tsolakoglou on April 20, without the authorization of the government. The British Expeditionary Force was quickly evacuated. By this time the Bulgarian army had gone into action. Relations with Yugoslavia were broken on April 15, and Skopje was occupied on April 19. After the conclusion of the campaign on the peninsula, German parachute troops in May captured Crete.

Meanwhile, the preparations for Operation Barbarossa continued. Although relations between Berlin and Moscow were still amicable on the surface, signs of disagreement between the two states multiplied. On April 5, after receiving news of the Belgrade coup, Stalin signed a nonaggression pact with the Yugoslav representative in Moscow, the principal significance of which

32  Ristić; *Yugoslavia's Revolution of 1941*, p. 123.

was its symbolic assertion of Soviet approval of Yugoslav resistance. On April 13, in an action that was very disadvantageous to Germany, Japan and the Soviet Union signed a nonaggression pact. This document allowed the Soviet government to turn its major attention to the West, and Japan to proceed with its plans of expansion at the expense of Britain and the United States.

Despite this setback, Germany secured the assistance of its other allies. Hitler sought the active cooperation of Finland and Romania in the invasion of the Soviet Union. On June 12 Antonescu was informed of the plans in detail; the Romanian army was then mobilized. On June 18 the German position in the Balkans was strengthened when a nonaggression pact was signed with Turkey that assured its continued neutrality. Italian participation in the attack on Russia was not requested; Italy was to concentrate its efforts in the Mediterranean theater.

Operation Barbarossa began on June 22, and Italy and Romania declared war on the Soviet Union on that date. Slovakia joined the next day, with Finland following on June 24 and Hungary on June 27. Bulgaria, because of the pro-Russian attitude of its people, was not required to act.

By the summer of 1941 the war had thus engulfed the Balkan peninsula. All of the states were involved. Albania, Greece, and Yugoslavia were under enemy occupation. Bulgaria was at war with Yugoslavia and Greece and in occupation of Macedonia and Thrace. Romania was fighting with Germany against the Soviet Union. The policy of neutrality adopted by the states in 1939 had thus proved impossible to maintain. As in the previous periods of European crisis, the strategic position of the peninsula made its domination a major prize in the struggle of the great powers.

## CONCLUSION

With the involvement of the entire peninsula in the war, the summer of 1941 marks the end of a major epoch in Balkan history. With the exception of Greece, all of the states were to emerge from this new catastrophe with different political institutions and another orientation in foreign policy. At this point it might be well to review the conditions in these nations to this point. As has been emphasized previously, most accounts of Balkan history, particularly of the internal developments, are uniformly critical. Too often the worst in the Balkans is compared with the best in the Western industrial countries. The failings of Balkan administration are contrasted with the alleged successes of wealthy and strong nations. Certainly a better comparison might be made with other similar regions – that is, not with Britain, Belgium, Denmark, or Holland, but with Spain and Portugal, which were Mediterranean countries with many problems in common with the Balkan States.

Even in comparison with the industrial West, the internal situation in the Balkans was not completely bleak. In this section the problem of the minorities has been discussed – for instance, the undoubted discrimination against

Transylvanian Romanians under Hungarian administration or against Croatians and Albanians in a Serbian-dominated state. Yet in a sense this pattern was repeated throughout the world. The record of Britain and France in their colonial domains is certainly no better. When France acquired Alsace-Lorraine in 1918, it instituted the principle of a centralized administration and oppressive language laws that we have seen previously in Hungary and elsewhere. In a region where the majority of the population was German-speaking, the French insisted that the language of education and administration should be exclusively French. Woodrow Wilson, without apparent consciousness of hypocrisy, could attack other nations for violations of self-determination when strict codes of segregation were applied in the southern states of his own nation. It is not fair to judge Balkan developments according to standards set by Western liberal intellectuals, which were in fact applied uniformly in no region of the world.

In their domestic political life, as we have seen, all of the Balkan states had authoritarian regimes in the 1930s. Previously, the governments had attempted to adopt Western institutions; this development was the result of a deliberate choice by the national leaders and by the European great powers who set up the first regimes. In the nineteenth century the preferred pattern was that of constitutional monarchy. Representative institutions and a centralized administration were thus introduced. The local political parties, usually called Liberal, Conservative, Radical, Progressive, and so on, were in many ways similar to their Western counterparts. After World War I, Communist and peasant parties assumed more importance; they were followed in the 1930s by factions with a more conservative orientation, although only Romania's Iron Guard had a truly fascist ideology. In general, throughout this entire period, no matter what the political theory being implemented was, the administrations and the politicians represented the interests primarily of the narrow social group that ran the state, which was composed of government officials, army officers, merchants, industrialists, large landowners, businessmen, and those in professions, such as the lawyers, doctors, and teachers, who had advanced educations. This group represented at the most 10 percent of the population. Despite the fierce competition among the political parties, the majority rested on a single base; there were few real ideological differences. The issue at the polls was who should control the government and the power and the spoils that went with it. Even the Communist, socialist, and agrarian parties were run by intellectuals. The peasant parties tended to represent the views of the more prosperous and not of the great impoverished majority. The Communists, of course, carried out the instructions, and were the tool, of the Soviet government working through the Comintern.

Although the failure to guarantee civil liberties may have been the most criticized aspect of the Balkan political systems, it is perhaps the corrupt, centralized administrations that deserve the major condemnation. In the nineteenth century, as we have seen, a centralized bureaucracy was regarded as the most modern and efficient way to run a state. The institution, however, did not transplant well into the Balkans, where a decentralized community and millet organization had previously been in effect. The necessity of referring all decisions, great and small, to the capital and of deferring to local administrators who were appointed by and who represented the central government caused much animosity and tension. The system also placed too much strain on the central authority. When it weakened or became corrupt, the entire state suffered. These regimes also made very difficult the amalgamation of new areas with other political traditions, such as Transylvania into the Regat or Macedonia into Greece, and centralization, of course, made particularly complicated the unification of developed regions, such as Slovenia and Croatia, with more primitive ones, in this case Serbia.

In this period the Balkan peninsula was considered the poorest and most backward region in Europe, although this judgment may in fact be unfair. The main economic problem of the entire peninsula was the impoverished condition of the peasantry, who constituted 80 percent of the population of the 16 million Romanians and 7 million Bulgarians; 75 percent of the 16 million Yugoslavs; 60 percent of the 7 million Greeks; and 90 percent of the 1 million Albanians.[33] The worst conditions were experienced by the small or dwarf landowner. In the 1930s, it has been estimated, 62 percent of the Bulgarian farms, 68 percent of the Yugoslav, and 80 percent of the Romanian were under 12.5 acres (5 hectares) in size.[34] Five acres for each member of the family were regarded as necessary for subsistence. The situation was made worse by the fact that the peasants often did not work consolidated holdings, but only scattered strips. Although these lands were difficult to cultivate, the system had been favored as a form of crop insurance and a way of ensuring a reasonably equitable distribution of the land.

As we have seen, the peasant's answer to his major problems was the acquisition of more land; reform had meant to him primarily the division of the great estates, an action that was largely accomplished after World War I. With the rise in the population and the repeated subdivision of the individual plots, there were soon simply far too many people for the land available. In 1930, 61.5 percent of Yugoslavia's rural population, 53 percent of Bulgaria's, 51.4 percent of Romania's, and 50.3 percent of Greece's were classified as underemployed.[35] This excess was itself a block to further improvements. Peasants with small holdings did not have the money to buy farm machinery or to introduce the modern techniques necessary for intensive cultivation; without these their yields remained very low and they had no means of improving

33   Robert Lee Wolff, *The Balkans in Our Time* (New York: Norton, 1978), p. 159.
34   Wolff, *The Balkans in Our Time*, p. 165.
35   Stavrianos, *The Balkans since 1453*, p. 595.

their conditions. The average Balkan peasant grew food for only 1.5 persons at a time when the Western European average was 1 for 4.

The Balkan peasant family not only had to support itself, but had to pay taxes and buy a few indispensable items, such as salt, matches, and some clothing and household goods that it could not itself produce. The tragedy for this class was the fact that although it had to carry the major weight of the state taxes and produce the recruits for the army, it received few benefits from state services. Most Balkan governments hesitated to institute large income taxes; instead, they placed the greatest tax burden on articles of consumption, such as shoes, salt, sugar, tobacco, fertilizers, textiles, and imported agricultural implements, all items the peasant bought. It has been estimated that income taxes provided from 19 to 25 percent of the government budgets, but taxes on these consumer goods from 55 to 65 percent.[36]

The plight of the peasant was recognized; the problem was how to relieve his conditions, given the situation of the time. The peasant solution had been to take out loans or to send members of the family out to do seasonal labor. Since agricultural credit was not easily available on fair terms, the peasants had been the victims of usurers and often had not been able to pay off their debts. Emigration had been a common means of relieving the local population pressure. After World War I, this alternative was no longer so easily available; the United States, the best outlet for these people, instituted strict immigration quotas that were prejudicial to Balkan nationals. Since it has been estimated that 400,000 people a year would have had to leave to meet the problem of overpopulation, emigration was in general not a practical solution.[37]

In Western Europe the excess agricultural population had provided workers for the industrial economies. Although all the Balkan states wished to industrialize, this action was not easily accomplished. The main problems here have been discussed previously: the lack of capital, natural resources, and a skilled managerial or working class. Efforts in this direction had, nevertheless, been made, particularly in Romania. Of necessity great reliance had to be placed on foreign loans and investments and on outside advisers and technicians. Before World War II only a small section of the population was employed in this sector of the economy; the figures are around 100,000 for Bulgaria, 289,000 for Romania, and 385,000 for Yugoslavia.

The situation in the countryside became even worse when, as a consequence of the Great Depression, the prices of agricultural goods fell even faster and further than those of industrial products. The governments were not prepared to handle the crisis. Moreover, Balkan bureaucrats were not agricultural experts. Most of those holding high office had benefited from a

36  Stavrianos, *The Balkans since 1453*, p. 599.
37  Wolff, *The Balkans in Our Time*, p. 179.

higher education, but they had followed a standard classical curriculum. Law, not agronomy, was regarded as the proper background for a career in the civil service. Moreover, the institutions of the representative government that had been adopted in the past did not provide the means for a massive intrusion in the life of the average citizen. Liberal theory was in strong contradiction to such practices. Yet without state intervention on a large scale very little could be accomplished. The peasants required irrigation projects and better transportation facilities so that they could market their crops where they could best be sold. They wanted financial assistance to improve their agricultural methods and to buy machines. In addition, they needed some sort of central guidance so that they could diversify their production and emphasize those crops which were in demand abroad. Some measures were taken in this direction when German orders and investments encouraged the growing of specialty crops like sunflowers, tobacco, sugar beets, and soya beans. Last, but equally important, the peasantry required an educational system that would enable them to enter into the modern world. At the beginning of World War II the figures for illiteracy were 27 percent for Greece, 32 percent for Bulgaria, 40 percent for Yugoslavia, 50 percent for Romania, and 85 percent for Albania.[38]

Of course, one of the major hindrances to government activity in aid of any section of the population after World War I was the continuing need to maintain a high level of military preparedness and an active foreign policy. Although a period of relative respite occurred in the 1920s, the next decade was a period of recurrent crises in foreign relations. We have seen how the dissolution of the Ottoman and Habsburg empires and the fall of the tsarist regime in Russia did little to lessen the tensions in the area. The French alliance system perpetuated the previous conflicts, although in another form. The subsequent rise in power of Fascist Italy, Nazi Germany, and Communist Russia revived many of the issues of the Eastern Question. All of the Balkan governments had to follow these developments with care and, certainly in the years immediately preceding their involvement in World War II, to give priority to external rather than internal problems. They had to choose, as the current saying went, guns over butter.

In looking back over the developments in the peninsula since the eighteenth century, it is obvious that the greatest single force in shaping the political life of the Balkan people was the national idea. By 1941 this principle had developed stronger negative than positive features. Its implementation had indeed resulted in the formation of the national states of Albania, Bulgaria, Greece, and Romania, but it had torn Yugoslavia apart. Certainly the most interesting development in the interwar years in this respect was the fate of the Yugoslav concept. Despite the hopes and beliefs of a generation of intellectuals and students – mostly, it is true, constituting a small minority

38   Stavrianos, *The Balkans since 1453*, p. 606.

among the Croats, Serbs, and Slovenes – a Yugoslav nationality had not come into existence. Serbian centralist policies had instead created feelings of enormous bitterness and hostility that would result in a series of incredible wartime atrocities.

As we have seen, Balkan passions were deeply involved in the question of the control of lands that were claimed on a historic or national basis. All of the states had territorial disputes with their neighbors. The issue of Macedonia among Bulgaria, Greece, and Yugoslavia and that of Transylvania between Hungary and Romania were perhaps the most serious, but there were also conflicts over Thrace, Epirus, Dobrudja, Bessarabia, Bukovina, Dalmatia, Istria, the Vojvodina, the Kosovo area, the Dodecanese Islands, Cyprus, and other smaller areas. The competition over these lands served both to divide the Balkan peoples and to provide excuses for great-power intervention. France, Britain, Italy, Germany, and the Soviet Union all played on these mutual animosities to further their own interests. This situation was to continue during the war and in the postwar world. The national question and outside intervention were to remain the major Balkan issues.

# PART II

*World War II and the postwar developments*

# 7

## The Balkan states in World War II

### THE MILITARY BACKGROUND

B Y THE TIME GERMANY INVADED the Soviet Union in June 1941 all of the Balkan states were involved in the hostilities: Romania and Bulgaria were Axis allies, whereas Greece, Albania, and Yugoslavia were under German, Bulgarian, and Italian occupation. The great influence exerted on Balkan affairs by external forces, in particular the Nazi–Soviet pact of August 1939 and the subsequent Axis victories, has been emphasized. This pattern was to continue throughout the war. Although Balkan conditions were always a concern of the great-power belligerents, the area was to remain during World War II, as during World War I, a sideshow to the decisive campaigns waged elsewhere. World War I, as we have seen, was won by the Allied victories in northern France in the summer and fall of 1918. The greatest influence on the outcome of World War II was undoubtedly the failure of the German campaign against the Soviet Union and this latter power's subsequent ability to launch a great offensive against Eastern and Central Europe. The British and American operations in North Africa, Sicily, and Italy, and, finally, the opening of the second front in Normandy, played a secondary role in the final defeat of Nazi Germany. Since the fate of the Balkan states was so closely tied to these battlefield decisions, a review of the major events on both the eastern and the western fronts is necessary. As will be noted later, this progress of events was closely reflected in developments within the individual Balkan states.

In their invasion of the Soviet Union the German armies were accompanied by Italian, Hungarian, Finnish, Slovak, Croatian, and Romanian detachments, as well as Spanish volunteers. At first the Soviet Union was supported only by Britain, although material aid was expected from the United States. The German leadership and that of most of the other countries expected a swift Nazi victory on the eastern front; all of the contemporary observers had been impressed by the unexpected ease of the campaigns in the west. It did indeed seem for a time as if this pattern would be repeated. The German forces quickly defeated the Soviet units concentrated near the border and then swept into the Russian heartland. They were able to occupy just about the same areas the German army had held before the Russian capitulation in 1917. They reached the outskirts of Moscow, but they failed to take either that city or Leningrad. At this point they suffered what was eventually to prove to be a fatal disaster. Winter came early in 1941. Overconfident of their abilities and blinded by previous successes, the German leaders had not prepared their troops adequately for Russian weather. The soldiers did not have proper uniforms, and, even worse, the mechanized equipment on which the Germans had depended heavily in the past was not prepared for the bitter temperatures. The trucks, tanks, cars, artillery, and all the other advanced weaponry simply did not function. Trained and outfitted for these conditions, the Russian troops were able to launch counterattacks while their opposition remained mired in ice and snow.

The war assumed a truly worldwide dimension when on December 7, 1941, Japan opened hostilities with the United States and Britain with a surprise attack on Pearl Harbor and bases in the Far East. On December 11 the other major members of the Tripartite Pact, Germany and Italy, declared war on the United States. The Axis allies and satellites, Romania, Bulgaria, Slovakia, Hungary, and Croatia, soon followed their example. The Soviet Union and Japan remained at peace, both because of the existence of the 1941 neutrality pact and because their individual interests were best served by such a course of action. Even though a front of Germany, Italy, and Japan had apparently been formed against Britain, the United States, and the Soviet Union, the Japanese belligerency was to have little real effect on the outcome of the war in Europe. The Western powers gave priority to the European theater, and Japan did not coordinate its campaign with its Axis partners. German interests would have been far better served by a Japanese attack on Russian Siberian cities than by the move southward and eastward.

During 1942 the chief attention remained on the Russian front. In the summer the German army and its allies launched a great offensive in the south. In August an attack on the strategically located city of Stalingrad commenced, and the troops reached its outskirts by September. In the next month the Soviet forces counterattacked; in February 1943, operating under favorable winter conditions, they were able to surround the German Sixth Army, concentrated in the city, and force its surrender. Although the German command organized another offensive elsewhere in the spring, Stalingrad was more than a military defeat. Until this time the apparent invincibility of the German army had been a major factor in the Axis diplomatic successes. In the summer of 1943 the German failure in the Kursk offensive brought about a shift of opinion. As we shall see, after this year the conviction grew stronger among the Balkan leaders, whether of the left or of the right, that the Allied powers would eventually win and that political preparations for this event had to be made. It was increasingly clear that the Axis did not have the

necessary reserves in manpower or the economic potential to carry a pro-
tracted conflict on to victory. Moreover, Germany, with its forces spread thin
in various areas, did not have strong and dependable allies: its closest partner
was soon to withdraw from the fighting. The tide had, in fact, turned; in
Europe it was the Soviet armies that were on the offensive.

With the major battles being waged on Soviet territory, the Western Allies
concentrated on other regions. Despite repeated and strong Soviet requests
for a second front in an area that would force the withdrawal of large numbers of German troops from the eastern front, Britain and the United States
chose first to occupy North Africa and then to advance to Sicily. Fighting
had already commenced in Africa in 1940. Although the Axis armies were at
first able to win important victories, they were forced on the defensive after
the beginning of the Russian campaign, when they no longer received adequate replacements in men and supplies. By November 1942 the British had
won control of Libya and Egypt. Cairo subsequently became the center of
their Middle Eastern operations. In the same month American, British, and
some French forces began the occupation of the French colonies of Morocco
and Algeria, which had previously been subject to the French government in
Vichy. By May 1943 the Mediterranean was under Allied control.

The Allied invasion of Sicily was to have major repercussions in the Balkans. The campaign was begun in July, and in the same month Benito Mussolini was overthrown and replaced by Marshal Pietro Badoglio. Negotiations for an armistice were immediately opened; the document was signed in
September. The Italian surrender had an immediate effect in the Balkan peninsula, where Italian troops had undertaken wide responsibilities in the administration and occupation of conquered territories. Although the German
command was able to keep effective control of these regions, it could not
prevent the transfer of huge quantities of Italian weapons into partisan hands.
The German forces were also able to hold most of Italy, including Rome,
until late spring 1944. Although the Allied armies crossed to the Italian mainland in October 1943, they did not occupy the capital until June 1944.

The invasion of Western Europe through the Normandy beachhead began
in that same month. The Soviet forces simultaneously continued to achieve
great victories in the east against the steadily weakening German army. In
August 1944 Soviet troops occupied Romania and continued on to Bulgaria,
which they entered in September. Belgrade was taken in a combined Russian
and Yugoslav partisan action in October. Even with these great Allied victories, the war in Europe did not come to an end until May 1945. Japan still
remained to be conquered. Despite the American fears that a long and costly
campaign would be necessary in the Pacific, the dropping of atomic bombs
on Hiroshima on August 6 and on Nagasaki on August 9 brought a quick
Japanese surrender. The armistice was signed on September 2, 1945.

## BALKAN PARTICIPATION IN THE WAR

These campaigns were followed closely in the Balkan capitals, where the governments based their decisions on the military and political situation in the rest of Europe.

### Romania

As the only Balkan state with troops actively fighting alongside those of a belligerent power, Romania suffered all of the tragedies of a nation at war. The initial decisions were not unpopular. The war against the Soviet Union was waged ostensibly for the recovery and defense of national lands. General Ion Antonescu, in full charge of the government, was at first convinced that Germany would win. In order to share in the spoils of victory, and also to forestall yet another partition of Transylvania, he felt that Romania would have to participate in the German campaign against Russia. In July 1941 the Romanian forces were again in possession of the Bukovinian and Bessarabian territory that had been lost in the previous year. Although there was general public acceptance of the need to fight for the return of these areas, there was much less enthusiasm about continuing the war thereafter. Despite the fact that, unless Germany won, Romania could not expect to hold these lands, many were fearful of the consequences of further military involvement.

One major consideration, however, kept the Romanian armies in the field. In joining with Germany, the Romanian government was really fighting for Transylvania. Throughout the war this region remained the center of extreme tension between Bucharest and Budapest, whose governments were in theory in alliance. Each accused the other of atrocities and of maladministration in its section of the partitioned province. Both took their complaints to Berlin, where the German authorities acted as arbiters. In this contest the Romanian diplomats felt themselves at a disadvantage. We have seen how, in the Vienna Award of 1940, at least some of the Hungarian claims received recognition. The Romanian representatives in Germany recognized that Hungarian propaganda was very effective; its emphasis on the "injustice of Trianon" was received with sympathy by Germans who judged that they too had been most unfairly dealt with at Versailles. The Romanians thus feared that if they did not support Germany, the rest of Transylvania would be awarded to Hungary on the day of victory. Conversely, the hope was never abandoned that if the Romanian armies fought well, the Vienna Award would be annulled. In fact, in March 1944, following an unsuccessful Hungarian attempt to leave the war, Hitler assured Antonescu that the territory in question would indeed be returned.

With these considerations in mind, the Romanian government undertook a major role in the German campaign. Thirty Romanian divisions participated in the initial invasion in 1941. Their main theater of operation was southern Russia, where they played an important part in the taking of Odessa and the Crimea. Romanian troops were also at Stalingrad; the Third and Fourth armies and the First Romanian Tank Division participated in this disaster. Romanian casualties in these actions were heavy; it is estimated that about eighty thousand died.

By the terms of an agreement signed with Germany in August 1941, Romania was given responsibility for the area between the Dniester and Bug rivers, amounting to about ten thousand square miles, which was called Transnistria by the Romanian authorities. A major propaganda campaign was inaugurated to justify future Romanian claims to the area. Postage stamps were issued, and there was an attempt to prove that these were indeed historically Romanian lands. Although the region was under Romanian military administration, Antonescu did not attempt a formal annexation. The Romanian leaders did not want to create a situation in which Transnistria would become a payment for the loss of Transylvanian territory.

During the war the relations of Germany and Romania were fairly typical of those between any similarly allied powers. In the past Romanian sympathies had always been directed more toward the Western European states, in particular France, than toward Germany. Most Romanians did not consider themselves at war with the Western allies in any real sense. Their animosity was directed against their Soviet neighbor and had its base in the historical conflicts and the recent Bolshevik issue. The feeling toward Germany lay somewhere in between these two attitudes. The Romanian army was well aware of the weakness of its military position; it was sadly lacking in modern equipment. Constant pressure was exerted on the German command for larger deliveries of war matériel. After Stalingrad, where Romanian soldiers fought to the German satisfaction, more arms were indeed supplied, but the amount was never sufficient. There was apparently some fear on the German side that arms delivered either to Romania or to Hungary might be used by the Axis allies to fight each other over Transylvania.

For Germany the chief significance of the Romanian alliance was the guarantee which it gave that the vast economic resources of the region could be utilized. Romanian oil and wheat were particularly important. However, during the entire war constant friction arose over the deliveries and, in particular, the method of payment. Since both states were in theory fighting for the same goals, the German negotiators hoped to obtain favorable terms, and they continually felt that the Romanian side could contribute more than it did. For their part, the Romanian representatives wished to profit from the exchange and, most important, to be compensated for their deliveries as soon as possible. They would accept payment in either goods or money. Naturally, during the war the German economy could not produce the necessary amount of goods. As far as money was concerned, the German economists wished to use the country's gold to buy strategic materials in neutral countries. A Romanian observer has commented on the German reaction:

Germany believed that a clique of old and malevolent politicians was at work in Bucharest, who sat like maggots in the National Bank and ruled this citadel of reaction – a clique of anti-German Romanian politicians (*Politikastertum*), who ruled the Romanian economic life and, in an indirect way, also the political scene and who were endeavoring to sabotage the Romanian efforts in behalf of the common struggle and victory.[1]

The relationship became even more strained after the failures on the Soviet front, when the Germans expected their ally to make major sacrifices. The Romanian attitude, however, remained the same: economic arrangements were a commercial affair even in wartime. In addition, the Romanian government had joined the German side to achieve territorial goals; there was no real ideological element in the relationship. Although some attempt had been made to mount an anti-Bolshevik campaign in the country, it had not been successful. The Romanian leadership had no desire to share in the consequences of a German defeat. Its terms thus became tougher as the German situation worsened. The Germans did send increased amounts of war matériel and also equipment for the maintenance of the railroads, but these supplies did not pay for more than a part of the raw materials they received.

As could be expected, disagreements also arose over the status of the Saxon German population of Transylvania, which the Nazi leadership wished to recruit for its military efforts. Since these men were Romanian citizens, they were taken into the Romanian army. Nevertheless, by the end of the war an estimated eighty thousand had entered into direct German service.

Once the fighting commenced, Antonescu was increasingly occupied with military affairs. As a result, his vice-premier and foreign minister, Mihai Antonescu (no relation to the general), played the major role in domestic affairs. He did not become a popular figure. As we have seen, Romania at this time was a military dictatorship rather than a fascist state. During the war, under extreme Nazi pressure, the government did take some further measures against the Jews. However, special laws were passed to protect the Jews of the Regat, in particular those who came from families whose members had served in the army in the previous wars. The situation in the Romanian-occupied lands of southern Russia, where there was a strong concentration of Jews, was quite different. Here the transportation of the Jewish population to concentration camps in Poland was expedited, and massive atrocities were witnessed.

Despite their strong political position, General Antonescu and his supporters were always well aware of the opposition to their rule that existed. As previously, this regime allowed a "tolerated opposition" to function. Although neither Maniu nor Constantine Brătianu could act openly as a party

---

1 Ion Gheorghe, *Rumäniens Weg zum Satellitenstaat* (Heidelberg: Kurt Vowinckel Verlag, 1952), p. 211.

leader, they did remain politically active, and they could make their opinions known. They had, for instance, opposed a continuation of the war after the winning back of Bessarabia and Bukovina. Despite their official disbanding, the Liberal and National parties still represented the opinion of the majority of the Romanian citizens. On the left of the political spectrum a Socialist Party and a very weak Communist Party functioned in association with some other factions – an organization to be discussed later in this chapter. During the war Antonescu and the traditional party leadership remained at the center of the political stage. Despite his ties with Berlin, the general appears to have worried chiefly about a possible revival of Iron Guard activity. Its leader, Horia Sima, was at this time again in prison, but in Germany. There was always a possibility that the German government might use him as a replacement for Antonescu, should the proper moment arise.

For the Romanians, as for other East Europeans, the year 1943 marked a turning point. After the Stalingrad debacle it was clear that the war might end in a disaster for Romania. In August 1943 the first Allied raids on the Ploeşti oil fields commenced. Until that time the country had been spared most of the horrors of the battlefield. The first attacks were followed by others directed toward Bucharest. Unprepared for such an event, the population was panic-stricken, and daily life was paralyzed.

Once it appeared that an Axis defeat was inevitable, official and unofficial efforts to conclude a separate peace with the Western Allied powers, which had been begun previously, were intensified. Throughout the war individual Romanians who, like their counterparts in the other Axis countries, had extensive connections in Western Europe, attempted to arrange an armistice, centering their activities in the neutral capitals. Some Romanians harbored unrealistic expectations that they could come to an agreement with the Western Allies and arrange terms that would allow them to keep Bessarabia and Bukovina. The events of the war had intensified the Romanian fear and dislike of the Soviet Union. Ideally, the Romanians would have liked the negotiations to be accompanied by the airlifting of Western troops into Romania. This action not only would serve as a check on Soviet actions, but would prevent a German occupation similar to that which occurred in Italy after the armistice there. The Western powers, however, would not agree to a separate peace, and they kept their Soviet partner informed of the peace negotiations.

The first major Romanian approach was made in March 1944, when Prince Barbu Ştirbei went to Cairo. Later, in July, Maniu sent Constantine Vişoianu on a similar mission. In these negotiations, which were known to the Soviet Union, the Romanian diplomats were informed clearly not only that Russia would keep the lands acquired in 1941, but that their government would have to declare war on Germany and pay reparations in return for any armistice agreement. The hope that northern Transylvania would be returned was, however, held out to them.

By the beginning of August 1944 it was obvious that Romania faced a catastrophe. The Soviet armies were fast approaching; the country would soon become a major battlefield. In this crisis the court finally took decisive action. During the war King Michael and his advisers had not enjoyed good relations with Antonescu. The court and the government formed two different circles, with the king excluded from the discussions on the important decisions. By this time Antonescu too had come to realize that Romania would have to withdraw from the war. He, however, preferred that his country follow the example of Finland, which first notified Germany of its intention. Recognizing that this course of action was not practical, since it would only delay matters and give the German troops the opportunity to occupy Bucharest, the king decided to act.

On August 23 Michael received Antonescu, who had just returned from Germany. The general was dismissed from his post, disarmed, and imprisoned. This royal coup was carried through with the cooperation of the king's aides, Baron Stârcea-Mocsonyi and Grigore Niculescu-Buzeşti, and there was no opposition to the action. Michael at once broadcast agreement to the armistice conditions previously set by the Allies. No special concessions were given. The Romanian desire for Allied airborne troops was impossible to fulfill, and it was quite clear that the Soviet army would occupy the country. It will be noted that the coup was carried through by the traditional leadership. Although there had been some Communist Party activity during the war, most of the prominent members were either in jail or in exile. The attempt to organize a Patriotic Front in 1943 had also met with little success.

The national government that was formed at this point thus resembled previous regimes, except that it contained representation from the left. General Constantine Sănătescu became premier; other army officers assumed major positions. Brătianu and Maniu, together with the Social Democratic leader C. Titel Petrescu, became ministers without portfolio. The vital post of minister of justice was given to Lucreţiu Pătrăşcanu, the most prominent Communist who was not either in prison or in the Soviet Union. The appointment was a clear recognition of the fact that political arrangements that would conciliate the Soviet Union would have to be made. The new government next faced the difficult task of shifting sides in the war and negotiating the terms of an armistice. On Allied insistence Romania declared war on Germany on August 24, but by this time the bulk of the German troops were already out of the country. Nevertheless, the Romanian soldiers still had to face months of fighting in Central Europe and to suffer a further 170,000 casualties.

Meanwhile, the Soviet army entered Romanian territory. On September 12 an armistice was signed in Moscow that obligated the Romanian government to pay $300 million in reparations and, in addition, the costs of the Soviet occupation. Although in theory the country was under the supervision of an Allied Control Commission, which had American and British as well as Soviet members, the Soviet government was in fact in full control. By this time the Western Allies had already conceded that Romania lay within the Soviet sphere. This decision, which will be discussed in detail later, was not known to the Romanian leaders.

## Bulgaria

Of the Axis allies, Bulgaria enjoyed perhaps the best conditions during the war. Unlike his Romanian counterpart, the Bulgarian soldier did not participate in the deadly campaign in the Soviet Union. His contributions to the war effort were limited to providing garrison service in territories conquered by German and Italian troops. Bulgaria was also an important source of raw materials for Berlin, especially grain. The Bulgarian occupation of Macedonia and Thrace was greeted initially with enthusiasm. The nationalists had thereby acquired what they regarded as the correct boundaries of their state. In May 1941 the Bulgarian government formally annexed some of the lands that it occupied; the Germans, who had already conceded Thrace, made no objection. With the acquisition of these territories, Bulgaria became the strongest Balkan state. The popular attitude was expressed by a Bulgarian politician:

> We were all intoxicated by the idea that for the first time in history we would get our just due, which we had demanded in vain for so long. To be sure, we had somewhat of a bad conscience because we had not fought for and conquered but rather received it as a gift.[2]

The occupation at first was also greeted with approval by many in Macedonia, where the former Serbian-dominated Yugoslav administration had aroused violent opposition. As one inhabitant commented later: "Of course we cheered, we had no way of knowing then that the Bulgarians would just repeat all the mistakes the Serbs had made."[3] Indeed, and unfortunately for the Bulgarian interests, the local population soon lost sympathy with the occupying forces, whose leaders acted like conquerers and who often proved to be corrupt and incompetent administrators.

Desiring to counter such unfavorable reactions, and expecting that these lands would be held permanently, the Bulgarian government inaugurated a massive propaganda effort to win support among the people and to convince them of their Bulgarian nationality. Attempts were made to raise the general cultural level of the region, which was one of the most backward areas of the Balkans. The Bulgarian authorities opened about eight hundred schools, as well as a library, a national theater, and a university. These establishments

---

2  Marshall Lee Miller, *Bulgaria during the Second World War*, (Stanford, Calif.: Stanford University Press, 1975), p. 55.
3  C. M. Woodhouse, *The Struggle for Greece, 1941–1949* (London: Hart-Davis, MacGibbon, 1976), p. 8.

were, of course, intended to serve as vehicles to ensure the bulgarization of Macedonia and Thrace. At the same time the Bulgarian Holy Synod took over the administration of all Orthodox church affairs.

The individual Bulgarian soldiers and officials, products of their own national education, were convinced that the inhabitants of Macedonia and Thrace, which they called Belomorie, were indeed co-nationals. Although there was a basis for this belief in Yugoslav, or Vardar, Macedonia, most of the lands formerly under Athens had undergone a radical change in national character in the interwar years. Whereas in 1912 the Greek population had comprised only 43 percent of the Macedonian lands and, in 1919, 17 percent of western Thrace, by the 1920s, largely as a result of the resettlement of refugees from Asia Minor, Greeks constituted 89 percent of the people in Aegean Macedonia and 62 percent of those in Thrace. Despite the fact that Slavic-language speakers thus constituted only a relatively small minority, the Bulgarian authorities proceeded to try to enforce their nationalizing policies.

After the occupation of Thrace the Bulgarian authorities closed the Greek schools and other public institutions. They also prepared measures directed to securing the expulsion of the Greeks and colonization by Bulgarian settlers. Their harsh measures resulted in a revolt in September 1941, which spread through Thrace and Greek Macedonia; it is estimated that 15,000 Greeks were killed during its suppression.[4] The deportation of Greek inhabitants occurred both in Thrace and in Macedonia. According to Greek figures, 200,000 of their nationals were removed; the Bulgarians admit to 70,000.[5] The Bulgarian actions led many Greeks to move into the areas under Italian or German occupation, where similar policies were not in effect. The Bulgarian repression at this time accounts for much of the bitter postwar tension between Bulgaria and Greece.

As might be expected, the German attack on the Soviet Union was greeted with dismay in Sofia. Expecting a short war, the German government did not ask for Bulgarian participation. Bulgarian troops were needed for guard duty in the Balkans, and the German officials recognized the pro-Russian sympathies of the people. Of course, when the war did not proceed as expected, the German representatives requested increasing economic and military assistance. It was, however, difficult for Berlin to put effective pressure on its ally. With the acquisition of southern Dobrudja, Macedonia, and Thrace, the Bulgarian government had achieved its maximum national program. Its leaders also had legitimate fears. The Bulgarian army was badly equipped; it had few modern arms. The commanders were constantly in dread of a Soviet invasion by way of the Black Sea ports of Varna and Burgas. Much apprehension was also felt concerning possible Turkish actions, despite the nonaggres-

4  Miller, *Bulgaria during the Second World War*, p. 117.
5  Nissan Oren, *Bulgarian Communism: The Road to Power, 1934–1944* (New York: Columbia University Press, 1971), pp. 190, 191.

sion pact that had been signed in February 1941. Although Turkey was still carrying on trade with Germany, the state was technically a British ally. Nevertheless, despite its fears, the Bulgarian government did not hesitate to join its Tripartite Pact partners and declare war on the United States after the Japanese attack on Pearl Harbor. America was far away, and Bulgaria was already at war with Britain.

Although Bulgarian relations with Germany remained good until September, 1944, much tension arose between Sofia and Rome. The Bulgarian court, it will be remembered, had close ties with Italy. Boris's mother was Marie Louise of Parma; his wife was the daughter of Victor Emmanuel III. The principal cause of the friction was the conflict of interest connected with the occupation zones in conquered territory. The Bulgarian government feared that Italy would seek to create a large Albanian state, including parts of western Macedonia, which it claimed. In August 1942 clashes took place between the Bulgarian troops and Albanian and Italian soldiers. A German mediation gave support to the Bulgarian claims. As in the conflict between the Romanian and the Hungarian positions in Transylvania, the German officials could use the rivalries over Macedonia for their own interests.

After Stalingrad the German government attempted to win a greater degree of support from Sofia in the Russian conflict. It sought, at the least, a severance of Bulgarian diplomatic relations with the Soviet Union, if not a declaration of war. Although the Bulgarian leaders refused these requests, they did agree to some other German desires. Since the Russian conflict made necessary the transfer of more German soldiers from the Balkans, and as partisan activity was rising in the region, the German command wished the Bulgarian army to undertake wider occupation duties. The Bulgarian government, which preferred to administer only the lands that it intended to annex, was at first reluctant, but it finally did extend its zone of occupation.

During the war King Boris remained the principal political figure; Bogdan Filov was prime minister. In June 1942 the government was reorganized; Filov became both premier and foreign minister, with General Nikola Mihov as war minister. A royal dictatorship rather than a fascist regime, Boris's government nevertheless did follow some German examples. As in Romania, measures were passed involving the Jews, but much opposition to their enforcement arose. The approximately fifty thousand Jews in the country had never been an issue in national life; the difficult minorities were the Turks and the Greeks. Because of this attitude, the deportation of the Jewish population, organized by the Germans, was resisted; the nation's Jews were instead dispersed to the countryside. The Bulgarian officials could not, however, stop the transportation of Jews from Thrace and Macedonia to European concentration camps, where almost all died.

In general, Boris got along well with the German representatives; Hitler thought him clever. The king appears to have been apprehensive that his authority might be challenged by those who were even more pro-German and who favored a closer collaboration with Berlin. Among the latter, the most prominent was Alexander Tsankov, who had been premier from 1923 to 1926. A fascist legionary movement under General Khristo Lukov had also been organized. In Bulgaria, as in Romania, a tolerated opposition was in existence. The political parties could not function as such, but individuals could express their opinions on points of policy. Despite much opposition to his personal rule, Boris remained the center of political life; in fact, his presence was necessary to hold the system together. The government was thus thrown in a state of crisis when the king died suddenly in August 1943. After returning from a visit to Germany, Boris climbed Mt. Musala, the highest peak in Bulgaria. Three days later he died from what was undoubtedly a heart attack, although, because of the wartime situation, rumors that he had been murdered abounded. The Bulgarian public appears to have thought that he had been poisoned by the Germans, but his death was actually a blow to German influence.

Since the heir to the throne, Simeon, was only six years old, a regency had to be established. According to the constitution a Grand National Assembly should have been convened to choose the members, but, owing to the wartime conditions, this procedure was not followed. Instead Filov, Mihov, and Boris's brother, Prince Cyril, became the regents, and their appointment was approved by the regular assembly. In September 1943 Dobri Bozhilov, the minister of finance, became premier. This new regime had to face a deteriorating military and political situation. Until this time Bulgaria had been left relatively undisturbed by the war, and economic conditions were good because of the German purchases. In November 1943, however, massive bombings of Bulgarian cities commenced. In the attacks of January 1944 thousands were killed or wounded. Unprepared for these events, the population reacted with general panic.

Like the Romanian, the Bulgarian government recognized that efforts would have to be made to withdraw from the war. There was no desire to share in the German ruin. Although attempts were indeed made to get in touch with Allied officials, the Bulgarian leaders did not enjoy the same favorable relations with the West as their northern neighbors. Moreover, certain practical problems arose. Foremost was the probability that if Bulgaria made peace, a German occupation would follow. In addition, most Bulgarians continued to be convinced that Thrace, Macedonia, and Dobrudja were rightfully theirs. Like the Romanian leaders in their attitude toward Bessarabia and Bukovina, the nationally minded Bulgarians found it difficult to contemplate the surrender of lands that they regarded as integral parts of their historical state.

The Agrarian Union remained at this time the strongest political organization among the tolerated opposition. Before the war it had divided into a right wing under Dimitŭr Gichev and a left wing, the Pladne group, under the leadership of Nikola Petkov and Dr. G. M. Dimitrov, who lived in France.

Both sections were pro-Western in their political orientation. A similar moderate position was held by the leader of the Democrats, Nikola Mushanov. There was also a small Communist Party, the membership of which had dropped from an estimated 30,000–35,000 in 1934 to 10,600 by mid-1941. It had, however, a youth organization with a membership of around 19,000.[6]

The fortunes of the party had thus not fared well during the war. As we have seen, during the period of the Nazi–Soviet Pact, following Comintern directives, it had concentrated its attacks on the "imperialist" Western Allies. After the commencement of Operation Barbarossa, this attitude had naturally changed. Although the party received clear directions from Moscow to adopt an active policy, the leadership was divided on the question whether it would not be wiser to wait until better preparations had been made. Soviet actions, however, forced the party into the open. In July and August 1941 some Bulgarian Communist emigrés were sent back to the country by submarine and parachute, with the mission of organizing an uprising. Of the fifty-eight people involved in the undertaking, twenty were captured and shot at once and the others were soon subdued. This action, which was easily suppressed, resulted in massive police reprisals against the party. Most of the members were arrested without difficulty. The local cells were large enough, with the average membership being around twenty, for the police to find informers who would identify the other participants. By the spring of 1942 there were very few Communists out of jail. In June General Vladimir Zaimov, who had connections with the Soviet government, was executed for treason, and Communist influence reached its lowest point.

Even without this setback, the Communist Party faced a difficult situation. Like the members of the other parties, the Bulgarian Communist was sincerely convinced that the population of Macedonia was truly Bulgarian. Before the war such convictions had received support from the Comintern, whose policy called for the establishment of an independent or autonomous Macedonian state. Such a move, which would separate the province from Yugoslavia and Greece, was in the Bulgarian interest. Most Bulgarian leaders expected that the government of an autonomous Macedonia would work closely with, or even choose to join, Bulgaria. These convictions brought the Bulgarian party into direct conflict with the Greek and Yugoslav parties both before and during the war. In this struggle, which will be recounted in greater detail later, the Bulgarian Communists found themselves at an increasing disadvantage. By the end of the war the Yugoslav Partisans were in control of the region, and they had won Soviet support.

One of the reasons for the relative weakness of the Bulgarian position was the party's failure, especially in comparison with its Yugoslav rival, to organize an effective resistance movement. The Bulgarian leadership, of course,

6  Oren, *Bulgarian Communism*, pp. 167, 168.

was working under very difficult conditions. Bulgaria was a German ally; the few German troops in the country caused no problems. As long as the Axis was winning, there was much popular satisfaction with this state of affairs. Historic lands had been occupied; the villages were prospering because of the increased demand for their agricultural products. Moreover, if guerilla actions were undertaken, they would have to be against Bulgarian soldiers or the police; there was no menacing foreign occupation. A Bulgarian account explains that events followed different courses in Bulgaria and in Yugoslavia "because the old state apparatus in Bulgaria was not crushed as in Yugoslavia, because the Bulgarian army had not been defeated and its arms had not passed into the hands of the people, and, finally, because the Germans had entered Bulgaria not as an open force of occupation."[7]

With this basic weakness in its program and with most of its members in jail, the party had difficulty fulfilling the Soviet call for the organization of bands and partisan activity. Moreover, the majority of the members recognized that it would be wiser to conserve their strength for the future. Thus, although some partisan groups were indeed formed, the emphasis was on urban terrorism, and after February 1943 a number of assassinations of prominent figures occurred. Communist political activities were not markedly successful. The small bands operating in the mountains were not received with sympathy by the villagers, who did not want to be involved in acts of violence against other Bulgarians, which would lead in turn to reprisals by the Bulgarian police. The bands thus faced a real problem with securing the food and fuel necessary to keep alive. It has been estimated that in September 1944, when the movement was at its height, there were between eight thousand and ten thousand partisans.[8] The German estimate was twelve thousand. Although the military contribution of these bands was small, their later political significance was great. Their activities became a part of postwar Bulgarian Communist mythology.

During the war the Soviet government favored not only the formation of partisan organizations, but also the continuation of the popular-front policy and Communist collaboration with certain other parties. In Bulgaria, the Communist Party, in conformity with this program, stood behind the organization of the Fatherland Front, which was a weak combination of political organizations that had often been antagonistic in the past. Formed in June 1942, the Front contained, in addition to Communist Party members, representatives from the Social Democrats, the Pladne Agrarians, and the Zveno group, headed by Kimon Georgiev. The Gichev Agrarians and Mushanov's Democrats did not participate.

In the spring of 1944, when it was clear that the war was lost, the national

---

7   Quoted in Oren, *Bulgarian Communism*, p. 196.
8   Oren, *Bulgarian Communism*, pp. 216–219.

leaders began to prepare the steps by which they intended to withdraw from the conflict. In June the government was reorganized, and Ivan Bagrianov, an Agrarian, became premier. The Bulgarian position was considerably weakened by the August coup in Bucharest and the subsequent Romanian surrender. Faced with certain defeat, Bagrianov prepared to take Bulgaria out of the war. On September 2 the ministry was again reorganized, and another Agrarian, Kosta Muraviev, who was associated with Gichev, became premier; the Fatherland Front refused to cooperate in the formation of the ministry. The new regime, which was pro-Western, declared that it was no longer at war with Britain and the United States.

Meanwhile, on August 31 the Soviet army had occupied Bucharest. Because it was not at war with the Soviet Union, the Bulgarian government apparently did not expect an occupation. The Soviet leaders were well aware of events in Sofia, since they had maintained a mission in the city throughout the war. On September 5 a Soviet declaration of war on Bulgaria was issued, and on September 8 Soviet troops entered the country. The action was taken without consultation with Britain or the United States and with very little prior notice. In a hopeless position, the Bulgarian government instructed its troops not to resist. Relations with Germany were immediately broken. On September 8 the war with the Soviet Union was concluded with the arrangement of a cease-fire.

At this point the leaders of the Fatherland Front prepared to take action. First, strikes were organized, and on September 9 the organization simply took over the government. There was no opposition; the police and the army cooperated fully. Another regency council, which included the Communist Todor Pavlov, was formed. The new Bulgarian government was based on the four parties of the Fatherland Front. Colonel Kimon Georgiev of Zveno became premier; his associate Damian Velchev, received the post of minister of war; and the Communist Party obtained the vital ministries of the Interior and Justice. Despite the armistice the war did not end for the Bulgarian soldiers, who were required for the first time actually to fight. Like the Romanians, they were to join with the Soviet forces in the advance against Germany; around thirty thousand died in the subsequent battles.

The political developments in Bulgaria were thus in contrast to those in Romania. After the death of Boris the traditional conservative political forces were in an increasingly vulnerable position. The declaration of war by the Soviet Union allowed a front organization composed of parties of the center and left, including the Communists, to take control. It should also be noted that the Soviet demand that the Romanian and Bulgarian armies take part in the war against Germany resulted in the removal of the bulk of these troops from their countries during a crucial period for the political future of the state. A traditional source of support for conservative regimes was thus effectively removed.

Map 10. The partition of Yugoslavia

## Yugoslavia

Following the surrender of the Yugoslav army and the flight of the king, the country fell under the control of the German and Italian victors, who partitioned the conquered territories into spheres of influence. The lines of division can best be understood by reference to Map 10. First, the Axis allies were able to satisfy some of the national ambitions. Most of Macedonia, as we have seen, fell under Bulgarian domination. Hungary for its share took its pre-1919 territories of Bačka and Baranja, together with some other small areas. The remainder of the Vojvodina, the Banat, was put under the control of its German minority. In the south, Italian-ruled Albania was given the Kosovo region, together with some Macedonian and Montenegrin lands. Germany and Italy each annexed a part of Slovenia. Italy, in its major gain, took most of the Dalmatian coast and the Adriatic islands. The remaining

Yugoslav territories were organized into Serbian, Croatian, and Montenegrin political authorities, under the supervision of Germany and Italy. Before Italy's Grecian debacle, it will be remembered, Rome had been assigned the predominant influence in the western Balkans in the Axis planning. Now, however, the German government exerted at least an equal influence in the administration of the conquered territory. It held first responsibility in Serbia, and it shared control of Croatia.

Serbia, because of its strategic location, was of particular importance to the German war effort. The first German consideration was thus to install a regime that could keep order in the region. General Milan Nedić, the head of the government during the period of German occupation, regarded it as his major task to act as caretaker until the end of the war and the possible return of the previous government; his administration thus had no ideological coloration. He had at his service a small military force. The Serbian fascist leader, Dimitrije Ljotić, was given some support by the occupying power, and he was allowed to organize a corps of about 3,600 men.

Montenegro, under Italian rule, underwent a more turbulent experience. At first the Italian government attempted to establish a puppet kingdom. The officials wished to encourage and win the allegiance of the small group of Montenegrin separatists, who yearned for the days of Nicholas, and to exploit the fact that the queen of Italy was the daughter of that ruler. Ideally the Italians would have liked to set up an autonomous Montenegrin administration that would run its own affairs. Their efforts were completely unsuccessful; by July 1941 the country was in revolt. Since some Montenegrin units had been allowed to keep their arms after the surrender, the rebels had adequate equipment. Nevertheless, Italian troops, with Albanian support, were able to retake the region by June 1942. Widespread reprisals followed, and this remote and mountainous area remained a center of unrest and rebellion.

The most controversial political creation of this period was the independent state of Croatia, whose formation was announced on April 10, even before the end of hostilities. In theory, the new nation was an ally of the Axis and on the same level as the other similarly situated East European countries, that is, Bulgaria, Romania, Hungary, and Slovakia. Although most of the Dalmatian coast was lost to Italy, the Croatian territories now included Bosnia and Hercegovina, long the goal of the nationalists. The acquisition of these lands, however, considerably complicated the ethnic basis of the state. Of its 6.5 million inhabitants, only 3.4 million were Croatian; there were also 1.9 million Orthodox Serbs, 700,000 Muslims, 150,000 Germans, 18,000 Jews, and some Italians. The Croatian government was recognized by Italy, Germany, Hungary, Bulgaria, Romania, Slovakia, Finland, Spain, Japan, Burma, and Manchukuo; it was a signatory of both the Tripartite Pact and the Anti-Comintern Pact.

Despite its alleged independence, the state was split into two spheres of influence, with the line of division running north to south; Italy controlled the western section adjacent to the Adriatic. Although a German military command was assigned to Zagreb, Hitler let Mussolini determine who would run the government. Given the opportunity, the Italian dictator naturally chose Ante Pavelić, the Ustaša leader whom he had been periodically supporting for the past twelve years. Pavelić returned with the few hundred of his followers, who had also been living in Italy. The regime had very weak foundations. Previously, the Ustaša movement had enjoyed no wide support within Croatian society. The administration lacked the services of experienced officials and trained army officers. Its subservient nature was underlined when in May 1941 the state was proclaimed a monarchy with Prince Aimone of Savoy, the Duke of Spoleto, as king. This ruler, who took the name Tomislav II, never visited his kingdom. The Ustaša regime was thus largely the creation of Fascist Italy. Hitler held a low opinion of the state; he tended to be more sympathetic toward the Serbs and the Greeks, who had fought.

Undoubtedly, the proclamation of an independent Croatia was greeted at first with much favor. As Maček later wrote: "A wave of enthusiasm pervaded Zagreb at this time, not unlike that which had swept through the town in 1918 when the ties with Hungary were severed."[9] A reaction soon followed, particularly when the Italian annexations in Dalmatia became known. During the period of Ustaša rule the two strongest political forces in the country, the Croatian Peasant Party and the Catholic church, remained largely passive, although many individual examples of both collaboration and opposition can be found. At first, both Maček and Archbishop Stepinac, the highest Croatian Catholic prelate, urged the population to support the new regime. Maček then retired to his farm; he was later interned. With the responsible leaders largely neutralized, the control of the state fell into the hands of a group of fanatics who gave free reign to all of the national passions of the past.

In discussing events in the region, it should first be emphasized that neither the German nor the Italian forces were large enough to keep order everywhere. The enlarged Croatian state contained some of the wildest and most remote areas of Yugoslavia, places where repeated rebellions had been centered in the past and where national antagonisms had always been particularly bitter. Regular administration soon broke down, and conditions of complete anarchy followed. This situation became worse when the new Croatian leadership embarked on a policy of annihilation of the Serbian third of the population. Muslims joined with Croats against the Serbs, who were often faced with the alternatives of extermination, expulsion, or conversion to Catholicism. Where they could, Serbian villages replied with reprisals against their Croatian and Muslim neighbors, often with Italian aid. In this situation of chaos and national civil war, it was inevitable that the casualties would be

9  Vladko Maček, *In the Struggle for Freedom* (University Park: Pennsylvania State University Press, 1957), p. 230.

high; it has been estimated, for example, that as many as 350,000 Serbs were killed at this time.[10]

At the same time, in line with the previous Croatian-nationalist creed that Serbs were simply apostate Croats, an effort was made to force conversions. About 200,000 to 300,000 Orthodox, only a small fraction of the total number, became Catholics. When this policy failed to produce the desired result, the government created a Croatian Orthodox church; its members were regarded as truly Croatian, but of another creed.

The chaotic conditions created by the massacres and the maladministration of the state produced a situation that was extremely unfavorable for the occupying powers. The Axis leaders would have much preferred a government under a responsible, traditional leadership. Although repeated approaches were made to Maček, he consistently refused to take an active part in political life. A division of opinion also existed among the German officials. The commander of the occupation forces, General Edmund von Glaise-Horstenau, wanted to end the terrorism and violence of the Ustaša regime, which he believed was damaging to the German military interests. He was opposed by the political officer, Siegfried Kasche, who had close connections with Ribbentrop and who was convinced that the Ustaša was the only Croatian group upon whom the Axis could rely.

The major German aim in the occupation was to protect the military communications and to obtain raw materials. Men were also needed for labor in German industry. Some were obtained from among the war prisoners and those scheduled to be deported; others volunteered. Extremely short of manpower to hold the extended frontiers, the Axis authorities sought the assistance of reliable local elements to keep order in the country and to put down any resistance to their rule. We have already seen how valuable garrison duties were performed by the Bulgarian army in Macedonia, in Thrace, and eventually in part of Serbia. The German command thus had an interest in strengthening the military arm of the Croatian state, the Home Guard, or *Domobranci*. Some of its members were sent to Germany for training, and the preparation of this force for action was rushed. Since a strong partisan movement made its appearance almost at once, these men never received an adequate training. The Ustaša regime thus did not have an experienced or reliable military support. Because all of the top commanders and most of the officers in the former Yugoslav army had been Serbs, there was, of course, a shortage of Croats with adequate military training and experience.

In Croatia, as elsewhere in the Balkans, the Axis was able to exploit national grievances and hatreds. After the surrender of Italy in 1943, the territory in Dalmatia that had been occupied by that country was handed over to

---

10   Jozo Tomasevich, "Yugoslavia during the Second World War," in Wayne S. Vucinich, ed., *Contemporary Yugoslavia: Twenty Years of Socialist Experiment* (Berkeley: University of California Press, 1969), p. 78.

the Ustaša regime. The Greater Croatia of this year was thus composed of all of the lands, except Istria and Rijeka, to which the Croatian nationalists had previously laid claims. Through the fulfillment of nationalist dreams and objectives that had been severely frustrated in the past, the Ustaša leaders did win some popular support. An example of the deep passion that could be aroused by such issues is given by Maček, who noticed that one of the guards assigned to him was obviously a devout Catholic. When asked if he did not fear the punishment of God because of the crimes he had committed, the guard replied: "Don't talk to me about that . . . for I am perfectly aware of what is in store for me. For my past, present and future deeds I shall burn in hell, but at least I shall burn for Croatia."[11]

The major centers of opposition to the Axis occupation and the affiliated regimes were from the resistance forces that were soon organized throughout the country. Moreover, after the conquest an official Yugoslav government-in-exile, which was recognized by the Allied powers, including the Soviet Union, was established in London by King Peter and his fellow emigrés. Separated from events in Yugoslavia and maintaining a Serbian-national bias, these men held what was to become an increasingly unrealistic view of the situation at home. Their main preoccupation was with past grievances and with the problems of the interwar period, the chief of which had been the bitter Croatian–Serbian controversies. Influenced by reports of the massacre of Serbs in Croatia, they did not wish to continue to observe the terms of the Sporazum of 1939, which had left large numbers of Serbs under Croatian administration. The first premier of the exile government was General Dušan Simović, who had led the coup of 1941. In January 1942 he was replaced by Slobodan Jovanović, a leading Serbian historian. In this cabinet Colonel Draža Mihailović was named minister for the army, navy and the air force. This officer, active within Yugoslavia, had organized the guerilla bands that were loyal to the government-in-exile.

From the first days of the Axis occupation conditions in Yugoslavia were almost ideal for the formation of an armed resistance. The very swiftness of the war and the surrender meant that the country was never completely occupied, nor was it possible for the conquerors to collect and destroy all of the available arms. As a result, after the armistice, armed men without leaders were in ready supply. The importance of the Balkan tradition of resistance and the romanticization of the role of the guerilla fighter and the bandit have been described throughout this account. After the collapse of the regular government, with the German and Italian forces unable to occupy the entire territory effectively, the general situation was most favorable for revolt. The actions of the Pavelić regime and the outbreak of violence between the nationalities also forced many to enroll in armed bands for self-protection. Conditions in Yugoslavia were thus in strong contrast to those in Romania and

11 Maček, *In the Struggle for Freedom*, p. 245.

Bulgaria, where the regular administration and army held control throughout the war, and there was no enemy occupation.

Immediately after the surrender in May 1941, Colonel Mihailović and a small group of Serbian officers went into the hills to organize a center of resistance. Mihailović called his forces the Chetnik Detachments of the Yugoslav Army; the term *chetnik* recalled to memory similar groups that had fought against Ottoman rule. Closely associated with the government-in-exile and King Peter, this organization attracted an almost exclusively Serbian following. Its members thus tended to be both anti-Croat and anti-Communist. The Chetnik army became primarily an association of individual bands under local leaders who confined their activities to their own territories. Because of this situation, Mihailović often did not have full control over his subordinates, and he lacked mobility. Throughout the war the Chetniks and their leader remained loyal to the old regime, that is, to the king and the previous Serbian-dominated Yugoslavia. They supported the traditional political and social system.

The major resistance movement, that of the Partisans, was of a very different nature. Its leader was Josip Broz Tito, the general secretary of the Yugoslav Communist Party. Although the Communist leadership of the organization was effective from the beginning, Tito and his followers appealed to all of the parties and nationalities for support. Following the popular-front idea, the Partisans called for the unity of all patriotic forces against the invaders. The chief support for this movement came at first from the peasant population of the mountain areas, where conditions were the harshest. Here guerilla bands composed of the local peasantry could operate with relative freedom and could obtain supplies, given willingly or unwillingly, from the local population.

The Partisan bands, who could, of course, not defeat the occupation forces by regular military tactics, used the guerilla actions that had proved so effective in the Balkans in the past. Their forces struck at the weak points in the Axis defenses or against small, isolated detachments of troops or individuals. Like all guerilla warfare, these methods led to high casualties and atrocities on both sides, but they were effective. The movement also benefited from the fact that the central leadership was tightly united, with a strong ideological base, and it could and did enforce discipline.

At first some attempts were made by the Partisans and the Chetniks to work together; both, after all, had the objective of expelling the enemy. The unification and cooperation of resistance forces in all occupied countries was also urged by the Western powers and the Soviet Union. A basic disagreement, however, soon arose on the conduct of the struggle. After the German invasion, it will be recalled, Soviet policy had shifted sharply. Where previously the Comintern instructions had emphasized opposition to the "imperialists," the Moscow directives now called for an open struggle against the Axis. The Communist parties were to engage immediately in actions that would distract the enemy and kill its soldiers, no matter what the cost to the participants. The safety of the motherland of socialism was to be the first consideration of the loyal party member, before his own life, property, or country. With these orders the Partisans did launch repeated actions against the occupying powers, and these attacks were difficult for both the Germans and the Italians to combat. Many German troops had to be removed to the Russian front, particularly after the failure of the first offensive. Vastly outnumbered and untrained in guerilla warfare, the occupation armies, whether German, Italian, or Bulgarian, adopted a policy of reprisal. For instance, according to a German directive of September 1941, a hundred hostages were to be executed for each German killed and fifty for each wounded. The measure was applied chiefly in Serbia, where the most extreme example of the implementation of the order occurred. In October 1941 ten Germans were killed and twenty-six were wounded in Kragujevac. In reprisal, seven thousand of the city's inhabitants were executed, including schoolchildren.

Although resistance, even with high casualties, fitted the Communist party line, the implications of this policy were difficult for many Serbian leaders to accept. Like French politicians before the war, some Serbs were obsessed by fears for the future of their nation. It appeared to them that, among the South Slavic people, they had suffered the greatest losses in the past. During World War I the Serbian nation had lost 20 percent of its population as a result of battle losses, disease, and privation. In the first period of the Axis occupation reports of massacres of Serbs came not only from the Croatian-controlled territories, but also from the Kosovo region, which was under Albanian and Italian rule. Preoccupied with fears of national suicide, the Chetnik commanders, who fully expected an eventual Allied victory, saw no point in actions that could not succeed and that would entail enormous losses. They therefore preferred to organize their forces and prepare for the expected Allied intervention. The danger of this policy, of course, was the difficulty of maintaining an active, enthusiastic guerilla organization when its members seldom went into battle. Many of Mihailović's forces were in fact disbanded to await future action; some of the members enlisted with the Nedić government.

Even more serious than the disagreement over tactics was the division between the Chetniks and the Partisans over the future of Yugoslavia. Closely connected with the London government, the Mihailović supporters were loyal to the king and the former system. As far as the organization of the country after the war was concerned, they expected an even stronger Serbian role in the government. Convinced that the Croats had betrayed Yugoslavia in 1941, they favored an increase in the territorial jurisdiction of Serbia and its absolutely preponderant position among the national regions. Although such a program might appeal to the Serbs, it had no attraction for the Croats, Macedonians, Albanians, Slovenes, and Bosnian Muslims – the people who, after all, composed the majority of the Yugoslav population.

In contrast, one of the principal attractions of the Partisan movement was its position on the national question. Tito, himself of a mixed Croatian–Slovenian peasant background, attempted to stand above these quarrels. The Communist position had been to defend the equal rights of all the constitutent nationalities of the Yugoslav state. The first major Partisan support came from the Serbian population under attack by the Ustaša forces. Later the movement recruited followers from all of the national areas. The Partisan political program called for the reorganization of the state on the basis of a federation of the nationalities, a position that was to attract wide popular support.

By November 1941 the early efforts to secure cooperation between the Chetniks and Partisans had failed. A very complicated situation arose. Although a German and Italian occupation had been established in the Yugoslav lands, the officials of the two powers did not always agree, and there were similar divisions of opinion on how the country should be treated within the governments of these two states. Collaborating regimes held power in both Belgrade and Zagreb, but their ability to control their administrative regions was always in doubt. In the countryside, two major resistance organizations had been formed, with opposing leaderships and different political, national, and social programs. It should be added that a similar division existed in the Slovene lands, where there were differences within the collaborating groups and between the right and left organizations of the resistance. In Macedonia the situation was further confused by the national rivalries and by the struggle between the Bulgarian and the Yugoslav Communist parties for control of the resistance. Needless to say, in this chaotic situation many combinations among their competing elements were possible. As it became increasingly apparent that the Axis would lose the war, each group concentrated primarily on assuring its position in the postwar world. Some strange alliances were thus made. Although instances of cooperation between members of all of the resistance forces and the occupying powers can be found, the most widespread collaboration, and that most easily documented, was established between the Chetniks and the Axis command.

After June 1941 the Soviet Union, as we have seen, supported strong resistance movements in all Axis-occupied lands in order to relieve the pressure on its own forces. Until the final surrender of the German army, it was in the Soviet interest to have partisan bands continue an active, aggressive policy. However, hard pressed in its own sphere of activity and never in possession of a surplus of war matériel, the Soviet government was unable to extend adequate military assistance to the guerilla organizations. In contrast, the British leaders, with their major interest in the future control of the Mediterranean and their particular interest in Greece, had both the ability and the desire to cooperate with Balkan resistance organizations. Although British missions were thus sent to both Tito's Partisan and the Chetnik headquarters, increasing evidence soon became available that Chetnik units were cooperating with the Axis and with the Nedić regime in operations against Tito. The British government therefore gradually shifted its policy until by the spring of 1944 all its assistance was being channeled to the Partisans. Yet despite this attitude toward Mihailović, British backing was still given to King Peter and his government-in-exile.

From the summer of 1941 on, the resistance movements were a major problem for the German and Italian military commands. Although their primary concern was to maintain the lines of communication to Greece, on the one hand, and along the Danube, on the other, the German occupation authorities could not allow the Partisan movement to gain such strength that it could literally take over the country. During the war years they therefore organized what postwar Yugoslav historians have designated as seven campaigns, in which they had at different times the cooperation of the Italians, the Ustaša, Nedić's forces, and the Chetniks. The aim of all of these undertakings was to surround and destroy the Partisan bands. Although they were able to inflict major casualties on their opponents, the Germans did not succeed in their basic objective of destroying the insurgent leadership and capturing Tito. Operating under extremely difficult conditions, Tito and his closest associates were able to avoid encirclement and to hold their organization together.

After the surrender of Italy in September 1943, the German position became even more difficult. Huge quantities of Italian arms fell into Partisan hands. The German command was continually apprehensive that an Allied force would land in the peninsula, and the guerilla bands would rush to its assistance. The growing conviction that the war would be won by the Allies also made it increasingly difficult for the German authorities to retain the cooperation of any local organization: all were concerned with the probable postwar conditions.

As the war drew to a close, it was apparent that the Partisans had established an advantage over any possible political opponent within Yugoslavia. The London regime, despite the fact that it held a strong international position, did not have an administrative structure within the country. In contrast, Tito was in fact in effective control of the state. Whenever the Partisans had occupied a region, they had organized committees of peasants to run local affairs and to maintain law and order. Even when the Partisans lost control of an area, these political auxiliaries remained active. In November 1942 the Partisan leaders held a conference at Bihać, where they established a central authority called the Anti-Fascist Council for the National Liberation of Yugoslavia, abbreviated as AVNOJ. This organization, an assembly of fifty-four representatives from different sections of the country, was set up on a broad political basis, but the Communist Party was the dominating force. The popular-front program, which was announced at the conference, called for the establishment of a freely elected government after the war and, most important, a federal organization for the state.

In November 1943 a second meeting was held in Jajce in Bosnia. AVNOJ was declared to be the government of Yugoslavia; a ministry was appointed, and Dr. Ivan Ribar became president. Tito received the title of marshal and remained in command of the armed forces. Most significant, the authority of the government-in-exile was repudiated. Elections were to be held to determine the question of the return of the king and his ministers. The federal organization was again reaffirmed.

Two separate Yugoslav authorities thus existed. Despite the continued Allied recognition of the London government, military assistance was being given to the Partisans. In May 1944 the German command launched an airborne attack on Tito's temporary headquarters at Drvar in Bosnia, and he barely escaped. He was subsequently evacuated to Italy, and from there to the British-occupied island of Vis. The British government had, of course, every interest in reconciling the two political centers. Extreme pressure was placed on King Peter to repudiate Mihailović and to form a government that could come to an understanding with the Partisans. Finally, in June 1944, Dr. Ivan Šubašić, of the Croatian Peasant Party, became the premier of the government-in-exile and immediately left to negotiate with Tito in Vis. On June 16 he signed an agreement that gave the chief advantages to the Partisan side. Its terms required the London government to recognize AVNOJ as the only political authority within Yugoslavia, and the Partisan army as the official armed force. The question of the monarchy would be decided after the war.

In the summer of 1944 it was obvious that the fighting in the Balkans would soon end; the German forces had begun to withdraw. In August Tito met with Churchill in Naples, and then in September, in a surprise action, he flew to the Soviet Union without informing the British government. Hitherto his closest relations had been with the British military mission. In the Soviet Union he came to an understanding with authorities there on the steps to be taken in the final liberation of the country. In October the Partisans, with Soviet assistance, took Belgrade. Thereafter the Soviet army passed through northern Yugoslavia and on into Central Europe. Tito's forces, in control of the country, were free to eliminate their domestic political adversaries, which they did with great ruthlessness.

Although the enemy armies had by the spring of 1945 left the land, the Partisans still faced internal opposition. First they had to deal with the remnants of the Chetnik detachments and the groups that had collaborated with the Axis, such as the Ustaša, the Croatian Home Guard, and the supporters of Nedić and Ljotić. The issues at this time were neither simple nor clear-cut. The majority of Yugoslavs were certainly not in favor of a Communist government; the party had won the sympathy of only a small minority of the population before the war. Its members, however, dominated AVNOJ and the armed forces; no rival political center was allowed to function. The Partisan leaders used the opportunities offered by the postwar situation not only to take revenge against the true collaborators, but also to assure that no political opposition was allowed to organize. The Chetnik forces, representing the former regime, caused no problems. By the end of the war they had been reduced to 10,000 to 12,000 troops, and most of these men were subsequently caught and killed. Mihailović himself was captured, tried, and executed in July 1946. The most bloody episode, however, involved the fate of the Croatian supporters of the Pavelić regime.

Although many Croats hastened to join the ranks of the victors at the end of the war, others were unable to take such an action either because they had been compromised by their activities during the war, such as membership in the Ustaša or the Home Guard, or because they opposed the Partisan political stand. Over 100,000 of these people, with their families and other refugees, decided to flee northward and surrender to the British army, an action that led to the last mass atrocity in Yugoslavia during the war. On May 15, at the Austrian village of Bleiburg, this group tried to surrender to the British command. Because of an inter-Allied agreement that prisoners were to be turned over to the government against which they had fought, the British handed these men over to the Partisans. Many, including civilians, died within the next weeks. It has been estimated that between 40,000 and 100,000 perished at this time.

Not only did the Partisans win over all other elements in the Serbian, Croatian, and Slovenian regions, but they were able to take full control in two areas of the old Yugoslav state, Macedonia and Kosovo, where the previous national policies had been under strong Comintern attack. The Yugoslav Communist Party was to show itself fully capable of defending and extending state interests even when its measures were in conflict with certain previous Communist declarations. Before the war, as we have seen, the Comintern had called for an independent or autonomous Macedonia that would include not only Aegean (Greek) and Vardar (Yugoslav) Macedonia, but also Pirin (Bulgarian) Macedonia. Bulgarians of all political parties had approved such a stand. Yugoslav Communists, however, although they had previously accepted the Comintern program, were soon shown to have other ideas.

The Communist parties of both Bulgaria and Yugoslavia were faced with the Macedonian issue when in the spring of 1941 Bulgarian troops occupied the region. If the Macedonians were indeed Bulgars, or if they formed a separate nationality, then the Bulgarian Communist Party could expect to exert its authority in Skopje. Metodi Šatarov, the secretary for the Macedonian Communist Party, which was a branch of the Yugoslav, tended toward such a Bulgarian orientation. In order to maintain its influence, the Yugoslav party sent Lazar Koliševski to the region in May 1941. Although the chief advantages were at first on the Bulgarian side, this situation changed when Germany attacked the Soviet Union and the Comintern called for armed risings to aid the Soviet cause. As has been shown, it was difficult for the weak Bulgarian party to organize partisan activities that would be directed against Bulgarian soldiers. In this situation the more militant Yugoslav organizers were able to launch the first actions, and in the fall of 1941 Partisan detachments were formed under Koliševski's direction. Their efforts, however, met with an early disaster. The Bulgarian occupation forces were able to break the party organization and crush the first Partisan actions.

In 1943 the Yugoslav Partisans again attempted to organize a resistance movement in Macedonia. They had by this time decided that the region would become a part of the future federal Yugoslav state. To implement their policies they sent an able organizer, Svetozar Vukmanović, also known as Tempo, to get in touch not only with Macedonian groups, but also with partisan units in Greece and Albania. The Yugoslavs thus held the initiative. In November 1943, at the Jajce congress, Macedonia was declared to be one of the six constituent republics of Yugoslavia. This action placed the Bulgarian Communist Party on the defensive, since it brought into question the status of Pirin Macedonia. After this time, the Bulgarian influence was effectively excluded. With the withdrawal of the Bulgarian occupation forces in 1944, the control of the area passed into Yugoslav hands. The Soviet government gave its support to this development.

The issue of Kosovo was decided by similar determined actions. During the war the region had been under Italian and Albanian occupation; the Partisan leadership solved the problem of its future by simply taking over the direction of the resistance forces in Albania.

## Albania

After the conquest of Albania in 1939 the Italian government introduced a new administration for the country. As in Montenegro and Croatia later, the Italian preference was for the establishment of a constitutional monarchy under the house of Savoy. The Albanian army and diplomatic corps were immediately amalgamated into those of Italy. Because relations between the two countries had been close in the past, the Italian officials did not have difficulty in finding collaborators. At first, Shefqet Verlaci, the largest landowner in the country, worked closely with them. Friction, however, soon developed, and he was replaced by Mustafa Kruja in December 1941.

The Italian invasion of Greece did not, as we have seen, produce any cooperation between Albanians and Greeks, despite their common opponent. In fact, it soon became clear that the Greek desire to annex southern Albania had not diminished; in a similar fashion, Albanian nationalists continued to claim a part of Greek Epirus. After the fall of both Yugoslavia and Greece in May 1941, Albania, although still, of course, under Italian domination, was given the control of the Kosovo region. Like Bulgaria and Croatia, Albania saw the realization of some of the chief nationalist aims during the Axis occupation.

Nevertheless, a resistance was organized there as well as in the neighboring Greek and Yugoslav lands. In 1940 Abas Kupi, representing the northern clans, had organized bands in support of King Zog. For the future, however, the most important groups were those that were formed by the Communist Party and the rival National Front, or Balli Kombëtar. The Communist Party, as we shall see, was largely a product of Yugoslav initiatives.

The weakness of Communist influence before the war has already been discussed. No formal organization existed. The Communist ranks were primarily composed of Western-trained intellectuals who felt that they had no place in the traditional, conservative Albanian society. They were joined by some landless peasants and other groups who were deeply dissatisfied with Albanian conditions. A major flaw in the intellectual leadership was its tendency to break into rival factions and quarrel on ideological points. It has been estimated that this minute organization in early 1941 was split into eight separate groups, two of which were Trotskyite, that is, in opposition to the Soviet regime. Observing the confusion in the Communist fold, Tito in October 1941 sent two delegates, Dušan Mugoša and Mladen Popović. They brought together the leaders and factions that they favored, and a regular Communist Party was organized. Enver Hoxha was appointed as party secretary, and a central committee of eleven was chosen. In November, after this meeting, 130 members were admitted officially to the party.

The Yugoslav guidance was thorough. The Albanian party was instructed on points of organization, on recruitment, and on how to work in the villages. A youth organization was also set up. Similarly, under Yugoslav direction, a popular-front political coalition was established in September 1942, which was called the National Liberation Movement, abbreviated in Albanian LNC. Although the Communists predominated, the body included some members of other political beliefs. By March 1943 its Army of National Liberation had authority over most of the partisan bands.

In October 1942 Balli Kombëtar, the second resistance movement, was formed. It was headed by Ali Klissura and Midhat Frashëri, the well-known national leader. Its members, who were liberal and nationalistic, opposed the return of King Zog and favored the establishment of a republic and a wide program of domestic reform. In contrast to the LNC, they were Western-oriented and anti-Soviet. They also wished to retain the boundaries of 1941, including the Kosovo district. In general, the LNC concentrated on the cities and Balli Kombëtar on the peasantry. They also differed on the methods to be used. Here, as in Yugoslavia, the Communist-led guerillas did not concern themselves about reprisals; they felt, in fact, that atrocities committed by the occupation aided their own recruitment. The Balli Kombëtar leaders favored more conservative actions, and they worried about reprisals against their peasant followers.

As in Yugoslavia and Greece, the British government through its military missions in the Balkans urged the two resistance groups to unite. Before the invasion of Sicily, the British agents wished to create the impression that an Allied landing in the Balkans was actually being planned. For reasons of security the local partisan groups had to be convinced that such an action would indeed take place. The Western governments also had a strong interest in securing the united backing of all of the partisan bands in the campaign against the Axis. Under Allied prodding the leaders of the two major organizations met in August 1943 at Mukaj, where they formed the Committee for the Salvation of Albania. A disagreement arose here over the future of Kosovo, which Balli Kombëtar wanted to retain after the war. Although both groups agreed that a plebiscite should be held in the region, the LNC soon repudiated this understanding under Yugoslav pressure. The Yugoslav Partisans had no intention of surrendering the district, despite the fact that the Communist Party had favored such an action in 1940. Tito's emissary, Vukmanović-Tempo, now arrived in Albania, and the Yugoslav ascendancy in the LNC was reinforced.

The Italian surrender in September 1943 had, of course, major repercussions in Albania. There as elsewhere the partisans acquired more weapons. A German occupation, however, was effectively established; a parachute division took Tirana. Thereafter the German authorities concentrated on holding the major cities and the coastline; the resistance forces were in control in the mountains. Interested primarily in securing a stable administration, the German government announced that it would recognize Albanian independence, and a regency was appointed. No opposition was expressed to the possible return of Zog. The state was declared neutral, and a national police and army were organized. With their major concern directed toward the defense of the lines of communication and invasion, the German authorities interfered little in the running of the Albanian administration. They did, however, give a great deal of ostentatious support to the Albanian acquisition of Kosovo. At the same time, Albanian groups cooperating with the occupation, notably the Skanderbeg S.S. Division, carried on a campaign of expulsion and extermination against the Serbian population in the disputed area.

Meanwhile, the resistance remained divided into competing groups. After the breakdown of the Mukaj agreement, members of Balli Kombëtar, as well as other nationalists, worked with the Tirana government. Abas Kupi, who had previously cooperated with the LNC, broke with this group and formed his own organization, called Legality, which opposed both the LNC and Balli Kombëtar. He had the support of the northern Gheg clans, who favored the restoration of Zog. The strongest political force, however, remained the Communist-dominated LNC. In May 1944 it held a congress at Përmët, and, again following Yugoslav examples, the representatives set up the Anti-Fascist Council of National Liberation, with Enver Hoxha at its head. At a second meeting, held in Berat in October 1944, a provisional government was formed.

The Albanian political future, of course, was to be decided by events taking place elsewhere. As during World War I, Albania's position was precarious. The claims of its neighbors on its territory were bound to be reasserted. The Allied powers had never recognized an Albanian government-in-exile or King Zog. In fact, the Albanian question was not discussed by the Allied statesmen at any of the major conferences. Because of the Yugoslav relationship to the LNC, there was a strong possibility that Yugoslavia would replace Italy as the Albanian protector. As far as the internal situation was concerned, the LNC clearly had control of the strongest armed force; it had established its authority over much of the country, and it had the backing of the victorious Yugoslav Partisan movement. When the German forces withdrew in November 1944 and their regime in Tirana collapsed, the LNC had little difficulty in establishing its ascendancy.

## Greece

In the months between the Italian attack in October 1940 and the German conquest in April 1941, the Greek government functioned as before. After the death of Metaxas, Alexander Koryzis became premier; the country did not return to constitutional rule. Most of the members of the Greek Communist Party, the KKE, were in jail, and the principal Republican leaders were in exile. During the previous period of crisis the nation had been united by the necessity of fighting the Italian invasion, and the king became a symbol of resistance. After the surrender George II, like King Peter, fled abroad and formed a government-in-exile in London, which received Allied recognition. A second center of Greek activity was established in Cairo after the British victories over the Axis in North Africa. Here a Greek army, navy, and air force that operated under the British command were organized.

Like their Yugoslav counterparts, the Greek politicians in exile tended to continue their controversies on prewar lines. Among the Yugoslavs the national question had predominated. For the Greek exiles the principal unresolved political issue remained the familiar conflict between the Republicans and the Royalists. This basic split weakened and divided the Greek emigrés. The first premier of the London-based government was Emmanuel Tsouderos, a Cretan of Republican and Venizelist political convictions. His government was subsequently widened to bring in more Republican representation. A great weakness of this regime was its isolation from events in Greece. In contrast to the Yugoslavs, the Greek royal regime never acquired the allegiance of an insurgent force in Greece; there was thus no Greek Mihailović. The government's relations with the resistance groups during the war were carried on through the intermediary of the British military mission in Greece, and the Greek forces in Egypt were its sole military arm.

After the conquest of Greece, the victor powers divided the responsibilities of administration (see Map II). Bulgarian troops, as we have seen, assumed occupation duties in most of Thrace and in part of Greek Macedonia. Athens and other major centers were held by German soldiers; Italian and Albanian garrisons controlled other regions. As in Serbia, an administration that cooperated with the Axis was organized in the capital; it was headed successively by General Tsolakoglou, I. Logothetopoulos, and D. Rallis, who con-

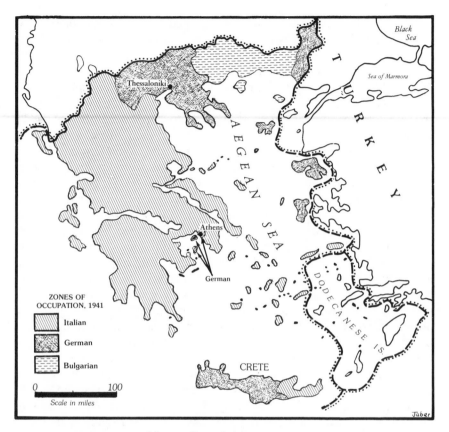

Map II. Occupied Greece, 1941

sidered it their primary duty to assure political order until the end of the war. Most of the former military and political leaders remained in Athens, where they maintained a passive attitude. The majority simply awaited the outcome of the war and what they expected to be an Allied victory. Some, such as Archbishop Damaskinos and Colonel Evert, the head of the police, stayed in office and were able to give secret assistance to the British. The first winter of the occupation was a national disaster. Prior to the war Greece had imported about 45 percent of its wheat; with the British blockade in force there was simply not enough food available, and widespread starvation resulted. Subsequently, the blockade was eased enough to allow Red Cross relief shipments.

As in other parts of the occupied Balkans, the Axis authorities did not attempt to administer the entire country: about two-thirds of the territory and half of the population were not under the effective authority of the central administration. Again, as in the neighboring states, anarchical conditions arose, particularly in the mountains; they created a favorable environment for the rise of resistance movements. Here, as elsewhere, the strongest forces were those under Communist direction.

Prior to the war the Communist Party had not played a major role in Greek political life except for the brief period when its actions had contributed to the establishment of the Metaxas dictatorship. The party itself had no wide appeal; its membership came from among unhappy intellectuals, the city middle classes, the aggrieved minorities, and in particular, the refugees from Anatolia. Its attraction had been gravely weakened by the Comintern position on an independent Macedonia. At this time the two most important leaders were Nikos Zachariadis, who led the party from 1931 to 1941 and again from 1945 to 1956, and George Siantos, who was the principal figure during the war years, when Zachariadis was in the Dachau concentration camp. Like their fellow Communists elsewhere, the Greek party had been confused by the signing of the Nazi–Soviet Pact in 1939 and the subsequent cooperation between the Axis and the Soviet Union. The leadership at this time instructed its members to follow the example of "the heroic fraternal people of Bulgaria," [12] who were, of course, cooperating fully with the Axis. The Communist position was simplified exceedingly after the German attack on the Soviet Union; a strongly nationalistic position could be adopted toward the occupying powers, and the former political agitation continued.

In the fall of 1941 guerilla organizations arose throughout the mountain regions of Greece. In September, under Communist leadership, the National Liberation Front, or EAM, was formed. Its membership included a wide spectrum of political opinion, not only of the left, but also of those factions and individuals that had opposed the Metaxas dictatorship and the king. The Republican element was particularly strong. Closely attached to this political center was the military arm, the National Popular Liberation Army, or ELAS, which became active first in the summer of 1942. Other resistance groups arose at the same time. The most important rival to EAM/ELAS was the National Republican Greek League, or EDES, which was formed in September 1941 under the command of Colonel Napoleon Zervas. It recognized the authority of General Plastiras, the Republican leader, who was living at the time in exile in France. A third, much smaller, group, the National and Social Liberation, or EKKA, led by Colonel Dimitrios Psaros, was not organized until early 1943. Liberal and Republican in political orientation, it played a lesser role than the other resistance organizations. It will be noted that the leadership in the resistance was Republican and Communist; there was no equivalent Royalist group. The former senior Greek army officers either had left the country or remained outside political life.

Greek events were to be profoundly affected by the British military and political decisions. Determined to maintain its imperial position and to con-

---

12  Woodhouse, *The Struggle for Greece*, p. 17.

trol the Mediterranean, the British government wished to exert the predominant influence in Greece after the war. The United States readily conceded a prior British role in military planning in the area. The major British concern was preventing Greece from falling into the hands of guerilla groups with a primary Communist, and thus presumably Soviet, direction. Although there was much disagreement on the correct course to pursue, strong support was given to the king's government as the best basis on which to build for the future. At the same time, the British leaders attempted to make use of the resistance forces within Greece, all of which had either a Republican or a Communist leadership, against the Axis enemy. The British government was thus faced with a difficult dilemma: its military and political objectives were in a sense in conflict.

Despite these problems, the attempt was made to implement what became a double line of policy. In the fall of 1942 the British army was preparing to launch a military campaign in North Africa. The major German supply lines for this area ran through the Balkans. In order to assure that the main railroad would be cut for a significant period, British parachutists were sent to Greece at the end of September 1942. They organized the existing partisans into a guerilla group that succeeded in blowing up the Gorgopotamos viaduct on this vital rail line. The British officers assigned to this operation subsequently remained in the country and worked with some of the resistance groups. Their aim was not the organization of an underground Greek army, but the establishment of a kind of federation of guerilla bands under British control. Such actions, however, obviously conflicted with the political objectives of the government. A member of the British mission at this time, C. M. Woodhouse, has commented on the difficult position of the British representatives, who were "required to safeguard the position of the King, which could only have been done by ensuring that there was no resistance at all. Such an alternative was illusory in practice, since resistance had already begun, mainly on the initiative of anti-monarchists, before any British officers arrived in Greece."[13]

In the summer of 1943 the Allies needed the cooperation of the guerilla groups in another major undertaking. On the eve of the invasion of Sicily, the Allied command wished to distract the Axis into believing that the main thrust would be against the Balkans. In June and July Operation Animals was thus begun. Because security was even worse in Greece than elsewhere, the Greek partisan leaders, as well as the Albanian, had to be convinced that a Balkan landing would indeed take place. Here too, as in Yugoslavia, a major attempt was made to unite the various resistance forces. In July 1943 the British effort met with success with the signing of the National Bands Agreement, in which the guerilla groups agreed to cooperate against the Axis. In order to strengthen the political front, the British mission in August arranged to fly six members of the resistance groups to Cairo to consult with represent-

13   Woodhouse, *The Struggle for Greece*, p. 37.

atives of the government-in-exile. Although the majority represented the EAM/ELAS interest, EDES and EKKA each had a delegate. Once in Egypt, the resistance leaders brought up the major dividing issue at once. They wished a coalition government to be formed in which they would have representation, and, most important, they did not want the king to return to Greece before a plebiscite was held on the question of the monarchy. After consulting with both Churchill and Roosevelt, George II refused this demand. He wanted to be in Athens before the plebiscite took place. As a result of this decision, the partisan representatives went back to Greece without an agreement.

The next major step in the developing Greek crisis occurred after the overthrow of Mussolini and the Italian surrender. The partisan bands, in particular EAM/ELAS, were in a much stronger position. EAM had acquired enough Italian equipment to assure its superiority over the other competing guerilla organizations. Less dependent on Allied supplies, the leaders could adopt a more independent attitude. They expected that the war would end soon, and they were convinced that an Allied force of a respectable size would be sent to Greece. Foreseeing that the British government would attempt to restore the old regime, the EAM leadership was determined to gain full control of the country before a British expeditionary force arrived. With this objective in mind, ELAS in October 1943 launched an attack on the rival partisan bands. This month marked the beginning of the first stage in the long Greek civil war that was to last until 1949. The main ELAS target was Zervas and his EDES band. ELAS had the services of about fifteen thousand fighting men; Zervas had only five thousand. In addition, ELAS had an advantage in weaponry, since after the Italian surrender it had acquired not only small arms, but also artillery, mortars, and machine guns. Despite this superiority, ELAS was able to subdue only the small independent guerilla units; EDES remained intact.

By Christmas it had become clear that there would be no Allied landing and that EDES would still be active. In February 1944 an armistice was arranged through British mediation. At this time, another armed force assumed significance. In the summer of 1943, largely as a reaction to the violent deeds of the partisans and their increasing political influence, some prominent Greeks, including the generals Pangalos and Gonatas, had joined the Security Battalions that had been formed under the German occupation regime. Their aim was to assure the maintenance of law and order in the threatened districts.

In March 1944 EAM established the Political Committee of National Liberation, or PEEA. Like AVNOJ this group was potentially a rival authority to the government-in-exile in London. Although many of the members of PEEA were not Communists, the party continued to play the leading role in the partisan movement. Its position was considerably affected by events that took place at this point in Egypt.

The major weakness of the Royalist government, as we have seen, was its lack of an armed force in Greece; its strongest asset was the support that it received from the British government and from Winston Churchill in particular. Obviously, it would be to the advantage of the British and their protégés if some sort of a unified regime could be established. There were in fact many efforts made to bring representatives of the resistance into contact with the emigré government. All of these foundered on the continued objections of the parties of the left to the immediate return of the king. The Royalist position was severely damaged when in April 1944 mutinies broke out in the Greek military and naval units in Egypt. Despite widespread suspicions at the time, these actions were not organized by either the EAM or the KKE, though members of the Communist Party as well as Republicans were among the leadership. Discontent had been widespread among these troops for a long time. Although the uprising was suppressed by the British army, the revolt meant that for a period the royal government was completely without an armed auxiliary. A thorough purge of the military forces had to be undertaken; about ten thousand officers and men were sent to concentration camps. New units were then formed of those who were considered completely trustworthy, those who would support the king and thus ultimately the British interests in Greece.

At the same time a major reorganization was undertaken in the composition of the London government, and a real attempt was made to reconcile the disputing factions. After the mutiny Tsouderos was replaced by Sofoklis Venizelos, but he soon resigned in favor of George Papandreou, who was to become the major political figure in this period. Papandreou, who called himself a Social Democrat and who had approved of the British suppression of the mutiny, organized a meeting that was held in Lebanon in May 1944. This conference was attended by twenty-five delegates representing all of the major political parties and resistance organizations, including PEEA, ELAS, EAM, and EKKA. It was decided that a new coalition government would be formed and that the left parties would receive positions in the ministry. Although this agreement was accepted by the PEEA and EAM delegates, their actions were repudiated after they returned home. As a result, the offices allotted to this group were not immediately taken up.

A radical change, however, soon took place in this negative attitude. As we shall see in the next section, the Soviet Union had by this time conceded the British predominance in Greece. In July 1944 a Soviet emissary, Colonel Gregory Popov, arrived in the country by way of Yugoslavia. Although it is not known precisely what he told the EAM leaders, he may have informed them that they should deal with Britain. In September they therefore took the posts assigned to them in the government. Even more important, in that same month they accepted the Caserta agreement, which provided that all of the partisan bands were to be placed under the authority of Papandreou's newly organized Greek Government of National Unity, and ultimately under the direct command of the British general, Sir Ronald Scobie. Thus, despite its overwhelmingly predominant military position, EAM/ELAS agreed to enter the coalition government and to subordinate its armed forces to British control.

In September 1944 the German troops began withdrawing from Greece. Athens was evacuated on October 12, and a British occupation force entered the city a few days later. The British command faced a potentially volcanic situation. Since there had been no invasion of the Balkans, there was no Allied army on the spot to enforce the authority of the Greek government. Britain could spare only a small contingent, at first just four thousand troops, most of whom were not trained for combat. ELAS, in contrast, had seventy thousand men in arms. An ideal situation thus existed should the resistance organization wish to seize power. Since both the British officials and the Greek authorities recognized the potential threat, they immediately took measures to disband the partisan bands and to form a national army to back their position. At the same time the British command brought in more troops, including air squadrons. By the middle of December it had fifty thousand soldiers available for action, and some reliable Greek units were also scheduled to return from abroad.

Although EAM had agreed to the demobilization, it demanded that all of the military formations, including the Greek units organized to support the government, be disbanded at the same time. General Scobie, however, was determined to proceed with the original plan of demobilization, which was to be applied to ELAS and EDES on December 10. On December 1 the EAM members withdrew from the government. At the same time the Central Committee of the EAM called for a mass demonstration on Sunday, December 3, to be followed on the next day by a general strike. Papandreou first agreed to and then refused to allow the demonstration. Nevertheless, thousands gathered in the central square of Athens. The police fired on the crowd, killing about fifteen people. For the next six weeks sporadic fighting took place throughout Greece, with attacks on the police and on public buildings. The positions of both the British forces and the official government were very difficult: the partisan armed forces controlled most of the countryside, and they were well armed.

The British determination to hold Greece was very strong. Churchill on December 5 sent a directive to Scobie in Athens ordering him not to "hesitate to act as if you were in a conquered city where a local rebellion is in progress."[14] More troops were rushed to the scene. On December 25 both Churchill and his foreign secretary, Anthony Eden, flew to Athens, where they met with the leaders of all of the parties, including those on the left. Some political concessions had to be made; thus George II was forced to agree that he

14   Woodhouse, *The Struggle for Greece*, p. 128.

would not return to Greece before a plebiscite was held on the question of the monarchy. Archbishop Damaskinos was appointed regent until this issue could be settled. Changes were also made in the government: Papandreou was replaced by General Plastiras, the nominal head of EDES, who was both Republican and anti-Communist.

Although ELAS still held three-quarters of Greece and had suffered no major military defeats, it had not achieved control of Athens. In contrast, the British position was becoming steadily stronger. ELAS could expect no assistance from the Soviet Union, which had appointed an ambassador to Athens, accredited to the regular government. Under these circumstances the EAM accepted an armistice, which took effect on January 15, and the Varkiza agreement, which was signed on February 12, 1945. This document provided for the demobilization of all the bands and the surrender of a specified number of weapons. In return, full political rights were guaranteed, and an amnesty was granted covering any political activities carried on during the previous period. This latter measure, however, did not include common-law crimes against life and property – a distinction that was to cause major problems later. Peace was restored, but the civil conflict had cost eleven thousand lives and property damage estimated at $250 million.

At the conclusion of World War II, Greece therefore had a coalition government, based largely on the prewar parties, which enjoyed British backing. It will be noted that the British policy toward Greece was in contrast to that pursued in Yugoslavia. In Athens the British gave full military and political support to the official government and were willing to fight to prevent the victory of a partisan-dominated regime. In Yugoslav affairs, however, the government-in-exile was pressed into accepting an arrangement that virtually ensured Tito's eventual full control. The difference in attitude toward the two countries is dramatically illustrated in a much-quoted conversation held between Churchill and Fitzroy Maclean, the head of the Allied military mission to Tito, at the end of 1943. As Maclean later described the occasion, he expressed it as his opinion, during a discussion of conditions in Yugoslavia, that the Partisans would be

> the decisive political factor in Jugoslavia after the war and, secondly, that Tito and the other leaders of the Movement were openly and avowedly Communist and that the system which they would establish would inevitably be on Soviet lines and, in all probability, strongly oriented towards the Soviet Union.
>
> The Prime Minister's reply resolved my doubts.
>
> "Do you intend," he asked, "to make Jugoslavia your home after the war?"
>
> "No, Sir," I replied.
>
> "Neither do I," he said, "And, that being so, the less you and I

worry about the form of Government they set up, the better. That is for them to decide. What interests us is, which of them is doing most harm to the Germans?"[15]

## THE INTER-ALLIED NEGOTIATIONS ON THE BALKANS

Churchill's attitude toward Balkan events and the Soviet failure to exploit the Communist position in Greece were in fact expressions of understandings that had been made by these governments. The future of the peninsula, as of the rest of Europe, was determined in the negotiations conducted during the war among Churchill, Stalin, and Roosevelt, three men whose visions of the postwar world differed considerably. Stalin and Churchill, both practical politicians, sought to gain advantages for their countries and to preserve their previous gains. Although the extent to which Soviet influence would extend into Central and southeastern Europe was at first not clear, it was evident that Stalin at a minimum expected to keep the territory acquired as a result of the Nazi–Soviet Pact of 1939. This determination brought up major problems for both the British and the American governments, particularly in relation to the Polish lands that were involved. The Polish issue had immediate repercussions in U.S. domestic politics, and Britain had, after all, gone to war to protect the territorial integrity of Poland, as well as to maintain the European balance of power. It would be ironic indeed if all of the efforts and sacrifices resulted in a direct Soviet domination of a major part of prewar Poland and a complete upset of the European political equilibrium.

In addition to the basic division of opinion between the Western powers and the Soviet Union, the American and British views were also in conflict on many points. Except for the brief participation of the United States in World War I and the U.S. influence exerted at the subsequent Paris conference, the American role in East European affairs had previously been quite peripheral. The chief connection had been through the streams of immigrants that came to the United States from that area. Since the majority of these did not rise to commanding positions in American society, and since the American public, aside from these immigrant groups, showed little interest in the events of the region, it is not surprising that the concern of the United States with the problems of the wide belt of territory from the North Sea to the Aegean was so limited. During the war the American officials made clear their wish that all political decisions be postponed until the fighting was over. It was then hoped that some international body, such as the United Nations, would assume a major responsibility. Prisoners of the Wilsonian

---

15  Fitzroy Maclean, *Eastern Approaches* (London: Jonathan Cape, 1949), pp. 402–403. Maclean, however, later did acquire a house in Korčula! Duncan Wilson, *Tito's Yugoslavia* (Cambridge: Cambridge University Press, 1979), p. 33.

liberal mythology on international affairs, these officials were in general strongly opposed to the drawing of spheres of influence or the negotiating of secret agreements. Their position was that territorial changes made during the war could be recognized only at the final peace conference. Regarding the Soviet demands, it was obvious that the annihilation of the Baltic states, the cession of Finnish territory, and the annexation of Polish territory, all of which had been accomplished as a result of the bargain with Hitler, might cause a strong political reaction from minorities in the American electorate with strong ties to these regions, despite their previous relatively passive stance.

The British attitude was more realistic; Churchill was certainly in every respect a traditional British statesman. He had no intention of presiding over the demise of the British Empire or of assisting in the delivery of the Continent to the control of one power. He recognized the necessity of reaching some sort of an understanding concerning southeastern Europe, particularly in view of the weakness of the British military position there. He had during the war favored an invasion through the Ljubljana Gap, an action that would have brought the Western armies to Vienna first. However, since British and American forces did not occupy the Balkan peninsula or the Danube valley, it was clear that the Soviet influence could be expected to predominate in the region. Extremely sensitive about the British position in the Mediterranean, Churchill, as we have seen, was most concerned about Greece. Although hampered by the refusal of the United States to make deals, he did attempt to come to some sort of an informal arrangement with Stalin.

As the Soviet armies approached the boundaries of the East European states, the need for an understanding among the Allies on their administration after the Soviet occupation became obvious. Until this time the Soviet Union had made no overt attempts to install purely Communist regimes. In the Communist-dominated partisan movements, preference had been given to the establishment of popular-front regimes. Despite this Soviet policy, the British government, Churchill in particular, wished to reach a clear agreement with Stalin that would define, and if possible limit, future Soviet influence. In May 1944 the British suggested that in the next months the principal responsibility for Romania be assigned to the Soviet Union, and that for Greece to Britain. Although Roosevelt accepted this limited arrangement, it was never formally in effect. In October 1944, when Churchill and Eden were in Moscow, and when Roosevelt was not present, the prime minister made further proposals in this direction. The most controversial section of these talks concerned the so-called percentages bargain. In his memoirs Churchill gave his version of his conversation with Stalin held on October 9:

> The moment was apt for business, so I said, "Let us settle about our affairs in the Balkans. Your armies are in Romania and Bulgaria. We have interests, missions, and agents there. Don't let us get at cross-purposes in small ways. So far as Britain and Russia are concerned,

how would it do for you to have ninety percent predominance in Rumania, for us to have ninety percent predominance in Greece, and go fifty-fifty about Yugoslavia?"

Churchill then wrote his proposed figures on a slip of paper, adding a 75 percent share of Bulgaria for the Soviet Union and an even split for Hungary.

I pushed this across to Stalin who had by then heard the translation. There was a slight pause. Then he took his blue pencil and made a large tick upon it, and passed it back to us. It was all settled in no more time than it takes to set down.

Of course we had long and anxiously considered our point, and were only dealing with immediate war-time arrangements. All larger questions were reserved on both sides for what we then hoped would be a peace table when the war was won.

After this there was a long silence. The pencilled paper lay in the centre of the table. At length I said, "Might it not be thought rather cynical if it seemed we had disposed of these issues, so fateful to millions of people, in such an offhand manner? Let us burn the paper." "No, you keep it," said Stalin.[16]

This conversation has been frequently cited as an example of the worst in great-power politics. The episode has been quoted here at length because it is typical in many respects of the manner in which European statesmen dealt with Balkan problems. It was a practical arrangement, designed to maintain a balance of influence and to prevent one government from dominating the entire area.

In subsequent talks between Eden and Molotov the percentage for Bulgaria was slightly altered to 80–20, but the figures remained 90–10 for Greece and 50–50 for Yugoslavia.[17] This distribution of influence, of course, represented only a convenient manner of expressing an informal understanding. No true agreement had been made. The percentages bound neither the Soviet Union nor Britain, and the United States would have nothing to do with such arrangements. The next months, however, did witness the practical implementation of part of the division. Britain, as we have seen, sent a military force into Greece and by February 1945 had suppressed a Communist-led revolt. At the same time the Soviet government gained subservient regimes in Bucharest and Sofia. The 50–50 arrangement on Yugoslavia was never tested, chiefly because Tito was soon to make it clear that he would accept domination from no outside power.

16 Winston S. Churchill, *The Second World War* (Boston: Houghton Mifflin, 1953), VI, 227, 228.
17 Albert Resis, "The Churchill–Stalin Secret 'Percentages' Agreement on the Balkans, Moscow, October, 1944," *American Historical Review* 83, no. 2 (April 1978): 377, 378.

In February 1945 Roosevelt, Churchill, and Stalin met in Yalta. The main subjects of discussion were the future of Germany, the war against Japan, the organization of the United Nations, and the composition of the Polish government, a matter that caused much friction. Roosevelt brought to this conference a general statement formulated by the State Department, entitled the Declaration on Liberated Europe. Accepted by the Soviet Union as well as Britain and the United States, it referred directly to the future political order in the Balkans. The text proclaimed "the right of all people to choose the form of government under which they will live" and "the restoration of sovereign rights and self-government to those peoples who have been forcibly deprived of them." The most important section stated:

> To foster the conditions in which the liberated peoples may exercise such rights, the three governments will jointly assist the people in any European liberated state or former Axis satellite state in Europe where in their judgement conditions require, (a) to establish conditions of internal peace; (b) to carry out emergency measures for the relief of distressed peoples; (c) to form interim governmental authorities broadly representative of all democratic elements in the population and pledged to the earliest possible establishment through free elections of governments responsive to the will of the people; and (d) to facilitate where necessary the holding of such elections.[18]

When the war in Europe ended in May 1945, no further general arrangements concerning the Balkan countries had been made. In the armistice agreements with Romania and Bulgaria provisions were included for the establishment of Allied Control Commissions in Bucharest and Sofia, composed of U.S. and British as well as Soviet representatives. British influence, as we have seen, was paramount in Athens. Although the Partisans were in full military control of Yugoslavia, Tito had agreed to a coalition government that would include some representatives from the former parties. How events would evolve in each of the states, however, was still uncertain.

## THE ESTABLISHMENT OF THE COMMUNIST REGIMES

As the war drew to a close, popular-front governments, with Communists in key positions, held power in all of the Balkan capitals except Athens. Full Communist control was not to be established throughout these countries until 1948. Complete Communist domination was gained first in Yugoslavia and Albania, where the Partisan forces had won military predominance during the war. In Romania and Bulgaria the party concentrated first on con-

18   Quoted in Robert Lee Wolff, *The Balkans in Our Time* (New York: Norton, 1978), p. 265.

trolling the vital ministries of the Interior and Justice; it then proceeded either to suppress the opposition parties or to infiltrate and divide them. The shift to a purely Communist rule was to take the longest in Romania.

## Romania

After August 1944 Romania was at war with Germany, and the government was in the hands of a ministry that was headed by General Sănătescu and contained representatives from the Peasant, Liberal, Social Democratic, and Communist parties, as well as army officers. The real power in the country, of course, was held by the Soviet occupation authorities. Although an Allied Control Commission was in existence, the British and American representatives were almost totally ignored. The situation was thus most favorable for Communist interests, but the party was in no position to exploit the opportunities fully. With a membership of less than two thousand, the organization also lacked a strong national leadership. As a result of the repression of the previous period, most of the prominent Communists had spent the past years in jail or had emigrated to the Soviet Union. This last group, the so-called Muscovites, at this point came back to Romania. The leading figures were Ana Pauker, whose father was a Moldavian rabbi; Emil Bodnaraş, who came from Bukovina and had a Ukrainian background; and Vasile Luca, a Transylvanian Szekler. Luca had been in Bukovina when it was annexed by Russia; he subsequently joined the Soviet army. After his return to Romania he edited the party newspaper, *Scînteia* (The Spark). The great weakness of this trio was their non-Romanian background in a highly nationalistic country. As we have seen, between the wars the appeal of the Communist program had been strongest among the discontented national minorities.

Among the Communists who had stayed in Romania during the war, the most important, aside from Lucreţiu Pătrăşcanu, was George Gheorghiu-Dej, a former railroad worker who had gained prominence during the Griviţa strike in February 1933 and who had subsequently spent much time in prison. Although limited in membership, the Communists were able to work with some other relatively small groups, among them the Ploughmen's Front, led by Dr. Peter Groza, whose base was the Transylvanian peasantry. At first, this organization represented the interests of the poorer peasants, as against the more prosperous element who formed the backbone of the National Peasant Party. Later it was infiltrated by Communists. In addition, the Communist Party could cooperate with the Union of Patriots, an organization of professional men; the Hungarian People's Union, or MADOSZ, representing Transylvanian Hungarians; the Society of Friendship with Russia, or ARLUS, which organized propaganda and cultural exchanges; and the Patriotic Defense, which collected money for charitable causes.

In October 1944, under Communist direction, a front organization, the National Democratic Front, or FND, was formed. The FND was composed of, in addition to the Communist Party, the Ploughmen's Front, some elements of the trade union organizations, a section of the Liberal Party led by Tătărescu, and a wing of the Social Democrats. The front program emphasized popular causes such as land distribution, the reacquisition of northern Transylvania, and increased workers' control in industry. At this time the party began a mass recruiting campaign under the direction of Ana Pauker; it attempted to attract all possible sections of the population, including former members of the Iron Guard.

The first Sănătescu ministry, which was composed largely of army officers, lasted from August to November 1944. It restored the constitution of 1923, which had been suspended in 1938. Its major task, however, was to establish good relations with the Soviet occupation. When it is considered that all of the traditional Romanian parties had been both anti-Russian and anti-Communist, the difficulties to be faced can be fully appreciated. After a disagreement with the Soviet authorities, Sănătescu reorganized this government in November. He remained premier, but the ministers were appointed from the political parties, including the Liberals and the National Peasants. Brătianu and Maniu, who remained the party leaders, did not assume posts. The FND was represented by Gheorghiu-Dej and Groza. The most controversial member of this regime was to be the minister of interior, Nicolae Penescu, of the Peasant Party. His office, which gave him control of the police, the militia, and the appointment of prefects and mayors, was naturally the first goal of the Communist leaders.

In December 1944 another ministry was appointed, this time under General Nicolae Rădescu, who had Soviet approval. Rădescu was to remain in office until March 1945. He personally took over the difficult post of the Interior, but one of his undersecretaries was Teohari Georgescu, a Communist who often acted independently of his superior. At this time the central government did not have full control of the Romanian territory: in Moldavia the Soviet army had set up its own administration, which was not under the authority of Bucharest, and a similar situation existed in northern Transylvania, still not returned to Romanian jurisdiction.

In January 1945 Ana Pauker and Gheorghiu-Dej went to Moscow, where they were evidently instructed to push for a government under full FND domination. Certainly attacks on the government increased at this time. Demonstrations of workers and peasants were organized, and the officials were harassed. The Communist and FND program continued to proclaim, not the establishment of a revolutionary regime, but agrarian reform, friendship with the Soviet Union, and the return of northern Transylvania. Meanwhile, although the front organization had full freedom to campaign, the activities of the other parties were severely curtailed, and a strict censorship was enforced. Since Communists controlled the printers' unions, they were able to block the appearance of Peasant and Liberal newspapers.

The continual harassment finally pushed General Rădescu too far. When some deaths resulted from a violent demonstration, held on February 24, he denounced Pauker and Luca as "horrible hyenas" and "foreigners without God or Country."[19] Three days later a Soviet emissary, Andrei Vyshinsky, who had gained a sinister reputation as prosecutor during the Soviet purge trials in the 1930s, arrived in Bucharest. He demanded that Michael dismiss the Rădescu government and gave the king a two-hour ultimatum. When Michael named Ştirbei as a possible premier, Vyshinsky refused and insisted that Groza be appointed to head a purely FND ministry. The acceptance of these demands by the king signified that Romania would be controlled by a front organization under full Communist domination. This Soviet action had been taken unilaterally, without consultation with the United States and Britain, and was in violation of inter-Allied understandings.

The Communist Party gained control of the two most important posts in the Groza ministry: Georgescu became minister of interior and Pătrăşcanu minister of justice. Tătărescu, who, it will be remembered, had joined the FND along with some other Liberals, became foreign minister. Since some individual Liberals and National Peasants were included, this government could claim that it was based on a wide representation. It was also able to announce the return of northern Transylvania to Romanian jurisdiction and the inauguration of some measures of land redistribution. As one of its principal tasks, this front government inaugurated a purge of the ranks of the bureaucracy and placed its supporters in important positions in the civil service. General Antonescu, Mihai Antonescu, and two other generals were tried in May 1945 and executed in June. During the proceedings, General Antonescu openly defended his past policies, declaring that his aim had been to defend Romania against the Soviet Union, which was the main national enemy.

In October 1945 the Communist Party held a national meeting. The success of the recruitment drive was impressive: from a membership of about 2,000 the organization had grown to 800,000 in the short period since the end of the war. It was obvious that the standards of selection had been anything but strict. Gheorghiu-Dej held the position of general secretary, with Pauker, Luca, and Georgescu sharing the principal influence in the party hierarchy.

The Soviet interference to force the downfall of the Rădescu government caused a strong reaction in London and Washington. Since the Groza ministry was obviously in violation of the Yalta principles, both the British and American governments refused to accept it. The Soviet representatives replied to all such objections by referring to British actions in Athens, which they interpreted in a similar light. In an attempt to secure an administration that would be acceptable to all of the Allied powers, King Michael requested Groza to resign. When he refused, the king left for his mountain home at Sinaia. He would not sign decrees, and for all practical purposes he withdrew from governmental affairs. Despite this setback the anti-Communist opposi-

19    Quoted in Wolff, *The Balkans in Our Time*, p. 282.

tion did not regard its position as hopeless, and it still expected Western aid. In November, on the occasion of the king's birthday, demonstrations were held in his favor.

Despite widespread expectations, neither the United States nor Britain had either the means or the intention of supporting the opposition parties against Communist pressure. In December 1945 the Allied foreign ministers met in Moscow. To settle the Romanian problem, they decided that one representative each from the Peasant and the Liberal parties should be added to the ministry and that elections should be held. The limited nature of this advice was a Soviet victory. There was little chance that two ministers would be able to influence the policy of a cabinet of twenty. Nevertheless, Emil Hațieganu of the Peasant Party and Mihail Râmniceanu of the Liberals were appointed. They were ministers without portfolio, and their position was weak. With this token measure, both Britain and the United States recognized the Groza government.

The elections held in November 1946 were characterized by a repressive atmosphere. Opposition newspapers were suppressed; harassment and intimidation made any regular electoral campaigning impossible. In the voting, as could be expected, the government list gained an overwhelming victory. In the assembly of 414 delegates, the Peasant Party won 32 seats and the Liberals 3, but all of the rest went to the FND and its supporters. Both Hațieganu and Râmniceanu resigned, and so the FND was in full control of the government.

With the signing of the final peace treaty between the Allies and Romania in February 1947, all Western diplomatic controls over Communist action were removed. The party could now move decisively against the remaining opposition. Before the war, the main political power had been held by the Liberal and Peasant parties, and their leaders still could exert a great deal of influence. In a move designed to break the Peasant Party, the government in July arrested Maniu and Mihalache; they were accused of conspiring with U.S. intelligence agents to organize a revolt and to establish American air bases. Both received life sentences. It will be noted that the point of attack against the opposition was no longer "fascist collaboration," but an allegedly treasonous connection with Washington.

The final Communist takeover was to come soon. In August 1947 the Peasant and Liberal parties were officially dissolved. In the next month the Social Democrats were forced into fusion with the Communist Party to form the United Workers' Party. At the same time, the foreign ministry, long a center of traditional views, was purged. Tătărescu was replaced by Pauker. In December, as a final step, Michael was compelled to abdicate. In March 1948 new elections were held in which the government list won 405 of the 414 seats. In addition to the United Workers' Party, the victorious coalition included the Ploughmen's Front, the National Popular Party (formerly the Union of Patriots), and the Hungarian People's Union. Groza was still at the head of the government, but Communists held all of the major posts: Pauker remained as foreign minister; Luca took the Ministry of Finance, Georgescu that of Interior, Bodnaraş that of Defense, Gheorghiu-Dej that of National Economy, and Bunaciu, who replaced Pătrăşcanu, that of Justice.

## Bulgaria

In Bulgaria the Communist leadership from the beginning was in a stronger position than its counterpart in Romania. It had played an important role in interwar Bulgarian politics, and it had won a popular following. It also had more influential allies. The Fatherland Front, although Communist-dominated, did represent a combination of strong parties, including the Social Democrats, the Pladne Agrarians, and the Zveno group, all of which had enjoyed considerable political prestige previously. Equally important, there was much genuine pro-Russian sentiment in the country. The Soviet occupation forces contributed to the basically friendly atmosphere by behaving there in a more disciplined fashion than in Romania or Yugoslavia. In addition, the party had the advantage of holding the ministries of Justice and Interior after the September coup. Its leaders could thus move at once to purge the administration and place party members and supporters in the commanding positions. The party, however, was still small. In September 1944 the membership was under 15,000, perhaps as little as 8,000. It still needed to cooperate with other political elements.

Despite its advantages, the Fatherland Front regime won for itself one of the worst records of terrorism of the postwar period. An enormous effort to eliminate any possible opposition was soon begun. A "people's militia" was formed, which proceeded to make mass arrests; the suspects were tried by "people's courts." Plentiful opportunities were thus opened for individuals to seek redress for past grievances and revenge for injuries, as well as to win political advantage. In December 1944 the government put the regents and members of past governments on trial. Prince Cyril, General Mihov, Filov, Bozhilov, Bagrianov, twenty-five members of wartime ministries, and sixty-eight deputies in the assembly were all executed. Muraviev received a life term; the Democrat Mushanov and the right Agrarian Gichev were given long sentences. The government admitted that 2,138 were executed out of 10,897 tried, but the true figures were undoubtedly much higher.[20] The illegality and brutality of these proceedings had an initial effect of terrorizing much of the population and encouraging an attitude of passive obedience.

The strongest opponent of full Communist control of the government was the Agrarian Union, still the most important popular party. Despite the Pladne group's cooperation with the Fatherland Front, some of its leaders tried to block a complete domination of the coalition by the Communists. In Sep-

20   Wolff, *The Balkans in Our Time*, p. 293.

tember 1944 Dr. G. M. Dimitrov returned from abroad and assumed the post of secretary of the Agrarian Union. In this office he attempted to encourage independent party action; he was also pro-Western in orientation. A victim of continual obstruction and harassment, he finally resigned in favor of Nikola Petkov. Dimitrov later took refuge with the American mission in Sofia and then eventually emigrated to the United States. At first, Petkov appeared to have a better background for cooperation with the Communist Party. He had worked with the Fatherland Front from the beginning, and he favored close association with the Soviet Union. He too, however, soon came into conflict with the Communists, whose objective was the total destruction of Agrarian influence.

Since the Communist leaders were unable to dominate the Agrarian Union directly, they next attempted to split it into factions and to take over a section of the dissident membership. In May 1945 the Union held a congress, at which the Communists produced their own candidate, Alexander Obbov, for party secretary. Using his powerful backers, he was able to oust Petkov and gain control of the central party organization, so that he and his followers represented the Agrarian Union in the Fatherland Front. Similar tactics were followed in relation to the Social Democrats, and again the Communists found individuals or factions that would work with them. Thus, although both Agrarian and Social Democratic members were still a part of the Fatherland Front, they no longer represented the majority opinion of their parties. Some socialist and agrarian groups, of course, still remained outside the coalition.

In March 1945 the Fatherland Front held a congress in Sofia, at which George Dimitrov was elected president of the central committee. A former head of the Comintern, Dimitrov had won a strong reputation in the international Communist movement. Long a resident of the Soviet Union, he had acquired Soviet citizenship, which he surrendered on his assumption of office in Bulgaria. After having spent most of his life in exile, he returned only in November 1945, eight months after his election. In the summer of 1945 the government announced that elections would be held. Disagreements arose at once within the coalition. The Communist leadership of the Fatherland Front wished to present a single list to the electorate. In contrast, Zveno and the Agrarian Union preferred to run their own candidates separately. The pressure on the dissident groups was so strong that Petkov appealed to the Western powers, charging a violation of the Yalta Declaration on Liberated Europe. Because of the protests, the government postponed the elections for three months, although this delay was to have no effect on the final outcome.

The elections, held in November 1945, were accompanied by widespread police interference and electoral fraud; the Fatherland Front won an 86 percent majority. The validity of elections conducted under these circumstances was brought up at the Moscow conference of foreign ministers held in December. As in the case of Romania, the ministers suggested that members of the opposition parties be added to the government, advice that was not taken. Instead, the Communist leadership continued its campaign against the remaining independent political elements, including those which had previously shown a cooperative attitude. In the summer of 1946 the target was Zveno. Velchev was removed as minister of war and ended his career as the Bulgarian representative in Switzerland. Kimon Georgiev remained, however, for a short period as premier.

By this time it was clear that the monarchy would have to be abolished. Burdened by two lost wars, the institution had become genuinely unpopular. After a plebiscite was held in September 1946, Simeon and his mother left the country. Since a major constitutional change was necessary, representatives for a Grand National Assembly had to be chosen. Again fraud and violence characterized the elections. Although the opposition parties did run separate lists, they could not conduct regular campaigns. The difficulty of their position was illustrated by the fact that

> in the summer of 1946 fifteen members of the central committee of the Socialist Party, seven out of twenty-two members of the "Presidium" of the Agrarian Union, and thirty-five out of eighty members of the Supreme Council of the Agrarian Union were in prison or concentration camps. An example of the grounds for arrest is the case of the agrarian journalist Kunev. The formal accusations stated that Kunev in an article had "in a truly criminal manner called the Bulgarian government political and economic dreamers."[21]

In the election held in October the Fatherland Front won 78 percent of the votes and the opposition 22 percent. In the new government George Dimitrov became premier, with Georgiev as vice-premier and foreign minister. Elected as a representative to the assembly, Petkov openly defied the Communist leadership and attacked Dimitrov as a tool of the Soviet Union. This opposition was allowed to continue for a while because the government wished to obtain Western approval of the peace treaty, which had finally been completed. The day after the U.S. Senate ratified the agreement, in June 1947, Petkov was arrested. He was tried in August, sentenced to death, and, despite Western protests, hanged in September. One week after this event the United States officially recognized the Bulgarian government. With the completion of the destruction of the Agrarian opposition, the Communists proceeded in similar manner against those Socialist Democrats who still attempted to maintain an independent position. By the end of 1947 Bulgaria was completely under Communist control, and a new constitution was in effect.

---

21   Hugh Seton-Watson, *The East European Revolution* (New York: Praeger, 1951), p. 216.

# The Balkan states in World War II

## Yugoslavia

The Communist regime of Yugoslavia, of course, was in the best position of all the socialist governments in East Europe. The Partisan forces, numbering 800,000 men, were in full military control. There was no Soviet or Allied occupation; so foreign interference was not a problem. Not only was the central government in the hands of AVNOJ, but an effective administrative structure, embracing the entire country, had been established during the war.

The single limitation on its power was the agreements made between Tito and Šubašić concerning the participation in the government of members of the London regime. On November 1, 1944, immediately after the capture of Belgrade, a second understanding was reached between these two men, which defined the future arrangements in greater detail. It was agreed that King Peter was not to return until a plebiscite was held on the question of the monarchy; until then a regency would hold the executive power. AVNOJ was to be enlarged with the addition of members from the last regular assembly who had not collaborated with the occupation. It was to be, at least temporarily, the national legislative body. King Peter was extremely opposed to these terms; he argued that the Yugoslav constitution did not provide for a regency when the king was able to rule. Under strong British pressure, however, he capitulated. In March 1945 three members of the government-in-exile joined Tito's government: Šubašić; Milan Grol, the leader of the Serbian Democratic Party; and Juraj Šutej, who was a close associate of Šubašić and a member of the Croatian Peasant Party.

At this time a regency including a Serb, a Croat, and a Slovene was established. In March, as could be expected, it named Tito as premier and charged him with the formation of a government. Tito took the posts of both premier and war minister; Šubašić became foreign minister. Of the twenty-eight cabinet posts, all but five were in Partisan hands. Nevertheless, the Allied governments recognized this regime. The provisions for the enlargement of AVNOJ in no way challenged or interfered with the Communist control. The last assembly had been elected in 1938 and dissolved in 1939; many of its members had died; others were now to be excluded for political reasons. Finally, thirty-nine previous delegates, together with sixty-nine members of six non-Communist parties and thirteen prominent individuals, were added to AVNOJ. In August 1945 this body became the national provisional assembly. Preparations were then made for an election.

Despite the great strength of its position, the Partisan regime resorted to the methods of terror and intimidation that we have seen practiced elsewhere. A strong secret police was established under the direction of Alexander Ranković. It was first called the Department of the Defense of the People, or OZNA, but the name was soon changed to the State Security Service, or UDBA. Police pressure, spies, and informers were used freely to destroy the political opposition, and the traditional parties soon found that they could not function. Moreover, the three members of the London government too found their position impossible: they could not carry out their duties, and they were not consulted on political decisions. Gröl resigned in August 1945, and his two colleagues followed his example in September. Šubašić was subsequently placed under house arrest. Prevented from conducting a regular political campaign and from issuing party newspapers, the opposition parties boycotted the election. Thus the Serbian Radicals, the Agrarians, and the Democrats, as well as the Croatian Peasant Party, withdrew from the campaign.

Elections were held in November 1945. Some voters were excluded because of their wartime activities. Although only the government list was available, it was possible to express disapproval. Voting was in theory secret, but electoral fraud and violence were common and a negative vote was difficult to cast. There was also a widespread conviction that the police would know how each individual voted. A great effort was made by the government to assure a wide participation and to secure a massive demonstration of approval. Of those eligible, 88 percent came to the polls, and of these 90 percent expressed their support for the government.

In November 1945 a constitutional assembly met. The monarchy was abolished, and the Federal People's Republic of Yugoslavia was proclaimed. Once a new constitution had been adopted, the assembly turned itself into a regular legislature. Full Communist control had thus been established. Although members of other parties continued to take part in the government, they held their posts as individuals and not as representatives of separate political organizations. There was certainly no tolerated or loyal opposition. The transition had been accomplished with relative ease. As a victor power, the Yugoslav Partisan government could not easily be influenced by Western opinion; it did not have to worry about peace terms, or the Yalta declaration. Under these conditions, and despite the agreement with Šubašić, there was little chance that the Partisan leaders would risk the return of the former political parties or would hold genuinely free elections.

Unlike the other Communist East European states, postwar Yugoslavia was organized on a federal basis (see Map 12). In an attempt to heal some of the bitter interwar national strife, the state was divided into six republics: Bosnia-Hercegovina, Croatia, Macedonia, Montenegro, Serbia, and Slovenia. Within Serbia two autonomous provinces were established: Kosovo, with an Albanian majority, and the Vojvodina, with a mixed Hungarian, Romanian, Serbian, Croatian, Slovak, and Ukrainian population. Four major languages, Croatian, Macedonian, Serbian, and Slovenian, were recognized; Albanian and Hungarian had an accepted place in the autonomous regions. The three major religious organizations, the Catholic, the Orthodox, and the Muslim, all continued to function, but with the limitations on their activities

Map 12. Postwar Yugoslavia: federal organization

common to states under Communist domination. Yugoslavia thus had a more complex internal organization than any of its neighbors.

## Albania

A situation similar to Yugoslavia's existed in Albania, where the LNC, soon to be renamed the Democratic Front, was in complete charge of the government after the German forces left Tirana in November 1944. As in the other states, the Communist leaders, with Hoxha at their head, immediately moved to strengthen their position and to eliminate any possible source of opposition, either within the front organization or from other political parties. Rival leaders and members of former governments who might challenge the Communist position were tried as "war criminals"; the minister of interior, Koci Xoxe, presided over these judicial travesties. These proceedings were also used as the occasion to attack the Western powers, in particular Britain, whose relations with the Albanian regime were very bad at this time.

In December 1945 an election was held with only members of the Democratic Front on the electoral list. Although means were provided to express opposition, the fears that we have seen elsewhere handicapped the use of this alternative. According to official reports, 92 percent of the electorate voted, and 93 percent of the voters chose the Democratic Front list. The new assembly met in January 1946 and proceeded with the reorganization of the state. The monarchy was abolished, and a people's republic was established. The constitution that was prepared at this point closely resembled those of Yugoslavia and the Soviet Union.

Despite the victory, the government found itself in a very difficult position, particularly in its relations with the outside world. The regime was not recognized by the major powers, and Yugoslav domination remained a fact of political life. Equally dangerous were the threats to national lands. Much concern was felt that the British, who were in control in Athens, would back Greek demands for southern Albania; in July 1946 the U.S. Senate passed a resolution supporting the Greek claims. The situation in Kosovo was also dangerous. After the German withdrawal, the Yugoslav Partisans had taken possession of the region, and massacres of Albanians by Serbs followed. Although the Yugoslav Communist Party in meetings held in Dresden in 1928 and in Zagreb in 1940 had supported the cession of the area to Albania, it was quite evident that, once in political power in Belgrade, the Partisan regime would insist on the retention of the prewar Yugoslav boundaries. Even though he was willing to allow the Albanian majority in Kosovo some rights within the federal state, Tito was certainly not about to favor "self-determination" when it involved a cession of Yugoslav territory. This issue was to remain a point of friction between the two states.

## PARTISAN WARFARE

During World War II, as we have seen, partisan bands were active in the mountainous areas of Albania, Greece, and Yugoslavia. Some comment should be made concerning the attractions and deficiencies of these organizations because of their significance for later Balkan developments. Although this guerilla activity did not play a vital part in determining the outcome of the war, it did supply the leadership for the Communist regime in Yugoslavia, in particular. Just as the nationalist leaders of the Balkan revolts in the nineteenth century often emerged as the political leaders of the new states, the so-called Club of '41 enjoyed a privileged position in postwar Yugoslavia. Partisan movements were regarded with so much respect in all of the Communist states that even the governments of Romania and Bulgaria, where significant resistance groups did not make their appearance until the enemy was clearly on the defensive, found it necessary to inflate the extent and importance of the limited actions that occurred in their lands. A cult of partisan warfare and heroism was thus built up to provide a background for regimes that needed to enhance their popularity. Such a development did not, however, occur in Greece, where the wartime resistance soon became identified with the Communist Party and the losing side in the civil war of 1946–1949.

The partisan movements during the war were very attractive to the young and idealistic, as well as to those who had no alternative but to join with the mountain bands. The Communist core offered an ideology that promised a pure and humane future society, one that would be in strong contrast to the corrupt and oppressive regimes of the past. Many observers were impressed by the idealism of the young fighters. C. M. Woodhouse, with the British military mission in Greece, has written that the KKE was "tough, disciplined, secretive, hardened by experience. Its rank and file were for the most part not the sinister conspirators of popular mythology, but patriotic and high-minded men and women, inspired by a vague idea of a new and better Greece."[22] Fitzroy Maclean has made similar observations concerning the Yugoslav Partisans and their pride in their achievements: "With this pride went a spirit of dedication, hard not to admire. The life of every one of them was ruled by rigid self-discipline, complete austerity; no drinking, no looting, no love-making. It was as though each one of them were bound by a vow, a vow part ideological and part military."[23]

Guerilla fighting also fitted in with the traditions of the mountain regions. An American historian who was in Greece in 1946 has commented on the role of economic necessity in the recruitment of village youths for EAM/ELAS; they left home when life

> in their parental households had become unendurable. The fact was that to have grown sons lounging at home when there was not enough food to go round was unacceptable to old and young alike. Young men were supposed to be breadwinners . . . Joining an armed band was, in effect, a simple variant of this age-old pattern. For when peaceable work was impossible to find – as assuredly was the case in 1941–44 – a man with a gun could still expect to feed himself by demanding a share of the harvest from peasants of the plain. With luck, he might even lay hands on a little extra booty to take back home. Since such actions were also patriotic and heroic, this avenue of escape from the futile idleness of mountain villages became irresistible.

This author has also noted the similarity of circumstances in Yugoslavia, the only other European country where partisan activities appeared at once: "Yu-

22  Woodhouse, *The Struggle for Greece*, p. 20.
23  Maclean, *Eastern Approaches*, pp. 324–325.

goslavia was also the only other country of Europe to have food-deficit mountain villages like those of Greece, where the same heroic tradition prevailed. Elsewhere resistance fighters became active in the field only when German power was about to collapse."[24]

Despite the idealistic aspects of these movements, they also had their grim side. The emphasis on comradeship, courage, discipline, and other noble virtues applied usually only to the relationship within the bands and among friends. Enemies, whether co-nationals or foreign occupiers, were treated with ruthlessness and cruelty, attitudes that were to be carried over into the postwar regimes and to affect policy toward any political opposition. The massacre of Albanians in Kosovo and Croatians in Bleiburg has been described. The guerilla warfare in the mountains, where no side would normally take prisoners or care for enemy wounded, was particularly brutal. Milovan Djilas, the most famous literary figure to arise from the Partisan movement, here describes his own treatment of two captured Germans:

> I unslung my rifle. Since I didn't dare fire, because the Germans were some forty yards above – we could hear them shouting – I hit the German over the head. The rifle butt broke and the German fell on his back. I pulled out my knife and with one motion slit his throat. I then handed the knife to Raja Nedeljković, a political worker whom I had known since before the war, and whose village the Germans had massacred in 1941. Nedeljković stabbed the second German, who writhed but soon was still. This later gave rise to the story that I had slaughtered a German in hand-to-hand combat. Actually, like most prisoners, the Germans were as if paralyzed, and didn't defend themselves or try to flee.[25]

24  William H. McNeill, *The Metamorphosis of Greece since World War II* (Chicago: University of Chicago Press, 1978), pp. 66, 67.
25  Milovan Djilas, *Wartime* (New York: Harcourt Brace Jovanovich, 1977), p. 283.

# 8

## The immediate postwar readjustments: the Greek civil war and the Yugoslav–Soviet conflict

### THE ALLIED COALITION BREAKS

BY THE TIME THE WAR CAME TO AN END in Europe, the victorious Allies, as we have seen, had failed to conclude any prior agreements on the shape of the future peace. The U.S. leaders continued to place much faith in the efficacy of the future United Nations and in such vague statements as the Yalta Declaration on Liberated Europe. Churchill, much more practical and experienced, had attempted to win an understanding on future spheres of influence, at least in the Balkans. With the lack of any previous arrangements, the political structure of the Eastern and Central European countries was in practice to be decided by the armies of occupation. This situation was recognized early by Stalin, who in April 1945 expressed to Tito his opinion on the "distinctive nature" of the situation: "This war is not as in the past; whoever occupies a territory also imposes on it his own social system. Everyone imposes his own system as far as his army can reach. It cannot be otherwise."[1]

In 1945, however, many aspects of the future peace settlement could not accurately be foretold. The massive decline in the power and influence of Britain and France and the emergence of the United States and the Soviet Union as the two great powers were not yet fully understood. All of the governments devoted their major attention to the immediate issues and the liquidation of the conflict in the Far East. The war had been fought and won by a coalition whose members did not have similar aims. As had been the case with all such combinations in the past, the divisions became increasingly apparent as the final days of the fighting approached. During the war the major decisions were made by Churchill, Roosevelt, and Stalin, with, of course, the advice of their staffs. Even during the war there had been obvious differences of outlook. Stalin was angered by what he saw as the continual postponement of the opening of a genuine second front; the suspicion was bound to arise that the Western powers were hoping that the German and Soviet

---

1 Milovan Djilas, *Conversations with Stalin* (New York: Harcourt, Brace & World, 1962), p. 114.

armies would destroy each other. Both the Soviet Union and the Western governments feared that the other would make a separate peace. In addition, quite different interpretations were given to the causes and significance of the war itself. In February 1946 Stalin in a speech discussed this question:

> It would be incorrect to think that the war arose accidentally or as the result of the fault of some of the statesmen. Although these faults did exist, the war arose in reality as the inevitable result of the development of the world economic and political forces on the basis of monopoly capitalism.
>
> Our Marxists declare that the capitalist system of world economy conceals elements of crisis and war, that the development of world capitalism does not follow a steady and even course forward, but proceeds through crises and catastrophes. The uneven development of the capitalist countries leads in time to sharp disturbances in their relations, and the group of countries which consider themselves inadequately provided with raw materials and export markets try usually to change this situation and to change the position in its favor by means of armed force.
>
> As a result of these factors, the capitalist world is sent into two hostile camps and war follows.[2]

In other words, the Soviet dictator saw World War II as having arisen, not from the German attack on Poland or the British and French determination to maintain the balance of power, but from the inevitable struggle between two capitalist camps, between which the differences in ideology were relatively insignificant.

The major immediate points of disagreement between the Western powers and the Soviet Union concerned issues outside the framework of this narrative; they were the political and territorial settlement for Poland and the entire question of the future of Germany. Although Stalin was to remain in power for another eight years, these issues were to be decided by new leaders in the West. In April 1945 Roosevelt died and was succeeded by Harry S Truman. Elections held in Britain in July 1945 resulted in a defeat for Churchill's Conservative Party and the victory of the Labour Party under the leadership of Clement Attlee, who became prime minister; the foreign secretary was Ernest Bevin. Although these men were at first relatively inexperienced in dealing with the current problems, they were to prove firmer and tougher in their attitude toward the Soviet Union than their predecessors.

In July and August 1945 the heads of government again met, this time at Potsdam. The United States, still fearing a lengthy war with Japan, hoped to obtain Soviet assistance in the Far East. The relationships, however, were strained. The Soviet government had added to its other demands a request

2 *New York Times*, February 10, 1946, p. 30.

for a naval base on the Bosphorus or the Dardanelles and a revised Straits settlement. At this time pressure was being placed on Turkey. Previously, in March 1945, the Soviet Union had denounced its treaty of friendship and nonaggression with Ankara and had put forward demands for Kars and Ardahan. The Soviet objectives in the Near East thus remained similar to those communicated to Hitler in November 1940. During the sessions of the Potsdam conference the war in the Far East was drawing to an unexpectedly swift conclusion. On July 16, at the beginning of the sessions, the United States tested the atom bomb; the first bomb was dropped on Hiroshima on August 6 and another on Nagasaki on August 9. Foreseeing a quick American victory and desiring a place in the future peace negotiations, the Soviet Union declared war on Japan on August 9. The Japanese surrender followed on August 14.

At the end of the hostilities in Europe and Asia, the United States was clearly the strongest power in the world. It had as many men in arms as the Soviet Union, and it alone had the world's greatest terror weapon, the atom bomb, a monopoly that it held until 1949. Yet at first the U.S. government proved extremely reluctant to use its military advantages. The American public was exerting great pressure to bring the soldiers home and to liquidate foreign commitments as far as possible. Hopes were still placed in the United Nations and in international negotiations. It was in this period that the principal Soviet advances in Eastern Europe were made. Despite the Yalta agreements, Communist-dominated coalitions, with Soviet backing, took full control in Albania, Bulgaria, and Yugoslavia in 1945; in Poland in 1947; and in Czechoslovakia, Hungary, and Romania in 1948. In each instance, Communist domination was achieved through fraudulent electoral procedures and the free use of police terror, actions that were in violation of inter-Allied understandings on the postwar regimes to be set up in Eastern Europe.

Until this period the United States had shown little interest in the fate of the countries of this region, except Poland, whose immigrant community had political significance. Previously, American officials had opposed the establishment of spheres of influence, but they had not suggested adequate alternatives to assure a diplomatic balance in the area. When the Communist parties used illegal methods to gain control, the leaders of the opposition frequently appealed to the U.S. representatives and inquired whether the United States intended to enforce the Yalta Declaration to ensure that the interim governments chosen were indeed "broadly representative of all democratic elements in the population and pledged to the earliest possible establishment through free elections of governments responsive to the will of the people."[3] Iuliu Maniu, for instance, asked that the Western states inform him if the United States intended to resist Soviet domination in Romania; if not, his party should make the best agreement possible with the occupying power.

---

3  Quoted in Robert Lee Wolff, *The Balkans in Our Time* (New York: Norton, 1978), p. 265.

The reply was that the United States was determined to assure that representative government was maintained, an answer given despite the fact that Washington had in fact no plans on how this objective could be secured against Soviet obstruction. A recent criticism of this policy states that

> American officials did not worry about the gap between ideal United States pronouncements and their limited actions to implement United States goals and were quite unprepared for later charges of American irresponsibility and betrayal . . . It was a surprise to State Department officials when opposition leaders and the American representatives in these countries misunderstood United States rhetoric for an intention to take strong initiatives to see these principles were implemented . . . They never attempted to communicate to the Soviet Union exactly what they could and could not tolerate in terms of Soviet actions in Eastern Europe. These officials regularly acknowledged to themselves that the Soviet Union would exercise "predominant" influence in Eastern Europe after the war and that the Soviet Union had "more direct" interests in this part of the world than the United States. They never defined, however, what they meant by these statements.[4]

The failure to formulate and carry through a clear and coherent policy in Eastern Europe, of course, reflected the general lack of concern over the area among the American public and its representatives in Congress, except on special issues that directly involved their interests. Eastern European questions were generally seen as peripheral, and the region was not considered politically or militarily vital to the United States. With this attitude there was little possibility that firm action would be taken to prevent Communist takeovers in the East European capitals. Yet without the implicit threat of force it is difficult to see how the Western powers could have prevented the political developments that took place in the area. Grandiose declarations simply confused those political elements which were friendly to the West.

Although Soviet-controlled regimes were established in Bulgaria and Romania, and Communist governments in Albania and Yugoslavia, at the end of the war, Greece followed a different path. This state too, however, was subject to foreign intervention. The first phase of the civil war ended in early 1945, and preparations were then made to hold elections. The basic domestic conflicts had, nonetheless, not been resolved. The United States, as well as Britain, was soon to be forced to make a clear decision on its policy in the Balkans and the Eastern Mediterranean. Similar questions were to be in-

4  Lynn Etheridge Davis, *The Cold War Begins* (Princeton, N.J.: Princeton University Press, 1974), pp. 390–391.

Map 13. The Balkans in the postwar era

volved when in 1948 Yugoslavia broke from the Soviet camp and the Balkan peninsula again faced a major crisis. The great controversies in the immediate postwar period, with the exception of the conflict over Trieste, were to concern political and ideological rather than territorial questions. The postwar map of the Balkans (Map 13) showed no radical changes. Although Romania lost Bessarabia and northern Bukovina to the Soviet Union and southern Dobrudja to Bulgaria, it retained Transylvania. Greece gained from Italy the Dodecanese Islands. As will be explained in this chapter, although Yugoslavia made important gains from Italy, the final boundary did not accord with Yugoslav expectations.

## THE GREEK CIVIL WAR, 1946–1949

During the period when the Communist Party and Communist-dominated coalitions took power in neighboring states, the political situation in Greece also deteriorated. As we have seen, in December 1944 the British government had acted decisively to maintain its influence in Athens. During the next months the general assumption remained that Britain would continue to be the predominant power in the Mediterranean, with a base of strength in Greece. In line with this policy, the British representatives devoted a great deal of attention to the political developments in Athens, and efforts were made to promote postwar reconstruction. British missions arrived to assist in the reestablishment of the financial institutions, the legal system, and the police, as well as to aid in economic and relief projects. General Scobie and the ambassador, Sir R. Leeper, wielded a great deal of influence; they were consulted on the composition of all eight governments that held power between January 1945 and April 1946. A close observer of these events has commented: "Up to 1947 the British Government appointed and dismissed Greek Prime Ministers with the barest attention to constitutional formalities. British experts dictated economic and financial policy, defense and foreign policy, security and legal policy, trade union and unemployment policy."[5]

In general, the British advisers worked with and encouraged the moderate and progressive elements in the Greek political scene, such as the parties led by Papandreou, Plastiras, and Sofoulis. At the same time, the right and the Royalists were able to strengthen their hold over the newly organized police and National Guard. The firm hand of Britain was observed with increasing criticism by the left and often by the United States, whose government still remained largely uninvolved in Greek events. American funds, however, were the basis of the massive relief provided by the United Nations Relief and Rehabilitation Administration, or UNRRA, which kept the country from starvation.

Meanwhile, the former political coalitions regrouped; the major influence was exerted by the Populists under Tsaldaris, the Liberals under Sofoulis, the National Liberals under Gonatas and Zervas, and the National Political Union, composed of the followers of Papandreou, Panagiotis Kanellopoulos, and Sofoklis Venizelos. As previously, the parties were centered around strong individuals. Such combinations were easily formed, but their basic instability lent an element of uncertainty to the political scene.

Although the center and right were divided into factions, the left presented an even more chaotic picture. By 1945 the EAM coalition had weakened. Many of its former members had been dismayed by the policies pursued in the December civil war and by the atrocities committed in some areas, ac-

---

5  C. M. Woodhouse, *The Struggle for Greece, 1941–1949* (London: Hart-Davis, MacGibbon, 1976), p. 149.

tions that included the large-scale execution of opponents and the taking of hostages. The Republican left, which was composed of a number of small groups, such as agrarians and socialists with differing programs, lacked a strong center. Their chief point of agreement was their opposition to the return of the king; they quarreled on most other matters. Of the left parties, the KKE remained the strongest, despite its internal tensions.

During the war the principal figure in the Communist Party had been George Siantos; political power had been securely in the hands of the local party members. This situation changed in 1945 when Nikos Zachariadis returned from imprisonment in Germany. With close affiliations to international Communist circles, the new leadership was extremely critical of previous policies. Although still in theory favoring a popular-front policy and willing to enter a government coalition, the party now adopted an active and aggressive stand against the political situation of the time. The British role in Greek affairs in particular was attacked, and the government was denounced as "monarcho-fascist." At the same time close relations were maintained with the Communist parties of Albania, Bulgaria, and Yugoslavia, which were in a position to aid the Greek movement.

As in wartime, collaboration with the Bulgarian and Yugoslav organizations was fraught with difficulty. The Greek partisans and the KKE had always found a great deal of support in Greek Macedonia. Despite the clearly Greek character of the majority of the population, Slavic-speaking Macedonians had played important roles in the resistance. With Yugoslav Partisan assistance, they had organized the Slavo-Macedonian National Liberation Front, or SNOF, later reorganized as NOF. The members were to be a major component of the Communist forces by the end of the civil war. Even before the outbreak of the renewed civil conflict, the links with the Yugoslav party, not only of this group, but also of the KKE, were close. Greek Communists could cross the border freely; in 1945 camps were formed inside Yugoslavia to house refugees and to provide some military training. This close association with the northern neighbor inevitably involved the problem of Macedonia and the question of the future status of its Aegean section. Since the issue involved a possible cession of Greek lands, it remained a serious hindrance to the KKE in its attempt to win public favor.

The Varkiza Pact of February 1945 did not bring stable conditions. Despite the British efforts, the Greek government was not strong enough to control events in the countryside. Although ELAS had surrendered the arms specified in the agreement, its members still retained many weapons. At the same time all of the old resentments and hatreds left from the war reemerged. Both the Communists and the Royalists, as well as other factions, had armed bands at their service. Traditional Greek brigandage also reappeared. The opportunities for private vengeance and reprisal were thus plentiful. The advantage, however, lay on the side of the right-wing elements and the government. The reestablished regular Greek army, whose members were conscripts, was commanded chiefly by the prewar officer corps, which was largely Royalist. Although the army had previously had a large, often predominant, Republican element, these officers had been largely eliminated after 1936. Similarly, the police force was composed primarily of men who had held their positions throughout the occupation and who were anti-Communist. In addition, the right could make use of the section of the Varkiza agreement that allowed the arrest of former partisans who had committed common-law crimes. The courts proved much more vigilant in the pursuit of these men than in judging crimes related to collaboration with the enemy. The major weapons of repression were thus in the hands of the center and the right, groups that at this time apparently also had the support of the majority of the Greek people.

Unlike conditions in much of the rest of Europe, the economic situation in Greece did not improve after the end of the fighting. The basic weaknesses of the Greek economy have been described in previous sections; the war intensified all of these problems. Eight percent of the population, or 0.5 million out of 7 million, had been killed. The country was beset by a huge inflation; wages at the same time remained low. There was a continuing balance-of-trade problem. Greece still had to import food to prevent starvation, and it did not have the means of payment. Although supplies were sent in by UNRRA, a considerable percentage ended on the black market. The obvious corruption and the prevalence of profiteering caused great social bitterness. The villages and mountain areas were in a particularly bad situation. They did not have the roads or other means of communication necessary to assure an efficient distribution of relief supplies, nor did they have the political influence to make certain that they received their fair share of the available food and clothing. The starvation, misery, and deep resentment that were present in the countryside form a background to the rebellion.

The first political question that had to be settled was that of the monarchy. Reversing a previous decision, over Soviet protests, the Western governments decided that elections for the assembly should precede the plebiscite on the king, a measure that was also disapproved by George II. British, French, and American missions were to be sent to observe the voting. Since the conditions in the countryside made campaigning difficult for the left parties, they requested a postponement. When a delay was not granted, the KKE and some other groups, including some in the center, abstained from the elections. This action was ultimately to be extremely damaging to their interests. Because of their failure to participate in the campaign and to present candidates, they were to have no representatives in the assembly during the next crucial four years. The Communist Party thus was deprived of the political influence that could be exerted through this means.

The elections, held as scheduled in March 1946, gave an absolute majority to the Populist Party of Tsaldaris, which supported the monarchy. With these returns the results of the plebiscite on the return of the king were a foregone conclusion. Held in September, the vote went as expected, and George II won the approval of 68 percent of the voters. Both of these elections, however, aroused controversy. The left claimed that huge numbers of their supporters abstained, so that the result did not truly reflect the will of the Greek public. Undoubtedly, their accusations of widespread police interference had much justification. It is, of course, impossible to predict accurately what the result would have been had the KKE and the rest of the left entered the contest.

Meanwhile, the situation in the countryside worsened. In 1946 increased incidences of political violence were reported: "Figures collected by a British observer showed that in a single week of July in Macedonia, ten murders could be attributed to bands of the Left, six to the Right and five were uncertain; in another week the record for the whole country was twenty-three for the Right, sixteen by the Left and two uncertain."[6]

In this chaotic atmosphere it is impossible to date the exact beginning of the renewal of civil war. Armed bands representing the entire political spectrum had remained organized since the war; their activity now simply increased, and incidents between government supporters and the left multiplied. The KKE forces, known as the Democratic Army of Greece, were under the command of Markos Vafiadis. Zachariadis stayed in Athens, where the Communist center remained intact and the press continued to publish until October 1947. The real strength of the KKE was still in the mountains; the chief recruits were peasants. In contrast, the movement did not receive the support of the city workers, at least not in an open or effective form. Throughout this crisis the government and the regular army were in control of the major cities, including Athens, Piraeus, and Thessaloniki. Estimates of the numbers on each side are difficult to make, but in the summer of 1946 it appears that the rebels had between 1,500 and 2,700 men; the numbers rose to between 8,000 and 13,500 by the end of the year. Opposing them were the government forces, consisting of the army of 90,000 and the police of 30,000,[7] which also had the advantage of supplies of heavy military equipment, including machine guns, armored cars, and tanks. The navy and air force, as well as the army, remained loyal to the government.

Despite this disparity in size and weaponry, the rebels held control of much of the country by the spring of 1947. Like partisan forces elsewhere, they had certain advantages. Using hit-and-run tactics, they made good use of their superior mobility. The army could not use its heavy equipment in primitive mountain areas, where much of the fighting took place. Although the number of active fighters was relatively small, the rebels were aided by an underground army of sympathizers in the villages and towns. The insurgent bands, unlike the regular army, were not hampered by the necessity of maintaining large support units; they lived off the countryside. In addition, since they

6  Woodhouse, *The Struggle for Greece*, p. 180.
7  Woodhouse, *The Struggle for Greece*, p. 186.

controlled the mountains, they had the advantage of interior lines of communication. The government, in contrast, held the large cities, the coastal areas, and the major roadways. The situation was thus in some respects similar to that of the 1820s, when the Ottoman army could not dislodge guerilla fighters from their mountain bastions.

Another major problem faced by the Greek government was the low morale of its troops, who did not fight well at first. The British military mission trained the soldiers along the lines that had won the war against Germany; these officers were not equipped to teach guerilla tactics. The Greek soldiers were thus not prepared to meet their opponents. They were also spread very thin: the army had to guard the frontiers, watch the lines of communication, and protect the loyal villages. Their effectiveness was further handicapped by repeated political interference in questions of strategy and the appointment of the commanders. The morale of the common soldier was also adversely affected by the ability of the sons of the rich to buy their way out of the service and by the failure to make adequate provision for the soldier's personal care and for that of his family.

The rebel control of much of Greece was bound to become a matter of international concern, particularly in view of the Communist victories elsewhere and the concurrent pressure exercised by the Soviet Union on Iran and Turkey. It appeared that the Soviet government was making a determined effort to gain a stronghold in the Aegean and Eastern Mediterranean region. At the Potsdam conference, Stalin had indicated his desire to acquire a naval base on the Aegean. The Soviet press at the time had launched a bitter campaign against the "monarcho-fascist" regime in Athens. It was also clear that the KKE was receiving assistance from Yugoslavia, Albania, and Bulgaria. The Western states naturally inferred that such actions could be carried out only as a result of Soviet approval or even initiative.

Meanwhile, the Greek government found itself in increasing difficulties. It was obviously not winning the civil war; at best, it could maintain the defensive positions. Since it soon became impossible for the British to continue their assistance, the Greek government turned to the United States. The resultant deep American involvement in Greek affairs came in gradual stages. At first, economic assistance was increased. The American government began to regard the events in Greece as an example of what appeared to be a pattern of Soviet aggression against weak and vulnerable regions; reflecting this viewpoint, Lincoln MacVeagh, the ambassador in Athens, wrote to the State Department in February 1947: "If Greece falls to communism, the whole Near East and part of North Africa as well are certain to pass under Soviet influence."[8]

---

8    Quoted in John O. Iatrides, "Greece and the Origins of the Cold War," in John T. A. Kou-
     moulides, ed., *Greece in Transition: Essays in the History of Modern Greece, 1821–1974* (London:
     Zeno, 1977), p. 237.

# The immediate postwar readjustments

The decisive turn of American policy came in March 1947. In February the British government informed the United States that it could no longer continue to meet its responsibilities in Greece. In response, President Truman requested from Congress that $400 million in assistance be granted to both Greece and Turkey. In a speech on March 12 he declared: "The very existence of the Greek state is today threatened by the terrorist activities of several thousand armed men, led by Communists, who defy the government's authority ... Greece must have assistance if it is to become a self-supporting and self-respecting democracy." In order to win support in Congress and with American public opinion, the president justified his actions with a general statement, which subsequently became known as the Truman Doctrine: "I believe that it must be the policy of the United States to support free peoples who are resisting attempted subjugation by armed minorities or by outside pressures."[9] This direct involvement in an area where American influence had not previously been exerted marked a major departure in U.S. foreign policy. It was a companion to the Marshall Plan for economic aid to Europe, which was announced in June 1947, and included Greece.

The U.S. government thus replaced the British as the major foreign influence in Athens. American missions and advisers undertook the same tasks as their British predecessors. As had been the case previously with other Greek protectors, American intervention caused much friction and was to be violently attacked later by many Greek politicians. The American presence introduced a new style and manner; it has been commented that the Greeks found their new patrons "more inflexible, less adaptable, less willing to make allowances, more inclined to impose American methods, regardless of national characteristics ... They were vigorous, resourceful and immensely efficient."[10] Despite the assurances of American assistance, it was clear that some time would elapse before the arrival of the promised supplies and military equipment. Meanwhile, in April 1947 George II died; he was succeeded by his brother Paul.

The year 1948 brought a military stalemate; both sides prepared for the future decisive conflict. With American aid the Greek army was increased in size from 132,000 in early 1948 to a final total in all the forces of 232,500 men. American officers and advisers were also sent to assist them. Although funds were allotted for economic assistance, the major part of the American aid went for the provision of military equipment and for strengthening the army. By September 1948 the United States had supplied 140 airplanes, 3,890 guns and mortars, 97,000 rifles, and 10,000 cars and trucks.[11] Despite Soviet protests, the United Nations supported this assistance.

9  Statement of Truman to Congress, March 12, 1947, in *Documents on International Affairs, 1947–1948* (London: Oxford University Press, 1952), pp. 2–7.
10 Woodhouse, *The Struggle for Greece*, p. 235.
11 Woodhouse, *The Struggle for Greece*, p. 247.

The KKE could not withstand the challenge. Although supplies were received from Yugoslavia and Bulgaria, the Soviet government gave no encouragement or support to the rebels. Stalin, in fact, wanted the revolt halted before it caused difficulties for Soviet policy elsewhere. In April 1948 he expressed his disapproval to visiting Yugoslav and Bulgarian leaders, arguing that the rebellion had

> no prospect of success at all. What do you think, that Great Britain and the United States – the United States, the most powerful state in the world – will permit you to break their line of communications in the Mediterranean Sea! Nonsense. And we have no navy. The uprising in Greece must be stopped, and as quickly as possible.[12]

This Soviet attitude brought neither an end to Yugoslav assistance nor a change in KKE policy. Nevertheless, it was apparent that the Balkan nations could not compete with the United States in the provision of military assistance. The Greek rebels were constantly disappointed in the level of the aid they received. In addition, it was soon clear that they could not win the support of the majority of the Greek peasants. Although at first they had been able to attract the village youth, Markos later admitted that by the middle of 1947 90 percent of their recruitment had to be by force.[13] Moreover, many of their actions caused deep resentment. For example, when they were compelled to vacate an area, they often took the local children with them. About 28,000 children were removed, and many of them were sent across the border; only 10,000 ever returned to their homes.[14]

The rebel camp was also weakened by a split in the leadership and a disagreement over strategy. Zachariadis had no personal experience in mountain fighting. Influenced by Marxist ideology, he believed that the victory would be won in the industrial cities. This attitude naturally led him into conflict with Markos, whose influence lay in the villages. Experienced in guerilla warfare, the military commander wished to continue these methods, but he was overruled by those who preferred to adopt principles of conventional warfare. In December 1947, again influenced by the Yugoslav experience, the rebels set up a Provisional Democratic Government of Greece, which resembled AVNOJ. Markos was the premier and minister of war. It is interesting to note that none of the East European governments recognized this regime.

During the civil war the Democratic Army, which had 25,000 men by the end of 1948, relied on supplies brought across the border and then carried throughout the mountains by mule train. Because of this dependence on

---

12  Djilas, *Conversations with Stalin*, p. 182.
13  Woodhouse, *The Struggle for Greece*, p. 212.
14  Woodhouse, *The Struggle for Greece*, p. 209.

foreign aid, the quarrel that broke out between Yugoslavia and the Soviet Union in the spring of 1948 was to prove a disaster for the rebel cause. The dispute involved not only Belgrade and Moscow: it resulted in a complete rupture in the relations between Yugoslavia and its neighbors – Albania, Bulgaria, Hungary, and Romania. Despite this crisis, Yugoslav aid continued throughout 1948, but the outlook was increasingly bleak for the KKE forces. By the end of the year Markos was convinced that the war was lost. In a report of November 1948 he gave as the principal causes of the failure the problem of finding new reserves, the lack of support in the cities, and the insufficiency of outside assistance. In February 1949 he was replaced as commander of the Democratic Army, and he left for Yugoslavia.

The rebel cause was further damaged by the KKE's approval of the formation of a Macedonian state. In March 1949 its radio station, operating in Romania, endorsed the idea. In the dispute that had arisen in the socialist camp, Zachariadis had supported the Soviet position and thus accepted the Bulgarian line on the Macedonian problem. It now appeared that a KKE victory might well lead to a loss of Greek territory. The Communist connection with the neighboring governments, all of which had claims on Greek lands, had always been a vulnerable point. It should also be noted that Slavic-speaking Macedonians, organized in NOF, formed a major portion of the KKE troops. One estimate sets the number at 11,000 at the beginning of 1948, and at 14,000 by the end of the revolution.[15]

The revolt was finally brought to a conclusion in 1949. In January General Papagos took command of the army; in Athens a stable, moderate center regime was in power. The full weight of U.S. aid was now placed in the balance. In the spring the army began to clear the rebel centers, beginning in the Peloponnesus and then moving northward. In July 1949 Tito closed the Greek border and thus interrupted the rebel lines of supply. The fighting came to an end in September; many of the defeated forces fled the country. In October the KKE leadership accepted the result and blamed the debacle on Tito.

The civil war was a disaster for the Greek nation. It is estimated that about 70,000 were killed on the government side and 38,000 on the rebel. The physical damage to the country was immense, far more than during the preceding European war. Moreover, the government had followed a policy of clearing the villages in threatened areas, an action that created an enormous refugee problem. By the end of 1947 there were about 400,000 of these people, and the number increased to almost 700,000 by 1949; all of them had to be cared for during the fighting and resettled afterward. Even worse, the conflict left a legacy of bitterness and hate. Like all civil wars, it was fought with violence and cruelty. A modern Greek author has given dramatic expression

15  R. V. Burks, *The Dynamics of Communism in Eastern Europe* (Princeton, N.J.: Princeton University Press, 1961), pp. 102–104.

in one of his novels to this atmosphere. In one village, he writes, the inhabitants

> were not surprised when the killing began, brother against brother. They were not afraid; they did not change their way of life. But what had been simmering slowly within them, mute and unrevealed, now burst out, insolent and free. The primeval passion of man to kill poured from within them. Each had a neighbor, or a friend, or a brother, whom he had hated for years, without reason, often without realizing it. The hatred simmered there, unable to find an outlet. And now, suddenly, they were given rifles and hand grenades; noble flags waved over their heads. The clergy, the army, the press urged them on – to kill their neighbor, their friend, their brother. Only in this manner, they shouted to them, can faith and country be saved. Murder, the most ancient need of man, took on a high mystic meaning. And the chase began – brother hunting brother.[16]

### THE YUGOSLAV DEVELOPMENTS

#### The Yugoslav objectives

At the conclusion of World War II Yugoslavia was clearly the strongest Balkan nation – in fact, the leading state outside the Soviet Union in Eastern Europe. It had a impressive army of 800,000 experienced fighters under a purely national command, and a revolutionary regime that had apparently close and friendly relations with Moscow was in power. Confident of their position the Partisan leaders had developed a wide and ambitious program for the future. In addition to the economic, social, and political changes they intended to effect within their country, they also wished to secure certain territorial objectives and foreign policy goals. As we have seen, they had already achieved a predominant position in Tirana. In addition, although they were in full control of Vardar Macedonia, they were to seek to unite the Pirin and Aegean sections to the Skopje government. This action was to be accomplished through negotiations with the Bulgarian government and the KKE and was to be part of an arrangement by which it was intended that Bulgaria would become the seventh Yugoslav republic. To the north the Yugoslav government hoped to acquire territory in the peace treaties that still had to be negotiated with Italy and Austria. The great prize here was the Istrian peninsula, with the city of Trieste, which was a major Yugoslav objective. In addition, it was hoped that the southern part of the Austrian province of Carinthia, which had a partly Slovene population, could be annexed.

Great obstacles, however, stood in the way of the achievement of this am-

---

16  Nikos Kazantzakis, *The Fratricides* (New York: Simon & Schuster, 1964), p. 8.

bitious program, particularly in regard to Istria and Carinthia. A major difficulty was caused by the fact that Yugoslavia did not have great-power backing for these plans. Soviet opposition was in the end to be particularly effective in blocking the attempts at Balkan federation. Western support was lost owing to certain Yugoslav actions that alienated Britain and the United States. During the war, as we have seen, the principal Partisan links with a foreign power had been those with Britain through the military mission. Churchill had expected to have at least a 50 percent influence in the area after the war. Instead, upon achieving victory, the Partisans had immediately demonstrated their faithfulness to the socialist camp by establishing close cooperation with the Soviet representatives and by making it clear that any Western interference would be rejected. The Tito–Šubašić agreements were violated, and nothing resembling the free elections required by the Yalta Declaration was ever held. Even worse, open conflict with the United States soon developed. In August 1946, after repeated protests over the violation of its air space, the Yugoslav airplanes forced down an American transport plane and then shot down another, with the loss of five lives. Although the government eventually paid an indemnity, the incident inaugurated a period of very bad relations with Washington. Certainly Yugoslavia could not expect assistance from the United States or Britain in the achievement of its more controversial territorial goals.

In addition to its negative attitude toward certain aspects of Balkan cooperation, the Soviet Union also had reservations on the Carinthian and Trieste questions. As far as Carinthia was concerned, the Western governments considered its retention necessary for the viability of the Austrian state, which they were fully determined to restore as an independent nation. The Soviet Union for its part was not interested in expediting a settlement. As long as a treaty was not made, it could keep troops in Austria and maintain lines of communication through Romania and Hungary, thus in fact keeping these states under military occupation. On the Trieste issue the Soviet government in the end proved unwilling to come into conflict with the West or to jeopardize its interests elsewhere in order to please Belgrade. The fate of the city played an important role in Italian politics, and the position of the Italian Communists also had to be taken into consideration.

In the peace negotiations Yugoslavia first claimed all of the former Italian province of Venetia Giulia. In May 1945 Partisan forces were in occupation of most of the area. Under strong United States–British pressure they were forced to withdraw from western Istria to a line that left the major cities of Pula, Trieste, and Gorizia in the hands of the Western allies. In the negotiations connected with the formulation of a peace treaty for Italy the Soviet Union at first supported the Yugoslav claims, including that to Trieste. The British and American governments, in contrast, wished to allow Italy to retain Trieste and western Istria. In July 1946 the Soviet Union, Britain, and the United States all accepted a French compromise proposal that gave Yu-

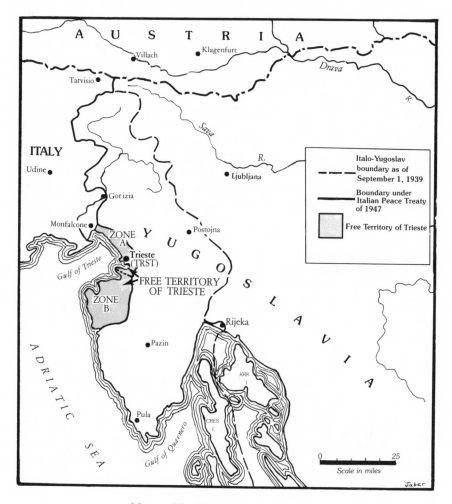

Map 14. The Trieste controversy

goslavia most of Istria, but also provided for the establishment of the "Free Territory of Trieste," composed of the city and certain surrounding lands; this territory in theory eventually would have an international government. The area was divided into two zones (see Map 14). The northern, which included Trieste and was to be known as Zone A, was given a British and American administration. Zone B, to the south, was placed under Yugoslav control. In the peace treaty signed with Italy in February 1947, Yugoslavia received 2,995 square miles of territory, with about 600,000 inhabitants. Despite these large gains, the Yugoslav government remained dissatisfied with the settlement concerning Trieste and bitter about what it regarded as a Soviet failure to give adequate support to its interests.

Although the northern borders of Yugoslavia were determined by the great powers, the territorial questions on the other frontiers were settled between the Balkan states and their national Communist parties. Here the Yugoslav government, with its military superiority, had the advantage. The Kosovo region was reoccupied. Measures of reprisal were taken against the Albanian population, and fierce fighting broke out. The area was subsequently joined to Serbia, but as an autonomous region with Albanian recognized as an official language. In practice, nevertheless, Serbian predominance was reestablished. In Albania proper the Yugoslav representatives simply assumed the former Italian role. Strong political influence was exerted; experts and advisers were sent into the country. Plans were made to exploit the local economic resources.

The really difficult question involved Macedonia. During the war, as we have seen, the Yugoslav Communist Party had been able to establish a preponderant position in the Vardar section, which became one of the six republics of the new Yugoslavia. The biggest problems involved the status of Pirin and Aegean Macedonia. Since the entire Macedonian controversy was to remain a major cause of tension among the Balkan states, the background of the issue, which has already been mentioned in various sections of this narrative, is here reviewed in detail.

### The Macedonian controversy: the "apple of discord"

The fate of the Macedonian lands, as we have seen, had been the principal cause of bitterness and controversy among the Balkan states since 1878. Even the Romanian government had put forward claims based on the Vlach population. In the Treaty of San Stefano of 1878 Bulgaria had been awarded the greater portion of these lands, as well as Thrace, a settlement corresponding to what was judged at the time to be the national character of the region. After the division of the Bulgarian state in the Treaty of Berlin, Bulgarian opinion remained convinced that the Macedonians were in fact Bulgarians. Thereafter, the area became the center of violent conflict. The Serbian, Greek, and Bulgarian interests organized cultural societies and terrorist bands. Some groups favored an independent Macedonia and argued for the distinct ethnic character of the population. It should be noted that the Bulgarian government was not unsympathetic to this latter standpoint. Should it prove impossible to annex the entire region directly, the Bulgarian leaders usually supported the creation of a separate Macedonian state; they were convinced that it would work closely with Sofia and that eventually a union would be accomplished. Instead of these alternatives, however, Bulgaria after the Balkan Wars of 1912 and 1913 had to agree to the partition of Macedonia, with the major share of the territory awarded to Serbia. The Pirin district, constituting only 10 percent of the total area, was a poor substitute for the wider Bulgarian objectives.

In the interwar years Macedonia remained a center of violence and controversy. Belgrade attempted to administer its lands as "southern Serbia" and to treat the inhabitants as Serbs. Although the national conflicts here did not assume the magnitude of those between the Serbs and the Croats, they did provide an element that further weakened the Yugoslav state. The Macedonian IMRO, now pro-Bulgarian, cooperated with the Croatian Ustaša, and both received Italian and Hungarian aid. In this same period a major change occurred in Greek Macedonia. The settlement of Greek refugees from Anatolia and the exchange of populations made this region and western Thrace predominantly Greek in population.

The Macedonian question, as well as the other national controversies, were discussed at length in the meetings of the Yugoslav Communist Party and the Comintern. The principal point at issue for the Yugoslav party was whether their state represented a union of three "tribes," that is, the Serbs, the Croats, and the Slovenes, or whether it was indeed based on one Yugoslav nationality. The Macedonians were at first not treated as a separate entity. In 1923 a party conference accepted the federalist position and even agreed that the component nations had a right to form separate states. Although the Macedonians and the Montenegrins were not placed on the same level as the three dominant peoples, they too were considered victims of Serbian "hegemony."[17] The right of each of the Yugoslav "nations" to self-determination and succession was accepted.

This decision reflected Comintern opinion. In the 1920s that organization adopted what was in fact a Bulgarian standpoint: the establishment of an autonomous Macedonia that would include the Vardar, Pirin, and Aegean regions, and its membership in a Balkan federation. The Comintern position appealed to IMRO, and it gained the support of the Croatian Peasant Party, which also favored a federal reorganization of Yugoslavia. It is important to note that Stalin took a major role in these Comintern discussions; he too supported the right of the component Yugoslav nationalities to secede and establish their own governments.

These issues continued, of course, to be hotly debated within the Yugoslav party circles. As in the Greek party organization, it was difficult for the membership to become enthusiastic about a loss of state lands. Nevertheless, when the third congress of the Yugoslav party was held in Vienna in May 1926, the Comintern stand was accepted. Yugoslavia was recognized as a multinational

17 Wayne S. Vucinich, "Nationalism and Communism," in Wayne S. Vucinich, ed., *Contemporary Yugoslavia: Twenty Years of Socialist Experiment* (Berkeley: University of California Press, 1969), p. 243.

state in which Macedonia was a separate component. The reorganization of the country into a federation of worker-peasant republics, based on the nationalities, was also supported. This policy was reaffirmed at the fourth congress, held in Dresden in 1928. Thus the breaking up of Yugoslavia into separate authorities was approved despite the devastating effects that such an action would have on general Yugoslav interests and on the balance of power in the Balkans.

A modification in this attitude toward the national question, and thus toward Macedonia, occurred in 1935. At this time the Comintern decreed a change to popular-front tactics on the part of its members and their cooperation with other parties to obstruct the advance of right-wing and fascist influences. The Yugoslav party henceforth adopted a more favorable attitude toward the state, which was described as a natural and not an artificial union. The objective was declared to be its reorganization into a federation of equal nationalities. More effort was also put into the strengthening of the Communist organizations in Bosnia, Hercegovina, and Macedonia, which had received less attention previously. In a party meeting held in Zagreb in 1940 the participants called for the application of the principle of self-determination in Bosnia, Hercegovina, Montenegro, Macedonia, and the Albanian regions. This program remained thereafter the basic Yugoslav Communist policy. The party no longer supported any measures leading to the breakup of the state or a cession of territory; "self-determination" was to be granted, but only within a Yugoslav federation. At Jajce the provisional government was organized on the basis of six constituent republics, of which Macedonia was one. Efforts were then made to enlarge the area to encompass both the Pirin and the Aegean regions.

These objectives were bound to bring the Yugoslav leaders into conflict not only with the governments of the neighboring states but also with their Communist parties. The problems that arose during the war have already been mentioned. The question who would dominate Macedonia depended, of course, on the outcome of the conflict. As we have seen, the Bulgarian government under King Boris had hoped to acquire this region and Thrace; success would have given his state the predominant position in the Balkans. After the Bulgarian coup in 1944 and the entrance of the Soviet army into the country, the Bulgarians could still hope to exert influence in Macedonia. The Fatherland Front government simply changed sides in the war; therefore the Bulgarian soldiers in occupation of Macedonia were in theory on the same side as the Partisans. This army, however, was soon withdrawn to fight in Europe. Nevertheless, no Bulgarian government, whether Communist or royalist, could abandon the Macedonian issue. There was still hope that an autonomous state could be formed – a solution that remained acceptable to Sofia. In 1943 the Fatherland Front, in protesting the Jajce decisions, issued a declaration reaffirming this position:

Macedonia is an apple of discord. Rivers of blood have been shed for it . . . It is the cradle of the Bulgarian renaissance . . . To avoid new historic mistakes and to give Macedonia lasting pacification, the Fatherland Front proclaims the watchword "Macedonia for the Macedonians" . . . The only saving solution is an integral, free, and independent Macedonia. Only thus can it cease to be an apple of discord and become a healthy unifying link between all the Balkan peoples.[18]

As we have seen, in the past century Balkan leaders of various parties and nations had found in the idea of federation an answer to the constant controversies among the states. This proposal had been a fundamental part of previous Communist programs for the area, but the major obstacle remained the lack of any general agreement on how such a federation should be organized. Each government put forward the proposals that would best protect its own individual interests. Yugoslavia's plans at this time were certainly designed to enhance the power of that state. A basic objective was to secure the union of Pirin Macedonia with Skopje. It was then proposed that Bulgaria join in a federation with Yugoslavia, but on a basis that would reduce it to a position similar to that of the other constituent republics. Bulgaria would thus be equal to Bosnia or Montenegro, and, of course, also to Serbia or Croatia.

Negotiations on Macedonia and on a possible federation were commenced between Bulgaria and Yugoslavia in November 1944. The Bulgarian position was comparatively weak. The Yugoslav proposal that Bulgaria join as a seventh republic was, of course, rejected. The Yugoslav government similarly could not accept a Bulgarian suggestion that the two countries unite on an equal basis. At the same time much pressure was placed on Bulgaria to cede Pirin Macedonia. In August 1946 the Bulgarian party went far toward meeting the Yugoslav proposals and agreed that close cultural relations should be established between the Pirin and the Vardar sections. Unification, however, should be considered only after other political ties linked Bulgaria and Yugoslavia, such as the conclusion of a treaty of alliance and the abolition of customs and frontier barriers. Nevertheless, despite this and other support that had been given to the concept of Macedonian autonomy, the Bulgarian authorities did not move toward granting a separate status to the Pirin area.

The height of the policy of cooperation was reached in August 1947 when Tito and Dimitrov met at Bled. There the foundations were laid for a gradual approach toward eventual federation. On the question of Macedonia it was agreed that Yugoslavia could carry on an active program of cultural propaganda in the Pirin region. As a result of this understanding, the Yugoslav

---

18  Quoted in Elisabeth Barker, *Macedonia: Its Place in Balkan Power Politics* (London: Royal Institute of International Affairs, 1950), p. 97.

government inaugurated a massive propaganda campaign, including the sending of

> ninety-three teachers . . . "to assist in the correct teaching of the Macedonian literary language and Macedonian history." The teachers, however, did not confine themselves to this task. They gave courses for illiterates and courses for adults in Macedonian language and history. They gave lectures on life in the Macedonian People's Republic. They founded a Macedonian National Theatre at Gorna Djumaja, to present Macedonian plays. They established a publishing concern called the "Macedonian Book," which in a few months issued over 80,000 copies of books, brochures and journals . . . The Government of the Macedonian People's Republic gave 149 scholarships for students from Pirin Macedonia, and established teachers' courses attended by 135 teachers from Pirin Macedonia.[19]

Despite the Bled agreement and the ostensibly friendly relations with Belgrade, the Bulgarian government was deeply disturbed by these activities. The wartime situation had been totally reversed. Whereas in 1941 an enormous Bulgarian propaganda campaign had been inaugurated in Vardar Macedonia, a pro-Skopje movement was now being carried on in Pirin Macedonia.

In November 1947 Tito visited Dimitrov in Sofia, where a Treaty of Friendship was signed. By this time, it will be remembered, both states were deeply involved in the Greek civil war, and they had close connections with the rebels, in particular with NOF. Both Bulgaria and Yugoslavia favored the eventual cession of Aegean Macedonia and its unification with the other two regions. In October 1945 Tito had taken a strong stand on Macedonian unity. The support given to Markos's forces and the maintenance of an open border to aid the rebels have already been discussed. The fate of Greek Macedonia, as well as that of the other two sections, was to be determined by the outcome of the Greek civil war and by the break that was to occur between Belgrade and Moscow.

### The Yugoslav–Soviet conflict

In the first years after the conclusion of World War II it appeared not only that Yugoslavia would remain the strongest Balkan state, but also that it would assume an important place in European affairs. Tito was certainly interested in playing a major role within the Communist camp. He negotiated treaties with Albania, Poland, and Czechoslovakia in 1946, with Bulgaria in 1946 and

---

19   Barker, *Macedonia*, p. 104.

321

1947, and with Romania in 1947. Yugoslav influence in the international Communist circles was also strong. The Soviet and Yugoslav parties now supported the formation of an international organization that would at least partially replace the Comintern, which had been abolished by Stalin in 1943. In September 1947 representatives of the parties of Bulgaria, Hungary, Romania, Czechoslovakia, Yugoslavia, the Soviet Union, France, and Italy met in Poland and formed the Information Bureau of the Communist Parties, the Cominform. As the title indicated, the main objective of the organization was to establish a center for the exchange of information. The headquarters were to be in Belgrade. A newspaper, *For a Lasting Peace, for a People's Democracy*, was subsequently issued.

Despite the relatively independent role that the Partisan leaders had assumed during the war, they all expected in the future to cooperate closely with the Soviet Union. The government was dominated at this time by four men in addition to Tito, who held dictatorial powers: Ranković for security, Edvard Kardelj for foreign policy, Milovan Djilas for propaganda, and Boris Kidrić for economic planning. All were firmly devoted to the Soviet Union. Djilas, expressing an attitude common among loyal party members, later wrote: "For I, too, like every other Communist, had it inculcated in me and I was convinced that there could exist no opposition between the Soviet Union and another people, especially not a revolutionary and Marxist party, as the Yugoslav Party indeed was." Yugoslav Communists, he wrote further, idealized Soviet conditions; for them

> Moscow was not only a political and spiritual center but the realization of an abstract idea – 'the classless society' – something that not only made their sacrifice and suffering easy and sweet, but that justified their very existence in their own eyes.

Stalin too became more than human:

> In the dungeons and the holocaust of war, and in the no less violent spiritual crises and clashes with the internal and external foes of Communism, Stalin was something more than a leader in battle. He was the incarnation of an idea, transfigured in Communist minds into pure idea, and thereby into something infallible and sinless. Stalin was the victorious battle of today and the brotherhood of man of tomorrow.[20]

Although Tito had spent a long period of time in Moscow before the war, he had remained in a subordinate position and he had not enjoyed the con-

---

20  Djilas, *Conversations with Stalin*, pp. 26–27, 11, 57.

fidence of the top Soviet party officials. He had, however, in September 1944, paid a secret visit to Stalin to negotiate the passage of the Soviet army through Yugoslavia. Despite the initial Yugoslav enthusiasm for cooperation with the great Communist power, problems arose at once. In its passage through the "liberated" countries, the Soviet troops caused great resentment by their violent and undisciplined behavior; friend and foe suffered alike. Although this army crossed through only the northeast corner of Yugoslavia, Djilas noted that there were, among other crimes, "121 cases of rape of which 111 involved rape with murder, and 1,204 cases of looting with assault." Unlike some other regimes that were in a weaker position, the Yugoslav officials made strong protests, but on a personal and unofficial basis. The charges were greatly resented by Stalin, who told a Yugoslav delegation that he did not see how complaints could be made if a Russian soldier, after years of fighting, had "fun with a woman" or took "some trifle."[21]

Another cause of friction came from the Soviet failure to show adequate appreciation for what the Partisans considered their major achievements during the war. Supremely self-confident, even arrogant, the Yugoslav leadership felt that it had made an important contribution to the Allied victory. Not only did the Soviet officials appear not to understand the special difficulties of the Partisan struggle, but Stalin was not above teasing Tito about the superior performance of the Bulgarian soldiers, commenting: "And yours, the Yugoslav – they are still Partisans, unfit for serious front-line fighting."[22]

Even more serious was the growing conviction of Yugoslavia's leaders that the Soviet government did not intend to back their demands in the international field. They were particularly disturbed by reports of understandings among the three great Allies on the division of the Balkans into spheres of influence, and by the lack of Soviet support on the Trieste and Carinthian issues. The uneasy feeling persisted that the country was once again to be the victim of great-power machinations. There was also much resentment over economic questions. Instead of aiding in Yugoslav economic development, it appeared that the Soviet Union was intent on preventing the rise of a potential rival. As one young Communist commented at this time:

> All through history Serbs and Croats have worked for others – well, we were as good as told that we were to continue to do just that. We were to dig our coal and ores, but not build plants to smelt our iron and make it into steel and make the steel into the machinery we needed ... No, we were to send our wealth abroad, raw, just as always – we were to be exploited, we were to be a colony, just as always. After the struggles in the old times against the Turks and

21 Djilas, *Conversations with Stalin*, pp. 88–89, 95.
22 Djilas, *Conversations with Stalin*, p. 112.

Austrians and Magyars, after our own fights with the Nazis and the Italians, we were to keep our muddy roads, walk on them in our peasant *opanke* [sandals] and step aside when the Russian engineers rode past in their motorcars just as Serbs used to do when the Turks rode by on their mules![23]

The Yugoslav authorities were similarly deeply disturbed by Soviet penetration of their country of two other sorts: through secret agents and through propaganda. They were quite aware that the Soviet representatives were seeking to recruit agents and friends in the vital centers of the army, the secret police, and the top economic administration. At the same time the Russian government pressed the Yugoslavs to fill their radio programs with Russian music, their theaters with Russian plays and films, and their press with articles concerning the glorious achievements of the Soviet Union. There was no reciprocity: the Yugoslav press published 1,850 Soviet books; in return 2 Yugoslav works appeared in Moscow.[24]

When judging the causes for the break that occurred between the Soviet and Yugoslav governments, the main evidence must come from Yugoslav sources. Some of the participants later published accounts of their experiences, and the government printed many of the basic documents reflecting the opinion of the two sides. From these accounts it appears that the main reason for the quarrel was the independent Yugoslav attitude and the failure to consult the Soviet government on every action, whether domestic or international. Certainly, in the past the Yugoslav leaders had made their major moves without asking Soviet advice. They had informed Moscow of the Jajce decisions only after they had been made; they had not installed a true popular-front government after the war, as the Soviet, the British, and the American governments had all desired. The intervention in the Greek civil war and the negotiations between Yugoslavia and Bulgaria on federation had all been undertaken on the Yugoslav initiative. The Yugoslav domination of Albania, or what Stalin referred to as the "swallowing" of that country, was a result of Belgrade's decision alone, although Stalin did not disapprove of it.

Despite the signs of friction that appeared regularly after the end of the war, a crisis in the Soviet–Yugoslav relationship did not come until the spring of 1948. In February Stalin summoned delegations from both Yugoslavia and Bulgaria to Moscow in order to lecture them on the mistaken policies of their governments. Kardelj, Djilas, and Vladimir Bakarić, the premier of Croatia, were the Yugoslav representatives. The Bulgarian delegation was even more impressive: it included George Dimitrov, by then premier; Traicho Kostov, the deputy premier; and Vasil Kolarov, the president of the People's Republic. At these meetings Stalin made clear his great displeasure with his visitors'

---

23 Hamilton Fish Armstrong, *Tito and Goliath* (New York: Macmillan, 1951), pp. 101–102.
24 Wolff, *The Balkans in Our Time*, p. 355.

independent actions, especially the recent dispatch of two Yugoslav divisions to Albania. When this move was justified as being necessary in case complications arose from the Greek civil war, the Soviet dictator expressed his strong disapproval of the intervention and his desire that the Greek revolt be brought to an end. He also opposed the Yugoslav and Bulgarian plans for a Balkan federation. Before returning home, Kardelj had to sign an agreement that in the future Yugoslavia would consult with the Soviet Union on matters of mutual concern in foreign policy.

Relations between Yugoslavia and the Soviet Union had reached a state of crisis. The issue facing the Yugoslav government was clearly whether it would maintain its independence or accept subservience to Moscow. Determined to maintain their freedom of action, the Yugoslav leaders made clear their refusal to accept a satellite relationship. Soviet retaliation commenced at once. In February 1948 the Soviet government halted negotiations in progress for a new trade agreement. In March Soviet military and civilian advisers were ordered home. The basic points at issue were stated in an exchange of correspondence that was subsequently published by the Yugoslav government. The letters were signed by Tito and Kardelj, on the one hand, and by Stalin and Molotov, on the other. The Soviet recriminations covered a wide spectrum, including denunciations of the Yugoslav party, the political organization of the state, the treatment of the Soviet advisers, and the "arrogant" attitude of the Yugoslav leaders, "who do not suffer from undue modesty and who are still intoxicated with their successes, which are not so very great." In a particularly wounding paragraph also from the Soviet letter of May 4, the Partisans' claims to particularly heroic conduct in the war were disposed of:

> We must also say that the services of the Communist Parties of Poland, Czechoslovakia, Hungary, Romania, Bulgaria and Albania are not less than those of the CPY. However, the leaders of these Parties behave modestly and do not boast about their successes as do the Yugoslav leaders, who have pierced every one's ears by their unlimited self-praises . . . Even though the French and Italian CPs have so far achieved less success than the CPY, this is not due to any special qualities of the CPY, but mainly because after the destruction of the Yugoslav Partisan Headquarters by German paratroopers, at a moment when the people's liberation movement in Yugoslavia was passing through a serious crisis, the Soviet army came to the aid of the Yugoslav people, crushed the German invader, liberated Belgrade and in this way created the conditions which were necessary for the CPY to achieve power. Unfortunately the Soviet army did not and could not render such assistance to the French and Italians CPs.[25]

---

25  *The Soviet–Yugoslav Dispute: Text of the Published Correspondence* (London: Royal Institute of International Affairs, 1948), p. 51.

In his replies Tito defended his party from the specific charges and justified the Yugoslav standpoint. As an expression of policy, his letter of April 13 is of particular significance. Here he stated: "No matter how much each of us loves the land of Socialism, the USSR, he can, in no case, love his country less, which is also developing socialism." In a later section of the same letter the theme of different roads to socialism, which was to become the basis of the Yugoslav position, was enunciated:

> We study and take as an example the Soviet system, but we are developing socialism in our country in somewhat different forms. In the given period under the specific conditions which exist in our country, in consideration of the international conditions which were created after the war of liberation, we are attempting to apply the best forms of work in the realization of socialism. We do not do this, in order to prove that our road is better than that taken by the Soviet Union, that we are inventing something new, but because this is forced upon us by our daily life.[26]

The Soviet point of view naturally received the full support of the Communist bloc governments. In June a Cominform meeting, which the Yugoslavs refused to attend, was held in Bucharest. On June 28, again the fateful date of the battle of Kosovo, the Cominform members expelled Yugoslavia and issued a strong statement that repeated the previous accusations and attacked Tito, Ranković, Kardelj, and Djilas personally. The Yugoslav party was openly invited to rid itself of its leadership: "The Information Bureau considers that such a disgraceful, purely Turkish terrorist regime cannot be tolerated in the Communist Party. The interests of the very existence and development of the Yugoslav Communist Party demand that an end be put to this regime."[27]

This outright, personal attack on the Yugoslav leaders gave them little choice: they had to resist or face demotion, imprisonment, or perhaps even death. They naturally chose to defy the Soviet Union and the Cominform. Immediate actions were taken within the country. The two highest officials with pro-Soviet sympathies, Andrija Hebrang and Sreten Žujović, had already been expelled from the party and imprisoned in May. In August General Arso Jovanović, the former Partisan chief of staff, was shot while trying to cross the Romanian frontier. Suspected Cominform adherents within the government or party were dismissed and imprisoned. In July, at the first party congress held since the war, Tito spoke for nine hours before 2,300 delegates. Although he defended his position, he still did not openly criticize Stalin or

---

26   *The Soviet–Yugoslav Dispute*, pp. 19, 27.
27   *The Soviet–Yugoslav Dispute*, p. 65.

the Soviet Union. This policy was to be maintained for another year. In this period the Soviet government attacked Yugoslavia through the Cominform and not directly.

The Communist states were now divided into two camps over the issue of relationships with the Soviet Union. In December 5, 1948, the Cominform journal stated: "The attitude toward the Soviet Union is now the test of devotion to the cause of proletarian internationalism."[28] These last two words were to remain the codewords for loyalty to Soviet direction. The campaign against Yugoslavia became more intense in 1949. In September the Soviet Union, followed by all of the Communist states, denounced its treaties with Belgrade. A resolution adopted at a Cominform meeting held in Bucharest in November 1949 had as its title a report given by Gheorghiu-Dej: "The Communist Party of Yugoslavia in the Power of Assassins and Spies." Throughout Eastern Europe Yugoslav representatives were harassed and insulted. The radio and press of the Cominform countries heaped on the Yugoslav party abuse of a type that was seldom previously used in relations between states, but that from this time on was to be a regular part of the Communist verbal arsenal. These abusive terms included:

"Criminal Tito clique," "Judas Tito and his abettors," "despicable traitors and imperialist hirelings," "bankrupt group of sharks," "traitors to proletarian internationalism," "sinister heralds of the camp of war and death, treacherous warmongers, and worthy heirs of Hitler," "gang of spies, provocateurs, and murderers," "dogs tied to American leashes, gnawing imperialist bones, and barking for American capital," "new Tsar of the Pan-Serbs and of the entire Yugoslav bourgeoisie."[29]

The break with the Soviet Union and the Communist states left Yugoslavia isolated and faced with grave military and economic dangers. The open and venomous attacks from the neighboring states, together with the numerous border incidents that occurred, brought up the possibility that military actions might be taken by the Cominform governments. Of more immediate concern, however, were the economic problems that arose. In January 1949 the Communist states formed the Council for Mutual Economic Assistance, known as Comecon, CEMA, or CMEA, as an answer to the Marshall Plan. Yugoslavia, despite its request to join, was excluded, and by the summer of 1949 an economic boycott of Belgrade was in full effect. All of the Comecon members had limited, ended, or failed to renew their trade agreements with Yugoslavia. These actions forced the Yugoslav government to make changes in its economic planning, but they did not lead to alterations in its basic

28  Armstrong, *Tito and Goliath*, p. 81.
29  Wolff, *The Balkans in Our Time*, p. 371.

policies. The nationalization and collectivization measures proceeded. Nevertheless, it was recognized that the nation's complete isolation in international affairs would have to be ended.

By 1949 the division between the Western powers and the Soviet Union, supported by its satellite allies, was clear. Organized into separate military and economic alignments, the two camps were indeed separated by what Churchill referred to as an "Iron Curtain." As we have seen, in 1947 in Greece the United States had come to the aid of a government faced with a Communist revolt. The Truman Doctrine had placed the action on the ideological base of the defense of "free peoples who are resisting attempted subjugation by armed minorities or by outside pressures." Since Tito made it very plain that he did not intend to abandon or alter any of his previous objectives or methods, the question naturally arose whether the United States and its allies would be willing to assist a Communist regime in defending an independent national position.

The controversy had already proved of great advantage to the Western allies; the thirty-three divisions of the Yugoslav army were neutralized. In 1949 the border with Greece was closed, an action that effectively ended the civil war there. The defense of Italy was considerably simplified, since Yugoslavia could be considered a neutral. Recognizing the advantages of the situation, the Western governments decided that the Yugoslav position should be supported and that efforts should be made to keep Tito in power. The major financial assistance came from the United States. In the first example of such aid being extended to a Communist regime, the American government granted a loan of $20 million in September, 1949. Other assistance was soon to follow. The Yugoslav situation was immensely complicated by severe droughts that hit the country in 1950 and 1952. In order to alleviate the Yugoslav plight, the American Congress in 1950 passed the Yugoslav Emergency Relief Act, which provided for $50 million in aid. From the middle of 1949 to 1955 Yugoslavia received a total of $598.5 million in economic assistance from all sources, and $588.5 million in military aid. In all, Tito thus obtained a total of about $1.2 billion (American billion), of which only $55 million were to be repaid.[30]

In return the Western powers received a great deal. The strategic advantages of a neutral Yugoslavia have been mentioned. In addition, although the country did not join the Western alliance system, understandings were reached with Greece and Turkey, which were a part of this alignment. In 1953 Yugoslavia, Greece, and Turkey signed a treaty of friendship and cooperation, which in 1954 was extended to become a twenty-year alliance. In October 1954 the status of Trieste was again negotiated. Italy took over the administration of Zone A from Britain and the United States; Yugoslavia retained control of

---

30 John C. Campbell, *Tito's Separate Road: America and Yugoslavia in World Politics* (New York: Harper & Row, 1967), pp. 27–29.

Zone B, with some minor border rectifications in its favor. Of even greater value to the Soviet adversaries was the effect of Tito's stand on the entire Communist bloc. The concept of national communism and separate roads to socialist goals was to have an enormous attraction for the leaders of other East European states, and the Yugoslav success in resisting Soviet domination was to encourage other governments to attempt similar actions. These policies were, however, to be adopted only in future years. As long as Stalin was alive, the other Communist regimes remained under firm Soviet control.

## THE REPERCUSSIONS IN THE SOVIET BLOC

The immediate effect of the Yugoslav resistance was the fall from power of various leaders in the neighboring Communist countries. In a period of declining health and mental competence, Stalin still held the supreme voice in determining Soviet policy. Under pressure from Moscow, the satellite parties were forced to rid themselves of members who could be suspected of Titoist or nationalist sentiments. "Proletarian internationalism," or blind loyalty to the Soviet Union, was the test for survival. In practice, this policy meant that the Communists who had risen to power and influence within their own countries were sacrificed in favor of those who had spent the war in the Soviet Union or who were close to the Soviet representatives. In all of the East European states the overbearing Soviet attitude, the interference in domestic affairs, and the economic exploitation caused much resentment among even the most convinced Communists. National sentiments were strong in left circles even before Tito made a stand on ideological principle. No other Communist state, however, had the strategic and military advantages of Yugoslavia. Resistance to directives from Moscow, which were, after all, backed by Soviet armed might, were obviously impractical elsewhere.

The purging of the nationalist opposition was accomplished through a series of demotions, expulsions from office, and show trials. The first such events occurred in Poland and Hungary. In Warsaw, Władislaw Gomulka, a supporter of nationalist policy, was first removed as party secretary in the fall of 1948 and then gradually deprived of all influence in the government by the end of 1949. More fortunate than his colleagues elsewhere, he was placed under house arrest, but not tried or executed. In Hungary, in contrast, László Rajk was the victim of one of the worst of the show trials. After spending the war years in prison, he had become the minister of interior in 1946. Dismissed in August 1948, he was finally brought to trial in September 1949 and accused of being a Titoist and a Trotskyite. In the course of truly farcical legal proceedings, he confessed to numerous crimes, including participation in a conspiracy with Yugoslavia against the Soviet Union. His evidence was used to justify the termination of the treaties between the Communist states and Yugoslavia. Rajk was executed in October.

Similar events occurred in Romania and Bulgaria. In fact, in Romania a purge of home Communists had already been accomplished. The principal native leader, Lucreţiu Pătrăşcanu, had, as we have seen, played a major role in the events that brought to power a front government. He was, however, opposed by the Muscovite Communists, that is, those who had spent the war in the Soviet Union, among whom were Ana Pauker and Vasile Luca. In February 1948, even before the Tito–Stalin controversy had come into the open, Pătrăşcanu was removed from office, although he was not tried and executed until 1954. In Bulgaria events followed the pattern of Poland and Hungary, and here the victim was Traicho Kostov, an outstanding local Communist. His experiences with the Soviet officials resembled those recounted by the Yugoslavs.

Although Dimitrov and Kolarov had far more prestige in international Communist circles, Kostov had more experience in internal Bulgarian affairs. With a long career of service to the party, he had been imprisoned and tortured repeatedly under the former regime. Along with the other home Communists Anton Yugov and Dobri Terpeshev, Kostov had been given important posts after the war. In charge of economic planning, he not only occupied a key position, but dealt with the Soviet representatives. Like his Yugoslav counterparts, he came to resent Soviet practices. A typical example of their methods occurred in 1946–1947: the Russian agents bought Bulgarian rose essence and tobacco at low prices set by their government; then, when the Bulgarians attempted to sell the rest of their supplies of these crops on the world market, they found that they were being undercut by Soviet agents, who were offering their Bulgarian purchases at bargain rates. Kostov made his objections known.

Kostov's subsequent downfall was closely tied to the internal struggle for power. The highest positions in the government were held by Dimitrov and Kolarov, both of whom were obviously approaching the end of their careers. The most ambitious and aggressive figure was Vulko Chervenkov, the brother-in-law of Dimitrov, who wished to inherit his power and position. In March 1949 the attack on Kostov commenced. In a meeting of the central committee of the party, he was accused of being anti-Soviet and nationalistic and of failing to cooperate with the Soviet Trade Mission. He was deprived of his positions as vice-premier and chairman of the Economic and Financial Commission and, at first, simply assigned to lower offices. With the demotion of Kostov, the principal power was held by Dimitrov, Kolarov, Chervenkov, and Yugov. In May 1949 new national elections were held. Thereafter, in June, even severer measures were taken against Kostov: he was expelled from the party, and he lost his seat in the national assembly. In July Dimitrov died and Kolarov succeeded to the position of premier. A major party purge followed. The most prominent victim, Kostov, was brought to trial in December and accused of a list of preposterous charges, including collaboration with the police and the British during the war, plotting to assassinate Dimitrov with American approval, and keeping the Yugoslav and Bulgarian federation plans secret from the Soviet Union. The judgment came quickly; Kostov was executed on December 16.

Having disposed of Kostov, Chervenkov directed his efforts toward eliminating Yugov, who lost the post as minister of interior that he had held since 1944. Chervenkov was by then the most powerful Bulgarian Communist; by 1950 he was both premier and party secretary. Under his leadership Bulgaria remained the closest to the Soviet Union of all of the satellite regimes.

## ALBANIA CHANGES DIRECTION

Yugoslavia's expulsion from the Communist bloc had an especially direct effect on the development of Albania. As we have seen, after the war the country was under strong Yugoslav influence. In July 1946 the two states signed a Treaty of Friendship, Cooperation and Mutual Aid, which supplemented other agreements on different aspects of their close relationship. Similar arrangements were made with Bulgaria, and plans for a federation of the three states were discussed. Meanwhile, relations with the Western powers became progressively worse. In the spring of 1945 the United States and in May Britain sent missions to Tirana, but they were withdrawn after a series of incidents, the most severe of which involved Britain. The Albanian government had declared that its jurisdiction in the Adriatic Sea extended up to three miles from its coastline, a provision that affected the status of the Corfu Channel in particular. Challenging the Albanian claim, the British government sent four destroyers through these waters; on October 22, 1946, two ships struck mines, and forty-four men were killed. British minesweepers then cleared the area. The question was referred first to the United Nations and then to the International Court of Justice, which decided that the Albanian government should pay reparations. Relations with the West deteriorated further when Britain and the United States opposed Albanian admission to the United Nations and when the United States Senate supported the Greek claims to territory in southern Albania.

Given these bad relations with the Western states and the Soviet acquiescence to Yugoslav domination, the Albanian leadership had no alternative but to cooperate with Belgrade. An extremely poor country, Albania desperately needed outside aid. The $26 million it received from UNRRA helped at first, but further and increased assistance was needed for economic recovery and development. At first, relations with Yugoslavia remained very close. The Albanian constitution of 1946 was similar to the Yugoslav, and Yugoslav advisers came in large numbers into the country. Very soon, however, the familiar problems arose. It appeared to many Albanians that, like Italy previously, Yugoslavia intended to turn its neighbor into an economic colony. Complaints were made that the Yugoslavs were paying unreasonably low prices for raw materials, that they were exploiting the country through the organization of joint companies, and that they were deliberately hindering the economic development of the country. The Albanians wanted aid in building consumer industries and in constructing an oil refinery. The Yugoslavs wished them instead to concentrate on improving their agricultural methods and on developing their mineral resources. The Albanian charges against the Yugoslav advisers and their policies thus closely resembled the reproaches made by Belgrade against similar Soviet economic practices. The Albanian officials also resented the actions and attitude of the Yugoslav experts and technicians.

As in the other Communist capitals, there was a division of opinion in Tirana concerning the future road that the country should take. One group, the moderates, favored an independent course and better relations with the West. They believed that the more extreme Communist measures should be postponed until the country had reached a higher level of economic development. Opposing them were the militants who wished to copy the Yugoslav pattern in both domestic and foreign policy. Enver Hoxha, holding the posts of premier, foreign minister, defense minister, and commander-in-chief of the army, as well as general secretary of the party, was the strongest Albanian leader; second to him in power was Koci Xoxe, the minister of interior. In December 1945 Hoxha gave his full support to the militants, and the moderates were expelled from the central committee in the following October.

Meanwhile, the resentment against Yugoslav influence was increasing. The leading critic was Nako Spiru, who, as the head of the state planning commission, was in direct contact with the Yugoslav officials and had to deal with their demands. He became convinced that the Yugoslav government wished to keep the country backward and to control it closely. Unable to change the Albanian policy, he committed suicide in 1947. Despite his failure, some attempts were made to limit Yugoslav control; for example, the proposal of a joint five-year plan was rejected. During this period Xoxe was the principal supporter of the Yugoslav tie, but Hoxha too, at least at first, accepted the financial advantages that the relationship offered: in July 1947 his government received from Belgrade a credit of $40 million, a sum that represented 58 percent of the Albanian budget.

In an attempt to find an alternative source of support, Hoxha in this same month traveled to the Soviet Union. Despite Stalin's agreement to Yugoslav control, the Soviet government promised to aid Albania in the building of factories and in general economic development. Albania, however, was not invited to become a member of the Cominform when it was organized in September. In addition, as we have seen, Stalin advised the Yugoslav representatives to "swallow" the country. Yugoslav influence was in fact at a height in Tirana as the break with Moscow approached. At party meetings held in February and March 1948 the pro-Yugoslav faction was able to expel prominent members, such as Kiri Belishova, the widow of Spiru, and Mehmet Shehu, the chief of staff of the army.

The situation changed radically after Yugoslavia's expulsion from the Cominform in June 1948. The realignment, carried out under Hoxha's leadership, was abrupt. In July 1948 the Yugoslav advisers were given forty-eight hours to leave the country, the economic agreements were denounced, and a violent press campaign commenced. Successful appeals were then made to the Soviet Union for economic assistance. The plans for a federation with Yugoslavia were violently denounced as a cover for annexation and a revival of former imperialist plans. Stalin became the Albanian hero; Hoxha assumed the mantle of a national leader defending his nation against foreign aggression. Thus, while Tito attacked the Soviet Union for interference and domination, the Albanian premier leveled the same charges against Yugoslavia.

The shift of alignment led naturally to changes in the Albanian leadership. In October Xoxe lost his position as minister of interior. Shehu was rehabilitated and took his place and also became again the chief of the General Staff of the army. In November 1948, at the first Albanian Communist Party congress ever held, Hoxha laid the principal blame for the Albanian difficulties on Xoxe and the Yugoslav government. In May 1949 Xoxe was tried for treason and sentenced to death. Albania, along with the Cominform members, was securely in the pro-Soviet, anti-Yugoslav camp.

## THE COLD WAR

Events in the Balkans in the years between 1941 and 1950 have been discussed in some detail because they established a pattern that was to remain constant in the following years. By the late 1940s Communist regimes tied closely to the Soviet Union had been established in Albania, Bulgaria, and Romania; Greece, under a constitutional monarchy, remained in the Western camp. Yugoslavia, with a Communist government, was henceforth to attempt to occupy a central, neutralist position. The political division of the Balkan peninsula paralleled that of the rest of Europe, which was similarly split into two military and ideological alignments. In the late 1940s the major controversy there concerned the fate of Germany. At this time the German territories were divided into zones of occupation, with the eastern sections under Soviet and Polish control and the rest under the Western governments. Austria was under a similar occupation. A major crisis occurred in the winter of 1948–1949 when the Soviet Union blocked the roads and railroads serving the Western-controlled sections of Berlin, and this city of 2 million found itself cut off from supplies of food and fuel. The Western allies solved the problem by the organization of a giant airlift.

During this period the occupation powers established political institutions in their zones of occupation that corresponded to their own patterns of government. The Western-backed German Federal Republic, with its capital in Bonn, was officially established in May 1949. In October 1950 the Soviet-sponsored German Democratic Republic was proclaimed. The last decision on the former German territories concerned Austria, and in 1955, after long negotiations and numerous delays, a treaty was signed that obligated it to refrain from joining either world alignment. It was henceforth to have a Western parliamentary political system, but to remain neutral in its foreign relations.

The European situation was further influenced by Communist victories in other areas of the world. The single greatest change occurred in China, where, after the final defeat of the Nationalist armies, the forces of Mao Zedong took complete control of the mainland in 1949. In 1950 a war broke out in Korea between the Communist-dominated north and the Western-allied government in the south; American and United Nations intervention resulted in the division of the country in a peace settlement reached in 1953. Asia, like Europe, was thus organized into two camps, with Japan, Taiwan, and South Korea allied to the West, and China and North Korea, with Communist regimes, tied to the Soviet Union. Most Western leaders, at least at first, assumed that the states with Communist governments would constitute a firm and lasting alignment.

During this period both the Western allies and the Soviet bloc concluded formal economic and military agreements joining their members in close association. In June 1947 the American secretary of state, George C. Marshall, announced proposals for economic assistance that would be open to all European states, regardless of their political systems. After the Soviet government blocked the Czech attempts at participation, however, the Marshall Plan was limited to the Western-allied nations. An enormous success, this program led to the rapid advance of its participants. Further efforts toward economic cooperation resulted in the establishment of the European Common Market in 1957. As a countermeasure, the Communist bloc in January 1949 established Comecon, which, given the relatively limited resources of its members, could not reach a similar level of achievement.

In April 1949 the Western powers concluded a formal military alliance, the North Atlantic Treaty, signed by Britain, France, Belgium, the Netherlands, Luxembourg, Denmark, Iceland, Norway, Italy, Portugal, Canada, and the United States. Greece and Turkey joined in 1952 and Western Germany in 1955. In May 1955 the Soviet bloc states joined together in the Warsaw Pact. In the meantime, in 1949, the Soviet Union exploded its first atomic bomb. With the advance of Soviet weaponry, the two camps were to achieve rough military parity by 1970.

By 1950 a standard pattern for the next years had thus been set. Except for a seven-year period of military dictatorship, Greece was to remain a parliamentary democracy allied with the West. The four other Balkan states, Bulgaria, Romania, Albania, and Yugoslavia, were to retain their Communist systems, but they were to develop in different directions. Yugoslavia and subsequently Albania were to show the most resistance to Soviet leadership and were to determine their international alignments by their evolving national interests. Bulgaria, Moscow's most loyal friend, was to remain in this position. In the 1960s a change was to occur in Romania, when attempts were made to assert independence from Soviet direction. As in the past, the five Balkan states were to prove unable to join together to resist great-power domination. All went their own ways and sought different means of adjusting to an international situation dominated by the two great military powers, the Soviet Union and the United States.

# 9

*The Communist governments,*
*1950–1980*

LTHOUGH THE CAMP of the Communist states began breaking apart scarcely three years after the Soviet vic:ory, the governments continued to share many attributes and to retain various interests in common. In the following pages the attempt is made to analyze, first, the political and economic systems of the states; second, their foreign relations both in regard to the rest of the world and within the Communist bloc; and, finally, their individual development. The sections dealing with the domestic developments in each nation emphasize the sharp divergence of the policies of Yugoslavia in both foreign and internal politics from those of the other Communist bloc countries.

## INTERNAL DEVELOPMENTS

### Theory: Marxism-Leninism

As we have seen, prior to 1945 most Balkan regimes had as their theoretical basis the national-liberal ideologies common to Western and Central Europe. To review briefly, liberal doctrines had been developed as a reaction to the autocratic and despotic governments in power and to the mercantile system. Although there was much disagreement on ultimate goals and methods, most liberals placed great emphasis on the introduction of political institutions that would free the individual from social, economic, and political constraints. They believed that citizens could best develop their own capabilities in an atmosphere of liberty and that society as a whole would benefit if government interference was reduced as much as possible. The constitutions of the French Revolution and the nineteenth century were seen as social contracts designed to provide a clear statement of the rights of the citizen against the state authorities. The separation of powers among the executive, judicial, and legislative branches of government – the system of checks and balances – was designed to assure that no individual or group could dominate the government. Private property was usually regarded as a "natural right" and as an additional assurance against tyranny. This political and economic system worked well in Western Europe and North America. By 1914 Britain, France, Germany, and the United States had become the world's strongest nations with wealthy industrial economies and a high standard of living for their citizens. Constitutional governments and a free-enterprise economic system allowed individuals to exploit fully the possibilities inherent in the industrial revolution; in addition, the Americans populated a continent.

Such a course of events, however, did not take place in the Balkan peninsula. At a time when Western Europe, despite its frequent political and economic crises, was making rapid strides forward, the Balkan states remained primitive, agrarian backwaters. Where modern improvements were introduced, they were confined to the capital cities and were enjoyed by a privileged minority. Moreover, despite the formulation of many constitutions, no Balkan government succeeded in approaching the standards of the Western democratic systems. There were very few honest elections. Even more serious were the increasingly grave social and economic conditions in the region. The ever-increasing population placed an intolerable pressure on the land and the resources; a level of industrialization sufficient to absorb the excess peasant population had not been reached. Before 1945 socialist and agrarian parties had been organized that sought to solve the burning domestic questions by radical reforms, most of which required a level of state intervention in economic affairs that was outside the previous liberal programs.

Of the alternative plans for political, social, and economic regeneration, the Communist program was certainly one of the most radical. An understanding of its teachings is most important because of the central role of theory in Communist political activity. Liberal-national doctrines as developed in the nineteenth century had many points in common, but they were never synthesized into a definitive program, nor were the leading proponents ever regarded as authorities whose words should be regarded as infallible. Writers and philosophers – for example, John Locke, Adam Smith, Thomas Jefferson, J. J. Rousseau, and Voltaire – contributed to Western thought in major ways, but despite the respect in which they are held, critics have never hesitated to tear apart their ideas or to comment negatively on their lives. Certainly their pictures do not adorn all of the post offices, train stations, schools, and other public buildings of the Western world. In contrast, the Communist governments have always regarded the persons and works of Karl Marx, Friedrich Engels, Vladimir Ilich Lenin, and, for a time, Joseph Stalin with the veneration accorded in previous centuries only to religious figures, holy texts, and semimythical national heroes. Their pictures and statues are conspicuous in all public places, where they serve the same functions as previous depictions of saints, monarchs, and heroes of the national movements. Any criticism of the working of the present Communist governments or of the relationships among the states must be made on the basis that the measure or program in question is not "truly Marxist" or does not express the real intent of Lenin. The idea that Marx or Lenin could be dead wrong on any issue is usually not an acceptable viewpoint. The Communist systems are all militantly atheistic; yet they endow these men with suprahuman attri-

337

butes. As long as Stalin was alive, this attitude was adopted toward his words and deeds, although it was later denounced in his case as the "cult of personality." Similar criticisms have not been made of Marx, Engels, or Lenin. An examination of their views is thus an essential first step in a study of the development of the Communist bloc states.

Marx based his theories to a large part on the works of such British political economists as David Ricardo, Adam Smith, and John Stuart Mill, and on those of German philosophers, in particular Georg W. F. Hegel. Both Marx and Engels were also greatly influenced by their observations of the social and political consequences of the industrial revolution in Britain and in the German Rhineland from the middle of the century until the 1880s, the period when the worst abuses of the capitalist system became apparent. Very simply stated, Marx believed that history was unfolding along a predetermined path, with economic phenomena as the basic element in the evolution. At any given moment, he taught, the means by which people produce the goods they need or exploit the available natural resources determine all other aspects of their lives. In each epoch of history the economic base, or substructure, calls for a given superstructure, which includes the social, political, cultural, and economic institutions proper for the period. Since these tend to remain fixed, or to change only slowly, whereas the economic basis evolves with the development of new means of production or a better exploitation of natural resources, the superstructure in time lags behind. This discrepancy can be corrected through the instrumentality of the class struggle. In each period, according to this theory, one class enjoys a privileged position, based on its ability to make use of the economic conditions of the time. It dominates society and creates state institutions in its own image, institutions that are designed to protect its individual interests. Simultaneously, an antagonistic class, consisting of those who are exploited or enslaved by the system, comes into being. At some time the two elements are brought into violent conflict, an event that produces a new dominating class, a new society, and yet another class struggle.

In Marxist literature the historical epochs have been few in number: history is divided into only five great periods. During the first, covering the earliest stages of human development, men supported themselves by hunting and fishing; property was held in common. The second, that of classical civilization, was marked by the prevalence of slave labor. The third age, feudalism, was characterized by serfdom. The fourth, modern capitalism, covers the industrial revolution. A fifth and final stage was to follow a complete Communist victory. As far as the class struggle is concerned, the conflict in the classical age was between slave and master, in the feudal era between serf and lord, and in the capitalist period between workers and the "bourgeoisie," defined as those who exploit or benefit from the opportunities offered by the industrial revolution. In the fifth period, when the workers come to power and the majority of the population controls the government, there will in theory be no class left to exploit, and the class struggle will come to an end. Since the state is by definition an instrument of class domination, it will fade away once a condition of complete social equality had been established.

Marx wrote in a period when it did indeed appear that society would be forced into two extreme camps, with a small number of rich and powerful opposed to the mass of impoverished workers. In fact, quite another development took place. Instead of polarizing into two antagonistic groups, the capitalist societies showed an increase in the numbers of moderately prosperous families in the center, including members of the professions, tradesmen, artisans, and even skilled workers. Moreover, the majority of the industrial proletariat was attracted not to militant Communist movements, but to the trade unions and the socialist parties that wished to work within the existing political systems. Recognizing the trend, "revisionist" socialist leaders accepted this development and sought to gain benefits for the workers by winning elections rather than by preparing for revolution. The more violent aspects of the class struggle and the seizure of power were either denied or seen as events of the distant future.

The revisionist viewpoint, which was predominant in European socialist circles prior to World War I, was sharply challenged by others who saw political change as coming through revolution rather than through gradual, moderate reform. Lenin was by far the outstanding leader and theoretician in this group. Recognizing that the working class was not ready for revolt, but that it preferred instead to put its trust in trade unionism and moderate socialist doctrines, Lenin placed his main emphasis on the Communist Party, not the proletariat, as the catalyst of radical political change. Arguing that only a minority of the workers, the "vanguard of the proletariat" organized in the Communist Party, were aware of the true situation, he called upon the party to prepare to take advantage of the opportunities offered by the recurrent world crises to seize the state. Political change was thus to come by revolution and not through the ballot box. Once victorious, the Communist leadership would at first be compelled to use forceful measures. It would, for instance, have to rid the state of the bourgeois police and army and substitute its own equivalent. This period, that of the "dictatorship of the proletariat," would last until the last "class enemy" was destroyed. The proletarian state and its institutions would then "wither away." For after the class opposition was liquidated, the instruments of coercion, including the government itself, would no longer be needed.

In this account, it should be noted, the words *Communist* and *socialist* are used interchangeably to refer to the governments of Albania, Bulgaria, Romania, and Yugoslavia. The leaders themselves call their systems "socialist." Tito in a previously cited letter referred to the Soviet Union as "the land of socialism" and to Yugoslavia as a country that was developing socialism. Used in this context, the word, of course, pertains exclusively to Marxist socialism and not to the other socialist programs that have been previously discussed.

The Balkan states in theory today have socialist systems, under Communist Party leadership, that are supposed to evolve toward a future "classless," communist society. All doctrinal questions of this kind, however, are at present being hotly debated among the world Communist Party organizations.

The weaknesses and deficiencies of this program do not need to be indicated here. Some aspects will appear in the next pages in relation to the debates carried on among the Communist parties of the socialist bloc. However, as an absolute system, Marxism-Leninism has certain advantages. It provides a relatively inflexible doctrine for those who need the security of a fixed world view, particularly one whose ultimate victory is regarded as certain. Although none of the "fathers" of communism produced a timetable, the establishment of the system is seen as the inevitable outcome of a predetermined historical evolution. On the negative side, there are two aspects of communism that were bound to clash violently with previous Balkan traditions: it is atheistic and it seeks the end of the system of private property. We have seen throughout this narrative the important role of the churches in national development and the close links between religious and state institutions. Communist theory, based on the Western experience, denies the entire Christian idea and considers the church another instrument by which the bourgeoisie enslaves the workers and keeps them mentally and emotionally tied to the capitalist system. The Balkan peasant people also considered private property a sacred institution; their aim was the acquisition of more lands and goods, not the surrender of their property to the state. This contradiction between party and peasant aims was, as we shall see, to cause great difficulties in all of the Balkan socialist states.

Despite the fact that these theories play a major role in socialist controversies and are taught in the schools, it is difficult to find individuals in Eastern Europe, particularly among the educated classes, who accept these ideas as embodying absolute truth. Nevertheless, many citizens of these states support the regimes for reasons other than the validity of the ideology on which they are based. Recognizing that the major problem in the peninsula is its economic backwardness and poverty, they consider state-directed socialism the best means of remedying this condition. Tight central control and an administration that has the power to compel obedience is seen as a necessary attribute of any government that wishes to introduce quickly the advantages associated with industrialization. Others, particularly those who were extremely critical of the former regimes, see Communism as a means of assuring social justice. Thus advocates of modernization and social equality can see advantages in a regime that at least states these ideals as its principal objectives. Balkan Communist parties contain, of course, a large number of opportunists, but also many members who, although they may not accept all points of Marxist doctrine, believe that the parties' practical programs are the key to the future happiness and prosperity of their countries and that the new political and economic institutions, to be described shortly, will indeed bring to their people the blessings of the industrial revolution without the attendant social evils believed present in the capitalist world.

Convinced Communists were, as we have seen, very few in number in prewar Eastern Europe. The postwar regimes came to power by force and violence. Communism was introduced in Bulgaria and Romania as a result of the Soviet military presence. In Yugoslavia, where the Partisans did indeed win a revolutionary war, their ultimate victory also rested on the fact that the Soviet Union won the war on the eastern front. Similar forceful methods have been needed to maintain the leadership of these states in power. Despite its relative liberality and popularity, the Yugoslav government has never dared risk the introduction of a multiparty system or the holding of a genuinely free national election. The most authoritarian Balkan regime, the Albanian, is the dictatorship of a small minority, kept in power by the police and the army. Adherents of the system would argue that these methods are necessary to achieve the stated social aims, that a radical transformation of society can only be achieved by revolutionary means – the establishment of the dictatorship of the proletariat and the concentration of power in the hands of the enlightened Communist minority.

## Practice: government and party organization

Since the new regimes were the product of the Soviet military and ideological preponderance, it could be expected that Soviet institutions would provide the model for the new governments, and indeed they did. Even in Yugoslavia the political institutions duplicated their equivalents in the Soviet Union. At first no attempt was made, or believed necessary, to modify forms that had been developed for the Soviet state, with its extensive territories and resources, when they were adopted by the small, impoverished Balkan states. The new institutions had some superficial resemblance to those of the previous regimes; all of the states, for example, still had constitutions and national assemblies. The radical shift was in the nature of the party system. Generally, under previous regimes, many parties had competed for power; their common goal was to capture the government. They had no real authority unless they won the elections, by fair means or foul, and set up their own administrations. Under the new system the power in the state lay in the hands of the only legal political parties, the Communists and their front organizations, rather than in the government offices. Elections could in no way modify their influence. The constitutions recognized the predominant position of the party. In addition these documents made no provision for checks and balances among the branches of the government. Thus in practice in each state the party leadership ran the country. The constitutions all guaranteed a standard program of civil rights, such as free speech, free press, and so on, but each one contained limiting paragraphs or sentences subordinating these rights to the "good of society" or the interests of the working people.

Although some variations developed, the governments and party institutions of the four states have remained similar. All have constitutions patterned after Soviet models, and these documents have been revised several times to record the theoretical advance toward communism. Each state has a national assembly elected by the people, but usually with a single party ticket. These bodies, which have little real authority, meet generally only twice a year. In three countries, the members approve the selection of a smaller body, called a Council of State in Romania and Bulgaria and a Presidium in Albania, which exercises the powers of the assembly when it is not in session. The Yugoslav assembly differs in that it is composed of two houses to reflect the federal nature of the state: The Federal Chamber and the Chamber of the Republics and Autonomous Provinces. In addition, each of the four governments has a Council of Ministers, consisting of the premier, his deputies, and the heads of the ministries. In Yugoslavia this function is filled by a Federal Executive Council of thirty-three members.

However, the real power in the state lies not in these government bodies, but in the councils of the Communist Party. Its organization follows Soviet examples and is similar in all the states. In theory, the highest body is the party congress, which is composed of delegates from the local units and usually meets every five years. Its main function is to listen to reports from the leaders on past accomplishments and to receive general indications of future directions in policy. The main decisions are made in the Central Committee, which is chosen to run party affairs between congresses, and, more specifically, in an even smaller group, usually given the name of Political Bureau, or Politbureau, after the Soviet counterpart. In practice, the socialist states are governed by the members of this committee. Since the party leadership nominates the candidates who run for the assemblies and the delegates to the party congresses, it can be seen that the states are in the hands of narrow oligarchies. Authority proceeds from the top down. This domination is made more effective by the fact that the major Communist figures usually hold the highest positions in both the state and the party organizations. These "interlocking directorates" reinforce the position of the party and assure that ultimate control remains in only a few hands. Despite the obvious drawbacks, the system has had the great advantage of assuring stable government. The major Balkan Communist leaders have enjoyed terms in office that compare favorably with those of hereditary monarchs; both Tito and Hoxha held power without interruption after the first days of the establishment of their Communist regimes in 1944. Tito's death in 1980 ended his long predominance; Hoxha in that year still enjoyed his.

With this concentration of power in the hands of a few men whose authority is checked neither by electoral processes nor by other state institutions, the question naturally arises of the role of the individual in the nation's political life and the extent to which popular pressure can determine policy. Almost all citizens are, of course, eligible to join the Communist Party. In

342

theory, this organization should recruit its membership primarily from the politically active members of the industrial working class. In practice, in the Balkans as in the Soviet Union after 1917, the low level of industrialization precluded the availability of a large number of politically conscious workers. The original parties, very small in membership, were run by intellectuals and contained a high percentage of poor peasants. Since 1944 the organizations have been dominated by the groups that participate in and benefit from the socialist system: the officials, the managers of enterprises, professional men, members of the police and security systems, and others who are generally designated in the statistics as "white-collar workers." Often well educated and enjoying a higher wage scale than the average worker or peasant, they are in a good position to exert influence. Although the attempt has been made to assure an adequate percentage of workers, in consonance with ideological standards, the Balkan Communist parties cannot be regarded as workers' organizations. In the 1970s the class composition of the parties was as follows: of the 789,796 members of the Bulgarian party in 1976, 41.4 percent were workers, 23 percent were peasants, and 30.2 percent were white-collar workers; the Romanian organization in the same year had 2,655,000 members, of whom 50 percent were workers, 20 percent were peasants, and 22 percent were white-collar workers; the relatively small Albanian Party of Labor, with 101,500 members, had 38 percent workers, 29 percent peasants, and 33 percent white-collar workers; in 1976 the Yugoslav League of Communists had 1,302,836 members, and its social composition was 41.8 percent white collar, 28.1 percent worker, and 5.1 percent peasant.

In addition to the party network, the socialist states have mass organizations that attempt to involve all of the citizens. In Bulgaria the Fatherland Front and the Agrarian Union have been active since the end of the war. The Romanian Front of Socialist Unity and the Albanian Democratic Front perform the similar function of serving as a channel through which government programs can be explained, popular enthusiasm aroused, and public approval won. Labor and youth organizations, naturally Communist-led, have similar important tasks. The labor unions have been used to attempt to maintain morale when pressures on the workers have been particularly heavy. The rapid pace of industrialization has affected in particular the working class, which has often had to spend long hours at hard labor at a time when consumer goods and even adequate food supplies were not available to compensate for these efforts.

Aside from participation in political and party organizations the individual citizen does and is expected to take part in the life of the community and the place of employment, whether it is a factory, a government office, or an agricultural association. The socialist states are bureaucratic societies. A multitude of minor decisions, seldom of political significance, are made through committees and at meetings of those directly involved. Discussions on matters of immediate concern and participation in various activities of this nature take up a great deal of the average citizen's time and energy. Here freedom is allowed for "criticism and self-criticism" as long as it does not involve the nature of Communist rule, the party itself, or major directives concerning political or economic matters. Moreover, under the concept of "democratic centralism," once a decision is reached by discussion, everyone is thereafter obligated to support it without further question.

### The economic system

With the ideological emphasis on modernization, social welfare, and class equality, the heart of the Communist program, and the basis on which its success or failure should be judged, is its blueprint for economic advancement. Like the political systems, the economic policies adopted after the war closely followed the Soviet patterns and were introduced with the assistance of Soviet experts and managers.

During the immediate postwar years all of the Balkan countries faced the necessity of rebuilding after the dislocation and destruction of the previous period. In addition, Romania and Bulgaria, as defeated nations, were forced to pay reparations and to support Soviet armies of occupation. At this time, the Soviet government was using the resources of the East European countries to assist in the recovery of its own devastated lands. The greatest burden usually fell on the former enemy states, but friendly regimes also had to pay a price. In addition to collecting occupation and reparation costs, the Soviet authorities followed a policy of what amounted to outright looting. They removed entire factories, railroad cars, and similar items, and shipped them back to the Soviet Union. In their relationship with all of the socialist bloc countries, they tended to charge high prices for their exports, but to pay prices below the world market for their purchases. They also established joint companies, in which the Soviet contribution usually consisted of confiscated German property. Enterprises of this sort gave the Soviet government control over important sections of these Balkan economies. It has been estimated that the total cost of this Soviet policy to all of the Eastern European socialist regimes to the death of Stalin in 1953 was about $14 billion (American billion), a sum roughly equivalent to that which the United States invested in European recovery under the Marshall Plan.[1] Of this amount, by far the heaviest burden was borne by East Germany, but Romania paid about $1.7 billion. The Soviet allies suffered too; Yugoslavia's complaints about economic exploitation have been recorded previously. Of the Balkan countries, Bulgaria appears to have received particularly favorable treatment. As a result of this Soviet policy, the Communist regimes started out with definite disadvan-

---

1 Paul Marer, "East European Economies: Achievements, Problems, Prospects," in Teresa Rakowska-Harmstone and Andrew Gyorgy, eds. *Communism in Eastern Europe* (Bloomington: Indiana University Press, 1979), p. 248.

tages: they had not only to repair their own wartime damages, but also to contribute substantially to Soviet reconstruction.

After 1947 the Communist states were ready to launch their own programs of industrialization and modernization. Despite the great differences in size and resources between the Soviet Union and the small states, Soviet policies, as developed in the 1930s during Stalin's dictatorship, were adopted. These were characterized by strong central controls and by an emphasis on large industries. In addition, instead of encouraging economic development on a regional basis, with each area concentrating on the production of what it could best manufacture, Soviet influence initially led all the states to establish similar and parallel industrial economies. Autarkical plans, practical in the Soviet Union, with its rich store of natural resources, were not to prove equally advisable in the Balkans, but once introduced they were difficult to change. The Stalinist pattern was adopted at first at least partially because the Soviet advisers and the local Communist leaders genuinely believed that the Soviet example was preferable to any other alternative. From the viewpoint of Moscow, the system had the advantage of providing for the production of goods needed at the time by the Soviet Union, and it kept the socialist states separated from each other. Each developed its own economic structure and kept its principal trade links with the Soviet Union.

The new economic systems adopted by the Communist states had at the outset many similar characteristics. The Yugoslav deviations, which came after 1950, will be discussed in detail later. The first objective was the securing of government ownership of all of the means of production, either through nationalization or, in the case of the land, through collectivization. The central state administration therefore took over the production and distribution of most goods and services. It had to determine such matters as what products should be produced, where they should be manufactured, their exact specifications, and their price, questions that had previously been determined by private businessmen and by the working of the free market. Foreign trade was also brought under government control. Henceforth, the import and export of goods were handled through special state offices, the foreign trade organizations. At first, extensive outside commercial relations were not encouraged; the early autarkical programs attempted to limit trade to the securing of those items that could not be produced at home.

New burdens were thus placed on the central government and on the state bureaucracy. Although many of the prewar Balkan regimes had attempted to aid economic development, they had intervened only in limited ways, such as by the imposition of tariffs or by preferential taxation. Now, however, the central authority was expected to make decisions that had previously been taken by many thousands of individuals on various levels of the economic system. Central planning became the principal task of the socialist state operating under a "command" economy. Henceforth, the preparation of the plans, usually made on a five-year basis, absorbed the major attention of the government and party officials. The Politburo, the Council of Ministers, and the special State Planning Commissions (SPCs) were all involved in this activity. Consultations and relations with all the links in the economic chain, of course, had to be maintained. Some of the problems that had to be dealt with are well illustrated by the following example:

> Suppose the SPC discovers that in the plan coming up from the enterprises, the projected supply of trucks falls short of the projected demand for trucks. The SPC can increase the targets for truck production, inform the Ministry of the Automotive Industry of the changes, and the Ministry can then tell the truck-producing enterprises how many more trucks must be produced. But then those enterprises will ask for more inputs, including more steel, glass, and tires. Assuming that there is no excess supply of those three products around, those production targets must be increased. But steel, for example, requires iron ore; so that production target must also be increased. But increased output of iron ore *requires more trucks* to haul the ore. And the process begins again.

Because of the details that had to be included, the plan sent to an enterprise by the central authorities could be the "size of a phonebook in a large American city."[2]

Following the Soviet example, the Balkan Communist governments placed emphasis almost completely on heavy industry, in particular on metallurgy and machine building. Socialist planners also preferred to devote their efforts to the construction of impressive enterprises, such as giant iron and steel complexes and hydroelectric projects, with the goal of acquiring a strong industrial base for the future. Since the Balkan states lacked the necessary capital, and since Soviet credits, although available, were small, this rapid advance in one part of the economy had to be paid for by the peasantry and the consumers. Not only was very little money put into agriculture, but the peasant producer carried much of the burden of the economic revolution. Similarly, the average citizen was forced to accept a reduced standard of living, because consumer industries and services were regularly sacrificed for the alternate goal. The argument was made that such measures were necessary for the future well-being of the nation, and that only when a sufficiently high level of industrial development had been attained could the state afford to turn to the production of consumer goods in an effort to raise living standards.

The centralized planned economies could and did achieve a great deal; they had marked successes in certain fields. They could mobilize resources, man-

2 Edward A. Hewett, *The Economies of Eastern Europe* (Lincoln, Nebr.: Cliff's Notes, 1978), pp. 22–23, 24.

power, and money and direct them toward the achievement of a given objective. They could also use hitherto unexploited labor reserves, such as the excess agricultural population and women. Advanced technologies, either from the Soviet Union or from the West, could in conditions of early industrialization be introduced more easily from above. Certain weaknesses, however, are inherent in the system, and they became increasingly obvious. Much, of course, depended on the ability of the planners and their access to the type of information that would enable them to make correct decisions. A major drawback of a plan is that it tends to be rigid and that adjustments cannot be made quickly. Mistakes in the original draft can thus be extremely costly and relatively difficult to correct. An example will be shown in the Bulgarian decision to build a large iron and steel complex at a location that may prove most unfavorable in the future. Although a restriction of present civilian consumption can be justified if indeed it will lead to better conditions later, it is another matter if the savings thus made are squandered in uneconomic enterprises.

Other problems have arisen because of the lack of incentives and competition within the system. Since a given enterprise did not have to make a profit, there was often no reason for it to operate at a high level of efficiency. If it lost money, the state would provide a subsidy. In the same manner, the relative equality of the wage scales, the lack of consumer goods on the market, and the virtual assurance that they would not be fired led many workers to exert only minimal efforts on the job. Similarly, the lack of competition has often led to the production of shoddy goods at a high cost. If a given product, say a pair of shoes, will be the only item of its kind available to the buyer, the manufacturer will have less reason to worry about either the style or the workmanship of his goods.

These weaknesses, of course, derived from the apparent failure of individuals to work as hard for state enterprises as they would for private owners or for themselves. In Marxist theory such a situation should not arise, or at least it should change in the future. Since human attitudes and values were judged to be the reflections of the social and economic conditions of any given epoch, it was argued that under socialism a "new man" would evolve who would think not of selfish interests, but of the general good of society. One of the major aims of the schools in the Communist states is to teach these values and to produce a different type of individual, an objective that is far from achievement.

Perhaps the greatest failure has been in agriculture. Before 1945, as we have seen, the Balkan states were primarily agrarian societies with peasant populations that worked the land by traditional methods. Marxist doctrine has always had difficulty dealing with the peasantry, whose independent and individualistic attitudes and life-styles are regarded as primitive and a hindrance to progress. The solution to the agrarian problems has been seen in the conversion of the peasantry into a kind of rural proletariat, a step that could be accomplished by the organization of either state farms, where the peasants would become the equivalent of workers in an industry, or collectives, where most of the lands and livestock would be pooled. Under either alternative the state planners would be able to dictate the details of production and adjust the levels to the general needs of the economy. In theory, this large-scale farming would be more efficient: mechanized equipment could be introduced, and modern improvements, such as better fertilizers, seed, and insecticides, could be provided. With full state control, irrigation and land-reclamation projects could also be implemented.

The major drawback to these schemes has been the violent opposition shown by the peasantry to the entire idea. Everywhere collectivization has been met with fierce resistance. Individuals have slaughtered their animals rather than surrender them to the state. The sentiment has been so strong that the entire effort has been abandoned for all practical purposes in both Yugoslavia and Poland, where the governments have been receptive to the feelings of their rural populations. Even in countries such as Romania and Bulgaria, where collectivization remains enforced, the peasants put more effort into their small individual holdings, which they are allowed to retain, than into their work elsewhere. One of the chief difficulties with the effort at collectivization has been the failure of the governments to invest adequately in agricultural improvements. Preferring to concentrate on industrial development, the planners have not provided the machines and modern techniques that might have made this form of agricultural organization more attractive to the rural population.

## Social transformation

The introduction of the socialist political and economic program obviously had a shattering effect on the existing social structure. Communist propaganda has usually directed its strongest attacks against the "bourgeoisie." Middle-class property owners, from the proprietors of small shops, or even marketplace stalls, to the great industrialists, were faced with the confiscation of their property and a drastic change in their occupations. Where fortunate, they were able to find places as managers in state-owned enterprises. Otherwise, they too joined the workers. The members of the professional classes – the lawyers, doctors, dentists, engineers, and those who provided similar services – became state employees, subject to the controls inherent in this status. They similarly found their incomes sharply reduced. Workers too found conditions changed, although not as drastically. As employees in state enterprises, they lost some of the rights they had previously enjoyed. For instance, they could not strike, and their ability to change jobs was curtailed. They were still under the control of "bosses," but these now represented the state and the party. At first, under the difficult conditions of the early years of the new system, their wages were low and their living standards depressed. The socialist regime, however, did guarantee employment and offer social services, such as health care. All workers also had the psychological advantage of being at least in theory the favored class in the new system. Government propaganda encouraged them to believe that, bad as conditions were at present, the future belonged to them.

Despite the radical changes made necessary by political events, the workers and the members of the professional, managerial, and commercial middle class had previously made the adjustment to modern life. They were a part of the urban society of their nation, and they had for the most part willingly accepted the attributes of an industrial civilization. The most difficult transformation was that faced by the peasant population. As we have seen, the aim of socialist planners was to turn peasant farmers into an agrarian proletariat working on a collective or a state farm. Such a move would mean a sharp break in the traditional pattern of life. Certainly, few if any Balkan peasants supported Marxist-Leninist plans for their future. Such changes would drastically alter their relationship to the three centers that had dominated their lives – the land, the family, and the village.

Previously, as we have seen, land and landownership played a major role in village society. When a man had extra money, he invested in land. His prestige was tied to his possession of property. When he lost control over his farm, as occurred in Bulgaria, Albania, and Romania, or when the size of his holding was limited, as in Yugoslavia, his attitudes had to change, although there was violent resistance to the new conditions everywhere. Since land could not be readily purchased, any surplus income was subsequently more likely to be spent on consumer goods. As industrial products became increasingly available, more of the peasant's income could be spent for the improvement of his personal conditions – for instance, on his house and for clothing. Except perhaps in Yugoslavia, this development did not go very far; material conditions in the rural areas in the socialist countries remained bad. The principal efforts directed toward raising living standards took place in the cities, just as under the previous regimes.

The breakup of the family farm naturally had an effect on its former members, although not as much as might be expected. Since landholding was no longer a prime means of transferring wealth from generation to generation, family ties could be expected to weaken. Moreover, the state took over many of the tasks once assigned to the family, including a primary responsibility for the care of the sick and the aged. The new conditions also brought certain changes in the family. Socialist doctrine proclaimed the equality of men and women. Equally important, economic conditions both compelled and encouraged women to seek jobs outside the home. The state similarly insisted on its right to interfere in the parent–child relationships, and the authority of the father and the eldest male in a family was thus diminished. Old habits and ways of thinking are, nevertheless, difficult to change. The family, in addition to being an economic and emotional relationship, had always provided assistance and defense against outside dangers. Certain conditions, such as the prevalent housing shortage and the need for grandparents for child care, encouraged three-generation households. Thus in many ways family ties and traditional bonds remained unimpaired in both the city and the country.

Although the family remained strong, the isolated village community was doomed, a development that, of course, was already under way in all of the Balkan countries before the war. With the improvement of roads and transport, and especially with the wide availability of radios and television, the outside world was brought into even the most remote Balkan area. The massive movement of the rural population into the cities, which occurred throughout the peninsula, depopulated the countryside and naturally disrupted traditional patterns. Unfortunately, no truly adequate substitute for the village association developed. The new working population, fresh from the countryside, at first faced great problems in finding any housing at all. To handle the problem, all of the socialist governments erected "new cities," consisting of mammoth barrackslike apartment complexes. Here the overcrowding of the countryside was continued, but these quarters were usually equipped with the modern conveniences of running hot and cold water, electrical appliances, modern bathrooms, telephones, and similar facilities that had not been widely available before. These changes, although they often brought increased material comforts, were extremely disruptive. Party and factory associations, moreover, could not fully replace the village church and community; the psychological readjustment from farm to city was often painful. Balkan societies, in the early 1980s, are still in a process of change and readjustment.

At the conclusion of this brief account of social transformation, some of the benefits that the Communist governments sought to bring to their people should be reviewed. It should first be emphasized that the new regimes in practice as well as in theory did pay far more attention to social welfare than the previous governments. After 1945 hospitals, rest homes, sports arenas, theaters, vacation centers, concert halls, and similar facilities were constructed to serve the general public. Attempts were made to bring modern health care into even the most backward areas. New pension schemes and provisions to cover sickness and accident were introduced. In Albania, Bulgaria, and Romania employment is guaranteed. Despite the many weaknesses in some aspects of the social welfare programs, their inauguration is among the most important accomplishments of the Communist Party leadership.

### Ideological controls

The major stated objective of the socialist regimes in their first years was to prepare the way for the Communist society of the future. Not only were new institutions to be introduced, but, equally important, it was felt necessary to suppress any organizations that were believed to be hostile to the government or that were bastions of the "class enemy," the bourgeoisie. This attitude has deeply affected the churches, schools, and universities, as well as individual writers and artists. All of the Communist governments, even to an extent the Yugoslav, have found it necessary to institute a strict censorship over national cultural life, including the press, education, and religion – a control that is enforced by the police and the courts.

The first to be affected by the Communist seizure of power were the religious communities, Catholic, Orthodox, and Muslim alike. All had played major roles in national life; the religious outlook was part of the Balkan national character. The churches controlled much property, and they had been a major support to the prewar political system. Because they were strongly anti-Communist and because atheism was doctrinally correct, the new leadership at first acted quite stringently toward them. Their property was confiscated, and they were forbidden to conduct schools. Strong efforts were made to discourage, or even prohibit, the population from attending services. Many churches and ecclesiastical institutions were closed or turned into "museums of atheism." Later, with the decline of revolutionary zeal, the political leaders came to realize the importance of the churches in national cultural life, and a partial reversal of attitude occurred. The Romanian government, for instance, has expended huge sums in the restoration of churches and monasteries, which it recognizes as an essential part of the cultural heritage of the people. Although the churches do not play the prominent roles they once did, religion is no longer suppressed as extensively as it was in the immediate postwar period. The religious institutions and the clergy are supported by the state and by the contributions of church members.

Similar radical changes were made in the prewar educational systems. As previously mentioned, Marxist theory taught that a change in human attitudes would accompany or be the result of the evolution to a communist society. The schools were thus not only to teach communist ideology, but also to train students in the pattern of the "new man." Naturally, a radical revision had to be made in all of the textbooks to reflect Communist doctrine. In addition, with the drive toward industrialization, the schools, in particular the higher institutions, had to devote more attention to science and technology.

Although this narrative will not deal with cultural history in detail, some comment must be made on attitudes toward art and literature. These generalizations apply to Albania, Bulgaria, and Romania only; the exceptional conditions in Yugoslavia are described in a later section. In general, the Communist regimes have required not only that their writers and artists adopt a positive approach toward the system, but that they extol its virtues. They are thus expected to be, in a sense, propaganda agents and to assist the government in its efforts to win the support of the general population for its political and economic programs. In addition, attempts have been made to limit relations with the Western countries. Foreign newspapers, books, and periodicals have only a limited circulation in these countries; close relationships between their citizens and foreign friends or colleagues are discouraged. These policies have not been uniformly implemented; they have varied according to place and time. In some years there has been relative laxity, in others strict regulation, in the sphere of cultural controls.

Closely associated with this supervision has been the attitude of these regimes toward the granting of visas for travel or emigration. One of the major fears of all of the socialist countries, except Yugoslavia, has been that the implementation of an easy travel policy would result in discontent with conditions at home or even in a large-scale emigration. Two examples of the latter occurred elsewhere in eastern Europe. Between 1949 and 1961 2.5 million people crossed the border from East into West Germany. A similar massive exodus occurred in 1956 when approximately 180,000 Hungarians left for the West. Since most of the emigrants came from the younger and usually best-educated elements of society, their defection was deeply felt. Until the living standards and the political liberties allowed in their countries approach those of the West, most Communist governments are convinced that they must retain a firm hold on their citizens.

## FOREIGN POLICY

### Theory: the imperialist wars

Communist doctrines also covered the field of international relations, and here the concepts of Lenin are particularly important. As we have seen, the polarization of society expected by Marxist theorists had failed to occur by 1914. Instead of living in conditions of increasing impoverishment, the working class shared in the benefits of the new industrial society. Revisionist socialist programs supported the idea of collaboration with the bourgeois state. Directing his attention to this problem, Lenin argued that the improving position of the worker was the result of the foreign policy of the capitalist states, which were in the highest stage of their development – that of imperialism. These governments, after seizing control of large stretches of territory in Asia and Africa, had exploited the resources and labor of these areas and made enormous profits. They were thus able to satisfy the demands of their workers, but at the expense of the backward peoples. However, since colonial lands were limited in extent, the capitalist nations would inevitably come into conflict over their division, and wars would result. Stalin's comments on the origins of World War II, previously quoted, are a good example of this reasoning.

The imperialist wars, despite the devastation they caused, were to be welcomed for the opportunity they provided for revolution. Conditions would be created that would allow the Communist Party, the vanguard of the proletariat, to seize power in a time of crisis. It will be noted that this is a revolutionary, not an evolutionary, program: it calls for violent action. The doctrines of peaceful coexistence and détente, which were to be supported by the Soviet Union after 1953, were to be challenged by Chinese and Albanian leaders, who preferred the classical interpretation of Marxist-Leninist doctrine.

After 1945 the governments of Albania, Bulgaria, Romania, and Yugoslavia were to become involved in foreign affairs on two levels: first, in their relationships with those who were outside the Soviet system, including the NATO allies and the new states of Asia and Africa; and, second, in their closer involvement with other Communist states, in particular with their East European neighbors and the Soviet Union. These matters will be examined in the next section, with especial attention devoted to the two socialist supranationalist institutions, Comecon and the Warsaw Treaty Organization.

### Practice: the Soviet Union and the Communist states in world affairs

In the years after 1945 the East European governments at first remained closely tied to the Soviet Union in foreign relations and were thus inevitably influenced by all issues involving that state and the rest of the world. The major events here were the relations between Moscow and Washington, the breakup of the great European colonial empires, and the spread of the revolutionary movement, in particular the victory of Mao Zedong in China. Continental European affairs and the fate of the German lands were also to remain important. In the three decades after the close of World War II, three Balkan states, Albania, Romania, and Yugoslavia, were able in one manner or another to obtain a degree of freedom in foreign policy. The ability of Albania and Romania to follow independent paths was affected by the changes that took place in the Soviet leadership, by the rise of the Chinese Communist Party to power, and by alterations in the world balance of power. Yugoslav independence was, as we have seen, obtained first and by the state's own efforts.

As long as Stalin was alive, international relations were dominated by the sharp conflict that existed between the Soviet-led bloc and the United States and its allies. The Western European democracies were joined in NATO. In 1948 the socialist camp was weakened by the defection of Yugoslavia, but apparently strengthened by the addition of China. After Mao's final victory, it was generally assumed that China would be as closely allied to the Soviet Union as were the East European nations. In February 1950 the two states signed a military alliance, and China was promised economic assistance. Thus at mid-century the world was split into two competing power blocs: the United States, the European powers participating in NATO, and Japan, together with their small allies, faced the Soviet Union, China, and their supporters in the socialist bloc.

Between 1950 and 1954 the principal area of confrontation between the two blocs became Asia. After the war Korea had been divided into two zones, with a Soviet-dominated government in the north. In June 1950 this regime launched an invasion of the south that was opposed by the United States, which had the support of the United Nations. Although at first the Western armies were successful, in October 1950 Chinese "volunteers" joined in the fighting. By the summer of 1951 the battle had reached a stalemate, with the division of forces roughly approximating the previous boundary between the zones. Finally, after long negotiations, in July 1953 an armistice was concluded, and the two Korean governments remained in control of their former territories. Soviet and Chinese support had thus allowed the north to maintain its position.

The center of conflict then shifted to Indochina, a French colonial area. The French attempts to establish an independent Vietnamese state, based on the former social system and linked closely with France, were opposed by a radical native movement under the leadership of Ho Chi-minh. His successful partisan activities forced the powers again to resort to a partition arrangement; in 1954 a Communist-dominated regime was established in the north, with a pro-Western government in the south. Another socialist state thus came into existence.

Meanwhile, however, Stalin had died in March 1953. The transition of power was not easy. At first the Soviet government was in the hands of three men: the premier, G. M. Malenkov; the foreign minister, Molotov; and L. D. Beria, the powerful head of the secret police. Nikita S. Khrushchev succeeded Malenkov as party secretary. These men supported the concept of a collective leadership, an idea that they also attempted to introduce into the other socialist states. The period of cooperation among them, however, was short. In the subsequent struggle for predominance, the first to be eliminated was Beria, who was shot in December 1953 in the last of such drastic actions to be taken against a top Soviet official. In February 1955 Malenkov was forced to resign and was replaced by N. A. Bulganin; it was clear by then that he and Khrushchev held the chief influence. In 1957 Malenkov and Molotov made an unsuccessful attempt to overturn the new leadership. In March 1958 in a further step, Bulganin was forced to resign. Khrushchev then took the post of premier, and he remained the head of the party, both positions that Stalin had previously held; the idea of collective leadership had thus been abandoned.

Khrushchev's accession to power had its chief impact on the East European leaders in 1956. In a secret speech delivered at the twentieth party congress of the Soviet Communist Party in February, Khrushchev made a violent attack on Stalin, criticizing in extreme terms both his internal and foreign policies and his conduct of the war. This denunciation, the text of which soon became available, was a tremendous shock to some of the East European Communist leaders. Many, like Djilas, had been taught to venerate Stalin, or a least to admire his strong leadership and his victories. In the quarrel with Tito, the

Stalinist viewpoint had prevailed in all of the Communist bloc states; the opposition had been purged from the party ranks, and many had been imprisoned or executed. Now the parties were expected to reexamine their positions and to criticize the previous decisions. They were in particular expected to denounce the "cult of personality," the assigning to individual leaders of unusual, even superhuman, characteristics.

Khrushchev also introduced some major changes in Soviet foreign relations. Under Stalin, as has been shown, a series of conflicts had taken place between the two great military alliance systems. In 1953, however, the Soviet Union, which had been armed with nuclear weapons since the late 1940s, also acquired the hydrogen bomb. With both sides in possession of devastating nuclear weapons, it soon became apparent to rational observers that a war between the great powers would be a major disaster for mankind; there might be no winners in a third world war. With these considerations in mind the new Soviet leadership adopted a policy of "peaceful coexistence" and the stand that a war with the "capitalist, imperialist" states was not inevitable. This attitude was reflected in a series of meetings held between Soviet representatives and their Western counterparts, during which an attempt was made to settle the outstanding issues in Europe. In 1955 the State Treaty with Austria was signed; Soviet troops withdrew from their sector. The problem of the two German regimes and the status of Berlin, however, remained difficult to negotiate.

Although East–West relations did indeed improve, a major confrontation between the Soviet Union and the United States occurred over the question of Cuba. Previously an American preserve, this island in 1959 fell under the control of a partisan movement, led by Fidel Castro, which subsequently turned for support to the Soviet Union and the socialist bloc. In April 1961, under Central Intelligence Agency (CIA) leadership, an unsuccessful attempt was made to overthrow the regime in the disastrous "Bay of Pigs" episode. A year later, in October 1962, American intelligence sources discovered that Soviet intermediate range missile bases were being constructed on the island. After a tense crisis, the Soviet government agreed to withdraw the missiles and destroy the sites. Nevertheless, Castro's regime was firmly in power, and another state was added to the socialist alignment.

In 1964 Khrushchev was forced from office, principally because of his failures in domestic policy. His position was taken by two men, Leonid Brezhnev and Alexei Kosygin, who made no major changes in Soviet policy in regard to either the Western nations or the Communist bloc. In the 1960s Soviet relations with the United States were greatly influenced by the American involvement in Vietnam. Despite the division of the country in 1954, a strong guerilla movement continued in the south, which was supplied by the north, which in turn was backed by the Soviet Union and China. After 1963 American troops and supplies were sent in ever-increasing amounts, but this massive support was not sufficient to save the pro-Western regime. In 1973, after prolonged negotiations, the United States withdrew from the region in an action that marked a grave defeat for the Southeast Asian policy of the American government. With the subsequent union of the north and south, the Communist bloc gained an important member.

Despite their conflicts in many areas, the American and Soviet governments continued negotiations in other fields, notably in connection with the limitation of nuclear weaponry and, after November 1969, in the Strategic Arms Limitation Talks, called SALT. Meetings were also held between heads of state; President Richard Nixon traveled to the Soviet Union in 1972, and Brezhnev returned the visit in 1973. The policy of détente was thus continued through the 1970s.

In the major conflicts between the Soviet Union and the NATO states, all of the socialist regimes stood firmly behind Moscow in its support of the friendly regimes in Korea, Cuba, and Vietnam, and behind East Germany on the Berlin issue. In contrast, however, numerous points of controversy arose within the bloc on major questions involving the attitudes of the governments to the Soviet Union and their economic and military interrelationships.

### Interbloc relations

Although Marxism-Leninism offered certain theories concerning the conflicts between the Communist and the capitalist systems, it gave no clear guidance on the relations among socialist states. The Soviet government naturally preferred the principle of "proletarian internationalism" – that is, the acceptance by all of the socialist states of Soviet predominance. This tenet was challenged not only by Yugoslavia, but also by other Communist regimes. As we have seen, in the three decades after the end of World War II, China, Cuba, North Korea, and Vietnam (and also Mongolia) joined the alignment. With this increase in membership and with the wide geographic separation of the members, stresses were bound to appear in the relationships of the governments and parties. Certainly Tito's successful defiance of Moscow had a great deal of influence on the attitude of the other socialist states. For the Soviet Union problems were to arise in its relationships both with China and with the neighboring Eastern European states. Three major crises occurred within the Communist bloc: the revolution of 1956 in Hungary, the Sino-Soviet dispute after 1960, and the Soviet intervention in Czechoslovakia in 1968. Although none of these events involved Balkan territory, their ramifications directly affected the socialist states there.

After 1953 the Soviet government modified the degree of control exerted over its own population and over the governments of the East European satellites. This period of relaxation allowed more differences of opinion to be expressed, and it gave those who were dissatisfied with the Communist system a better chance to air their views. How far the Soviet government would allow dissent to go, however, remained an open question. In all the socialist countries the economic conditions associated with the centralized plans had imposed heavy burdens on the entire population. There was thus a great deal of dissatisfaction and unrest. In June 1953 workers in the Soviet zone of Berlin struck in protest against their working conditions; the strike spread throughout East Germany, and restoring order required the intervention of Soviet troops stationed in the country. Riots also took place in Czechoslovakia.

The impact of the post-Stalin Soviet policy was to be particularly strong in Poland and Hungary, where the conflict between Tito and Stalin had resulted in the purging from the parties of alleged pro-Yugoslav elements. Attempts were now made to rehabilitate these men, including those who had been executed, and to adopt more independent policies. The attraction of the Yugoslav idea of separate roads to socialism was very strong indeed. The first outward signs of unrest occurred in Poland, where riots broke out in June 1956. At the same time, the Polish Communist Party requested that Władislav Gomulka, who had been purged, be placed at the head of the party. After a period of tension during which Soviet divisions in Poland advanced on Warsaw, Khrushchev accepted the Polish desires. They involved, of course, no threat either to the Polish Communist regime as such or to Soviet control in the region. Further reform subsequently introduced in Poland included the disbanding of such collectives as had been organized, wider privileges for the Catholic church, and a general easing of controls.

Events were to follow quite a different path in Hungary. In October 1956, after student riots and popular demonstrations broke out, a new government under the leadership of Imre Nagy made it clear that it intended to take Hungary out of the Warsaw Treaty Organization, to introduce a multiparty system, and to move toward Western constitutional forms. Since these actions offered a clear challenge to both its military position and its ideological control in the region, the Soviet government acted quickly. In November 1956 Soviet troops entered Budapest, put down the revolutionary movement, and installed a subservient regime under János Kádár. Nagy was executed in 1958.

This intervention made a great impression on the Western European countries and within the bloc. In the Balkans the action was applauded by the Albanian, Bulgarian, and Romanian governments and even accepted by Tito. After the death of Stalin, his successors had made a great effort to improve relations with Yugoslavia. In 1955 Khrushchev and Bulganin paid a visit to Belgrade, where they placed the major blame for the previous conflict on the recently purged Beria. Thereafter, as we shall see, Soviet–Yugoslav relations pursued an uneven course. Although no break equivalent to the 1948–1949 crisis occurred, Yugoslavia did not rejoin the socialist alliance system. After the suppression of the Hungarian revolution, relations among the bloc states resumed their regular course until 1964, when Romanian resistance to attempts to strengthen Comecon and the Warsaw Treaty Organization became an open issue. By this time, however, a major upheaval in the Communist camp had been caused by China, which sought a position within the bloc commensurate to its claims to great-power status.

After the victory of Mao, relations between Peking and Moscow remained friendly until about 1958. During these years the two countries were in alliance, and the Soviet Union made some efforts to aid Chinese industrialization. Problems began, however, after the rise of Khrushchev, and especially after the commencement of his attacks on Stalin. The Soviet dictator had been greatly admired in Chinese party circles, and Mao was certainly a practitioner of the cult of personality carried to an extreme degree. Despite the Chinese approval of the Soviet intervention in Hungary, a series of controversies arose between the two states whose details were discussed in various party conferences. Gradually it became apparent that the Soviet Union had a rival for leadership in the socialist world.

Like Tito previously, the Chinese leaders not only disputed Soviet predominance in the socialist camp, but also offered doctrines that they argued were superior to any Soviet equivalent. In 1958 the Great Leap Forward, the objective of which was to bring China directly into the communist epoch without passage through the intermediate stage of socialism, was inaugurated. At the same time, the government adopted an ideologically militant position on world affairs. Whereas Khrushchev and the Soviet leaders were calling for a policy of peaceful coexistence, Mao supported a continuation of an open conflict with the "imperialist" powers. The Chinese frightened some of their allies by their statements that they did not fear nuclear warfare or its accompanying huge casualties. In Europe the Chinese position was supported by Albania, which in 1961 shifted to Peking's side.

Although Chinese–Soviet relations improved slightly after the ouster of Khrushchev, they worsened again when it became apparent that the Brezhnev–Kosygin leadership would continue the policy of coexistence with the Western states. Beginning in 1966 there was a major crisis in their relations. Faced with growing opposition within the Chinese party, Mao decided to use the army and the militant youth, organized in the Red Guard, to bring down his critics. In addition to radical internal changes, the resulting Cultural Revolution was accompanied by a violent propaganda campaign against the Soviet Union and by clashes on the Manchurian border. The Soviet–Chinese conflict had reverberations throughout the Communist world; their differences were debated in the party meetings held during the sixties. Although more normal relations were restored after 1968, the two states remained rivals for influence within the socialist bloc. The Chinese position was affected by a change subsequently made in its attitude toward the Western states, in particular the United States. In 1972 President Nixon visited China, marking a high point in the Chinese attempt to gain more flexibility in its foreign policy.

By the late 1960s Soviet dominance among the socialist states had been questioned by China, Yugoslavia, and – in a less dangerous manner – Albania and Romania. Nevertheless, all of these states, despite their criticisms of Soviet policy, were firmly Communist in their ideological convictions. Despite his resistance to Soviet dictation, Tito was always a loyal Communist; the leaders of the other dissident socialist states – China, Romania, and Albania – were Stalinist in their internal policies. By 1968, however, a situation had arisen in Czechoslovakia which was in some respects similar to that in Hungary in 1956. The regime began a series of reforms, particularly in cultural matters, which caused apprehension among its neighbors that the state might leave the socialist fold. Protests were made in Moscow, particularly by the East German and Polish governments, which feared the effects in their own countries. In August 1968 the Soviet Union, accompanied by Warsaw Pact troops from East Germany, Poland, Bulgaria, and Hungary, occupied Czechoslovakia and forced a change of government. This action, which was taken despite the fact that the Czechoslovak government had not threatened to leave the Warsaw Pact or to alter the socialist basis of the state, was strongly denounced by both the Yugoslav and the Romanian leaders, who prepared to resist any similar military intervention in their own countries. The justification of the Soviet action, which became known as the Brezhnev Doctrine, stated that the Soviet Union had the right and duty to act whenever socialism was in danger. Such intervention did not have to be requested; the Soviet government would decide when it was necessary.

Despite the wide implications of the doctrine, no further use was to be made of it until the invasion of Afghanistan in 1980. In fact, no major crises of international significance occurred in East Europe in the next decade. In this period, as before, Bulgaria and Romania were associated with the other East European countries in the two alignments, Comecon and the Warsaw Pact. Although Yugoslavia did not join the military alliance, its government did maintain close economic links with the Comecon members. Albania, as we shall see, went its own way.

### Comecon and the Warsaw Pact

The predominant position of the Soviet Union in the conduct of international relations among the Communist bloc nations was reflected in the economic and military associations formed among them. In January 1949 the Soviet Union, Poland, Czechoslovakia, Hungary, Bulgaria, and Romania, together formed Comecon; they were soon joined by Albania and the German Democratic Republic. Membership was extended to Mongolia in 1962, to Cuba in 1972, and to Vietnam in 1978. Yugoslavia, North Korea, China, Laos, and Angola were each granted observer status. As we have seen, the organization was intended as a counterweight to the Marshall Plan and later to the European Common Market.

As long as Stalin was alive, Comecon did not play a major role in bloc affairs. Each state followed a policy of building up its own economy on competing rather than complementary lines. All were dependent on the Soviet Union, and the emphasis was on bilateral trade between each nation and the Soviet center. It will be remembered that during this period the Soviet Union also used the resources of the entire region for the restoration of its own economy; it exploited the area through the extraction of reparations, the removal of factories and other capital goods, the organization of joint companies on an unequal basis, and an unfair price system in commercial transactions. At the same time a limited amount of credit and access to Soviet raw materials was offered.

After new policies were introduced in 1953, there were attempts to improve the economic relationships. Soviet assistance was increased; the outright exploitation came to an end; and proposals were drawn up to make Comecon a more effective association. By this time many of the disadvantages of the Stalinist pattern of economic development had become apparent. The small states had undertaken overly ambitious programs, and they were in competition with each other. As Khrushchev commented:

> It is impossible to develop everything everywhere simultaneously . . .
> Hungarians, Poles, Romanians and the others have tried to build up
> everything by themselves . . . As regards tractor or motor vehicle
> production, for example, the situation today is that tractors and mo-
> tor vehicles are produced not only in the Soviet Union, but by Po-
> land, Czechoslovakia, Hungary and Romania. Thus production is
> not always profitable. The sooner and the better we develop the di-
> vision of labor between our countries, the stronger will our econo-
> mies be.[3]

In line with this reasoning, the Soviet government called for what was termed a "socialist division of labor": each country was to concentrate on what it could best produce. Unfortunately for the Balkan countries, any rational plan of regional specialization would leave them in what they regarded as a disadvantageous position. The plan that was supported at this point called for a concentration of industry in the more highly developed states, particularly East Germany and Czechoslovakia; Albania, Bulgaria, and Romania were expected to remain primarily agricultural. Another objection was that implementation of this type of organization would require the creation of supranational agencies that would have much authority over the central plans of the individual national economies. The proposal caused particular indignation in Romania, whose government had no intention of seeing the

---

3  Quoted in Michael Kaser, *COMECON: Integration Problems of the Planned Economies* (London: Oxford University Press, 1967), pp. 64–65.

state reduced to being the supplier of food and raw materials to the rest of the bloc. It must also be remembered that the entire Communist program had placed much weight on the idea of modernization through industrialization; agrarian states were in general regarded as backward and weak. The Romanian objections were supported in one manner or another by Albania, China, and Yugoslavia, who saw the whole project as simply another Soviet attempt to gain a tighter control over the socialist states.

Although Romanian opposition prevented economic integration or the establishment of effective central planning agencies for the bloc, some moves were made toward closer cooperation. Plans were developed for a common transportation network, an oil pipeline, and an electric grid system. Some agreements were made providing for specialization in limited fields. There was also an increased exchange of information, industrial blueprints, and experts; financial problems connected with interbloc commerce were dealt with by joint commissions.

By the 1970s these states, including the Soviet Union, showed less interest in a further integration of the bloc economies. They were by then primarily concerned with developing closer ties with the Western nations, which produced superior goods and had the advantage of being able to provide advanced technology. Largely owing to Romanian insistence, the Comecon members had agreed that each should be free to participate in or to withdraw from joint projects. Moreover, the earlier problems were still present. Each state had developed according to the original Stalinist model, and their industrial economies continued to produce competitive products. The governments remained convinced that modern socialist states should have large industries. They were particularly proud of their giant enterprises and more spectacular projects, no matter how high the cost.

By the 1970s this condition had caused an interesting reversal in the Soviet economic relations with the bloc countries. When developing their industrial economies, the states had become heavily dependent on Soviet supplies of raw materials and energy. In return, they had offered the products of their new industries. However, as prices for basic materials, particularly oil, rose on the world market, the Soviet government began to find itself on the losing end of the arrangement. Manufactured goods from the bloc industries were often not of a high quality; there were frequent Russian complaints that the Soviet Union was becoming a dumping ground for defective merchandise, as is shown in the following assessment written in 1974:

> Regrettably, there is much evidence that the Socialist countries . . . supply low quality consumer goods, including clothes, knitwear, footwear, fabrics, leatherwear, and furniture . . . There are also latent defects . . . the assortment of goods does not always satisfy the Soviet people's needs, since modern fashions and models are sometimes

disregarded . . . suppliers sometimes violate contracts by shipping goods which neither meet the contractual terms nor correspond to the selected samples.[4]

Despite these considerations there was little that the Soviet government could do. The socialist states needed the Soviet Union both as a source of raw materials and energy and as a market. The political consequences of a shift of trade or a drastic change in the terms of the commercial agreements could not be faced. The Soviet government was thus forced to pay a high economic price to assure its political goals.

Similar problems, particularly in regard to questions of national sovereignty, arose in connection with the Warsaw Pact. This treaty was signed in May 1955 by the Soviet Union, Albania, Bulgaria, Czechoslovakia, the German Democratic Republic, Hungary, Poland, and Romania. The official reason for the formation of the alignment was given as the rearmament of West Germany and its admission to NATO, although, as we have seen, the pact provided the additional advantage of allowing the Soviet Union to maintain troops in Hungary and Romania after the signing of the Austrian treaty. The German question, however, was also vital to the Soviet government, and the threat of German "revanchism" was useful to hold the bloc together.

In the years after the end of the war, the Soviet Union, of course, had no need of a formal alignment of the socialist states. The Soviet army held full military control of the region; it had no interest in increasing the military capabilities of the satellite states. However, efforts were made to assure that the command of their armies was securely in the hands of Communist or pro-Communist commanders. Much attention was devoted to the building up of the security forces, which were seen as the main support of the socialist regimes. After 1948 the Soviet Union signed a series of bilateral military treaties with the individual states and maintained a close liaison with their army commands. Soviet advisers played a major role in all military matters; the Soviet military organization was the model for the bloc, and officers from the East European armies were brought to train in the Soviet Union. In 1949 conscription was introduced in all the bloc countries except East Germany, where it was delayed until 1962.

Once the Warsaw Pact was signed, many of the problems that we have seen with Comecon arose. All the signatories wished to participate in military planning, but they were also most concerned about protecting their sovereignty. Their leaders thus worried about supranational authorities and the presence of foreign troops on their soil. The Soviet domination was obvious

---

4  V. Zoloyev, "Soviet Foreign Trade in the First Half of the Decisive Year," *Foreign Trade* (Moscow), November 1974, quoted in Paul Marer, "Has Eastern Europe Become a Liability to the Soviet Union? The Economic Aspect," in Charles Gati, ed., *The International Politics of Eastern Europe* (New York: Praeger, 1976), p. 70.

from the beginning. The commander-in-chief of the joint forces and the chief of the General Staff were always Russians; Soviet liaison officers were attached to the bloc armies and their war ministries, but similar representatives were not sent by the member states to Moscow. The pact provided for the establishment of a Political Consultative Committee composed of representatives of the signatories. It, however, met only fifteen times between 1956 and 1976, although it was supposed to hold sessions twice yearly. The principal fear of the Warsaw Pact participants has been that the Soviet Union would exploit its position in the organization to enforce political decisions within the bloc, rather than concentrate on the defense of East Europe from outside attack. These apprehensions are justified; as we have seen, the Soviet Union has intervened unilaterally in the internal affairs of the member states, and, in the case of Czechoslovakia, it did use the troops of other socialist bloc nations.

In the twentieth century, as in the nineteenth, Russian military strategy has been primarily concerned with the German and Polish territories that are the road into the Russian heartland. The Soviet leaders have thus always been more watchful of internal events in Poland, East Germany, Czechoslovakia, and Hungary than of those in the Balkan states. No military intervention like those which occurred in East Germany, in Hungary, and in Czechoslovakia resulted from the strong defiant attitudes assumed by Albania and Yugoslavia. The firm control of the northern tier of states is seen as a military necessity. Both Soviet and NATO military planners see World War III as commencing with a Soviet offensive launched from this region into West Germany. Whether as a base for an attack on the West or as a buffer against outside aggression, the northern states in the bloc are of crucial importance to the Soviet Union.

During the Khrushchev era and under the later Brezhnev regime attempts have been made to tighten the organization of the alliance. The chief opposition to closer military cooperation, as to economic integration, has come from Romania, whose attitude became even firmer after the invasion of Czechoslovakia. The other states in the alignment have similarly criticized the Soviet predominance and the burden that defense expenditures place on their economies. They have, however, no alternative but to remain in the alignment. One of the major reasons for the Soviet intervention in Czechoslovakia was the fear that it might leave. Although Albania has withdrawn from the organization, there is little chance that any other member would be allowed to follow its example.

Despite the attempts made to protect their autonomy, the armies of the Soviet bloc states in any future war would undoubtedly fight under the direct authority of the Soviet command. This system was used in the final phase of World War II when, it will be remembered, the Romanian, Bulgarian, and Yugoslav armies, as well as smaller units representing other East European states, fought together with the Soviet Union. When Warsaw Pact troops were used in the invasion of Czechoslovakia, they were deployed and commanded by Soviet officers. There was no formal consultation among the military leaders of the pact members before the action was taken; it was a Soviet decision alone.[5]

## CONTRASTING COMMUNIST REGIMES:
### BULGARIA, ROMANIA, ALBANIA

Although the socialist states, as has been shown, did indeed share many general characteristics, they also differed in important respects. Here the internal history of Bulgaria, Romania, and Albania is reviewed, both to describe domestic developments and to determine the reaction of each to the major events of the epoch.

### Bulgaria

By 1950 Vulko Chervenkov, who held the posts of both premier and party secretary, had become the most powerful man in Bulgaria. The son of a noncommissioned officer in the Bulgarian army, he had spent his youth in Communist Party activities. In 1925 he went to the Soviet Union, where he attended both military and party schools. In close association with George Dimitrov, his brother-in-law, he took a prominent part in Comintern affairs. He returned to Bulgaria in 1945, having been absent twenty years, and rose to a commanding position after Dimitrov's death in 1949. Since Chervenkov was an adherent of the Stalinist system, his position was weakened after 1953. Following the direction of Moscow, he too was compelled to relax the strict measures of control and to place more emphasis on "socialist legality." At this time attempts were made to improve conditions in the countryside, in particular on the collectives. Members of the subservient Agrarian Union were sent to try to convince the peasantry of the advantages of collectivization and to argue that this policy followed the doctrines of Stamboliski. More attention was given to housing and to the production of consumer goods. In another adherence to Soviet examples, the party and state posts were separated. Chervenkov chose to keep his position as premier; Todor Zhivkov became party secretary. Coming to this office in 1954 at the relatively young age of forty-three, Zhivkov was at first not seen as a possible successor to Chervenkov. George Chankov, the head of the State Planning Commission, had a higher reputation.

After 1944 Bulgaria maintained the closest relations with the Soviet Union of all the East European states. The government and its leaders were henceforth to copy any changes in the Soviet internal system and to follow Mos-

---

5    A. Ross Johnson, "Has Eastern Europe Become a Liability to the Soviet Union? The Military Aspect," in Gati, *International Politics.*, p. 51.

cow's direction in foreign policy in exact detail. The Stalinist economic system, which placed the chief attention on the building of large industrial enterprises, to the neglect of light industry and agriculture, had already been adopted with enthusiasm. As in other states, the objectives were plotted out in a series of plans, the first being the two-year plan for 1947 and 1948; a series of five-year plans followed. As we have seen, Bulgaria is an extremely poor country and lacks the basic coal, iron, and oil needed for industrial development. Almost all of these vital resources had to be imported from the Soviet Union. Moreover, the country lacked experienced technicians and managers, a deficiency that was partially filled by Soviet experts, whose salaries ran about four times higher than those of their Bulgarian colleagues.

Although Bulgaria was treated more favorably than any other bloc state, it did suffer from a degree of Soviet exploitation after the war; for instance, high prices were charged for Soviet products, and Bulgarian exports were undervalued. Most of these policies were abandoned after 1953, and the joint companies were closed in 1954 and 1955. With the emphasis placed on industry, the Bulgarian economy did show some improvement in this field; the basis for an iron and steel industry was established. The electrification of the country also made rapid progress. Housing in the cities and consumer goods were still, however, in extremely short supply.

Agriculture in Bulgaria, as in the other socialist states, was the weak point in the system. Previously the Bulgarians had enjoyed a general European reputation as small farmers and gardeners. As a land of peasant farms, the state had formerly had a good agricultural base. Following the Soviet example, the government made an effort to collectivize the land rapidly, but sufficient funds were not invested in the mechanized equipment and the modern improvements needed to make the collectives efficient. Farm production declined significantly. The peasants were allowed to utilize for their own needs small plots, of from .5 to 1.3 acres (2 to 5 decares). This land was in theory still under state ownership, but any livestock raised on the plots was the private property of the individual. Here production was high. In 1958 a third of the sheep, 38 percent of the cattle, and 40 percent of the pigs came from this source; 52 percent of the meat and 40 percent of the milk was provided by private holders and not by the collectives. Although these percentages changed in subsequent years, the individual plots were still cultivated with more care and concern than the land on the collectives. Nevertheless, collectivization was never abandoned, and it changed the face of the countryside. With the emphasis placed on large units, Bulgarian farmland was organized by the end of the 1950s into 932 large collectives whose average size was 42,000 decares (10,378 acres).[6] A new pattern of village and agrarian life thus emerged despite the continued peasant resistance to this form of agricultural organization.

6  J. F. Brown, *Bulgaria under Communist Rule* (New York: Praeger, 1970), pp. 205–208.

Meanwhile, Chervenkov's position continued to deteriorate. After he surrendered his post of party secretary to Zhivkov, his influence weakened. Furthermore, in the struggle for power that was going on in the Soviet Union, he became associated with the losing Malenkov faction. Khrushchev, steadily gaining in influence, showed a dislike for the Stalinist East European leaders; since he sought a reconciliation with Tito, he also tended to disapprove of those who had been prominent in attacking the Yugoslav leader. Taking advantage of the situation, Anton Yugov, the minister of interior from 1944 to 1948, was able to regain his lost influence. In addition, those who had been imprisoned because of their alleged connections with Kostov were released and rehabilitated. Chervenkov thus faced a growing opposition. The final blow came in 1956 with Khrushchev's secret speech. The implications of the address were particularly damaging to Chervenkov, who had been closely identified with the cult of personality. In April the Central Committee of the Bulgarian party met to consider its future in the light of the new Soviet course. In the same month Chervenkov was forced to resign as premier, though he remained in the government as deputy premier.

Yugov became the new premier. Although some changes were introduced, the essentially conservative party leadership never favored reform. The Soviet repression of the Hungarian revolt in 1956 came as a relief to them. Chervenkov, still active despite his demotion, became minister of education and culture in February 1957 and implemented a policy of strict state control. In the spring and summer of that year, during the period when Khrushchev moved against Molotov and Malenkov, party purges also occurred in Bulgaria, and Chankov lost his previous influence.

The only departure from the conservative, steady policy of the Bulgarian leadership came in 1958. The third Bulgarian Five Year Plan, drawn up for the years 1958 to 1962, was moderate in its objectives; it placed more stress than previous plans on developing light industry and food processing. However, in October and November a delegation visited China. There were obvious similarities between the two countries, both of which had primarily peasant populations and the desire to modernize. Under the influence of the Chinese example the Bulgarian government decided to emulate some of the aspects of the Great Leap Forward. It was thus announced that the plan was to be completed in three or four rather than five years. Attempts were made to mobilize the population for a great effort; mass meetings were held to awaken enthusiasm. Nevertheless, the entire undertaking was a failure. Although the government announced a success, it was able to justify its claims only by changing the definition of the objectives to be accomplished. No similar programs were to be introduced in the future. After the Sino-Soviet split became definite, Bulgaria ceased to be attracted by Chinese ideas.

Meanwhile, factional disputes continued to divide the party, and Chervenkov and Yugov remained hostile. A new crisis was precipitated by the events of the twenty-second congress of the Soviet party, held in October 1961, at which Khrushchev launched a new anti-Stalinist campaign. In Bulgaria Chervenkov was still an obvious target, and at the end of the year he was removed from the Politburo. At this point Yugov and Zhivkov were the principal figures in Bulgarian politics. In May 1962 Khrushchev paid an extensive visit to the country, his first since 1958. During his tour he indicated his preference for Zhivkov, and the choice was confirmed at a party conference held later in the year. Yugov not only lost his position as premier, but was expelled from the party for violations of "socialist legality." Chervenkov suffered a similar fate. In firm control, Zhivkov added the post of premier to that of party secretary.

Todor Zhivkov, born in 1911, came from a poor peasant background. He joined the party in 1932 and was later active in the partisan movement. He became a member of the Central Committee in 1948 and, as we have seen, party secretary in 1954. With the elimination of Chervenkov, Chankov, and Yugov, he faced no other powerful opponents. His supporters dominated the party hierarchy. In the next years there was to be only one challenge to his position, and that was not serious. In April 1965 Major General Ivan Todorov-Gorunya shot himself in his apartment in Sofia. Nine men, including three generals, were subsequently arrested, of whom the most important was Major General Tsviatko Anev, the commander of the Sofia garrison. All were convicted of involvement in an alleged pro-Chinese conspiracy. Anev was given the relatively mild sentence of twelve years; the others received only three to fifteen years.[7] Except for this limited disturbance, Bulgarian internal affairs remained tranquil. The regime kept its conservative stance in political, cultural, and economic affairs.

Bulgarian economic planning was, as noted, Stalinist in organization and outlook. The enormous barrier to industrial advancement remained the weak base of essential raw materials, in particular coal and iron ore, which had to be imported almost entirely from the Soviet Union. Oil was another major problem. These deficiencies, however, did not prevent the Bulgarian government from undertaking the construction of the Kremikovtsi Metallurgical Combine. This giant iron and steel complex, supported by a great deal of Soviet aid, was constructed near Sofia and opened in November 1963. Designed as a showpiece for the Communist regime, it absorbed a fifth of the total capital investment in industry in 1962 and 1963. Often called "the graveyard of the Bulgarian economy," it was constructed in an area where both the iron and coal supplies were of a poor quality and in a limited supply.[8] In the future most of the necessary coal and iron ore will have to be imported by sea; the inland location makes the transportation extremely expensive. Varna would have been a better choice. The enterprise is a good illustration of the pitfalls of central planning and the Stalinist economic concepts. It also helps

7   Brown, *Bulgaria under Communist Rule*, pp. 175–177.
8   Paul Lendvai, *Eagles in Cobwebs* (New York: Doubleday, Anchor Books, 1969), pp. 311, 312.

to explain the comment of a Bulgarian citizen: "No nation is working so hard and so strenuously as ours, yet none lives so miserably."[9]

In foreign relations the Bulgarian government maintained the loyalty to Soviet direction that we have seen in internal policy. One major problem, however, came with Khrushchev's determination to improve relations with Yugoslavia. Despite Soviet urging, the Bulgarian attitude toward Belgrade remained critical and distrustful. The major problem was still Macedonia, a region to which Bulgaria could never abandon its claims. In fact, the old quarrel was to become even more bitter. Previously, as we have seen, the Bulgarian government had recognized the existence of a Macedonian nationality and had been willing to accept the creation of a Macedonian state, but as part of a Balkan federation. The issue had a particular significance for the Petrich district, also called Pirin Macedonia. In the census of 1956 the existence of 187,789 Macedonians in Bulgaria was duly recorded, with the majority living in this one region. Subsequently, there was a radical change in policy. With the increase of hostility over the question, the Bulgarian government decided that another approach was necessary; henceforth, the existence of a separate Macedonian nationality was to be vigorously denied. In the census of 1965 only 8,750 declared themselves Macedonians. The question was extremely complicated: two of the chief figures in the Communist movement, Blagoev and Dimitrov, were born in Macedonia. Bulgarian historical writing has been based on the assumption that Bulgarians and Macedonians were one people, that is, Bulgarians. Moreover, should a Macedonian nationality indeed be judged to exist, then the Bulgarian control of Pirin Macedonia could be brought into question.

As far as relations with the other neighbors were concerned, Bulgaria's attitude toward Romania became less cordial after Bucharest began to resist Soviet control in the economic and military fields. Bulgaria always supported the Soviet position, no matter what it was. There was also considerable friction with Turkey, particularly in the immediate postwar years. Southern Dobrudja, which Bulgaria had acquired in 1940 and kept after 1945, had a large Turkish population. The Bulgarian government put great pressure on these people to force them to emigrate, since it wanted their lands for its collectivization program. Although about 150,000 Turks left in the early 1950s, there were still around 750,000 in the country in 1965.[10] In addition, soon after the war about 45,000 Jews left for Israel. The number of minorities in Bulgaria was thus further reduced.

A major improvement took place in respect to Greece. As could be expected, in the first years after the conclusion of the Greek civil war, relations

---

9   Quoted in Lendvai, *Eagles in Cobwebs*, p. 321.
10  Nissan Oren, *Revolution Administered: Agrarianism and Communism in Bulgaria* (Baltimore: Johns Hopkins University Press, 1973), p. 122.

were strained. Moreover, according to the peace treaty signed by Bulgaria in 1948, Greece was to receive $45 million in reparations. In addition, although this same agreement limited the Bulgarian army to 65,000 men, it had been increased to between 150,000 to 200,000.[11] Controversy was also caused by the Bulgarian nationalization of Greek property. During the 1950s, because of these conflicts, the border between the two countries remained closed; direct road, rail, and telephone communications were cut. This condition was changed in the 1960s when a new Greek government under George Papandreou took office in Athens. In 1964 the two nations signed a series of agreements concerning trade, diplomatic relations, and cultural cooperation. At this time the Greek representatives abandoned many of their previous claims; the Bulgarian government thus paid only $7 million in goods against its reparations account.

As has been emphasized, the main distinguishing feature of Bulgaria's policy after 1945 was the closeness of its relationship with the Soviet Union and the special favors that this attitude won. In many respects the country functioned at this time as another Soviet republic. The Bulgarian ambassador to Moscow had the position of an ex-officio member of the government in Sofia; the Soviet ambassador accompanied the Bulgarian premier on tours of the country and sat with the ministers on public occasions.[12] The Soviet representatives also encouraged a servile attitude and obviously expected frequent expressions of devotion, such as Zhivkov's declaration after Khrushchev's visit in 1962 that the Bulgarian "political watch dial is exact to the second with the watch of the Soviet Union . . . our watch is working toward Moscow time. This is a matter of great pride for all Bulgarian people."[13]

Although this attitude can be strongly criticized, as it certainly was in other socialist capitals where a more independent stand toward Moscow was adopted, the Bulgarian position can be understood. Certainly no other power could then or later replace the Soviet Union as a support to the country. Bulgaria needs raw materials, and its manufactured goods are not of a quality to compete on the world market. In 1974 Bulgarian trade with the Soviet Union amounted to 46.9 percent of the total.[14] It would be difficult to find a substitute commercial partner. As far as the international position of the country is concerned, the situation is very similar. Like all of its neighbors, the Bulgarian government is serious about its national goals, and it needs a great-power patron. Here too no other state could render similar assistance and protection. The relationship, nevertheless, raises serious questions. One authority has commented: "Has the national ego of this small people been impaired in

11  Brown, *Bulgaria under Communist Rule*, p. 275.
12  Lendvai, *Eagles in Cobwebs*, pp. 255, 256.
13  Quoted in Brown, *Bulgaria under Communist Rule*, p. 129.
14  Robert R. King, "Bulgaria," in Rakowska-Harmstone and Gyorgy, *Communism in Eastern Europe*, p. 183.

the process? A sanctified theology of 'second-best,' which states that the Bulgarians are great, but which reminds everyone from the cradle on that the Russians are even greater, continues unabated."[15]

## Romania

Like the Bulgarian, the Romanian leaders after 1948 devoted their attention to the construction of a socialist economy. They had more difficulties than their neighbor, since Romania, unlike Bulgaria, had been thoroughly plundered. It has been estimated that war damages, together with reparations to the Soviet Union, amounted to three and a half times the national income in 1938.[16] This economic exploitation took the familiar forms of the expropriation of factories and industrial equipment, the levying of high occupation costs, the establishment of joint companies, and the unequal price system that we have seen elsewhere. Moreover, in contrast to the other Balkan countries, Romania had lost a large section of its prewar land. Bessarabia and northern Bukovina, annexed by the Soviet Union in 1940, and southern Dobrudja, returned to Bulgaria, amounted to a fifth of the former national territory and contained 15 percent of the previous population.

Although Romania thus lost lands to two neighbors, it received back the part of Transylvania that had been transferred to Hungary in 1940. Once more in possession of the prewar Transylvanian lands, the Romanian government again faced the problem of dealing with the Hungarian minority. This sensitive issue was to remain a subject of dispute with Hungary, despite the fact that the two states were members of the same diplomatic and military alignment. Thus both Bessarabia and Transylvania continued to be potential sources of international controversy.

In April 1948 a new constitution was adopted, and the government proceeded to implement massive economic changes. In June 1948 the banks, industries, insurance companies, mines, and all means of transportation were nationalized. By 1950, 1,060 enterprises – 90 percent of the productive capacity of the country – had been taken over.[17] The Soviet joint companies, naturally, could not be seized; they continued to operate under Soviet managers with special extraterritorial privileges, including exemption from taxation. In July 1948 central state planning was inaugurated. In introducing these measures, the Romanian authorities met with the usual problems. Although the prewar regime had taken a strong interest in industry, it had done little beyond enacting protective tariffs and special tax regulations. Like the Bulgarian, the Romanian government had to rely strongly on the Soviet Union for

---

15 Oren, *Revolution Administered*, p. 172.
16 Lendvai, *Eagles in Cobwebs*, p. 345.
17 Ghita Ionescu, *Communism in Rumania, 1944–1962* (London: Oxford University Press, 1964), p. 162.

technical advice and other assistance. The adoption of the Soviet economic model caused difficulties here too. Romania had oil, but not iron, which had to be imported from the Soviet Union at an initially high cost. Nevertheless, the emphasis continued to be placed on the construction of large industrial complexes.

Collectivization, however, proceeded at a slower pace than in Bulgaria. Faced with violent peasant opposition, the government introduced its policies gradually. At first the large units of land were confiscated and their owners evicted. The land was not divided among the peasants, but instead organized into state farms or collectives. In the winter of 1949–1950 a policy of forced collectivization was introduced, which at first was not successful. Since very little was invested in the undertaking, the collectives lacked the necessary machinery and other equipment to allow them to operate efficiently. When production dropped, the government retreated and shifted to a policy of levying quotas for deliveries from private land. Nevertheless, collectivization remained the goal, and the peasants were almost fully collectivized by 1962.

Despite the fact that it had been forced to cede territory, Romania still had a large number of non-Romanian citizens, principally Hungarians, Germans, Serbs, Turks, and Jews, who together represented over 12 percent of the total population. As in Bulgaria, the majority of the Jews who remained at the end of the war emigrated to Israel. Many Turks left for Turkey, and the Romanian officials, like the Bulgarian, encouraged the emigration in order to acquire more Dobrudjan land. The extent of this demographic change is shown in the following figures: in 1930 there were 728,115 Jews in the country, but the number was 146,264 in 1956 and 42,888 in 1966; the Turkish population fell from 154,772 in 1930 to 14,329 in 1956.

The major minority problem, however, still concerned Transylvania. The German element had been greatly reduced during and after the war, when tens of thousands of the former Saxon population were killed, were forced to emigrate, or chose to leave with the German army. Of the 745,000 Germans living in Romania in 1930, 385,000 remained in 1956. As in the interwar period, this minority caused no great political problems. The major difficulties lay in the Romanian relationship with the large Hungarian group, numbering about 1.6 million in 1956, the majority of whom lived in the center of Transylvania. The bitter conflicts during the war only served to aggravate earlier controversies. In an attempt to moderate the situation, the constitution, passed in 1952, provided for the creation of a Hungarian Autonomous District in Transylvania, composed of lands in which 77 percent of the population was Hungarian. Although Jews and Turks had been allowed, even encouraged, to emigrate immediately after the war, this policy was not applied to the Hungarians. Moreover, soon all emigration – that of the Romanians as well as of the national minorities – was blocked.

Immediately after the war, as we have seen, the power in the state lay in the hands of the Muscovite group, consisting of Ana Pauker, Vasile Luca, and Teohari Georgescu, the minister of interior. The most influential native Communist was George Gheorghiu-Dej, who had been party secretary since 1944. Another important local Communist, Lucreţiu Pătrăşcanu, was purged during the anti-Tito agitation. By May 1952 Gheorghiu-Dej was in a strong enough position to move against his three rivals. He had not only the backing of the party, but the approval of Stalin; Pauker, Luca, and Georgescu all lost their high positions. Luca was tried and condemned to death in 1954, a sentence that was later commuted to life imprisonment. Pauker was merely demoted to a lower position.

In June 1952 Gheorghiu-Dej assumed the post of premier, while remaining at the head of the party. Born in Moldavia in 1901, Gheorghiu-Dej had participated in revolutionary activities in his youth. In 1933 he was arrested and sentenced to twelve years in prison because of his participation in the Griviţa railroad strike of that year. A Stalinist in internal policy, he was able to support enthusiastically the denunciations of Tito's national deviation. The death of Stalin and the subsequent shift of Soviet policy, which occurred almost simultaneously with the consolidation of his own power, was naturally unsettling. He and his followers did not like the idea of a collective leadership, but he was forced to make some gesture in this direction in view of the attitude in Moscow. In 1954 he thus resigned his post as party secretary, but remained as premier. In the next year he took back the party position and made his supporter Chivu Stoica premier. Fearing any possible opposition, he had already had Pătrăşcanu executed in April 1954.

As a Stalinist in a period of de-Stalinization, Gheorghiu-Dej found himself in a difficult position. Since he needed a scapegoat, he blamed the previous excesses on Pauker, Luca, and Georgescu, who were denounced as "Stalinists." He still faced opposition from within the party, in particular from Iosif Chisinevschi and Miron Constantinescu, but they were removed from the Politburo in a purge conducted in July 1957. Later Constantinescu became minister of culture and education. By this time Gheorghiu-Dej's policies in internal affairs had been considerably strengthened as a result of the revolt in Hungary and the subsequent Soviet intervention, of which he thoroughly approved. His tough line seemed justified by the events in Budapest, which appeared to prove that a liberal line would indeed endanger Communist control.

The outbreak of the Hungarian revolution naturally caused a strong reaction in Romania, where great sympathy for the rebels was shown, in particular by the Transylvanian Hungarians. The expression of national feeling at this time led to a narrowing of their cultural rights. A major move in this direction occurred in July 1959, when the Hungarian Bolyai University in Cluj was merged with the Romanian Babeş institution. The result was a reduction in the number of classes conducted in Hungarian. Further anti-Hungarian actions were to follow. In 1960 the boundaries of the Hungarian Autonomous District, now called the Mureş-Hungarian Autonomous Region, were gerrymandered to bring more Romanians into it and thus reduce the percentage of Hungarians to only 62.

Once securely in power, Gheorghiu-Dej proceeded with the full collectivization of the peasantry; the accomplishment of this objective was announced in 1962. The main emphasis remained, however, on industrialization. As a convinced Stalinist and Marxist, Gheorghiu-Dej was particularly interested in the industrial development of the country, and his determination to pursue this objective was soon to lead the Romanian government into controversies with its neighbors. In the field of foreign affairs, he worked closely with Ion George Maurer, who became foreign minister in 1957 and premier in 1961 and thus was the second man in influence in the government. Gheorghiu-Dej and Maurer adopted a policy of resistance to Soviet efforts to achieve bloc economic integration through Comecon and a tighter military unity through the Warsaw Treaty Organization.

At first, during the 1950s, Romanian foreign policy was closely associated with that of Moscow; the intervention in Hungary was supported. Despite their lack of sympathy with de-Stalinization measures, the Romanian leaders found that the new Soviet policies brought advantages. Less interested in asserting full domination, the Soviet government sold most of the joint companies, but not those dealing with oil and uranium, to Romania by 1954. Although economic pressure lessened, Soviet troops were not finally withdrawn from the country until 1958. During this period Romanian officials not only cooperated with the Soviet Union, but took a leading role in forwarding Soviet objectives in the Balkans. In 1957 the Warsaw Pact members stood sponsor for a plan to create a nuclear-free zone in Central Europe and the Balkans, a proposal that was bound to win wide popular support as well as to provide advantages for Soviet military strategy. In September 1957 Stoica sent notes to Albania, Bulgaria, Greece, Turkey, and Yugoslavia, suggesting a conference to discuss their mutual problems, including the question of nuclear weapons. Reflecting their positions in world diplomatic affairs at the time, Bulgaria and Albania accepted at once, and Greece and Turkey refused. The Yugoslav government agreed only in principle. In 1958, after Yugoslavia introduced a new and much more liberal economic reform program, the relations of that state with the rest of the bloc once again deteriorated. Nevertheless, in June 1959 when the United States was installing rocket bases in Greece, Stoica again called for the establishment of a neutral zone in the area and a ban on rockets and nuclear weapons. The Soviet government even suggested that nuclear disarmament be extended to the Adriatic and thus cover similar installations in Italy.

The assertion of Romanian independence in foreign affairs and in interbloc relations was to come only slowly. The adoption of a position of resistance to Soviet pressure was, of course, bound to be much more popular in Romania than, for instance, in Bulgaria. Romania had no tradition of pro-Russian or pro-Slavic friendship. In fact, as we have seen, the Romanian national movement had been directed as much against Russian domination as against Ottoman sovereignty. Nor had the events of the past two decades improved relations. The Soviet seizure of Bessarabia and northern Bukovina in 1940 was still deeply resented. The conduct of the Soviet armies of occupation and the subsequent economic exploitation had simply intensified previous harsh resentments.

As a first step toward a more independent stand the Romanian government began to participate more actively in world diplomacy; it was particularly interested in developing ties with the new nations in Asia and Africa. These Romanian efforts were aided a great deal by the Yugoslav defiance of Moscow. Despite previous Romanian denunciations of Tito's actions, Romania's relations with Yugoslavia were improved with relatively little difficulty, particularly since the two states, even with their ideological differences, had many interests in common and no territorial disagreements. In the 1960s they engaged in a joint hydroelectric project at the Iron Gates on the Danube. In the same manner the Chinese challenge to Soviet leadership of world Communism assisted the Romanians. In this controversy they attempted to stay in the middle and to mediate between the two great powers: they supported China's insistence on the equality of Communist parties, but not its hostile attitude toward the capitalist world. At this time the Romanian government was actively seeking better relations with Western Europe.

The immediate cause of the Romanian conflict with the Soviet Union did not, however, involve questions of general diplomatic relations, but rather issues of internal economic development and the right of the socialist bloc states to pursue their own programs without outside intervention or direction. The Romanian Communist leadership was determined to proceed on its program of industrialization. The Comecon plan, sponsored by the Soviet Union, for a "socialist division of labor" was a direct threat to this policy. The Romanian government opposed not only a program that reduced the country to the role of a supplier of raw materials and agricultural products, but also the establishment of supranational supervising institutions that would be able to interfere in the internal policies of the Comecon states. The entire concept, in the Romanian opinion, was demeaning and dangerous. National and ideological sensibilities were affronted by the idea of Romania's being relegated to the permanent position of an agrarian state; progress was still seen as industrialization. As a predominantly agricultural country, Romania had been weak and backward. By 1963 the Romanian government had made clear its firm opposition to central planning within Comecon, to specialization within the bloc, and to the establishment of supranational authorities. The immediate question at issue was the fate of a gigantic iron and steel enterprise that was under construction at Galaţi.

In April 1964 the Romanian party published the text of a resolution stating the official position toward Comecon and the proposals for integration. Entitled "A Statement on the Stand of the Romanian Workers' Party concerning the Problems of the World Communist and Working Class Movement," it is the most important Romanian declaration on foreign policy in the postwar period. Its chief attack is directed against the idea of a supranational authority:

> *The idea of a single planning body for all Comecon countries has the most serious economic and political implications.* The planned management of the national economy is one of the fundamental, essential and inalienable attributes of the sovereignty of the socialist State – the State plan being the principal means by which the socialist State achieves its political and socio-economic objectives, establishes the direction and rates of development of the national economy, its basic proportions, the accumulations and the measures for raising the people's living standard and cultural level. The sovereignty of the socialist state requires that it takes full and effective advantage of these means and retains in its hands all the levers for the management of economic and social life.
>
> To hand over these levers to the competence of some super-State or extra-State bodies would be to turn sovereignty into a concept without any real content.[18]

Romania took a similar attitude in the discussions concerning the Warsaw Treaty Organization. Here too a strong stand was made against the establishment of a central military authority with wide powers of intervention in internal affairs.

The task of implementing this policy was to be undertaken chiefly by a new leadership. In March 1965 Gheorghiu-Dej died, his position as party leader was inherited by his close associate, Nicolae Ceauşescu. Born in January 1918 of a family of peasant origin, Ceauşescu joined the party in 1936. After the Communist victory, he was active in party organization and military affairs. He became a member of the Central Committee in 1952 and of the Politburo in 1955. After 1965 he shared power with Stoica and Maurer, but by the end of 1967 he and his supporters were in control of the major government and party positions. Under his leadership, state power remained concentrated in the hands of a very small group. In January 1974 a new body called the Permanent Bureau of the Political Executive Committee was placed at the head of party affairs. In 1977 its membership consisted of nine people, including Elena Ceauşescu, the wife of the Romanian leader. Ceauşescu took for himself the principal posts, including the office of president, created in 1974. By the mid-1970s he thus held positions as

the President of the Republic, the President of the State Council, the President of the Supreme Council of Economic and Social De-

---

18  Quoted in David Floyd, *Rumania: Russia's Dissident Ally* (New York: Praeger, 1965), p. ix.

velopment, the President of the Defense Council, Supreme Commander of the Romanian Armed Forces, and Secretary General of the Romanian Communist Party. Therefore, he occupied all of the important posts in the country and coupled with the incredibly extensive and intensive personality cult he promoted, he made the phrase *l'état c'est moi,* quite valid in Romania.[19]

Although his personal power was thus secure in internal affairs, Ceauşescu walked a tightrope in the international arena. In addition to the new ties with the African and Asian nations, the Romanian government made great efforts to improve relations with the West European states, especially with the traditional friend, France. In January 1967 formal diplomatic relations were established with West Germany, a move that was important for Romanian foreign trade. Great care had to be taken in the treatment of the Soviet Union, even though Romania opposed certain of its policies. Soviet military predominance was overwhelming. Despite the Comecon disputes, the largest percentage of Romanian trade was with the socialist bloc. The Soviet Union was still the major single trading partner and the source of essential raw materials, particularly iron ore, whose loss would have disastrous repercussions for the industrial economy. Moreover, like Bulgaria, Romania had few alternatives in international relations; no other great power would assist the state. The United States, in spite of its previous moves to aid Tito, was obviously not about to challenge the Soviet Union for Romanian interests. The Chinese made it perfectly clear that they could not offer military assistance to their friends in Eastern Europe.

In resisting economic integration the Romanian government had opposed policies endorsed in particular by Khrushchev. His fall from power in 1964, however, brought no basic change in the relationship between the two countries. In addition to the economic and military differences, another issue had arisen. The Romanian government, backed by public opinion, had never recognized the justice of the cession of Bessarabia, the majority of whose population was, after all, Romanian. There was no similar resentment about the surrender of northern Bukovina, which did have a predominantly Ukrainian population. Although it was quite apparent that the Soviet Union would never willingly return the territory, the question did become an issue in international politics. In 1964 Mao in a press interview mentioned the region as one of the territories unjustly seized by the Russians in the past. The entire problem was made much more complicated by the Soviet stand. Under government encouragement, some historians and writers in the Moldavian Soviet Republic, most of whom had a Slavic and not a Romanian background, began to assert the existence of a unique Moldavian nationality with a lan-

19  Aurel Braun, *Romanian Foreign Policy since 1965: The Political and Military Limits of Autonomy* (New York: Praeger, 1978), pp. 200–201.

guage and a history distinct from that of Romania. Not only did this effort involve some very strange interpretations of past history, but the implications were dangerous: if the Moldavians were indeed a separate nationality, then the fate of Romanian Moldavia could be brought into question. Again the territorial integrity of the state could be under attack. Although in 1965, during a visit to Moscow, Ceauşescu formally recognized the Romanian boundary with the Soviet Union, the Moldavian question remained a source of controversy.

Meanwhile, the old disputes over Transylvania continued. Here the issues remained the status of the Hungarians in Romania and the effect of this question on relations between Bucharest and Budapest. Although the Romanian government did attempt to promote Hungarian cultural activity and to appoint Hungarians to posts in proportion to their numerical strength in the country, many aspects of this nationality problem were handled in a manner that caused much resentment. Despite many fine statements about the equality of all its citizens, the fact remained that the Romanian officials simply did not trust this segment of the population, whose national ties were obviously still with the Hungarian state. In 1968, after a major administrative reorganization of the country, the autonomous area was abolished altogether and replaced by three ordinary counties. Although Hungarian-language books, newspapers, and radio and television programs produced in Romania were made available, publications from Hungary were not imported. The exchange of visits across the border was discouraged, and cultural exchanges were few in number. The problem was compounded by the fact that living standards were higher in Hungary, a condition that added to the attraction of this state for the Romanian Hungarians. The question of the German population has not caused similar controversies. Although its members had difficulty emigrating, many in fact did. Their grievances did not receive firm support in either of the two German states.

A major shock to Romanian–Soviet relations came with the invasion of Czechoslovakia in 1968. Since such an intervention in the internal affairs of a bloc state was exactly what the Romanian leaders feared most, they joined with the Yugoslavs in a strong denunciation of the action. Both states made clear their determination to resist any threat to their own countries, and troops were mobilized. Romania could not accept the implications of the Brezhnev Doctrine. Relations with Moscow, however, subsequently improved, and in July 1970 Romania signed a new treaty of friendship and mutual aid. Its text went far in its concessions toward the Romanian position on military autonomy and noninterference in internal affairs.

Throughout the 1970s a balance was maintained in Soviet–Romanian relations. Despite the points of friction that remained, no major crisis occurred. Although the Romanian attitude caused annoyances, the Soviet government could afford to remain calm. It had, after all, complete military control of the situation. Moreover, at no time did the Romanian government challenge the

Communist system. Ceauşescu and his supporters were loyal members of a Soviet-style party; never liberalizing, they maintained a firm control over their country. As long as they were in power, there was little likelihood that Romania would follow a path of real internal reform or emulate Yugoslav examples.

### Albania

The most doctrinaire and rigid regime was to be established in the smallest and poorest of the socialist states. By the end of the 1970s the Albanian government was still rigorously Stalinist in spirit and firmly convinced of the validity of the principles of the cold war in international relations. In 1948, it will be remembered, the country shifted from a close alignment with Belgrade to a similar dependency on the Soviet Union. The support of this great power lessened only slightly the government's fears for its political survival and its ability to defend the territorial integrity of the state. The old dangers were still present. The former Greek claims to southern Albania remained alive; it could also be expected that the Yugoslav government would back any serious attempt to overthrow Hoxha. In addition, the British and American secret services joined in a complicated plot to overthrow the regime.[20] During the war, as we have seen, the British had been active in organizing the resistance forces in the area; they thus had experience with Balkan guerilla operations. After 1946 plans were developed to encourage and equip anti-Communist and royalist forces within Albania. It was hoped that a revolt could be instigated that would spread to other countries within the Soviet bloc. There was no difficulty in finding volunteers for such activities in the refugee camps and in emigré circles. In 1947 some of these were trained and sent into Albania.

In 1949 the operation became more serious, and the CIA became deeply involved. The Balkans now seemed open to Western influence. The Greek civil war was almost over, and Tito had broken with Stalin. Albania, although in the Soviet camp, was isolated. The British and U.S. secret services worked with King Zog, and they used members of his guard. Albanian refugees in Italy, Egypt, and Greece were recruited and then trained in Cyprus. The first of this group was sent into Albania in 1950, the last in spring 1952. All of the efforts met with disaster: the guerillas were either killed or captured. The Albanian army and police seemed to be expecting them, as indeed they were. The major defect in this entire conspiracy was that all of the plans were known to H. A. R. (Kim) Philby, a British double agent. Employed in the British secret service, he was sent in 1949 as a liaison officer to the CIA. In Washington he played a major role in organizing the Albanian adventure, and he

---

20 Bruce Page, David Leitch, and Phillip Knightley, *The Philby Conspiracy* (Garden City: Doubleday, 1968), pp. 196–203.

transmitted the information to Moscow. About three hundred people were killed in the operation. This fiasco discredited any further ideas in Britain or the United States about fomenting anti-Communist uprisings. These activities, of course, also had a profound effect on the Albanian government, which blamed not only the British and Americans, but also the Greek, Yugoslav, and Italian secret services. Although the attempts at outside interference were blocked, it can be understood why the Albanian leaders thereafter kept a defensive attitude and were convinced that they were "building socialism under conditions of a fierce encirclement by imperialist and revisionist enemies."[21]

Despite its many unique features, the Albanian government was one of the most stable in the postwar years. From 1956 to 1971 only one member of the Politburo, Kiri Belishova, and five members of the Central Committee were removed for political reasons.[22] Enver Hoxha maintained a firm hold on the state. Born in 1908, Hoxha came from a middle-class Muslim family. He was unusual among the East European Communist leaders because of the high level of his education and his extensive experience in Western Europe, particularly in France, where he lived from 1930 to 1936. Thereafter, he returned to Albania and became a French teacher in a secondary school. At the same time he was active in the Communist Party, and he later joined the partisan movement. As we have seen, he became premier in the government organized in 1944. He worked closely with Mehmet Shehu, who had a similar wide European experience. Born in 1913 in a Muslim family, Shehu had attended an American school in Tirana and later an Italian military college. Expelled from the latter for his Communist activities, he went back to Albania and entered an officers' school there. He then participated in the Spanish civil war. After a period in a French internment camp and in Italy, he returned to Albania during the war to become a leader in the resistance. In 1945–1946 he attended a military academy in Moscow.

Primarily of middle-class Tosk background, the Albanian ruling circles were not only tightly unified, but well known for their prevailing nepotism. In February 1962, at a time when Soviet relations with Albania were particularly bad, the Moscow radio described the network of relationships: only a part of the list is quoted here:

> Half, or more, of the 53 members of the Central Committee of the Albanian Party of Labor are related. First, we have four couples: Enver Hoxha and his wife Nexhmije Hoxha; Mehmet Shehu and his wife Fiqrete Shehu; Hysni Kapo and his wife Vito Kapo; and Josif

21 Quoted in Peter R. Prifti, *Socialist Albania since 1944: Domestic and Foreign Developments* (Cambridge, Mass.: MIT Press, 1978), p. 42.
22 Nicholas C. Pano, "Albania," in Rakowska-Harmstone and Gyorgy, *Communism in Eastern Europe*, p. 202.

Pashko with his wife Eleni Terezi. The wives of Manush Myftiu, Politburo member, and of Pilo Peristeri, candidate-member of the Politburo, are sisters. Kadri Hasbiu, candidate-member of the Politburo and Minister of Internal Affairs, is the husband of Mehmet Shehu's sister. The brother of Hysni Kopo's wife is Piro Kondi, also a member of the Central Committee.[23]

In addition to the dangers from the neighboring states, this Albanian regime faced perhaps the most difficult internal situation of any of the socialist states because of the backward conditions and the low standard of living. Nevertheless, the Communist leadership attempted to deal with this situation by adopting the familiar Stalinist methods. A highly centralized planned economy was introduced, with an emphasis on independence in heavy industry. Collectivization was considered the answer to the agricultural problems. In December 1944 the state took control of industry, banking, and transportation. The first economic plan, introduced in 1947, had a nine-month duration; the second covered the two years 1949 and 1950. During this period immense difficulties were caused by the break with Yugoslavia and the withdrawal of its economic aid. Soviet assistance, however, soon arrived. The first five-year plan commenced in 1951.

Albanian economic development was aided by the fact that, despite its extreme poverty, the country did have a rich store of certain minerals. After 1950 an emphasis was placed on the exploitation of the chrome, copper, nickel, oil, and coal resources, as well as on industrial growth. Attention was also given to light industry and food processing. Like the other socialist states, the Albanian government proceeded with an ambitious electrification program.

Agriculture had always been an Albanian weakness. With only 10 percent of the land suitable for the growing of crops, and another 31 percent adequate for pastureland, the major problem was the production of enough food to feed the population. Moreover, the richest farmland lay on the coast, an area characterized by the prevalence of marshes and malaria. Despite its doctrinaire character, the government at first proceeded slowly toward the ultimate goal of full collectivization. In August 1945 the large estates were confiscated, an action that ended the economic power of the previously predominant class. In 1955 about 87 percent of agricultural production still came from private lands. Collectivization was then accelerated until by 1960 87 percent of the produce came from the collectives or the state enterprises.[24] Here as elsewhere the process was very unpopular with the peasantry.

In its agricultural policy the government made a great effort to increase food supplies. This move was particularly necessary because Albania had the

23  William E. Griffith, *Albania and the Sino-Soviet Rift* (Cambridge, Mass.: MIT Press, 1963), pp. 319–320.
24  Prifti, *Socialist Albania since 1944*, pp. 65, 66.

highest birthrate in Europe. The successive five-year plans put an emphasis on mechanization and the introduction of modern improvements such as the use of fertilizers and insecticides. By 1976 it was claimed that the country was self-sufficient in grains; a target date of 1980 was set for other foodstuffs.

After the break with Yugoslavia in 1948, Albania was closely aligned with the Soviet Union. Although there were complaints about the Soviet failure to lend sufficient support to plans for industrialization, relations remained very good while Stalin was alive. The political systems were similar, and there was genuine admiration for the Soviet leader among the Albanian Communists. After 1953 there was pressure in Tirana, as in the other socialist capitals, to copy the new revisionist trends. Some moves were indeed made in the direction of establishing a collective leadership. Hoxha surrendered the Foreign and Defense ministries, but at first he retained his posts as premier and party secretary. In 1954 he gave the premiership to Shehu. Thus, despite some disagreements, Albania remained close to Moscow and the socialist bloc. In 1955 the state was one of the founding members of the Warsaw Treaty Organization. The country had not before been part of any military alliance system; this pact gave it some security.

Many aspects of Khrushchev's program, however, clashed sharply with Hoxha's policies. The Albanian leadership particularly disliked the decisions of the Soviet twentieth party congress. Little enthusiasm was shown for such concepts as peaceful coexistence and different roads to socialism. Considering Yugoslavia a continuing threat, the Albanian government had scant sympathy with Khrushchev's efforts to secure a reconciliation with Tito. Despite the Soviet desire, it refused to rehabilitate Koci Xoxe, who had been executed in 1949 for leading the pro-Yugoslav faction, as a gesture of goodwill to Belgrade, although some improvements in the relations of the two nations were indeed made. As could be expected, the Soviet suppression of the Hungarian revolution was greeted with favor; the events in Hungary were seen as the logical outcome of Tito's revisionist ideas. Once again relations with Yugoslavia declined, and recriminations about conditions in Kosovo were again exchanged. This problem, which is discussed in the next section, remained a constant subject of controversy between the states.

In addition to the general discontent felt with Khrushchev's policies, the Albanian government, like the Romanian, did not approve of plans for Comecon integration. Like the other Balkan states, Albania was to be a source of agricultural products and raw materials. The Albanians too did not want to be suppliers of grapefruit and similar items, while the more fortunate nations built cars and airplanes. Moreover, by 1960 Albania had discovered an alternate ally, and the country did not need to follow Soviet directions.

The increasingly important role played by China in Communist affairs and its growing rivalry with the Soviet Union have already been discussed. Many of the Chinese arguments were received with great sympathy by the Albanian Communists. They had never lost their feeling of admiration for Stalin, and they were extremely critical of the policy of coexistence. China and Albania shared a dislike of Tito and his revisionist stand. By 1960 relations with Moscow were also deteriorating. In addition to the disagreements over foreign policy and doctrine, there was also friction in economic matters. The differences first became public in June 1960 at a party meeting held in Bucharest, where in an open clash between the Chinese and the Soviet representatives the Albanians supported China. Soviet reprisals followed at once; much-needed grain shipments were halted. In addition, Soviet support was given to the formation of an anti-Hoxha conspiracy led by Kiri Belishova and Koco Tashko. Hoxha, in control of the army and the security forces, had no difficulty in dealing with this challenge. China also responded immediately and provided wheat shipments to replace those cut off by the Soviet action.

In November 1960, when representatives of eighty-one Communist parties met in Moscow, the Chinese–Soviet conflict was the center of attention. The Chinese delegates directly attacked the Soviet position of leadership in the socialist camp, declaring that there could be no superior or inferior Communist parties. In this debate the Albanians once again sided with China. In the meetings the two great Communist powers conducted their battles through proxies. The Soviet representatives leveled their criticisms at the Albanians, although they really meant the Chinese. The latter replied by denouncing the Yugoslavs in words intended for Moscow. The continued Chinese enmity toward Tito was based primarily on Yugoslav internal policy, which by this time had deviated strongly from the Stalinist pattern still espoused by Mao.

After this conference, diplomatic relations between Albania and the Soviet bloc deteriorated rapidly. In December 1961 the Soviet Union formally broke relations with Albania, a step that was not, however, taken by the other bloc states. Nevertheless, by this time Albania could not count on aid from the Soviet Union or its supporters in the socialist camp. The consequences were very serious for the Albanian economy. Not only were the Soviet advisers withdrawn, but deliveries of supplies from the Soviet Union, including spare parts for the equipment already received, were halted. Although Chinese assistance was promised, it was obvious that it could not arrive at once. Nevertheless, the Albanians remained firm. Moreover, the Chinese did honor their assurances: they provided credits and other assistance that covered about 90 percent of what Albania had expected to receive from the Soviet bloc. Most important was the delivery of 430,200 tons of wheat and corn during the critical period from 1960 to 1963. There were also some advantages to Chinese aid. The loans, which totaled $500 million between 1954 and 1975, were granted on a more favorable basis than those from the Soviet Union.[25] The Chinese technicians received the same pay as the Albanians and lived in similar conditions. In late December 1963 Zhou Enlai and a delegation arrived for a ten-day visit to the country. Meanwhile, Albanian relations with the East Euro-

---

25  Prifti, *Socialist Albania since 1944*, pp. 80–82.

pean socialist countries remained very bad. The bloc representatives were summoned home, and Albania did not participate in further Warsaw Pact or Comecon activities. The fall of Khrushchev in 1964 did not alter this tense situation. In 1968, after the invasion of Czechoslovakia, Albania officially withdrew from the Warsaw Pact.

Just as the Albanian party had previously followed Yugoslav and Soviet examples, it now copied the Chinese. As we have seen, from 1965 to 1969 China went through the period of the Cultural Revolution. Albania had a similar movement, but it was quite different in certain respects. Hoxha was in complete control of his party, and there was no need to mobilize the youth or the army. Nevertheless, the opportunity was used to try to drum up more enthusiasm for the system and to arouse more revolutionary ardor among the young. Renewed attacks were directed against religion, as well as against backwardness and superstition. As in China, programs were developed in which students worked part time in addition to their studies.

By 1970 relations between Albania and China had begun to decline. There had been obvious difficulties from the beginning. The Chinese leadership was realistic; it had indicated clearly that socialist states, including Albania, Romania, and Yugoslavia, could not expect military assistance in their defiance of the Soviet Union. In economic matters too China could not be the equivalent of the Comecon powers. A poor country itself, it could not supply goods of a sufficient amount or quality without a real sacrifice. Also, by this time China had less need for Albania. The alignment had given the Chinese government a foothold in Europe and a stage from which to present its views; but as China emerged from isolation and increased its relations with other states, its leaders were bound to reassess their Albanian commitments. In 1970 China resumed relations with Yugoslavia, a step that Albania took in the next year. Even more significant was the commencement of the negotiations with the United States that led to the visit of President Nixon to China in 1972, an event that Tirana strongly disliked. By this time Albania, too had begun to widen its contacts with the outside world. Trade and diplomatic negotiations were carried on with, for example, France, Italy, Greece, and the new states of Asia and Africa.

Albanian–Chinese relations were also affected by the deaths in 1976 of Mao and Zhou Enlai. Their successors were to follow quite different paths in foreign policy and to seek to broaden Chinese links with the capitalist world. Although the Albanian government had widened its horizons as well, its ideological outlook was still comparatively inflexible. In its eyes the Soviet Union and the United States were still the primary enemies; it wished no close relations with "revisionist" and "imperialist" states. The leaders were bound to feel betrayed when China established relations with the United States and renewed ties with Yugoslavia. Relations between Tirana and Peking became increasingly strained until, in July 1978, the Chinese ended their programs of assistance.

It can thus be seen that, of all the socialist states, Albania made the fewest changes in doctrine. Stalin was still a hero. The party paper, *Zëri i Popullit* (Voice of the People), in November 1961 praised the Soviet dictator in these words: "J. V. Stalin was and remains a titanic figure in the history of mankind, in the history of the international Communist and workers movement, and in the struggle for the liberation of the peoples from imperialist subjugation . . . Current history knows J. V. Stalin as an indomitable revolutionary, a great theoretician, and a brilliant organizer."[26] This attitude was to remain constant. In internal policy Hoxha continued to support Stalinist concepts. There was no relaxation in cultural matters, and the country with few exceptions was closed to the outside world. Although relations were established with France and Italy, Albania was the only European socialist country that did not have regular diplomatic links with Britain and the United States. This intransigent leadership did, however, bring about significant changes in national life.

### THE YUGOSLAV VARIANT

As we have seen, from 1945 the Yugoslav Communist leadership enjoyed a much more favorable position than those of other parties. Since the Partisans were in control of the country, there was no need of a transition period before full political power could be obtained and a Communist program for internal development introduced. As a victorious state, Yugoslavia, unlike Romania and Bulgaria, did not have to negotiate a peace treaty or pay reparations. No foreign army was in occupation, and the Soviet Union did not have the opportunity to remove large quantities of industrial goods as it did in other areas. The country had, however, suffered enormous wartime devastation, and the first task of the government was to repair this damage. From 1945 to 1949 the state followed closely the Stalinist models that we have seen introduced elsewhere. Again the emphasis was placed on the development of large industries and on electrification projects. Until his death in 1953 Boris Kidrić was in charge of central planning. Unlike their counterparts in the Soviet Union and the other socialist states, the Yugoslav planners had to take national and regional problems into consideration. New industries were thus placed in backward areas, such as Bosnia-Hercegovina, Macedonia, and Montenegro, which had been, incidentally, the center of previous Partisan activity. Although the intention was to equalize the economic conditions in the Yugoslav republics, these "political factories" were to cause many difficulties later.

The nationalization policy met with few initial major obstacles. The German occupation authorities had taken control of most of the Yugoslav indus-

---

26  Griffith, *Albania and the Sino-Soviet Rift*, p. 240.

tries, mines, and banks, as well as the transportation and communications network. Many of the remaining private owners could be accused of collaboration either with the Axis or with Mihailović, or simply of being "class enemies." By the middle of 1947 most of Yugoslav industry and the retail trade, as well as all transport, were under government control.

Collectivization was to prove to be more difficult. At first, radical measures were restricted to the confiscation of large holdings and of farms formerly belonging to ethnic Germans and others who had worked with the Axis authorities. Nevertheless, despite its social base in the peasantry, the Yugoslav Communist leadership was at the outset extremely doctrinaire on agricultural questions. Collectives were seen as the best means of raising production and of improving life in the countryside. In January 1949, six months after the commencement of the quarrel with the Soviet Union, the government began a policy of forced collectivization, partly to meet Soviet doctrinal criticisms. As elsewhere, the peasants resisted violently. They killed their livestock, and they evaded deliveries of produce. The situation was made worse by the severe droughts that devastated the country in 1950 and 1952. In 1950 agricultural production dropped to 73 percent of the prewar level, with grain deliveries falling to 43 percent.[27] The Yugoslav government did not have the means to make the collectives function as intended; they could not invest enough in them or supply the mechanized equipment and modern technology they required. The resistance and violence of the peasants were difficult for the regime to handle, since most of the party members were from this class.

The Yugoslav government was at this time under the control of a small group consisting of Tito and the members of the Politburo, called at this time the Presidium. In addition to Djilas, Ranković, Kardelj, and Kidrić, who have already been mentioned, there were at the head of the government also Moša Pijade for legal affairs, Franc Leskošek for heavy industry, General Ivan Gošnjak for the army, and Blagoje Nešković, who was chairman of the State Control Commission.

Tito retained his overwhelmingly predominant position. Born in May 1892 in Kumrovec, Croatia, he was the seventh in a family of fifteen children. His father was Croatian, his mother Slovene. He attended the village school and was then apprenticed to a locksmith. He worked subsequently as a mechanic in Croatia, Austria, and Germany. In World War I he became a noncommissioned officer in the Austro-Hungarian army. Severely wounded, he was taken prisoner by the Russians in 1915, and he remained in that country during the revolutionary period until 1920. He then returned to Yugoslavia, where he was active in Communist Party affairs and served a term in prison from 1928 to 1934. Thereafter he spent periods in the Soviet Union and in other Euro-

27  Dennison Rusinow, *The Yugoslav Experiment, 1948–1974* (Berkeley: University of California Press, 1977), p. 36.

pean countries working for the Comintern. After his appointment in January 1939 as general secretary of the party, he returned to Yugoslavia. His career during the war has been recounted previously.

Of Tito's close associates, Kardelj, Djilas, and Kidrić were most concerned with questions of doctrine. The break with the Soviet Union was particularly difficult for convinced Communists. Feeling that they must justify their actions on an ideological basis, the party leaders sought to demonstrate that their policies represented true Marxist thinking and that it was the Soviet position which was out of line. They thus restudied the Marxist texts to find a justification for their criticisms. Their attacks centered on obvious flaws in the Soviet system, in particular the extreme centralization of government, the size and influence of the bureaucracy, and the nature of the relationship with the bloc states. The charge was made that the Soviet government was in fact a form of state capitalism rather than socialism: the state was not withering away, but growing ever stronger; the bureaucracy was exploiting its position, and a great gulf had come into existence between it and the people. Moreover, in its attitude to other nations, the Soviet Union was imperialistic. It used other states as sources of raw materials and markets, and it made profits from the dependent areas.

Having thus denounced the Soviet government in its most sensitive areas – its centralized system and its relationship with the states under its influence – the Yugoslav theorists proceeded to present ideas of their own. As far as the other Communist bloc states were concerned, the most important concept was that of the necessity of separate roads to socialism. It was argued that, since material conditions differed among the East European states, it was logical that each should develop according to local needs its own institutions and strategies to attain the common goal. Thus Yugoslavia attacked the Stalinist model of economic and political development.

The Yugoslav theoreticians also offered alternative ideas on the organization of state life. Since they had principally denounced the centralization and bureaucratization of Soviet socialism, they were naturally led toward decentralization and a return of political control to the "people." The implications of their theories involved the entire field of government and party organization, but the most immediate effect was on the economic system. In June 1950 the National Assembly passed the law on the Management of State Economic Enterprises and Higher Economic Associations by the Work Collectives, a measure that one authority has called the "most famous legislative act of the postwar era in Yugoslavia."[28] Based on the principle of "workers' self-management," the new system in theory took away from the state the ownership of the means of production, which were declared "social property." The workers were now considered trustees for the management of the individual enterprises. The producers were thus to control their product. In each

---

28  Rusinow, *The Yugoslav Experiment*, pp. 57–58.

factory the workers were expected to exercise their influence through councils, consisting of from fifteen to two hundred representatives, depending on the size of the enterprise, who would be elected by secret ballot. The council in turn would choose a managing board. The most important single position was that of director. Named by the workers' council in consultation with the trade union and administrative officials of the locality, he was responsible to the community as well as to his individual enterprise. The Yugoslav party has been extremely proud of this new concept, which is described as a higher form of socialism, a return to Leninism, and a corrective to Stalinist deviations.[29]

At first, the councils did not function as the theory implied. In 1950 economic conditions were still very difficult. The Cominform blockade was in effect, and the drought had reduced agricultural production. Moreover, the system had obvious drawbacks. Since the majority of the workers in the factories were illiterate peasants or workers with a low level of education, they often could not understand the complicated technological and financial aspects of a large enterprise. They thus tended to approve whatever the management put before them. Where they exerted influence, it was usually to raise wages, even when such an action could not be justified. Moreover, in practice the workers' councils proved to have relatively little power. The real control lay in the hands of the managers, who were usually close to the local party or were in fact its appointees.

The establishment of workers' councils was, of course, in direct contradiction to the principle of central planning. Many major decisions in theory were now to be made on a lower level. Central plans were still to be formulated, but they were to serve as general guides rather than as programs whose stipulations had to be fulfilled. The contradiction between the existence of a central planning mechanism and the theoretical local control was never satisfactorily resolved. In addition, the Yugoslav system started to move slowly toward a market economy. As we have seen, enterprises had not previously had to show profits: if they lost money, they would be subsidized by the state. This situation changed in the 1960s, when subsidies were cut off. Under the new system an industry was expected to make money; at least a percentage of a worker's wage was to be determined by the profit the factory earned.

After 1951 changes were also made in the policy of forced collectivization. Peasant opposition had become too strong to resist. In March 1953 measures were passed to allow the peasants to leave the collectives and take with them what they had brought in originally, as long as it did not exceed 24.7 acres (10 hectares). Thereafter the collectives dissolved rapidly. By 1957 the socialist sector of the total arable land had declined to 9 percent from a height of 25 percent in 1952.[30] However, at the same time a law was passed that called for

29  Rusinow, *The Yugoslav Experiment*, p. 58.
30  Rusinow, *The Yugoslav Experiment*, p. 78.

the limitation of private holdings to 24.7 acres. Yugoslavia thus continued to remain a country of small farms, with all the disadvantages attendant on that condition.

The emphasis on decentralization naturally had an effect on party and government organization. In 1952 the Communist Party changed its name to the League of Communists of Yugoslavia. Henceforth the party was in theory to have as its main task the political education of the population and the formulation of general programs. Communists were expected to exert influence primarily as citizens and individuals, and local organizations were given more authority within the party structure.

Changes were also made in the administration of the state to conform to the new direction. Most important, the republics received increased power. More authority was also given to the communes, the basic administrative unit of local government. Here, as in the economic and party reorganization, the stated objective was to establish a type of socialist direct democracy and to involve the population in the making of the decisions that would affect their lives. Individual influence was to be exercised by the participation of the citizen in workers' councils, in local government, and in the party and Communist-controlled mass organizations. Although many of the new schemes did not function as intended, and although Communist Party control remained effective, these experiments had much to commend them. Certainly in the next years the Yugoslav system showed much more flexibility and freedom than the governments in the other socialist countries. Moreover, despite the attention paid to doctrine, the Yugoslav leaders were concerned with adopting institutions that worked in practice, and they were thus willing to modify or discard practices that proved unsuccessful, no matter what their ideological basis.

One obvious result of the Yugoslav reforms was the freer cultural atmosphere that emerged. In contrast to the neighboring socialist governments, the Yugoslav did not attempt to enforce rigid standards in art and literature as long as certain boundaries were not overstepped. A similar attitude was shown toward religion; relations between the state authorities and all of the religious institutions became much better. Similar improvements were seen in the law courts and the system of justice. Henceforth there was a concern for legality, except in cases involving challenges to the party control of the state or suspected external subversion.

The limits on political freedom were soon to become apparent. In October 1953 Djilas commenced the publication of a series of articles in the party paper, *Borba* (Struggle), in which he criticized the party and the government and called for less bureaucracy and more democracy. At first his commentaries were well received as an example of self-criticism on the highest Communist level. Soon, however, his attacks became more pointed and centered on the party itself. In fact, he appeared to be arguing for its disbanding. For instance, he wrote:

The League of Communists would change from the old Party into a real and vital union of ideologically united men . . . The present League of Communists would "weaken," "wither way" as a classical party . . . [It] would gradually take on the character of a strong, ideological, widely-diffused nucleus, but would lose its party character. It would merge with the Socialist Alliance, and the communists would merge with ordinary citizens.[31]

Djilas also criticized the soft life of the Communist leaders. Like their colleagues in other countries, the former revolutionaries had indeed rewarded themselves for their sacrifices. With good housing, special shops, and vacation retreats, they enjoyed far better conditions than the average citizen despite the egalitarian socialist ideals, and many abused their positions of power. Any criticisms on this basis were bound to arouse a violent reaction from the group against whom the attacks were leveled.

In January 1954 the Djilas question was considered by the Central Committee of the League of Communists. Although Djilas was one of Tito's closest comrades from Partisan days, that did not stop the Yugoslav leader from condemning these heresies. At this meeting Tito addressed himself directly to the question of the reduction of party influence:

I was the first to speak of the withering away of the Party, the withering away of the League. However I did not say that that ought to happen within six months or a year or two, but that it would be a long process. Until the last class enemy has been rendered incapable of action, until socialist consciousness has penetrated all layers of our citizenry, there can be no question of the withering away of the League of Communists or of its liquidation.[32]

Djilas was subsequently expelled from the Central Committee; he then resigned from the party. Despite this judgment, he continued to write in a critical tone. His works were published widely in Europe and the United States, where his best-known books were *The New Class* (1957) and *Conversations with Stalin* (1962), a book that has been quoted extensively in this volume. Djilas was to spend the next years in and out of prison.

The death of Stalin and Khrushchev's subsequent attempts to end the tension between the two governments have been noted previously. The height of the Soviet policy of rapprochement was reached in May 1955, when the Soviet leader visited Belgrade. At the airport he read a statement in which he in effect accepted the Yugoslav position on separate roads to socialism. A document on the mutual relations of the two states, issued in June, stated the

31  Quoted in Rusinow, *The Yugoslav Experiment*, p. 84.
32  Quoted in Rusinow, *The Yugoslav Experiment*, pp. 85–86.

principles that both would observe: "mutual respect and noninterference in one another's internal affairs for whatever reason, whether of an economic, political, or ideological nature, inasmuch as questions of internal organization, difference of social systems, and difference in the concrete forms of socialist development are exclusively the concern of the peoples of the respective countries."[33] This formal reconciliation was thus based in theory on a mutual recognition of the equality of socialist nations, on peaceful coexistence, and on noninterference in one another's internal affairs. Despite the reestablishment of amicable relations with Moscow, the Yugoslav government did not join the socialist alignment in either military or economic affairs. Although it was later to have an observer status in Comecon, it did not sign the Warsaw Pact. The rest of the bloc followed the Soviet example in restoring relations with Belgrade, but there was resentment over the policy, particularly among those who had most vigorously supported Stalin's denunciations of the Yugoslav deviation. It appeared that Tito was being rewarded for his independent attitude, whereas those who had remained loyal were being discredited.

Despite the improvement in relations with the other socialist states, the Yugoslav government did not wish to join the Soviet alignment any more than it wanted to be a part of NATO. It therefore attempted to follow a policy of neutrality or nonalignment in foreign affairs. Tito worked with Nehru of India, Sukarno of Indonesia, and Nasser of Egypt to try to form some sort of "third world" force that could serve as a counterweight to the American and Soviet blocs. In recognition of Yugoslavia's role, the first summit meeting of the heads of state of the nonaligned movement was held in Belgrade in 1961, with Tito as host. Special efforts were made to establish close ties with the new Asian and African nations. A limited amount of economic aid was sent to some of these countries, and students were brought to study in Yugoslavia's universities and technical schools.

Khrushchev's secret speech of February 1956 contained a further justification of Tito's position. In his address Khrushchev made specific reference to the previous break as an example of Stalin's willfulness and incompetent diplomacy:

> It was a shameful role which Stalin played here. The "Yugoslavia affair" contained no problems which could not have been solved through party discussions among comrades. There was no significant basis for the development of the "affair"; it was completely possible to have prevented the rupture of relations with that country. This does not mean, however, that the Yugoslav leaders did not make mistakes or did not have shortcomings. But these mistakes and

---

33  Quoted in Paul E. Zinner, ed., *National Communism and Popular Revolt in Eastern Europe* (New York: Columbia University Press, 1956), p. 6.

shortcomings were magnified in a monstrous manner by Stalin, which resulted in a break of relations with a friendly country.[34]

In April the Cominform was dissolved. In June, when Tito visited Moscow to return Khrushchev's visit of May 1955, party relations between the two countries were also reestablished. However, no sooner did it seem that the former Stalinist policies of intimidation and intervention had been abandoned than the reform movements in Poland and Hungary caused a major crisis in bloc relations. At first Tito supported the moderate reform measures in both countries, but his attitude changed sharply when it appeared that Hungary would proceed to a multiparty system and other radical changes. In November, after the Soviet intervention, Tito gave a speech at Pula, in which he blamed the original causes of the Hungarian revolt on Stalinist policies, but gave a surprisingly strong defense of the Soviet crushing of the movement:

> It is clear, and we have said so and will continue to say it, that we are against interference and the use of foreign armed forces. Which was now the lesser evil? There could be either chaos, civil war, counterrevolution, and a new world war, or the intervention of Soviet troops which were there. The former would be a catastrophe and the latter a mistake. And, of course, if it meant saving socialism in Hungary, then, comrades, we can say, although we are against interference, Soviet intervention was necessary . . . the intervention of Soviet troops was also bad, but if it leads to the preservation of socialism in Hungary, that is, to the further building up of socialism in that country, and to peace in the world, then one day this will become a positive thing, provided that the Soviet troops withdraw the moment the situation in that country is settled and quiet.[35]

Despite these words of support, Yugoslav relations with the bloc again deteriorated. Although nothing equivalent to the dramatic events of the 1940s occurred, renewed friction arose. The party program adopted by the seventh congress of the League of Communists in 1958, which called for a further liberalization, met with criticism and distrust in the other socialist states. Relations with the West remained much as before. In 1957 the major American military assistance ended, but economic aid continued.

The rise of Chinese influence in Communist world circles was to have particularly strong repercussions for Yugoslavia. After 1958 the Chinese leaders regarded Tito as the major heretic and the cause of many of the problems

---

34  Quoted in Dan N. Jacobs, ed., *The New Communist Manifesto and Related Documents* (New York: Harper Torchbooks, 1965), pp. 150–151.
35  Quoted in Zinner, *National Communism and Popular Revolt*, p. 529.

in the Communist camp. They thus leveled their strongest attacks against Belgrade. The shift of Albania to the Chinese camp meant, of course, that relations between that state and Yugoslavia again worsened. By the time Khrushchev was removed from office in 1964, not only Yugoslavia but also Albania and China had assumed an openly independent attitude toward Moscow, and Romania had also resisted Soviet attempts to tighten its control. At the beginning of the 1960s the Yugoslav position was thus in general favorable as far as foreign relations were concerned. There was no longer a single Communist camp; Albania, China, and to a lesser extent, Romania had each asserted an independent policy. Yugoslavia had satisfactory relations with the Western nations, the Afro-Asian states, and most of the Communist bloc. Despite the hostile attitude of Albania and China, neither of these states was a real threat. With no serious outside pressures, attention could be turned to internal affairs.

Throughout the 1950s the general trend, not without opposition, had been toward liberalization in economic affairs. The 1960s were to be characterized by a more intense and constant struggle between the liberal and the conservative viewpoints. The liberals wished to continue even further in the same direction: they wanted to allow the individual enterprises more control over their earnings, to close factories that failed to show a profit, to base prices on supply and demand, and to adopt other measures more common to a market than to a centrally planned socialist economy. At the same time, they argued that increased attention should be paid to the production of consumer goods and to raising living standards. In party and government affairs they stood for further decentralization and more civil liberties. In contrast, the conservatives wanted to maintain party authority and central control of the economy. They were also deeply concerned about some aspects of the reforms. One of the original intentions of the Communist program had been to develop the backward regions; the political factories had been built for this purpose. Yet it was exactly these enterprises, often set up on a weak economic base, that were failing to meet the test of profitability. In fact, under the new system the rich republics were becoming richer and the poor relatively poorer. In the same manner, if factories that did not show favorable financial returns were to close and if wages were to be based on the earning power of an enterprise, then greater variations in average income among the republics, as well as widespread unemployment, might result – evils that were supposed to be confined to the capitalist states. The conservatives thus emphasized general social goals and the assurance of equality among the Yugoslav citizens of the different republics. Many problems had already arisen. Despite the efforts made, the economic situation in the backward areas did not show relative improvement. The rise of unemployment resulted in the emigration to Western Europe of a large and increasing number of young, able-bodied workers, until by 1973 over a million Yugoslavs and their dependents were working abroad. In 1975, for every hundred workers employed in Yugoslavia, twenty worked outside the country. Yugoslavia was the only Communist country, it should be noted, that permitted worker emigration.

Despite the many problems, the political power remained with the reformers. In 1965 new laws eliminated state control over most investments, and changes were made that limited special aid to backward regions. Measures were also passed to aid the independent small farmer. At this time 2.6 million peasants held 88 percent of the arable land and 91 percent of the livestock; they accounted for 76 percent of the agricultural production.[36] As in the other Communist states, the agrarian sector of the economy lagged behind the industrial. Whether the lands were collectivized or not, the socialist governments did not devote as much attention to agriculture as to industry; peasant conditions and farm problems were not high among Communist priorities.

The decentralization of the economy, the administration, and the party organization was to have a largely unexpected result. The six federal republics were based on the former national and historic divisions. With the loosening of the central bonds, more authority was transferred to the capitals of the republics, the majority of which had been, and still were, strongholds of fervent nationalist sentiments. When disputes arose over economic or political questions, the local leaders tended to dust off all the old flags and symbols and return with enthusiasm to the battles of the past. The national question was to become once again the predominant issue in Yugoslav internal politics and to lead to a series of crises. A basic conflict between the developed areas, Slovenia and Croatia, and to a lesser extent, Serbia, and the backward regions, Macedonia, Montenegro, and Bosnia, had already commenced. However, the really vicious disputes were to involve the old adversaries, the Serbs and the Croats, and, within the Serbian republic, the Serbs and the Albanians.

In 1966 an issue arose that involved the sensitive questions of opposition to the liberal reforms, the power of the secret police, and the strong position of the Serbian republic within Yugoslavia. The Serbs, according to the census of 1971, comprised 8.4 million of the 20.5 million inhabitants of Yugoslavia, and, as in the past, they again aroused the jealousy of the other nationalities. Since the capital of the Serbian republic and the nation were both in Belgrade, there was a strong tendency to identify centralization in the government with Serbian domination. Not only Croats, but also Albanians, Bosnian Muslims, Macedonians, and Slovenes, looked with suspicion on Serbian actions. There was some justification for their attitude: the army, the police, and the security forces were indeed predominantly Serbian. It will be remembered that during the war the major sources of Partisan recruitment had been from the Serbian population of Montenegro, Bosnia, and Croatia. Moreover, the Serbs appeared to have a strong leader in Alexander Ranković, who as vice-president of Yugoslavia after 1963 was the second man in the state and widely regarded as Tito's successor.

---

36    Stevan K. Pavlowitch, *Yugoslavia* (New York: Praeger, 1971), p. 305.

Ranković, in addition to being popularly identified with the Serbs, was conservative in economic policy. To the liberals it appeared that this former head of the security forces was using his connections with the secret police to block the reforms of 1965. He thus stood as a barrier to further economic advancement. Fortunately for his opponents, Ranković was vulnerable to attack. Under his administration UDBA, the State Security Service, had used terrorist methods; its record was particularly bad in Kosovo. Moreover, it had inaugurated some very risky procedures. In the summer of 1966 it was discovered that security agents had placed wiretaps and bugs in the homes and offices of the leading political figures – even in Tito's residence. Although Ranković had much influence in the security section and much Serbian nationalist support, he did not have the backing of the army or the majority of the party. When Tito was informed of the surveillance of his premises, he too turned against his former Partisan comrade. In July 1966 the party Central Committee met at Brioni to consider the case. Ranković was accused of building a personal power base in UDBA. Moreover, the organization was shown to be a center of corruption and police brutality. Ranković was forced to resign from all his offices, but he was not put on trial. He and his close associates were simply retired on pensions. Both Serbs and non-Serbs saw his case as a national issue; the Croats and the other nationalities felt that they had gained a victory.

The relative freedom enjoyed by Yugoslav citizens in comparison with their socialist neighbors was shown in many aspects of their lives in the second half of the 1960s. Most important was the fact that Yugoslavs could travel with almost complete freedom. Visas were also given to foreign visitors with few restrictions, or not required at all. No attempt was made to limit tourist travel in the country, except in military zones. In fact, all of the regions sought to profit from holiday visitors. Foreign books, periodicals, and newspapers were allowed to circulate in the country with little hindrance. Workers who went abroad seeking jobs were similarly free to come and go at their own convenience.

In the economic field the reforms continued, and there was a similar liberal trend in politics. Although nothing like a multiparty system arose, the voter often did find that he had more than one name to choose from on the ballot. Yugoslavia also had a much better record on civil liberties than other Communist-dominated states. Although full freedom of the press did not exist, the controls were more leniently administered than elsewhere. An example was the controversy surrounding the journal *Praxis*, a publication started in Zagreb in 1964 that appeared twice a month. Although the writers associated with it declared themselves Marxists, their articles were openly critical of the social and political conditions in the country. Despite constant attacks by the party establishment and by Tito himself, the journal was not suppressed until 1975. A strike by students and intellectuals in Belgrade in June

1968, which was called to express dissatisfaction with some aspects of the system, was also dealt with in a moderate way; Tito met this problem by speaking on television and in a fine paternal manner expressing his sympathy with many of the demands.

The Soviet intervention in Czechoslovakia did much to contribute to the popularity of the Yugoslav government. Its citizens were clearly shown the advantages that they enjoyed, and the rise in party membership reflected the favorable sentiment. In 1968, 100,000 new members, mostly under the age of twenty-five, joined the party, with the majority entering after the Soviet invasion of Czechoslovakia in August.[37] Despite his statements at Pula in 1956, Tito strongly denounced the new Soviet action; this time he did not feel that an intervention was justified. Military precautions were immediately taken, and Yugoslavia made it clear that it would fight if necessary. Subsequently, additional laws were passed for the defense of the country, with an emphasis on training for partisan warfare. All Yugoslav men from the ages of eighteen to sixty-five and women from nineteen to forty were to be prepared to fight in any future war. Arms were distributed to factories and offices.

Although international questions and domestic economic and political issues were to continue to command attention, the most sensitive problem remained that of the national conflicts. The next crisis was to center in Croatia. The fears of the Croatian people for their national future were strong. In the 1960s this republic had the highest number of emigrants and one of the lowest birthrates. In 1971, 5.2 percent of the population worked abroad; of these, 50.7 percent were below the age of thirty and 63.2 percent were men.[38] There was also widespread apprehension about Serbian influence in the government. That the deep antagonisms of the past were still alive is clear from this quotation concerning the Croatian attitude:

> The metaphor for all that was outdated, centralist and authoritarian was "Belgrade." Belgrade, the capital of Serbia. Serbia, whose notorious "Serbian bourgeoisie" had ruled and ruthlessly exploited richer, more sophisticated Croatia and Slovenia in prewar Yugoslavia, and who had recently attempted a repeat performance with Ranković and a Serbian-dominated Party and police bureaucracy. Serbian politicians, primitive by education, hardfisted by training, and therefore "neo-Stalinist" or at least "dogmatic Communist" by definition. Serbian hegemony, exploitative and authoritarian, the primary – perhaps the only – reason why Croatia was not already as rich and democratic as . . . Denmark?[39]

37 Rusinow, *The Yugoslav Experiment*, p. 239.
38 Fred Singleton, *Twentieth-Century Yugoslavia* (New York: Columbia University Press, 1976), p. 226.
39 Rusinow, *The Yugoslav Experiment*, p. 249.

The first major sign of a Croatian national reaction came in 1967. At this time 130 intellectuals, including the foremost Croatian author, Miroslav Krleža, signed a petition demanding that Serbian and Croatian be recognized as two separate languages, with Croatian used in the schools of the republic. The Serbs immediately countered with the request that the 700,000 of their people living in Croatia receive reciprocal rights. The revival of the language problem, which also occurred in other parts of the country among other national minorities, marked the decline, if not the fall, of the hopes that some had once held for the creation of "Yugoslav" national sentiment. In 1967 facilities for simultaneous translation were installed in the Federal Assembly.

Although the language question was important, the major Croatian grievances were economic. As members of a wealthy republic, the Croats had previously supported democratic and decentralizing trends in economic as well as in political and cultural affairs. They thus wished as much authority as possible concentrated in the governments and party organizations of the republics. Despite the relative health of their economy, Croats claimed that Belgrade, meaning Serbia, was exploiting the other republics. They pointed out that the large banks, the major insurance companies, and the most prosperous enterprises had their headquarters in the capital. The financial life of the country still centered there. The Croatian officials were particularly concerned about the foreign trade situation; they were convinced that their republic was not receiving its fair share of the foreign currency. They argued that a large amount was earned by the tourist industry on the Dalmatian coast and that 80 percent of the Yugoslav foreign trade went through Croatian ports. There were also complaints that 30 percent of the Croatian state income was drained away for the advantage of other parts of the country.[40]

An important section of the Croatian Communist Party was sympathetic to these accusations. Led by Miko Tripalo and Savka Dabčević-Kučar, this group called for a further political decentralization of the government and a reform of the banking and currency regulations. At the same time there was a strong upsurge of Croatian national feeling, which reached a climax in the final months of 1971. A leading role in this movement was played by the *Matica Hrvatska*, which became in effect a nationalist political party. A cultural organization founded in the 1840s, it encouraged a revival of the memories of past Croatian history, including the grievances as well as the heroes and national accomplishments. By the end of the year the Croatian nationalists had presented extreme proposals, which, as summarized by an authority on Yugoslav affairs, called for a change in the Croatian constitution that was to include

> a straightforward definition of Croatia as "the sovereign national state of the Croatian nation" . . . with its sovereignty based on "the

40 Singleton, *Twentieth-Century Yugoslavia*, p. 225.

right to self-determination, including the right to secession." Croatian was to be the sole official language, Croatian authorities would exercise full control over all tax revenues collected in Croatia . . . there would be a separate Croatian monetary policy and bank of emission. Croatian recruits with the Yugoslav People's Army would normally serve only in the Republic, and there would be an autonomous Croatian territorial army.[41]

Meanwhile, Tito had been watching the events in Croatia carefully. In July 1971 he had spoken in strong terms to the Croatian party leadership about the dangers in the situation, warning that nationalism had "run wild . . . in some villages because of nervousness the Serbs are drilling and arming themselves . . . Do you want to have 1941 again?" He was also apprehensive about foreign, meaning Soviet, intervention, declaring: "Others are watching. Are you aware that others would immediately be present if there were disorders? But I'll sooner restore order with our army than allow others to do it."[42] In December, after a further intensification of nationalist activities and after the Croatian party leaders had failed to act upon his warnings, Tito intervened decisively. On December 2 his statement, read on national radio and television, attacked the Croatian nationalists and blamed the crisis primarily on the ideological problems within the party, the lack of a proper Marxist education, and the toleration of pro-Western ideas in the schools and universities. The subsequent suppression of nationalist activities was aided by the fact that the Croatian party was badly split. Tripalo and Dabčević-Kučar were forced to resign. Over four hundred nationalist leaders and their sympathizers were dismissed or resigned from their official positions. The Matica Hrvatska was reorganized, and its activities were severely curtailed.

The dismissal of Ranković had involved the issue of the control of the security forces as well as those of economic policy and Serbian nationalism. The Croatian movement brought up the extent to which a party in one of the republics could follow an independent policy. After this experience Tito supported a strengthening of the central organization; he also approved the intervention by the central authorities in the affairs of the republics should the Communist system, as he defined it, be in danger. Thus, although favoring self-determination and noninterference as standards governing relations among socialist states, he did not intend to apply these principles to the Yugoslav republics. There were to be no separate roads to socialism within Yugoslavia. Not only Croatia, but also other republics, felt the weight of his decisions. The Croatian nationalists had stood for liberal economic policies and decentralization in politics. Action was now taken against "liberal" elements in Slovenia, Macedonia, and Serbia. In October 1972 the head of the

41  Rusinow, *The Yugoslav Experiment*, p. 305.
42  Quoted in Rusinow, *The Yugoslav Experiment*, p. 299.

Serbian Communist Party, Marko Nikezić, lost his position, and other changes in party and state personnel were made. The motives for the individual actions were not always clear, but Tito had shown that he could take stern measures in Serbia as well as in Croatia.

Although Serbian and Croatian national rivalries were most dangerous for the state as a whole, the Albanian problem continued to cause international as well as internal difficulties. Until the 1960s the Albanian population in the Kosovo district undoubtedly suffered great disadvantages in comparison with the Serbs, who held a disproportionate number of the top state and party positions and dominated cultural and economic life. Serbian officers also controlled the local police and security forces, whose abuses were part of the charges made against Ranković. This situation was modified after 1966 and further after November 1968, when riots occurred in the region. Thereafter Kosovo and also the Vojvodina were made almost equivalent in status to the republics. Kosovo gained its own flag and anthem, and an increased emphasis was placed on the use of the Albanian language in administration and education. In 1970 what had been in effect a branch campus of the university of Belgrade at Priština became a separate university, with most of the instruction in Albanian.

The Albanian population in Yugoslavia may provide some demographic problems for the future. With the highest birthrate in the country, the Albanians are at some time expected to pass the Slovenes in numbers. In 1971 there were 1.3 million Albanians in Yugoslavia, or more than half as many as in Albania proper. Of this number the majority, or 920,000, lived in Kosovo, where they formed 74 percent of the population. They were also 17 percent of population of Montenegro and 7 percent of Macedonia, in each of which they live in a compact group near the Kosovo frontier. The basis thus exists for the creation of a separate Albanian Yugoslav republic, or for a unification of these lands with neighboring Albania. The contrast in conditions between Yugoslavia and Albania, however, may limit the attraction of a possible union. As a Yugoslav citizen, the Albanian peasant can farm his own land and practice his Muslim religion. Severe irredentist demonstrations that occurred in April 1981 and later may, nevertheless, indicate that the neighboring Albanian state exerts a strong influence on the Kosovo population.

The Macedonian problem provided even more difficulties than the Albanian for Yugoslav foreign policy and stood as a barrier to good relations with Bulgaria. In domestic politics, however, the republic caused no major crises. As we have seen, Macedonia had been included as one of the six republics in the organization set up at Jajce in 1943. In 1944 party and state institutions had been established. The leadership then devoted its attention to building up a Macedonian nationality. The process resembled that which we have seen with other national groups in the past: the first emphasis was on formulating a standard literary language. In August 1944 the government in Skopje declared Macedonian to be the language of the republic; a commission was set up to determine its form. Its members had to select a single local dialect and approve a standard vocabulary, and the choice fell on the Macedonian dialect that was least like either Bulgarian or Serbian. A vocabulary was produced that contained as few foreign words as possible, though more attention was given to the removal of Russian and Bulgarian than to the excision of Serbian words. The Bulgarian government subsequently attacked the official language as an artificial and serbianized form of the Bulgarian language.

The establishment of a literary language was just one step in the building of a Macedonian nationality. It was also felt necessary to provide the proper historical background, and here serious problems arose. It was exceedingly difficult to distinguish Macedonian from Bulgarian history. Similar difficulties arose in connection with literature, when the Skopje authorities tried to separate the Macedonian from the Bulgarian writers. In an effort to bolster the movement, the Macedonian Orthodox church was removed from the jurisdiction of Belgrade in 1968 and granted autocephalous status. The Macedonians, with a standard language, an official history, and their own national church, thus acquired many of the attributes of a modern nation.

Although much attention has been given to the Yugoslav–Bulgarian conflict over the region, it should be emphasized that the Macedonian leaders in Skopje were almost as adamant in their rejection of Serbian influence as of Bulgarian. However, after 1945 the issue was confused by the fact that Macedonia, as a backward region, was strongly in favor of central economic assistance and wanted political factories constructed in the republic. Although it did receive considerable aid, the population continued to feel that it was being exploited. This attitude was well expressed by the premier of the republic, Nikola Mincev, in 1966:

> Every factory can be called a political factory but in our republic there are none; only one cigarette factory had losses last year . . . Despite federal aid, our relative position in Yugoslavia has not improved but on the contrary become worse. If you take the over-all Yugoslav average national income as 100, then Macedonia stood at 68 after the war, but dropped to 62 percent last year.[43]

The head of the Macedonian Communist Party in the late 1960s, Krste Crvenkovski, held a similar opinion:

> The main danger lies in Great Serbian hegemony . . . We are also allergic to the economic hegemony of Slovenia. One should not always talk only about aid, but also about the fact that we had to pay

43  Quoted in Lendvai, *Eagles in Cobwebs*, p. 174.

40 percent higher prices for machines delivered by Yugoslav con-
tractors for our steelworks here than the prices in the world market.[44]

Although national controversies did arise in areas other than Serbia, Croatia, the Kosovo region, and Macedonia, they were less open and acute. As
under the former kingdom, the Slovenes adjusted relatively well to the Communist regime. Their distinct language, which received full recognition, and
their lack of a practical alternative political solution made them firm supporters of the Yugoslav federation. However, they joined the Croatians in complaints about the financial support given to the building of political factories,
and they expressed fears about the large numbers of emigrants who left to
work abroad. On the other end of the economic scale, the inhabitants of
Montenegro have been relatively content. Usually considering themselves Serbs,
they have no fears about Serbian domination. Moreover, since the region was
a center of Partisan activity in the war, Montenegrins subsequently received
a disproportionate share of positions in the state. The area also benefited
from the attempts to build up backward regions.

In two areas of mixed nationality, Bosnia-Hercegovina and the Autonomous Region of the Vojvodina, there was an attempt to avoid major national
frictions by maintaining careful balances. In 1971 the predominant group in
Bosnia-Hercegovina was the Muslim, with 39.6 percent of the population, as
against 37.2 percent for the Serbs and 20.6 percent for the Croatians. Having
decided by 1968, after vacillation and compromise, to regard the Serbo-Croatian–speaking Muslims as a sixth separate and equal South Slav "nation," on
the grounds that Islam is a culture as well as a religion, the state authorities
encouraged their further development. In the Vojvodina, which had a Serbian majority of 55.8 percent, the strongest minority was the Hungarian, with
21.7 percent of the population; the region also had Slovaks, Romanians, and
Croats. Particular care was given to conciliating the Hungarians and also to
granting cultural rights to all groups. Thus, the languages of the major nationalities were all recognized as official.

In the 1970s the Yugoslav leadership was faced with a continuation of the
issues that have been previously discussed; the most serious problems still
involved the economic and national conflicts. The national controversies were
dealt with by the maintenance of a careful balance: appointments to state and
party posts were determined by an "ethnic key" to assure that each people
secured an influence in proportion to its numbers. After the suppression of
the Croatian movement, Tito, as we have seen, moved toward tightening the
central authority. Liberalism could be discredited by associating it with nationalism. At the tenth party congress, held in May 1974, emphasis was placed
on "democratic centralism" and on the assertion of party authority through-

---

44  Quoted in Lendvai, *Eagles in Cobwebs*, p. 175.

out the political system. Although some alterations were made, the eleventh congress of June 1978 also emphasized centralism and the role of Tito.

Nevertheless, despite the renewed criticism of nationalism in the republics, there was no attempt to alter the federal basis of the state. In fact, many of the objections of the Croatian nationalists in the economic field were met. Croatia acquired the right to keep a larger share of the foreign currency that it earned, and the influence of the great banks and enterprises, with their headquarters in Belgrade, was reduced. Most important, the new constitution of February 1974 included provisions giving the federal republics and provinces virtual veto power over the most important state matters. This long and complicated document further emphasized the role of self-management and the party in the Yugoslav system.

The majority of the economic problems that have been previously discussed also remained. Before we review them, it must be emphasized once again that despite the many problems inherent in the system, Yugoslav consumers enjoyed a far wider and better choice of products than their counterparts anywhere else in the Communist bloc, including the Soviet Union. The country as a whole gave the impression of much greater prosperity than its neighbors. Nevertheless, the ideal of workers' self-management still contained many internal contradictions. Within the enterprises the workers often remained more interested in their own benefits and their working conditions than in matters of general policy. As one former director commented: "Our system of self-management, instead of meaning self-management of and for the enterprise and society as a whole, means to most people self-management of one's self – working only when and as hard as one wants, but with assurance that one's job will go on and one's pay will continue to increase."[45]

Other economic difficulties were equally troublesome. Although agricultural production was still chiefly in the hands of small farmers, it did not show a rate of growth sufficient to fulfill the role that the planners intended. Even more controversial was the continued inequality in wealth between the favored republics, chiefly Slovenia and Croatia, and impoverished Macedonia, Montenegro, and Kosovo. Some of the other economic problems were shared with the rest of the world. Yugoslavia too suffered from a high inflation rate, which had risen to 30 percent by 1980. Like the rest of the European powers, Yugoslavia found its economic position severely damaged by the rise of oil prices, which contributed to the already bad foreign deficit. In 1980 this stood at over $15 billion; the debt repayments used up 25 percent of the foreign currency earnings. At the same time unemployment passed 800,000.

In foreign affairs the government maintained its previous policy of nonalignment, although this position became increasingly difficult to sustain. Whereas previously the principle had commanded a wide degree of unity among the undeveloped Asian and African nations, this loose alliance devel-

45 Quoted in the *New York Times*, May 11, 1980, p. 2E.

oped serious fissures. In Yugoslav eyes nonalignment meant an equal separation from both great-power blocs – from Soviet "hegemonism" as well as from American "imperialism." This neutral stance was increasingly combated by the Soviet Union, whose diplomats worked through Cuba to turn the movement solely against the Western powers. In 1979 Tito took a leading role in the conference of nonaligned powers at Havana in the attempt to keep the alignment truly neutral.

Nevertheless, relations with the Soviet Union remained at the center of Yugoslav foreign policy. Yugoslavia was, after all, still a socialist state; Soviet allies were its close neighbors. In August 1971 Brezhnev visited Belgrade, and in July 1972 Tito returned the visit. The estrangement following the invasion of Czechoslovakia in 1968 was thus formally at an end. Yugoslav suspicions of Soviet intentions, however, remained strong. Recognizing these feelings, Brezhnev, during a visit to Belgrade in November 1976, denounced the "authors of such fairy tales [who] try to present Yugoslavia as a helpless Little Red Riding Hood, whom the terrible bloodthirsty wolf – the aggressive Soviet Union – is preparing to dismember and devour."[46] Moreover, despite the exchange of visits, Tito remained a firm opponent of Soviet attempts to dominate world Communist parties. He insisted that they should form an association of equal partners and that all should recognize the principle of different roads to socialism. Strongly opposing Soviet military intervention in other countries, he denounced the invasion of Afghanistan in December 1979.

To the Soviet dismay, Tito also mended his fences with China. Relations had, in fact, started to improve after 1969. In 1977 Tito visited China; in August 1978 premier and party chairman Hua Guofeng was his guest in Yugoslavia. Good relations were maintained also with most of the Comecon states, who remained important trade partners. As could be expected, Tito approved of Ceauşescu's attempt to maintain an independent stand. Friction over Macedonia continued to arouse strong feelings in both Bulgaria and Yugoslavia and prevented close cooperation between the governments.

As far as the West was concerned, trade with the Common Market countries was particularly important for the Yugoslav economy. Moreover, these states employed many Yugoslav workers and sent masses of tourists to expand this now flourishing industry. In 1973 6.15 million tourists came to Yugoslavia, a figure that dropped to about 5.6 million in 1976 and 1977. On the formal diplomatic level no major controversies occurred in what was a relatively uneventful decade for the Continent.

Perhaps the central political problem of the 1970s – certainly the one that commanded the most interest and attention – was that of finding a successor to Tito, who was in his eighties. As we have seen, the previous stresses and

---

46 Quoted in Dennison I. Rusinow, "Yugoslav Domestic Developments," *American University Field Staff: Reports*, no. 25, 1978, p. 19.

strains in the Yugoslav system had largely been ameliorated by the fact that Tito had the power and prestige to force a solution whenever a real crisis arose. He was also an unusually able leader. As a former British ambassador to Belgrade has written: "One of his greatest strengths has been pragmatism. He has not been a doctrinaire intent on imposing his views about the ideal political structure, in conditions where they clearly could not be realized."[47] Throughout his period in power Tito did indeed usually employ his great authority to enforce compromises and to mediate among the competing forces within his multinational and combative population.

There was no obvious successor. By the end of the 1970s Tito had outlived most of his contemporaries. Of his former close Partisan companions, one of the last, Kardelj, died in February 1979. Ranković, although still alive, was in disgrace and apparently out of the political picture. During the decade attempts were made to deal with the situation and to find a solution that would be acceptable to all of the nationalities. Tito was state president from 1953 until 1971, when a constitutional amendment established a collective presidency of twenty-three members, with Tito as president for life. The constitution of 1974 reduced the membership to nine: one representative for each republic and autonomous province, together with Tito. After his death, the leadership was to rotate on an annual basis among the members. Similar arrangements were made for the party. In January 1980 Tito became severely ill; he finally died in May at the age of eighty-seven. As previously arranged, Lazar Koliševski, representing Macedonia, became the head of the state presidency; Stephen Doronjski, from the Vojvodina, was in charge of the League of Communists. The orderly transmission of power did much to calm fears about the Yugoslav future after the removal of the man who had undoubtedly been the strongest and most successful of the East European socialist leaders.

Despite the many difficulties faced by the Yugoslav government after 1945, certain marked successes must be recorded. First, the state did hold together. A federation of national groups, with differing languages, religions, historic associations, and economic resources, Yugoslavia was exposed to greater stresses than its Balkan neighbors with more homogenous populations.[48] Second,

---

47  Duncan Wilson, *Tito's Yugoslavia* (Cambridge: Cambridge University Press, 1979), p. 259.
48  In March 1981 a new census was taken in Yugoslavia, whose results were published in part a year later. In this survey 1,215,000 people declared their nationality as Yugoslav, a 450 percent increase from 1971. The significance of this change has been variously interpreted. The population showed a 9.2 percent rise, with the greatest growth (27.47 percent) in the Kosovo autonomous district. In the entire country the Albanians showed the greatest increase – from 1,309,000 in 1971 to 1,730,000 in 1981. The republics had the following increases: Bosnia and Hercegovina – 10.11 percent; Croatia – 3.95 percent; Macedonia – 16.07 percent; Montenegro – 10.08 percent; Slovenia – 9.49 percent; Serbia (without the autonomous provinces) – 8.36 percent. The autonomous province of the Vojvodina had a low 3.87 percent growth, which reflected the decrease in the Hungarian population from 477,374 in 1971 to 425,000 in 1981. Radio Free Europe Research, RAD Background Report/59 (Yugoslavia), March 10, 1982.

and equally important, the association was strong enough to permit social and political experimentation. Unlike their colleagues in the other bloc nations, the Yugoslav Communist leaders could try different forms of socialist organization. Moreover, they could allow their people a wider range of civil liberties than any other Communist government permitted. Yugoslav citizens have been free to travel, to work outside the country, and to emigrate. Third, the state has been able to maintain a neutral position between the Soviet camp and the West and to resist interference in its internal affairs.

## CONCLUSION

In this chapter the internal development of the four socialist Balkan states has been discussed. After the conclusion of the war in 1945 they had many attributes in common. All adopted governments based on Marxist-Leninist theory, and with the exception of Albania, which was at first under Yugoslav direction, all were at the outset subject to strong Soviet influence. Each nation had a one-party political system; civil liberties were suspended. The major effort of the government was directed to a total reorganization of the economic life of the country. Stalinist Soviet models were adopted. The emphasis was on industrialization; agriculture, a sort of Communist stepchild, was to be the responsibility of state or collective farms.

Despite these similar beginnings, differences soon appeared. Of the four, Bulgaria was to show the least change. This state has with relatively little deviation followed the original pattern adopted after the Communist victory and has remained close to the Soviet Union in foreign affairs. Although Romania too has retained a rigid internal system, the government was able to assert an element of independence in foreign policy after 1964. Albania has similarly maintained a doctrinaire domestic organization, but it has pursued a contentious course in international relations. The closest Albanian friendships have indeed been within the socialist bloc – that is, with Yugoslavia, the Soviet Union, and China – but the state has not hesitated to enter into the bitter controversies within the camp.

Among these four states, Yugoslavia stands apart. Not only has this country pursued a highly independent foreign policy, but it has allowed a great deal of freedom within the country. While retaining a one-party system and ideological controls, it has nevertheless not maintained the same tight hold on the lives and persons of its citizens as have the neighboring states. Moreover, with a complex national organization, its leadership has at least attempted to find a system that would allow its nationalities, each with its own past history and its unique economic disabilities, to live together in relative harmony. Past grievances have in no manner been laid to rest, but at least the problems have been recognized.

Because of the general international situation, these states have since 1945 been spared from the burdens of war and national revolt that were such a major drain on their resources in the previous centuries. They could thus devote their energies to internal development, and the goals and the difficulties encountered in each state have been described here. By the 1980s the Balkan nations could look back on their record of the past thirty-five years with mixed feelings. Undoubtedly much had been achieved, but the difficult world economic conditions, whose effects limited the development and curtailed the prosperity of even the wealthiest states, were bound to cause added difficulties for this relatively poor region. Here, as elsewhere, the expectations for the economic future of the people have become less optimistic.

# 10

## *The Greek alternative*

### ECONOMIC PROBLEMS: AMERICAN
### INTERVENTION

FOR THE GREEK PEOPLE the years after World War II were a repetition of a previous experience. In 1918 the war ended for most of Europe, but the Greek army fought almost continuously until 1922. Again, although continental Europe was at peace in May 1945, the Greeks were engaged in a bitter civil war until 1949. Both periods resulted in a massive resettlement and a disturbance of Greek population patterns. In the 1920s, as a result of the Anatolian disaster and the exchange of populations, approximately 1.3 million Greeks found new homes. The civil war after 1946 created a group of around 700,000 refugees, who had to be either returned to their villages or given other employment. Those who owned their own farms or workshops had the least trouble in resuming a normal existence. Many never returned to their poverty-stricken mountain homes: some emigrated; others moved into the cities.

World War II and the civil war had, of course, caused enormous economic destruction. Moreover, wartime conditions had intensified the basic economic problems, which have been discussed previously. The limited amount of arable land and the lack of many of the basic requirements for an industrial economy remained the great impediments to Greek economic progress. In 1950 agriculture was still the major employment of half of the Greek population. As previously, the fragmentation of individual holdings, caused primarily by inheritance customs, made the introduction of modern methods difficult. Industrial development remained limited, with the small factory and the workshop predominant. Most of the firms were family-owned; they supplied a small group of local clients, and they were not designed to compete on international markets. Previously protected by high tariffs, they needed the continuation of such policies in order to survive. It was difficult for these businesses to adopt new technological advances or to purchase expensive modern equipment. They relied instead on cheap labor. Greeks were also still reluctant to invest in industry. They continued to prefer to buy real estate or to engage in commerce. In these years many Greek families chose to buy houses or apartments rather than invest in local enterprises even on a small scale.

The outcome of the civil war had, of course, determined the course for the future; Greece would retain its Western European political and economic system. However, the country was now to come under a new and highly controversial influence – that of the United States. In the previous chapters the Soviet interference in the Communist bloc countries and the British influence in Athens after 1944 have been discussed, and the extreme sensitiveness of all of these states to foreign intervention has been emphasized. It was thus inevitable that any attempt made by American officials to influence Greek internal affairs would be greeted with great suspicion, and, unfortunately, American interference was often blatant. In addition, whereas the Soviet government was usually able to cover its activities in Eastern Europe with a veil of secrecy through the strict censorship enforced, American actions received full publicity, not only in the Greek opposition press, but throughout Europe and in the United States.

The most obvious sign of American involvement was the large amount of money provided, without which Greece could not have recovered. Between 1947 and 1966, $1,895 million in economic aid and $1,854 million in military assistance, a total of $3,749 million, were given to this nation of approximately 8 million people. In 1966–1967 approximately $65 million were given in military aid, with similar amounts to follow later.[1] When supplying this money, the American government insisted that its officials serve as consultants or participate in the programs funded by the grants. This demand arose from the American concern over the extensive corruption in Greek politics. American experts were also needed to give technical assistance on certain projects. Thus American officials and missions supervised many Greek activities and checked expenditures, in particular in connection with the work of the Ministry of Coordination, which included the offices of Finance and Commerce. American intervention was also especially thoroughgoing in military affairs. American officers were on the Greek general staff, and they were attached to Greek units down to the divisional level. The presence of American representatives in so many important positions naturally drew them deeply into Greek domestic affairs and into the political quarrels. Since they became associated with the parties and individuals in power, those out of office – or those whose national pride had been wounded – naturally attacked the foreign influence. In addition, once the American embassy in Athens became involved in the making or breaking of cabinets, it could expect to carry the blame for the failures and weaknesses of the regimes it supported.

Many problems were to plague the Greek–American relationship, most of

1  Jane Perry Clark Carey and Andrew Galbraith Carey, *The Web of Modern Greek Politics* (New York: Columbia University Press, 1968), p. 213.

them the familiar frictions that we have seen arise whenever a European great power tried to guide and control a Balkan state. Although the United States, unlike the Soviet Union in East Europe in the years immediately after the war, did not make a profit out of its position, there were many difficulties, some of them on the personal level. Previous British missions had been staffed by officials with classical educations; most were Philhellenes who genuinely admired the ancient Greek civilization. They also had more experience with and understanding of the Greek mentality than their American counterparts. The American advisers came from a different background. Although many worked with great good will and devotion, others stamped on sensitive Greek toes. The full force of the resentment was not to be expressed until the 1960s, when the United States became identified, justly or not, with unpopular regimes.

The American position was, of course, also influenced by changing world conditions. With the defection of Tito and the apparent waning of the danger in the north, Greece had less need for a protector. As far as gratitude for previous aid was concerned, some argued that the United States had acted in its own interest in the matter and that, in fact, most of the assistance had arrived after the need for it had passed. In the years after the civil war, when the American presence remained strong, United States policy in the eastern Mediterranean, as could be expected, was based on American interests rather than on the needs and concerns of the Greeks themselves. Particularly in the question of Cyprus, the single major problem in Greek foreign relations, American objectives did not always coincide with those of Greece.

## PAPAGOS AND KARAMANLIS: GREEK GOVERNMENTS TO 1963

During the civil war Liberal and Populist leaders had worked together. The ministries were composed of representatives from the center and right of the political spectrum; the Populists were the strongest party in the assembly. At the same time the influence of the right increased in the army and the police. Measures of punishment and retribution were taken, as might be expected, against the rebel leaders and their supporters after the conclusion of the fighting. Between June 1946 and October 1949 there were 3,150 sentences of death, of which 1,223 were actually carried through. Thousands received prison terms.[2] These judgments and the continued confinement of political prisoners were to become major political issues during the next years.

After the civil strife was over, Greek politics returned to normal. Once again a large number of factions, built around strong individuals, fought for power. The fragmentation of political life was clearly illustrated in the elections of March 1950, in which forty-four parties competed for 250 seats. The

---

2 John Campbell and Philip Sherrard, *Modern Greece* (London: Benn, 1968), p. 249.

system of proportional representation, introduced in 1946, assured that a large number of these groups would win places. Although the Populists emerged as the single largest party, with 62 seats, the most votes were given to center Liberal candidates split into several groups under different leaders. Thus the Venizelos faction won 56: Papandreou's supporters 35; and Plastiras, at the head of the National Progressive Union, or EPEK, gained 45. The Communist Party had been outlawed in 1948, but its members could enter the elections as part of the New Democratic Front, which received 18 seats. This balance of parties made it difficult to form a stable government. Using the threat of the termination of assistance, the American officials attempted to bring the center and right-wing parties together, but the situation remained fluid. In the next eighteen months five weak coalition ministries were formed, four of them headed by Venizelos and one by Plastiras. By the fall of 1951 this system had failed, and new elections had to be scheduled.

The American desire for a stable government had thus not been satisfied; the center parties had been unable to work together to assure a smoothly functioning administration. After the outbreak of the Korean War, in which Greek troops participated as part of the United Nations contingent, American policy shifted from backing Liberal coalitions to preferring more conservative ministries. Support was thus given to Alexander Papagos, who had won a national reputation in the Greek campaign against Italy and had been in command of the army at the end of the civil war. Since he had spent most of World War II in German prison camps, he had not been part of the intricate political maneuvering of that period. Primarily a military man, who became Greece's only field marshal in 1949, he had little regard for professional politicians. He now formed a coalition of right-wing parties, known as the Greek Rally, that was deliberately patterned after the Rally of the French People organized by General Charles de Gaulle. Papagos succeeded in gaining the support of four men who were to play a major role in Greek affairs in the future: Panagiotis Kanellopoulos, Stephen Stefanopoulos, Constantine Karamanlis, and Spyros Markezinis. This new political front was not immediately successful. In elections held in September 1951, which were based on a modified system of proportional representation, the Greek Rally won 114 out of 258 seats. It succeeded in dealing a crushing blow to the Populists, who gained only 2 places, but it did not win a majority. This election gave 10 seats to a new coalition, the United Democratic Left, or EDA, which was to remain a stable combination for the next years. It absorbed the former Communist Party members, who played an important, perhaps the predominant, role in its activities. Of the remaining seats, Plastiras's EPEK and Venizelos's section of the Liberals had 131 together. Since Papagos refused to enter a coalition, the government was based on the two last-named parties, with Plastiras as premier.

This new government took some important actions. A revised constitution came into effect in January 1952, and Greek association with NATO was negotiated. Some action was taken in favor of those who were jailed for their activities during the civil war. Almost all the death sentences were commuted; other prisoners received reduced sentences or pardons. The government, however, faced constant opposition, and the economic situation was declining. Even though it had American backing, the coalition was too weak to hold the situation together. To try to secure the basis for a stable government, Papagos proposed that the majority system, which is that used in the United States, be adopted instead of proportional representation for the next elections. Plastiras also favored the change. At this time the United States Embassy again intervened in Greek politics, warning that aid would be ended unless a stable political situation was established. In addition, the ambassador, John E. Peurifoy, issued a public statement supporting a change in the electoral rules that declared:

> Because the American Government believes that the reestablishment of the "simple-proportional" election method, with its unavoidable consequences of the continuation of governmental instability, would have restrictive results upon the effective utilization of American aid to Greece, the American Embassy feels itself obliged to make its support publicly known for the patriotic position of the Prime Minister Plastiras with regard to this subject.[3]

This declaration is generally quoted as illustrating the extent of American pressure in Greek politics. Although it certainly went beyond the limits of normal diplomatic procedure, and it certainly was unwise, it was in no sense the equivalent of the Soviet interference within the socialist bloc. The Greek voter did, of course, have the alternative of simply voting for anti-American parties and thus rejecting the American dollars. The United States could not enforce its desires by military means: it did not have an army in occupation, although it did have much influence in the Greek police and military.

Different voting procedures were indeed adopted, and elections were held in November 1952. The change, as expected, benefited the Rally, which won 49 percent of the votes and 247 of the 300 seats in the assembly. The former government parties, the Liberals and EPEK, took 34 percent of the votes and were reduced to 51 representatives. EDA and the Populists received no places at all. The power in Greek politics thus passed into the hands of the right, although some Liberals, including at first Papandreou, supported the new regime.

With a conservative leadership in control and Papagos as premier, Greece was to enjoy eleven years of political stability, from 1952 to 1963. The main attention could be shifted from factional squabbling to meeting internal problems. Great efforts were made to improve general economic conditions,

3   David Holden, *Greece without Columns* (Philadelphia: Lippincott, 1972), pp. 177–178.

and some measures achieved a high degree of success. In the countryside much attention was given to the improvement of agricultural methods. The introduction of better seed resulted in higher yields, and irrigation projects, including the draining of swampland, brought more land into use. In the past, it will be remembered, Greece had not been able to feed its own population. By 1957 the country grew enough wheat to fill domestic demands; 31 percent of the cultivated land was devoted to this purpose. Although this achievement was important, it also meant that less land was available for the growing of the export crops that were so important for the Greek balance of payments. As in previous years, these remained primarily tobacco, cotton, and fresh and dried fruits. In the middle of the 1960s these products accounted for 51 percent of the value of Greek exports.[4]

In addition to the agricultural improvements, advances were made in other sections of the economy. Markezinis was placed in charge of the Ministry of Coordination, and although he left his post in 1954, his policies were continued. Like his American supporters, he favored an open, free-enterprise economy, but with stringent reforms in certain areas. For instance, he reduced the size of the civil service and attempted to make it more efficient. In the interest of securing a stable currency, he devalued the drachma in 1953 by 50 percent. During this period strong support was given to plans for economic development, such as the building of new power stations and the exploitation of Greek mineral resources. With American assistance a national electrical system came into operation in 1955; within the next fifteen years even remote mountain villages were to receive the advantages of this modern convenience. A road network, commenced during the civil war for military purposes, bound the country closer together.

During this period American influence remained strong, but the objectives of the Papagos ministry coincided with those of the United States. Immediately after the conclusion of the civil war the principal goal of the American advisers was to restore normal conditions as quickly as possible. At this time the obvious reforms to be introduced involved a reduction of the inflated bureaucracy, an emphasis on the collection of taxes, and a cutting of the size of the army, which absorbed much of the national budget. The measures to aid agriculture were also important. The reforms pressed on the Greek government were largely in the spirit of the New Deal of the Roosevelt era in the United States. Equating Greeks with their own citizens, the American advisers hoped to introduce a change of attitude and to end the traditional patronage relationships, which they regarded as corrupt. The expectation was that the American financial assistance would not last long; the Marshall Plan aid was scheduled to end in 1952. However, after the outbreak of the Korean War and the attendant deterioration in relations between the United States and the Soviet Union, the American intentions shifted. The American gov-

4  Campbell and Sherrard, *Modern Greece*, p. 299.

ernment henceforth placed greater weight on the Greek role in NATO and its place in the policy of containment of Soviet influence. The American representatives cooperated well in this endeavor with the Papagos government, which also wished to retain a strong army and was firmly opposed to Communism. The military aspects of the Greek–American relationship thus took on new importance, and it was clear that financial assistance would have to be continued.

In October 1953 the two countries signed an additional agreement on military cooperation. This pact gave the United States extraordinary privileges in Greece, going far beyond those normally granted to another government by a state not under its direct colonial rule. American personnel could use the Greek roads and railroads; they could build and run military bases. They also had wide rights of extraterritoriality, always an extremely sensitive subject. This increased American military presence was bound to arouse hostility. Attacks on the American influence soon became a basic part of the political programs of the left parties. Moreover, when Greek relations with Yugoslavia and Turkey improved, the need for the American army appeared less. In August 1953, it will be remembered, Greece signed a military alliance with these two states: former enemies were now allies. Although this alignment was soon to break down, it did give a feeling of security for the moment.

The Papagos government, of course, represented a conservative influence in Greek life. Much of the legislation of the civil war period, the years from 1947 to 1949, remained in effect; in fact, it was not to be changed until 1974. The police held a great deal of authority; they could jail or deport an individual without a trial. The prisons were still full of those who had been convicted on political grounds. Also left from the civil war were the official Certificates of Social Beliefs, which people needed for employment in any state office, for admission to institutions of higher learning, and for documents such as drivers' licenses and passports. Such documents stated that neither the holder nor his or her relatives were associated with an "antinational" organization.

In October 1955 Papagos died. Faced with the necessity of appointing a successor to the post of prime minister, King Paul made the unexpected decision to nominate Constantine Karamanlis, a man who was to exert a major influence on Greek politics henceforth. Born in Serres in northern Greece in 1907, Karamanlis came from a poor family; his father had been a village schoolteacher. He had nevertheless been able to finish his education and to become a lawyer. After holding secondary government posts, he became minister of public works in 1955. Abrupt and forthright in manner, he gained the respect of those who worked with him. He was also liked by the American advisers, who came to know him in connection with the road-building projects.

The appointment did not win the approval of all of the members of the Rally. Papagos himself had designated Stefanopoulos as his successor. The disappointed candidate, with twenty-nine of his supporters, left the coalition, Karamanlis then organized his own party, the National Radical Union, or ERE, which he dominated. From this time until 1963, and then again after 1974, Karamanlis was the predominant figure in political life. By making repeated readjustments in the voting procedures, he won elections in 1956, 1958, and 1961, and he lost by only a small fraction in 1963. He was returned to power in 1974. He thus has held office longer than any previous Greek premier. Although in the 1950s he was a new man in the field, he gained at once the support of the elements that counted: the most influential politicians of the center and right, the American representatives, and, at first, the court, which retained much influence.

The opposition, of course, tried constantly to bring down the government. In the elections of February 1956 the center and left, including EDA, formed the Democratic Union, a combination that broke up immediately after the voting. At this time ERE gained 47.3 percent of the vote and 165 out of the 300 seats. Elections were held again in May 1958. In this campaign the opposition parties had great difficulty in forming a united front. Although Venizelos and Papandreou could cooperate, others could not. Once again ERE won a majority of 171 places, but its share of the vote was reduced to 41 percent. The great change in this election was the strength shown by EDA, which received a quarter of the votes and 79 seats.

The ERE victories were undoubtedly assisted by the fact that it was the party in power. As such, it could use the police, and it had the support of its members, who held the majority of posts in the civil service and the military. In addition, economic conditions were good; the life of the average citizen was improving. Unfortunately for Karamanlis, an issue in foreign policy was to arise that was to plague all of the Greek governments after 1955. The center of the dispute was Cyprus, but the fate of the island was linked closely to the question of the American relationship and the participation in NATO.

## THE CYPRUS DISPUTE

Although Greece had been on the winning side in World War II, the victory had not brought a satisfaction of territorial objectives. The Dodecanese Islands, formerly in Italian possession, were annexed, but international conditions precluded changes in the northern frontier. The claims against Albania could not be enforced. Alteration of the northern boundaries would have been difficult in any case, because Greece had reached its ethnic frontier in Europe. In fact, the island of Cyprus was the only territory inhabited in the majority by Greeks that was not under the control of Athens. Events that occurred on Cyprus in the mid-1950s were to make this region the focus of Greek national passions and in a sense an outlet for the frustrations of war and postwar turmoil. Every succeeding Greek ministry, no matter what its foreign policy orientation, had to deal with this major problem.

In 1878, it will be remembered, Britain took over the administration of Cyprus from the Ottoman Empire. When the empire joined Germany in World War I, Britain annexed the island. This action was confirmed in the Treaty of Lausanne. In 1950 the population of approximately 600,000 was 80 percent Greek and 18 percent Turkish. As elsewhere in the Balkans, the two people lived apart, each in villages of its own nationality. In the past, successive Greek governments had demanded enosis, or union. The basic difficulty was that the island lay only forty miles off the Turkish coast, but five hundred miles from Greece. The violent Turkish opposition to a Greek annexation was motivated by considerations of national security and perfectly justified fears about the possible fate of the Turkish inhabitants under Greek rule. As we have seen in the past, whenever a Balkan Christian administration was established in a former Ottoman region, the treatment of the Muslim population had been harsh. The experiences of the Turkish population in Romania and Bulgaria after 1945 have been noted. There was certainly nothing in the Cypriot situation that served to quiet Turkish apprehensions.

The island's Greek population, of course, supported the viewpoint of Athens. National organizations were formed whose objective was the expulsion of the British and union with Greece. Once again the Orthodox church took a leading role in the struggle for a national goal. The archbishop of Cyprus, Makarios, became the principal figure in island politics and the leader of the Greek community; he also maintained contact with the armed bands that were formed to try to force the British to leave. The foremost guerilla leader was Colonel George Grivas, who had been active in Greece during the war as the leader of the rightist X (or Khi) group. In Cyprus he headed the National Organization of Cypriot Fighters, or EOKA.

The Greek nationalists had some hope of success. Papagos was sympathetic with their aims, although he did little to aid them during his term in office. Moreover, at first the British government seemed to be liquidating its colonial commitments. However, it soon became apparent that, quite to the contrary, Britain intended to remain a Mediterranean power and to shift its base of operations to Cyprus. The British authorities made it clear that they did not intend to give independence to the island or to alter its status in any important manner. Similarly, Cypriot appeals to the United Nations went unheeded.

Since their goals could obviously not be obtained by negotiations, many Greek Cypriots turned to terror. Grivas, who had adopted the pseudonym Digenis Akritas, became the leading figure. The bands carried out acts of violence not only against the British occupation, but also against the Turkish population. These events, as might be expected, caused a strong reaction from Turkey, which was willing to accept continued British rule, but not the transfer of the island to Greece. The quarrel that arose over Cyprus caused extreme animosity between these two NATO partners and thus involved American policy in the eastern Mediterranean. Thereafter, largely because of the passions aroused among the people by the issue, neither the Turkish nor the Greek government could retreat from its position of giving firm backing to its section of the island population. Both nationalities resorted to violence. Whereas Greek Cypriot terrorists attacked local Turks, the Turkish population of Istanbul in September 1955 turned against the approximately 100,000 Greeks who still lived in the city. As a result of riots there, the majority of the Greeks were compelled to emigrate.

Acutely embarrassed by the situation, the British diplomats attempted to mediate between the Greek and Turkish governments and between the respective communities on Cyprus. In March 1956 the British authorities exiled Archbishop Makarios to the Seychelles Islands; he remained there until April 1957, when he went to Greece. The Turkish government, at this time and later, was willing to agree to a partition of the island with Greece, a solution that Athens would not consider: Greek public opinion demanded control of the entire territory. A stalemate thus resulted. On the island Greek and Turkish armed bands fought intermittently; their community leaders could not control the situation. Arms from Turkey were delivered secretly to the greatly outnumbered Turkish combatants.

With both partition and enosis eliminated as possibilities, one other solution remained – independence. Britain was willing to surrender control, but only under certain specific conditions. In February 1959 Karamanlis met with the Turkish premier, Adnan Menderes, in Zürich to try to work out an understanding. Their proposals, which were backed by their governments and Britain, were then presented for approval, but without the option of emendation, to Makarios and Dr. Fazil Küçük, the leader of the Turkish Cypriot community. All of those involved in the negotiations agreed that the island should become an independent republic linked to neither Greece nor Turkey. An elaborate system was worked out to preserve a national balance, but with the Turkish minority receiving a numerical advantage. The president was to be Greek, the vice-president Turkish. A house of representatives was to be elected, consisting of fifty members of whom thirty-five would be Greek and fifteen Turkish. The offices in the administration were similarly to be apportioned on a national percentage basis. In August 1960 Cyprus thus became an independent state, with Makarios as president and Küçük as vice-president.

Despite the island's theoretical independence, the powers remained deeply involved in Cypriot affairs. Britain kept two air bases, and some British and Turkish troops were still in occupation. The island was also placed under a formal British, Greek, and Turkish guarantee, the terms of which allowed any of the protectors to intervene unilaterally. These three states also agreed that there was to be no partition and no enosis.

This moderate and intelligent solution satisfied neither side. The Greeks of both the mainland and the island were particularly incensed; enosis remained their objective. Because the United States supported the new settlement, the issue directly affected the American influence in Athens. EDA naturally attacked the agreement. This party wished Greece to adopt a neutralist stand, to develop more connections with the socialist bloc, and to leave NATO. The opposition to Karamanlis used the issue to weaken his government and to make him appear an American tool. The entire episode increased the numbers of those opposed to the American presence. Even friends of the United States felt that Washington should have given more support to the Greek position on Cyprus, thus ignoring the obvious fact that Turkey, as the larger and stronger nation, was more valuable to NATO as an ally.

This anti-American sentiment was expressed when the proposals for the creation of a neutral zone in the Balkans were presented by the socialist bloc and even more intensely when, in December 1957, the placement of intermediate range ballistic missiles was discussed. Not only the left, but many in the center, opposed their installation. The danger for Greece of having atomic weapons on its soil was debated and the value of the American alliance attacked. In addition, many responsible Greeks had come to question the need for the huge expenditures that were being made for national defense. Greece at this time was devoting a proportionately higher percentage of its budget to the military than any other NATO country. American assistance funds had also been sharply curtailed, so this source of funds was reduced.

The growing feeling of disillusionment with the United States led many moderate Greeks to favor a tightening of relations with the continental European countries and a loosening of ties with Washington and London. In line with this view, the Greek government in June 1959 applied for membership in the European Economic Community (EEC), which Britain had not yet joined. In July 1961 an agreement was signed which provided that full Greek participation would come only in 1984. During this period the Greek economy could prepare for the association with the more-developed industrial countries.

## SOCIAL AND ECONOMIC CHANGES

This period of relative political stability, despite the rise of opposition to Karamanlis and the controversy over Cyprus, was marked by great changes in Greek life. Most important was the growing prosperity: in 1951 the average per capita income was $112, but it had risen by 1956 to $270, and by 1964 to $500 – still, of course, low by European standards. The economic and social improvements brought with them the tensions and dissatisfactions commonly associated with a period of rapid change. Most obvious at this time was the displacement of the population. The emigration from the poor rural districts, which we have seen in the past, continued. Many Greeks left permanently to find homes and employment overseas, in particular in the United States, Canada, and Australia; a height in this movement was reached in 1965, when 117,167 emigrated. It has been estimated that 850,000 persons, constituting 25.9 percent of the Greek work force, emigrated between 1951 and 1970.

Of these, 666,000 remained abroad. In addition, many others found work in the industrial centers of Europe, especially in West Germany. Their status was regulated in agreements between the German and Greek governments defining the working conditions of these so-called guest workers: their wages were to accord with the regular German pay scales, and they were to receive social benefits; but they were expected eventually to return to Greece. The remittances of the guest workers helped decisively with the Greek balance of payments.

In addition to the emigration abroad, a massive movement from the countryside into the cities took place. Between 1951 and 1961 Athens grew from 1.37 million to 1.85 million in population; thus almost a quarter of the 8 million Greek citizens lived in the capital. By 1961 the Greek city and rural population balanced. The effect of this movement on the countryside can well be imagined. As a result of internal and external migration, in many villages only the very old and the very young remained, and a shortage of farm labor resulted.[5]

The new populations in the cities met great problems in adjusting to urban life. For many, conditions in the city failed to meet their expectations. Moreover, even when their personal conditions improved, city life brought them in touch with those who benefited most from the political and social system. They saw the life of the privileged class and the luxury items in the store windows. The unrest and discontent that naturally resulted increased the political opposition to the government in power.

The Karamanlis ministry, like the socialist regimes, had to face the question of choosing the best means to secure better economic conditions. Greeks of all parties favored modernization; they too wished their state to enjoy all of the advantages of the industrialized nations of Western Europe. Yet the problem of industrial investment had not been solved. The government, of course, could not use the methods of the centrally planned socialist economies. In addition, individual Greeks still hesitated to invest their money in industrial enterprises. As an alternative, attempts were made to attract foreign capital, but these efforts immediately became a matter of political controversy. The Péchiney aluminum works, under French control, and an oil refinery and petrochemical plant built in Thessaloniki by Standard Oil of New Jersey were the targets of particular criticism. Both enterprises were granted special concessions, and it was widely believed that they were involved in political corruption. Many Greeks, refusing to recognize that their country did not have the capital, resources, or techniques for a completely independent economic development, were very suspicious of all foreign investors. They had a similar mistrustful attitude toward those Greek citizens who amassed great fortunes – for example, Stavros Niarchos, who constructed shipyards near

5 William H. McNeill, *The Metamorphosis of Greece since World War II* (Chicago: University of Chicago Press, 1978), pp. 105, 106, 117.

Athens, and Aristotle Onassis, who took over the national airlines, among other enterprises.

The large foreign concessions and the local millionaires were easy targets of attack from the left, even though in fact foreign investment was relatively small. A picture could be painted of a country at the mercy of foreign exploiters who worked in connivance with a corrupt government. The Karamanlis regime was particularly vulnerable to this type of criticism. As in the past, the spoils system was in full effect; ERE supporters held the important posts in the administration, and there was still much corruption. Moreover, the government had put its major effort into economic development, and it had neglected social services. The rich had indeed benefited more than the poor. Not only did the latter receive very little from the state, but the tax system weighed more heavily on them. Indirect taxes still accounted for the major portion of the state income. The privileged sections of society were skilled in tax evasion, and they were able to avoid paying a proportionate share of the national expenses.

The educational system, desperately in need of a thorough reform, was also a cause of particular bitterness. The schools and institutions of higher education suffered from the fact that the state invested only 2.1 percent of its income in education. Only a small proportion of the population was able to acquire a higher education. The opening of this door to social and economic advancement was a major issue in the opposition attacks on Karamanlis.

By 1960 the government faced all of the difficulties that can be accumulated by a regime that has been too long in power. The economic policies and the Cyprus dispute had caused much dissatisfaction. Moreover, a significant number of the opposing political parties were finally able to overcome their differences and to unite in the common goal of the overthrow of Karamanlis. The 1960s, in contrast to the 1950s, were to be years of political change.

## THE PAPANDREOU ERA

### The formation of the Center Union

The long period of ERE domination had been made possible at least partly by the fragmentation of the center and the handicaps under which the left suffered as a result of the civil war. Whereas ERE on the right and EDA on the left were stable political combinations, the middle ground was divided into competing splinter parties. This polarization had obvious dangers. As the opposition to Karamanlis increased, the possibility existed that EDA, which was widely believed to be under Communist control, would benefit from being the only stable political alternative to ERE and would win a future election. The disadvantage of the lack of a strong center was also recognized in Washington. In 1960 an administration under John F. Kennedy took office. Less sympathetic with the right, the new leaders also recognized that it was not wise to have American influence identified with only one party. A similar position was taken by the court circles. Pressures for the formation of a center coalition thus came from forces outside the party system as well as from within.

Recognizing the necessity of the move, the leaders of the center took steps to form a common front. In discussions lasting from February to September 1961, the heads of nine parties under the guidance of Papandreou, working with Venizelos, composed their differences so that they could at least cooperate in the elections. Since they differed in aims and leadership, they could not present a single program to the electorate. Nevertheless, their political coalition, the Center Union, did enter the elections of October 1961 as a united party. It did not win a victory: ERE gained 50.8 percent of the votes and thus controlled 176 seats in the assembly. The Center Union, together with Markezinis's Progressive Party, received 100 seats; EDA had 24.

The defeated Center Union immediately embarked upon an active and aggressive campaign against Karamanlis's government, which had remained in power. Papandreou, the main spokesman for the Union, was an orator of great talent who could hold and convince a large crowd, and he challenged the validity of the past election. Whether his charges of fraud and violence were justified or not is open to question, but undoubtedly the ERE candidates had benefited from the traditional advantages of the party in power and their ability to use the police. Moreover, the electorate could well believe that the government officials had falsified the returns, since this had been done in the past. In addition to calling for new elections, Papandreou struck at those weaknesses in the Karamanlis administration which have been discussed previously: the American influence, the failure to annex Cyprus, the prominence of foreign investors, and, most important, the lack of social services and the growing inequality between the social classes. As a skilled popular speaker, he appealed to the restless and the discontented. His program was not revolutionary; he did not call for a dropping of the NATO alliance or a basic change in the political system. He simply emphasized the issues that had caused the most discussion and that would attract the majority of the electorate. His personal popularity was also important:

> Nor was it only Papandreou's unrivalled ability to talk to the masses which held them captive. He had simply caught the yearning of the working people, and particularly of the peasantry, for some social justice. Whereas the government were proud to announce impressive rates of economic growth, their ideology as well as their connexions with profiteering business made them unwilling to think about income redistribution. Papandreou, by contrast, realized that rapid economic growth meant growing inequality, particularly for the masses of the agrarian poor, who started the move towards foreign emigration during this period. What were in a sense no more

419

than slogans, such as pensions for old peasants, higher price support for their products, free medical treatment, and most persistently education for their children, thus became for the rural masses what no cool-headed political program could ever become. For a whole year, and while sophisticated politicians doubted whether the game was a winner, the old man was trekking the countryside in a curiously enthusiastic yet almost mystical communion with the people.[6]

The crisis that brought the downfall of the Karamanlis government, however, was precipitated from another direction. As we have seen, the premier had been the choice of the king, and thereafter the influence of the court had been behind his government, although there had been disagreements. The continuation of the monarchy, despite the plebiscite of 1946, remained a matter of open debate. Much criticism was directed at the person of the king and, in particular, at his wife, Queen Frederika, a strong-minded woman who took part in political affairs and obviously exerted a great deal of political influence. Critics could also point out that, for a poor country, the monarchy cost a great deal of money. For instance, in 1964 Paul received $566,000, of which $313,000 went to the upkeep of his staff, his palaces, his trips to other countries, and similar expenses.[7] There were also continual questions concerning the handling of the Queen's Fund, a charitable foundation whose money came from public sources, such as taxes on imported automobiles, but whose accounts were never open to scrutiny. Suspicions were bound to arise that this money was used to support the personal interests of the monarch and political corruption.

This question of royal expenditures caused major disagreements between Karamanlis and the royal family. In 1962 Princess Sophia, Paul's elder daughter, married Don Juan Carlos of Spain. According to established custom, a dowry had to be provided, and $300,000 of government funds were used. The court wished a similar dowry to be available for the younger daughter, Irene. The use of tax money for such a purpose was highly unpopular; it will be remembered that the average per capita annual income at this time was $500. The final break between the premier and the court came over a relatively trivial matter. In April 1963, when Queen Frederika was on a private visit to London, she was the target of a small but highly publicized demonstration organized to protest the continued incarceration of political prisoners from the time of the civil war. An official visit of both the king and queen was scheduled for later in the year. Karamanlis asked that it be postponed because he feared further incidents that might react unfavorably on Greek interests. When Paul refused, Karamanlis resigned on June 11, 1963. He then left for Paris, where he was to remain for a decade.

6 Constantine Tsoucalas, *The Greek Tragedy* (Baltimore: Penguin Books, 1969), pp. 174–175.
7 Carey and Carey, *Web of Modern Greek Politics*, p. 168.

With the resignation of the premier, a caretaker government had to be appointed and new elections scheduled. The king first asked Panagiotis Pipinelis to serve; when the opposition objected that he was both an ERE supporter and a royalist, he was replaced by Stylianos Mavromichalis, the president of the supreme court. The outcome of the elections could be foretold. The forces opposed to ERE had become strong, and the attacks on the repressive and corrupt nature of that administration were given new weight by the Lambrakis affair. In May, prior to Karamanlis's resignation, Dr. Grigorios Lambrakis, an extremely popular socialist leader in the EDA coalition, was assassinated in Thessaloniki after a peace rally. He was killed by a three-wheeled motor vehicle, and evidence pointed to police connivance. He immediately became the symbol of official repression and a hero of the left.

The elections, held in November 1963, were conducted with strict regard for legality. The Center Union won 138 seats; ERE, a close second, gained 132. EDA received 28, and Markezinis's Progressives 2. Papandreou formed a government, but he was unwilling to depend on the left for support. He thus resigned so that new elections could be held. In the voting, which took place in February 1964, the Center Union won a decisive victory, with 53 percent of the votes and 171 representatives. ERE and Markezinis together received 107 seats, and EDA 22. The Center Union victory had been aided by EDA's decision not to enter candidates in about half – that is, twenty-four out of fifty-five – districts so that the vote opposing ERE would not be divided.

### Papandreou in power

As the head of the new Center Union government, Papandreou had a clear mandate from the voters to proceed with internal reforms. He had aroused great expectations. His program had been relatively moderate, but he had promised social reform. He was personally very interested in education, and he became minister of education as well as premier. It was obvious that the entire system needed a complete reorganization; the books and curricula were long outdated. The institutions of higher education were in a particularly bad condition. The emphasis was still placed on the classical education that was believed the best preparation for future lawyers, civil servants, and other professional men. The secondary schools and universities did not properly prepare students in the mathematics and science necessary for a modern technological society. Moreover, the continued use of katharevousa, the artificial written language, was an obstacle for students from poor families. Although reform was needed, Papandreou was able to accomplish only a limited number of changes. Three years of secondary education were added to the six elementary levels open to all students. There was also some reorganization in the universities and other institutions.

Other measures were also introduced in line with the campaign promises. Attempts were made to gain wage increases and higher social welfare benefits for the workers. To aid the peasants, the minimum price for wheat was raised until Greek prices stood at 80 percent above the world price. A new and more equitable contract concerning the refinery at Thessaloniki was negotiated with the Standard Oil Company. There were attempts to improve relations with the socialist countries; the agreement with Bulgaria negotiated at this time has already been discussed. Political prisoners who were still in jail were released. Despite these accomplishments, the Center Union could inaugurate only a relatively modest program. Greece remained a poor country; it could not afford costly social welfare reforms. Even with these limited changes, the economic repercussions were felt by mid-1965. The Greek balance of payments, always a major problem, worsened, and inflation again became a problem.

The great weakness of the Papandreou government was not, however, to be in its political program, but in the predominance that personal passions and interests were to assume in public affairs. The major public attention was soon to center not on the immediate social and economic issues, but on these conflicts. The Greek political scene acquired all of the elements of high drama, with the premier, his son, the king, and Archbishop Makarios assigned the major roles.

During the campaigns Papandreou and the Center Union candidates had strongly attacked Karamanlis on his Cyprus policy and his apparent failure to support Greek interests adequately. Once in power, the Center Union government was faced immediately by a crisis on the island, which broke out in December 1963. As we have seen, neither the Greeks of the mainland nor those of Cyprus liked the settlement reached in 1959. Their goal remained either enosis or, at the least, the assumption by the Greek community of full control over the island. With this goal, Makarios and his Greek supporters attempted to assert their authority over the Turkish population, and they acted in violation of the previous agreement. Once again the Greeks were the aggressors and the Turks the victims. The armed bands were active, and the casualties mounted. As previously, the Turkish government came to the defense of the threatened minority. Negotiations were resumed among Greece, Turkey, and Britain, while sporadic fighting continued on the island. The problem remained almost impossible to settle. The Turkish side would accept the retention of the 1959 agreement or the partition of the region on the basis of nationality; the Greeks demanded enosis or full control of the administration. In February Britain placed the issue before the United Nations, which eventually sent a peace-keeping force.

Meanwhile, the fighting continued. Although at a great numerical disadvantage, the Turkish population was strengthened by arms and volunteers that arrived from Turkey. In August 1964 the Greek bands, which had heavy equipment, launched a major attack on the Turkish enclave of Kokkina in the northwest section of the island. The Turkish government was able to save this threatened point only with the use of its air force. A major crisis had now developed between the NATO partners. Despite its criticism of the actions of the previous regime, there was little that the Papandreou government could do. Turkey was a much stronger state than Greece. The United States government was willing to caution Turkey, but it certainly was not about to enforce the Greek demand for enosis. As a result of this crisis the Greek and Turkish communities became even further separated; each remained concentrated in its own areas, and partition, for all practical purposes, had been accomplished. A United Nations force was in occupation, along with the Greek and Turkish troops.

At this point a change took place in the attitude of Makarios. Since he did not obtain what he considered adequate help from the West during the crisis, he appealed to the Soviet Union. Thereafter, still nursing a sense of grievance, he attempted to win support from the socialist bloc and from the Asian and African nations. Because he was also angry with Athens, he no longer supported enosis, but rather the maintenance of Cypriot independence. His goal became a neutralized Cypriot state under the control of the Greek element of the population. This shift toward the socialist camp made the archbishop very popular with the Cypriot Communists and with the Greek EDA. The Center Union policy on Cyprus thus not only had brought no advancement, but had led to great tension between Athens and Nicosia. The lack of success in the Cyprus question was to remain an embarrassment for the Center Union government.

Whereas Cyprus was the major problem faced by Papandreou in foreign policy, his deteriorating relations with the court and the problems caused by his son were his chief domestic weaknesses. When Papandreou first took power, certain changes took place that seemed to his advantage. In February 1964 his old rival in the Liberal camp, Sofoklis Venizelos, died. In March King Paul also died and was succeeded by his twenty-three-year-old son, Constantine II, who in that same year married a Danish princess. At first, it seemed that the Center Union government would be able to cooperate with the court and that the issue of the monarchy would not again become acute. Indeed, the major problem of personal relations that the premier faced was within his own family. Papandreou was the head of a coalition, rather than a party based solely on his own followers. Such organizations are always difficult to hold together, and much friction was caused by actions and attitude of the premier's son Andreas. George Papandreou was seventy-six years old, and it appeared to many that he was treating his son as a crown prince designated to acquire his father's position and honors. Such a succession was not contrary to Balkan custom: the Venizelos and Brătianu families, among many others, had become political dynasties. Andreas, however, had a background and certain ideas that made him intensely unpopular with many Greeks. For almost twenty years he had lived in the United States, and he had become an American citizen. Educated at Harvard, he had been a professor of economics at the University of California in Berkeley. In 1959 he returned to Greece, where he worked at a research center financed by the Ford Foundation. He thus lacked experience in Greek politics, and he had not participated in the events of the crucial war and civil war years. Not only was his appearance on the political stage sudden, but he started at the top. He was first elected to the assembly from his father's safe district. After the victory he was appointed deputy minister of coordination, an action that won Andreas the name "the parachutist of politics." Once in office, he took controversial positions. Identified with the left wing of the Center Union, he often disagreed with his father, who nevertheless gave him full backing. His rapid rise was bound to cause jealousy, and he was often not tactful in dealing with his colleagues. If necessary, he would go above them and appeal to his father. Moreover, although he strongly attacked corruption and misgovernment, he was obviously the beneficiary of a policy of nepotism and favoritism.

Notwithstanding these criticisms, Andreas Papandreou had many supporters in his own right. Despite his American experience, he made the United States the scapegoat for many of the Greek problems. This theme was to be a major element in his political program thereafter and was to appeal to those who hated foreign interference. With a strong reform program and a faith in "social engineering," he found particular favor among the educated youth, who shared similar ideas. His appeal has been described as follows:

> His reputation as an academic economist with a preference for planning, his fashionably liberal turn of mind, going back to Trotskyist flirtations in his youth, combined with the power of his Papandreou ancestry to make him a natural leader for the young, largely disestablished men of the managerial and professional class who had grown up after the war on American money and American opportunity and had come to resent American domination. To them, he was more than just one of themselves – he was a "new" man who had both the intellectual grasp and the political connexions with which to shape the "new" Greece; and through him they sought to capture his father's party and Government and turn it into an instrument of radical reform.[8]

The question of Andreas's political doctrines was soon to become a major Greek political issue. In June 1964 George Papandreou sent Grivas back to Cyprus with the mission of checking on Makarios's activities and keeping the idea of enosis alive. Grivas, intensely nationalistic and conservative, soon uncovered a conspiratorial group, called *Aspida*, or Shield, among the Greek troops assigned to the island. Its political program called for the establishment of a socialist and neutral regime in Athens; it thus opposed the monarchy and Greek participation in NATO. The scandal occurred when it was

---

8  Holden, *Greece without Columns*, p. 226.

alleged, though never proved, that Andreas was involved in its activities. The opposition thus had an ideal weapon with which to attack the government, and it used the Aspida affair as others had used the Lambrakis assassination against Karamanlis. The results of these attacks were out of proportion to the issue at hand. Investigations were conducted, and after eighteen months of study, twenty-eight officers were charged, of whom fifteen were convicted in March 1967 of high treason and the attempt to overthrow the government. Meanwhile, however, the question was to bring down the Papandreou government.

The Aspida affair naturally caused great concern within the army. The major role that the military has played historically in Greek political life has been repeatedly emphasized. In the past the army had supported at different times alternate royalist and republican policies. In the 1920s the predominant trend had been republican, but thereafter it became royalist and conservative. During the Karamanlis years the army had provided a major support to the regime and to the NATO and American ties. Once the Center Union came into office, this political coalition was naturally concerned about the political coloration of the military forces. There were few officers with Center Union connections, and the party wished to remedy the situation. This policy caused understandable alarm among the officer corps. The attacks on the United States and on NATO, the failures in Cyprus, and, finally, the Aspida conspiracy made many fear not only for their positions, but for the future direction of their country.

The entire question came to a crisis in July 1965. The minister of defense, Peter Garoufalias, was closely attached to the court and to the right in politics. When Papandreou gave him a list of officers whom he wished retired or transferred, the minister refused to make the changes or to resign from his office. The premier then went to Constantine II, demanded that Garoufalias be dismissed, and presented himself as the best candidate for the defense post. The king refused, arguing that Papandreou was already premier and minister of education. He also pointed out that, as long as Andreas was under investigation in connection with the Aspida plot, it would not be proper for his father to be minister of defense. The king was willing to take any alternate candidate. What happened next is open to dispute. Papandreou evidently offered to resign and the king agreed. No written document was involved.

A brilliant political tactician, Papandreou used all of his talents as an orator to attack the king. He announced that in fact he had been dismissed and that Constantine had acted outside his constitutional rights. The ousted premier, arguing that the premier had the right to appoint whomever he wished, reduced the entire question to the issue of who should in fact govern Greece, the king or the man who represented the majority in the assembly. Papandreou organized political demonstrations against the king and made full use of his abilities as a street orator. From this time on the political situation deteriorated rapidly.

Constantine II was a young, inexperienced, and not very popular ruler. The situation was indeed dangerous. Papandreou demanded either his reappointment as premier or a new election. Constantine could agree to neither. An election, it was recognized, would become another plebiscite on the monarchy, and the king might well lose. After two unsuccessful attempts, Stefanopoulos was able to form a government with the backing of ERE, Markezinis's party, and forty-five dissident members of the Center Union. This ministry lasted eighteen months. During this time Papandreou and his supporters campaigned throughout the country. Their principal argument remained that a premier with a majority in the assembly had the right to appoint his ministers without the interference of the king. Strikes and demonstrations, all of which had the support of EDA, were organized to support Papandreou.

In December 1966 the government fell when ERE withdrew its support. There was obviously no alternative left but new elections. Papandreou agreed that they should not be turned into a plebiscite on the monarchy. It was, nevertheless, very difficult to form a caretaker government for the election period. The first, under Ioannis Paraskevopoulos, fell over the difficult question of the status of Andreas Papandreou. An investigation of his role in Aspida was under way, but since he had parliamentary immunity as a representative in the assembly, he could not be arrested. If, however, this body were dissolved for the election, he could go to prison. When the Center Union tried to extend the period of immunity to cover the election, the caretaker ministry resigned. After great difficulty, another was formed by Kanellopoulos. Meanwhile, preparations proceeded for the elections, which were scheduled for May 28, 1967. There were general expectations that Papandreou would win, but rumors of a possible military revolt were also prevalent.

## THE MILITARY DICTATORSHIP

### The colonels take power

The situation was bound to cause extreme unease among the military and the right-wing political parties. Should the Center Union win as expected, radical changes in the army command and the forced retirement of many officers could be expected. In addition, George Papandreou's advanced age aroused fears that he would not be able to remain long as the head of the government. His son was then a logical successor. Andreas could be expected to keep most of his father's following. With this group, his own supporters, and the left parties, he could form a government that would most certainly take any measures necessary to assure that he had control of the army. A change to a neutralist foreign policy and a withdrawal from NATO might also occur.

Faced with this real or imagined threat to their position, a small group of officers made plans for revolt. They were aided by the existence of a military contingency plan designed to protect the government from a Communist takeover. This plan was not unique; there were similar projects in other countries. Under the provisions of the Greek version, if such a danger were imminent, the king and the generals would assume full power. They could then call the Greek military forces into action to protect the country against internal revolt or outside invasion. Martial law would be proclaimed and the constitution suspended. The decision to put the plan into effect would be signaled by the code word Prometheus. This scheme was known to the king, the military commanders, some NATO officers, and the American ambassador.

By April 21, 1967, the conspirators were prepared to seize the government. The action was carried through by relatively junior officers, and only a small number were involved. Colonel George Papadopoulos, Colonel Nikolaos Makarezos, and Brigadier Stylianos Pattakos were the leaders. In command of the tank and security units in Athens, the officers first moved to gain control of the major government and military offices and the communications network. Of these, their major objective was the army headquarters in Athens, called the Pentagon after the American Defense Department building. It was seized by a company of paratroopers. The officers then issued the code word Prometheus, which was the signal for the army to occupy other public buildings, close the frontiers and the airports, and immediately enforce martial law. The military were similarly to proceed with the arrest and detention of persons considered potentially dangerous, whose names were on a previously prepared list.

The implementation of the plan required the approval of Constantine II and the chief of staff, General Grigorios Spandidakis, neither of whom were involved in the first stages of the coup. Papadopoulos met the problem by simply using the name of the king without his knowledge and by persuading Spandidakis to join the action. Pattakos, in charge of the tank corps in Athens, had little difficulty in securing the capital, and the coup proceeded without outright opposition or bloodshed. Constantine too accepted the event. He wanted a civilian at the head of the government, however, and he suggested Constantine Kollias, a royalist who was close to the court. Accepting this nomination, the officers set up a government with Kollias as premier, Spandidakis as deputy premier and minister of defense, and Makarezos as minister of coordination. Papadopoulos, contenting himself with holding the real power, took the office of minister in the prime minister's office.

### Military rule

Thus, once again, as in 1843, 1862, 1909, and the 1920s, the army had intervened in Greek politics. The new military leaders had many common attributes. They shared a village background, and they had no real experience outside Greece. From poor families, they came from that part of Greek society which sent its sons into the army to secure their advancement. In school during the Metaxas era, they had absorbed the ideas of that period. Later they had fought against the Communists in the civil war. Some belonged to rightist societies, such as the Sacred Union of Greek Officers, or IDEA. Like their counterparts in the Metaxas regime, they were to emphasize the virtues of loyalty, religion, and nationalism; they declared that the revolt had prevented a Communist seizure of power.

This claim, as well as a strong disapproval of the previous constitutional regime, was expressed by Kollias in a speech delivered on April 21. Here the premier referred to the past crimes that he believed had been committed against the Greek people:

> the unhesitant and shameful party dealing, the misconduct of a great part of the press, the methodical assault against all the institutions, their corrosion, the debasement of Parliament, the slandering of everything, the paralysing of the State machinery, the complete lack of understanding of the burning problems of our youth, the ill-treatment of our students, the moral decline, the confusion and the blurring, the secret and open cooperation with the subversives and, finally, the continuous incendiary slogans of unscrupulous demagogues: all these have destroyed the peace of the country, have created a climate of anarchy and chaos, have cultivated conditions of hatred and division and have led us to the brink of national disaster. There was no other way of salvation left than the intervention of our Army.[9]

Armed with these convictions, the government proceeded to carry out the measures of repression that we have seen associated with similar regimes. Martial law, which was declared in April, remained in effect. Some articles of the constitution, such as the sections on civil rights, were suspended. The political parties were abolished, and strikes were forbidden. It is estimated that over 6,500 people were arrested; many of those who had been freed under the previous government were returned to prison. The political prisoners were often sent to island camps, whose bad conditions gained international attention. The police were able to make arrests without warrants; a person could be kept in jail for an unlimited term without a trial. A strict press censorship was instituted, which naturally forbade criticism of the political conditions; meetings of more than five people were prohibited. With these measures in force, the military rulers faced little internal opposition.

Constantine II, however, continued to cause difficulties for the regime. Although he had accepted the revolution, his relationship with the new lead-

---

9 Quoted in Kenneth Young, *The Greek Passion: A Study in People and Politics* (London: Dent, 1969), p. 341.

ers was bad. Once again the question of the army command precipitated a crisis. The coup had been carried through by lower-rank officers; many of their superiors had not participated in the action and remained unsympathetic. The government wished to retire or transfer some of these senior officers, many of whom were close to the court. Constantine, correctly understanding that the true issue was the control of the army, agreed to some but not all of the changes, and he was supported by Spandidakis. At the same time the king began to organize a surprise coup of his own. After making totally inadequate preparations, he and his family flew on December 13 to Kavalla, from where he called on the country to rise in his support. The major portion of the army was concentrated in northern Greece because a new crisis had arisen with Turkey over Cyprus. The king expected that the commanders of these troops would join him, but in fact, no such action occurred. After fifteen hours of futile maneuvering, Constantine II, accompanied by his family and Kollias, fled into exile.

With the king out of the country, a regent had to be named to perform the official functions of the monarch. General George Zoitakis took the position, and the government was reorganized. The king's supporters, Kollias and Spandidakis, also had to be replaced. Papadopoulos had himself appointed to the posts of both premier and defense minister. No attempt, however, was made to abolish the monarchy. There was, instead, constant communication with the king, who was in Italy, and his income was maintained. In the constitution that was drawn up at this time the monarchy was retained. As could be expected, this document provided for a conservative, authoritarian regime. The assembly was to be composed of members who were to be in part elected and in part appointed. Severe limitations were placed on civil rights, and the military forces were given special privileges. In the plebiscite held in September 1968 to approve the document, the government won a vote of 92 percent in its favor. Needless to say, this result was obtained by the traditional methods of dictatorial governments. Although the constitution came into effect in November 1968, seven of its provisions were suspended and the country remained under martial law. In 1973, when Papadopoulos decided that the monarchy should be abolished, a second plebiscite was held, with predictable results. Greece thus became a republic; Papadopoulos was elected president for eight years.

The program of the military dictatorship was largely negative. The Papandreou educational reforms were abolished, and many in government posts, such as teachers, civil service personnel, and judges, whose loyalty to the regime was suspected, were dismissed. These actions, of course, had characterized previous changes of government. The press and radio were used for propaganda in support of the Revolution of April 21, 1967, as the movement was called. Like Metaxas, the army leaders attempted to develop an ideology based on vague ideals of a new Helleno-Christian civilization.

Although the regime faced no dangerous opposition within the country, it did not win support among any large section of the population. The leaders came from the section of the army that had no powerful foreign or domestic connections. They were also not a part of the traditional Greek political and intellectual establishment to which, of course, Papandreou and most of the prominent politicians belonged. To these circles the new ministers appeared crude, stupid, and uneducated. The military coup in fact failed to produce any popular figures; Papadopoulos did not attract a following. In addition, the regime became the focus of a strong criticism from abroad among those whose political sympathies ranged from moderate to Communist. Attacking in particular the suppressions of civil liberties and the conditions in the prisons, these groups used the full weight of their influence to discredit the Athens government, which was far more vulnerable to such action than the Communist regimes, where conditions were worse.

This period of military rule became associated not only in left-wing thinking, but also in general Greek opinion, with American influence. A large section of the public held the CIA responsible for the original success of the colonels and their continuation in power. Since Papadopoulos had been associated with the Greek equivalent of this intelligence organization, and since he did have ties with American officials, the connection seemed obvious. Moreover, the conviction was widespread that American power was so pervasive that no change could occur in Athens without the approval of Washington. It has been commented that "Greeks of all classes believe that little of major importance can happen in Greece that is not the result of American action, pressure, or at least acquiescence. It has been considered axiomatic that no military coup could occur without American complicity, particularly because of the close ties between the Greek and American military establishments."[10]

Certainly the military leaders sought friendly relations with the United States. Militant anti-Communists, they felt entitled to special consideration, and they were disappointed at the cool American reaction to the coup. In fact, the United States did little one way or another. It protested the overthrow of the constitutional government and for a while suspended the delivery of heavy military equipment, but never of the small arms that are needed for civil control. There was, in fact, very little that the United States could do one way or another. Since the massive economic assistance of the past had ended, this method of pressure was eliminated. During the Nixon presidency relations improved. Vice-President Spiro Agnew visited his family village in 1971 and made a few favorable remarks about the regime. Moreover, after the Soviet intervention in Czechoslovakia in 1968, the United States and the NATO allies wanted a stable government in this Mediterranean stronghold. Fears about Soviet intentions had again been aroused. The support given by the United States to Israel in 1967 and 1973 dictated a similar Mediterranean pol-

---

10  Keith R. Legg, *Politics in Modern Greece* (Stanford: Stanford University Press, 1969), p. 229.

icy. It is interesting to note that many of the Greek groups that had most strongly attacked American interference previously now wished active measures to be taken against the military regime.

In addition to the repressive measures and generally negative program, the military government made some efforts to aid the poorer sections of the population. In order to assist the peasants, debts owed to the Agricultural Bank were canceled. Although strikes and labor union activities were suppressed, workers' wages were increased. From 1967 to 1973 per capita income increased from $700 to $1,200, a rise largely offset by a dangerous inflation that, at 30 percent in 1973, was the highest in Europe. Despite its desire to create a populist image, the regime favored the interests of the middle class and those who had previously held power. Much damage was done to the government by the passage of measures that aroused ridicule, particularly among intellectuals at home and abroad. The regime passed laws regarding such matters as the length of skirts and hair and the breaking of glasses in taverns. In an attempt to return to an emphasis on basic values, the school textbooks were reviewed and alterations made; among the improvements was a change in one of the elementary chemistry textbooks that "went so far as to declare that God had made ice to float on the water out of His solicitude for the fish."[11]

Despite their growing unpopularity, the military leaders were aided by the inability of the party leaders to form a united front. Even the Communists had split into two warring factions whose major points in common were limited to opposition to NATO and to American influence. The center presented its usual fragmented face. The right was divided between those who considered the colonels better than any practical alternative and those who looked to other leaders, such as Karamanlis or Constantine II. None of the traditional parties appeared capable of providing the leadership for a revolt. The incident that caused a shakeup of the regime came from the students. In November 1973 a group barricaded themselves in the Athens Polytechnic Institute, with the support of a large number of sympathizers gathered in the street. In suppressing this demonstration the army killed at least thirty-four participants and wounded hundreds of others. This incident caused a split within the ruling group.

On November 25 a new coup forced the resignation of Papadopoulos, who was put under arrest. Once again a group of military leaders claimed that they had acted to save the country from chaos. At their head was General Dimitrios Ioannidis, who was in command of the military police; another general became president, but the ministry was in civilian hands. This regime proved to be even more conservative than its predecessors; no attempt was made to restore regular constitutional rule. After a short eight months in power, from November 1973 to July 1974, this government was brought down by another crisis in Cyprus.

11    Holden, *Greece without Columns*, p. 267.

## The Cyprus question and the fall of the military regime

While these events were taking place in Greece, conditions in Cyprus had again become dangerous. Archbishop Makarios still supported the continuation of the independent status of the island, of course under his firm control, but he made efforts to improve relations between the Greek and the Turkish communities. He was opposed by those who still sought enosis, a position that had powerful military support. During the Papandreou period more Greek soldiers had been sent to the island, so that by 1967 these forces numbered about 12,000, although a limit of 950 had been set by international agreement. In addition, Grivas, a firm adherent of enosis, was in command of the Cypriot National Guard, and he could count on the support of many sympathizers who were also armed. To oppose him, Makarios attempted to strengthen the police, which he controlled. The archbishop also had the backing of the left-wing factions on the island; they did not want union with Greece, where the Communist Party was now illegal. In fact, the island had become a refuge for those fleeing from the military regime.

Three factions thus existed: Makarios with his supporters, Grivas with his armed bands, and the Turkish community, which received weapons from Turkey. In 1967 Grivas's bands, aided by the soldiers sent from Greece, began to attack the Turkish villages. Completely outnumbered, the Turkish population suffered heavy casualties. Once again the Turkish government prepared to intervene to support the Turkish Cypriots. In November 1967 the experienced politician Pipinelis became foreign minister in Athens. Greece seemed to be on the verge of a war with its neighbor, an action that could have been suicidal: Turkey had a population of 34 million and an army of 390,000; Greece, with about 9 million people, had 118,000 soldiers. In this situation the Greek government had no choice but to retreat. It agreed to reduce the number of its troops in Cyprus to 950 and to pay compensation for the Turkish Cypriots who had been killed. Grivas was summoned back to Athens. The United States warned Ankara not to act.

The situation, however, remained much as before; there were bad relations between Athens and Nicosia. In January 1974 Grivas died and received a hero's funeral. Despite its retreat in 1967, the Greek government still wished to take over the island. In an extremely rash action, in July 1974, it backed a revolt against Makarios that was carried through primarily by the Cypriot National Guard, joined by the Greek troops stationed on the island. The archbishop was overthrown and replaced by a new president, Nikos Sampson, an EOKA terrorist who had won a bad reputation as a killer and a thug. Only Athens recognized the new Cypriot regime. Greece was isolated in diplomatic affairs; no other state approved this violent act. Moreover, the military leaders had precipitated an action without adequate preparation for the inevitable reaction of Turkey.

According to the agreement of 1959 the Turkish government, as a protecting power, had a legal right of unilateral intervention. On July 20 a Turkish army landed on the island to protect the Turkish population. The Greek government replied with a call for mobilization, an order that resulted in massive confusion. Despite seven years of military rule, the country was not prepared for war. The army did not have the necessary weapons or supplies. Recognizing the hopelessness of the situation, the army commanders in northern Greece simply defied their superiors in Athens. They refused to risk a war, since they recognized that such an action could lead to a national catastrophe. Another military coup followed, and another set of army officers forced the retirement of Ioannidis. Once in power they called for the reestablishment of constitutional government. Karamanlis was summoned back from Paris, where he was still living, to take control of the deteriorating situation.

## KARAMANLIS RESTORED

Returning on July 24, 1974, Karamanlis gave immediate assurances that constitutional government would be restored, but he had to move carefully. He had, after all, been brought back to power by a section of the army. Military control was still firm throughout the state, and the maintenance of civilian rule depended on the cooperation of the army. Moreover, the enormous problem of Cyprus remained. As long as war with Turkey was a possibility, no measures could be taken that would weaken or demoralize the armed forces. At first, therefore, no attempt was made to purge its ranks or to bring to trial those who had collaborated with the Papadopoulos regime.

Meanwhile, the situation in Cyprus had declined further. Although a provisional cease-fire had been arranged on July 23, only a few weeks later, on August 14, the Turkish army began another advance. It now occupied the entire northern section, or 38 percent, of the island, a region that contained the major economic resources of the island and around 200,000 Greek inhabitants. A massive stream of 170,000 refugees poured out of the area. Though another cease-fire was arranged, Turkey was in possession of the richest part of the country (see Map 15). Makarios was restored to his old office, and negotiations were recommenced. This time, however, the Turks were in a favorable position, and they had no reason to seek a quick solution.

In his first months as premier Karamanlis thus had to deal with major external as well as internal problems. The Cyprus affair caused an extremely strong reaction against the United States. Once again, most Greeks thought that Washington should have intervened in their favor and should have halted the Turkish invasion, despite the role that the Ioannidis regime had played in precipitating the crisis. Although the United States did suspend military assistance to Ankara for a period, since American weapons had been used in violation of previous agreements, this act did not satisfy Greek public opin-

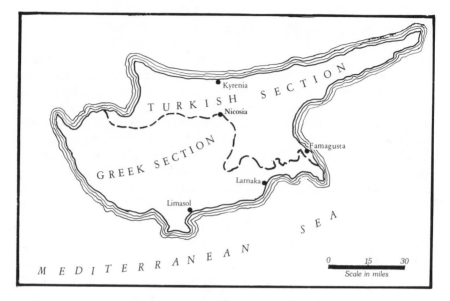

Map 15. The partition of Cyprus, 1974

ion. To meet the popular sentiment, Karamanlis withdrew the Greek forces from the military organization of NATO and brought up the question of the continuation of American bases in Greece.

In internal affairs, the Karamanlis government restored the constitution of 1952 and lifted martial law. Those who had lost their positions under the previous regime were reinstated; political prisoners were released. Some measures were then taken against the leaders of the 1967 coup, but there were no executions and no extreme measures of reprisal. The three colonels, imprisoned on an island, were not brought to trial until after the elections. They and the chief figures in their government received life sentences.

In order to obtain a stable government, Karamanlis scheduled elections for November 1974, that is, only four months after the restoral of constitutional government; a plebiscite on the monarchy was to follow. With the end of the military dictatorship, politics as usual resumed its course. A new spectrum of political coalitions made its appearance. On the far right, the National Democratic Union was the only party that supported the monarchy and was sympathetic to the past regime. Next, on the moderate right, stood Karamanlis's party, the New Democracy, which was the successor to ERE. The former Center Union retained its name; its new leader was George Mavros. To the left a new party led by Andreas Papandreou, the Panhellenic Socialist Movement, or PASOK, advocated a socialist and neutralist program. The Communist Party (KKE), now legal, stood on the far left. In 1968 it had split into the Communists of the Exterior, who followed the Moscow line, and the

Communists of the Interior, who were advocates of Eurocommunism and who espoused a more independent stand. Now that the Communists could campaign openly, EDA declined rapidly. In the elections Karamanlis's party won 54 percent of the votes and thus 219 seats. The Center Union, with 21 percent, received 60 seats. PASOK won 14 percent and 13 places. Other left parties, running in a United Left coalition, gained 9 percent and 8 seats. The National Democratic Union, with only 1.1 percent, had no representation at all. In December the plebiscite on the monarchy resulted in a 69 percent vote against the return of the king. A major problem from the past had thus been settled; Greece remained a republic.

With his authority confirmed by a popular mandate, Karamanlis could proceed with changes in the government. In 1975 a new constitution was issued, one that gave the president strong powers. He could appoint and dismiss ministers, including the premier; dissolve the assembly; and veto bills. A three-fifths' majority of the assembly was required to override his action. Constantine Tsatsos was chosen for the position, but Karamanlis as premier retained the principal influence in the government. Greece did not rejoin the military organization of NATO, but its continued Western orientation was reflected in the decision to press toward full membership in the European Economic Community even before the previously set date of 1984.

In the next years Karamanlis was able to maintain his strong position in Greek political life, although with some losses. In elections held in November 1977 his New Democracy party was reduced to 42 percent of the votes and 172 of the 300 seats in the assembly. The most interesting change was the increased strength shown by PASOK, which won 25 percent of the vote and 93 seats; the Center Union, with only 12 percent of the vote, took only 15 seats. The Communist Party remained split, with the Moscow wing receiving 9 percent, or 11 seats. The remaining places were won by splinter parties of the right and left. In May 1980, in presidential elections in the assembly, Karamanlis, seventy-three years old at the time, won on the third ballot. The 93 PASOK members, hoping to force new elections before the scheduled date of November 1981, did not vote. George Rallis, the new prime minister, announced his intention of retaining close ties with Western Europe and trying to improve the embittered relations with the United States.

Foreign affairs, in particular the Cyprus question, which involved also NATO and the United States, still proved difficult for the government to handle. Makarios died in August 1977 and was succeeded as president by Spyros Kyprianou. Although negotiations proceeded between the Greek and Turkish governments, and between the communities on the island, no mutually acceptable formula for settlement could be found. In other questions Karamanlis was more successful. Relations with the Balkan states remained good. Formal diplomatic ties with Albania had been restored in 1971. Karamanlis traveled to the other Balkan capitals, and he encouraged visits to Greece by their leaders. His greatest success, however, was the acceptance by the Greek assembly in June 1979 of an early entry into the European Economic Community. Once again the principal opposition came from PASOK. Although this party and the Moscow wing of KKE walked out of the assembly, the action was accepted by 193 votes, more than the three-fifths' majority necessary for ratification. The tenth member of the association, Greece entered formally on January 1, 1981. Ties with Western Europe were further strengthened when, in October 1980, the country rejoined the integrated command structure of NATO.

## ANDREAS PAPANDREOU: THE ELECTIONS OF OCTOBER 1981

The second term of the New Democracy government, with Rallis as premier but with Karamanlis as the major figure, met increasing problems. Economic difficulties and the ever-present Cyprus issue remained unsolved. Moreover, this administration, like so many of its predecessors, became the target of accusations of corruption and favoritism. This situation was used to advantage by Papandreou and his PASOK followers. Previously, Papandreou had called for strong actions in foreign policy. He took a firmly nationalist position on the Cyprus question. Extremely critical of the influence of the United States in Greece, he wished the American bases dismantled. Even further, he called for Greek withdrawal from NATO and the EEC. In internal affairs the PASOK program called for radical reforms, including the nationalization of some Greek industries. However, just prior to the elections, Papandreou softened his position on some critical issues in what was to be a successful endeavor to win votes among the moderates.

The elections, held on October 18, 1981, gave PASOK 48.06 percent of the votes and 172 seats; the New Democracy, with 35.8 percent, was reduced to 115 representatives. The Communists of the Exterior made slight gains, receiving 10.9 percent of the votes and 13 seats. The new administration was under the strong personal direction of Papandreou; Karamanlis, of course, remained as president. The constitution of 1975, it will be remembered, had endowed that office with strong powers, and he could provide a restraining hand. In its first months in power, the PASOK government certainly initiated no drastic changes in Greek policy. Despite previous declarations, Papandreou made no move to take Greece out of NATO or the EEC, and the American bases were not closed. Relations with Turkey remained tense. The disagreements concerned not only Cyprus, but the conflict of claims of jurisdiction over the waters of the Aegean Sea, in particular in the areas around the Greek islands.

In domestic policy the changes were similarly limited. Some reforms were enacted: civil marriage was made legal, and plans to improve health care were introduced. The government declared its intentions of doing something about bureaucratic inefficiency and of allowing local government more power. Despite its stated intention of introducing an ambitious program of social improvement, PASOK faced great difficulties, caused at least in part by the world economic problems. With a high inflation and a slowing rate of economic growth, the country could not easily pay for the social reforms endorsed by PASOK. Although tourism remained profitable, with 5.6 million visitors in 1981, another mainstay of the economy, shipping, faced great difficulties. Papandreou thus, despite his strong electoral victory, at the beginning of his term in office faced formidable practical obstacles to the realization of his program.

## CONCLUSION

After 1945, as we have seen, Greece had the most varied political experience of all the Balkan states. Although the basic economic and social system remained stable, the political changes were dramatic. After the civil war Greece first had a moderate conservative government under Papagos and Karamanlis, and then the center liberal regime of George Papandreou; this government was overthrown by a military coup, with the leadership held first by Papadopoulos and then by Iaonnidis. In 1974 a return was made to the first stage when Karamanlis restored the constitutional system. In 1981 PASOK, under Andreas Papandreou, won the election. Although it was a socialist party, it did not share the ideological base of the Marxist socialist regimes in the neighboring Balkan states.

During the entire postwar period, Greece retained a Western orientation in foreign policy, but the country also experienced many conflicts with its allies. Britain regained its traditional dominant influence immediately after the war, but was forced to surrender it in 1947 to the United States. Greece thus became a part of the NATO defense system in the eastern Mediterranean. This alignment weakened during the Cyprus crisis of 1974, when the Greek government felt that it had not been given adequate support by the United States. The disenchantment with the American association led the Greek leaders to seek closer ties with the Western European countries; Greece joined the European Economic Community and also sought better relations with its Balkan neighbors. The Cyprus issue remained the center of foreign policy. Although Papandreou campaigned in 1981 on a program attacking Greek membership in NATO and the EEC, he took no immediate action once he assumed office.

Despite the fact that Greece in the postwar period usually retained a Western constitutional government – with the seven-year military dictatorship as the exception – the country experienced enormous changes. Like its neighbors, Greece underwent a demographic revolution. After the conclusion of the civil war, a massive movement into the cities occurred; the prewar emigration continued until 1975, when a reverse trend began. Removed from their traditional villages, the former rural populations had to make adjust-

*tie to loss of control (social demo.)*
*and avoidance of inf. stigma?*

437

ments to new conditions, but they, like all Greeks, could enjoy the advantages offered by new technology and by the conscious efforts made to raise the economic level of the country. The continuing social and economic problems of the first years of the 1980s were at least to some extent shared by other nations and reflected the difficult world conditions of the time.

consumerism

# *Conclusion*

THIS NARRATIVE, which comes to an end in the early 1980s, has covered the successive transformations in the lives of the Balkan people since the end of the seventeenth century. At that time the majority lived under the jurisdiction of the Ottoman Empire and were members of the Orthodox church; their faith and their common subjection to Ottoman rule were the major sources of unity among them. A minority, Catholic Croats and Slovenes and Orthodox Romanians and Serbs, were under Habsburg rule. The Balkan people, largely peasants, shared certain experiences. Their chief ties were to their families and to their local communities; they supported themselves principally as farmers, herdsmen, or fishermen. Some were merchants and artisans, and an even smaller number rose to become a part of the political leadership. Largely illiterate and speaking dialects of the major languages, these people nevertheless had similar views about their lives and the society to which they belonged. With their outlook shaped by the church and by a complex heritage of local traditions handed down generation after generation, they formed settled and ordered societies whose basic concepts and rules of behavior were accepted by their members. Since they lived in an age when central governments were not expected to provide social services, they depended upon the village and family units, which offered protection for a population with a subsistence economy and which sheltered the aged, the sick, the young, and those who could not otherwise deal with the problems of these violent times. In normal circumstances the local authorities, together with the church, handled most of the problems of village life and the maintenance of order. Justice was administered on the basis of church and customary law.

Under attack from without and within, the Ottoman Empire became in the eighteenth century an increasingly unstable political organization. The central government failed both to repel foreign invaders and to maintain its authority within its own domains. During the course of this century some Ottoman lands were lost to Russian and Habsburg conquest. Later, at the time of the French Revolution and the Napoleonic Wars, the French, British, Russian, and Habsburg forces competed for control of the Ottoman government or parts of its territories. Even worse for internal stability, local Muslim notables, the ayans, were able to challenge the central authorities successfully

439

and to gain control in some regions. All of these events were extremely detrimental to the welfare of the Balkan Christian population. Faced by the dual catastrophes of foreign invasion and increased anarchy in the countryside, the local communities were forced to take upon themselves even larger responsibilities. Already certain sections of the empire, such as the Greek islands, the Peloponnesus, and Montenegro, were virtually self-governing. The Serbian revolution, as we have seen, had its origins in such circumstances.

These events in the Balkan peninsula paralleled the rise of nationalism in Western and Central Europe. The liberal and national ideology of the European revolutionaries influenced Balkan leaders so strongly because it was immediately applicable to local conditions. Following in the path of European romantic nationalism, Balkan intellectuals too became concerned with their national languages and, most important, with their past history and its heroes. With roots in classical Greece, Rome, Byzantium, and the medieval Serbian and Bulgarian empires, Balkan nationalists had as strong claims to historic glory as any contemporary European movement. Although these aspects of the national revivals were closely connected with native institutions and traditions, the Balkan leaders accepted certain political institutions from Europe, in particular the constitutional monarchy and the centralized state administrative system. This choice, which did in fact reflect Balkan opinion, was also made necessary by the enormous direct influence of the great powers on events in the peninsula.

The national liberation movements of all of the nationalities were made more complex by the frequent intervention of the European governments. The central strategic position of the peninsula and of the Ottoman Empire itself made the area the focus of the imperial drives of Britain, France, Russia, the Habsburg Empire, and later united Italy and Germany. Although the Balkan leaders were often able to exploit this situation – since in effect Russian wars won Balkan freedom from Ottoman control – the new national governments were forced to endure constant interference in their internal affairs by outside powers. The Eastern Question did indeed turn the Balkans into the "powderkeg of Europe," but the responsibility for this situation lay as much with the great powers and the principle of the balance of power as with the Balkan states.

By the end of the nineteenth century, as we have seen, independent or autonomous Bulgaria 1, Greek, Romanian, Serbian, and Montenegrin governments had been established, and an Albanian national movement had commenced. Moreover, the nationality question within the Habsburg Empire had become acute with the rise of political consciousness among the Croatian, Romanian, Serbian, and Slovene population, as well as among the other peoples of that state. The leaderships usually supported both the national idea as the basis for political organization and the principle of constitutional, representative government. Where national states were established, the population enjoyed certain advantages; freedom from Ottoman control was unquestionably the great popular demand. Yet the new regimes introduced problems of their own. Their establishment did indeed end the former imperial control, but it also led to a curtailment of local government, where much authority had rested in the hands of peasant notables. Adopting Western, principally French, administrative practices, the national leaderships preferred to concentrate political power in the capitals and to send government representatives to administer the countryside, thus breaking traditional bonds and loyalties. The new political system, although conforming in its outer aspects to contemporary liberal ideals, in practice gave the control of each nation to a small minority.

The establishment of the national governments, unfortunately, did not serve to lessen the problems of the peninsula as a pawn in international relations. In fact, in many respects the situation became worse. With the intensification of imperial world rivalries at the turn of the century, the Balkans became of ever increasing diplomatic significance. To the historic rivalries of great powers were now added the bitter conflicts among the nationalities, which had been largely submerged in the Ottoman period. Boundaries for the Balkan states were most difficult to draw; under both Habsburg and Ottoman rule the population had intermingled. As a result, all of the new states were to a greater or lesser extent multinational. Moreover, no national leadership was content with its frontiers; each state had some claims on its neighbors. The individual governments thus devoted a disproportionate amount of attention to foreign policy and to military preparedness. They also sought foreign alliances that would advance their aims. The great powers in turn attempted to use the situation to their advantage and to find client states that would work in their interests. Oppressed minorities and militant nationalists assigned to an alien authority still looked to terror and revolutionary action as the best hope for the future. World War I, with its immediate origins in Balkan events and its massive destruction of lives and property, marked the culmination of this explosive situation.

The peace treaties following this conflict, despite the numerous problems that they caused, at least established political boundaries that have remained relatively stable. The outward shape of the Balkan national states was thus set. The great issues of internal organization and economic development, however, were still unresolved. Although the peninsula had a thoroughly agrarian economy, the political power in all of the capitals lay in the hands of a relatively small percentage of the population, whose outlook was often quite different from that of the peasant majority. This group was composed primarily of those who were able to obtain university educations and who subsequently entered the government, the army, the professions, business, or similar middle-class occupations. The political parties that competed under the parliamentary systems represented the divergent interests within this group. Concentrating on the pursuit of their own ambitions, the traditional parties paid comparatively little attention to what was transpiring in the countryside.

Balkan governments regarded their rural populations primarily as a source of taxes and of recruits for the army; few attempts were made to provide compensatory benefits.

Despite their blindness toward some aspects of their national life, the Balkan leaderships were competitive and proud. Recognizing the backward nature of their societies, they envisioned a radical transformation in the future. Most wished to emulate conditions in the advanced Western European states. Industrialization and modernization were common goals, but formidable barriers stood in the way. The lack of adequate capital, sufficient raw materials, and trained personnel has been mentioned. Even more difficult to meet were the revolutionary social and political implications of a radical economic transformation. Very little was in fact accomplished before the peninsula was drawn into another devastating period of warfare. Meanwhile, the agrarian problems became even more acute, particularly with the continuing rise of the population and the limitations that had been placed on external emigration. The Great Depression, bringing with it the collapse of world grain prices, had a particularly devastating effect on this fragile situation.

The short period between the two world wars was a curious interlude. All of the difficulties of the national division of the Balkans became clearly apparent. Not only did the states continue to fight among themselves, but in internal politics national issues often threatened to bring regular government to a standstill. The bitterest conflicts occurred within Yugoslavia, but the Macedonian issue also played havoc in Bulgarian politics. Nor had relations with the great powers improved. The French postwar system of alliances kept alive the bitterness over the peace settlements and reinforced the resentment of the nationalities who felt that they had been unjustly treated. The Italian and later the German diplomats could make use for their own advantage of the Hungarian indignation over the Transylvanian settlement, the Croatian resentment of the Serbian dominance in Yugoslavia, and the Bulgarian determination to keep the Macedonian question prominent. These and other historic grievances thwarted any attempts to secure Balkan unity or to organize united efforts to block great-power interference.

The Balkan political situation became drastically worse when the Great Depression seriously undermined the stability of the world economy. Beset by increasing social and economic problems, the Balkan states, like their German and Italian neighbors, could not maintain their former parliamentary systems. In each an authoritarian regime was established, with the monarchy and the army as the center. The main aim of each of these governments was the assurance of internal order and the maintenance of the existing social structure. The royal dictatorships were emergency measures; they served to protect the domestic status quo, and they sought to defend national interests at a time of increasing international danger. When Europe once more plunged into war, these regimes maneuvered frantically but in vain to keep the fighting away from their lands.

# Conclusion

Once again warfare among the great powers led to major changes in the peninsula. Most important was the diplomatic revolution that came with the peace. With Germany and Italy defeated and France and Britain severely weakened, the Soviet Union and the United States emerged as the only two surviving powers that could lay claims to a first rank. Neither of these states had been intimately involved in Balkan events in the interwar period. After the war, however, they were able to exert the major influence in determining the forms of government in the states and even in the nomination or approval of the leaders. First Britain and then the United States held the preeminent place in Greek politics; the Soviet Union, at least at the outset, enjoyed a special position in the other countries, but after 1948 it was able to control the situation directly only in Bulgaria, Romania, and until 1960 in Albania.

After the conclusion of the Greek civil war and the stabilization of Yugoslav relations with the Soviet Union, the Balkan peninsula ceased to be a major focal point of international conflict. World attention shifted to the former colonial areas of Asia and Africa and the struggle for control there. In Europe the most important issues were economic unification within both blocs, the German question, and, as far as the Communist states were concerned, the Soviet military intervention in Hungary and Czechoslovakia. Although all of the Balkan states took an active part in world affairs, they had to an extent lost their freedom of action. Despite the continuation of many of the former inter-Balkan controversies, it was unlikely that any government could have gone to war without at least the tacit approval of its great-power patron. Even theoretically nonaligned Yugoslavia had to keep a sharp watch on both great powers. Moreover, in contrast to the situation in the nineteenth century, it was no longer possible for the Balkan nations to draw their great-power allies into war over strictly local issues. This shift, together with the change in the strategic significance of the Balkans, was in part caused by the revolutionary changes that occurred in military technology. Small Balkan states had neither the finances nor the skills to construct hydrogen bombs or elaborate missile systems. The age of the Balkan guerilla fighter, armed with rifles and grenades and dependent on local villages for supplies, had perhaps passed, although this generalization is still open to question.

More important than the shifts in the international status of the Balkan nations were the radical alterations in domestic policy that occurred in the postwar years. These changes often had a more radical effect on the everyday life of the individual than any we have seen in the previous three centuries of Balkan development. The great wars and revolutions of the past had indeed caused much material damage and loss of life on the local level; there had also been shifts of population within the peninsula, as well as overseas emigration. However, these events had left the basic social structure relatively undisturbed. In this agrarian society family and village relationships were of principal importance; the ideal of most of the peasant population was ownership of a prosperous farm. After the national revolutions, the central governments had attempted to assert more political control over the countryside, but the changes in traditional patterns of life were relatively superficial. Moreover, revolutionary doctrine in the nineteenth century was liberal as well as national. The new constitutional systems were intended to free individuals to choose their own paths; they were directed toward individual liberation and not social betterment. They were not intended to provide absolute guidelines for the future or to indicate to the citizen his role in a larger plan. In contrast, the socialist systems had the goal of social advancement and economic modernization; their leaders supplied a plan of action that indeed did constrain the individual and assign each citizen a place in a general scheme. The stated aim was equality and not liberty. Both the ultimate goals and the instruments clashed with the traditions and ideals of patriarchal village life. The real revolution in the Balkans was thus not the Communist seizure of political power, but the subsequent slow destruction of patterns of life that had held for centuries. Similar changes, of course, occurred in Greece, where economic advancement was inevitably accompanied by radical changes in the countryside. These processes, which are continuing, are not easy to characterize, nor can their final results be clearly pictured.

That radical changes were necessary had, of course, been recognized before 1945. The monarchical governments had made repeated if largely unavailing attempts at economic development. Their efforts were hampered by the conditions of the times and the nature of their regimes, but also by the fact that they lacked the ability to make truly violent alterations in old patterns. Their armies could suppress political opposition, but not compel, for instance, measures leading to industrialization. Prewar Balkan politicians, despite their many abuses of their positions, could not push around large groups of people, nor could they assign hundreds of "volunteers" to unpleasant tasks – except, of course, in wartime. The new socialist leaderships were under no such restraints. They had a plan provided by the Soviet Union. Backed by the armed power of that state and in full control of agencies of coercion and propaganda, they could implement programs without concern for public opinion. They could thus carry through measures, such as those providing for a sharp curtailment in living standards to pay for factories, or laws aimed at crushing all expression of political opposition, that would not have been possible under previous regimes.

Although the harsher aspects of the Communist systems have received wide publicity, particularly in the United States and Western Europe, it would perhaps be best to judge them by their own standards. The national governments they replaced based their justification to rule on their role in the establishment of the independent states and on their constitutional regimes, which in turn rested, at least in theory, on the concept of individual liberty and political, if not social and economic, equality. The socialist leaders have instead emphasized economic modernization and social equality. They have, of course, also attempted to replace the Christian view of human destiny with

Marxist doctrine, which sees each individual life as inevitably bound up with a preordained pattern of historical development. On the positive side, the Communist regimes have undoubtedly brought many material benefits to their citizens, particularly in Yugoslavia, which is the least doctrinaire of these governments. In comparison with their predecessors, the Communist leaders can point to significant achievements in the field of social services, including the introduction of national health programs, educational systems open to all, subsidized housing, paid vacations, and pensions for the sick and aged. Full employment has also been assured in Albania, Bulgaria, and Romania. Where such measures have been well administered, they have provided a cushion for the radical changes that have occurred, and they have brought these benefits to many who did not previously enjoy such protection. The socialist planners have at least attempted to construct modern housing for as many as possible, and they have been successful in providing some of the most prized consumer goods, notably radios, television sets, and even automobiles, to a large segment of their populations.

Despite the obvious advances, the Communist governments face major problems. Some of these are shared with the rest of the world, whereas others are indigenous to Balkan or socialist conditions. Like other nations, the Balkan states suffered from the rise in world oil prices in the 1970s; other basic raw materials, such as coal and iron, remain in short supply. The multitude of problems that beset all industrialized societies are difficult to solve within the framework of the relatively poor Balkan economies. In political life, the disadvantages of one-party rule and the stifling effects of an entrenched bureaucracy must still be met. Although political stability has been achieved, the price has been the imposition of much individual and social control. Moreover, like their predecessors throughout Balkan history, all the governments, including Greece's, depend on the loyalty of their armed forces, a matter that is always in question.

Judging contemporary societies is singularly difficult; predicting their future is almost impossible. For the Balkans the effects of the recent changes, in particular the economic transformation, the movement of population, and the adoption of new social patterns, will certainly be lasting. Traditional bonds have been broken; whether new loyalties of equal stability will take their place has yet to be seen. It will also be interesting to watch how successful the governments will be in fulfilling the assurances that they have given their people; certainly one problem faced by the Communist regimes, in particular, is that of enhanced expectations. Socialist propaganda has presented a utopian view of the future and one that raises hopes not only for better social relationships, but also for a rise in living standards that may be disproportionate to the resources of the peninsula. All Communist Party programs contain an implicit assurance that eventually the citizens of socialist states will enjoy living conditions equal to or even better than those of their counterparts under the Western capitalist systems. With the Greek alternative path open for examination, at least a rough comparison should be possible. Balkan citizens, however, have the tendency to compare themselves, not with their neighbors, but with the most successful of the European states, especially with France or the German Federal Republic. Of course, for all of the Balkan nations external factors, largely beyond their control, will probably determine their future. Because they are part of a closely bound human community, their fate also depends on world economic conditions and on the relations between the heavily armed great powers.

# Bibliography

T HE BIBLIOGRAPHY for the second volume of this Balkan history is limited to books in English that may interest a reader who would like more information on the subjects covered in the text. It does not attempt to include all of the excellent books that are available on Balkan history. All articles and works in other languages are omitted. Although the emphasis is on history, the final sections list some studies on village life and travel accounts, in addition to a selection of surveys of Balkan literature. For further information on studies in all disciplines, the reader is referred to Paul L. Horecky, ed., *Southeastern Europe: A Guide to Basic Publications* (Chicago: University of Chicago Press, 1969), and to the bibliographical essays in volumes VIII and IX of *A History of East Central Europe*, edited by Peter F. Sugar and Donald W. Treadgold, cited herein. A discussion of American scholarship on Balkan studies is to be found in Charles Jelavich, ed., *Language and Area Studies: East Central and Southeastern Europe* (Chicago: University of Chicago Press, 1969). Publications that appeared in the decade after the completion of that book are reviewed in the journal *Balkanistica* 4 (1977–1978), in an issue devoted to the question.

## GENERAL HISTORIES OF THE BALKANS

Berend, Iván T., and György Ránki. *Economic Development in East-Central Europe in the Nineteenth and Twentieth Centuries.* New York: Columbia University Press, 1974.

Djordjevic, Dimitrije, and Stephen Fischer-Galati. *The Balkan Revolutionary Tradition.* New York: Columbia University Press, 1981.

Hösch, Edgar. *The Balkans: A Short History from Greek Times to the Present Day.* Translated by Tania Alexander. New York: Crane, Russak, 1972.

Jelavich, Charles, and Barbara Jelavich. *The Balkans.* Englewood Cliffs, N.J.: Prentice-Hall, 1965.

Jelavich, Charles, and Barbara Jelavich, eds. *The Balkans in Transition: Essays on the Development of Balkan Life and Politics since the Eighteenth Century.* Reprint ed., Hamden, Conn.: Archon Books, 1974.

Lampe, John R., and Marvin R. Jackson. *Balkan Economic History, 1550–1950.* Bloomington: Indiana University Press, 1982.

Ristelhueber, René. *A History of the Balkan Peoples*. Edited and translated by Sherman David Spector. New York: Twayne, 1971.

Schevill, Ferdinand. *The History of the Balkan Peninsula*. New York: Harcourt, Brace & Co., 1933.

Seton-Watson, Robert W. *The Rise of Nationality in the Balkans*. London: Constable, 1917.

Stavrianos, L. S. *The Balkans, 1815–1914*. New York: Holt, Rinehart & Winston, 1963.

*The Balkans since 1453*. New York: Rinehart, 1958.

Stoianovich, Traian. *A Study in Balkan Civilization*. New York: Knopf, 1967.

Sugar, Peter F., and Ivo J. Lederer, eds. *Nationalism in Eastern Europe*. Seattle: University of Washington Press, 1969.

Sugar, Peter F., and Donald W. Treadgold, eds. *A History of East Central Europe*. Seattle: University of Washington Press. Vol. VIII, *The Establishment of the Balkan National States, 1804–1920*, by Charles Jelavich and Barbara Jelavich, 1977; Vol. IX, *East Central Europe between the Two World Wars*, by Joseph Rothschild, 1974.

## NATIONAL AND IMPERIAL HISTORIES

### *Balkan nationalities*

#### ALBANIANS

Frasheri, Kristo. *The History of Albania*. Tirana: n.p., 1964.

Logoreci, Anton. *The Albanians: Europe's Forgotten Survivors*. Boulder, Colo.: Westview Press, 1977.

Marmullaku, Ramadan. *Albania and the Albanians*. Translated by Margot Milosavljević and Boško Milosavljević. London: Hurst, 1975.

Swire, Joseph. *Albania: The Rise of a Kingdom*. London: William & Norgate, 1929.

#### BULGARIANS

Kossev, D., H. Hristov, and D. Angelov. *A Short History of Bulgaria*. Sofia: Foreign Languages Press, 1963.

Macdermott, Mercia. *A History of Bulgaria, 1393–1885*. London: Allen & Unwin, 1962.

Michew, D., *The Bulgarians in the Past: Pages from the Bulgarian Cultural History*. Lausanne: Librairie Centrale des Nationalités, 1919.

#### GREEKS

Campbell, John, and Philip Sherrard. *Modern Greece*. London: Benn, 1968.

Clogg, Richard. *A Short History of Modern Greece*. Cambridge: Cambridge University Press, 1979.

# Bibliography

Forster, Edward S. *A Short History of Modern Greece, 1821–1956*. London: Methuen, 1960.

Heurtley, W. A., H. C. Darby, C. W. Crawley, and C. M. Woodhouse. *A Short History of Greece*. Cambridge: Cambridge University Press, 1965.

Kousoulas, D. George. *Modern Greece: Profile of a Nation*. New York: Scribner, 1974.

Miller, William. *Greece*. New York: Scribner, 1928.

Sophocles, S. M. *A History of Greece*. Thessaloniki: Institute for Balkan Studies, 1961.

Woodhouse, C. M. *The Story of Modern Greece*. London: Faber & Faber, 1968.

### ROMANIANS

Chirot, Daniel. *Social Change in a Peripheral Society: The Creation of a Balkan Colony*. New York: Academic Press, 1976.

Giurescu, Dinu C. *Illustrated History of the Romanian People*. Bucharest: Editura Sport-Turism, 1981.

Oţetea, Andrei, ed. *The History of the Romanian People*. New York: Twayne, 1970.

Seton-Watson, Robert W. *A History of the Rumanians from Roman Times to the Completion of Unity*. Cambridge: Cambridge University Press, 1934.

### SERBS, CROATS, AND SLOVENES

Auty, Phyllis. *Yugoslavia*. New York: Walker, 1965.

Clissold, Stephen, ed. *A History of Yugoslavia from Early Times to 1966*. Cambridge: Cambridge University Press, 1966.

Dedijer, Vladimir, Ivan Božić, Sima Ćirković, and Milorad Ekmečić. *History of Yugoslavia*. Translated by Kordija Kveder. New York: McGraw-Hill, 1974.

Gazi, Stephen. *A History of Croatia*. New York: Philosophical Library, 1973.

Temperley, H. W. V. *History of Serbia*. New York: Fertig, 1969.

Tomasevich, Jozo. *Peasants, Politics, and Economic Change in Yugoslavia*. Stanford, Calif.: Stanford University Press, 1955.

## The Ottoman Empire

Davison, Roderic H. *Turkey*. Englewood Cliffs, N.J.: Prentice-Hall, 1968.

Lewis, Bernard. *The Emergence of Modern Turkey*. London: Oxford University Press, 1961.

Miller, William. *The Ottoman Empire and Its Successors, 1801–1927*. Cambridge: Cambridge University Press, 1936.

Shaw, Stanford J., and Ezel Kural Shaw. *History of the Ottoman Empire and Modern Turkey*. 2 vols. Cambridge: Cambridge University Press, 1967, 1977.

Vucinich, Wayne S. *The Ottoman Empire: Its Record and Legacy*. Princeton, N.J.: Van Nostrand, 1965.

### The Habsburg Empire

Kann, Robert A. *A History of the Habsburg Empire, 1526–1918*. Berkeley: University of California Press, 1974.
   *The Multinational Empire: Nationalism and National Reform in the Habsburg Monarchy, 1848–1918*. 2 vols. New York: Columbia University Press, 1950.
Macartney, C. A. *The Habsburg Empire, 1790–1918*. London: Weidenfeld & Nicolson, 1968.
May, Arthur J. *The Habsburg Monarchy, 1867–1914*. New York: Norton Library, 1968.
Tapié, Victor. *The Rise and Fall of the Habsburg Monarchy*. Translated by Stephen Hardman. New York: Praeger, 1971.
Taylor, A. J. P. *The Habsburg Monarchy, 1809–1918*. New York: Harper Torchbooks, 1948.

## SELECTED STUDIES FOR THE PERIOD BEFORE WORLD WAR I

### Economic developments

Blaisdell, D. C. *European Financial Control in the Ottoman Empire: A Study of the Establishment, Activities, and Significance of the Administration of the Ottoman Public Debt*. New York: Columbia University Press, 1929.
Evans, Ifor L. *The Agrarian Revolution in Roumania*. Cambridge, Mass.: Harvard University Press (Belknap Press), 1962.
Feis, Herbert. *Europe the World's Banker, 1870–1914*. New York: Norton, 1965.
Hočevar, Toussaint. *The Structure of the Slovenian Economy, 1848–1963*. New York: Studia Slovenica, 1965.
Sugar, Peter F. *Industrialization of Bosnia-Hercegovina, 1878–1918*. Seattle: University of Washington Press, 1963.

### General studies on diplomacy

Anastassoff, Christ. *The Tragic Peninsula: A History of the Macedonian Movement for Independence since 1878*. St. Louis: Blackwell & Wielandy, 1938.
Anderson, M. A. *The Eastern Question, 1774–1923*. New York: Macmillan, 1966.
Brailsford, H. N. *Macedonia: Its Races and Their Future*. London: Methuen, 1906.
Dedijer, Vladimir. *The Road to Sarajevo*. New York: Simon & Schuster, 1966.
Georgevitch, Tihomir R. *Macedonia*. London: Allen & Unwin, 1918.

# Bibliography

Geshov, Ivan E. *The Balkan League.* Translated by Constantin C. Mincoff. London: Murray, 1915.

Helmreich, Ernst C. *The Diplomacy of the Balkan Wars, 1912–1913.* Cambridge, Mass.: Harvard University Press, 1938.

Jelavich, Barbara. *The Habsburg Empire in European Affairs, 1814–1918.* Reprint ed., Hamden, Conn.: Archon Books, 1975.

*St. Petersburg and Moscow: Tsarist and Soviet Foreign Policy, 1814–1974.* Bloomington: Indiana University Press, 1974.

Remak, Joachim. *Sarajevo: The Origins of a Political Murder.* New York: Criterion Press, 1959.

Rossos, Andrew. *Russia and the Balkans: Inter-Balkan Rivalries and Russian Foreign Policy, 1908–1914.* Toronto: University of Toronto Press, 1981.

Thaden, Edward C. *Russia and the Balkan Alliance of 1912.* University Park: Pennsylvania State University Press, 1965.

Wilkinson, H. R. *Maps and Politics: A Review of the Ethnographic Cartography of Macedonia.* Liverpool: University Press of Liverpool, 1951.

## National development

### ALBANIANS

Great Britain, Office of the Admiralty, Naval Intelligence Division. *Albania: Basic Handbook.* 2 pts, 1943, 1944.

Skendi, Stavro. *The Albanian National Awakening, 1878–1912.* Princeton, N.J.: Princeton University Press, 1967.

Stickney, Edith Pierpont. *Southern Albania or Northern Epirus in European International Affairs, 1912–1923.* Stanford, Calif.: Stanford University Press, 1926.

### BULGARIANS

Beaman, A. Hulme. *M. Stambuloff.* London: Bliss, Sands & Foster, 1895.

Hall, William W. *Puritans in the Balkans: The American Board Mission in Bulgaria, 1878–1918.* Sofia: Cultura Printing House, 1938.

### GREEKS

Augustinos, Gerasimos. *Consciousness and History: Nationalist Critics of Greek Society, 1897–1914.* Boulder, Colo.: East European Quarterly, 1977.

Coulumbis, T. A., J. A. Petropulos, and H. J. Psomiades. *Foreign Interference in Greek Politics: An Historical Perspective.* New York: Pella, 1976.

Dakin, Douglas. *The Greek Struggle in Macedonia, 1897–1913.* Thessaloniki: Institute for Balkan Studies, 1966.

*The Unification of Greece, 1770–1923.* London: Benn, 1972.

Kaltchas, Nicholas S. *Introduction to the Constitutional History of Modern Greece.* New York: Columbia University Press, 1940.

# Bibliography

Koumoulides, John T. A. *Greece in Transition: Essays in the History of Modern Greece, 1821–1974.* London: Zeno, 1977.

Levandis, John A. *The Greek Foreign Debt and the Great Powers, 1821–1898.* New York: Columbia University Press, 1944.

Papacosma, S. Victor. *The Military in Greek Politics: The 1909 Coup d'état.* Kent, Ohio: Kent State University Press, 1977.

Vlastos, Doros. *Venizelos: Patriot, Statesman, Revolutionary.* London: Lund Humphries, 1942.

### ROMANIANS

Constantinescu, Miron, et al., eds. *Unification of the Romanian National State: The Union of Transylvania with Old Romania.* Bucharest: Academy of the Socialist Republic of Romania, 1971.

Eidelberg, Philip Gabriel. *The Great Rumanian Peasant Revolt of 1907: Origins of a Modern Jacquerie.* Leiden: Brill, 1974.

Jowitt, Kenneth, ed. *Social Change in Romania, 1860–1940.* Berkeley: Institute of International Studies, 1978.

### SERBS, CROATS, AND SLOVENES

Djilas, Milovan. *Land without Justice.* New York: Harcourt, Brace & Co. 1958.

Petrovich, Michael Boro. *A History of Modern Serbia, 1804–1918.* 2 vols. New York: Harcourt Brace Jovanovich, 1976.

Rogel, Carole. *The Slovenes and Yugoslavism, 1890–1914.* Boulder, Colo.: East European quarterly, 1977.

Seton-Watson, Robert W. *The Southern Slav Question and the Habsburg Monarchy.* London: Constable, 1911.

Vucinich, Wayne S. *Serbia between East and West: The Events of 1903–1908.* Stanford, Calif.: Stanford University Press, 1954.

### THE OTTOMAN EMPIRE

Ahmad, Feroz. *The Young Turks: The Committee of Union and Progress in Turkish Politics, 1908–1914.* Oxford: Oxford University Press (Clarendon Press), 1969.

Berkes, Niyazi. *The Development of Secularism in Turkey.* Montreal: McGill University Press, 1964.

Ramsaur, Ernest E. *The Young Turks: Prelude to the Revolution of 1908.* Princeton, N.J.: Princeton University Press, 1957.

## WORLD WAR I AND THE PEACE SETTLEMENTS

Adams, John C. *Flight in Winter.* Princeton, N.J.: Princeton University Press, 1942.

Dallin, Alexander, ed. *Russian Diplomacy and Eastern Europe, 1914–1917.* New York: King's Crown Press, 1963.

# Bibliography

Djordjevic, Dimitrije and Stephen Fischer-Galati, eds., *The Creation of Yugoslavia, 1914–1918*. Santa Barbara, Calif.: Clio Books, 1980.

Evans, Laurence. *United States Policy and the Partition of Turkey, 1914–1924*. Baltimore: Johns Hopkins Press, 1965.

Frucht, Richard C. *Dunărea Noastră; Romania, the Great Powers, and the Danube Question, 1914–1921*. Boulder, Colo.: East European Quarterly, 1982.

Genov, Georgi P. *Bulgaria and the Treaty of Neuilly*. Sofia: Danov, 1935.

Helmreich, Paul C. *From Paris to Sèvres: The Partition of the Ottoman Empire at the Peace Conference of 1919–1920*. Columbus: Ohio State University Press, 1974.

Howard, Harry N. *The Partition of Turkey: A Diplomatic History, 1913–1923*. New York: Fertig, 1966.

Lederer, Ivo J. *Yugoslavia at the Paris Conference: A Study in Frontier-Making*. New Haven, Conn.: Yale University Press, 1963.

Leon, George B. *Greece and the Great Powers, 1914–1917*. Thessaloniki: Institute for Balkan Studies, 1974.

Mamatey, Victor S. *The United States and East Central Europe, 1914–1981*. Princeton: Princeton University Press, 1957.

Pallis, Alexander A. *Greece's Anatolian Venture and After: A Survey of the Diplomatic and Political Aspects of the Greek Expedition to Asia Minor, 1915–1922*. London: Methuen, 1937.

Petsalis-Diomidis, N. *Greece at the Paris Peace Conference, 1919*. Thessaloniki: Institute for Balkan Studies, 1978.

Seton-Watson, Hugh, and Christopher Seton-Watson. *The Making of a New Europe: R. W. Seton-Watson and the Last Years of Austria-Hungary*. Seattle: University of Washington Press, 1981.

Smith, C. Jay. *The Russian Struggle for Power, 1914–1917: A Study of Russian Foreign Policy during the First World War*. New York: Greenwood Press, 1969.

Smith, Michael Llewellyn. *Ionian Vision: Greece in Asia Minor, 1919–1922*. London: Allen Lane, 1973.

Spector, Sherman David. *Rumania at the Paris Peace Conference: A Study of the Diplomacy of Ioan I. C. Brătianu*. New York: Bookman Associates, 1962.

Theodoulou, Christos. *Greece and the Entente, August 1, 1914–September 25, 1916*. Thessaloniki: Institute for Balkan Studies, 1971.

Živojinović, Dragan R. *America, Italy and the Birth of Yugoslavia, 1917–1919*. Boulder, Colo.: East European Quarterly, 1972.

## THE INTERWAR YEARS

Bell, John D. *Peasants in Power: Alexander Stamboliski and the Bulgarian Agrarian National Union, 1899–1923*. Princeton, N.J.: Princeton University Press, 1977.

Hoptner, J. B. *Yugoslavia in Crisis, 1934–1941*. New York: Columbia University Press, 1962.

Macartney, C. A., and A. W. Palmer. *Independent Eastern Europe*. New York: St. Martin's Press, 1966.

Maček, Vladko. *In the Struggle for Freedom*. Translated by Elizabeth Gazi and Stjepan Gazi. University Park: Pennsylvania State University Press, 1957.

Mitrany, David. *The Land and the Peasant in Rumania: The War and Agrarian Reform, 1917–1921*. London: Oxford University Press, 1930.

Nagy-Talavera, Nicholas M. *The Green Shirts and the Others*. Stanford, Calif.: Hoover Institution Press, 1970.

Pearton, Maurice. *Oil and the Roumanian State, 1895–1948*. Oxford: Oxford University Press (Clarendon Press), 1971.

Pentzopoulos, Dimitri. *The Balkan Exchange of Minorities and Its Impact on Greece*. Paris: Mouton, 1962.

Pribichevich, Stoyan. *World without End: The Saga of Southeastern Europe*. New York: Reynal & Hitchcock, 1939.

Ristić, Dragiša N. *Yugoslavia's Revolution of 1941*. University Park: Pennsylvania State University Press, 1966.

Roberts, Henry L. *Rumania: Political Problems of an Agrarian State*. New Haven, Conn.: Yale University Press, 1951.

Rogger, Hans, and Eugen Weber, ed. *The European Right: A Historical Profile*. Berkeley: University of California Press, 1966.

Rothschild, Joseph. *The Communist Party of Bulgaria: Origins and Development, 1883–1936*. New York: Columbia University Press, 1959.

Seton-Watson, Hugh. *Eastern Europe between the Wars, 1918–1941*. New York: Harper & Row, 1967.

Sugar, Peter F., ed. *Native Fascism in the Successor States, 1918–1945*. Santa Barbara, Calif.: ABC-Clio, 1971.

## WORLD WAR II AND THE POSTWAR PERIOD

### *General studies*

Barker, Elisabeth. *Macedonia: Its Place in Balkan Power Politics*. London: Royal Institute of International Affairs, 1950.

Brzezinski, Zbigniew K. *The Soviet Bloc: Unity and Conflict*. Cambridge, Mass.: Harvard University Press, 1971.

Burks, R. V. *The Dynamics of Communism in Eastern Europe*. Princeton, N.J.: Princeton University Press, 1961.

Davis, Lynn Etheridge. *The Cold War Begins*. Princeton, N.J.: Princeton University Press, 1974.

Fejtö, François. *A History of the People's Democracies: Eastern Europe since Stalin*. Translated by Daniel Weissbort. New York: Praeger, 1971.

# Bibliography

Gati, Charles, ed. *The International Politics of Eastern Europe*. New York: Praeger, 1976.

*The Politics of Modernization in Eastern Europe: Testing the Soviet Model*. New
York: Praeger, 1974.

Gianaris, Nicholas V. *The Economies of the Balkan Countries*. New York: Praeger, 1982.

Hewett, Edward A. *The Economies of Eastern Europe*. Lincoln, Neb.: Cliff's
Notes, 1978.

Hoffman, George W., ed. *Eastern Europe: Essays in Geographical Problems*.
London: Methuen, 1971.

Höhmann, Hans-Hermann, Michael Kaser, and Karl C. Thalheim, eds. *The
New Economic Systems of Eastern Europe*. Berkeley: University of California Press, 1975.

Ionescu, Ghita. *The Break-Up of the Soviet Empire in Eastern Europe*. Baltimore: Penguin Books, 1965.

Kaser, Michael. *Comecon: Integration Problems of the Planned Economies*. London: Oxford University Press, 1967.

King, Robert R. *Minorities under Communism: Nationalities as a Source of
Tension among Balkan Communist States*. Cambridge, Mass.: Harvard
University Press, 1973.

Kostanick, Huey Louis, ed. *Population and Migration Trends in Eastern Europe*. Boulder, Colo.: Westview Press, 1977.

Lendvai, Paul. *Eagles in Cobwebs*. New York: Doubleday, Anchor Books, 1969.

Maclean, Fitzroy. *Eastern Approaches*. London: Jonathan Cape, 1949.

Mastny, Vojtech. *Russia's Road to the Cold War*. New York: Columbia University Press, 1979.

Mellor, Roy E. I. *Eastern Europe: A Geography of the COMECON Countries*.
New York: Columbia University Press, 1975.

Orlov, Dietrich. *The Nazis in the Balkans: A Case Study of Totalitarian Politics*.
Pittsburgh: University of Pittsburgh Press, 1968.

Pounds, Norman J. G. *Eastern Europe*. Chicago: Aldine, 1969.

Rakowska-Harmstone, Teresa, and Andrew Gyorgy, eds. *Communism in Eastern
Europe*. Bloomington: Indiana University Press, 1979.

Remington, Robin Alison. *The Warsaw Pact: Case Studies in Communist Conflict Resolution*. Cambridge, Mass.: MIT Press, 1971.

Seton-Watson, Hugh. *The East European Revolution*. New York: Praeger, 1951.

Shub, Anatole. *An Empire Loses Hope: The Return of Stalin's Ghost*. New York:
Norton, 1970.

Staar, Richard F. *Communist Regimes in Eastern Europe*. Stanford, Calif.: Hoover
Institution Press, 1977.

Triska, Jan F., and Paul M. Cocks. *Political Development in Eastern Europe*.
New York: Praeger, 1977.

Wolff, Robert Lee. *The Balkans in Our Time*. New York: Norton, 1978.

# Bibliography

Van Creveld, Martin L. *Hitler's Strategy, 1940–1941: The Balkan Clue*. Cambridge: Cambridge University Press, 1973.

## Albania

Amery, Julian. *Sons of the Eagle: A Study in Guerilla War*. London: Macmillan, 1948.
Griffith, William E. *Albania and the Sino-Soviet Rift*. Cambridge, Mass.: MIT Press, 1963.
Hamm, Harry. *Albania: China's Beachhead in Europe*. Translated by Victor Anderson. New York: Praeger, 1963.
Pano, Nicholas C. *The People's Republic of Albania*. Baltimore: Johns Hopkins Press, 1968.
Prifti, Peter R. *Socialist Albania since 1944: Domestic and Foreign Developments*. Cambridge, Mass.: MIT Press, 1978.
Thomas, John I. *Education for Communism: School and State in the People's Republic of Albania*. Stanford, Calif.: Hoover Institution Press, 1969.

## Bulgaria

Brown, J. F. *Bulgaria under Communist Rule*. New York: Praeger, 1970.
Chary, Frederick B. *The Bulgarian Jews and the Final Solution, 1940–1944*. Pittsburgh: University of Pittsburgh Press, 1972.
Dellin, L. A. D. *Bulgaria*. New York: Praeger, 1957.
Miller, Marshall Lee. *Bulgaria during the Second World War*. Stanford, Calif.: Stanford University Press, 1975.
Oren, Nissan. *Bulgarian Communism: The Road to Power, 1934–1944*. New York: Columbia University Press, 1971.
    *Revolution Administered: Agrarianism and Communism in Bulgaria*. Baltimore: Johns Hopkins University Press, 1973.

## Greece

Athenian [pseud.]. *Inside the Colonels' Greece*. Translated by Richard Clogg. New York: Norton, 1972.
Carey, Jane Perry Clark, and Andrew Galbraith Carey. *The Web of Modern Greek Politics*. New York: Columbia University Press, 1968.
Clogg, Richard, and George Yannopoulos, eds. *Greece under Military Rule*. London: Secker & Warburg, 1972.
Couloumbis, Theodore A. *Greek Political Reaction to American and NATO Influences*. New Haven, Conn.: Yale University Press, 1966.
Holden, David. *Greece without Columns*. Philadelphia: Lippincott, 1972.
Iatrides, John O. *Revolt in Athens: The Greek Communist "Second Round," 1944, 1945*. Princeton, N.J.: Princeton University Press, 1972.

# Bibliography

Koumoulides, John T. A., ed. *Greece in Transition: Essays in the History of Modern Greece*. London: Zeno, 1977.

Kousoulas, D. George. *Revolution and Defeat: The Story of the Greek Communist Party*. London: Oxford University Press, 1965.

Legg, Keith. *Politics in Modern Greece*. Stanford, Calif.: Stanford University Press, 1969.

McNeill, William H. *The Metamorphosis of Greece since World War II*. Chicago: University of Chicago Press, 1978.

Stavrianos, L. S. *Greece: American Dilemma and Opportunity*. Chicago: Henry Regnery, 1952.

Tsoucalas, Constantine. *The Greek Tragedy*. Baltimore: Penguin Books, 1969.

Woodhouse, C. M. *Apple of Discord*. London: Hutchinson, 1948.

*The Struggle for Greece, 1941–1949*. London: Hart-Davis, MacGibbon, 1976.

Young, Kenneth. *The Greek Passion: A Study in People and Politics*. London: Dent, 1969.

Xydis, Stephen G. *Greece and the Great Powers, 1944–1947*. Thessaloniki: Institute for Balkan Studies, 1963.

### Romania

Braun, Aurel. *Romanian Foreign Policy since 1965*. New York: Praeger, 1978.

Fischer-Galati, Stephen. *The New Rumania: From People's Democracy to Socialist Republic*. Cambridge, Mass.: MIT Press, 1967.

*The Socialist Republic of Rumania*. Baltimore: Johns Hopkins Press, 1969.

Floyd, David. *Rumania: Russia's Dissident Ally*. New York: Praeger, 1965.

Gafencu, Grigore. *Prelude to the Russian Campaign*. London: Frederick Muller, 1945.

Gilberg, Trond. *Modernization in Romania since World War II*. New York: Praeger, 1975.

Ionescu, Ghita. *Communism in Rumania, 1944–1962*. London: Oxford University Press, 1964.

Jowitt, Kenneth. *Revolutionary Breakthroughs and National Development: The Case of Romania, 1944–1965*. Berkeley: University of California Press, 1971.

King, Robert R. *History of the Romanian Communist Party*. Stanford, Calif.: Hoover Institution Press, 1980.

Montias, John Michael. *Economic Development in Communist Rumania*. Cambridge, Mass.: MIT Press, 1967.

Tsantis, Andreas C., and Roy Pepper. *Romania: The Industrialization of an Agrarian Economy under Socialist Planning*. Washington, D.C.: World Bank, 1979.

### Yugoslavia

Apostolski, Mihailo, and Haralampié Polenakovich. *The Socialist Republic of Macedonia*. Skopje: Macedonian Review Editions, 1974.

457

# Bibliography

Armstrong, Hamilton Fish. *Tito and Goliath*. New York: Macmillan, 1951.

Auty, Phyllis. *Tito: A Biography*. London: Longman, 1970.

Avakumovic, Ivan. *History of the Communist Part of Yugoslavia*. Aberdeen, Scotland: University Press of Aberdeen, 1964.

Campbell, John C. *Tito's Separate Road: America and Yugoslavia in World Politics*. New York: Harper & Row, 1967.

Deakin, F. W. D. *The Embattled Mountain*. London: Oxford University Press, 1971.

Dedijer, Vladimir. *The Battle Stalin Lost: Memoirs of Yugoslavia, 1948–1953*. New York: Viking, 1971.

*Tito*. New York: Simon & Schuster, 1953.

Denitch, Bogdan Denis. *The Legitimation of a Revolution: The Yugoslav Case*. New Haven, Conn.: Yale University Press, 1976.

Djilas, Milovan. *Conversations with Stalin*. Translated by Michael B. Petrovich. New York: Harcourt, Brace & World, 1962.

*The New Class: An Analysis of the Communist System*. New York: Praeger, 1957.

*Tito: The Story from Inside*. Translated by Vasilije Kojić and Richard Hayes. New York: Harcourt Brace Jovanovich, 1980.

*Wartime*. Translated by Michael B. Petrovich. New York: Harcourt Brace Jovanovich, 1977.

Hoffman, George W., and Fred Warner Neal. *Yugoslavia and the New Communism*. New York: Twentieth Century Fund, 1962.

Kofos, Evangelos. *Nationalism and Communism in Macedonia*. Thessaloniki: Institute for Balkan Studies, 1964.

Johnson, A. Ross. *The Transformation of Communist Ideology: The Yugoslav Case, 1945–1953*. Cambridge, Mass.: MIT Press, 1972.

Marković, Mihailo. *From Affluence to Praxis: Philosophy and Social Criticism*. Ann Arbor: University of Michigan Press, 1974.

Mates, Leo. *Nonalignment: Theory and Current Policy*. Dobbs Ferry, N.Y.: Oceana Publications, 1972.

Mićunović, Veljko. *Moscow Diary*. New York: Doubleday, 1980.

Milazzo, Mateo J. *The Chetnik Movement and the Yugoslav Resistance*. Baltimore: Johns Hopkins University Press, 1975.

Milenkovitch, Deborah D. *Plan and Market in Yugoslav Economic Thought*. New Haven, Conn.: Yale University Press, 1971.

Palmer, Stephen E., and Robert R. King. *Yugoslav Communism and the Macedonian Question*. Hamden, Conn.: Archon, 1971.

Pavlowitch, Stevan K. *Yugoslavia*. New York: Praeger, 1971.

Roberts, Walter R. *Tito, Mihailović and the Allies, 1941–1945*. New Brunswick, N.J.: Rutgers University Press, 1973.

Rubinstein, Alvin Z. *Yugoslavia and the Nonaligned World*. Princeton, N.J.: Princeton University Press, 1970.

# Bibliography

Rusinow, Dennison. *The Yugoslav Experiment, 1948–1974*. Berkeley: University of California Press, 1977.

Schrenk, Martin, Cyrus Ardalan, and Nawal A. El Tatawy. *Yugoslavia: Self-management Socialism and the Challenges of Development*. Baltimore: Johns Hopkins University Press, 1979.

Sher, Gerson S. *Praxis: Marxist Criticism and Dissent in Socialist Yugoslavia*. Bloomington: Indiana University Press, 1977.

Shoup, Paul. *Communism and the Yugoslav National Question*. New York: Columbia University Press, 1968.

Singleton, Fred. *Twentieth Century Yugoslavia*. New York: Columbia University Press, 1976.

Stojanovic, Svetozar. *Between Ideals and Reality: A Critique of Socialism and Its Future*. Translated by Gerson S. Sher. New York: Oxford University Press, 1973.

Tomasevich, Jozo. *The Chetniks: War and Revolution in Yugoslavia, 1941–1945*. Stanford, Calif.: Stanford University Press, 1975.

Ulam, Adam. *Titoism and the Cominform*. Cambridge, Mass.: Harvard University Press, 1952.

Vucinich, Wayne S., ed. *Contemporary Yugoslavia: Twenty Years of Socialist Experiment*. Berkeley: University of California Press, 1969.

Wilson, Duncan. *Tito's Yugoslavia*. Cambridge: Cambridge University Press, 1979.

Zaninovich, M. George. *The Development of Socialist Yugoslavia*. Baltimore: Johns Hopkins Press, 1968.

Zukin, Sharon. *Beyond Marx and Tito: Theory and Practice in Yugoslav Socialism*. Cambridge: Cambridge University Press, 1975.

## TRAVEL BOOKS AND SOCIOLOGICAL STUDIES OF BALKAN LIFE

Adamic, Louis. *My Native Land*. New York: Harper & Bros., 1943.

Campbell, John K. *Honour, Family, and Patronage: A Study of Institutions and Moral Values in a Greek Mountain Community*. Oxford: Oxford University Press (Clarendon Press), 1964.

Erlich, Vera St. *Family in Transition: A Study of 300 Yugoslav Villages*. Princeton, N.J.: Princeton University Press, 1966.

Friedl, Ernestine. *Vasilika: A Village in Modern Greece*. New York: Holt, Rinehart & Winston, 1962.

Garnett, Lucy M. J. *Turkish Life in Town and Country*. New York: Putnam, 1904.

Graves, Sir Robert. *Storm Centres of the Near East*. London: Hutchinson, 1933.

# Bibliography

Halpern, Joel M. *A Serbian Village*. New York: Columbia University Press, 1958.

Halpern, Joel M., and Barbara K. Halpern. *A Serbian Village in Historical Perspective*. New York: Holt, Rinehart & Winston, 1972.

Lodge, Olive. *Peasant Life in Jugoslavia*. London: Seeley, Service, n.d.

Sanders, Irwin T. *Balkan Village*. Lexington: University of Kentucky Press, 1949.

*Rainbow in the Rock: The People of Rural Greece*. Cambridge, Mass.: Harvard University Press, 1961.

Trouton, Ruth. *Peasant Renaissance in Yugoslavia, 1900–1950*. London: Routledge & Kegan Paul, 1952.

West, Rebecca. *Black Lamb and Grey Falcon: A Journey through Yugoslavia*. 2 vols. New York: Viking Press, 1941.

Winner, Irene. *A Slovenian Village: Zerovnica*. Providence, R.I.: Brown University Press, 1971.

## HISTORIES OF BALKAN LITERATURE

Barac, Antun. *A History of Yugoslav Literature*. Translated by Peter Mijušković. Ann Arbor: Michigan Slavic Publications, 1973.

Dimaras, C. Th. *A History of Modern Greek Literature*. Translated by Mary P. Gianos. Albany: State University of New York Press, 1972.

Mann, Stuart E. *Albanian Literature: An Outline of Prose, Poetry, and Drama*. London: Quaritch, 1955.

Moser, Charles A. *A History of Bulgarian Literature, 865–1944*. The Hague: Mouton, 1972.

Munteano, Basil. *Modern Romanian Literature*. Bucharest: Editura Cuvântul, 1943.

# Index

461

# Index

# Index

# Index

# Index

# Index

Spiru, Nako, 332
Sporazum of 1939, 203–4, 266
*Srbobran*, 67
*Srpski List*, 57
Stadler, Josip, archbishop of Sarajevo, 62
Stalin, Joseph: and the Aegean, 310; and Albania, 333, 381, 384; and Balkan affairs, 231; and Communist theory, 337–8; denunciation of, 354–5, 358; and Greek revolt, 312; and post–World War II occupations, 301; and Romania, 220, 372; Soviet policy under, 195, 353, 359; and World War II, 220, 221, 223, 284, 285, 301–2, 352; and Yugoslavia, 318, 322–7, 329, 330, 332, 357, 378, 389, 390
Stalingrad, 248, 253
Stamboliski, Alexander, 39, 125, 137, 166, 167, 168, 169, 170, 364
Stambolov, Stephen, 8, 37
Stârcea-Mocsonyi, Baron, 254
Starčević, Ante, 58, 66, 167
State Planning Commissions, 346
State Security Service, *see* UDBA
Stefanopoulos, Stephen, 409, 412
Stepinac, Aloysius, archbishop of Croatia, 264
Ştirbei, Barbu, 253, 290
Stoica, Chivu, 372, 373, 375
Stoilov, Constantine, 37–8
Stojadinović, Milan, 202, 203, 214, 215, 216
Straits, 128, 131–3; *see also* Dardanelles
Strategic Arms Limitation Talks, *see* SALT
Strossmayer, Josip Juraj, bishop of Djakovo, 68, 69
Struma River, 89
Sturdza, Dimitrie, 24
Styria, 54, 55
Šubašić, Ivan, 204, 271, 295, 296, 313
Sukarno, Achmed, 390
Supilo, Frano, 124, 144
Supreme Committee, Supremists, 94
Šutej, Juraj, 295, 296
SVEA (Albania), 181
Szeged, 119

Taaffe, Count Eduard von, 54, 56
Talat, 126
Tanzimat, 5, 82, 85
Tătărescu, George, 204, 206, 289, 290, 291
Temesvar, *see* Banat of Temesvar
Tempo, *see* Vukmanović-Tempo, Svetozar
Tenedos, 125
Terazija, 47
Terezi, Eleni, 380
Terpeshev, Dobri, 330
Tevfik Pasha, 129, 132
Thessaloniki: and Allied forces, 118, 120, 121, 128; as free zone, 170; as goal of Greek and Bulgarian armies, 98; as great Balkan center, 46; as IMRO headquarters, 93; as major port, 89–90; Serbian consulate in, 92; as Young Turk headquarters, 83; as Yugoslav free port, 177
Thessaly, 18, 40, 79
Thrace: and Bulgaria, 117, 118, 255–6, 258; and Greece, 40, 120, 125, 129, 131, 206; 1941 revolt in, 256; and Ottoman Empire, 13, 79, 98, 127; population of, 256; and Turkey, 132
Three Emperors' Alliance, 9
Timișoara, 74
Timok River, 31
Tirana, 177, 178, 275
Tirol, 54
Tisza, Kálmán, 64, 73
Tisza, Stephen, 64, 113
Tisza River, 119, 124
Tito, Josip Broz, 269–71, 274, 301, 330, 339, 342, 357, 394, 397, 408; career of, 385–6; independence of, 286, 333, 354–5, 359, 366, 372, 374, 378, 381, 389–91, 402–3; as Partisan leader, 267; as Yugoslav leader, 287, 295, 298, 313, 320–9, 376, 389, 395
Todorov-Gorunya, Ivan, 367
Tomislav II, king of Croatia, 264
Toptani, Esad, 101, 103, 179, 180
Topulli, Bajo, 87
Transnistria, 251
Transylvania, 71–6; and Apponyi Laws of 1907, 73; franchise in, 72, 73, 74, 75, 158; Germans in, 72, 73, 77; and Grand National Assembly (1918), 157; and Grand National Council, 158; Hungarians in, 72, 73, 77; and Hungary, 72, 225; political parties in, 74–6, 157 (*see also names of individual parties*); population of, 72, 73; as potential source of controversy, 135, 370, 371, 377; and Romania, 26, 119, 122, 225, 226, 250, 305; Romanians in, 72, 73–5, 76, 77, 239; status of population of, in World War II, 252; Szeklers in, 72, 77; and Vienna Award, 225–6
*Transylvania*, 76
Transylvanian National Party (Romania), 161
Trentino, 117
Trialist solution, 67–8, 71, 144, 145
Trianon, Treaty of (1920), 122–4
*Tribuna*, 76
Trieste, 117, 314–17, 328
Trikoupis, Charilaos, 41, 43, 176
Tripalo, Miko, 396, 397
Tripartite Pact (1940), 230–6, 263
Triple Alliance, 9, 95, 106
Triple Entente, 95, 106
Tripoli, 84, 89, 96, 97
Triune Kingdom, 57, 66, 68, 69
"True National" Party (Montenegro), 36

# Index